How Will *Odyssey* Help Improve Your Writing?

***Odyssey* is organized into seven parts to help you build your writing skills.**

PART 1: **Starting Out (Chapters 1–4).** This section focuses on writing as a means of exploration and discovery, and on the stages of the writing process—generating ideas, composing, and refining.

PART 2: **Using the Patterns of Paragraph Development (Chapters 5–13).** This part focuses on the rhetorical modes, which are the specific techniques that help a writer fulfill the purpose of a paragraph. Examples of these modes are narration, description, example, and process.

PART 3: **Moving On to the Essay (Chapters 14–16).** In this part, you will learn to apply the principles you encountered in Part 1 (writing process) and Part 2 (rhetorical modes) to essay writing.

PART 4: **Developing Sentence Sense (Chapters 17–20).** These four chapters focus on the mechanics of writing correct sentences and avoiding common sentence errors, such as fragments, comma splices, and run-ons.

PART 5: **Understanding Subjects and Verbs (Chapters 21–24).** In these chapters, you will gain practice with subject–verb agreement, and with various verb tenses of both regular and irregular verbs.

PART 6: **Keeping Your Writing Correct (Chapters 25–31).** This part focuses on many important aspects of word usage and mechanics: working with nouns, pronouns, and modifiers; maintaining parallelism; spelling correctly; and using commas, other punctuation, and capitalization.

PART 7: **Connecting: Responding to Reading.** Professional writers always say that in order to write better, you need to read more. Thus, in Part 7 you will find 15 readings from both professional writers and student authors. The student writings grew out of assignments like those presented in *Odyssey*. This part also provides guidelines for careful reading and questions that promote critical thinking, discussion, and further writing.

A Conversation with
William J. Kelly

Q. *What is the biggest stumbling block for new or developing writers?*

A. By far, it is just plain fear.

Q. *How can new or developing writers overcome their feelings of inhibition and anxiety as they face the blank page or computer screen?*

A. It may sound simplistic, but one of the best ways is to try to lessen their expectations of the finished product. I'm not suggesting that anyone plan to write ineffectively. But many people focus too much on what the finished product should look like and as a result become discouraged and intimidated. A better idea, then, is to assume that the first words you write won't yet be in their best or most complete form. They will serve as the foundation you need to fulfill the promise of their ideas.

Q. *Do you think that everyone can learn to express their ideas clearly in writing?*

A. Absolutely. If people can think and say their ideas so that others can understand them, then they can write them.

Q. *What is the one most important lesson you'd like students to remember from this book/course?*

A. The most important lesson is this: People have difficulty with writing not because they lack ability but because they lack practice. Be patient and keep writing. You will get better. You won't be able to avoid it. The truth is that I was not a good student in high school. It wasn't that I lacked ability—in fact, I had been an honor student up until the end of the ninth grade. But after that, I made the ridiculous, conscious decision not to work at my studies anymore. Instead I turned my attention to athletics and socializing. In my senior year, I applied to two local colleges, and fortunately for me, one of them took a chance on me. At that point, I was ready to turn my attention to academics once more, but after my three high school years of self-imposed academic inertia, I struggled greatly. It wasn't until the second semester of my sophomore year in college that I began to reach the level of my true capability again. Throughout my teaching career, I've tried to remember what that struggle was like, how it felt to want to do something but to be unable to reach it immediately. I learned that if I was patient with myself, if I was persistent, if I learned from my mistakes, I could succeed. These lessons form the foundation for my teaching and this book.

Q. *Is there anything else you would like to say to students who are about to begin using this book?*

A. I don't believe that a book has to be tedious to be rigorous. Students who lack knowledge or haven't had practice with writing need a text that talks to them simply, directly, conversationally, with a tone that is encouraging, respectful, and, lighthearted. That's what I want you to find here.

Odyssey

From Paragraph to Essay

Fourth Edition

Annotated Instructor's Edition

William J. Kelly

Bristol Community College

Deborah L. Lawton

Bristol Community College

PEARSON

Longman

New York   San Francisco   Boston
London   Toronto   Sydney   Tokyo   Singapore   Madrid
Mexico City   Munich   Paris   Cape Town   Hong Kong   Montreal

Senior Acquisitions Editor:	Susan Kunchandy
Development Editor:	Lai T. Moy
Senior Marketing Manager:	Melanie Craig
Senior Supplements Editor:	Donna Campion
Media Supplements Editor:	Jenna Egan
Production Manager:	Donna DeBenedictis
Project Coordination, Text Design, and Electronic Page Makeup:	Elm Street Publishing Services, Inc.
Senior Cover Designer/Manager:	Nancy Danahy
Cover Art:	Getty Images
Photo Researcher:	Photosearch, Inc.
Senior Manufacturing Buyer:	Dennis J. Para
Printer and Binder:	Webcrafters, Inc.
Cover Printer:	Coral Graphic Services, Inc.

For permission to use copyrighted material, grateful acknowledgment is made to the copyright holders on p. 614, which is hereby made part of this copyright page.

Library of Congress Cataloging-in-Publication Data

Kelly, William J. (William Jude), 1953–
    Odyssey: from paragraph to essay / William J. Kelly, Deborah L. Lawton.—4th ed.
    p. cm.
    Includes bibliographical references and index.
    ISBN 0-321-33057-9 (annotated instructor's ed. : alk. paper)—ISBN 0-321-29081-X (student ed. : alk. paper)
    1. English language—Rhetoric—Handbooks, manuals, etc. 2. English language—Grammar—Handbooks, manuals, etc. 3. Report writing—Handbooks, manuals, etc. I. Lawton, Deborah L. II. Title.

PE1408.K475 2005
808'.042—dc22

                                                                        2004063812

Please visit us at http://www.ablongman.com/kelly

ISBN 0-321-29081-X (Student Edition)
ISBN 0-321-33057-9 (Annotated Instructor's Edition)

1 2 3 4 5 6 7 8 9 10—WC—08 07 06 05

Dedication

To Matthew and Amy—
With love . . .

To Michelle—
My life couldn't possibly be better—thanks to you.

Detailed Contents

PART 4
Developing Sentence Sense   257

PART 5
Understanding Subjects and Verbs   325

PART 6
Keeping Your Writing Correct   395

CHAPTER 27   Adjectives, Adverbs, and Other Modifiers: Using Describing and Modifying Words Effectively   440

CHAPTER 28   Parallelism: Presenting Related Items in a Similar Form   463

CHAPTER 29   Spelling: Focusing on Correctness   479

CHAPTER 30 Commas   507

CHAPTER 31 Other Punctuation and Capitalization   524

PART 7
Connecting: Responding to Reading   549

Preface

According to scholars, the Greek poet Homer first sang about the wondrous, fantastic travels of the legendary hero Odysseus some time during the eighth century B.C. Over time, the story of Odysseus' adventures had so much impact that its title—*The Odyssey*—came to mean a great journey. Writing is also a great journey, a voyage of self-expression through the world of ideas, which is why this book is titled *Odyssey: From Paragraph to Essay,* Fourth Edition.

The writing adventure begins with a few ideas scribbled on paper or typed across a computer screen. As you write, you tap into your creativity and draw on stored reserves of experience and knowledge. At the same time, you come into contact with the world, learning from the interactions with and reactions of others. Gradually your original ideas evolve and grow. The end result of this journey is a piece of writing that expresses your ideas in simple, clear, direct, complete, and correct terms. Think of *Odyssey* as a guidebook for all the journeys—and all the promise—that writing involves.

Three fundamental beliefs about writing form the foundation for *Odyssey:*

- **Confidence leads to competence.** The more people write, the more comfortable and confident they become with the process. As their confidence grows, so does their competence as writers. Therefore, the best way to learn to write is by writing.
- **Writing well combines sound critical thinking and creativity.** Effectively expressing ideas about a subject on paper involves not only the ability to understand that subject, but also the ability to analyze it from different perspectives. In addition, it also involves articulating key ideas about that subject in an engaging, original voice.
- **Good writing combines engaging content and correct form.** Writing successfully means expressing interesting, universal ideas in accordance to the rules of Standard American English.

To emphasize these three fundamental principles, we have designed a number of special features to help you achieve a greater mastery of writing.

Favorite Features

GETTING STARTED . . .

CW 1.1 Chapter basics

Q: Why do I often find it so much harder to write down something than to say it?

A: Writing often seems harder than speaking because, in most cases, it is. When you write, you face many challenges that you don't face when you speak. For instance, when you talk, you don't need to worry about things like correct spelling or punctuation. Also, if what you say aloud doesn't make sense, your listener can ask you questions. When you write, you don't have that advantage, and that makes the process harder.

"Getting Started" Q&A

All students have questions about writing and the English language. Many students never ask these questions, however, because they think their questions are too simple or too basic to ask. "Getting Started" showcases real questions asked by real students and focuses on the essence of the chapter.

FAST FACT The history of written language extends back at least 5,000 years to the ancient Sumerians.

Fast Facts

Learning about language and writing shouldn't be all hard work. Even the hardest-working writers need playful, entertaining moments to keep them going. "Fast Facts," located at several points in each chapter, fulfill this need and are tied to the chapter content, broadening perspectives about writing and language.

✔ Reader Evaluation Checklist

☐ What does the average reader need to know about _____?

☐ What does the average reader already know about _____?

☐ What information would help the average person better understand _____?

☐ What did I find the hardest to understand about _____ at first?

☐ What helped me to figure out _____?

☐ What's the best example or explanation I can give the average person about _____?

Checklists

Writers don't automatically know how to evaluate their own work or the work of others. Evaluation is a skill that has to be learned. That's why *Odyssey* provides numerous checklists—concrete tools for students to evaluate their own and others' work. Checklists cover proofreading, spelling, each of the rhetorical modes, and many other aspects of writing.

RECAP Ensuring Success in Writing

New terms in this chapter	Definitions
the writing process	the series of stages in writing, including prewriting, composing, revising, and editing
prewriting	when you generate ideas to develop into a piece of writing
composing	when you select and then express in sentence and paragraph form some of your prewriting ideas
revising	when you create new drafts through reexamining, improving, and polishing your initial version

Steps to Writing Effectively

• Understand the stages of the writing process: **prewriting, composing,** and **revising.**

• Understand how the four elements of writing—**writer, reader, topic,** and **means**—interact.

• Focus in particular on the **reader.**

Recaps

These visual summaries appear at the end of each chapter. They review terms presented in the chapter and offer graphic explanations of key concepts.

ESL Note
See "Writing Paragraphs," especially the section on unity, and "Writing Essays" on pages 601–603.

ESL Notes

These cross-references, appearing at relevant points in the margin, direct students to a specialized appendix, full of grammar and usage tips specifically for ESL students, but useful for native speakers as well.

CHAPTER QUICK CHECK Sentence Basics

CW 17.11 Sentence-level editing In each sentence in the following passage, identify all subjects and verbs. Underline each complete subject, and then circle each simple subject. With any compound subjects, circle each of the simple subjects within it. Double underline all verbs, verb phrases, and compound verbs. Put an X in front of any sentence in the imperative mood. Use the example to guide you.

EXAMPLE The (lawyer) with her briefcase and her client with a small notebook had been stopped and searched by the police officer at the door.

(1) Because of a recent technological development, a complete book can be produced in less than an hour. (2) Experts in this field refer to this innovation as Print on Demand and believe strongly in its future. (3) With this tech-

Quick Checks and Summary Exercises

These exercises provide students with all the concepts from a chapter in a single drill. These exercises are found at the end of each chapter in Parts 4, 5, and 6 of the book—where the sentence skills are taught. Quick Checks comprise ten items each and are intended to prepare students for the longer Summary Exercises, which instructors may use to assess student mastery of the chapter material.

CHALLENGE 1.1   Exploring the Writing Process

1. How do you feel about writing? On a separate sheet of paper, briefly explain what you like about writing—and what you don't.

2. Now compare your response with a classmate's. On the following lines, briefly summarize what the two of you have in common regarding writing.

_____

_____

_____

Collaboration

Because writers need feedback, and because two heads are often better than one, this book encourages collaboration. When you see this icon accompanying an exercise, you are asked to work with a partner.

In short, everything you need to master writing is here. Chapter after chapter, you'll find clear explanations and examples, plenty of opportunities to increase your knowledge of grammar and usage and to develop paragraphs and essays, and numerous self-evaluation tools. All will ensure that your journey—your writing odyssey—will be both enjoyable and rewarding.

Organization of the Text

Odyssey's organization fosters cumulative learning. **Part 1, Starting Out**, consists of four chapters that employ various enticing activities to focus on the writing process. Chapter 1, "Ensuring Success in Writing," discusses the essential elements of the writing process and the primary purposes of writing. Chapter 2, "Generating Ideas through Prewriting," introduces and provides facsimile examples of five prewriting activities, and Chapter 3, "Composing: Creating a Draft," discusses and illustrates the entire composing stage of writing, from topic sentence to completed draft, emphasizing the difference between writer-centered and reader-centered ideas. Chapter 4, "Refining and Polishing Your Draft," explains and illustrates each step of the revision stage by showing how a first draft becomes an effective final draft. Presented in sequence, these four chapters provide a solid background in and practice with the writing process.

Part 2, **Using the Patterns of Paragraph Development**, deals with writing paragraphs that feature the traditional rhetorical modes or organizing strategies: narration, description, example, process, definition, comparison and contrast, cause and effect, and division and classification. Chapters 5 through 12 explain and illustrate the specific characteristics of the various modes while also emphasizing the **purpose** or aim in a piece of writing. Chapter 13 covers argument, not as a mode but as a purpose, one that writers use a combination of modes to fulfill.

The three chapters making up **Part 3, Moving On to the Essay**, apply the principles of paragraph writing presented in the first two sections to this more complex and detailed form. Chapter 14, "Developing an Essay," focuses on a single essay, shown at every stage from prewriting ideas to polished final draft. Chapter 15, "Examining Types of Essays," discusses ways to use the rhetorical modes to develop entire essays, with argument again presented as a purpose. Chapter 16, "Adjusting Your Process: Timed Writing and Summaries," presents simple, clear, logical steps to perform well on such writing tasks as taking an essay exam, completing a timed writing assessment, and preparing a summary.

The four chapters in **Part 4, Developing Sentence Sense**, focus on writing correct sentences and avoiding the three most serious sentence errors: fragments, comma splices, and run-on sentences. The four chapters in **Part 5, Understanding Subjects and Verbs**, focus on subject–verb agreement as well as different aspects of verb use. The seven chapters comprising **Part 6, Keeping Your Writing Correct,** deal with other aspects of usage and mechanics. Specific topics include working with nouns, pronouns, and modifiers; maintaining correct parallelism and spelling; using commas and other punctuation; and capitalizing words properly.

Part 7, Connecting: Responding to Reading, is a brief anthology of fifteen readings, including seven pieces by professional writers such as Amy Tan, Judith Ortiz Cofer, and Deborah Tannen and eight writings by students, each accompanied by questions that promote critical thinking, discussion, and writing.

Two practical appendices supplement the lessons in the text. Appendix A, "Tips for ESL Writers," intended for nonnative speakers of English, but useful also for native speakers, covers selected aspects of grammar and usage that ESL students often find confusing. Appendix B, "Exploring the Dictionary," emphasizes good dictionary and vocabulary-building skills through use of a sample dictionary entry as well as stimulating exercises.

New in This Edition

Beginning with the first edition of *Odyssey,* we have had one primary goal: to create the most accessible, practical, efficient, and appealing writing text possible. To make this Fourth Edition even better than the previous volumes, we used and evaluated the text ourselves. We also considered what our students had to say in order to find the best way to meet their needs to an even greater degree. Of course, we also queried colleagues across the nation for their reactions and guidance. This collective wisdom has led to a number of significant changes in this edition of *Odyssey,* including

- Revised and redesigned chapter introductions for even greater clarity.
- Strengthened attention throughout the text to the importance of *purpose* in writing.
- More than double the number of opportunities for writing at the paragraph and essay level—individually and collaboratively—than in the previous edition.
- Revamped exercises on all aspects of writing, grammar, and usage.
- Revised Challenge exercises, offering the opportunity for critical thinking, application of writing principles, and collaboration.
- Five new reading selections, including three new student writings.

New and revised features include

- **Navigating This Chapter.** Gives an overview of the chapter's main points.
- **"Going Forward" Q&A.** Intended to complement the chapter-opening "Getting Started" Q&A, this new chapter-closing question reviews the material students have just learned in the chapter and answers the question, "How will what I just learned in this chapter help me in the next chapter?"

Navigating this Chapter

This chapter will explore the basic requirements for writing an effective narrative paragraph:

- providing a topic sentence that establishes a context
- explaining the events in the story in chronological order
- recognizing the most effective point of view

GETTING STARTED . . .

Q: I want to tell the story of something that happened to me. What's the best technique to use to tell someone else this story?

A: When you want to tell about an experience you have had—or, for that matter, an experience that you witnessed someone else have—the answer is **narration,** the organizing strategy through which you relate a series of events.

GOING FORWARD...

CW 5.9
Narration
review

Q: How can I make the story of what happened to me clear and easy for my leader to follow?

A: To ensure that your reader understands the story you are telling, first identify the specific incident and then tell it as fully as you recall it and in the order in which it happened. Once you do, you'll be all set.

QUICK STUDY | **Student Example**

This chapter focuses on three common applications of writing. Two involve dealing with the pressure of time. The third involves condensing something without losing the essence of the original. Here is a paragraph on a related subject—an experience when a shortage of time led to a serious mistake:

FOR FURTHER EXPLORATION

CW 1.14
Writing
processes

Focus on one of the following writing topics. Consider the subject, thinking what someone else might need in order to understand what you are thinking, and write down these examples and details. At the same time, identify and write down what you expect your primary purpose would be. Save this work for possible later use.

- the difficulties that a first-year college student might face
- a funny incident that happened to you or that you witnessed
- the ideal way to spend a rainy day

COMPREHENSION AND PRACTICE 1.2 | **Considering the Roles of Reading and Purpose in Writing**

1. How does understanding the purposes underlying a piece of writing help you as a writer?

CHALLENGE 1.2 Focusing on the Importance of Reading and Purpose in Writing

1. Of all the different documents you've read in your life—novels, magazine or newspaper stories, plays, essays, children's books, textbooks, and so on—which one stands out the most? On a separate sheet of paper, identify this document and the approach and techniques the writer followed to make the text so memorable for you.

2. Take another look at the paragraph on Reality Television on pages 4–5. On a separate sheet of paper, identify its main purpose and any secondary purposes, explaining what examples and details led you to these conclusions.

▶ **DISCOVERING CONNECTIONS**

What do you think of when you look at this picture? The scene captured in this picture is from a celebratory event. Based on the details in the picture, how would you classify the type of event being celebrated? Is it a holiday of some kind? Is it someone's birthday? Is it a cultural celebration? What makes you think so? The picture depicts five large masks striking slightly different poses or decorated differently. In the center is a single man. Why do you think the elements in this image are separated the way they are?

For this assignment, consider one of these questions or some other question the picture suggests. Using the information in this chapter to guide you, write a paragraph of at least five to ten sentences in which you employ division and classification to examine your topic in detail. As you create your paragraph, concentrate on key factors such as a logical method of analysis, a consistent presentation, and distinct and complete groupings. ◀

- **Quick Studies.** Also new to the Fourth Edition of *Odyssey,* these student paragraphs appear just before the Chapter Quick Checks in the grammar chapters (Chapters 16–31) and serve as models of correct grammar usage. They also provide several topics for *paragraph* development.

- **For Further Exploration.** These new writing assignments provide several topics for *essay* development and appear at the end of every chapter of the book. Both the Quick Studies and For Further Exploration assignments offer opportunities for individual and collaborative work as well.

- **Comprehension and Practice.** These activities, called simply "Exercises" in the Third Edition of *Odyssey,* have been renamed to help students and instructors distinguish between two types of exercises. Comprehension and Practice activities are intended to check students' understanding of a concept and to provide stimulating practice with the principles just presented. Almost all comprise complete pieces of discourse—brief writings with a clear opening, supporting details, and an effective closing. Therefore, they have the added advantage of serving as models for good writing.

- **Challenges.** The second type of exercise, "Challenge," has been revised to be consistently collaborative and to emphasize the keys to becoming successful writers: critical thinking, drafting, and revising. These writing activities give students the opportunity to apply what they've learned *up to that point in the book* by doing their own writing, thus giving them the opportunity to move to the next level of expertise.

- **Discovering Connections.** Located in the writing process and rhetorical modes chapters (1–15), these writing activities have been revised to always include a travel- or culture-related photo prompt, which is then followed by provocative questions to help students generate ideas for paragraphs and essays based on the material in the given chapter.

CW 9.4
Understanding
the pattern of
an effective
definition

- **Odyssey Online.** The technology advantage of the previous edition is now available in one convenient location: online! Annotated compass icons direct students to diagnostic tests, peer collaboration forms, additional exercises on important grammatical topics, editing tests, ESL worksheets, and Internet activities. Log onto **www.ablongman.com/odyssey4e** for video tutorials as well.

Supplements

For Instructors

The Annotated Instructor's Edition (AIE). The answers to all exercises in the student text are printed directly in the textbook itself for ease of use.

The Instructor's Manual and *Test Bank.* This supplement was prepared by Nadine Roberts, Three Rivers Community College, and offers teaching tips, sample syllabi, and a wealth of additional material for instructors of developmental English. Reproducible, easily graded quizzes for each chapter in the text are also provided.

The Longman Instructor's Planner. This planner includes weekly and monthly calendars, student attendance and grading rosters, space for contact information, Web references, an almanac, and blank pages for notes.

Printed Test Bank for Developmental Writing. Features more than 5,000 questions in all areas of writing, from grammar to paragraphing through essay writing, research, and documentation.

Electronic Test Bank for Developmental Writing. Features more than 5,000 questions in all areas of writing, from grammar to paragraphing through essay writing, research, and documentation. Instructors simply choose questions from the electronic test bank, then print out the completed test for distribution OR offer the test online.

Diagnostic and Editing Tests, **Seventh Edition.** This collection of diagnostic tests helps instructors assess students' competence in standard written English to determine placement or to gauge progress.

For Students

www.ablongman.com/odyssey4e. Log onto the Companion Website for diagnostic tests, additional exercises, video tutorials, and much more.

MySkillsLab 2.0 (www.ablongman/myskillslab). This exciting new Web site houses all the media tools any developmental English student will need to improve his or her reading, writing, and study skills, and all in one easy-to-use place. MySkillsLab 2.0 is available with any Longman title. MSL 2.0 contains the following for writing instruction:

Writing Diagnostics. Students can take a general Writing Voyage diagnostic that shows them which level of Writing Voyage to begin on, or take a Writing Skills diagnostic that targets specific areas for development, such as grammar, punctuation, reasoning, style, etc.

Writing Voyage. is an exciting new online writing resource, suitable for use with virtually any developmental writing text. Students develop their critical writing skills as they learn about the world, visiting exciting cities and viewing extraordinary landscapes. Students can read along as they listen to other students' writing strategies; watch animated video of other students as they write, revise, and edit; check their understanding of each concept with "Quick Check" quizzes on each page; and, as they progress from one lesson to the next, practice with numerous writing exercises designed to strengthen their writing skills with sentences, paragraphs, and essays.

Longman Online Handbook. This is a concise online handbook that provides in-depth explanations for the grammar points tested in Writing Voyage and ExerciseZone, as well as "Check Your Understanding" activities.

ExerciseZone. This is an interactive test bank of practice exercises designed to help college students improve their grammar, punctuation, mechanics, and usage skills. Key features include more than 2,500 exercises in ten practice topics that most frequently give students difficulty; diagnostic self-tests for each of the ten topics to identify individual strengths and weaknesses; and automatic grading to provide immediate feedback.

ESL ExerciseZone. For students whose first language is not English, or students who grew up in a multilingual environment, ESL ExerciseZone contains nearly 1,000 entries organized into ten question practice sets, targeted at areas most troublesome for speakers of multiple language.

Longman Study Skills Web Site. This site offers self-assessment quizzes to identify specific study and organization skills in need of development; learning style assessment to help students identify how they learn; helpful checklists, weekly schedules, and time management outlines; and more.

Exchange. This is Longman's online peer and instructor writing review program, and it allows instructors to comment on student papers at the word, sentence, or paper level or have students review each other's work in peer review groups.

Penguin Discount Novel Program. In cooperation with Penguin Putnam, Inc., Longman is proud to offer a variety of Penguin paperbacks at a significant discount when packaged with any Longman title. Excellent additions to any Developmental Reading or English course, Penguin titles give students the opportunity to explore contemporary and classical fiction and drama. The available titles include works by authors as diverse as Toni Morrison, Julia Alvarez, Mary Shelley, and Shakespeare. To review the complete list of titles available, visit **http://www.ablongman.com/penguin**, the Longman-Penguin-Putnam Web site.

***The Oxford American Desk Dictionary and Thesaurus,* Second Edition.** From the Oxford University Press and Berkley Publishing Group comes this one-of-a-kind reference book that combines both of the essential language tools—dictionary and thesaurus—in a single, integrated A-to-Z volume. The 1,024-page book offers more than 150,000 entries, definitions, and synonyms so you can find the right word every time, as well as appendixes of valuable quick-reference information including signs and symbols, weights and measures, presidents of the United States, U.S. states and capitals, and more.

The Longman Writer's Portfolio and Student Planner. This unique supplement provides students with a space to plan, think about, and present their work. In addition to the yearly planner, this portfolio includes an assessing/organizing area (including a grammar diagnostic test, a spelling quiz, and project planning worksheets), a before- and during-writing area (including peer review sheets, editing checklists, writing self-evaluations, and a personal editing profile), and an after-writing area (including a progress chart, a final table of contents, and a final assessment).

The Longman Writer's Journal, **by Mimi Markus.** Provides students with their own personal space for writing and contains helpful journal writing strategies, sample journal entries by other students, and many writing prompts and topics to get students writing.

State-Specific Supplements

For Florida Adopters

Thinking Through the Test: A Study Guide for the Florida College Basic Skills Exit Tests, with Answers. Featuring both diagnostic tests and exit exams, this study guide helps lessen student anxiety and strengthens their skills as they prepare for the exit tests. This guide is also available without answers.

Writing Skills Summary for the Florida State Exit Exam, **by D. J. Henry.** An excellent study tool for students preparing to take the Florida College Basic Skills Exit Test for Writing, this writing grid summarizes all the skills tested on the Exit Exam.

For Texas Adopters

The Longman THEA Study Guide, **by Jeannette Harris.** Created specifically for students in Texas, this study guide includes straightforward explanations and numerous practice exercises to help students prepare for the reading and writing sections of the THEA Test.

For New York/CUNY Adopters

Preparing for the CUNY-ACT Reading and Writing Test, **edited by Patricia Licklider.** This booklet, prepared by reading and writing faculty from across the CUNY system, is designed to help students prepare for the CUNY-ACT exit test. It includes test-taking tips, reading passages, typical exam questions, and sample writing prompts to help students become familiar with each portion of the test.

Acknowledgments

We would like to thank a number of people who offered their guidance and direction as we worked on this Fourth Edition of *Odyssey: From Paragraph to Essay.* First, we say thanks to John M. Lannon, University of Massachusetts, Dartmouth (retired); Robert A. Schwegler, University of Rhode Island; and Paul Arakelian, University of Rhode Island, for being such great teachers, great writers, and great friends.

We also offer thanks to a number of people at Bristol Community College for their ongoing support. We are particularly grateful to our students for all that they have taught us over the years. We offer special thanks to the students who allowed us to include their work in this text. We are particularly grateful to the students who allowed us to include their work in this edition: Greg Andree, Stephanie Jezak, Lori Ann Moyer, Erica Nardi, Jane Palenaude, Diane Riva, Josh Trepanier, and Naihsin Weng. Thanks also to our colleagues at BCC for their continuing interest in our work, including Catherine Adamowicz, Debra Anderson, Sally Cameron, David Feeney, Tom Grady, Jeanne Grandchamp, Penny Hahn, Jerry LePage, Arthur Lothrop, Diana McGee, Linda Mulready, Joe Murphy, and Michael Vieira. Thanks also to Jack R. Warner, Commissioner of Higher Education for Rhode Island. In particular, we offer thanks to Paul F. Fletcher, Professor Emeritus of English and retired Assistant Dean for Language, Humanities, and the Arts. During our careers, Paul has taught us so much about teaching and about treating both students and colleagues with kindness and respect.

Of course, suggestions made by a number of top professionals across the country have greatly improved *Odyssey,* and we sincerely thank them for their help. They include Gloria Bailey, Santa Ana College; Cynthia Catherwood, Metro Community College; Ray Foster, Scottsdale Community College; Larry Speight, Three Rivers Community College; and Mary N. Stchur, Luzerne Community College.

We also salute the fine team at Longman who have devoted their considerable talents to make this Edition of *Odyssey* so attractive. We thank Senior Acquisitions Editor Susan Kunchandy for her enthusiasm and desire to make *Odyssey* the best book of its type. We are particularly grateful for the work of Development Editor Lai Moy, who has worked so hard to make our work look so good. In addition, Donna DeBenedictis, Production Manager, and Sue Nodine, Project Editor for Elm Street Publishing Services, Inc., have done a superb job of transforming the manuscript into its final form. All in all, the Fourth Edition of *Odyssey* couldn't have been in better hands at any stage in its development.

And finally, we would like to thank our friends and family for supporting us and our work. Debbie Lawton would like to thank her Border friends, Mary Beth, Judy, Tom, Barbara, and Michele, for their friendship and support. Above all, she would like to thank her family for their love and encouragement. Her parents,

Charles and Virginia Soucy, and her mother-in-law, Elizabeth McCleskey, have always been nearby to lend a helping hand or to give a pat on the back. She has learned much watching her children, Matthew and Amy, grow to adulthood. Her husband, Kevin, continues to be the spirit that guides her in both her work and in life and to him she owes her greatest thanks.

Bill Kelly would first like to offer thanks to his parents, the late Mary R. and Edward F. Kelly, for the love and support they offered Bill and his three brothers. The education that they worked so hard to provide established a foundation for future success. His parents-in-law, Flo and Leo Nadeau, also deserve great thanks for their continued and consistent belief in Bill and in his work. He offers special thanks to his sons-in-law, Timothy Matos and Jeremy Wright, and his daughters, Nicole Matos and Jacqueline Wright, for their love, inspiration, and hours of mirth. But he reserves the greatest thanks for his wife, Michelle Nadeau Kelly. She entered his life more than 33 years ago and transformed it. Her love and support have made this text—and the rest of his work—possible, a debt impossible to calculate or repay.

WILLIAM J. KELLY
DEBORAH L. LAWTON

About the Authors

William J. Kelly earned his Ph.D. in English from the University of Rhode Island. He also received an M.A. in English from Rhode Island College and a B.A. in English from Southeastern Massachusetts University (now the University of Massachusetts, Dartmouth). A classroom teacher since 1975, he began his career teaching junior high school and high school English in the Fall River (MA) Public Schools. In 1984, he joined the English Department at Bristol Community College and five years later became the youngest full professor in the history of the college. In addition to his teaching at BCC, he has enjoyed a three-year stint writing a weekly newspaper column and presented numerous teacher training workshops and graduate courses in the teaching of writing. In 1997, the Carnegie Foundation for the Advancement of Teaching and the Council for Advancement and Support of Education named him Massachusetts Professor of the Year, the first and only time a community college professor in the state has received this prestigious award. He is the author of several other texts, including Longman's *Discovery: From Sentence to Paragraph; Strategy and Structure: Short Readings for Composition;* and *Intersections: Readings for College and Beyond.* A runner for more than 30 years, he is also an avid handball player. He lives in Fall River with his wife, Michelle; they are the parents of two daughters, Nicole C. Matos, an instructor of college literature and writing (and co-author of *Intersections*), and Jacqueline M. Wright, a flutist and graduate student in music, concentrating on conducting.

Deborah L. Lawton has been an advocate of the community college mission for more than 20 years. Her professional life at Bristol Community College has included 5 years as a student affairs professional and 20 years as an instructor of writing, literature, and communication. She is currently Associate Professor of English, and as Assistant Dean, she leads the college's Division of Language, Humanities and the Arts. She holds an M.A. in English from Western Michigan University, a B.A. in English from the University of Massachusetts, Amherst, and an A.A. in Liberal Arts from Greenfield Community College in Greenfield, Massachusetts. She and her husband, Kevin, residents of Swansea, Massachusetts, are the parents of Matt and Amy.

Odyssey

Annotated Instructor's Edition

PART 1

Starting Out

USING ODYSSEY ONLINE

All the multimedia activities once available on CD are now available online! Annotated compass icons throughout the book direct you to the improved and expanded Companion Website. Here you will find diagnostic tests, additional grammar exercises, peer collaboration forms, Internet activities, and much more.

CHAPTER 1
Ensuring Success in Writing

▶ Navigating This Chapter

On this first leg of your excursion into the world of ideas, you will discover the basic elements of writing:

- the three stages of the writing process—prewriting, composing, and revising
- the four interacting components of writing—writer, reader, message, and means
- the purposes of writing—to inform, to entertain, and to persuade

GETTING STARTED...

CW 1.1
Chapter basics

Q: Why do I often find it so much harder to write down something than to say it?

A: Writing often seems harder than speaking because, in most cases, it is. When you write, you face many challenges that you don't face when you speak. For instance, when you talk, you don't need to worry about things like correct spelling or punctuation. Also, if what you say aloud doesn't make sense, your listener can ask you questions. When you write, you don't have that advantage, and that makes the process harder.

Overview: Understanding the Importance of Good Writing Skills

CW 1.2
Overview of good writing skills

Odyssey, an extended, adventurous journey, is the ideal word to describe what happens when you write. On this odyssey, you will discover the power of your ideas and the connections between them. You'll also learn to express your ideas more effectively and to develop greater skills in terms of usage, spelling, and punctuation. When you express your good ideas clearly, directly, and correctly in the classroom, you will earn better grades. When you do the same thing at work, you will inspire the respect of your colleagues and supervisors, ensuring your success as a professional. It's that simple.

FAST FACT The history of written language extends back at least 5,000 years to the ancient Sumerians.

Recognizing the Stages of the Writing Process

A successful piece of writing is much more than the words you see on a piece of paper. Writing is more than the final product. It is a *process,* one that consists of three stages: *prewriting, composing,* and *revising.*

Prewriting is the first stage of the writing process. Think of prewriting as planning. No one would expect a musician, artist, or athlete to perform at top level without some kind of rehearsal, exploration, or warm-up. The same is true of a writer. When you prewrite, you generate ideas on a subject that you can then develop into a piece of writing. Any activity that enables you to examine a subject more closely, for example, thinking, reading, talking to or observing others, can be a good technique. Chapter 2, "Generating Ideas through Prewriting," discusses and illustrates a number of other, more structured prewriting activities.

The next stage of the writing process is **composing.** During composing, you take the ideas generated during prewriting, express them in correct sentences, and then arrange them in paragraph form. Chapter 3, "Composing: Creating a Draft," explains this part of the writing process.

The third stage of the writing process is **revising.** As Chapter 4, "Refining and Polishing Your Draft," illustrates, a final piece of writing actually develops from several earlier versions, called **drafts.** Think of revising as **reseeing.** When you revise, you reexamine and then return to the earlier stages of the writing process, each time creating a more effective draft.

The following figure illustrates the process:

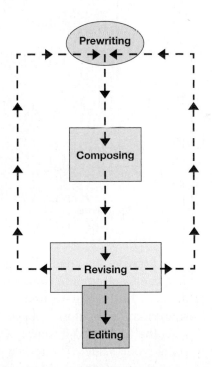

When you write, you begin with prewriting, move to composing, and shift to revising. As you can see, however, the arrows in the illustration flow back from revising to prewriting. Then the arrows continue through composing, leading eventually through revising and editing. That's because the writing process is *recursive.* In other words, as you write, you may move back as well as forward through the process in order to make a piece of writing as effective as possible. For example, if during revision you notice that your draft needs more detail in order to make your point clearer and easier to understand, you return to prewriting to generate new ideas and then move again to composing to develop those ideas into supporting sentences.

Understanding the Dynamics of Writing

CW 1.3
Understanding academic writing

Writing involves four interacting components: (1) a **writer,** the person expressing ideas; (2) a **reader** or **audience,** the person or persons receiving the ideas; (3) a **message,** the writer's **topic** and supporting ideas about it; and (4) the **means,** the expressive form the message takes—written language. The following communications triangle illustrates the interaction among these four components:

CW 1.4
The communication triangle

In this triangle, the shaded portion on the left half represents what you as the writer know and want to communicate about your message. Your job as the writer is to use the means—written language—to communicate what you want your reader to know about the subject.

As the triangle also shows, when you write, a division always exists between you and your reader. The reason for the separation is simple: You have a specific degree of knowledge about your subject, a level of understanding and insight that your reader probably won't have. To overcome this division, you have to figure out what your reader doesn't know, and then include examples and details that will help your reader understand your subject.

CW 1.5
Summarizing the communication triangle

So how do these four elements interact in a piece of writing? Imagine you have written the following paragraph on the subject of reality television shows:

> A successful and controversial innovation in television programming is Reality TV. Reality shows feature so-called ordinary people as they interact in situations and locales arranged by the producers. MTV is

sometimes credited with beginning this trend with its show The Real World. On this show, several people from diverse backgrounds were brought together to share a house and try to get along. But reality television hit the mainstream with the introduction of Survivor, which involved teams of people of different ages and experiences living in some deserted area. They engaged in staged events while they tried to avoid being voted off the island by the other participants. The popularity of the first series led to additional editions of Survivor as well as other shows based on the same theme such as Fear Factor and The Apprentice. Some people have criticized reality shows, saying that they highlight people's greed and bad behavior. But right now, the popularity of reality shows means they will be around for a while.

CW 1.6
The principle
of composition

You've written the piece, so you are the **writer.** Your **message** is the information you have included about the popularity of Reality TV and the controversy it has sparked. The **means** of communicating your ideas is written language—the words, examples, and details you have included. And your **reader** is the person or persons to whom you are directing this information.

Focusing on the Reader

As a writer, you need to concentrate primarily on your reader. If your writing doesn't communicate to a reader, then it's not effective. It's that simple.

Sometimes you will know exactly who your reader is. For example, if you are writing a follow-up letter after a job interview, you know that the reader will be the person who interviewed you.

However, for much of the writing you'll do, your reader won't be so clearly identified. In these cases, you must imagine a reader. It may help to think of a specific person, someone you know slightly but not well. The danger in using someone close to you is that you share too much common knowledge. Unless you assume that you are writing to a stranger, you may omit information necessary to communicate with your actual readers.

CW 1.7
Focusing on
the reader

CW 1.8
Considering
the audience

Sometimes you may find it easier to focus on **the average reader.** Think of yourself *before* you learned detailed information about your subject. The average reader is just like you were. What kinds and degree of information did you need to know? The average reader needs the same type of examples and details.

For example, imagine that you have just signed up for high-speed broadband Internet service. Before you signed up, you didn't really understand the difference between high-speed service and dial-up Internet service. After doing a little research, you discovered that unlike dial-up service, high-speed Internet service doesn't rely on a personal telephone line. This difference means that a high-speed user won't face the kinds of interruptions of phone use and disconnections that frequently occur with dial-up service. In addition, high-speed service means instant access to the Internet and much faster download speeds. Of course, you also discovered that high-speed service costs more—in some cases, more than twice as much per month. Such details help the average reader make the right choice of Internet service. As this scenario demonstrates, the average reader needs as much detailed information as possible to fully understand a given situation.

It's especially important to keep the needs of the average reader in mind when your subject is personal, unusual, or complex. These topics may seem easy or ordinary to you, but that's because of the background knowledge you've already developed. Personal, unusual, or complex subjects won't be so familiar for most readers, however. To help reduce this unfamiliarity, you, as a writer, should provide the kinds of details and examples that enabled you to understand the subject in the first place.

CW 1.9
Understanding different audiences

COMPREHENSION AND PRACTICE 1.1

Considering the Stages and Dynamics of Writing

1. Why do writers move back and forth through the stages of the writing process as they develop a piece of writing?

   Writing is a recursive activity. As writers discover gaps or problems in their writing,

   they return to prewriting to generate information to address these problems and then

   to composing to transform these new ideas into sentences.

2. How do you overcome the barrier in terms of level of knowledge that separates writer and reader?

   You need to consider what the average reader needs to know in order to understand

   the topic. You can think of your own needs when you first learned about the subject or

   focus on the average reader.

3. Why is focusing on the average reader often a better choice than writing for a close relative or friend?

   It's better to think of the average reader than a close relative or friend, because a

   close relative or friend shares some of the same knowledge as you. As a result, you

   might not include things you should.

CW 1.10
Why do students write?

4. Look again at the paragraph about Reality Television on pages 4–5. What level of understanding about this kind of programming do you think the writer has about the reader of this document?

   The writer has a good understanding of this kind of programming, as evidenced by

   the many specific references.

CHALLENGE 1.1 Exploring the Writing Process

1. How do you feel about writing? On a separate sheet of paper, briefly explain what you like about writing—and what you don't.

2. Now compare your response with a classmate's. On the following lines, briefly summarize what the two of you have in common regarding writing.

Answers will vary.

_____

_____

3. Working with a classmate, make two lists on a separate sheet of paper. In one column, write down at least four things that strong writing skills would enable you to do. In the second, list at least four problems that you or others would face because of weak writing skills.

4. Consider everything you understand about the topic *the Internet*. On the following lines, list three details you have thought of that you feel most readers would know, and explain why you think they would know these things.

Answers will vary. Likely choices will include such characteristics as communicating

rapidly, downloading pictures and music, and gaining access to information on any

subject.

Examining the Purpose behind Your Writing

CW 1.11
Finding the purpose of a writing assignment

When people write, they fulfill three main **purposes** or aims: *to inform, to entertain,* or *to persuade.* A paper explaining the effects of lead poisoning in children, for example, would inform. So would a paper spelling out how to build a stone wall.

A paper about attending a concert or sporting event would clearly entertain. Not all writing that entertains makes you laugh, however. A story about the break-up of a relationship would also entertain because it would arouse your reader's interest and emotions.

An essay suggesting that world powers should work together to reduce harmful emissions from fossil fuels would be persuasive. So would one suggesting that the United States should have a national health care program. As a college writer, you'll frequently be called upon to prepare persuasive writings or *arguments.* Writing that persuades can be particularly challenging. For this reason, Chapter 13 is devoted entirely to ways to develop an effective argument paragraph. In addition, a section of Chapter 15 explains ways to write an effective argument essay.

CW 1.12
Using verbs to identify purpose

Often your purposes in writing overlap. An informative paper on lead poisoning might also entertain if it draws in the reader by describing specific cases. It might also be persuasive if it claims that more research money should be devoted to discovering ways to reverse the effects of the poisoning. Although one purpose may be primary, most papers fulfill more than one purpose.

Often students don't think much about the primary purpose of their writing because it is dictated by the assignment. However, you should always take a moment to identify that purpose, because purpose determines what you include and also influences the style and tone you adopt.

For example, imagine that your instructor asks you to write a paper that outlines some of the difficulties a first-semester college student might encounter. The primary purpose is to inform. If you instead write a paper in which you assert that college students today have greater opportunities to explore careers than ever before, the paper won't fulfill the primary purpose. Moreover, it won't meet the needs of your reader, who expects different content.

FAST FACT When it comes to spoken and written communication, the world is becoming smaller every day, as many languages begin to disappear from use. In fact, among the world's 6,800 languages spoken today, linguists believe that 50 to 90 percent could be extinct by the end of this century.

Understanding the Important Relationship between Writing and Reading

One of the best ways to improve as a writer doesn't actually involve writing anything. Rather, it has to do with reading. When you read, whether it is an essay, a textbook, a newspaper or magazine, and so on, you immerse yourself in the world of words. As Part 7, "Connecting: Responding to Reading" (pages 594–588), indicates, reading actively enables you to uncover the significance or importance of what a writer is saying.

But just as important, reading critically puts you in the position to notice the way other writers present their ideas. You'll begin to notice how they arrange their sentences, how they structure documents, and how they begin and end them. Once you begin to identify different strategies, you'll be in the position to use them yourself. Just by reading carefully, you'll develop a **writing awareness** that will result in more effective papers.

CW 1.13 Analyzing the writing situation

COMPREHENSION AND PRACTICE 1.2

Considering the Roles of Reading and Purpose in Writing

1. How does understanding the purposes underlying a piece of writing help you as a writer?

Understanding the purposes underlying a piece of writing helps you as a writer

because it simplifies the task of choosing the appropriate information to include.

2. How would you explain the relationship between reading carefully and improving as a writer?

When you read carefully, you see how writers develop and present their ideas. In

other words, you will develop a greater writing awareness.

3. Read the following paragraph:

> Recent statistics indicate that more than 50 percent of all marriages in the United States end in divorce. This phenomenon has far-reaching implications, especially for the children of these broken families. In particular, many of these children experience trouble in school. Guidance counselors have reported cases in which elementary school children became distant and cold after their parents divorced. High school students who have experienced divorce often challenge authority and demonstrate increased aggression at school and at home. Overall, divorce usually spells at least a temporary drop in classroom productivity.

    a. What is the *primary* purpose of this paragraph? What details and examples in the paragraph led you to this answer?

The primary purpose of the paragraph is to inform, as illustrated by the various

statistics about divorce and children.

    b. Does it fulfill other purposes as well? Explain your reasoning on the following lines.

The paragraph also persuades. It provides much evidence indicating that divorce

can be harmful to children.

CHALLENGE 1.2　Focusing on the Importance of Reading and Purpose in Writing

1. Of all the different documents you've read in your life—novels, magazine or newspaper stories, plays, essays, children's books, textbooks, and so on—which one stands out the most? On a separate sheet of paper, identify this document and the approach and techniques the writer followed to make the text so memorable for you.

2. Take another look at the paragraph on Reality Television on pages 4–5. On a separate sheet of paper, identify its main purpose and any secondary purposes, explaining what examples and details led you to these conclusions.

COLLABORATION

3. Working with a partner, choose one of the following three subjects:
   - a New Year's Eve party
   - a job interview
   - a popular vacation destination

Now, list details and examples you might include in a paper on this topic that fulfills each of the following purposes:

a. to inform

Answers will vary. If students choose a New Year's Eve party, they might describe

how to prepare for one or how the party evolved or the party's purpose.

b. to entertain

Answers will vary. Students might describe some amusing incidents from New

Year's Eve parties, or they might describe the most unusual party they ever

attended.

c. to persuade

Answers will vary. Students could use examples of successful or unsuccessful

parties to persuade readers to give or not to give their own New Year's Eve party.

FOR FURTHER EXPLORATION

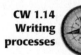

CW 1.14 Writing processes

Focus on one of the following writing topics. Consider the subject, thinking what someone else might need in order to understand what you are thinking, and write down these examples and details. At the same time, identify and write down what you expect your primary purpose would be. Save this work for possible later use.

- the difficulties that a first-year college student might face
- a funny incident that happened to you or that you witnessed
- the ideal way to spend a rainy day

▶ **DISCOVERING CONNECTIONS**

What comes to mind when you look at this picture? Do you think of the past in general and what we can learn from it? Does the image inspire you to imagine what life was like in a country in a time and a location far away from your own? Does it make you think of the power of art—or of religion? Or does it make you wish you could head out on an odyssey to explore this or some other exotic country?

For this assignment, consider one of these questions or some other one that the picture suggests. Using the material in this chapter to guide you, jot down what you think an average reader would need to know in order to understand your thoughts. At the same time, write down the primary purpose you expect your paper would fulfill. Then, drawing on the ideas you've developed, prepare a draft paragraph of at least five to ten sentences. ◀

RECAP Ensuring Success in Writing

New terms in this chapter	Definitions
the writing process	the series of stages in writing, including prewriting, composing, revising, and editing
prewriting	when you generate ideas to develop into a piece of writing
composing	when you select and then express in sentence and paragraph form some of your prewriting ideas
revising	when you create new drafts through reexamining, improving, and polishing your initial version
draft	version of a paper
writer	the person expressing ideas through the written word
reader	the audience to whom a paper is directed
topic	the subject of a paper
message	the supporting examples, details, and explanations that represent your understanding of the topic
means	the written language used to express ideas
purpose	the intent or aim of a paper
average reader	a device to help you meet the needs of a reader that involves envisioning your level of knowledge before you learned what you now know about a subject
writing awareness	a recognition as you read a document of devices and strategies that other writers have used

(continued)

Steps to Writing Effectively

- Understand the stages of the writing process: **prewriting, composing,** and **revising.**

- Understand how the four elements of writing—**writer, reader, topic,** and **means**—interact.

- Focus in particular on the **reader.**

- Recognize the **purpose** of any writing assignment.

    to *inform*—as in a paper explaining how a movie special effect is created
    to *entertain*—as in a paper recalling the first time you drove a car
    to *persuade*—as in a paper asserting that recycling should be mandatory throughout the United States

GOING FORWARD...

**CW 1.15
Ensuring
success in
writing
review**

**CW 1.16
Writing as a
process**

Q: So what can I do to feel as comfortable with writing something as I am with saying it?

A: A great way to start is to focus on the points discussed in this chapter—the **stages of the writing process,** the **dynamics of writing,** the **purpose of writing,** and the **relationship between writing and reading.** In particular, think of your **reader.** If you *anticipate* the questions your audience will have about your subject and answer them, you'll find that communicating your ideas in writing becomes much easier.

CHAPTER 2
Generating Ideas through Prewriting

Navigating This Chapter

On this portion of your odyssey, you will learn how to use the following prewriting techniques:

- freewriting
- brainstorming
- clustering
- branching
- idea mapping
- keeping a journal

GETTING STARTED...

**CW 2.1
Chapter
basics**

Q: I want to write—I really do. I'm just not sure how to start. Why can it seem so hard to begin?

A: Beginning to write can seem difficult for several good reasons. Some people feel as if they have too much to say on the subject, much more than they could ever organize and express in a piece of writing. Other people find that the vision they hold of the final writing—a completed, effective paper—contrasts so much with the rough ideas from which they will develop the paper that they become overwhelmed and intimidated. Still others feel that they have nothing to say.

Overview: Seeing Prewriting as a Way to Explore Ideas

**CW 2.2
Overview of
prewriting**

As Chapter 1 discusses, writing is an odyssey through the world of ideas, an excursion to explore the world around you and your relationship to it. As you develop your writing skills, you also develop your creativity and powers of analysis. Through writing, you discover the significance of your ideas and explore the connections among them. This chapter will explore the most creative stage of writing: **prewriting**—the launch of an exciting journey to a new place.

Understanding Prewriting

**CW 2.3
Understanding
prewriting**

Actually, you have already begun to explore *prewriting*. In the exercises of Chapter 1, you thought of ideas to communicate what you know about a topic. That activity was one form of prewriting.

**CW 2.4
Getting
started with
writing**

Prewriting is the first stage in the writing process. When you write, you begin with prewriting and proceed to the other two stages, *composing* and *revising*. The real work for any piece of writing, however, always begins with prewriting. In order to explain your understanding of a topic, you have to generate ideas that will express that understanding for your reader. Through prewriting, you can discover what you think and know and develop these ideas about your subject.

Most writers use a number of informal prewriting activities, such as talking (either with other people or alone into a tape recorder), doodling, and thinking. However, experienced writers also use other, more specific techniques, including *freewriting, brainstorming, clustering, branching, idea mapping,* and *maintaining a journal.*

As you read about the different techniques, try them all out. That way, you'll know which technique—or which combination of techniques—is best for you.

Freewriting

**CW 2.5
freewriting
advantage**

Freewriting is a no-holds-barred prewriting technique that involves writing down all your ideas on a subject for a set period of time. Ten minutes is a typical period. To freewrite, simply write everything that comes to your mind, even if it contains errors, drifts from the original subject, or doesn't immediately make sense. Don't stop, even if you get stuck. Instead, write something like, "I can't think" or "I'm stuck here," or find a rhyme for the last word you've written until a new idea comes to your mind. The strength of this method is its ability to help you overcome inhibitions and concerns and to get your ideas starting to flow.

If you do your writing on a computer, you will discover that it is an excellent tool for freewriting. First, set up your program to triple-space your document. If you'd like, darken the screen so that you cannot see what you write. This may make you feel less inhibited. Now you can simply type away on your keyboard for ten minutes. When you are finished, print out what you have written.

A freewriting on a subject such as *a souvenir* might look like this:

A souvenir-weird word it sounds French-I'll have to look it up to see. I know it means a special memento. I'm a packrat-save everything, so lots for me to consider. T-shirt from first music festival I was in in middle school-doesn't even fit me anymore, but I keep it shoved in my drawer anyway-reminds me of the good times we all had. How about that little toy truck-my Gramma gave it to me when I was little. Remember *a lot from that time period—I wonder why? Mom had taken me to Gramma's apartment—Grampa had died and Gramma was moving and she gave me the truck—it's funny—can barely remember Grampa now, but I can still see Gramma's face when she put the car in my hand. OK, what else—what do I say now? All right, some people would probably think it's stupid, but I have a small paper napkin—came from the restaurant where I went on my first date—kind of goofy thing to keep. And Terry brought me a can of Sunshine from Florida last year—laugh every time I see the label—wonder if anybody ever opens the cans to see what's inside?*

CW 2.6
The
freewriting
advantage

As you can see, some parts of this freewriting are highlighted. No matter what prewriting technique you use, highlighting, underlining, or circling your best ideas is important. That way you can easily find them later if you want to develop them as topics. The highlighted areas here indicate many promising ideas.

Although these promising ideas are in very rough form, they represent *potential* for constructing a good piece of writing later on. You would then need to develop these ideas by writing additional details about them and drawing connections among them.

FAST FACT   In writing and in life, what lies beneath the surface is usually much more than we expect. Mauna Lau and Mauna Kea, volcanoes in Hawaii, are nearly 14,000 feet high, less than half the height of Mt. Everest. But when measured from the floor of the Pacific—the base—the Hawaiian volcanoes are actually some 56,000 feet, meaning that only one-fourth of the mountains are above sea level.

COMPREHENSION AND PRACTICE 2.1

Trying Freewriting

1. Now it's your turn. On a separate sheet of paper, freewrite for ten minutes on one of the following topics: *childhood, money, loneliness.*

CW 2.7
Freewriting online

2. Identify the most promising ideas in the freewriting by highlighting, underlining, or circling them.

CW 2.8
Writing on
another
recursive
process

3. Of the ideas you have identified, which one has the most potential for development? List it on your paper, and then generate three additional details about it.

CHALLENGE 2.1 Evaluating Freewriting

1. Which detail or idea from the freewriting about *a souvenir* holds the most potential for development as a topic for writing? Explain why you would want to explore this topic.

   Answers will vary.

   _____

   _____

COLLABORATION

2. Exchange your freewriting with a classmate. On the freewriting you receive, put a ✓ next to the idea that you find the most interesting. Return the freewriting to the writer, and explain why you identified this idea. Put your own work aside for possible later use.

CW 2.9
Online
writing
assignment

3. What do you like best about freewriting as a prewriting technique? What do you like least?

   Answers will vary.

   _____

   _____

Brainstorming

CW 2.10
Brainstorming

Brainstorming is a more focused prewriting technique than freewriting. To brainstorm effectively, you should concentrate on a subject and then make a list of every idea directly connected to the topic. Brainstorming is also an excellent technique when you are working with a partner or a group. Other people's ideas will start sparking your own creative thoughts, and soon you will find that the ideas come more quickly. A set time limit isn't necessary, although some people prefer to work with one. Remember, though, that you list only ideas directly related to the subject. After brainstorming, you may have fewer notes on paper than you do when you freewrite, but the ideas you generate are likely to be more obviously connected.

You can also brainstorm with your computer, if you wish, darkening the screen so that you cannot see what you write. Then type your list, letting your mind lead you easily from one idea to another. When you are finished, print out your list.

After you brainstorm, highlight, underline, or circle ideas that you think have potential as writing topics.

Here is a brainstorming on the subject of *vacation:*

Vacation-Camping

- Cheap compared to staying in a hotel
- borrow or rent a tent and sleeping bags
- food cooked outdoors tastes great
- swimming, fishing, hiking
- many campsites have individual electrical and water hookups
- trailer camping and SUVs-popular choice but really different from tent camping
- even some small RVs cost more than a luxury car or SUV
- everything in these RVs-microwaves, TVs, showers, air-conditioning-more like a hotel
- great to wake up with the sun warming the tent
- aroma of the pine trees is great
- some people are such pigs-leave litter everywhere
- state and national camping areas-good maintenance and security

As this example shows, once you complete a brainstorming, you should identify the most promising ideas by highlighting, underlining, or circling them.

**COMPREHENSION AND PRACTICE
2.2**

Trying Brainstorming

1. Now try brainstorming. On a separate sheet of paper, brainstorm on one of the following topics: *exercise, stereotypes, relaxation.*

**CW 2.11
Brainstorming
group activity**

2. Go through your brainstorming, and highlight, circle, or underline the ideas that are especially promising.

3. What single idea in your brainstorming seems most suited for further discussion? List it, and add three details you could use to develop the idea.

CHALLENGE 2.2 Evaluating Brainstorming

1. Which element or item of this brainstorming would you enjoy reading more about? Why?

Answers will vary.

2. Exchange the brainstorming you have completed with a classmate. On the brainstorming you receive, put a ✓ next to the idea or area about which you'd like to know more. Then return it to the writer, and explain why you identified this particular point. Save your own brainstorming for possible later use.

3. What do you like best about brainstorming as a prewriting technique? What do you like least? Explain.

Answers will vary.

Clustering

CW 2.12
Clustering

Clustering is a prewriting technique that visually emphasizes connections among the ideas you develop. To create a clustering, write a general idea in the middle of the page and circle it. As you think of related ideas or details, write them down and circle each one. Then draw lines to connect the new ideas to the ideas from which they developed. Continue this process until you have thoroughly examined the subject. The result is a series of ideas and examples, with lines showing how they relate to each other. You can then highlight or underline the ideas that hold the most promise.

Look at this clustering on the subject *habits:*

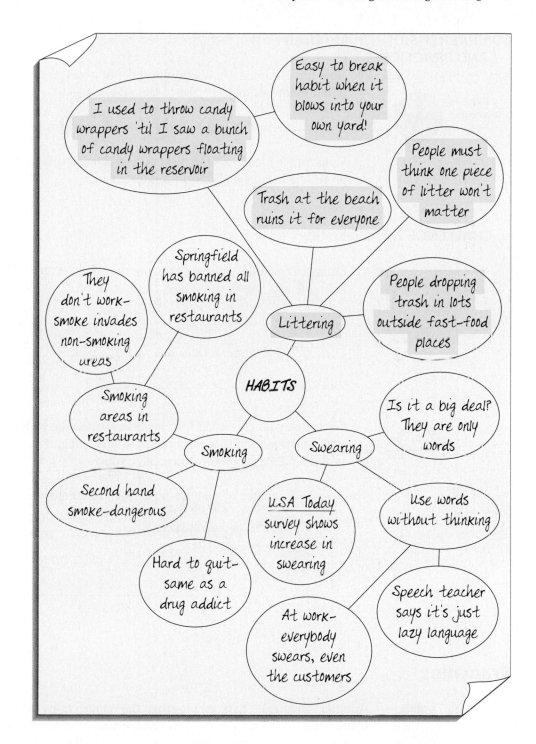

As this example shows, this prewriting technique emphasizes the various connections among related ideas in the material.

FAST FACT The late Fred Rogers, known to millions as Mr. Rogers in PBS's *Mr. Roger's Neighborhood*, was clearly low-tech when it came to his writing. "I always use a yellow pad and a blue Flair pen," he once told a reporter. The other thing that Mr. Rogers preferred when he wrote was silence.

COMPREHENSION AND PRACTICE 2.3

CW 2.13 Invention

Trying Clustering

1. Now try clustering. On a separate sheet of paper, create a clustering on one of the following subjects: *sports, humor, pride.*

2. Circle, underline, or highlight the ideas or examples that interest you most.

3. What single idea holds the most potential for development? Write that promising idea, and add three details about it.

CHALLENGE 2.3   Evaluating Clustering

1. Consider again the sample clustering on *habits* on page 19. Which section or item interests you most? Why?

   Answers will vary.

   _____

   _____

2. Exchange your clustering with a classmate. On the paper you receive, put a ✓ next to the portion that you find most interesting. Return the clustering to the writer, and explain your choice. Save your own paper for possible later use.

3. What did you like best about clustering? What did you like least?

   Answers will vary.

   _____

   _____

   _____

Branching

CW 2.14 Branching

Another technique that emphasizes the connections among related ideas is **branching.** To create a branching, first list your topic on the left side of a piece of paper. Next, write ideas inspired by this topic to the right of it, and connect them to it with lines. As these new ideas lead to related thoughts and ideas, add these to the right again. Working from left to right across the page, let your ideas branch out, with lines showing relationships. Once you complete the branching, highlight, underline, or circle any promising ideas for later development.

Look at this branching on the subject of *competition:*

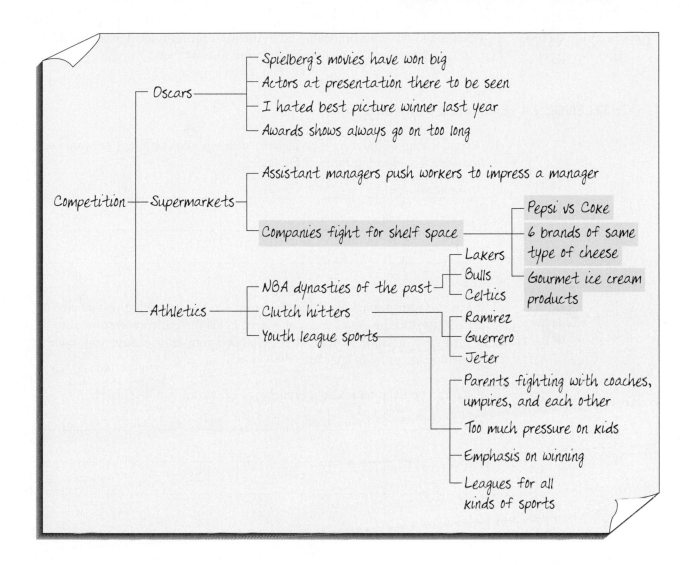

Branching leads you from one aspect of a topic to other, more specific aspects. As an added advantage, each branch holds an arrangement of related ideas. This focused organization allows you to concentrate on one area of your topic now and save the other areas for development later on.

COMPREHENSION AND PRACTICE

2.4

Practice with Branching

1. Now give branching a try yourself. On a separate sheet of paper, complete a branching on one of the following topics: *power, frustration, a holiday celebration.*

CW 2.15 More branching

2. Highlight, circle, or underline the portions of your branching that might be further developed.

3. What section in your branching holds the most promise for development? List it, and then add three details about this idea or section.

CHALLENGE 2.4 Evaluating Branching

1. Which section of the sample branching on *competition* on page 21 would you find easiest to develop further? Explain.

   Answers will vary.

   _____

   _____

2. Exchange your branching with a classmate. On the branching you receive, put a ✓ next to the detail or example that holds the most interest for you. Return the branching to the writer, explaining your choice. Save your own branching for possible later use.

3. What did you like most about branching? What did you like least?

   Answers will vary.

   _____

   _____

   _____

Idea Mapping

CW 2.16 Idea mapping

Idea mapping is a freewheeling prewriting technique that attempts to stimulate multiple aspects of your creativity. When you idea map, you write words *and* create images such as icons, scribbles, sketches, and symbols. According to the theory underlying this technique, the words you include flow from the areas of your brain responsible for logic and analysis. The sketches and doodles you create arise from the areas of your brain responsible for creativity.

To try idea mapping, start anywhere on the page, writing a word or drawing a picture representing the general topic. Then let your mind range freely on the subject, recording your associations in images or words, as seems natural. After you finish, identify the ideas and images that have the most depth and meaning to you; highlight or circle them.

Here is an idea map on the subject *frustration:*

The final step in idea mapping is to translate key images into words. For example, you might translate the scribbled sketch of the traffic light this way: "All the road construction makes the downtown streets seem more like a parking lot." You might convert the rough drawing of the computer to something like this: "Last night my computer crashed again. This time, I lost almost all my documents." The written version of the image can then serve as an idea to be used in a paper.

COMPREHENSION AND PRACTICE 2.5

Trying Idea Mapping

CW 2.17 Using two prewriting techniques

1. Look at the scene you see from your vantage point in the classroom, and create an idea map of your thoughts and feelings about the scene. Or, if you prefer, complete an idea map on one of the following subjects: *advertising, a perfect weekend, deadlines.*

2. Highlight, circle, or underline the ideas in your map that you feel you can develop further. Remember—translate key images into words.

3. What particular image or idea on your map holds the greatest potential for later development? Write it down, and add three details about it.

CHALLENGE 2.5   Evaluating an Idea Map

1. In the sample idea map about *frustration* on page 23, what image most interests or intrigues you? Why?

Answers will vary.

_____

_____

COLLABORATION

2. Exchange your idea map with a classmate. On the map you receive, put a ✓ next to the idea or image you'd most like to see developed. Return it to the writer with an explanation for your choice. Save your own idea map for later use.

3. What do you like most about idea mapping? What do you like least?

Answers will vary.

_____

_____

_____

Maintaining a Journal

CW 2.18
Maintaining
a journal

A journal is an idea book, a place for you to use writing informally to explore different subjects. How you set up your journal is up to you. It can be a notebook that you devote entirely to this purpose or a separate section of a notebook you use for other purposes as well. A computer is also an ideal place for journal entries. Simply open a file and enter the date at the start of each entry.

Writing, like any other activity, becomes easier the more you do it. Writing in your journal every day is one of the best ways to make writing seem as natural as talking and thinking. Use it to respond to discussions and books or articles you read for your classes or for personal enjoyment. Use it to sort out your feelings about another person or an issue that is important to you. You can be sure of one thing: This extra practice will translate into improved writing for you.

When you don't already have a subject to write on, focus on one of the following topics:

Internet spam
creativity
legalized gambling
favorite study spot
personal security
ways to waste time
dating adventures
stressful experiences
performance enhancement
   drugs and sports

dieting
impolite behavior
roller coasters
sports on TV
a fashion disaster
the power of music
questioning authority
a special keepsake
abuses of power

ideal vacation destinations
the best profession
a day at the mall
discrimination
hearing versus listening
entertaining advertising
difficulties with a boss
personal responsibility
secret ambition

true justice
nightmares
pet problems
credit cards
bullying
courage
testing worries
plastic surgery
physical fitness

Here is a sample journal entry on the subject *television violence:*

> Violence on TV—there's a lot of it, that's for sure. Wrestling. It's so obviously fake but do all the people watching know it? Cartoons? The old ones, like the Road Runner, were violent, but the new ones seem to be different. Even the news is violent. It's like the television stations have a camera at every terrible accident or school shooting or riot. Over and over they show that stuff. We talked about this subject in psychology class just yesterday. The big problem is that kids are exposed to this stuff, not just adults. My professor says nobody is sure yet. But some experts say kids just become accustomed to the violence. Then when they have problems, they react with violence themselves. I wonder how all the TV and movie violence I've seen has affected me.

**CW 2.19
Keeping a
journal for
one week**

Whenever you write in your journal, devote at least ten to twenty minutes to each session. After you complete each entry, reread what you've written, highlighting, circling, or underlining any ideas that you might want to develop into more formal writings later.

So which prewriting technique—freewriting, brainstorming, clustering, branching, idea mapping, or maintaining a journal—should you use? The answer, of course, depends on what works for you and makes you feel most comfortable. The best way to find out is to explore each technique a few times. Feel free to adapt or combine any of them to suit your own unique style.

COMPREHENSION AND PRACTICE 2.6   **Trying Journal Writing**

1. Now try journal writing yourself. On a separate sheet of paper, write a page on one of the following topics: *teamwork, fame, pets.*

2. Reread your journal entry. Circle, underline, or highlight the material you would like to explore in greater detail.

3. What section holds the most promise? Why? On your paper, briefly explain.

CHALLENGE 2.6   Analyzing Your Writing Rituals

**CW 2.20
What are
your writing
rituals?**

1. Take another look at the sample journal entry about *television violence* on page 25. What portion of it do you find most interesting? Why?

Answers will vary.

_____

_____

**CW 2.21
Analyzing
your writing
rituals**

2. As you worked on your journal entry, what did you notice about your writing habits or rituals? Is the time of day or the place where you write important to you? Do you need noise or silence? What do you use to write—pen, pencil, word processor? Begin your own journal by focusing on one aspect of your writing rituals, and then explore this subject for a page or so.

COLLABORATION

3. Now exchange your journal entry with a partner to compare answers.

FAST FACT   As you work through the writing process, you might find it helpful to consider how a pearl develops. It happens this way: A grain of sand or some other tiny piece of debris irritates an oyster. The oyster reacts by coating the irritant with a lustrous, smooth substance. In other words, the oyster turns a tiny thing that initially irritates it into something beautiful.

FOR FURTHER EXPLORATION

Focus on one of the following topics for further development. Using the prewriting technique—or combination of techniques—best suited to your style, examine the possibilities that the subject holds. Once you have completed your initial prewriting, highlight, underline, or circle the key ideas. Save your work for possible later use. Consider the subject, focusing on what someone else might need in order to understand what you are thinking, and write down these examples and details. At the same time, identify and write down what you expect your primary purpose would be. Save this work for possible later use.

- things you should throw away
- middle school or high school gym class
- the key to good friendship

▶ DISCOVERING CONNECTIONS

When you look at this photo, what comes to mind? Does it make you think of a letter you received recently or long ago? Who was it from? What was it about? Why do you remember it? Perhaps the image makes you remember a letter you have written—or wished you had. Or does it make you think of how communication has changed? Now that we have e-mail, does sending a letter seem old-fashioned?

Using the prewriting technique with which you are most comfortable, explore some of this subject's possibilities. Then highlight, underline, or circle the ideas that seem most promising. Save this material for possible later use. ◀

RECAP Generating Ideas through Prewriting

New terms in this chapter	Definitions
prewriting	the initial idea-generating stage of the writing process Prewriting techniques include freewriting, brainstorming, clustering, branching, idea mapping, and maintaining a journal.
freewriting	writing freely about a subject for a set period of time without stopping or worrying about correctness or completeness
brainstorming	focusing on a subject and listing all related ideas that come to mind
clustering	writing and circling an idea in the middle of the page, developing and circling related ideas around it, and drawing lines to connect related clusters of ideas
branching	listing a subject on the left side of the page, writing ideas inspired by that subject to the right, and connecting the branching ideas with lines
idea mapping	writing words and drawing images about a topic in a random manner across a page and then translating the images into words
maintaining a journal	writing several times a week in a separate notebook to explore or discover new ideas, respond to points raised in classes, or explore issues important to you

GOING FORWARD . . .

CW 2.22
Prewriting
review

Q: What can I do to overcome the anxiety of dealing with that blank page or computer screen?

A: Identifying the correct prewriting technique—or combination of techniques—appropriate for your own working style will definitely help you feel less overwhelmed and intimidated. So will reminding yourself that the final version of anything always starts out as something far less complete and polished. Keep your focus on what you are doing now—developing the details and examples that you will shape as you work through the rest of the writing process.

CHAPTER **3**

Composing: Creating a Draft

Navigating This Chapter

On this part of your odyssey, you will focus on how to create the two components that make up an effective paragraph:

- the topic sentence
- the supporting sentences

GETTING STARTED . . .

CW 3.1 Chapter basics

Q: I have good ideas about the subject, but right now they only make sense to me. How do I get my ideas in a form that would make sense to a reader?

A: Good ideas form the foundation for effective writing. Building on that foundation means taking the time to identify what someone else—your reader—would need to understand your good ideas and then expressing those ideas in correct sentence form.

Overview: Understanding Composing

CW 3.2 Overview of composing

Chapter 2 discusses the first stage in the writing process, showing you various techniques for generating preliminary ideas. This chapter focuses on the next stage: **composing.** If prewriting is the launch of your odyssey, then composing is the main leg of that journey. During this part of your journey, you focus on an aspect of a topic that you believe is manageable. Then you organize your relevant ideas into a coherent message. In this stage of the writing process, you also begin to pay attention to **correct form.** In other words, you express your good ideas in complete, correct sentences that support, explain, or illustrate your topic.

At this stage, your goal is to translate your good ideas into writing that communicates clearly to your reader. The following pages will discuss how to transform your prewriting material into a complete draft that meets your reader's needs. In other words, you will see how to limit your subject and identify the strongest details, examples, and illustrations for support.

FAST FACT **Compose** means much more than you might think. This versatile word has separate definitions in relation to such fields as music, art, and printing. So if you feel tired after composing for a while, maybe the fatigue has to do with the meaning of the word that is associated with writing: "To *construct* (in words)."

29

Recognizing the Structure of a Paragraph

CW 3.3
Paragraph structure

ESL Note
See "Writing Paragraphs," especially the section on unity, and "Writing Essays" on pages 601–603.

A **paragraph** is a series of sentences that work together to develop one main idea. Paragraphs vary in length, depending on the point you are trying to make. Longer pieces of writing may contain multiple paragraphs, some consisting of as few as three sentences. Generally, however, paragraphs run between five and ten sentences.

What is the role of a paragraph? The answer depends on the type of paragraph you are talking about. With longer, multi-paragraph documents, like **essays,** paragraphs are building blocks of words and ideas. As you expand your discussion, covering a subject in increasing detail, you move from paragraph to paragraph. (For more on the essay, see Chapters 14 and 15.)

Sometimes a paragraph functions in another way, as a miniature version of an essay. Like an essay, this kind of paragraph contains several items of support for its main idea. In the paragraph, however, the scope of the discussion is more limited than it would be in an essay.

The following figure shows how a paragraph is arranged:

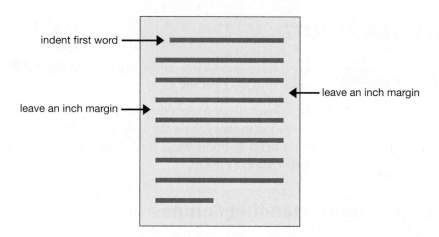

As this figure shows, the first sentence in a paragraph is *indented* about a half-inch on the page, with each subsequent sentence following it flush left to the margin. In multi-paragraph documents, this indentation provides a visual cue for the reader that the writer has moved from one idea to another.

Here's a sample paragraph that illustrates how you should structure the **content** or message of a paragraph:

> *A sunset two years ago at Horseneck Beach was the most beautiful sight I have ever seen.* During most of the day, the sky was full of clouds, but the temperature was a comfortable 80 degrees. At about 6 P.M., just after I had packed up all my stuff, the sky cleared completely. Instead of heading home, I decided to take a walk to the end of the beach. As I reached the point where the

Westport River flows into the bay, I looked out across the water to see a beautiful rose-colored sun. For the next twenty minutes I watched as the softly glowing sun seemed to melt into the water. I had never seen anything so wonderful, and I probably never will again.

CW 3.4 Topic sentence practice

The first sentence of this paragraph—the **topic sentence**—states the main idea. This topic sentence answers the reader's unstated question, "What's the point?" The other sentences are the supporting sentences, which make up the *body* of the paragraph. They elaborate on the topic through details and examples. Together, the supporting sentences communicate to the reader why the sunset was so beautiful.

COMPREHENSION AND PRACTICE

3.1

Working with Topic Sentences

1. Below are five topic sentences. Choose two of them, and on a separate sheet of paper, list three ideas that you would use to support each. If you need help to generate ideas, use the prewriting technique you prefer.

   a. Consumers have to be careful to avoid telemarketing scams.

   b. An insensitive teacher can have a terrible effect on young children.

   c. In most cases, the families of Alzheimer's patients suffer more than the patients themselves.

   d. The behavior of adults at youth league games is often offensive.

   e. The public is often more honest than the media would have us believe.

2. The following paragraphs lack topic sentences. Read each passage, and then, on the lines after it, write a suitable topic sentence.

   a. For example, using the tools of a word-processing program, you can easily produce attractive, error-free documents and letters. With money management software, you can keep track of all your financial transactions and plan for the future. You can choose from hundreds of entertaining and challenging games and programs for fun and learning on CD or online. Even more exciting, through the Internet, you can shop for everything from software to softballs, communicate with people around the globe, and find fascinating information about any topic you can imagine. Increasingly, the personal computer is becoming a one-stop business and entertainment center in American households.

   Answers will vary. Sample answers are given.

   Computers enable people to perform a wide range of both routine and entertaining

   activities quickly and efficiently.

b. Rent costs me $500 a month, a big chunk of my pay. In addition, I have to pay for my utilities: heat, lights, electricity, and telephone. That's usually $175 a month. Then I have to pay for food. Between the groceries I buy and the few meals I eat out, food costs me $400. My school expenses are enormous, too. I receive some aid, but I'm still responsible for $1,000 per semester plus the cost of books. At the end of the month, I have about $10 left.

After I pay my monthly expenses, I don't have much money left.

_____

_____

c. Many of my jobs involve cutting lawns and raking. On some jobs, I also tend gardens. This means regular watering, weeding, and fertilizing of the flower beds, and turning the mulch. I also have to dig up and reseed any problem spots in the lawns. On most days in the spring and summer, I work ten hours straight.

My yard care business keeps me busy with a variety of tasks.

_____

_____

CHALLENGE 3.1 Considering Topic Sentences and Supporting Details

1. The following passage consists of two paragraphs run together. After reading the entire passage, put a / at the point where the first paragraph ends. Then, on the lines that follow, explain what leads you to believe that the second paragraph begins at that point.

It was so much fun last summer watching the traveling circus set up the big top. First, the twenty members of the circus crew spread out the yellow-and-white-striped canvas, half as long as a football field. They hammered enormous spikes into the ground and tied off one end of the tent. Next, they laid the main tent pole flat, with the center of the tent attached to the top of the 35-foot post. Once this was set, they put several more spikes along each side and tied these sections off./Then came what everyone was waiting for: the elephants. The canvas seemed almost to come to life as the elephants strained to pull up the pole. The handlers quietly urged the elephants on while the crowd cheered. After five minutes of work, the pole was up, and the crowd applauded while the elephants enjoyed their reward, an extra bale of hay and a shower.

The first section is about the circus crew beginning to set up the big top. A new

section starts when the elephants are introduced. The whole section focuses on the

elephants' role in raising the big top.

COLLABORATION

2. Look again at the paragraph on pages 30–31 about the beautiful sunset. Working with a partner and using a separate sheet of paper, explain how the rest of the sentences in the paragraph support or explain the topic sentence.

3. Choose one of the following topics. On a separate sheet of paper, list five ideas that could support it. Try your hand at a paragraph, putting your ideas into sentence form. Save the paragraph for possible later use.
   a. the perfect night out
   b. a dangerous activity
   c. dieting

Identifying an Effective Topic

**CW 3.5
Identifying
an effective
topic**

Sometimes you know right away what part of a subject you want to focus on. In many cases, however, you will need to work through and evaluate your prewriting material to decide your focus. (See Chapter 2 to review prewriting techniques.)

For instance, imagine you have been asked to write about *childhood*. The general topic appeals to you. Like many people, you often think about your own childhood, so you certainly have plenty of ideas on the subject. However, *childhood* is far too broad a subject to cover in a paragraph. You aren't sure what aspect of the subject to focus on, so you do the following clustering on the subject:

CLEAR AND SPECIFIC   A sunset two years ago at Horseneck Beach was the most beautiful sight I have ever seen.

This version of the topic sentence is effective because it clearly and specifically identifies when the event occurred and why it was special.

You develop a topic sentence from the prewriting details that you identify as most promising or interesting. Your topic sentence must encapsulate the significance of those ideas and also provide a direction for the rest of the paragraph.

For example, look again at the highlighted material in the clustering on *childhood* (page 34). This information relates to matters of child rearing. The details all involve things that parents should do to provide children with a greater sense of love and security. Once you determine your attitude and reaction to this topic, you are ready to formulate a topic sentence:

EXAMPLE

┌────── topic ──────┐   ┌────── writer's attitude or reaction ──────┐
Through their own behavior, parents can *lay the groundwork for their children's*

happiness.

This topic sentence is effective because it is clear and specific and because it answers the reader's implied question, "What's the point?"

COMPREHENSION AND PRACTICE

Analyzing Topic Sentences

3.2 In each of the following topic sentences, circle the topic, and underline the writer's attitude or reaction to it. Use the example as a guide.

EXAMPLE   The (many costs of owning a car) make automobile ownership a luxury some

students cannot afford.

1. Most people don't spend enough time (planning for their future.)

2. (Poor highway design) is a major reason for auto accidents.

3. (Both major political parties in the United States) seem out of touch with the average person.

4. (Not all top high school athletes) are poor students.

5. (The fierce winter weather) is particularly hard on the poor and elderly.

6. (Better communication) is the key to an improved personal relationship.

7. (Raising the driving age to eighteen) may be one way to reduce the number of car accidents.

8. A (thorough employee training program) translates into a far better environment for workers and customers.

9. (Popular music today) is stale and unimaginative, with each new artist sounding like the others.

10. (A laptop computer's size and portability) make it a great choice for college students.

COMPREHENSION AND PRACTICE

3.3

Turning Topics into Topic Sentences

Below are ten topics. On a separate sheet of paper, turn each topic into a topic sentence by adding an attitude or opinion about it. Use the example as a guide.

EXAMPLE | melanoma, the most serious type of skin cancer

Melanoma, the most serious type of skin cancer, continues to increase because of our love affair with sunbathing.

1. an increase in the number of fatal auto accidents

2. special effects in movies

3. investing in the stock market

4. a better understanding of world geography

5. an increase in the minimum wage

6. a course in public speaking

7. the amount of money the federal government spends on education

8. life as a vegetarian

9. interest in astrology

10. the unique landscape of the desert

COMPREHENSION AND PRACTICE

CW 3.9 Revising topic sentences

Revising Topic Sentences

3.4 The following topic sentences are general and vague. On the lines provided, rewrite them, making sure they clearly focus on a specific topic and express a definite attitude. Answers will vary. Sample answers are given.

1. I enjoy physical activities.

   Physical activities can improve your mental health.

2. Being laid off is bad.

   Being laid off is particularly hard on men over age fifty.

3. Computers are amazing.

   Computers can put you in touch with people all over the world.

4. Television programming isn't challenging.

   Network television programming offers few shows dealing with important issues such as education, government, or the environment.

5. Science is interesting.

   Science interests many people because of the constant potential for discovery in a variety of fields.

6. Skateboarding is exciting.

   Over the past few years, skateboarding has become one of the most exciting spectator sports around.

7. Public transportation is important.

   Public transportation holds great potential to reduce pollution and congested streets and highways.

8. Personal counseling can be helpful.

Personal counseling can help people learn to understand themselves and their

behavior.

9. Energy conservation is important.

Energy conservation is important in order to ensure an adequate supply of power for

everyone.

10. Working as a construction laborer is hard.

Working as a construction laborer is physically demanding, especially on your back

and legs.

CHALLENGE 3.3 Evaluating and Developing Topic Sentences

1. Here are several potential topic sentences. Working with a partner, label the effective topic sentences with an *E* and the weak ones with a *W*.

    E _____ a. Working in a nursing home has helped me learn the true meaning of dignity.

    W _____ b. Housebreaking animals is necessary.

    E _____ c. My uncle's best decision ever was to get his general equivalency diploma (GED).

    E _____ d. Oil spills are environmental nightmares affecting the world for years.

    W _____ e. Many of today's movies are bad.

    W _____ f. Golf has increased in popularity.

    E _____ g. I trace my decision to major in music education to Ms. Souza, my first music teacher.

    W _____ h. The parking situation on campus needs attention.

    W _____ i. Winter can be a difficult time.

    E _____ j. My friend Alexei knows the secret to having a great party.

2. With the same partner, select one of the topic sentences that you identified as weak.

    a. On a separate sheet of paper, rewrite it. Be sure it focuses clearly on a *specific* topic and expresses a definite reaction.

b. On the same paper, develop at least three supporting sentences for this topic sentence.

3. In Challenge 3.2 (page 35), you identified the most promising idea in a prewriting on *greeting cards* and focused on it as a topic. Now, on a separate sheet of paper, write a draft topic sentence for this topic and at least three ideas you could use as support.

Providing the Best Support for the Topic Sentence

CW 3.10 Best topic sentence support

After you have developed a clear, specific topic sentence, you need to develop additional sentences that will support, illustrate, or explain it. You can draw much of your raw material from the related prewriting ideas you generated.

Here again is the highlighted clustering on *childhood* from page 34:

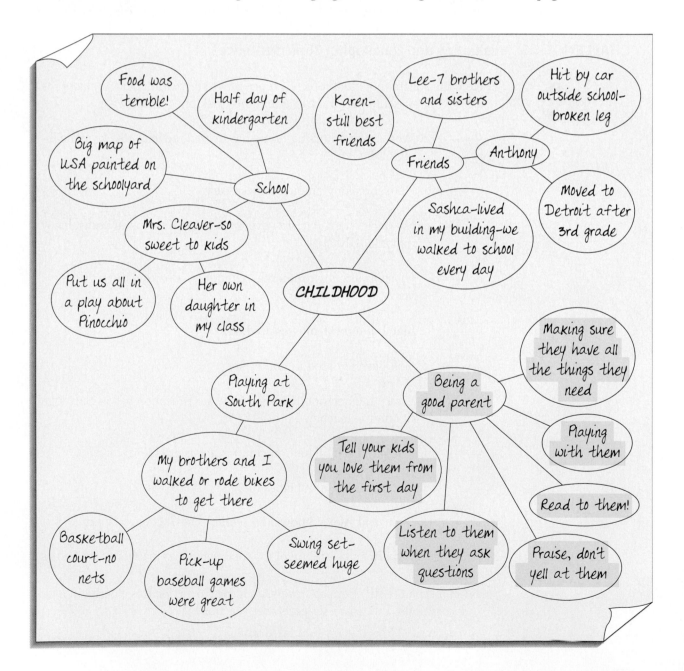

And here again is the proposed topic sentence inspired by the highlighted material.

EXAMPLE | Through their own behavior, parents can lay the groundwork for their children's happiness.

With your main idea clearly stated, you need to look back at your prewriting material with a selective eye. You've already identified the most promising section of the clustering. Now your job is to decide which of all the details and examples in that section supply the best support for the topic sentence.

To find out, first list the ideas you have highlighted:

Being a good parent

Tell your kids you love them from the first day

Making sure they have all the things they need

Playing with them

Read to them!

Praise, don't yell at them

Listen to them when they ask questions

These are all ways that parents should behave as they raise their children, so all the ideas support the thesis. If you were developing a longer piece of writing, you would probably use them all. Because you are working on a single paragraph, however, you must select the strongest and most complete items.

You've probably noted that the most compelling details are the following ones. They all concern ways that parents can provide their children with a blueprint for success and a sense of love and emotional well-being:

Tell your kids you love them from the first day

Read to them!

Praise, don't yell at them

Listen to them when they ask questions

Of course, in this form, these ideas aren't ready for use as support for the topic sentence. To make them more effective, you need to spell out these promising points in greater detail. Just as important, you need to express them as correct sentences.

FAST FACT   To compose the famous word game "Scrabble," out-of-work architect Alfred Mosher Butts relied upon the front page of the *New York Times*. Butts developed the game he first called Criss-Cross Words by identifying the frequency of use of the various letters of the alphabet. And what was the letter that appeared most frequently? **E.**

COMPREHENSION AND PRACTICE

3.5

Analyzing the Relationship between Topic Sentence and Body

1. Choose a paragraph of five to ten sentences from a reading in Part Seven, and identify its topic sentence.

2. On the lines that follow, explain the connection between this topic sentence and its supporting sentences. (Record the page number of the paragraph so you can locate it again easily.)

_____
Answers will vary.

_____

_____

3. Here is a list of details from an idea map on credit card purchases:

birthday presents	new coat
shoes	books
CDs	stereo equipment
graduation gifts	pants

Arrange the details in related categories on a separate sheet of paper. Add more specific details as you wish and pinpoint the topic they cover. Then, on a separate sheet of paper, write a clear, specific topic sentence.

CHALLENGE 3.4 **Evaluating a Topic Sentence and Grouping Details**

COLLABORATION

1. Exchange the topic sentence you drafted on *greeting cards* (page 40) with a partner. Check the topic sentence you receive to make sure it is clear and specific. Return the topic sentence and any suggestions for changes to the writer. Then make any necessary changes to your own topic sentence.

2. Group the ideas from the prewriting you completed for Discovering Connections at the end of Chapter 2 (page 27). Save this work for later use.

Deciding on the Most Effective Arrangement

Once you select the details and examples that will best support your topic sentence, you must arrange them in a logical, effective order. Ask yourself this question, "How can I present this information so that I hold my reader's attention?"

In the case of the clustering material on child rearing, you believe the following arrangement will accomplish this aim:

2   Listen to them when they ask questions
1   Read to them!
3   Praise, don't yell at them
4   Tell your kids you love them from the first day

Reading to children is important because it sets them up for success in school and beyond. Listening to children is even more important, however, because it tells them that they are important to their parents. But making sure that children hear praise and regular reminders that they are loved is most important of all. As you see it, this order of presentation, working up to your most important point, best lays the groundwork for a convincing paragraph.

Taking the time to sort out your ideas and establish a tentative order is an important step in creating an effective piece of writing. Your final decisions about how to order the details should always depend on what arrangement best draws and holds the reader's attention. In many cases, building from strong to stronger example helps to hold the reader's attention.

ESL Note
See "Writing Paragraphs" on page 601–602.

CHALLENGE 3.5   **Arranging Supporting Details in Your Writing**

1. Of the examples of good child-rearing practices listed on page 41, which do you think is the strongest? Why?

    Answers will vary
    _____

    _____

    _____

2. Choose one grouping of details you created on credit card purchases in Comprehension and Practice 3.5 (page 42). On a separate sheet of paper, arrange this list in an order you could use to support the following topic sentence: *Credit cards make it easy to spend more than you really want to.*

3. Exchange your list with a partner.

    a. On the list you receive, evaluate the order of the details and make any suggestions you think would help the writer develop a better paragraph. Return the list to the writer.

    b. After considering your reader's comments, make any changes you feel are necessary. Put this list aside for later use.

Making Your Material Reader Centered

CW 3.11
The audiences in your life

In order for your reader to understand your ideas, you must present them as **reader-centered writing**. In other words, you must express those ideas fully and in complete sentences, so that the average reader will understand them.

You generally don't express prewriting ideas completely or in correct sentence form. They are expressed as **writer-centered writing**, that is, in a raw, unpolished form that makes sense to you but not necessarily to another person.

To understand the difference between writer-centered and reader-centered material, think of your notes for one of your classes. In a psychology class, for example, you might have written the following notation:

WRITER-CENTERED | *Personality types/Jung-way you behave?*

These words have a specific meaning to you because you were present in class when your instructor explained the material, and you participated in the class discussion that followed. However, a reader who was not in that class would no doubt have trouble interpreting your notes.

Now, look at this reader-centered version of the same material:

READER-CENTERED | *Carl Jung's theories about personality types raise some questions about the way we behave.*

**CW 3.12
Making
your
material
reader
centered**

As you can see, this version expresses the ideas more thoroughly in complete sentence form. With the ideas spelled out this way, even a reader unfamiliar with psychology can understand what the note actually means.

In addition to expressing your good ideas in correct sentence form, one other step to make your writing more reader centered is to *amplify.* When you amplify, you provide additional specific examples and details to support your ideas. As a way to cue yourself to amplify, you might even consider including the expressions *for example* or *for instance.* When you write one of these expressions, you make a commitment to your reader to provide additional specific details about the information.

Consider the reader-centered example about personality types, but this time with the additional supporting information:

EXAMPLE | Carl Jung's theories about personality types raise some questions about the way we behave. **For example, some people prefer to work independently, while others prefer the company of co-workers. These preferences are connected to a person's personality type, which is identified by an instrument called the Myers-Briggs Type Indicator.**

As you can see, the idea becomes even more reader centered once the information introduced by *For example,* shown in boldface, is added. Even when you don't use *for example* or *for instance,* make sure to supply information to support or explain the point you are making.

CHALLENGE 3.6 Evaluating and Developing Reader-Centered Sentences

COLLABORATION

1. Make a copy of a page of notes you took for another class. Exchange this copy with a partner. On a separate sheet of paper, try to change the writer-centered notes you receive to reader-centered sentences.

2. Return the notes and your reader-centered version to the writer. Review the papers returned to you and circle any detail that your reader failed to understand. Explain the point you meant to communicate.

3. Return to the material you developed for exercise 2 in Challenge 3.4 (page 42). On a separate sheet of paper, identify and transform all your writer-centered details about writing to someone into reader-centered sentences.

COLLABORATION

4. Exchange your reader-centered sentences with a partner. On the page you receive, put a + next to each sentence that is reader centered and a ✓ next to any sentence that is still writer centered. Return the page to the writer, and suggest a way to improve the sentences marked with a ✓. Save your own work for later use.

Using a Reader Evaluation Checklist

CW 3.13
Outlining with a word processor

The secret to success in writing is to meet the needs of your reader. In most cases, you can assume that your reader knows a little bit about many subjects but not necessarily a great deal about most subjects. Using a **reader evaluation checklist** is one way to make sure that your supporting information meets the needs of your reader.

To use the reader evaluation checklist below, simply insert the name of your topic in the blanks, and then write your answers to the questions.

✓ **Reader Evaluation Checklist**

☐ What does the average reader need to know about _____?

☐ What does the average reader already know about _____?

☐ What information would help the average person better understand _____?

☐ What did I find the hardest to understand about _____ at first?

☐ What helped me to figure out _____?

☐ What's the best example or explanation I can give the average person about _____?

As you answer these questions, you will also focus on the examples or explanations that your reader will need to see your point.

COMPREHENSION AND PRACTICE 3.6

Analyzing Your Reader's Needs

1. On the lines below, list three subjects that you know a great deal about and then three subjects that you wish you knew more about.

I know a great deal about . . .   *I wish I knew more about . . .*

a. Answers will vary.   a. _____

b. _____   b. _____

c. _____   c. _____

2. Choose one item from each column in number 1, and then answer the following questions.

    a. What details would help you communicate to a reader what you know about the subject you understand well?

    Answers will vary.

    _____

    _____

    b. What details would help you understand more about the subject you want to explore?

    Answers will vary.

    _____

    _____

CHALLENGE 3.7 Evaluating How Well a Paragraph Meets a Reader's Needs

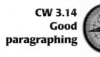

CW 3.14 Good paragraphing

1. Working with a classmate, assess the following paragraph. Use the questions below the paragraph as guidelines.

> Coffee bars are gaining popularity in cities and towns throughout the country. The trend began a while ago. The shops serve several varieties of coffee and food, and they offer a pleasant atmosphere. Some coffee bars have begun to include various activities to make patrons feel comfortable as they enjoy their favorite brand of coffee.

    a. Did the writer do a good job of providing information the average reader might not know?

    b. What did the writer assume the average reader *did* know?

    c. Are there areas on which the writer still needs to focus?

2. On a separate sheet of paper, write to the writer of the paragraph, suggesting ways to improve this paragraph.

COLLABORATION

3. Exchange the note you wrote above with a partner. Using the comments to guide you, rewrite the paragraph on a separate sheet of paper.

4. Exchange your rewritten paragraph with a partner. Use the reader evaluation checklist on page 45 to assess the paragraph you receive. Make a note next to any point that still needs work, and return the paragraph to the writer.

Developing a Complete Draft

ESL Note
See "Writing Essays"
on pages 602–603.

CW 3.15
Comparing
word
processors

The final part of the composing stage of writing is developing a **complete draft.** This draft combines your topic sentence with selected reader-centered examples and details in the order you have chosen.

As you develop this initial version, remember that it doesn't have to be perfect. (The next chapter will show you how to revise—to refine and polish—your writing.) At this point, focus your energies on stating your ideas completely and clearly.

You should make your draft look clean and readable, too. If you have access to a computer, learn how to use it to do your writing. You'll find the flexibility of writing with a computer especially helpful in making changes as you revise. Whether you use a computer or a typewriter, make sure to double-space to leave room to make corrections and additions. If you write by hand, write on every other line. Either way, you'll have room to make corrections and additions as you revise your work.

CW 3.16
Composing
a draft

Here's a completed draft of a paragraph on the importance of some aspects of child rearing, developed from the original clustering on childhood. The key ideas from the section on being a parent are underlined:

> Through their own behavior, parents can lay the groundwork for their children's happiness. <u>Reading to children</u> every day is important. Parents also need to spend time interacting with their children <u>and responding to their questions</u> patiently. They count on their parents to help them make sense of the world around them. Most of all, parents should regularly <u>tell their children that they love them</u> and <u>praise them when they do something well</u>. Nothing is more important to children's future success than the support and interest of their parents.

As you can see, the original writer-centered prewriting ideas from page 41 are all now reader-centered supporting sentences. You can also see that the material has been **amplified** a bit. Additional supporting ideas, all expressed in sentences, offer further clarification and explanation of the key points.

The general arrangement of the information follows the order indicated on page 42, with a significant example of good parenting behavior leading to increasingly significant examples. In addition, the final sentence serves as the conclusion, reiterating the main point of the paragraph.

COMPREHENSION AND PRACTICE 3.7

Analyzing a First Draft

1. On the following lines, explain what you like most about the first draft paragraph on child rearing.

Answers will vary.

_____

_____

_____

2. On the following lines, list any examples in this first draft that need improvement.

Explain why reading to children is important. Explain how parents should interact with

their children and respond to questions. Explain ways parents should show their love.

_____

CHALLENGE 3.8   Creating a First Draft

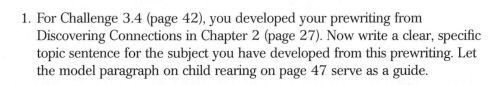

**CW 3.17
Explaining
something
you know
well**

1. For Challenge 3.4 (page 42), you developed your prewriting from Discovering Connections in Chapter 2 (page 27). Now write a clear, specific topic sentence for the subject you have developed from this prewriting. Let the model paragraph on child rearing on page 47 serve as a guide.

2. Identify your best details from the reader-centered sentences you developed in Challenge 3.6 (page 44), and turn them into your supporting sentences for a first draft. Save your draft for later use.

FOR FURTHER EXPLORATION

Focus on one of the following topics as the basis for a draft paragraph (at least five to ten sentences). Use the prewriting technique—or combination of techniques—that you prefer to generate some preliminary ideas. Then identify a specific topic and compose a first draft paragraph, using the material in this chapter to guide you through this process.

- biggest mistake you have ever made
- class clowns
- the one thing that all people need

FAST FACT   If you feel frustrated at the time it takes to complete a first draft, keep this point in mind: It took 70 years to produce the first version of the *Oxford English Dictionary*.

▶ DISCOVERING CONNECTIONS

What do you think of when you look at this picture? The people living and working in this area can use boats like the one in the forefront of the picture to get around. How about you? What method of transportation do you use? If you could, how would you change things to improve how you commute and travel? Do you look at this scene, which is from Amsterdam, and wish you could visit the Netherlands or some other country in the so-called Old World? What makes this kind of trip attractive to you?

For this assignment, consider one of these questions or some other one that the picture inspires. Using the material in this chapter to guide you, develop a complete draft of a paragraph (at least five to ten sentences long). In particular, concentrate on making your paragraph reader centered. ◀

RECAP Composing: Creating a Draft

New terms in this chapter	Definitions
composing	the stage of writing during which you focus on a topic and provide supporting ideas drawn from your prewriting material
paragraph	a series of sentences that work together to develop one main idea
topic sentence	the sentence stating the main idea, or topic, of a paragraph and setting the tone or direction for the writing
	The topic sentence expresses the topic, limits it to a manageable size, and usually reveals the writer's attitude or reaction to the topic.

EXAMPLE	┌──────── topic ────────┐ The new biography of former President Carter is ┌─ attitude or reaction ─┐ fascinating reading.

reader-centered writing	ideas expressed thoroughly and in complete sentence form so that they make sense to the reader
writer-centered writing	raw, unpolished ideas that provide enough clues to make sense to the writer but not necessarily to the reader
reader evaluation checklist	series of questions designed to help writers ensure that their supporting information meets their readers' needs
amplifying	the act of supplying additional specific examples and details
complete draft	the first complete version of a piece of writing, including a clear, specific topic sentence plus supporting sentences

(continued)

The Process of Composing a Draft

Focus on a topic.

↓ ↑

Create a **topic sentence.**

↓ ↑

Organize **prewriting ideas** and **examples.**

↓ ↑

Develop **supporting sentences.**

↓ ↑

Restate **topic sentence.**

GOING FORWARD...

CW 3.18
Composing
review

Q: Sometimes, even when all my prewriting ideas are expressed in sentences, my first draft paragraph doesn't really capture what I am trying to say. What am I doing wrong?

CW 3.19
Composing
your writing

A: At this point, you aren't doing anything wrong, except for being a little impatient. You've made your paper as good as you could make it—for now. That's the role of composing in the writing process, to create a complete draft. But it's a rare occurrence indeed when the first draft of a piece of writing is the best it could be. Relax and let your first draft sit for a little while. Then you'll be in a better position to make your paper say what you want it to say.

CHAPTER 4
Refining and Polishing Your Draft

Navigating This Chapter

On this leg of your writing odyssey, you focus on refining and polishing your initial draft so that it most effectively expresses what you mean through the following aspects of revision:

- reassessing
- redrafting
- editing

GETTING STARTED . . .

CW 4.1 Chapter basics

Q: I've already spent a lot of time on this paper, and I don't really understand what good can come of working on it anymore. Why should I spend any more time on my paper when it's already as good as I can make it?

A: Your initial draft was as good as you could make it—at that time. You worked hard, and when you work hard, you get tired and are less likely to see other possibilities for changing or improving things. But consider this: Haven't you ever had a discussion and then, after the discussion was long over, remembered something else you wish you had said? That's how it is with writing, too. After a little time away from your draft—and with some reactions from another reader or two—you will probably see several ways that you could make your good paper even better.

Overview: Understanding the Revising Stage

CW 4.2 Overview of revising

One sure truth about writing is that you won't write a masterpiece on the first try. Your best writing takes thought, time, and patience. A good first draft is only the beginning. Once you have completed a solid draft, you must *revise*—or refine and polish—your draft. This chapter explains how revising your writing will turn something good into something even better.

 Revising actually involves three interrelated steps: reassessing, redrafting, and editing. **Reassessing** means checking for *unity, coherence,* and *effective language.* It also involves seeking feedback from an objective reader. **Redrafting** means rewriting to eliminate any problem spots and add needed material. You may actually reassess and redraft more than once in order to achieve the results you want. **Editing** involves making any last-minute adjustments and proofreading your final draft to eliminate any remaining errors. It ensures that your paper is as correct in form as it is complete in content.

Reassessing: Reseeing Your Work

By the time you complete a draft, you will probably feel that you've taken your paragraph as far as you can. Let a little time pass, though, and you will undoubtedly find areas that still need work. Putting away your initial draft for a day or two will create a distance and enable you to *resee* your paragraph. When you look at it again with a fresh eye, you'll be better able to reassess it for unity, coherence, and effective language.

**CW 4.3
Gaining
revision
confidence**

Maintaining Unity

**CW 4.4
Maintaining
unity**

In order for your reader to understand your point, you need to make sure all your examples and details relate directly to your main idea. In other words, you need to keep your writing unified. When you reassess for **unity**, you eliminate any material that is not clearly connected to your subject.

Take a look at the following paragraph about a stressful experience—a road test for a driver's license. As you read, identify which information is not relevant to this topic.

**CW 4.5
Achieving
paragraph
unity**

Getting my driver's license was the most stressful experience I have ever faced. During my final road lesson that morning, I had no problems. In fact, my instructor told me that it was the best of my six training sessions. But as soon as the inspector from the Registry of Motor Vehicles stepped into the car, I could feel my heart racing. Stress contributes to the number of people who suffer heart attacks each year in the United States. Bad diet is one of the major contributing factors to the number of heart attacks. Heredity is another major cause. By the time the inspector sat down and put on her seat belt, I could feel my shirt becoming damp. When she told me to start up the car, for a moment I couldn't even think what to do. After a couple of seconds, I remembered to turn the key. For the next ten minutes, I felt like I was watching someone else pull out into traffic, turn left and right, complete a three-point turn, and parallel park. After I parked the car back at the Registry parking lot, the inspector turned to me and said that I had passed. At that point, I was exhausted, but I was happier than I had ever been.

You probably identified the fifth, sixth, and seventh sentences. They deal with heart attacks, which are related to stress, but this information is irrelevant to the specific experience of getting a driver's license. Once you eliminate these sentences, the paragraph is unified.

COMPREHENSION AND PRACTICE 4.1

Eliminating Unrelated Sentences

1. Check the following paragraph for unity. Circle any sentences that do not belong with the others.

Last summer, I had a great experience working as a soccer coach for the day camp at a local Boys and Girls Club. I was in charge of the indoor soccer games for the youngest group of campers, ages five to seven. (In many countries, soccer is called football.) During the first week of camp, I assigned the fifty kids to different teams and had practice games. They didn't really understand how to play the game, so I spent the first two weeks teaching them basic things like passing and playing defense. (Soccer is the world's most popular sport.) (So far, professional soccer has not been especially successful in the United States.) For the rest of the summer, I was able to watch the children as they improved and learned to love soccer. At the end of the summer, all the players gave me a plaque naming me "Most Valuable Coach." I never would have guessed that a simple summer job could have been so rewarding.

2. Use the following lines to explain why the sentences you've circled do not belong.

That soccer is also called football is not related to the topic. Soccer's popularity is not

relevant here. The fate of professional soccer in the United States has nothing to do

with the point of the paragraph.

CHALLENGE 4.1 Focusing on Unity

COLLABORATION

1. Below is a topic sentence, followed by several possible supporting ideas. Working with a classmate, choose at least three of the ideas and, on a separate sheet of paper, identify why you think these ideas, developed fully, would be directly relevant to the topic sentence.

CW 4.6
Identifying unity problems

For most people, life regularly presents the chance to perform little acts of heroism.

- being polite
- checking on old or infirm neighbors
- becoming a foster parent
- being a positive role model for younger family members
- running for elective office
- squeezing time from your schedule to listen to a friend's problems.

COLLABORATION

2. Take one item from the list that you didn't think was connected to the topic sentence, and, on the same paper, explain why, at least now, this detail isn't sufficiently related.

3. Choose one of the ideas you have identified as relevant, and, on the lines that follow, express that idea in a complete sentence that supports the topic sentence.

Answers will vary depending on the idea chosen.

_____

_____

Providing Coherence

CW 4.7
Transitions between ideas

If your paragraph is going to communicate your ideas to your reader, the information must be easy to follow. In other words, it must be **coherent.** Writing is coherent when it features plenty of **transition** and an **effective order of presentation.** When you reassess for coherence, you zero in on these aspects, making sure that the ideas flow smoothly and are arranged in a way that is most appropriate to communicate your point to your reader.

Transition   Connecting your supporting sentences smoothly is a matter of supplying *transition*. Writers use three techniques to relate sentences to one another.

1. Repeat key words and phrases or rename them with pronouns.

2. Substitute **synonyms,** words that have similar meanings, for key words.

3. Insert transitional expressions to connect ideas.

The repetitions and substitutions provide a thread of continuity that keeps the main idea uppermost in the reader's mind. Look at the italicized words in the following sentences.

EXAMPLE

The manager came out of *the movie theater* to talk to *the crowd* waiting to get into the *building. She* told *the angry people* that a smoke alarm had gone off. *Her* staff was checking to make sure the *facility* was safe.

In the second sentence, *She* takes the place of *The manager, the angry people* re-names *the crowd,* and the synonym *building* substitutes for *the movie theater.* In the third sentence, *Her* refers to *She,* and another synonym, *facility,* replaces *building.*

Perhaps the most useful technique for showing the relationships among sentences is adding **transitional expressions** to connect ideas. Here is a listing of common transitional expressions. Note the italicized words in the sentences following each list. These words provide a sense of connection between the ideas expressed.

Common Transitional Expressions to Illustrate or to Show Cause and Effect

accordingly	consequently	indeed	particularly
after all	for example	in fact	specifically
as a result	for instance	of course	therefore
because	for one thing	overall	thus

EXAMPLE

In-line skating injuries have risen dramatically over the past few years. *As a result,* sales of helmets and other safety equipment have also increased.

Common Transitional Expressions to Add, Restate, or Emphasize

again	finally	in conclusion	on the whole
also	first (second, last, etc.)	in other words	too
and	further	moreover	to sum up
besides	in addition	next	

EXAMPLE

Last week, people in the central part of the state faced intense temperatures and high humidity. *Finally,* a cold front brought three days of much-needed rain.

Common Transitional Expressions to Show Time or Place

above	beyond	lately	soon	until
after	currently	now	then	when
as soon as	earlier	once	there	whenever
before	here	presently	to the left (or right)	where
below	immediately	since	under	

EXAMPLE The golden retriever raced toward the open gate. *When* its owner shouted, the dog came to a dead stop.

Common Transitional Expressions to Compare or to Contrast

although	despite	in the same way	similarly
and	even though	likewise	still
as	however	nevertheless	though
both (neither)	in contrast	on the other hand	whereas
but	in spite of	regardless	yet

EXAMPLE Small stores can't compete with the prices of the giant home improvement centers. *However,* they can provide more personalized service.

As you can see, the italicized words in each of these example sentences signal the connection between ideas.

Consider the boldfaced and italicized words in the following paragraph:

> Good time management is the key to success in college. Setting up **an hour-by-hour breakdown** is the first step. *As* you make your **time plan,** don't forget to include time for meals and for nonschool activities such as exercise. *Once* you establish your **schedule,** you *then* need to follow it closely. *For example, if* you set aside Mondays from 12 to 2 for study time in the library, make sure to follow through on your **commitment.** *If* you follow your **schedule** carefully, you will find the quality of your work improving.

As you can see, transition holds this paragraph together. For example, **time plan** renames **hour-by-hour breakdown.** In the remaining sentences, two other synonyms, **schedule** and **commitment,** also replace **time plan.** In addition, a number of transitional expressions, including *as, once, then, for example,* and *if,* emphasize the connections between the points.

COMPREHENSION AND PRACTICE 4.2

Working with Transition

1. Read the following paragraph on the subject of relaxation. As you read, circle all transitional expressions and underline synonyms or pronouns that rename other words in the passage.

> (When) I want to relax, I get in my car and take a ride to Phoenix Park next to the Rodman River. (Once) I get there, I head over to the benches, which sit above the river. The bench I prefer is at the far end of the <u>park.</u> Because this bench is almost a quarter of a mile from the parking lot, <u>it</u> is al-

most always deserted. (Most) times, it's quiet enough for me to hear the <u>water</u> washing against the rocks along the <u>shore</u>. No matter how bad my day has been, problems seem to melt away as I close <u>my</u> eyes and listen to the <u>water</u> go by. (On the whole,) an hour or so in Phoenix Park is like a mini-vacation.

2. Choose two of the transitional expressions you have underlined and, on the following lines, explain how these expressions help to keep ideas in the paragraph unified.

   Answers will vary depending on the words chosen. Sample answers are given.

   Once, from the second sentence, indicates that the writer has arrived at the special

   spot. *Most times,* from the fifth sentence, specifies specific times.

CHALLENGE 4.2 Focusing on Transition

1. Write a draft paragraph of at least five sentences about what you do to relax.

COLLABORATION

2. Exchange your draft with a classmate. On the paper you receive, underline any transition you find. At the same time, put a ✓ at any spot where you feel transition is still needed and then return the paper.

3. Check your reader's evaluation and make any necessary changes to your paragraph.

FAST FACT   Be careful not to let your work in developing an effective paper overwhelm you, as it did novelist John Steinbeck. Disappointed in the tone of an early version of his Nobel prize-winning novel *The Grapes of Wrath,* Steinbeck destroyed the entire draft.

CW 4.8 Organizing sentences effectively

Organizing Sentences Effectively   Another crucial aspect of coherence is **effective organization.** As the previous chapter shows, the order you use to present your ideas affects how easily your reader is able to understand your point. Therefore, as you reassess, you need to check that you've effectively arranged your ideas. Three common methods of organization include *chronological order, spatial order,* and *emphatic order.*

CW 4.9 Chronological order

Using Chronological Order   You should employ **chronological order**—or order of time—whenever you are recalling a series of events as they occurred in sequence.

Look at this paragraph about dealing with jury duty:

> Being called for jury duty proved to be a waste of time for me. When I arrived at the courthouse at 8:30 A.M., I joined about twenty other people in the main courtroom. The court clerk then addressed us, explaining our duties as jurors. After the clerk was done, we watched a brief video about proper conduct in the courtroom. Next, the clerk told us to wait in that room until we were summoned. Sitting with nothing to do wasn't easy for me because of a problem I was having at work. Two days before, my boss had given me a huge new project with a tight deadline. I had been working like mad from that point on. Now I had to watch the minutes tick by. After about forty minutes, another court officer came into the room, told us that we were dismissed, and thanked us for our time. At that point, I picked up my jacket and headed to the door, thinking about my lost morning.

In this paragraph, chronological order and transitional words help the reader keep the events straight. *When* the writer arrived, she went into a courtroom and *then* the court clerk addressed them. *Once* the talk was over, they changed rooms, and *then* they were told to wait. *After* some time passed, the prospective jurors were told that they could leave, and *at that point* the writer thought about the time she had wasted.

Incidentally, as a writer, you will sometimes intentionally break the sequence of events by using a *flashback.* This device involves presenting information that occurred *before* the event under discussion in order to clarify or emphasize some point. In this paragraph about jury duty, for example, you probably noticed that sentences 7, 8, and 9 concern a situation at work that occurred before the day of jury duty. In this case, the flashback underscores how much of an inconvenience a day as a juror can be. The secret to using a flashback effectively is to provide sufficient transition so that your reader recognizes that you have switched the order of events.

COMPREHENSION AND PRACTICE 4.3

Considering the Uses of Chronological Order

1. List three types of subjects that would be best organized in chronological order—for example, an explanation of a date or party that went badly.

   Answers will vary. Students might choose subjects like their first meeting with

   someone who became significant in their lives, their first day in the military or in a

   foreign country, or their recollection of a particular sports event.

2. Choose one of the subjects you listed in number 1 and, on the following lines, list at least three steps in that sequence of events.

   Answers will vary.

CHALLENGE 4.3   Focusing on Chronological Order

COLLABORATION

1. Read the following paragraph. Then, working with a classmate, note where transition would help the flow of the paragraph. On a separate sheet of paper, rewrite the paragraph, inserting appropriate transitional expressions.
   Answers will vary.

> One of my best childhood memories is of my first trip to New York City with my godmother when I was 12. We arrived at Penn Station at 8 A.M. and after checking our subway map, we began our adventure. We took the subway down to Battery Park to board the ferry to the Statue of Liberty where we spent an hour. My aunt and I boarded the subway to head uptown to Central Park. We walked for a while along the different paths of this beautiful park, and we went across the street to the Museum of Natural History. We were really hungry. We went to the cafeteria for a quick lunch. We went into the museum and for the next two hours viewed the different exhibits, including my favorite ones, the dinosaurs. We got back on the subway and rode down to see the Empire State Building. It was 4 P.M., and we had to go back to Penn Station for the train to take us home. I've been back to New York City, but my first trip is the one I remember best.

2. Imagine that you had written this paragraph and had decided to revise it to include a flashback. On a separate sheet of paper, indicate what kind of information you might include, why you would include such information, and where in the paragraph it would appear.

CW 4.10
Spatial
order

Using Spatial Order   When you need to explain where one object, place, or person exists in relation to other objects, places, or people, you rely on **spatial order.** This method of arrangement helps a reader visualize a particular scene. Spatial order enables items, locales, and individuals to be viewed in an organized, natural way: top to bottom, left to right, near to far.

Look at this paragraph about a newly decorated apartment:

> The biggest transformation I have ever seen in a space was my Aunt Monique's last apartment. When I first saw the place, it was in terrible shape. The wallpaper throughout was torn and stained, with piles of trash in each room. When I returned a month later, the change was unbelievable. The living room was now painted off-white, with a stenciled pattern along the edge of the ceiling. Next to the living room was the kitchen, now decorated with pastel-colored striped wallpaper. Above the new sink and counter, a flowering plant hung. Under the counter were new cabinet doors. Through the door at the far corner of the kitchen was her bedroom. On the floor in front of her bed was a small blue area rug, with matching blue curtains decorating the window next to her bed. It was hard to believe that this apartment was the same place I had seen just a month earlier.

CW 4.11
Describing a
scene using
spatial
order

In this paragraph, spatial order helps the reader more accurately envision the apartment. After the renovation, the living room walls were newly painted, with stenciling *along the edge* of the ceiling. The kitchen, *next to* the living room, was also newly wallpapered, with a plant hanging *above* the sink and counter and new cabinet doors *under* the counter. The bedroom, which was *through the door* at *the far corner* of the kitchen, was also newly decorated and painted. The curtains on the window *next to* her bed matched the small area rug *on the floor in front* of the bed. As these italicized words illustrate, spatial cues make the scene easier to visualize.

COMPREHENSION AND PRACTICE 4.4

Reviewing Spatial Order

1. On the following lines, list at least five landmarks of some kind—stores, offices, signs, traffic lights, and so on—near your home.

   Answers will vary.

   _____

   _____

   _____

2. On a separate sheet of paper, make a list of at least five transitional expressions that would be appropriate to suggest the location of these places in relation to each other (for example, *next to*).

3. On the same sheet of paper, use spatial order to explain where your home is located in relation to three of the five landmarks you have listed.

CHALLENGE 4.4   **Focusing on Spatial Order**

COLLABORATION

1. Ask a classmate to give you a verbal tour of a room with which the classmate is very familiar, on campus, at work, at home, and so on. As your classmate describes this room, sketch its layout on a separate sheet of paper. Switch roles and then exchange sketches.

2. On a separate sheet of paper, assess the accuracy of your classmate's sketch. In your view, what aspects of spatial order affected your classmate's comprehension of your description?

CW 4.12
Ordering for
emphasis

Ordering for Emphasis   As discussed in relation to the child-rearing paragraph in Chapter 3 (pages 42–43), another way to organize your ideas is **emphatic order** or order of significance. In many cases, especially if you are trying to persuade readers, emphatic order means saving your strongest example for last. In other words, you build from less important to most important ideas. In this way, the examples or details build to a high point and sustain the reader's interest, much the way a story or play does.

Look at this paragraph about mandating the use of seat belts:

Everyone who drives or rides in a car should be required by law to wear a seat belt. One important reason is that seat belts prevent injuries in minor crashes because they keep the driver and passengers from bouncing around on impact. Even more important, not wearing a seat belt in a car equipped with air bags can lead to serious injuries. Recent studies have shown that unless a person is wearing a seat belt, the sudden expansion of an air bag can slam that person up against the roof of the car. Most important of all, children without seat belts are particularly vulnerable because they are generally too small to brace themselves for any crash. Seat belts keep children from being thrown against the windshield or out of the car in the most serious crashes. Clearly, because seat belts reduce injuries and save lives, wearing seat belts should be mandated by law.

The paragraph begins with a strong reason to mandate the wearing of seat belts: that they keep driver and passengers from bouncing around during minor crashes. This reason is followed by a stronger one: that air bags can be especially dangerous for those not wearing seat belts. This point is followed by an even stronger reason: that they help keep children safe. As you can see, emphatic order sustains the reader's interest as it accentuates the topic sentence.

COMPREHENSION AND PRACTICE 4.5

Working with Emphatic Order

1. Consider the following topic sentence:

   The parents of juveniles convicted of crimes like vandalism, shoplifting, and auto theft should be held legally responsible for the actions of their children.

   Now decide whether you are in favor of this statement or against it. Then, on a separate sheet of paper, generate at least four reasons to support your stand.

2. On the lines that follow, list your supporting reasons in *emphatic order,* moving from strong to stronger to strongest order.

   Answers will vary. Sample answers supporting the proposal are given.

   1. Knowing that their parents will be drawn into the legal issues may cause kids to rethink becoming involved in illegal activity.

   2. Kids generally have no income and are not in the position to make restitution.

   3. Juveniles aren't always aware of the full significance of their actions, but their parents should be.

   4. Parents are supposed to shape and monitor the behavior of their children, and if they don't do their job, they should be held responsible.

3. Read the following paragraph and, as you do, underline transitional expressions and phrases that help to illustrate degree of importance of each point in the argument.

American public schools should adjust the current school calendar and hold classes year round. A schedule calling for ten-week sessions of education followed by two-week vacation periods makes more sense. <u>For one thing</u>, this arrangement allows for a concentrated period followed by a rest period. As a result, students and teachers avoid the fatigue they face under the traditional calendar. <u>In addition</u>, the ten-week sessions would help with matters of discipline and order in the schools. For instance, more frequent breaks from school would minimize tensions among students. <u>More important</u>, though, adjusting the schedule would eliminate the long break in summer. When farming had a larger presence in the United States, the long summer break was necessary so that children could work. In today's world, however, the long summer break creates child-care problems for working parents. <u>Even more important</u>, the long break away from the classroom means students have a greater opportunity to forget what they have worked so hard to learn. Nobody would ever disagree that education is vital to success. Therefore, we should follow a calendar that will give students the best opportunity for sustained learning.

CHALLENGE 4.5   Working with Emphatic Order

1. Here are three topic sentences on controversial issues:
   a. People convicted of drunk driving should lose their licenses for five years.
   b. States should raise the minimum driving age from sixteen to eighteen.
   c. The FCC should more actively restrict the content of radio and television broadcasts.

   Choose one of the statements, decide whether you are in favor of or against it, and generate at least four supporting reasons. Then, on a separate sheet of paper, write a draft paragraph in which you include the topic sentence and use emphatic order to present at least three of the supporting examples you have generated.

2. Exchange your paragraph with a classmate. Evaluate the paragraph you receive, making sure the supporting examples are arranged in emphatic order. If you think any part of the presentation should be adjusted, make a note in the margin of the paper and return it to the writer.

3. Consider any suggestions your reader has made and make all necessary adjustments to your paragraph.

Choosing Effective Language

CW 4.13
Improving
diction

The words you choose to make a point can make all the difference in how successful you are in making it. Therefore, when you reassess, you must also reevaluate the language you've used. Your choice of words plays a direct role in how effectively your ideas come across for your reader. It's important to make sure that you use **effective language**—in other words, language that is specific and concise.

CW 4.14
Keeping
your writing
specific

Keeping Your Writing Specific To help your reader picture things as you picture them, you must keep your language specific, that is, detailed and to the point. When you write *sports car,* for example, you are probably visualizing a particular car. But *sports car* is a general expression, one that can mean different things to different people.

If you want to communicate your exact vision to your reader, you need to make all general terms specific. For example, instead of *sports car,* identify a particular type and brand of vehicle: *a brand new, metallic red Mitsubishi GT Eclipse Spyder convertible.* This way, your reader will have no question of what you mean when you write *sports car.*

Keeping your writing specific is particularly important when you deal with abstract concepts or ideas. Expressions like *highly talented* or *charismatic* are *abstract terms.* They *suggest* a broad array of possible meanings to a reader, but the concepts or ideas they name have no physical shape or equivalence. Therefore, when you use an abstract word, your audience might draw a different meaning from the one you intend.

The way to avoid difficulties with abstract terms is to support them with concrete examples. If you use *highly talented* to describe a person, include a *concrete* example to explain what you mean, as this example shows:

EXAMPLE

┌─ abstract term ─┐   ┌──── concrete supporting example ────

Jacqueline is a *highly talented* musician. *In high school, she placed first in every regional and state solo flute competition. Her breath control is so strong that every note is clearly audible, even during long, complicated pieces.*

Consider the specific details in the following paragraph about a special childhood play area:

> When I was young, one of my favorite spots was in the back of a closet at my grandmother's house. This closet was in the small second bedroom next to her living room. She kept all the toys and games for her grandchildren there, and I thought of it as my private hideaway. The paint on the door was shiny white, and it had been repainted so many times that I really had to tug on it to pull it open. Right at the front of the closet, hanging from a rod that ran across the width of the closet, was a row of my grandfather's clothes. My special spot was at the very back of the closet, so I had to push through this forest of clothes to get there. Then I would pull the string to put on the light, sit against the back wall underneath the rows of storage shelves, and be in my own four-foot-by-four-foot paradise. Even on the hottest day of the summer, this area was always cool, and I would happily read or color in there for hours. When I helped my grandmother move to a smaller apartment a few years ago, she and I laughed about all the times she had to come knocking on the closet door to find me.

FAST FACT If a word is used often enough, it eventually makes it into the dictionary as a legitimate part of the language. And so it happened that the favorite expression of cartoon dimwit Homer Simpson, "Doh!", was added to the *Oxford English Dictionary*'s online edition. Homer's frequently used saying is defined as "expressing frustration at the realization that things have turned out badly or not as planned or that one has just said or done something foolish. Also implying that another person has said or done something foolish." Doh!

Information like the exact location of the closet (*in the small second bedroom next to her living room*) and the description of the closet door (*shiny white, and it had been repainted so many times that I really had to tug on it to pull it open*) no doubt help you visualize the area. In addition, specific details about the inside of the closet (*this forest of clothes, the rows of storage shelves,* and *my own four-foot-by-four-foot paradise*) and the activities involved (*would happily read or color in there for hours*) bring this special place alive.

Keeping Your Writing Concise When you revise, you also need to make sure your writing is *concise*—brief but clear. One way to keep your writing concise is to eliminate deadwood. Deadwood means words and expressions that have no value and add no real meaning. For example, nonspecific words like *a lot, definitely, extremely, quite, really, somewhat,* and *very* combined with weak, vague terms such as *good* or *bad* may make your paper longer, but they do not help you communicate.

At the same time, concentrate on choosing the best word or two to express your meaning. The English dictionary is filled with words of precise meaning and almost endless variety. Don't write *really, really hot and humid* if you have a single word like *sultry* that provides the exact description you need. Take a look at the following two lists. The list on the left contains needlessly wordy phrases and expressions. The list on the right contains variations of these same phrases and expressions that are brief but to the point.

CW 4.15
Keeping your writing concise

CW 4.16
Learning new vocabulary

Convert these wordy expressions . . .	*into these concise words*
due to the fact that	because
a large number of	many
in the near future	soon
prior to	before
completely eliminate	eliminate
come to the realization that	realize
with the exception of	except for
in order that	so
at the present time	now
take action	act
the month of January	January
give a summary of	summarize
mutual cooperation	cooperation
make an assumption	assume

As you read the following paragraph, identify areas that you think need to be made more concise:

> My job last summer as a flagger for a construction company was harder than I really expected it to be. When I first heard about the opening, I figured that earning $7 to direct traffic around construction sites would be very easy. I soon found out how wrong I was. On the first morning in the month of June, I reported to the site at 8:15. Due to the fact that I needed to be highly visible to oncoming traffic, the boss handed me a hard hat, a safety vest, and a large orange flag. My station was next to the excavation in the road, and for the next four hours I had to stand in the extremely blazing sun directing traffic with my flag. Minutes seemed like hours as I stood there, sweating, and breathing in dust. By lunchtime, I felt that I had been on the job for a week instead of four hours. That's when I came to realize that I was in for a long summer.

As you can see, several sentences need to be made more concise. In the first sentence, *really* can be eliminated, as can *first* and *very* in the second sentence and *extremely* in the sixth. *The month of June* in the fourth sentence can be shortened to *June,* and *Due to the fact* in the fifth sentence can be changed to *Because.* Finally, *came to realize* in the last sentence can be shortened to *realized.*

Here's the same paragraph, this time with the changes:

> My job last summer as a flagger for a construction company was harder than I expected it to be. When I heard about the opening, I figured that earning $7 to direct traffic around construction sites would be easy. I soon found out how wrong I was. On the first morning in June, I reported to the site at 8:15. Because I needed to be highly visible to oncoming traffic, the boss handed me a hard hat, a safety vest, and a large orange flag. My station was next to the excavation in the road, and for the next four hours I had to stand in the blazing sun directing traffic with my flag. Minutes seemed like hours as I stood there, sweating, and breathing in dust. By lunchtime, I felt that I had been on the job for a week instead of four hours. That's when I realized that I was in for a long summer.

This version expresses the same idea, but thanks to the changes, it is more direct and concise.

COMPREHENSION AND PRACTICE 4.6

Working on Specific, Concise Language

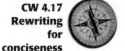

**CW 4.17
Rewriting
for
conciseness**

1. On a separate sheet of paper, take each of the following general words and transform them into concrete, specific terms.

   a. a vacation spot

   b. a DVD

   c. a sports team

2. On the lines that follow, make each of the following sentences more concise.

   a. A large number of tourists travel to New England during the months of October and November.

   Many tourists head to New England during October.

   _____

   b. The weather forecast calls for really cold temperatures in the near future.

   The forecast calls for cold temperatures soon.

   _____

   c. Michelle eventually came to the realization that cutting class definitely had the potential to create problems for her.

   Michelle eventually realized that cutting class could create problems for her.

   _____

CHALLENGE 4.6   Focusing on Effective Language

COLLABORATION

1. Read the following paragraph. Then, working with a classmate, underline the details that you agree are too general. On a separate sheet of paper, create details and write versions of these sentences that are more specific.
   Answers will vary.

**CW 4.18
Using
sentence
variety**

My first job, as a member of the staff at Mac and Al's Diner, was really fun. I worked every weekend for a long time when I was in high school. On Friday nights, I worked very long hours. On Saturdays and Sundays, I worked a lot of the day. I never knew what to expect when I went to work. Sometimes

I'd be the dishwasher, and other times the boss would have me do other things. The people I worked with were very nice. Many of the customers came in a lot, so they seemed like family. One couple originally met at the diner, so when they got married, they invited everyone to the wedding.

2. On a separate sheet of paper, complete the following topic sentence by filling in the blank:

The thing that I liked best about my first job was _____Answers will vary_____ .

Do some prewriting to generate ideas to support this topic sentence. Then, on the same piece of paper, create a draft paragraph of five to ten sentences on this subject.

COLLABORATION

3. Exchange your draft paragraph with a classmate. As you read the draft you receive, pay particular attention to the language, making note of any general or abstract words and expressions that need to be made more specific. Return the draft to the writer.

4. Consider any spots that your reader thinks should be more specific and make any adjustments in language that you agree are necessary.

Getting Feedback from an Objective Reader

CW 4.19
Getting
feedback
from an
objective
reader

An especially helpful step in reassessing is to seek feedback from an objective reader. Anybody who will read your work and then respond intelligently and honestly to it—a classmate, a family member, a friend—is a potential reader.

To make the task easier for your reader, provide the following reader assessment checklist. This series of questions will guide your reader through an evaluation of your writing. More important, the answers will help you to see how effectively you communicate.

CW 4.20
Understanding
peer editing

✓**Reader Assessment Checklist**

☐ Do you understand the point I am making? (topic sentence)

☐ Do I stick to that point all the way through? (unity)

☐ Are all my ideas and examples clearly connected and easy to follow? (coherence)

☐ Are the words I've used specific and concise? (effective language)

☐ What changes do you think I should make?

Here is an example of what a peer response to these questions might look like, in this case about the draft paragraph on good parenting presented earlier:

> *I like your paper—it really made me think. I think the topic sentence is good, and the other sentences are unified and coherent. I think the language you use is one of the best features because it is simple and anybody could understand your point. The only thing I wish is that you gave some specific examples to explain what you mean. Why exactly is it important that parents read to kids? How can parents help their kids make sense of the world? These are the kinds of questions your writing made me wonder about. If you add this kind of material, your paper would be even better.*

As you can see, comments like these can be very helpful in zeroing in on problem spots remaining in a draft.

COMPREHENSION AND PRACTICE 4.7

Evaluating the Feedback Process

1. On the following lines, explain what you find most difficult about evaluating another writer's paper and why you find this part hard.

   Answers will vary. Some students may find it most difficult to come up with specific

   suggestions for improving someone else's writing.

   _____

   _____

2. On the following lines, identify the question on the reader assessment checklist (page 67) that you think is most important to help writers improve their papers, and explain why, in your view, this question is more important than the others.

   Answers will vary. Many students will choose the first question: "Do you understand

   the point I am making?" They may reason that if their message isn't clear, most of the

   other questions won't matter.

   _____

CHALLENGE 4.7   Working with the Reader Assessment Checklist

COLLABORATION

1. So far, you have completed a number of draft paragraphs. After consulting with your instructor, choose one of these drafts and make a copy of it. Exchange your paper with a reader who has not previously seen it. Complete the following steps with the draft you receive:

a. Put a + next to the topic sentence if it provides a clear direction. Put a **?** next to it if the main point isn't clear.

b. Check the paragraph for unity and coherence. Underline any portion of a sentence or any complete sentence that disrupts the unity of the paragraph, and put a ✓ at any point where additional transition would help. Also, note any problem with the order of sentences, indicating how you think things should be changed to improve the paragraph.

c. Check the paragraph for effective language. Circle any general or abstract words and overly wordy phrases and expressions. Write suggested substitutes above the circled words and phrases.

2. Return the draft to the writer. Save your draft and your reader's comments for later use.

Redrafting

**CW 4.21
Tips for
revising**

After you have identified what still needs work in your writing, the next step is redrafting, or writing a new version or draft of your paper. As you work through later drafts, you will correct any flaws you've discovered. In addition, you will fill any gaps in content. As page 44 in Chapter 3 indicates, to do this you **amplify**—provide additional, specific details.

Here is a first draft paragraph dealing with medical explorations:

> Research has led to dramatic changes in medical treatment. Technological innovations have helped to turn ideas from science fiction into fact. In addition, researchers continue to develop new devices and treatments designed to prolong life.

Apply the reader assessment checklist to this paragraph and you will quickly uncover its strengths and weaknesses. The paragraph is largely unified, coherent, and organized, but, right now, it is far too general and it lacks supporting details and examples. To fill these gaps, you need to amplify by supplying information that answers the kinds of questions a reader might have about this subject. For instance, what *specific* changes in medical treatment have occurred? What *particular* innovations have made the impossible real? What *exactly* are medical researchers working on now?

Now consider this amplified version of the same paragraph:

> Research has led to dramatic changes in medical treatment. **For example, serious surgical procedures such as heart and brain surgery are now commonplace.** Technological innovations have helped to turn ideas from science fiction into fact. **Today, burn victims enjoy faster healing because of the development of artificial skin. Replacement knees, hips, and knuckles mean that people suffering from degenerative joint conditions can now regain greater mobility.** In addition, researchers continue to develop new devices and treatments designed to prolong life. **Prototypes of a completely self-contained artificial heart, powered by a rechargeable battery the size of a book, already exist. Within the next few years, researchers hope to make available a number of other bodily parts, including artificial kidneys and retinas.**

As you can see, the new information, shown in italics, clearly improves the paragraph. This new material specifies the progress that medical researchers have achieved as well as the changes that are on the horizon.

Redrafting is different with every paper you write. With some papers, you'll need to make minor adjustments in several areas. With other papers, you may have to concentrate to a greater degree on one particular point. No matter what you need to add, delete, or correct, however, remember that your goal for redrafting is always the same: to improve your writing.

FAST FACT   According to some estimates, the average sentence in American English is about twenty-two words.

COMPREHENSION AND PRACTICE 4.8

Amplifying for Effectiveness

1. The sentences below are too general to be effective. On the lines that follow each, add details or examples—in complete sentence form—that amplify the information. Answers will vary. Sample answers are shown.

a. That party was exciting. For example,

   my friends Tatiana and Carmella brought along a karaoke machine and set up a

   singing contest that lasted for three fun-filled hours.

b. My neighborhood is interesting. For instance,

   all the old manufacturing buildings have been turned into small shops and

   restaurants.

c. My high school had problems. For example,

   the new gym couldn't be used for two years because of problems with mold.

2. Choose one of the sentences you have just amplified. On a separate sheet of paper, write three additional supporting sentences, making sure that they are amplified so that they answer questions your audience might have.

CHALLENGE 4.8   **Employing the Reader Assessment Checklist to Identify Weaknesses**

COLLABORATION

1. Read the following paragraph:

> One thing that college students can be sure of is that their money won't stay in their wallets very long. For one thing, they have to pay tuition, which costs a lot. Financial aid and scholarships help, but many students still have to struggle to pay for other things. Different living expenses add up to quite a bit, and transportation is a big issue. Students also have to pay for supplies they need for their classes. College may be an investment for the future, but when it comes to paying for it, most students are much more worried about the present.

Now, working with a classmate, prepare an evaluation of the paragraph on a separate sheet of paper, using the reader assessment checklist (page 67).

2. On the same paper, make a list of at least five details that would help to improve the paragraph.

Acknowledging Your Sources

If in your writing you support your own ideas with information from some other source, you need to acknowledge that source. Otherwise you would be guilty of **plagiarism,** the act of taking or stealing someone else's work and passing it off as your own.

Whenever you come across material in another source that would help you make your point, you can include it with your own words in one of three ways. You can present it word for word as it appears with quotation marks around it. This is called **direct quotation.** A second way to record information from a source is to express the point in your own words and include an explanation or interpretation, which is called **paraphrase.** A third way to present information from a source is to provide, in your own words, a greatly reduced version of the original, which is called **summary.**

Regardless of the way you present information you take from another source, you must acknowledge *where it originally appeared* in two spots in your paper. To do so, you follow one of the standard methods of documentation. The **Modern Language Association (MLA) system** and the **American Psychological Association (APA) method** are the two most common methods.

The first place to acknowledge your source is immediately after the information you have included. At that point, insert a set of parentheses containing the author's last name. If you are following MLA, you also include the page number, as these examples show:

MLA parenthetical documentation

From a book

The people who make their living at sea clearly understand its tremendous power. In particular, they recognize and fear what can happen as a result of storm-driven waves. "On a steel boat the windows implode, the hatches fail, and the boat starts to downflood" (Junger 173).

From a newspaper, magazine, or other periodical

The goal had been to tell the story as accurately as possible. The best of intentions aren't enough with some stories, however, as she found out when she saw the article in print: "But later in the day, when I saw the magazine, the article seemed different to me from the version I had approved with my editor" (Szalavitz 76).

The second place that you must acknowledge your source is at the end of your paper, in a section called "Works Cited," as these examples show. Note that the second (and each subsequent) line of each entry is indented.

Works Cited

For a book   Junger, Sebastian. *The Perfect Storm: A True*
                              Story of Men against the Sea. New York:
                              HarperCollins, 1997.

For a newspaper,   Szalavitz, Maia. "12 Steps Back." *Brill's Content*
magazine, or   Jan. 2001: 72–78.
other periodical

If you use the APA method, you record the information in the text of your paper
in a slightly different way—the author's last name plus the *year of publication, pre-*
ceded by a comma, rather than a page number—as these examples show:

APA parenthetical documentation

From a book   The people who make their living at sea clearly
                              understand its tremendous power. In particular,
                              they recognize and fear what can happen as a
                              result of storm-driven waves. "On a steel boat
                              the windows implode, the hatches fail, and the
                              boat starts to downflood" (Junger, 1997).

From a newspaper,   The goal had been to tell the story as accu-
magazine, or   rately as possible. The best of intentions aren't
other periodical   enough with some stories, however, as she
                              found out when she saw the article in print:
                              "But later in the day, when I saw the magazine,
                              the article seemed different to me from the ver-
                              sion I had approved with my editor" (Szalavitz,
                              2001).

And your notations at the end of the paper, presented under the title "References,"
would also look slightly different from the MLA style. Initials rather than first
names are used, and the name is followed by the date of publication, in parentheses, plus a period. Also, you capitalize only the first word of the title of the work as
well as any subtitle and proper nouns, as these examples show. Again, make sure
to indent the second line (and any other subsequent lines) of each entry.

References

For a book   Junger, S. (1997). *The perfect storm: A true story*
                                  of men against the sea. New York: HarperCollins.

For a newspaper,   Szalavitz, M. (2001, January). 12 steps back.
magazine, or   *Brill's Content,* 72–78.
other periodical

Of course, you have many other types of documents from which you might draw
information to support your own ideas, including the Internet. The reference section of your college library contains complete explanations and thorough illustrations of how to acknowledge the source for these kinds of documents following
the MLA, APA, and other systems of documentation. If you have questions or
need additional guidance, stop by the reference desk for help.

COMPREHENSION AND PRACTICE
4.9

Working with Documentation

1. Find a source of a least five paragraphs from a book, magazine, or newspaper. On the lines below, write the parenthetical documentation for the source as well as a full citation for the end of a paper using both the MLA and APA styles of documentation. Use the examples above to guide you.

Answers will vary.

_____

_____

2. On a separate sheet of paper, prepare both a paraphrase and a summary of your five-paragraph passage.

Editing

Once you have eliminated the weaknesses in your draft, you are ready for the final step in revising: *editing.* When you edit, you polish that draft to correct errors in your use of English. This means you need to *proofread,* to identify and eliminate any errors in grammar, spelling, and punctuation.

Developing a Personal Proofreading System

CW 4.22
Revising, editing, and proofreading

The secret to effective proofreading is timing. Plan your time so that you proofread your paper when you are rested. That way, fatigue and familiarity with the content won't cause you to see what you *meant to write* rather than what you *have actually written.* When you are tired, for example, you may see *receive* even though you've actually misspelled it as *recieve.*

Also, concentrate on the types of errors that most often appear in papers. Focus on the following proofreading checklist, and you'll eliminate the mistakes that most trouble writers and distract readers.

✓ Proofreading Checklist

☐ Have I eliminated all sentence fragments (*frag*)? (Chapter 18)

☐ Have I eliminated all comma splices (*cs*)? (Chapter 20)

☐ Have I eliminated all run-on sentences (*rs*)? (Chapter 20)

☐ Is the spelling (*sp*) correct throughout? (Chapter 29)

☐ Is the verb tense (*t*) correct throughout? (Chapters 22, 23, 24)

☐ Do all subjects agree with their verbs (*subj/verb agr*)? (Chapters 17, 21, 25)

☐ Do all pronouns agree with their antecedents (*pro/ant agr*)? (Chapter 26)

Of course, this checklist doesn't cover all the errors writers make. You may have trouble with some other aspect of writing such as double negatives (Chapter 27) or apostrophe use (Chapters 29 and 31). Don't worry if you don't yet understand why some of these errors occur. Other chapters in this book will explain how to watch for and eliminate them. The Sentence Skill Locator on the inside back cover shows you where to look for help.

Another secret to effective proofreading is to tailor your checklist to suit your own needs. Concentrate on the items listed above that you find most difficult. Add others that especially trouble your writing. Then you'll have your own personal proofreading checklist that focuses on your particular areas of concern.

Teaming up with a proofreading partner is another way to eliminate errors in your paper. Once you have proofread your paper, exchange it with another reader. This proofreading partner will not be as invested or involved with the writing as you are and so may be better able to find any remaining errors. You can perform the same duties for your partner. The result will be better papers for both of you.

Using Computer Tools to Your Advantage

CW 4.23
Revising
with a word
processor

If you are using a computer to do your writing, you probably have an additional proofreading tool: the spell check command. This function checks your spelling against the computer's dictionary and points out words that appear to be misspelled. Sometimes the computer offers a list of words that you might have intended rather than the misspelled word. To eliminate the error, simply select the correctly spelled version. If the computer doesn't offer a possibility, look up the word to find the correct spelling, and then make the changes yourself.

CW 4.24
Computers
and revising

Don't trust the computer to find all your spelling errors, however. Imagine that you have written this sentence: "Suddenly the room became deathly *quite.*" The computer doesn't read and reason as you do, so it won't be able to tell that you meant to write *quiet,* not *quite.* Therefore, take full advantage of the spell checker on your computer, but do a final check yourself to make sure, for example, that you don't use *dose* when you really mean *does.*

COMPREHENSION
AND PRACTICE
4.10

Employing a Proofreading Checklist

1. Of the areas of concern noted in the proofreading checklist on page 73, which one has given you the most trouble in the past? Why do you think you have difficulty with this area?

   Answers will vary.
   _____

   _____

2. Proofread the following paragraph. Correct the errors you find. In the margin beside each error, write the abbreviation from the proofreading checklist on page 73 to identify the type of error (*frag, sp,* and so forth).

   The hardest thing I ever has to endure was my parents' divorce. I was ten

   when it happened, I had always thought I had the perfect family. A few days before Christmas, my mother sat down in front of my brother and me and told us that my father was moving out to live with another woman. Every kid wants to have someone they can look up to, and for me that used to be my father. But when I saw how sad my mother looks, I hated my father I wished he were dead. He kept calling the house to talk with me, but I wouldn't talk to him. Two years later, after the divorce was final. I met him by accident downtown. When he seen me, he started to cry and said he was sorry. I couldn't forgive him then and I can't forgive him now. He ruined my prefect family.

Now check your answers against the corrected version on page 77.

CHALLENGE 4.9   Editing to Complete a Final Draft

CW 4.25
Computers and editing

1. For Challenge 4.7 (pages 68–69), you and a classmate exchanged draft paragraphs you had been working on. You used the reader assessment checklist (page 67) to evaluate the draft relative to the topic sentence, unity, coherence, and effective language and returned the paper to the writer. Now take this paragraph and redraft it to eliminate the weaknesses you and your reader have identified.

COLLABORATION

2. Exchange your redrafted paragraph with a classmate who has not previously seen it. Using the proofreading checklist (page 73) to guide you, edit and proofread the draft you receive. Put a ✓ before anything you believe to be an error. Then return the paragraph to the writer.

3. After considering your reader's evaluation, make any necessary corrections to your paragraph.

FAST FACT   As you write and revise, focus on time and patience. Michelangelo worked three years to create his massive statue, *David,* and four years to paint the ceiling of the Sistine Chapel.

Examining a Revised Draft

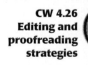

CW 4.26
Editing and proofreading strategies

So what happens when you follow the revising guidelines presented in this chapter? Here again is the completed draft version of the paragraph on being a good parent that appeared at the end of Chapter 3 (page 47).

Through their own behavior, parents can lay the groundwork for their children's happiness. Reading to children every day is important. Parents also need to spend time interacting with their children and responding to their questions patiently. They count on their parents to help them make sense of the world around them. Most of all, parents should regularly tell their children that they love them and praise them when they do something well. Nothing is more important to children's future success than the support and interest of their parents.

Now consider this revised version of the same paragraph:

> Through their own behavior, parents can lay the groundwork for their children's happiness. Reading to children every day is important. **It teaches them the basics of the language, from ABCs to sentences and paragraphs. It also makes them familiar with what books can do for them. As a result, when they enter school they'll have a head start that they'll never lose.** Parents also need to spend time interacting with their children and responding to their questions patiently. They count on their parents to help them make sense of the world around them. **For example, if they ask why the sun shines or why cats and dogs fight, parents should do their best to give an honest answer in terms the children can understand.** Most of all, parents should regularly tell their children that they love them and praise them when they do something well. **The consistent reinforcement when they pick up their toys or share with others helps provide a sense of love and security.** Nothing is more important to children's future success than the support and interest of their parents.

Thanks to the additional supporting material developed during revising, shown here in boldface, this version is far more specific and thorough. This final draft version is clear proof of the power of revision, as the following instructor's comments indicate:

> Congratulations—you have done a fine job revising your paper. You have made a number of improvements since I saw the first draft a week ago. I especially like the specific examples you've added. Now in addition to just <u>saying</u> what parents should do to help their children, you explain why through those new examples and therefore <u>show</u> exactly what you mean. When we move on to writing essays, you should consider expanding this paper. All in all it's an excellent first paper.

FOR FURTHER EXPLORATION

Focus on one of the following topics as the basis for a draft paragraph (at least five to ten sentences). To generate ideas for further development, use the prewriting technique—or combination of techniques—that you like. After identifying a specific topic, compose a first-draft paragraph. Then, using the material in this chapter to guide you, work your way through the different steps in revising to complete a final draft.

- superstition
- what constitutes physical beauty
- wireless phone annoyances

▶ **DISCOVERING CONNECTIONS**

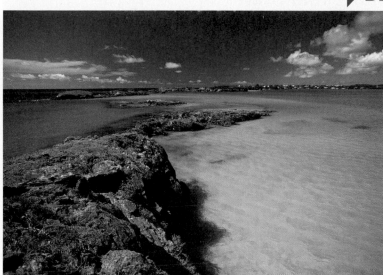

When you see this photo, what comes to mind? Do you wonder what it would feel like to step or dive into the inviting water on a hot day? Does it remind you of a time when you headed to the beach to escape the summer heat? Does the picture serve as a reminder of how beautiful—and vital to our survival—our oceans, lakes, and other waterways are? Or does it make you think of the beginning or end of a journey by sea as ancient mariners did? How difficult do you imagine these kinds of odysseys were? How do you think you would have fared?

For this assignment, focus on one of these questions or another one that the picture suggests. Referring to the material in this chapter as a guide, create a draft of at least five to ten sentences. Using the material in this chapter to guide you, develop a complete draft of a paragraph. Then, following the process outlined in this chapter, thoroughly revise the paragraph. ◀

Corrected Version of Comprehension and Practice 4.10, Number 2

t & subj/verb agr — The hardest thing I ever ~~has~~ *had* to endure was my parents' divorce. I was

cs — ten when it happened, I had always thought I had the perfect family. A few

days before Christmas, my mother sat down in front of my brother and me

and told us that my father was moving out to live with another woman. Every

pro/ant agr — ~~kid~~ wants to have someone ~~they~~ *he or she* can look up to, and for me that used to be

t/rs — my father. But when I saw how sad my mother ~~looks,~~ *looked* I hated my father I

wished he were dead. He kept calling the house to talk with me, but I

frag — wouldn't talk to him. Two years later, after the divorce was final, I met him by

t — accident downtown. When he ~~seen~~ *saw* me, he started to cry and said he was

cs — sorry. I couldn't forgive him then and I can't forgive him now. He ruined my

sp — ~~prefect~~ *perfect* family.

RECAP Refining and Polishing Your Draft

New terms in this chapter	Definitions
revising	the stage of writing during which you refine and polish a draft Revising means (1) reassessing, (2) redrafting, and (3) editing.
reassessing	looking closely at a draft to find and correct errors and weaknesses
redrafting	creating a new version of a piece of writing by correcting problems and incorporating new material
editing	polishing and proofreading a piece of writing to eliminate errors in grammar, spelling, and punctuation
unity	quality achieved in writing when all sentences relate to the main idea
coherence	quality achieved in writing when sentences hold together well Coherence comes from logical order and connections that show how ideas interrelate.
synonyms	words with similar meanings
transitional expressions	words that connect ideas and show relationships between them
chronological order	organization in sequence on the basis of time
spatial order	organization based on location of parts in relation to a whole
emphatic order	organization based on order of significance, or importance
effective language	language that communicates well because it is specific (detailed) and concise (brief but clear)
amplification	the addition of specific details and examples
plagiarism	appropriating someone else's work
direct quotation	presenting information word for word within quotation marks as it appears in an original source
paraphrase	presenting information from a source in different words with an interpretation or explanation
summary	presenting information from a source in a greatly reduced form
MLA system of documentation	the Modern Language Association's method of acknowledging sources
APA system of documentation	the American Psychological Association's method of acknowledging sources

The Process of Revising

1 Reassess ⟶ **2 Redraft** ⟶ **3 Edit**

Check for ⟵
- unity
- coherence
- effective language

Seek feedback from objective reader

Add new material ⟵

Improve existing material

Delete irrelevant material

Proofread for errors in
- spelling
- grammar
- punctuation

GOING FORWARD...

CW 4.27
Refining and
polishing
review

CW 4.28
Using spell
checkers

CW 4.29
Desktop
publishing
resources

Q: But what happens if I revise and I'm still not happy with my paper?

A: Actually, more often than not, you won't be completely satisfied with your first revision. Remember—writing is a *recursive* act, a process that you will cycle through, sometimes several times, before you've made your paper as good as it can be. The good news is that each time you revise, you will be focusing on fewer spots. In this sense, think of an artist, sketching or painting a scene. Rarely does the first pencil or brushstroke remain unchanged. The artist just continues to build on it, patiently and confidently. That's what you need to do when you revise: be patient enough to carry on and be confident that the work will be worth it.

PART 2

Using the Patterns of Paragraph Development

CHAPTER 5
Narration

Navigating This Chapter

This chapter will explore the basic requirements for writing an effective narrative paragraph:

- providing a topic sentence that establishes a context
- explaining the events in the story in chronological order
- recognizing the most effective point of view

GETTING STARTED...

CW 5.1
Chapter
basics

Q: I want to tell the story of something that happened to me. What's the best technique to use to tell someone else this story?

A: When you want to tell about an experience you have had—or, for that matter, an experience that you witnessed someone else have—the answer is **narration**, the organizing strategy through which you relate a series of events.

Overview: Understanding the Modes, Purposes, and Importance of Telling Your Story

CW 5.2
Overview of
narration

If you've looked ahead in this book or through the table of contents, you've seen names such as *description, example, process, definition, comparison and contrast, cause and effect,* and *division and classification.* These are the **modes,** organizing or developmental strategies or techniques that you can use to express your point on a subject. Each of these organizing strategies enables you to approach and cover a topic in a different way.

As Chapter 1 (pages 7–8) shows, you write to fulfill one of three purposes: to *inform,* to *entertain,* or to *persuade.* The organizing strategies are the devices you use to fulfill those purposes. **Narration,** the focus of this chapter, is the mode that people use to tell stories, from "Once upon a time . . ." fairy tales to personal experiences to autobiographies and memoirs.

CW 5.3
The
rhetorical
modes

This chapter and the seven that follow examine the modes one by one. As you read this material, you will learn and practice the characteristics of each developmental strategy. When you do, keep this point in mind: Most writing relies on a combination of modes to communicate ideas to readers. One mode will dominate and one or more of the others will support it. The longer a piece of writing is, the more likely this will be the case.

Imagine, for example, that you wanted to write about the problem of beach erosion affecting states such as North Carolina, New York, and Florida. In such a writing, you would rely heavily on cause and effect, which focuses on reasons underlying events. However, you might also use process to explain how the ocean gradually claims more and more of the shore. In addition, you might employ description to illustrate the changes and comparison and contrast to detail different solutions to the problems.

The focus of Chapter 13 is *argument.* Argument is different in that it doesn't refer to a single mode but to a purpose: to persuade a reader of the validity of your position on a subject. Simply put, argument is writing that persuades. As Chapter 13 shows, you use whatever combination of modes is necessary to fulfill that purpose.

The focus of this chapter, however, is narration. You use narration whenever you relate a series of events or incidents. For instance, with a story about a date gone wrong, you would focus on narration, as you would with a paper about a prank or the discovery of a family secret. Mastering this mode will also enable you to create longer documents that focus on narration.

Writing a Clear Topic Sentence That Establishes a Context

ESL Note
See "Sentence Basics" on pages 589–590 and "Word Order" on pages 591–592.

**CW 5.4
Establishing
a context**

In order to help readers understand the point of a narrative paragraph, the writer must establish a clear direction, or point, for the story he or she is about to tell. The part of the paragraph that provides this needed direction is the topic sentence. The topic sentence establishes a context for the sequence of events that follows. In other words, it sets the scene and orients the reader. As Chapter 3 showed, a typical topic sentence pinpoints both the *topic* and your *attitude* or *reaction* to it. In the narrative paragraph, the topic is the incident, or story. Your reaction is the "spin," or slant, you put on the events you relate.

Look at the topic sentence in this narrative paragraph from *Bird by Bird* in which author Anne Lamott discusses her father:

> I'm sure my father was the person on whom his friends relied to tell their stories, in school and college. I know for sure he was later, in the town where he was raising his children. He could take major events or small episodes from daily life and shade or exaggerate things in such a way as to capture their shape and substance, capture what life felt like in the society in which he and his friends lived and worked and bred. People looked up to him to put into words what was going on.

**CW 5.5
Providing
topic
sentences**

The topic sentence is *I'm sure my father was the person on whom his friends relied to tell their stories, in school and college.* As you can see, it prepares the reader for the focus of the rest of the paragraph. The opening sentence states that her father was the one whom acquaintances counted on to present their experiences, and the other sentences explain why.

Relying on Chronological Order

CW 5.6
Chronological
order

Narration is the mode that focuses on a series of events. For this reason, how effectively you present the sequence will influence how your reader understands it. With narration, **chronological order** is often the ideal choice. As Chapter 4 (pages 57–58) explains, this method of arrangement involves presenting the series of incidents in the order in which they happened. Consider the use of chronological order in the following narrative paragraph from John Monczunski's essay, "Cornered," in which he discusses an encounter with a stranger who, he fears, intends to harm him:

CW 5.7
Overview of
narration

> Then the spell breaks. Two blocks ahead, a solitary figure emerges from a building. He wheels around and begins walking toward me. When I see him my stomach knots. I am not sure if he is even aware of me, but I know I do not want to meet him. I decide on a tactical evasive maneuver and cross to the other side of the street. The man counters my move. Apparently he is intent on meeting me and he reestablishes our collision course. We mirror each other's movements all the while slicing the gap between us. His long-distance telegraphed intentions add to my unease. Am I paranoid or prudent?

Here, Monczunski makes it easier for his reader to understand the experience by relating it in the order in which it occurred. First, he noticed the man leave a building, turn and walk toward him. He then crosses the street to avoid the man, but the man crosses the street as well and continues heading toward him.

When you write a narrative, you will find certain transitional expressions helpful to show the sequence of events. Some of them are listed below.

Transitional Expressions for Narratives

after	during	later	soon
before	first (second, etc.)	meanwhile	then

Sometimes writers employ a **flashback,** an incident deliberately presented out of sequence, often to give the reader some important background information. Imagine, for example, you were writing about how you finally overcame terrible stage fright in your public speaking course. You had originally developed the stage fright in the first grade when you forgot your lines in the spring play. Including this flashback in your paper would make it easier for your reader to understand how difficult overcoming your anxiety was.

COMPREHENSION AND PRACTICE

5.1

Considering Topic Sentences and Chronological Order

1. Read the following paragraph by Helen Keller from her autobiography, *The Story of My Life,* in which she discusses learning some basic signs of communication without understanding their significance:

The morning after my teacher came she led me into her room and gave me a doll. The little blind children at the Perkins Institute had sent it and Laura Bridgman [the first deaf and blind person to be educated in the United States] had dressed it; but I did not know this until afterward. When I had played with it a little while, Miss Sullivan slowly spelled into my hand the word "d-o-l-l." I was at once interested in this finger play and tried to imitate it. When I finally succeeded in making the letters correctly I was flushed with childish pleasure and pride. Running downstairs to my mother I held up my hand and made the letters for doll. I did not know that I was spelling a word or even that words existed. I was simply making my fingers go in monkey-like imitation. In the days that followed I learned to spell in this uncomprehending way a great many words, among them *pin, hat, cup,* and a few verbs like *sit, stand,* and *walk.* But my teacher had been with me several weeks before I understood that everything has a name.

On the lines below, briefly explain how the topic sentence sets the direction and context for the supporting sentences.

The topic sentence identifies that this day was special because her teacher had given

her a doll. The rest of the paragraph discusses how her teacher taught her to sign,

with *doll* the first word she learned.

2. Choose one of the supporting sentences and briefly explain how it specifies the point made in the topic sentence.

Answers will vary somewhat depending on which sentence is chosen, but each is

related to signing words, *doll* being the first word Keller mastered.

3. On the lines that follow, briefly explain how chronological order helps you understand what Keller experienced.

Chronological order presents the events as they occurred, thus making it easy to

understand Keller's experiences.

Choosing the Most Effective Point of View

**CW 5.8
Narrating
from
different
points of
view**

Any time you tell a story, you select a **point of view,** the perspective from which you relate the experience. Often when you use narration, you will write from a *first person point of view,* that is, from your viewpoint as you participated in or experienced the event. With first person point of view, you use *I, me,* and other words that refer to yourself. Other times, you will write from a *third person point of view,* that is, as an observer rather than as a participant. Because you focus on others with third person narration, you use *he, she, her, they,* and so on.

Consider this narrative paragraph from "They All Just Went Away," an essay by writer Joyce Carol Oates, which features first person point of view:

> I must have been a lonely child. Until the age of twelve or thirteen, my most intense, happiest hours were spent tramping desolate fields, woods, and creek banks near my family's farmhouse in Millersport, New York. No one knew where I went. My father, working most of the day at Harrison's, a division of General Motors in Lockport, and at other times preoccupied, would not have asked; if my mother asked, I might have answered in a way that would deflect curiosity. I was an articulate, verbal child. Yet I could not have explained what drew me to the abandoned houses, barns, silos, corncribs. A hike of miles through fields of spiky grass, across outcroppings of shale as steeply angled as stairs, was a lark if the reward was an empty house.

It's clear from the use of words like *I, my,* and *me* that this passage concerns an incident in which Oates was a participant.

Now, consider this paragraph from Peter Griffin's biography of Ernest Hemingway, *Less Than a Treason.* It describes Hemingway's first encounter with flying.

> Ernest first saw the plane from the window of the taxi he and Hadley took to the field. It was a silver biplane with a tiny cabin with portholes, and a seat for the pilot in the rear. Ernest bought the tickets at a counter in the plane shed, and had them checked by an attendant who stood just ten feet away, by the door to the field. Then, with cotton stuffed into their ears, Ernest and Hadley climbed aboard the plane and sat one behind the other. The pilot, a short, little man with his cap on backwards, shouted contact, and the mechanic gave the propeller a spin.

In this case, the paragraph is related from the third person point of view. In other words, the writer is not a participant but a witness.

FAST FACT   Narrative writing has more staying power than you at first might think. The *Guinness World Records 2001* reports that the best-selling diary of all time is *The Diary of Anne Frank,* which has been translated into fifty-five languages and has sold more than twenty-five million copies.

COMPREHENSION AND PRACTICE 5.2

Considering Point of View

1. Read the following paragraph from "Ruby Bridges and a Painting." In it, Robert Coles recounts what he witnessed as a girl named Ruby Bridges became the first African-American child to attend a desegregated New Orleans school in 1960, a scene captured by famed American illustrator Norman Rockwell:

A fateful coincidence changed my life in the fall of 1960—and gave me, eventually, an unforgettable acquaintance with a Norman Rockwell painting. I was on my way to a medical conference in New Orleans when suddenly a police barricade confronted me and others trying to make our way toward that cosmopolitan city. All of us were told that because a nearby school was being desegregated by federal court order, we were not gong to be allowed further travel—a blockade had been established to give the police control over some of the city's neighborhoods. Suddenly, unexpectedly, I had a lot of time on my hands. I could have turned around and returned to Biloxi, Mississippi, where I then lived as an Air Force physician, in the military under the old doctors' draft law. Instead, I walked a few blocks, and soon enough I was in the presence of a large crowd of men, women, and children, who were not only milling around but occasionally uniting in a shouted refrain: "Two, four, six, eight, we don't want to integrate!"

On the following lines, briefly explain how, in your view, the impact of this paragraph would be changed if it were presented in third person point of view rather than first person.

This paragraph would be less likely to draw in the reader and be more clinical if third

person had been used rather than first person.

2. The final sentence of this paragraph includes a direct quotation from the people protesting the desegregation. On the lines that follow, briefly explain why you think that Coles chose to include the actual words the people chanted.

Coles chose to use direct quotation to heighten the intensity and create a greater

sense of realism.

CHALLENGE 5.1   Considering Purpose in Narration Paragraphs

COLLABORATION

This chapter features several sample narrative paragraphs. The names of the authors of these paragraphs, with the appropriate page numbers, are listed below. Working with a partner, take another look at the paragraphs. Then, on the lines next to the names, list the primary purpose and any secondary purposes for each paragraph.

1. Anne Lamott, page 83

Most students will agree that Lamott's primary purpose is to entertain and her

secondary purpose is to inform.

2. John Monczunski, page 84

Most students will agree that Monczunski's primary purpose is to entertain and that

his secondary purpose is to inform.

3. Joyce Carol Oates, page 86

Most students will agree that Oates's primary purpose is to entertain and her

secondary purpose is to inform.

4. Peter Griffin, page 86

Most students will agree that Griffin's primary purpose is to inform and his secondary

purpose is to entertain, although a few students may argue for the opposite view.

FOR FURTHER EXPLORATION
···

1. Choose one of the following topics and, selecting one of the strategies that
   you practiced in Chapter 2, prewrite on that topic. Let your mind revisit the
   events of that episode:

   - an occasion when you lost your temper
   - a good childhood playground experience
   - an experience with terrible weather
   - a particular holiday celebration
   - a visit to someplace unfamiliar
   - an embarrassing incident
   - a time when you witnessed someone's kindness

2. This chapter features several sample paragraphs:

   - a discussion of a father's special quality (Anne Lamott, page 83)
   - the story of an unwanted encounter with a stranger (John Monczunski,
     page 84)
   - the adventures of a child, exploring on her own (Joyce Carol Oates,
     page 86)
   - the account of Ernest Hemingway's first flight (Peter Griffin, page 86)

For this assignment, think of an experience you have had or witnessed similar to the events discussed in one of these paragraphs. Prewrite on the experience, identify a specific focus, and create a paragraph of at least five to ten sentences in which you use narration to discuss the event. Use the material in this chapter to guide you through this process.

▶ **DISCOVERING CONNECTIONS**

What do you think of when you look at this photo? What story do you think this ancient bas-relief is trying to tell? For example, where might the figures in the sculpture be marching to and for what purpose? What do you imagine they were feeling as they marched? The amount of work involved in creating the work of art must have been enormous—what's the biggest task you've ever taken on yourself? What was the outcome? Does seeing this artwork remind you of a visit you made—or wish you had made—to a museum of history or art?

For this assignment, turn your attention to one of these questions or another one that the picture makes your think of. Using the material in this chapter as a guide, develop a paragraph of at least five to ten sentences that draws on the power of narration. Remember to pay close attention to chronological order and appropriate point of view. ◀

✔ **Narrative Paragraph Checklist**

☐ Does the topic sentence establish a context?

☐ Is the material arranged in chronological order?

☐ Is the point of view used to present the paragraph appropriate?

☐ In your judgment, the best part of this paragraph is _____. Explain.

☐ Which detail or example would be even better if it were expanded? Why?

RECAP Narration

New terms in this chapter	Definitions
narration	the writing technique used to relate a series of events or incidents
flashback	a past event deliberately presented out of sequence to provide background information
point of view	the perspective a writer uses to tell a story

Using *first person point of view* makes the writer a participant (I, me, my, mine).

EXAMPLE	Suddenly, I heard a car stop outside my window.

Using *third person point of view* makes the writer an observer (she, he, they, him, her, his, them, their, it, its).

EXAMPLE	The old woman stood up and reached for her cane.

Writing a Narrative Paragraph

Focus on a subject that includes a **sequence of events**.

↓ ↑

Develop a **topic sentence** that establishes a **context** for the reader.

↓ ↑

Present the events through **chronological order**.

↓ ↑

Choose the most effective **point of view—first person** or **third person**.

GOING FORWARD...

**CW 5.9
Narration
review**

Q: How can I make the story of what happened to me clear and easy for my leader to follow?

A: To ensure that your reader understands the story you are telling, first identify the specific incident and then tell it as fully as you recall it and in the order in which it happened. Once you do, you'll be all set.

CHAPTER 6
Description

Navigating This Chapter

This chapter will explore the basic requirements for writing an effective descriptive paragraph:

- providing a topic sentence that previews your description
- drawing upon sensory details
- relying on both objective and subjective description
- considering spatial order

GETTING STARTED...

CW 6.1
Chapter
basics

Q: The experience was so vivid—it was like it was full of electricity. How can I capture that sense of energy and life for my reader when I write about it?

A: Whenever you need to record in words the vivid sensations you have seen or witnessed, the solution is **description**. Through description, you recreate and animate subjects so that a reader can feel the same energy and life associated with a subject that you feel.

Overview: Creating a Picture in Words

CW6.2
Overview of
description

When you write, think of your words as a camera lens through which your reader views the situations or experiences you are presenting. The mode that is perhaps the best to bring into focus the scene in your camera lens of language is **description.**

You use description whenever you try to capture a particular setting, individual, experience, or object in words. A paragraph detailing the feeling of speeding along on a motorcycle would call for description. So would a writing about the frenzy of last-minute holiday shoppers and one dealing with a schoolyard full of children on the first day of school. With the basics of description mastered, you will be prepared to write longer essays that use description.

Previewing the Focus of Description through the Topic Sentence

CW 6.3
Focusing
your
description

Your reader depends on you to clarify the focus of your writing early on. Your descriptive paragraph will create a vivid impression of an object, person, or place in the reader's mind. To begin it, you need a topic sentence that previews what will be described and suggests your point of view. That way your reader can make sense of the specific details and examples that follow.

Consider the italicized topic sentence in this paragraph from "Total Eclipse," an essay by writer Annie Dillard:

**CW 6.4
Composing
patterns:
narrative
and
descriptive**

> *The second before the sun went out we saw a wall of dark shadow come speeding at us.* We no sooner saw it than it was upon us, like thunder. It roared up the valley. It slammed our hill and knocked us out. It was the monstrous swift shadow cone of the moon. I have since read that this wave of shadow moves at 1,800 miles an hour. Language gives no sense of this sort of speed—1,800 miles an hour. It was 195 miles wide. No end was in sight—you saw only the edge. It rolled at you across the land at 1,800 miles an hour, hauling darkness like plague behind it. Seeing it, and knowing it was coming straight for you, was like feeling a slug of anesthetic shoot up your arm. If you think very fast, you may have time to think, "Soon it will hit my brain." You can feel the deadness race up your arm; you can feel the appalling, inhuman speed of your own blood. We saw the wall of shadow coming, and screamed before it hit.

The italicized topic sentence tells the reader that the paragraph will describe an experience of great darkness. It also prepares the reader for further discussion of that great darkness (a solar eclipse) that will so swiftly fall upon her and the other observers. The body of the paragraph then provides details and examples that make the scene come alive for the reader.

Using Sensory Details

**CW 6.5
Using
sensory
details**

Vivid experiences create vivid memories. Think for a moment of the aroma the last time you walked into a bakery or of the sensation the last time the sound of the phone woke you from a sound sleep. **Sensory details**—what you perceive by seeing, hearing, tasting, smelling, and touching—enable you to communicate these experiences to your reader. To write sensory details, choose concrete language that draws in the five senses.

Look at this paragraph from writer Richard Rodriguez's "Aria: A Memoir of a Bilingual Childhood," which features sensory details:

> There were many times like the night at a brightly lit gasoline station (a blaring white memory) when I stood uneasily hearing my father talk to a teenage attendant. I do not recall what they were saying, but I cannot forget the sound my father made as he spoke. At one point his words slid together to form one long word—sounds as confused as the threads of blue and green oil in the puddle next to my shoes. His voice rushed through what he had left to say. Towards the end, he reached falsetto notes, appealing to his listener's understanding. I looked away at the lights of passing automobiles. I tried not to hear any more. But I heard only too well the attendant's reply, his calm, easy

tones. Shortly afterward, walking toward home with my father, I shivered when my father put his hand on my shoulder. The very first chance that I got, I evaded his grasp and ran on ahead into the dark, skipping with feigned boyish exuberance.

As you can see, the passage contains a number of sensory details. When Rodriguez notes the brightness of the lights, the sound of his father's voice, and the shiver he felt, he fills the paragraph with a sense of vivid life.

FAST FACT   Tests have shown that, of the five senses, smell creates the most complete, lasting memories. Females have the advantage in this regard, because on the whole, females have better olfactory systems than males.

COMPREHENSION AND PRACTICE

6.1

Considering Topic Sentences and Sensory Details

1. Read the following paragraph from "The Inheritance of Tools" by Scott Russell Sanders in which he thinks back on his relationship with this father, memories that often involved the tools his father taught him to use:

CW 6.6
Using sensory details

> As the saw teeth bit down, the wood released its smell, each kind with its own fragrance, oak or walnut or cherry or pine—usually pine because it was the softest, easiest for a child to work. No matter how weathered and gray the board, no matter how warped and cracked, inside there was this smell waiting, as of something freshly baked. I gathered every smidgen of sawdust and stored it away in coffee cans, which I kept in a drawer of the workbench. When I did not feel like hammering nails, I would dump my sawdust on the concrete floor of the garage and landscape it into highways and farms and towns, running miniature cars and trucks along miniature roads. Looming as huge as a colossus, my father worked over and around me, now and again bending down to inspect my work, careful not to trample my creations. It was a landscape that smelled dizzyingly of wood. Even after a bath my skin would carry the smell, and so would my father's hair, when he lifted me for a bedtime hug.

On the lines that follow, briefly explain how the topic sentence prepares you for the details that follow.

The topic sentence discusses how sawing the wood released sawdust, which

becomes the focus of the supporting sentences that follow.

2. In your view, which sentence in Sanders's paragraph provides the strongest support for his topic sentence? What makes you come to this conclusion?

Answers will vary depending on the sentence chosen. Likely choices will include the

second sentence, which compares the smell to something baked, the fourth sentence,

which discusses his activities with the sawdust, and the final sentence, which

discusses the long-lasting aroma.

CW 6.7
Things to
consider in
writing
descriptions

3. On a separate sheet of paper, list the sensory details from this paragraph and briefly explain the role they play in the paragraph.

Relying on Objective and Subjective Description

CW 6.8
Objective
and
subjective
description

Descriptive writing can be divided into two basic types. **Objective description** concerns actual details and sensations. **Subjective description** focuses on the impressions those details and sensations create. Rarely is a paper completely objective, as a lab report is, or completely subjective, as an essay dealing with a nightmare or intense spiritual experience would be. Most descriptive writing contains a combination of both types.

Take a close look at the details in this paragraph from E. B. White's essay "Once More to the Lake," which concerns a trip he took with his young son to a vacation spot of White's youth. Here, he focuses on the lake itself, remarking on how unchanged it seems from his own childhood:

CW 6.9
Using
objective
description

> We caught two bass, hauling them in briskly as though they were mackerel, pulling them over the side of the boat in a businesslike manner without any landing net, and stunning them with a blow on the back of the head. When we got back for a swim before lunch, the lake was exactly where we had left it, the same number of inches from the dock, and there was only the merest suggestion of a breeze. This seemed an utterly enchanted sea, this lake you could leave to its own devices for a few hours and come back to, and find that it had not stirred, this constant and trustworthy body of water. In the shallows, the dark, water-soaked sticks and twigs, smooth and old, were undulating in clusters on the bottom, against the clean ribbed sand, and the track of the mussel was plain. A school of minnows swam by, each minnow with its small individual shadow, doubling the attendance, so clear and sharp in the sunlight. Some of the other campers were in swimming, along the shore, one of them with a cake of soap, and the water felt thin and unsubstantial. Over the years there had been this person with the cake of soap, this cultist, and here he was. There had been no years.

White employs both objective and subjective description to capture the scene at the lake. The number and type of fish, how he and his son killed them, the still and clear waters, the sunken sticks and twigs, the other people in the lake are all examples of objective description. The words used to discuss how they caught the fish—*briskly, in a businesslike manner*—constitute subjective description, as do the descriptions of the weather at the time—*merest suggestion of a breeze*—and the lake itself—*utterly enchanted sea, constant and trustworthy body of water,* and *the water . . . thin and unsubstantial.* Unlike the objective details, these subjective ones express abstract characteristics or qualities, ideas that lend themselves to different interpretations.

Using Spatial Order

CW 6.10 More on writing descriptions

As Chapter 4 indicates, writers often rely upon **spatial order** to organize descriptive writing. Spatial order locates the described elements logically in relationship to each other. It directs the reader's attention, for example, from left to right, from near to far, or from top to bottom. Spatial order helps your reader to visualize the details of the scene as they actually exist.

Consider the order of details in this paragraph from *The Diving Bell and the Butterfly,* in which Jean-Dominique Bauby describes how his father looked on their last visit:

> Hunched in the red-upholstered armchair where he sifts through the day's newspapers, my dad bravely endures the rasp of the razor attacking his loose skin. I wrap a big towel around his shriveled neck, daub thick lather over his face, and do my best not to irritate his skin, dotted here and there with small dilated capillaries. From age and fatigue, his eyes have sunk deep into their sockets, and his nose looks too prominent for his emaciated features. But still flaunting the plume of hair—now snow white—that has always crowned his tall frame, he has lost none of his splendor.

Here, Bauby's use of spatial order brings his father's face into clear focus. The description follows a logical order. He first discusses his father's neck, then moves his way up his father's face to describe his eyes, and finally ends up zeroing in on the hair at the top of his head.

Where spatial order is used to organize a descriptive paragraph, transitional expressions that show location help your reader. A few of these transitions are shown below.

Transitional Expressions Showing Location

above, below	in front of, behind	toward, away
close, far	next to, near, between	up, down

COMPREHENSION AND PRACTICE 6.2

Focusing on Objective and Subjective Description and Spatial Order

1. Read the following paragraph from "Final Cut," an essay by Atul Gawande in which he describes a room where an autopsy is to take place:

CW 6.11
Using
subjective
description

Not long ago, I went to observe the dissection of a thirty-eight-year-old woman I had taken care of who had died after a long struggle with heart disease. The dissecting room was in the sub-basement, past the laundry and a loading dock, behind an unmarked metal door. It had high ceilings, peeling paint, and a brown tiled floor that sloped down to a central drain. There was a Bunsen burner on a countertop and an old-style grocer's hanging scale, with a big clockface red-arrow gauge and a pan underneath, for weighing organs. On shelves all around the room there were gray portions of brain, bowel, and other organs soaking in formalin in Tupperware-like containers. The facility seemed rundown, chintzy, low-tech. On a rickety gurney in the corner was my patient, sprawled out, completely naked. The autopsy team was just beginning its work.

On a separate sheet of paper, make two lists, one of the subjective details and one of the objective ones. Then, on the lines that follow, explain whether you think the objective details or examples or the subjective ones do more to capture what the dissecting room was like and why you feel this way.

Answers will vary somewhat. Some students will discuss how the subjective details

affected their emotional reaction to the scene, while others will mention how the sheer

volume of objective details created a greater sense of what the room was like.

2. On the following lines, explain the role you think spatial order plays in Gawande's paragraph.

Spatial order presents the room as someone walking in might see it, thus making it

easier for a reader who has not seen the room to visualize it.

CHALLENGE 6.1 Considering Purpose in Description Paragraphs

COLLABORATION

CW6.12
Descriptive
writing
techniques

This chapter features several sample description paragraphs. The specific focus or names of the authors of these paragraphs, with the appropriate page numbers, are listed below. Working with a partner, take another look at the paragraphs. Then, on the lines next to the names, list the primary purpose and any secondary purposes for each paragraph.

1. Annie Dillard, page 92

Most students will agree that Dillard's primary purpose is to entertain and her

secondary purpose is to inform.

2. Richard Rodriguez, pages 92–93

   Most students will agree that Rodriguez's primary purpose is to entertain and his

   secondary purpose, although limited, is to inform.

3. E. B. White, page 94

   Most students will agree that White's primary purpose is to entertain and his

   secondary purpose is to inform.

4. Jean-Dominique Bauby, page 95

   Most students will agree that Bauby's primary purpose is to entertain and his

   secondary purpose, although limited, is to inform.

FOR FURTHER EXPLORATION

1. Select one of the following topics. Then, following one of the strategies that you practiced in Chapter 2, prewrite on that topic. Consider sensory details and location of parts of the scene (or person).

   - a memorable meal
   - the best-looking person you've ever met
   - a thunderstorm
   - an accident scene
   - the feeling of physical exhaustion
   - a vivid dream
   - a scene at the beach, park, or pool on a hot day

2. This chapter features several sample paragraphs:

   - a description of a natural phenomenon, a full solar eclipse (Annie Dillard, page 92)
   - the story of a youngster's embarrassment at a parent's lack of knowledge (Richard Rodriguez, pages 92–93)
   - the recounting of a special place enjoyed by parent and child (E. B. White, page 94)
   - the description of the face of a special person (Jean-Dominque Bauby, page 95)

For this assignment, consider a similar scene or situation that you have experienced or witnessed. First prewrite on this subject and identify a specific focus along with key supporting ideas. Then create a paragraph of at least five to ten sentences in which you use description to recreate it for your reader. Use the material in this chapter to guide you as you write.

▶ DISCOVERING CONNECTIONS

What ideas come to mind when you look at this picture, from Tuscany, an area of Italy steeped in history, art, and culture? This place seems to have escaped the passage of time, looking much as it probably did 400 or more years ago. What do you imagine life was like for the people living on this estate in those long-ago days? In terms of the scene the photo captures, what kind of day do you suppose it was, weather-wise? What do you think the air would feel like? What sounds and scents would you experience? If you were to travel to this part of Tuscany, what would you most look forward to? Why?

For this assignment, consider one of these questions or another that the picture inspires. Then, using the information in this chapter to guide you, create a paragraph of at least five to ten sentences in which you employ description to help your reader visualize the scene. Make sure you consider such key aspects as sensory details, objective and subjective description, and spatial order. ◀

✔ Descriptive Paragraph Checklist

☐ Does the topic sentence preview the description?

☐ Does the paragraph use sensory details? List them.

☐ Does it make effective use of both objective and subjective description? Write an *S* above every use of subjective description and an *O* above every use of objective description.

☐ Is it effectively arranged in spatial order or some other order? Explain.

☐ In your judgment, what is the best part of this paragraph? Explain.

☐ Which detail or example would be even better if it were expanded? Why?

RECAP Description

New terms in this chapter	Definitions
description	the writing technique used to paint a picture in words of a scene, individual, object, or experience
sensory details	information perceived through sight, sound, taste, smell, and touch
objective description	writing that focuses on actual details and sensations

> **EXAMPLE** The restaurant featured wood paneled walls and candlelit tables.

subjective description	writing that focuses on the impressions that details and sensations create within the writer

> **EXAMPLE** The atmosphere in the restaurant was warm and cozy.

Writing a Descriptive Paragraph

Develop a **topic sentence** that previews the object to be described in the paragraph.

↓ ↑

Include **sensory details** to bring the scene into focus.

↓ ↑

Use a combination of **objective** and **subjective description**.

↓ ↑

Present the details through **spatial order** when appropriate.

GOING FORWARD . . .

CW 6.13
**Description
review**

Q: So what's the best way to make sure that my description communicates my subject effectively to my reader?

A: Ensuring that your description is vivid and alive for your reader is easy. First provide a topic sentence that expresses your main point. Then include specific sensory details and objective and subjective description, presented in spatial order or some other appropriate method of arrangement.

CHAPTER 7
Example

Navigating This Chapter

This chapter will explore the basic requirements for writing an effective example paragraph:

- providing a topic sentence that clearly states the point you will illustrate
- choosing examples that are specific
- selecting examples that are relevant
- providing an effective arrangement

GETTING STARTED . . .

CW 7.1
Chapter basics

Q: I want to make sure that anyone reading my paper understands my subject the way I do. What's the best way to make sure I do this?

A: Whenever you want someone to understand something the way you do, **example** is the organizing strategy to use. An illustration or two can bring your topic into focus for your reader, increasing the odds that your reader will understand the point you are making as well as you understand it.

Overview: Illustrating Your Point

CW 7.2
Overview of example

You've probably said it hundreds of times yourself as you explained something: "For example, ..." We use examples to ensure that our points or statements are fully understood. In writing, **example** refers to the use of specific instances to illustrate, clarify, or back up a point.

As a writing technique, example is valuable. Well-chosen examples help make a point powerfully. A paragraph outlining types of fads could be developed through example. A paragraph about college challenges might also use example. Once you have mastered the basics of an example paragraph, you will also begin to understand how to write longer essays that use example.

Providing a Topic Sentence That States the Point You Will Illustrate

CW 7.3
Stating the point

In an example paragraph, the topic sentence identifies the general idea that the examples will then clarify and illustrate. It should clearly state the point to be illustrated.

**CW 7.4
Stating the
main point
clearly**

Look at this paragraph from "The Marginal World," an essay by environmentalist and writer Rachel Carson, in which she discusses an area at the edge of the sea:

> The flats took on a mysterious quality as dusk approached and the last evening light was reflected from the scattered pools and creeks. Then birds became only dark shadows, with no color discernible. Sanderlings scurried across the beach like little ghosts, and here and there the darker forms of the willets stood out. Often I could come very close to them before they would start up in alarm—the sanderlings running, the willets flying up, crying. Black skimmers flew along the ocean's edge silhouetted against the dull, metallic gleam, or they went flitting above the sand like large, dimly seen moths. Sometimes they "skimmed" the winding creeks of tidal water, where little spreading surface ripples marked the presence of small fish.

As you can see, the topic sentence indicates the focus of the paragraph: the change in the tidal flats as dusk approaches. The sentences that follow then provide specific examples of the various creatures that create the "mysterious quality" she speaks of. When you write, keep in mind that, like Carson, you may need to supply more than a single sentence to make each of your supporting examples clear for your reader.

Incidentally, with example you will often use the transitional expressions *for example* and *for instance*. Although Carson does not use either one in this particular paragraph, you will often final them good cues to use. They remind you of the commitment you have to your reader: to provide a convincing illustration of your point.

In addition to these two transitional expressions, you might want to consider the following words when you create a writing that features example. Like *for example* and *for instance,* these other transitional expressions will help you emphasize the significance of the illustrations and details you include.

Transitional Expressions for Example Writing

after all	in addition	moreover	particularly
indeed	in other words	of course	specifically

Providing Specific Examples

**CW 7.5
Composition
patterns:
examples**

Specific means detailed and particular. Writing **specific examples** means providing enough information so that your reader understands their meaning and significance. Generally, the more specific the information you supply is, the more convincing your examples are.

Imagine you are writing a paragraph about problems in today's schools, such as poor reading skills, lack of discipline in the classroom, students' personal difficulties, and unmotivated teachers. Supplying statistics or specific background about each of these examples would help your reader understand the problems. Simply stating that all of these things are problems would be less helpful and convincing.

Take a look at the following paragraph from the introduction to Eric Schlosser's *Fast Food Nation:*

CW 7.6
Providing
specific
examples

Over the last three decades, fast food has infiltrated every nook and cranny of American society. An industry that began with a handful of modest hot dog and hamburger stands in southern California has spread to every corner of the nation, selling a broad range of foods wherever paying customers may be found. Fast food is now served at restaurants and drive-throughs, at stadiums, airports, zoos, high schools, elementary schools, and universities, on cruise ships, trains, and airplanes, at K-Marts, Wal-Marts, gas stations, and even at hospital cafeterias. In 1970, Americans spent about $6 billion on fast food; in 2001, they spent more than $110 billion. Americans now spend more money on fast food than on higher education, personal computers, computer software, or new cars. They spend more on fast food than on movies, books, magazines, newspapers, videos, and recorded music—combined.

Here, Schlosser provides a number of specific examples to support his main idea: that fast food is an inescapable part of today's world. These examples include the many places where fast food is available as well as the astounding amount of money Americans spend on it in the twenty-first century—$110 billion, up from $6 billion thirty-one years earlier. Other examples point out a specific variety of other items that Americans spend less money on than fast food, including books, cars, college, and entertainment.

FAST FACT Here are examples of some English words for groups of things—**collective words**—that you don't hear too often: a *bale* of turtles, a *rout* of wolves, a *gam* of whales, a *leap* of leopards, a *crash* of rhino, a *cete* of badgers, and a *dray* of squirrels.

COMPREHENSION AND PRACTICE 7.1

Considering Topic Sentences and Specific Examples

1. Read this paragraph from Leslie Heywood's article, "One of the Girls," in which she discusses women and sports:

There are some great Nike ads out there that are a gateway to my vanished world, where I used to win races and everyone knew. In the black-and-white images, dreams, possibilities beckon to girls, welcome them into the world. Sports can give us that place, but a lot of work needs to be done before we've finished that race. Female athletes fight the same unrealistic images everyone fights, and researchers are only beginning to understand the relationship between those images and the "female athlete triad"—eating disorders and exercise compulsion, amenorrhea [abnormal cessation of menstruation]—that had me training until my bones fractured, my tendons ripped, and I stuck my fingers down my throat or simply didn't eat to stay lean. Nobody's been quite loud enough in saying that the female athlete triad is almost surely connected to all the old negative ideas about girls—girls trying to prove beyond a shadow of a doubt that they are not what those ideas say they are: weak, mild, meek, meant to serve others instead of achieving for themselves.

On the lines that follow, explain the connection between the topic sentence and the supporting sentences.

The topic sentence mentions the images in Nike advertisements and also indicates

that the days of her greatest athletic achievements are behind her. Then the

supporting sentences illustrate the damage that visual images and expectations for

achievement can create for female athletes.

2. On a separate sheet of paper, make a list of the specific details that Heywood supplies.

3. On the lines that follow, identify the specific detail that you think provides the strongest support for Heywood's main point.

Answers will vary depending on the detail chosen. Likely selections will include

information from the fourth sentence: fractured bones, ripped tendons, and intentional

vomiting.

Ensuring That Your Examples Are Relevant

CW 7.8 Adding specifics

Relevant means appropriate and connected. **Relevant examples** are directly associated with the topic. For a paper on frustrating household chores, examples such as dusting, vacuuming, and washing windows would be relevant. These tasks are all frustrating because they must be repeated so frequently. However, an example about sweeping up at work would not be relevant. Although this task may indeed be frustrating, it is an on-the-job duty, not a household chore.

Take a look at the following paragraph from "Gray Area: Thinking with a Damaged Brain," an essay by Floyd Skloot, in which he discusses ways that his thinking has been affected because of a brain virus:

ESL Note
See "Writing Paragraphs" on pages 601–602.

I am so easily overloaded. I cannot read the menu or converse in a crowded, noisy restaurant. I get exhausted at Portland Trailblazers games, with all the visual and aural imagery, all the manufactured commotion, so I stopped going nine years ago. My hands are scarred from burns and cuts that occurred when I tried to cook and converse at the same time. I cannot drive in traffic, especially in our standard-transmission pickup truck. I cannot talk about, say, the fiction of Thomas Hardy while I drive; I need to be given directions in small doses rather than all at once and need those directions to be given

> precisely at the time I must make the required turn. This is, as Restak explains, because driving and talking about Hardy, or driving and processing information about where to turn, are handled by different parts of the brain, and my brain's parts have trouble working together.

As you can see, Skloot's topic sentence indicates that the focus of the paragraph is how parts of his day-to-day living now overwhelm him. The examples that follow are all relevant because they detail a number of ordinary things that now "overload" him.

Providing an Effective Presentation

Once you've chosen the specific, relevant, and varied examples to fulfill the purpose of your document, you need to present this information so that it will have the most impact. Deciding on a method of arrangement always requires some careful thinking about your aims and the needs of your audience. No single right way to arrange a series of examples exists. One common method that you might find particularly useful, however, especially when your aim is to convince an audience of a point of view, is **emphatic order.** This method presents less important examples first and the most important ones later. Examples become increasingly convincing, with the very best—the final point your reader will remember—saved for last.

Take a look at the following paragraph about hand gestures from a psychology text by Carol Tavris and Carole Wade:

> Even the simplest gesture is subject to misunderstanding and offense. The sign of the University of Texas football team, the Longhorns, is to extend the index finger and the pinkie. In Italy and other parts of Europe this gesture means a man's wife has been unfaithful to him—a serious insult! Anita Rowe, a consultant who advises businesses on cross-cultural customs, tells of a newly hired Asian engineer in a California company. As the man left his office to lead the first meeting of his project team, his secretary crossed her fingers to wish him luck. Instead of reassuring him, her gesture thoroughly confused him: In his home country, crossing one's fingers is a sexual proposition.

Emphatic order helps Tavris and Wade make their point that serious consequences can result when simple gestures are misunderstood. The first example—that a gesture familiar to some U.S. sports fans indicates infidelity in some European countries—is surprising. Even more surprising is that an even more common gesture—crossed fingers indicating a hope for good luck—represents a proposition in some Asian countries. Moving from a strong example to a stronger one underscores how innocent actions can send a far different meaning than the one intended.

COMPREHENSION AND PRACTICE
7.2

Considering Relevant Examples and Appropriate Order

1. Read the following paragraph from Henry Petroski's *To Engineer Is Human: The Role of Failure in Successful Design,* which discusses unacceptable failures in product design:

> As the consequences of failure become more severe, however, the foresight we must give to them becomes more a matter of life and death. Automobiles are manufactured by the millions, but it would not do to have them failing with a snap on the highways the way light bulbs and shoelaces do at home. The way an automobile could fail must be anticipated so that, as much as possible, a malfunction does not lead to an otherwise avoidable deadly accident. Since tires are prone to flats, we want our vehicles to be able to be steered safely to the side of the road when one occurs. Such a failure is accepted in the way light bulb and shoelace failures are, and we carry a spare tire to deal with it. Other kinds of malfunctions are less acceptable. We do not want the brakes on all four wheels and the emergency braking system to fail us suddenly and simultaneously. We do not want the steering wheel to come off in our hands as we are negotiating a snaking mountain road. Certain parts of the automobile are given special attention, and in the rare instances when they do fail, leading to disaster, massive lawsuits can result. When they become aware of a potential hazard, automobile manufacturers are compelled to eliminate what might be the causes of even the most remote possibilities of design-related accidents by the massive recall campaigns familiar to us all.

On the following lines, briefly explain how the examples Petroski includes are relevant to his main point.

The examples Petroski includes are relevant to his main point because they all involve

issues stemming from or related to product failure.

_____

2. On a separate sheet of paper, identify the order Petroski uses to present his ideas and how this method of arrangement affects the impact of his paragraph.

CHALLENGE 7.1   **Considering Purpose in Example Paragraphs**

COLLABORATION

This chapter features several sample example paragraphs. The names of the authors of these paragraphs, with the appropriate page numbers, are listed on the next page. Working with a partner, take another look at the paragraphs. Then, on the lines next to the names, list the primary purpose and any secondary purposes for each paragraph.

1. Rachel Carson, page 101

   Most students will agree that Carson's primary purpose is to inform and her

   secondary purpose is to entertain.

2. Eric Schlosser, page 102

   Most students will agree that persuading barely edges out informing as the primary

   purpose in this paragraph.

3. Floyd Skloot, page 103–104

   A few students may note that Skloot's piece persuades because it suggests that

   people don't consider the far-reaching effects a brain injury can have.

4. Carol Tavris and Carole Wade, page 104

   Most students will agree that entertaining barely edges out informing as the primary

   purpose in Tavris and Wade's paragraph.

FOR FURTHER EXPLORATION

1. Select one of the following topics. Then, employing one of the strategies you practiced in Chapter 2, prewrite on that topic. Concentrate on useful, effective illustrations or examples.

   - good role models
   - difficulties in job hunting
   - distinctive style of dress
   - entertaining advertisements
   - bad social habits
   - ways that computers can entertain
   - ways to spend a day off from work or school

2. This chapter features several sample paragraphs:

   - a close examination of an area at dusk (Rachel Carson, page 101)
   - a discussion of American's love affair with fast food (Eric Schlosser, page 102)

- the consequences of a serious injury (Floyd Skloot, pages 103–104)
- the ways that signs and gestures can be misinterpreted (Carol Tavris and Carole Wade, page 104)

For this assignment, think of a condition, situation, or locale like those portrayed in these paragraphs. Do some prewriting on this subject, identifying a specific focus and key supporting ideas. Create a paragraph of at least five to ten sentences in which you rely on example to explain and illustrate your subject for your reader. Use the material in this chapter as a guide.

▶ DISCOVERING CONNECTIONS

When you look at this picture, what thoughts come to mind? Does the photo make you think of the wonders of nature, of beautiful and powerful wild animals living as they have for thousands of years, far away from human influence? Does it instead remind you how important companionship and comfort can be? Or does it make you dream of traveling to the Serengeti or some other wilderness area to observe and experience nature unspoiled by humans? What aspects of such a trip would excite you the most? How do you think it would affect your life?

For this assignment, tackle one of these questions or another that the photo suggests. Using the information in this chapter to guide you, write a paragraph of at least five to ten sentences in which you turn to example to give your reader a full view of the point you are making. As you develop your paragraph, be sure that the examples you include are specific and relevant. ◀

✓ Example Paragraph Checklist

☐ Does the topic sentence clearly state the point to be illustrated?

☐ Does the paragraph provide specific examples? Underline any example that you feel needs to be made more specific.

☐ Are all the examples relevant? Put an * next to any example that you feel is not directly connected to the main idea of the paragraph.

☐ Are the examples effectively arranged?

☐ In your judgment, what is the best part of this paragraph? Explain.

☐ Which detail or example would be even better if it were expanded? Why?

RECAP Example

New terms in this chapter	Definitions
example	the writing technique that uses specific instances to illustrate, clarify, or back up the point being made
specific examples	illustrative material that is detailed and particular
	EXAMPLE In the center of the room was *the old, dusty, mahogany roll-top desk.*
relevant examples	illustrative information that is appropriate and directly connected
	EXAMPLE The *household chores* I find most annoying are *dusting, vacuuming,* and *washing windows.*

Writing an Example Paragraph

Identify the **subject** that you wish to **illustrate**.

Provide a **topic sentence** that indicates the **specific idea** to be **illustrated**.

Keep all examples **specific**.

Make all examples **relevant**.

GOING FORWARD...

CW 7.9 Example review

Q: But how do I make sure that I include the right kind of examples so that my reader understands my point?

A: To meet the needs of your reader when you use example, always rely on examples that are specific and relevant to support your topic sentence. Also, pay close attention to how you arrange the examples so that they have the greatest impact on your reader.

CHAPTER 8
Process

Navigating This Chapter

This chapter will explore the basic requirements for writing an effective process paragraph:

- including a topic sentence that clearly states the procedure or technique
- using the imperative mood (you) when it's appropriate
- dividing the process into simple, logical steps
- relying on linear order

GETTING STARTED . . .

**CW 8.1
Chapter
basics**

Q: I know how this thing works, how to use it, too. But to explain so someone else understands it—now that I'm not so sure of. How do I write about it so another person will understand the steps involved?

A: Whenever you have to explain a process or procedure for somebody else, **process** is your answer. Process takes action or function and puts it into slow motion, making it easy for a reader to comprehend.

Overview: Explaining How It Happens or How to Do It

**CW 8.2
Overview of
process**

Whenever you explain how something occurs or how to do something, you are using **process.** There are basically three types of process writing. One type, called *process analysis,* explains such matters as how tornadoes form or how certain foods contribute to cholesterol problems. A second type, called *process narrative,* explains how you as the writer did something, such as organizing a weekend park cleanup or establishing a fitness routine. The most common type, however, often called *how-to writing,* presents instructions for filling out a financial aid form or assembling a gas grill. Once you have mastered the basics of process, you will begin to understand how to write longer papers involving process as well.

Including a Topic Sentence That Clearly States The Process

**CW 8.3
Process
writing**

An effective topic sentence for a process paragraph must focus on something that can be adequately explained in a brief space. It must clearly state the specific process—procedure, technique, or routine—to be explained and set a direction that the other sentences in the paragraph will cover.

Take a look at the relationship between the topic sentence and the supporting sentences in the following paragraph from a book on solving children's sleep problems written by Richard Ferber, M.D.:

CW 8.4 Listing processes

> Bedtime means separation, which is difficult for children, especially very young ones. Simply sending a toddler or young child off to bed alone is not fair and may be scary for him. And it means you will miss what can be one of the best times of the day. So set aside ten to thirty minutes to do something special with your child before bed. Avoid teasing, scary stories, or anything that will excite your child at this time. Save the wrestling and tussling for other times of the day. You might both enjoy a discussion, quiet play, or story reading. But let your child know that your special time together will not extend beyond the time you and he have agreed upon, then don't go beyond those limits. It is a good idea to tell your child when the time is almost up or when you have only two or three more pages to read, and don't give in for an extra story. Your child will learn the rules only if you enforce them. If both you and he know just what is going to happen, there won't be the arguments and tension that arise when there is uncertainty.

Ferber's topic sentence indicates that the paragraph concerns bedtime for children, specifically how difficult it can be. The rest of the paragraph lays out a procedure that will make a difficult time far easier for both parents and children.

Using the Imperative Mood: You

CW 8.5 Using the imperative mood

With instructions, it makes sense to address the reader directly, using the **imperative mood,** often called the **command.** When you use the imperative mood, the subject is not stated but *understood* to be the person reading the piece. When you write, "Close the kitchen window," you are actually saying, "*You* close the kitchen window."

Note the use of the imperative mood in this paragraph from a textbook on study skills by James F. Shepherd, which concerns identifying a person's level of concentration:

> When you begin to study, make a note of the time. Then, when you first become aware that your attention is not focused on studying, record the time again. Compare the two times and make a note of how many minutes you studied before you lost your concentration. Next, spend a few minutes doing something other than studying; you might stand up and stretch or look out the window. When you begin to study again, make another note of how long you concentrate.

The use of imperative order in this paragraph means that Shepherd *directly* relates the instructions for maintaining concentration to you as the reader. In fact, the subject is the word *you,* even though it isn't always stated.

COMPREHENSION AND PRACTICE   Considering Topic Sentences and Imperative Mood

8.1

1. Read the following paragraph, an explanation of how to insert a contact lens:

**CW 8.6
Defining
special terms
as part of
how-to
writing**

> Inserting a contact lens is a simple process. First, take the lens out of the fluid it is stored in and rinse it off. Next, place the cleaned lens on the tip of the index finger of your dominant hand. Check the edge of the lens to make sure the lens hasn't turned inside out. It should look like the top of an opened umbrella. Using your other index finger, pull down gently on your lower right eyelid to expose more of the white of the eye. Then carefully place the lens over the iris, or colored part, of your eye. Blink once to make sure the lens is securely in place. If you can see clearly though that eye, repeat these steps for your other eye.

On the following lines, briefly explain how the topic sentence prepares the reader for the discussion to follow.

The topic sentence prepares the reader for the discussion to follow because it

indicates that the process is easy to accomplish, and the sentences that follow

demonstrate that this statement is accurate.

2. On a separate sheet of paper, make a list of the steps involved in this process.

3. How does the use of the imperative mood help make this process clear for a reader? Briefly explain on the lines that follow.

The imperative mood used in this paragraph directs the reader to act in a specific,

step-by-step fashion. As a result, the entire process is easier to understand.

Dividing the Process into Simple, Logical Steps

The key to successful process writing is to separate the process into small, manageable steps and then to spell out these steps in detail. For example, although blood circulates through the human body in a highly complex process, you can describe it fairly accurately in four basic steps: (1) The heart pumps oxygenated blood to body tissues through the arteries and capillaries. (2) The veins carry the blood back to the heart. (3) The heart pumps the blood to the lungs to be oxygenated again. (4) The blood returns to the heart to be circulated through the body again. Breaking the process down into discrete steps, each with its own function, makes the complex process easier for the reader to understand.

Consider how the steps are presented in this paragraph from Simon Winchester's book, *The Professor and the Madman: A Tale of Murder, Insanity, and the Making of the Oxford English Dictionary:*

The volunteers' duties were simple enough, if onerous. They would write to the society offering their services in reading certain books; they would be asked to read and make wordlists of all that they read, and would then be asked to look super-specifically, for certain words that currently interested the dictionary team. Each volunteer would take a slip of paper, write at its top left-hand side the target word, and below, also on the left, the date of the details that followed: These were, in order, the title of the book or paper, its volume and page number, and then, below that, the full sentence that illustrated the use of the target word. It was a technique that has been undertaken by lexicographers to the present day.

This paragraph breaks down a process—the one that participants in the dictionary project followed—into distinct, easily completed steps. Because each step is explained in specific detail, a reader can understand the process that eventually produced the massive multivolume text that is among the most well-known and most often used reference works of all time.

FAST FACT Before any new word is added to the *Webster's New World Dictionary,* it is first put on "word watch" and its use is then monitored by a thirteen-member editorial team. The word must be widely used for at least three years before it will actually be considered for adoption. Words currently under examination include *irritainment,* entertainment of some kind that is both annoying and compelling, and *starter marriage,* a brief first marriage that ends in divorce, without kids, property, or, presumably, regrets.

Relying on Linear Order

Effective process writing often depends on **linear order,** or the arrangement of steps in the order they occur. Writing about the process of taking a photograph with a 35-millimeter camera would call for linear order: (1) adjust the focus; (2) change the setting to allow the proper amount of light through the lens; (3) push the shutter button to take the picture. Unless the steps are performed in this order, the photograph would probably not turn out well.

Consider the order of the steps in this paragraph concerning preparing a still-life scene from John Garrett's *K.I.S.S Guide to Photography:*

When you start composing still-life pictures, I suggest you begin by just placing objects together in a random way—to see if they will work together. When you are putting props together on a background, try to see them not as what they are but simply as colored shapes of various sizes and volumes. That will help you with the composition. Once you are happy that the colors and shapes are well placed, build the picture around one dominant object. This is what I do, and, as I add each prop, I make sure it relates comfortably to the others. The purpose of this exercise is to combine all the individual objects together to form an aesthetically pleasing whole. Learn to look carefully at negative space. This is the space between objects that leads the eye from one item to another and connects the objects to form one composition.

Linear order plays an important role in this paragraph. To prepare a scene—a composition—you must follow each step as Garrett lays them out. If you do the steps out of order, you risk not being able to create the composition.

Process writing places events in time order sequence. Therefore, transitional expressions that signal that order help your reader. See the list below for transitions useful in a process paragraph.

Transitional Expressions for Process Writing

Beginning	*Continuing*				*Ending*
begin by	as soon as	second step, etc.	until		finally
initially	next	then	while		last

Keep in mind that if you are explaining an unusual or specialized process, you may need to define special terms. In any how-to process paragraph, you will need to specify the materials or tools needed to carry out the process. In most cases, this information should come right after the topic sentence so that the reader will be fully prepared to complete the process.

COMPREHENSION AND PRACTICE 8.2

Considering Carefully Divided Steps and Linear Order

1. Read the following paragraph from Carla Stephens' "Drownproofing," in which she explains how to teach children a technique that even non-swimmers can use to stay afloat:

> When teaching your children, it's advisable to stand with them in shoulder-deep water. Have them bend forward to practice the breathing and arm movements. If they swallow water, be patient and encourage them to try again. Once they're comfortable with the procedure, move into deeper water near the side of the pool to coordinate the floating, breathing and body movements. Water just deep enough for them to go under is sufficient. Remember, all movements should be easy and relaxed.

On a separate sheet of paper, make a list of the steps involved in teaching children this technique. On the lines that follow, briefly explain how the presentation of steps acknowledges that the reader will be teaching children.

The presentation includes several cautions about fears and concerns that children

may have.

2. On the lines that follow, briefly explain why Stephens has used strict linear order to present this process.

Stephens uses linear order because the steps must be followed in a particular order

to achieve the ends—and to keep children safe and secure.

CHALLENGE 8.1 Considering Purpose in Process Paragraphs

COLLABORATION

This chapter features several sample process paragraphs. The specific focus or names of the authors of these paragraphs, with the appropriate page numbers, are listed below. Working with a partner, take another look at the paragraphs. Then, on the lines next to the names, list the primary purpose and any secondary purposes for each paragraph.

1. Richard Ferber, page 110

Most students will agree that Ferber's primary purpose is to inform and his secondary

purpose is to persuade.

2. James F. Shepherd, page 110

Most students will agree that Shepherd's purpose is to inform.

3. Simon Winchester, page 112

Most students will agree that Winchester's primary purpose is to inform and his

secondary purpose is to entertain.

4. John Garrett, page 112

Most students will agree that Garrett's primary purpose is to inform and his secondary

purpose is to persuade.

FOR FURTHER EXPLORATION

1. Select one of the following topics. Then, using one of the strategies that you practiced in Chapter 2, prewrite on that topic. Concentrate on the steps in the process involved:

   - how to gift wrap a package
   - how to braid hair in a particular style
   - how an accident occurred
   - how to stop in inline skates
   - how to write a check
   - how to iron a shirt
   - how to perform a basic task at your current (or most recent) job

2. This chapter features several sample paragraphs:

   - an explanation of helping adults deal with an issue involving children (Richard Ferber, page 110)
   - steps to take to work on improved concentration and performance (James F. Shepherd, page 110)
   - an explanation of the process followed to create an elaborate project (Simon Winchester, page 112)
   - the process to follow in order to complete an art or craft project (John Garrett, page 112)

   For this assignment, think of a process or procedure you understand that is similar to these. After completing some prewriting, identify and express your focus in a clear topic sentence. Then isolate the ideas that do the best job of explaining the process or procedure for your reader, using the material in this chapter to guide you.

▶ DISCOVERING CONNECTIONS

What does this picture, a shot from the area surrounding the Tower of London in England make you think? Does the image make you wonder how someone envisions and creates a distinctive form like these buildings? The officers in the center of the photo are marching in step, movements that require great discipline—what steps can the average person take to maintain personal discipline? How about if you wanted to travel to London in the next few days to see this scene in person—what steps would you have to take to prepare for this kind of last-minute trip?

(continued)

For this assignment, consider one of these questions or another inspired by the picture. Then, referring to the information in this chapter as a guide, write a paragraph of at least five to ten sentences in which you use process to explain the steps underlying the subject you are discussing. As you write, concentrate on expressing the process in simple, logical steps, with the appropriate use of the imperative mood and linear order. ◀

CW 8.7
Process
analysis

✓ Process Paragraph Checklist

☐ Does the topic sentence clearly state the procedure or technique to be presented?

☐ Does it use the imperative mood (you)?

☐ Is the process divided into simple, logical steps? Do you feel any step should be further subdivided to make it easier for the reader to perform the process? Put a ✓ next to any step that needs to be divided.

☐ Are the steps presented in linear order? Underline any step that is out of linear order, and then draw a line to the spot in the paragraph where it actually belongs.

☐ In your judgment, what is the best part of this paragraph? Explain.

☐ Which detail or example would be even better if it were expanded? Why?

RECAP Process

New terms in this chapter	Definitions
process	the writing technique that explains how to do something or how something occurs Three types of process writing include 1. *process analysis* (how something is done or occurs) 2. *process narrative* (how you did something) 3. *a set of instructions* (how to do something)
imperative mood	designating verb usage that expresses commands The subject of the sentence in the imperative mood is understood as the reader (you) rather than stated directly. **EXAMPLE** (*You*) Move your books and papers into the other room, please.
linear order	an arrangement of steps in the order of their occurrence

Writing a Process Paragraph

Write a clear **topic sentence** that specifies the process to be explained.

↓ ↑

Directly address the reader through the **imperative mood** when it's appropriate.

↓ ↑

Present the process in **simple, logical steps**.

↓ ↑

Introduce the steps in **linear order**.

GOING FORWARD...

**CW 8.8
Process
review**

Q: I understand the process. That's not the point. My concern is about making sense of it for another person, somebody who doesn't know the process—how do I do that?

A: That you understand the process or procedure means you are in great shape. Now think back to what it was like before you understood the subject. Present the steps with that perspective in mind, and you should be fine.

CHAPTER 9
Definition

Navigating This Chapter

This chapter will explore the basic requirements for writing an effective definition paragraph:

- providing a topic sentence that highlights the term to be defined
- understanding the elements of an effective definition
- recognizing all the possible meanings of the term defined
- enhancing definition through synonyms, negation, and etymology

GETTING STARTED...

**CW 9.1
Chapter
basics**

Q: Even though my topic is a little complex and abstract, I have a good understanding of it. But how do I explain it so another person will also understand it I the way I understand it?

A: When you need to communicate your understanding of a topic—the *meaning* that you understand or have assigned to something—**definition** is the organizing strategy to use. That's because definition establishes borders or distinctions of meaning for a reader, enabling you to seize control of important concepts in your writing, interpreting and translating them for your audience.

Overview: Making Meaning Crystal Clear

**CW 9.2
Overview of
definition**

No matter what your topic is, your job is to communicate your ideas about that topic clearly and precisely. One writing mode that will help you achieve this goal is **definition.** Through definition, you can specify the meanings of actions, ideas, places, and things.

For example, a paragraph featuring definition could spell out the qualities of a good boss. This mode would also be a natural choice to explain what makes a house a home. Once you have mastered the basics of definition, you will also be prepared to write longer papers involving this organizing strategy.

Providing a Topic Sentence That Highlights the Term to Be Defined

**CW 9.3
Highlighting
the term to
be defined**

An effective definition paragraph begins with a topic sentence that highlights the term to be defined. In fact, the topic sentence of a definition paragraph is often a brief definition itself. For example, if you were defining your view of what an *optimist* is, you might begin this way:

EXAMPLE   An optimist is a person who sees good even in the worst situations and believes that, somehow, things will always work out for the best.

As you can see, the topic sentence provides a brief definition of the term, setting the direction for the sentences that will follow.

Look at this paragraph from Robert Jourdain's book, *Music, the Brain, and Ecstasy: How Music Captures Our Imagination,* in which he offers a definition of the musical scale:

> Like the scale found at the bottom of a road map, a musical scale provides units of measure, but for pitch space rather than geographical space. The basic unit is called a *half-step* (or a *semitone*). Every key along a piano keyboard represents a half-step. From C to C-sharp is a half-step, and so is from E to F. In the scale system we're accustomed to in the West, there are twelve half-steps (and twelve piano keys) in any octave, say, from middle C to the C above.

The topic sentence clearly states the term to be defined, the musical scale. It also refers to another familiar scale—the scale at the bottom of a map—as a way to make this aspect of music easier to understand. The supporting sentences in the paragraph then develop the definition further, explaining the half-step's function within this musical scale.

Understanding the Pattern of an Effective Definition

CW 9.4
The pattern of an effective definition

A dictionary definition follows a simple pattern. It first identifies the general class to which the term belongs. Then it gives the special, or distinguishing, characteristics that set the word apart.

EXAMPLE

┌── class ──┐   ┌────── distinguished characteristics ──────┐
A zip drive is a *computer device* that *enables a user to store large amounts of information on special disks.*

CW 9.5
Listing characteristics of a best friend

Paragraphs that define should also follow this **pattern of an effective definition.** However, most definition paragraphs call for greater elaboration. Especially with abstract subjects such as fear, you will need to express personal interpretation or experience. For such words, in addition to class and distinguishing characteristics, you should also provide specific, concrete examples and details for support.

Note the elements of definition in the following paragraph from "The Search for Marvin Gardens," by writer John McPhee. In this article, he discusses the classic board game *Monopoly* and the actual by-ways of Atlantic City, New Jersey, the names of which make up the blocks on the game board:

> Marvin Gardens is the one color-block Monopoly property that is not in Atlantic City. It is a suburb within a suburb, secluded. It is a planned compound of seventy-two handsome houses set on curvilinear private streets under yews and cedars, poplars and willows. The compound was built around

1920, in Margate, New Jersey, and consists of solid buildings of stucco, brick, and wood, with slate roofs, tile roofs, multi-mullioned porches, Giraldic towers, and Spanish grilles. Marvin Gardens, the ultimate outwash of *Monopoly*, is a citadel and sanctuary of the middle class.

The elements of an effective definition are at work here. The opening sentence indicates that, unlike the other locales on the *Monopoly* game board, Marvin Gardens isn't actually in Atlantic City, New Jersey. The next two sentences specify the distinguishing characteristics of this area. Marvin Gardens is a small planned compound of seventy-two houses on tree-lined private streets in a suburb near Atlantic City. The other sentences then provide additional specific details, including the name of the city that is home to Marvin Gardens. Together this information leads to a complete picture of this small neighborhood made famous by a simple board game.

COMPREHENSION AND PRACTICE
9.1

Considering Topic Sentences and the Elements of Definition

1. Read this paragraph from "Weasel Words" by William Lutz:

CW 9.6
Writing a topic sentence for your definition

What makes a product "new"? Some products have been around for a long time, yet every once in a while you discover that they are being advertised as "new." Well, an advertiser can call a product new if there has been "a material functional change" in the product. What is "a material functional change," you ask? Good question. In fact, it's such a good question it's being asked all the time. It's up to the manufacturer to prove that the product has undergone such a change. And if the manufacturer isn't challenged on the change, then there's no one to stop it. Moreover, the change does not have to be an improvement in the product. One manufacturer added artificial lemon scent to a cleaning product and called it "new and improved," even though the product did not clean any better than without the lemon scent. The manufacturer defended the use of the word "new" on the grounds that the artificial scent changed the chemical formula of the product and therefore constituted "a material functional change."

On the lines that follow, briefly explain how the topic sentence contributes to the description of *new*.

The topic sentence raises the question of what makes a product new, suggesting that

the answer isn't as obvious as one might think. It also prepares the reader for a

discussion of how companies use the term even when the difference is minimal.

2. On a separate sheet of paper, explain the role that the elements of an effective definition play in Lutz's paragraph.

3. In each sentence of definition below, underline the word that is being defined. Then circle the class to which the word belongs, and double underline the distinguishing characteristics that set it apart. Use the example as a guide.

EXAMPLE   A diplomat is a (government representative) who conducts relationships involving trade, treaties, and other official business with the government of another nation.

a. A gecko is a (tropical lizard) with soft skin, a short, stout body, a large head, and suction pads on its feet.

b. A democracy is a (form of government) in which the people hold ruling power through elected officials.

c. The nuclear family is a (social unit) that consists of parents and the children they raise.

Recognizing the Full Effect of the Term Defined

CW 9.7 Denotation versus connotation

Preparing an effective definition paragraph may also mean taking into account all the possible meanings for the term you are defining. To do this, you need to consider both the **denotation,** or literal meaning of the word, and its **connotations—** all the associations that also come with the word.

For example, the denotation of *clever* is its literal meaning, *quick-witted* and *intelligent.* When we say a child is clever, that is a compliment. When we say a politician or a criminal is clever, we may imply something negative, such as the person's ability to manipulate or take advantage of others. It is important to keep these kinds of connotations in mind when you are writing a definition paragraph.

Consider the following paragraph from Esther Dyson's article, "Cyberspace: If You Don't Love It, Leave It," in which she offers another way to define *cyberspace:*

> In the same way, you could think of cyberspace as a giant and unbounded world of virtual real estate. Some property is privately owned and rented out; other property is common land; some places are suitable for children, and others are best avoided by all but the kinkiest citizens. Unfortunately, it's those places that are now capturing the popular imagination: places that offer bomb-making instructions, pornography, advice on how to procure stolen credit cards. They make cyberspace sound like a nasty place.

In this paragraph, Dyson takes the term *cyberspace,* an electronic arena that has no real permanent form or structure, and makes it more concrete for the reader by comparing it to a more familiar concept, *real estate.* Her definition works well in part because of what people understand real estate to mean. As she indicates, in terms of denotation, people do think of real estate in terms of land and buildings, property that is owned, rented, or shared. But in terms of connotation, people also think of real estate as something valuable, that can be a source of pride when it is well-maintained and a source of annoyance and fear when it isn't. Through this use of denotation and connotation, Dyson emphasizes that the virtual real estate has the same attributes and qualities as its actual equivalent. As a result, the term that she is using real estate to explain, *cyberspace,* is a bit easier to understand.

One way to ensure that the point you are making is clear for your reader is to supply transition. With definition writing, you may find the following transitional expressions useful:

Transitional Expressions for Definition Writing

accordingly	in addition	in other words	on the whole	therefore
indeed	in fact	in the same way	specifically	thus

FAST FACT   Who would have thought that simple definitions could cause any trouble, but that's what happened recently in a New London, Connecticut, court. A Superior Court judge ordered a new trial for a man convicted of felony murder, first-degree robbery, first-degree arson, second-degree arson, and tampering with evidence. The judge made this decision after the jurors admitted that they had consulted a dictionary for definitions of *robbery* and *burglary,* which, according to the judge, amounted to introducing "extraneous material."

Enhancing Definition through Synonyms, Negation, and Etymology

As you develop a definition paragraph, you might find several additional strategies useful. These techniques include *synonyms, negation,* and *etymology.*

Synonyms are words that hold a similar meaning. Using a synonym as a means of explanation of a term is a great way to add clarification to the meaning you are providing. If you are explaining that your best friend is *naïve,* noting that by *naïve* you mean *unsophisticated* will prepare your reader for the other supporting examples and details to follow.

In some cases, you may find that the best way to define something is to explain what it *isn't,* a technique called *negation.* By writing that *intelligence* isn't merely the knowledge of a great volume of facts, you also suggest that being intelligent involves much more, such as understanding the significance of and connections among these facts.

You may also occasionally find a word's origin and historical development—its *etymology*—useful. The etymology of a word is generally available in any collegiate dictionary, although an unabridged dictionary such as *Oxford English Dictionary (OED)* is the best place to find extensive etymological information. If you've ever wondered, for example, whether the world is slanted against left-handed people, consider the etymology of two words, *gauche* and *adroit. Gauche* is defined as "lacking tact or social graces." It comes from a French word, *gauche,* which means *left. Adroit* is defined as "deft and skillful," and it too is derived from a French word, *droit,* which means *right.* What is gained by an examination of the etymology of these two words is the implication that left-handed people are somehow awkward or unrefined, whereas right-handed people are capable and proficient.

Consider this paragraph from *Thereby Hangs a Tale: Stories of Curious Word Origins* by Charles Earle Funk:

> The Greek *schole,* which was the original source of *school,* once meant just the opposite from what the schoolboy of today thinks of that institution. It meant vacation, leisure, rest. The education of a Greek boy was by private teachers in reading, writing, arithmetic, singing, and gymnastics. But no man ever considered his education to be completed. His leisure time was spent in listening to the discussions of learned men, and thus this product of leisure, this use of one's spare time came also to be called *schole.* Eventually the Greeks used the term for the lectures or discussions themselves, and ultimately it included as well the place wherein the instruction was given. It was the latter sense, which descended to English use.

Here, by turning to the surprising etymology of the common word *school,* Funk adds another dimension of meaning.

COMPREHENSION AND PRACTICE 9.2

Considering Denotation, Connotation, and Other Aspects of Definition

1. Read this paragraph from Francine Prose's "Gossip":

> I'm even fond of the word [gossip], its etymology, its origins in the Anglo-Saxon term "godsibbe" for god-parent, relative, its meaning widening by the Renaissance to include friends, cronies and later what one does with one's cronies. One gossips. Paring away its less flattering modern connotations, we discover a kind of synonym for connection, for community, and this, it seems to me, is the primary function of gossip. It maps out ties, reminds us of what sort of people we know and what manner of lives they lead, confirms our sense of who we are, how we live and where we have come from. The roots of the grapevine are inextricably entwined with our own. Who knows how much of our sense of the world has reached us on its branches, how often, as babies, we dropped off to sleep to the rhythms of family gossip? I've often thought that gossip's bad name might be cleared by calling it "oral tradition"; for what, after all, is an oral tradition but the stories of other lives, other eras, legends from a time when human traffic with spirits and gods was considered fit material for gossipy speculation.

On the following lines, briefly explain what you think Prose means in the second sentence when she refers to the "less flattering modern connotations" of gossip.

Prose is referring to the commonly accepted view that gossip is a bad habit,

something that is potentially hurtful to others and therefore to be avoided.

2. Take another look at the explanations of denotation, connotation, etymology, and synonyms that appear on the previous pages. Then, on a separate sheet of paper, explain the role they play in the impact of Prose's paragraph.

CHALLENGE 9.1 **Considering Purpose in Definition Paragraphs**

COLLABORATION

This chapter features several sample definition paragraphs. The names of the authors of these paragraphs, with the appropriate page numbers, are listed below. Working with a partner, take another look at the paragraphs. Then, on the lines next to the names, list the primary purpose and any secondary purposes for each paragraph.

1. Robert Jourdain, page 119

Most students will agree that Jourdain's primary purpose is to inform and his

secondary purpose is to entertain.

2. John McPhee, pages 119–120

Most students will agree that McPhee's primary purpose is to inform and his

secondary purpose is to entertain.

3. Esther Dyson, page 121

Most students will agree that Dyson's primary purpose is to entertain and her

secondary purposes are to inform and to persuade (to convince the reader to

reconsider how cyberspace is perceived).

4. Charles Earle Funk, page 123

Most students will agree that Funk's purpose is to inform.

FOR FURTHER EXPLORATION

1. Select one of the following topics. Then, relying on one of the strategies that you practiced in Chapter 2, prewrite on that topic. Focus on the qualities of the term.

   - charisma
   - maturity
   - a genius
   - a slob
   - stress
   - hypocrisy
   - courage

2. This chapter features several sample paragraphs:

   - an explanation of an aspect of a performing art (Robert Jourdain, page 119)
   - a source for a name of a ordinary object, in this case, part of a board game (John McPhee, pages 119–120)
   - an explanation of a real space or area that can be difficult to comprehend (Esther Dyson, page 121)
   - the background and origin of a commonly-understood word (Charles Earle Funk, page 123)

   For this assignment, consider a concept, object, situation, word, or phrase similar to the ones discussed in these paragraphs. Then prewrite on this topic. Once you have identified a specific focus and strong supporting ideas, create a paragraph of at least five to ten sentences in which you use definition to help your reader share your understanding of the subject. Use the material in this chapter to guide you.

▶ DISCOVERING CONNECTIONS

When you look at this picture, a shot of section of the Great Wall of China, what comes to mind? The Great Wall, running more than 4,000 miles from east to west across China, is often described as a wonder of the world. Many people would term China as an exotic destination for a journey. When you use or hear *exotic,* what does it mean to you? And, in your view, what characteristics or elements qualify something as a wonder of the world? Why do you think it is called "The Great Wall"?

For this assignment, consider one of these questions or another the photo suggests. Using the information in this
(continued)

chapter to guide you, write a paragraph of at least five to ten sentences in which you employ definition to identify the special qualities of your topic. As you develop your paragraph, make sure you have taken into account the elements of an effective definition and the full meaning of the term and made appropriate use of synonyms, etymology, and negation. ◀

CW 9.8 Paragraphs that define

✓ Definition Paragraph Checklist

☐ Does the topic sentence highlight the term to be defined?

☐ Does it include the elements of an effective definition? What are they?

☐ Does it take into consideration both the denotation and connotations of the term?

☐ Are there any examples or details that are too general or too abstract to be effective? Underline and suggest a concrete example that might be used instead.

☐ Have appropriate uses been made of synonyms, negation, and etymology?

☐ In your judgment, what is the best part of this paragraph? Explain.

☐ Which detail or example would be even better if it were expanded? Why?

RECAP Definition

New terms in this chapter	Definitions
definition	the writing technique used to specify the meanings of both concrete and abstract objects, ideas, events, or persons
pattern of an effective definition	two-step method of defining by first identifying the general class to which the term belongs and then listing its distinguishing characteristics

		distinguishing
	word	class	characteristics
EXAMPLE	A *convertible* is a *car* with a *retractable top*.

denotation	the direct, specific meaning of a word, as listed in the dictionary
connotations	the additional, subjective meanings a word suggests, deriving from the associations or emotional overtones it has

Writing an Example Paragraph

Choose a topic whose meaning needs **clarification** or **delineation**.

↓   ↑

Provide a **topic sentence** that indicates the term to be defined.

↓   ↑

Focus on the **elements of an effective definition**.

↓   ↑

Consider the **denotation** and **connotations** of the term you are defining.

GOING FORWARD...

**CW 9.9
Definition
review**

Q: How can I make sure that my reader can make sense of the meaning I give? I understand it, but is it realistic to expect that my reader will understand it?

A: It *is* realistic to expect your reader to understand the meaning you express. The key is to identify the essence of your subject in a topic sentence and then supply supporting sentences that elaborate on and illustrate it.

CHAPTER 10
Comparison and Contrast

▶ Navigating This Chapter

This chapter will explore the basic requirements for writing an effective comparison and contrast paragraph:

- providing a topic sentence that specifies the subjects and indicates the focus
- establishing a basis for comparison
- providing a thorough presentation
- arranging ideas effectively

GETTING STARTED . . .

**CW 10.1
Chapter
basics**

Q: I want to talk about two subjects that are related. What's the best way for me to write about subjects that have similarities or differences?

A: When you have to show how two subjects are similar or different, the mode of **comparison and contrast** is your answer. Through comparison and contrast, you clarify the subjects by matching them or pitting one against the other.

Overview: Expressing Similarities and Differences

**CW 10.2
Overview of
comparison
and contrast**

Because we often make decisions after considering alternatives, mastering the writing technique that examines alternatives, **comparison and contrast**, is important. To compare is to examine *similarities;* to contrast is to examine *differences.* When you use comparison and contrast, you organize your explanation of one thing relative to another, on the basis of common points.

**CW 10.3
Paragraphs
that
contrast and
compare**

Comparison and contrast would dominate in a piece of writing discussing similarities and differences between two computer game systems. This mode would also be useful to explore the similarities and differences between two eras in history or two characters in a play. You may find, in fact, that you rely on comparison and contrast a great deal in academic writing, especially with essay examinations. Once you have mastered the basics of writing comparison and contrast paragraphs, you will be prepared to write longer papers featuring this developmental strategy.

Providing a Topic Sentence That Specifies Both Subjects and Indicates the Focus

CW 10.4 Specifying two subjects

The topic sentence of a comparison and contrast paragraph specifies the two subjects to be examined. It also indicates whether the focus is on similarities or differences.

Take a look at this paragraph from Amy Tan's "Mother Tongue":

> Recently, I was made keenly aware of the different Englishes I do use. I was giving a talk to a large group of people, the same talk I had already given to half a dozen other groups. The nature of the talk was about my writing, my life, and my book, *The Joy Luck Club.* The talk was going along well enough, until I remembered one major difference that made the whole talk sound wrong. My mother was in the room. And it was perhaps the first time she had heard me give a lengthy speech, using the kind of English I have never used with her. I was saying things like "The intersection of memory upon imagination" and "There is an aspect of my fiction that relates to thus and-thus"—a speech filled with carefully wrought grammatical phrases, burdened, it suddenly seemed to me, with nominalized forms, past perfect tenses, conditional phrases, all the forms of standard English that I had learned in school and through books, the forms of English I did not use at home with my mother.

Tan uses the topic sentence to indicate her subject—two levels of English—as well as to signify that her focus will be on contrast. The supporting sentences then follow through on that contrast. They explain in detail how the English she uses when she is speaking professionally is far more formal and sophisticated than the English she uses when she speaks with her mother.

Establishing Your Basis for Comparison

Whenever you use comparison and contrast, you need to establish your **basis for comparison.** In other words, once you have chosen your subjects and your focus, you must specify the characteristics or elements you are going to examine.

For example, in a paragraph examining two brands of personal computers, you might examine *purchase price, warranties, types and availability of software,* and *ease of use.* Once you have established this basis of comparison, the next step is to discuss each brand in relation to these features. To be sure you include comparable information for both brands on every point, you may find it helpful to construct a planning chart first.

	Computer 1	Computer 2
Price		
Warranty		
Software		
Ease of use		

Look at this paragraph by N. L. Gage and David C. Berliner, which contrasts experienced physicists with newcomers to the field:

> How do expert physicists differ from novices? One difference is that experts take more time than novices in studying a problem. But once they start to work, they solve problems faster than novices do. The experts also seem more often than novices to construct an abstract representation of the problems in their minds. That is, in their working memory they hold mental representations of the blocks, pulleys, inclined planes, levers, or whatever they need to solve a problem. Expert physicists also tend to classify new problems more frequently. They may decide a problem is a type-X problem, to be solved by using the laws of inclined planes. Or they may see the problem as belonging to the type that deals with forces, pulleys, and blocks, which are always solvable by using some variation of Newton's second law, F = MA (Force = Mass Acceleration).

As you can see, the basis for comparison is clear. Expert physicists differ from novices in terms of how much time they spend solving problems and how they study, visualize, and classify problems.

FAST FACT Consider this contrast: Even though this black and white, odoriferous rodent is immediately recognizable to anyone who sees it, not everyone in the United States calls it by the same name. In the North, people refer to it as a *skunk*. People in the South, however, knowing its appetite for *poultry*, may refer to it as a *polecat*.

COMPREHENSION AND PRACTICE
10.1

Consider Topic Sentences and a Clear Basis for Comparison

1. Read the following paragraph from *Language and the Sexes* by Francine Frank and Frank Ashen:

**CW 10.5
Focusing on
similarities
and
differences**

> Consider the following claim: Women and men don't speak the same. Admittedly, in the United States of America, most people speak English. But they speak it differently, and the differences between women's and men's speech go beyond the variations in regional speech which we call dialects. Everybody knows that men and women *sound* different when they speak. Women have high-pitched voices, which we may sometimes find to be shrill. They speak rapidly and often sound "emotional." Men, on the other hand, have deep resonant voices; they speak more slowly than women. It is true that children of both sexes sound more or less alike, but when boys' voices change at puberty, the differences become clearcut. In matters of usage, women's speech tends to be more polite and more "grammatical" than that of men.

On the following lines, briefly explain the relationship between the topic sentence and the supporting sentences that follow it.

The topic sentence indicates that men and women communicate in different ways,

and then the supporting sentences discuss the differences.

_____

_____

2. On the lines that follow, list the ideas that represent the basis for comparison in this paragraph.

a. Differences in the way men and women sound

b. Differences in the speed with which men and women speak

c. Differences in the degree of politeness and grammatical correctness that

characterize the speech of men and women

3. In the eighth sentence, Frank and Ashen include details about children's voices. On a separate sheet of paper, explain why you think they included this information in a discussion otherwise devoted to adults.

Providing a Thorough and Specific Presentation

To develop an effective comparison and contrast paragraph, you need to examine the subjects fully. Of course, no rule sets an automatic number of points of comparison you should establish. Common sense indicates, however, that the more thoroughly you examine the subjects, the more likely your reader will understand your point. Therefore, regardless of the number of points you are discussing about your subjects, present them in thorough detail.

Consider this paragraph from Elizabeth Wong's "To Be an All-American Girl," in which she discusses how, as a child, she wished to reject her Chinese culture, which in this case was represented by her grandmother:

> The language was a source of embarrassment. More times than not, I had tried to disassociate myself from the nagging loud voice that followed me wherever I wandered in the nearby American supermarket outside Chinatown. The voice belonged to my grandmother, a fragile woman in her seventies who could outshout the best of the street vendors. Her humor was raunchy, her Chinese rhythmless, patternless. It was quick, it was loud, it was unbeautiful. It was not like the quiet, lilting romance of French or the gentle refinement of the American South. Chinese sounded pedestrian. Public.

Here, Wong lays out in detail the many ways that the Chinese language she heard every day from her grandmother and others in her community differed from the other languages that she perceived as superior.

Arranging Your Ideas Effectively

CW 10.6
Using block
format

When you write a paragraph in which the comparison and contrast mode dominates, you can choose between two organizational plans. The first alternative, the **block format,** examines all the elements of subject A and then all the same elements in the same order for subject B. Imagine, for example, you were writing a paragraph about two bosses for whom you've worked. If you used the block format, you would first examine one boss in terms of knowledge of the job, patience with workers, and basic fairness. Then you would examine the same criteria in the same order for the second boss.

The other method of arrangement is the **alternating format.** When you follow this method, you switch back and forth between subjects as you examine each point. With the paragraph about your two bosses, you would first discuss how well boss 1 understood the job and then how well boss 2 understood it. Next you would explain how patient boss 1 was and then how patient boss 2 was, and so on.

Note the organizational plan of this paragraph from "Dazzled in Disneyland," an article by Aubrey Menen:

> There are two kinds of legends: with one sort we can get inside them; with the other we are always spectators. I suppose there can be no American male who has not, at some time in his life, found himself alone in the countryside and explored Tom Sawyer island, or fought Indians, or crept on his belly up to a paleface fort. But nobody, I think, at any age plays Water Rat and Toad, or goes into Mole's house, or plays Prince Charming or Cinderella (unless driven to it by sentimental elders). These stories are too complete to have room for the outsider. We would know what to say to Pinocchio if we met him, or the Three Ugly Sisters. But we do not imagine ourselves being these people. A lesser man than Disney would not realize this. But here Tom Sawyer's island is big enough for children to play on; and Pinocchio's village is so small there is not even room in its streets to put one's foot. Once again Disney shows himself a master of the use of proportion.

As you can see, this paragraph is arranged in the alternating format. First Menen discusses the type of fantasies that one participates in, such as the story of Tom Sawyer. Then, for contrast, he brings in imaginings associated with children's stories like *The Wind in the Willows* and Cinderella in which one is a spectator. Then he discusses the size of Tom Sawyer's Island in Disneyland and contrasts it with the size of Pinocchio's village.

Now here is an example of a paragraph from an astronomy textbook by Jay M. Pasachoff:

> Venus and the Earth are sister planets: their sizes, masses, and densities are about the same. But they are as different from each other as the wicked sisters were from Cinderella. The Earth is lush; it has oceans and rainstorms of water, an atmosphere containing oxygen, and creatures swimming in the sea, flying in the air, and walking on the ground. On the other hand, Venus is a

hot, foreboding planet with temperatures constantly over 750 K (900°F), a planet on which life seems unlikely to develop. Why is Venus like that? How did these harsh conditions come about? Can it happen to us here on Earth?

This paragraph is arranged in the block method. First, the writer discusses various characteristics of Earth, and then he notes the contrasting characteristics of Venus. For information on using these formats in an essay, see "Using Comparison and Contrast to Develop an Essay" on page 218 in Chapter 15.

Transitional expressions are a great help to readers as they follow your organizational plan. A paragraph of comparison will, of course, use different sorts of transitions than a paragraph of contrast. The list below shows some of the transitional expressions you will find useful for each of these techniques.

Transitional Expressions for Comparison and Contrast Writing

Contrast		*Comparison*	
although	however	also	just as
but	on the other hand	both, neither	like
in contrast	unlike	in the same way	similarly

COMPREHENSION AND PRACTICE 10.2

Considering a Thorough Presentation and an Effective Arrangement

1. Read the following paragraph discussing two variations of the same sport: baseball and slow-pitch softball:

Even though the rules for both games are the same, baseball and slow-pitch softball are definitely different games. Baseball is played on a large diamond. Softball, however, is played on a smaller field, more like a little league field. A baseball is pitched fast, more than ninety miles per hour in the major leagues, and overhand. In contrast, a slow-pitch softball is lobbed underhand. Because of the speed of the pitching and the variety of pitches, a .300 batting average for a baseball player is good. Because a softball is pitched more slowly, batting averages of .500 or more are common. Also, in baseball, players are allowed to steal bases. In softball, though, a runner can't leave the base until the ball is hit. One thing both sports share, however, is a high level of interest among people in all areas of the United States.

In your view, are the subjects covered in thorough detail or would you include additional information? Use the lines that follow for your answer.

Answers may vary somewhat. Many students will agree that the paragraph provides

thorough detail about each point discussed. Some students may suggest adding

information about the significance of the size of the field and base stealing for each

sport.

2. On a separate sheet of paper, identify the organizational plan used in this paragraph. Explain also whether or not you think the order was a good choice and what leads you to this conclusion.

CHALLENGE 10.1   Considering Purpose in Comparison and Contrast Paragraphs

COLLABORATION

This chapter features several sample comparison and contrast paragraphs. The names of the authors of these paragraphs, with the appropriate page numbers, are listed below. Working with a partner, take another look at the paragraphs. Then, on the lines next to the names, list the primary purpose and any secondary purposes for each paragraph.

1. Amy Tan, page 129

   Most students will agree that Tan's primary purpose is to persuade and her secondary

   purposes are to inform and to persuade.

   _____

2. N. L. Gage and David C. Berliner, page 130

   Most students will agree that Gage and Berliner's primary purpose is to persuade and

   the secondary purpose is to inform.

   _____

3. Elizabeth Wong, page 131

   Most students will agree that Wong's primary purpose is to entertain and her

   secondary purpose is to inform.

   _____

4. Aubrey Menen, page 132

   Most students will agree that Menen's primary purpose is to persuade and the

   secondary purposes are to entertain and inform.

   _____

5. Jay M. Pasachoff, pages 132–133

   Most students will agree that Pasachoff's primary purpose is to inform and his

   secondary purpose is to entertain.

   _____

FOR FURTHER EXPLORATION

1. Select one of the following topic pairs. Then, using one of the strategies that you practiced in Chapter 2, prewrite on that topic pair. Focus on the similarities and differences between the two people, places, or items.

   - two instructors
   - love and infatuation
   - two aunts, uncles, or cousins
   - two vacation spots
   - two kinds of exercise
   - advertisements for two brands of the same kind of product
   - way you reacted to a situation in the past and the way you would react now

2. This chapter features several sample paragraphs:

   - a discussion of the ways someone speaks to different audiences (Amy Tan, page 129)
   - an explanation of how experts handle things versus how newcomers perform (N. L. Gage and David C. Berliner, page 130)
   - a discussion of two cultures (Elizabeth Wong, page 131)
   - a discussion of two types of fantasies from childhood (Aubrey Menen, page 132)
   - an examination of two places, one close and familiar, the other far away and mysterious or unknown (Jay M. Pasachoff, pages 132–133)

   For this assignment, think of related subjects similar in some way to those presented in these paragraphs. After prewriting, identify your focus and isolate strong supporting examples and details. Then create a paragraph of at least five to ten sentences in which you use comparison and contrast to make your point about your subjects. Refer to the material in this chapter as a guide.

▶ DISCOVERING CONNECTIONS

What do you think of when you see this picture? Seattle's ultra-modern Space Needle, in the center of the photo, and majestic Mt. Rainier, in the background, represent two different concepts of beauty. How would you compare and contrast these two magnificent structures? Seattle is considered one of the gateway cities to the Pacific Northwest, one of several regions of the United States, which also includes the South, the Far West, the Midwest, and so on. If you were to travel to any of these areas from the one where you are currently living, how similar—or different—would these two regions be?

(continued)

For this assignment, address one of these questions or another the photo inspires. Using the information in this chapter to guide you, write a paragraph of at least five to ten sentences in which you turn to comparison and contrast to evaluate the subjects you are examining. As you write, make sure to establish a basis for comparison, provide a thorough presentation, and arrange the information effectively. ◀

CW 10.8
More on
comparison
and contrast
writing

✓ **Comparison and Contrast Paragraph Checklist**

☐ Does the topic sentence specify the subjects and indicate the focus?

☐ Does the paragraph establish a basis for comparison? Make sure that each characteristic or element is discussed in equal detail for each subject.

☐ Is the presentation thorough? Write *amplify* above any point that should be discussed in greater detail.

☐ Are the ideas arranged effectively? Would the paragraph be more effective if the ideas were arranged differently or a different format were used? Explain.

☐ In your judgment, what is the best part of this paragraph? Explain.

☐ Which detail or example would be even better if it were expanded? Why?

RECAP Comparison and Contrast

New terms in this chapter	Definitions
comparison and contrast	the writing technique that examines similarities and differences between subjects
	Comparison may be used to develop similarities between subjects; *contrast,* to develop differences.
basis for comparison	the aspects, characteristics, or elements to be examined for both subjects in a paragraph of comparison and contrast
block format	a method of arranging elements for comparison and contrast in which all ideas about one subject are presented first, followed by all ideas about the second subject
alternating format	a method of arranging elements for comparison and contrast in which each of the elements or characteristics is discussed for both subjects on a point-by-point basis

Writing a Comparison and Contrast Paragraph

Choose subjects with evident **similarities** or **differences**.

↓   ↑

Provide a topic sentence that specifies the **focus—comparison** or **contrast**.

↓   ↑

Determine the **basis for comparison**.

↓   ↑

Consider either the **block format** or the **alternating format** to arrange your ideas.

The Block Format

Introduction

Subject A
Point 1
Point 2
Point 3

Subject B
Point 1
Point 2
Point 3

Conclusion

The Alternating Format

Introduction

Point 1
Subject A
Subject B

Point 2
Subject A
Subject B

Point 3
Subject A
Subject B

Conclusion

GOING FORWARD...

**CW 10.9
Comparison
and contrast
review**

Q: I'm worried that my reader might not understand the relationship I want to show between the subjects. How can I make sure to explain these common points so my reader can understand them?

A: The answer is simple. Make sure you include a topic sentence that expresses your subjects and the focus—on comparison or contrasts. Then lay out a clear basis for comparison and arrange your supporting ideas so that they have the most impact on your reader. That's all there is to it.

CHAPTER 11

Cause and Effect

▶ Navigating This Chapter

This chapter will explore the basic requirements for writing an effective cause and effect paragraph:

- providing a topic sentence that focuses on either cause or effect
- distinguishing between direct and related causes and effects
- avoiding oversimplification of causes and effects
- providing an effective arrangement

GETTING STARTED...

CW 11.1 Chapter basics

Q: I need to explain what made this situation happen and what happened as a result of it. How can I explain the reasons and outcomes so that they make sense to someone else?

A: Whenever you want to explain the *why*—whether suspected or proven—that leads up to or stems from a particular event, the organizing strategy that answers your needs is **cause and effect.** This mode enables you to examine the often complex relationships between an event or experience and what led up to it or resulted from it.

Overview: Explaining Reasons and Consequences

CW 11.2 Overview of cause and effect

Nothing happens without a reason or without some kind of consequence. When you explain why things happen and what occurs when they do, the mode you use is **cause and effect.** *Cause* is the *reason* something occurred; *effect* is the *result* of what occurred. Effects always have causes and causes always lead to effects, so in writing, you rarely find one without the other. Often, however, the bulk of the writing focuses on either cause or effect.

A paragraph explaining why NASCAR racing has become so popular would call for a cause and effect approach. So would a writing dealing with the results of a severe drought and one explaining the recent increase in certain antibiotic-resistant bacterial infections. Once you have mastered these basics of writing cause and effect paragraphs, you'll be prepared to use cause and effect to write longer papers.

CW 11.3 Paragraphs that show results

Providing a Topic Sentence That Focuses on Cause or Effect

**CW 11.4
Focusing on
cause and
effect**

With cause and effect writing, an important function of the topic sentence is to make clear if the focus will be on cause or on effect. Consider the following paragraph by writer Alice Walker from her essay, "Looking for Zora":

> There are times—and finding Zora Hurston's grave was one of them—when normal responses of grief, horror, and so on do not make sense because they bear no real relation to the depth of the emotion one feels. It was impossible for me to cry when I saw the field full of weeds where Zora is. Partly this is because I have come to know Zora through her books and she was not a teary sort of person herself; but partly, too, it is because there is a point at which even grief feels absurd. And at this point, laughter gushes up to retrieve sanity.

The topic sentence specifies that the paragraph will focus on cause. It states that Walker's reaction to seeing the unmarked and untended grave of African-American writer Zora Neale Hurston did not match her profound sadness. The supporting sentences then specify why she reacted as she did.

Remember—transitional phrases will help you to clarify which of your supporting statements express causes and which express effects.

Transitional Expressions for Cause and Effect Writing

Cause		Effect	
because	since	as a result	if
cause	so that	consequently	therefore
reason	unless	effect	thus

Distinguishing between Direct and Related Causes and Effects

**CW 11.5
Understanding
coincidence**

Some causes and effects are more directly connected than others. For example, the primary cause of an automobile accident might be bad weather. However, excessive speed and lack of experience on the part of the driver may be contributing factors. You must distinguish between **direct causes** and **effects** and **related** ones so that you don't overstate a particular cause and effect relationship.

You must also make sure not to confuse cause and effect with **coincidence**, which refers to events, ideas, or experiences that occur at the same time but purely by accident. For example, just because the power went off in your next door neighbor's apartment while you were using your hair dryer, you cannot assume that one event caused the other.

Consider this well-constructed cause and effect paragraph from *The Autobiography of Malcolm X* written by Malcolm X and Alex Haley, which outlines what happened when Malcolm began to copy a dictionary by hand, one word at a time:

I was so fascinated that I went on—I copied the dictionary's next page. And the same experience came when I studied that. With every succeeding page, I also learned of people and places and events from history. Actually the dictionary is like a miniature encyclopedia. Finally the dictionary's A section had filled a whole tablet—and I went on into the B's. That was the way I started copying what eventually became the entire dictionary. I went a lot faster after so much practice helped me pick up handwriting speed. Between what I wrote in my tablet, and writing letters, during the rest of my time in prison I would guess I wrote a million words.

The opening sentence specifies his action—copying pages from the dictionary. The direct effects of his action, which the supporting sentences in the paragraph explain further, are an increased level of knowledge, greater speed in recording information, and a continued desire to learn even more.

FAST FACT Failure to pay attention to details can occasionally cause embarrassing effects, particularly when it concerns language. A few years ago, graduates of a prestigious New York City high school specializing in science and mathematics received diplomas noting the school's prominence in "science and *mathemetics*." After the error was discovered, corrected versions of the diplomas were made available. Presumably they were prepared by the New York City high school specializing in language arts.

COMPREHENSION AND PRACTICE

Considering Topic Sentences and Cause and Effect Relationships

11.1

1. Read the follow cause and effect paragraph from a chemistry textbook by Cynthia Hahn:

When a hot object is placed in contact with a cold object, energy is transferred from the hot object to the cold object by means of heat flow. The *temperature* of the hot object decreases because its *internal energy decreases*. The *temperature* of the cold object *increases* because its *internal energy increases*. The amount of energy lost by the hot object is equal to the amount of energy gained by the cold object. You know that heat flows spontaneously from hot objects to cold, but not from cold to hot.

On the lines that follow, briefly explain the connection between the topic sentence and the supporting sentences.

The topic sentence indicates an effect—the transfer of energy from a hot to a cold

object through heat flow. Then the supporting sentences spell out the reason the

transfer occurs.

2. On the lines that follow, identify whether the focus in Hahn's paragraph is on cause or on effect and what in the paragraph makes you think this.

The focus in this paragraph is on cause, as evidenced by the explanation in the

supporting sentences of how the transfer occurs.

_____

3. On a separate sheet of paper, explain whether you think the cause and effect relationship Hahn outlines in this paragraph is direct or related and upon what information you base your conclusion.

Avoiding Oversimplification of Causes and Effects

CW 11.6
Avoiding over-simplification

When you write about causes and effects, be sure to avoid **oversimplification** of either one. Rarely does an event or situation have a single cause or a single effect.

Think of a serious problem such as juvenile delinquency. If you were to state that children whose parents are lenient will end up as juvenile delinquents, you would be *oversimplifying* a situation that is quite complex. Certainly a lack of discipline in childhood can contribute to bad behavior later in life. But to claim that one situation automatically leads to the other would not be accurate. Other outcomes are possible. (We all know people who were raised in undisciplined environments but who became solid citizens. We all also know individuals who had strict upbringings but still ended up in trouble.)

This paragraph, from Steven Pinker's *Words and Rules,* discusses why identifying the exact pronunciation of a word in English at a particular time in history is difficult:

> We can never say for sure what the pronunciation of a given word at a given time actually was. Just as there are regional accents today (London, Boston, Texas, and so on), there were regional varieties of English centuries ago; indeed, many more of them, because people did not move around as much as we do, did not send their children to melting-pot schools, and had no dictionaries to consult. Also, the written record is haphazard. Most words and pronunciations were in use long before the first literate person chanced to write them down, and many others went to the grave along with their speakers.

As you can see, tracing the exact pronunciation of an English word throughout the history of the language is not a simple matter. To illustrate the difficulty, Pinker provides several reasons for the complexity.

Providing an Effective Arrangement

Regardless of whether the focus of your paragraph is on cause or effect, you should consider the best way to provide the supporting information. For example, chronological order would be useful with a paragraph that discusses the *causes* of acid rain, which are both gradual and cumulative. Spatial order would be the best way to arrange a paragraph on the *effect* of a water leak in an apartment: the collapse of a portion of the living-room ceiling, stains across the wall below it, and warping of the hardwood floor.

With many subjects, however, you will probably find that emphatic order—beginning with a strong example and building to more serious examples—the best choice. Take a look at the paragraph from *Concepts of Chemical Dependency,* in which Harold E. Doweiko uses emphatic order to arrange some of the effects of addiction:

> At this point in the continuum, the person demonstrates the classic addiction syndrome. Multiple social, legal, financial, occupational, and personal problems become worse. The person also will demonstrate various medical complications associated with chemical abuse and may be near death as a result of chronic addiction. This individual is clearly addicted beyond any shadow of a doubt in the mind of an outside observer. It should be noted, however, that the addicted individual may try to rationalize away or deny problems associated with his or her alcohol or drug use even at this late stage. More than one elderly alcoholic, for example, has tried to explain away an abnormal liver function as being the aftermath of a childhood illness.

First, addiction leads the individual to ignore worsening problems that disrupt every aspect of the person's life. Worse, addiction leads the abuser to ignore health concerns—some potentially deadly—resulting from substance abuse. Worst of all, addiction leads to serious self-delusion: that substance abuse had nothing to do with health problems, despite clear evidence to the contrary.

COMPREHENSION AND PRACTICE 11.2 — Considering Complex Cause and Effect Relationships and Effective Arrangement

1. Read the following paragraph from *The Western Heritage* in which Donald Kagan, Steven Ozment, and Frank M. Turner discuss the economics aftermath of the Black Death in Europe:

> As the number of farm laborers decreased, their wages increased and those of skilled artisans soared. Many serfs now chose to commute their labor services by money payments or to abandon the farm altogether and pursue more interesting and rewarding jobs in skilled craft industries in the cities. Agricultural prices fell because of lowered demand, and the price of luxury and manufactured goods—the work of skilled artisans—rose. The noble landowners suffered the greatest decline in power from this new state of affairs. They were forced to pay more for finished products and for farm labor but received a smaller return on their agricultural produce. Everywhere their rents were in steady decline after the plague.

In your view, how well does this paragraph explain the relationship between the Black Death and the economic changes that resulted from it? On a separate sheet of paper, evaluate the effectiveness of the paragraph, supporting your answer with specific details and examples from the paragraph.

2. On the lines that follow, identify the order followed in this paragraph and explain what in the paragraph leads you to this conclusion.

The paragraph follows chronological order. The supporting sentences lay out the

events, one after another, that occurred as a result of the Black Death's enormous

death toll.

CHALLENGE 11.1 Considering Purpose in Cause and Effect Paragraphs

COLLABORATION

This chapter features several sample cause and effect paragraphs. The names of the authors of these paragraphs, with the appropriate page numbers, are listed below. Working with a partner, take another look at the paragraphs. Then, on the lines next to the names, list the primary purpose and any secondary purposes for each paragraph.

CW 11.7
Reviewing a
difficult
decision

1. Alice Walker, page 139

   Most students will agree that Walker's primary purpose is to entertain and her

   secondary purpose is to inform.

2. Malcolm X and Alex Haley, page 140

   Most students will agree that Malcolm X and Haley's primary purpose is to entertain

   and their secondary purpose is to inform.

3. Steven Pinker, page 141

   Most students will agree that Pinker's primary purpose is to inform and his secondary

   purpose is to entertain.

4. Harold E. Doweiko, page 142

   Most students will agree that Doweiko's primary purpose is to inform. Some students

   will also see persuasion as a secondary purpose.

FOR FURTHER EXPLORATION

1. Select one of the following topics. Then, following one of the strategies that you practiced in Chapter 2, complete a prewriting on that topic.

   - cheating in the classroom
   - raising the driving age to 18
   - the appeal of a type of clothing or music
   - peer pressure
   - your choice of academic major
   - an insulting comment
   - failure in a class

2. This chapter features several sample paragraphs:

   - The feelings after a long, involved task has been completed (Alice Walker, page 139).
   - The reward and motivation resulting from seeking self-improvement (Malcolm X and Alex Haley, page 140)
   - What causes people to communicate or express themselves in different ways (Steven Pinker, page 141)
   - The consequences of dangerous or self-destructive behavior (Harold E. Doweiko, page 142)

   For this assignment, consider a connection or relationship you have experienced, witnessed, or learned about similar to those indicated and explained in these paragraphs. After prewriting on this subject, identify a focus and then create a paragraph of at least five to ten sentences that makes the connection or relationship clear for your reader. Refer to the material in this chapter as you write.

▶ DISCOVERING CONNECTIONS

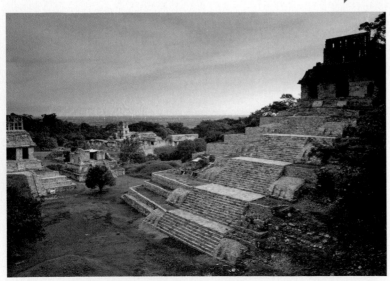

When you look at this picture of ancient Mayan ruins, what comes to mind? Does it make you wonder what eventually led the people who lived there to abandon the area? What would force you to pack your bags and leave an area for good? What effect does preserving the signs of the past—or obliterating them—have on society? If you were to journey to Mexico to visit this site, how would being around ruins of structures that are thousands of years old make you feel?

For this assignment, focus on one of these questions or another the picture makes you think of. Using the information in this chapter to guide you, write a paragraph of at least five to ten sentences in which you use cause and effect to explain your topic. As you develop your paragraph, be sure to recognize the differences between direct and related causes and effects, to avoid oversimplification, and to provide an effective arrangement. ◀

✔ Cause and Effect Paragraph Checklist

☐ Does the topic sentence focus on either cause or effect?

☐ Does the paragraph distinguish between direct and related causes and effects? Underline any details that seem like coincidences rather than true causes or effects.

☐ Does the writer provide a sufficient number of causes or effects to support the main idea? If you feel more specific details are required, write "I'd like to know more about _____" in the margin next to the appropriate sentence or passage.

☐ Is the supporting material effectively arranged? Indicate any suggested changes in the margin of the paper.

☐ In your judgment, what is the best part of the paragraph? Explain.

☐ Which detail or example would be even better if it were expanded? Why?

RECAP Cause and Effect

New terms in this chapter	Definitions
cause and effect	the writing technique that explains why things happen (**cause**) and what occurs when they do (**effect**)
direct causes	primary or main reasons
direct effects	primary or principal results
related causes or effects	contributing reasons or results
coincidence	events, ideas, or experiences that occur by accident at the same time
oversimplification	error in reasoning that causes one to overlook the complexity in a cause and effect relationship
	EXAMPLE "She doesn't want a career because her mother was never home when she was a child."

(continued)

Writing a Cause and Effect Paragraph

Identify a **subject** that focuses on the **reasons for** or the **results of** an event or phenomenon.

↓ ↑

Establish the **focus—cause** or **effect**—in a clear topic sentence.

↓ ↑

Be sure the reader will understand the differences between **direct** and **related** causes and effects in your paragraph.

↓ ↑

Provide details to convey the **complexity** of the cause and effect relationship you are describing.

GOING FORWARD...

CW 11.8
**Cause and
effect
review**

Q: The cause and consequences of what I am writing about make sense to me, but I'm not sure I am making the relationships clear for my reader. What should I do to make sure I write a cause and effect paragraph that communicates my meaning to my reader?

A: You are already in good shape because you understand the cause and effect relationship you are writing about. Now all you need to do is identify your focus in a clear topic sentence and then distinguish between direct and related causes and effects. At the same time, avoid oversimplifying your cause and effect relationships and be sure to arrange the paragraph so that the ideas come across most clearly for your reader.

CHAPTER 12
Division and Classification

> ### Navigating This Chapter
>
> This chapter will explore the basic requirements for writing an effective division or classification paragraph:
>
> - providing a topic sentence that defines the scope of the discussion and indicates an emphasis on either division or classification
> - establishing a logical method of analysis
> - maintaining a consistent presentation
> - using distinct and complete groupings

GETTING STARTED...

CW 12.1
Chapter basics

Q: The topic I've chosen is really complicated, involving a number of aspects and elements. I'm worried that my reader might not understand the subject unless I find a way to simplify it and present it in manageable parts. What's the best way for me to do that?

A: Whenever you have to simplify a complicated subject, the secret is to *analyze* it—to scrutinize its components to gain a better understanding of the whole topic—through **division** and **classification.** Whether your subject calls for a separation into parts (division) or an arrangement of elements into smaller groups (classification), this organization strategy makes it easy for your reader to understand the complicated issue you are presenting.

Overview: Analyzing the Whole in Terms of the Parts

CW 12.2
Overview of division and classification

Writing often involves simplifying complex subjects in order to communicate them clearly to a reader. The organizing strategy of **division** and **classification** is the one to turn to with these kinds of subjects. Although division and classification are separate processes, they are usually discussed together and often appear together in writing. Both processes involve **analysis**, looking at something large or complex by breaking it down into parts. *Division* refers to the separation of a subject into component parts. *Classification* refers to the arrangement of component parts into groups on the basis of some principle or characteristic.

CW 12.3
Paragraphs that analyze

Division and classification would dominate in a paragraph about weekend activities available in your city, including cultural events, wellness presentations, and dance clubs. A paragraph discussing an effective sales presentation would also employ division and classification, focusing on the *pitch, product demonstration, summary of benefits* and *close*. Once you have mastered the basics of using division and classification, you'll be prepared to use division and classification to write longer papers.

Specifying Scope and Emphasis through a Topic Sentence

**CW 12.4
Specifying
scope and
emphasis**

In a division or classification paragraph, the topic sentence specifies the scope of the subject that the writer will examine. It also often indicates whether the emphasis in the paragraph will be on division or classification.

A typical topic sentence for a classification paragraph will name the large group to be divided and then specify the *basis of classification*. This is the principle or characteristic used for making subdivisions or *classes*. The topic sentence may also name the classes, as in the following example:

EXAMPLE

large
group   basis for classes
We can classify *any rock* into one of three groups *according to the way in which*

classes
it was formed: igneous, sedimentary, or metamorphic.

Take a look at this paragraph from William Zinsser's *American Places: A Writer's Pilgrimage to 15 of This Country's Most Visited and Cherished Sites,* in which he discusses Niagara Falls:

> One misconception I brought to Niagara Falls was that it consisted of two sets of falls, which had to be viewed separately. I would have to see the American falls first then go over to the Canadian side to see their falls, which, everyone said, were better. But nature hadn't done anything so officious, as I found when the shuttle bus from the Buffalo airport stopped and I got out and walked, half running, down a path marked FALLS. The sign was hardly necessary; I could hear that I was going in the right direction.

Here the topic sentence identifies the subject—Niagara Falls—as well as the focus to be discussed in the paragraph—the misconception that this natural wonder is actually two separate waterfalls. The supporting sentences then use division to explain the way people often divide Niagara into the American Falls and the Canadian Horseshoe Falls, at the same time indicating that such a division isn't accurate.

Establishing a Logical Method of Analysis

Whether your focus is division or classification, you need to establish a logical method of analyzing the group or subject you choose. Any subject can be presented in a variety of ways. You need to choose divisions or categories that will enable your reader to understand your subject.

Imagine that you are writing about e-commerce—doing business on the Internet. You could approach this broad topic from a number of directions. One promising way is to use division and classification to detail different types of e-commerce the average consumer might use. As one category, you could talk about completing applications online, such as license renewal, financial aid forms, and tax returns. Then you could discuss using the Internet to complete banking transactions, and finally, to purchase various goods, from books to vacations. You could also use division and classification to discuss types of companies that have attempted to sell their products over the Web. Such a paragraph could focus on grocery sales services, gasoline sales programs, personal counseling centers, and pet food delivery services.

Consider this paragraph from "Risk" by Paul Roberts, in which he discusses the kinds of dangerous outdoor activities that Americans are seeking:

> Risky business has never been more popular. Mountain climbing is among America's fastest growing sports. Extreme skiing—in which skiers descend cliff-like runs by dropping from ledge to snow-covered ledge—is drawing wider interest. Sports like paragliding and cliff-parachuting are marching into the recreational mainstream while the adventure-travel business, which often mixes activities like climbing or river rafting with wildlife safaris, has grown into a multimillion-dollar industry. "Forget the beach," declared Newsweek last year. "We're hot for mountain biking, river running, climbing, and bungee jumping."

The method of analysis that Roberts employs here is clear and logical. He identifies his general subject as "risky business," and then he uses classification to identify the various kinds of activities: extreme skiing, paragliding, cliff-parachuting, river rafting, mountain biking, mountain climbing, and bungee jumping.

Certain words and phrases will help you to stress the divisions or classifications you establish in your paragraph. The list below gives you some possibilities.

Transitional Expressions That Show Division or Classification

can be categorized (classified)	the first type (kind), second type, etc.
can be divided	the last category

COMPREHENSION AND PRACTICE 12.1

Considering Topic Sentences and a Logical Method of Analysis

1. Read the following paragraph from Bernice Kanner's "Love for Sale: You Gotta Have Cards" in which she discusses the popularity of greeting cards:

> [In 1983], Americans exchanged 900 million valentines, 2.7 billion Christmas cards, 1.5 billion birthday cards—and 7 billion cards altogether. We sent bushels of Easter cards, Mother's and Father's Day cards, Thanksgiving cards, and cards commemorating lesser holidays as well as anniversaries, deaths, and other, less permanent departures. We dispatched cards in honor of Grandparents Day (the first Sunday after Labor Day, declared a national holiday in 1978—guess who lobbied for that?), cards that said, "Get well," "Sorry," or "Keep in touch," even cards that offered congratulations on buying a new car or sticking to a diet.

On the lines that follow, briefly explain how the topic sentence establishes the focus of the paragraph and prepares the reader for the rest of the discussion.

The topic sentence identifies that the focus of the paragraph is the number of greeting

cards Americans purchase yearly. It therefore prepares the reader for the explanation

and illustration in the supporting sentences.

2. In her topic sentence, Kanner includes statistics on the specific numbers of cards sold in 1983. Why do you think she chose to include these figures to open her paragraph? Do you agree with her strategy? Use the following lines for your answer.

Most students will agree that Kanner includes these statistics because of the impact

that the total number of cards purchased will have on the reader, and most will agree

with her strategy because the statistics have the effect Kanner intended.

3. Analyze the method of analysis Kanner uses to discuss greeting cards. Then on a separate sheet of paper, indicate whether, in your view, the method is logical, identifying what in the paragraph leads you to your conclusion.

Maintaining a Consistent Presentation

CW 12.5
Revising for consistency in presentation

As you decide on the focus of your division or classification paragraph, you also need to maintain **consistency** in the component parts or classes you establish. A **consistent presentation** involves divisions or classes established on a set basis, with no unrelated categories.

Imagine you were writing a paragraph about your expenses. You would be likely to discuss such items as *rent, food, clothing, savings,* and *entertainment.* You wouldn't discuss an upcoming raise or an expected tax return because these are *sources of income,* not *expenses.*

Take a look at this well-constructed classification paragraph about reinforcement from a psychology textbook by Zick Rubin, Letitia Anne Peplau, and Peter Salovey:

> **Reinforcement** is the process of using rewards—or reinforcers—to strengthen particular responses. A *reinforcer* is any event that strengthens the response it follows—that is, that increases the likelihood of that response occurring again. One of the most important challenges for anyone trying to teach something to an animal or person is to figure out just what things are reinforcing to that individual. Some things, such as food, water, and affection, seem to be naturally reinforcing; these are called **primary reinforcers.** Other things or events become reinforcing as a result of their association with primary reinforcers; these are called **secondary reinforcers.** Secondary reinforcers play a big part in shaping our behavior. Think of all the behaviors we engage in to earn awards, pats on the back, and grades. We have learned that the awards, pats, and grades are rewarding because they tend to go along with other more basic rewards, such as affection and esteem.

As you can see, this paragraph divides reinforcers into two similar categories: primary reinforcers and secondary reinforcers. It defines and explains each type through closely related examples: Food and water are primary reinforcers; awards and pats on the back are secondary reinforcers. Therefore, both the types it establishes and the details about those types are consistent.

> **FAST FACT**   Right now there are thirty million plus registered Web addresses ending in *.com, .org,* or *.net.* To alleviate the continuing demand for Web addresses in these classifications, the following seven new top-level domains are on the way: *.biz, .info, .museum, .aero, .coop, .name,* and *.pro.*

Using Distinct and Complete Groupings

CW 12.6 Using distinct groupings

As you develop a division and classification paragraph, you also need to use **distinct and complete groupings.** When a grouping is *distinct,* it is clearly distinguished from others. When it is *complete,* it is expressed in full detail.

Imagine that you are writing a paragraph on community theater that focuses on the people who attend the plays. If you were to divide these people into only two groups—family members of the cast and other people from the community—the second category would be too general. Your groupings would be incomplete. In fact, *other members of the community* is actually composed of several groups: senior citizens, invited city officials, high school students, families with young children, and so forth. None of these groupings overlap; each one has a distinctive set of members. In order to make your analysis complete, you would want to be sure that these categories did not overlook anyone who attends the plays.

Consider the way this paragraph from "Cellular Divide," an article about stem cell research by Sharon Begley, discusses types of cells:

> The cells that make up days-old embryos embody a world of potential. Four days after fertilization, the embryo is a hollow ball of cells called a blastocyst. Cells in the outer layer are destined to become the placenta. Those in the inner layer have not yet decided what they will be when they grow up: they are "pluripotent," able to differentiate into any of the 220 cell types that make up a human body, from the kidney, heart and liver to the skin, neuronal and pancreatic. These are the famous embryonic stem cells. For a few short days they are blank slates waiting for destiny (or the complex interplay of genes and biochemistry) to write their future.

In this paragraph, Begley ensures that her groupings are distinct and complete. To do so, she divides the types of cells constituting a human embryo in the first days after conception into two groups. The first group includes those on the outer layer, which become the placenta. The other group is made up of the *stem cells:* the undifferentiated cells that will become one of the 220 human cell types.

COMPREHENSION AND PRACTICE 12.2

Considering Consistency in Presentation and Distinct and Complete Groupings

1. Read the following paragraph from *Gifts Differing* by Isabel Briggs Myers and Peter B. Myers, in which they discuss how people perceive the world around them:

> Of the two very different kinds of perception, sensing is the direct perception of realities through sight, hearing, touch, taste, and smell. Sensing is needed for pursuing or even causally observing hard facts; it is equally essential to enjoying the moment of a sunrise, the crash of surf on a beach, the exhilaration of speed, and the smooth workings of one's body. Intuition is the indirect perception of things beyond the reach of the senses, such as meanings, relationships, and possibilities. It translates words into meaning and meaning into words whenever people read, write, talk, or listen; people use intuition when they invite the unknown into their conscious minds or wait expectantly for a possibility, a solution, or an inspiration. Intuition works best for seeing how situations might be handled. A thought that starts "I wonder if" is probably intuition, and the thought "Aha!" indicates that intuition has brought to mind something enlightening and delightful.

On the lines that follow, identify the components that Myers and Myers include, and then explain whether you think the paragraph maintains the focus on these subjects only.

The authors include two components, sensing and intuition. Most students will agree

that the paragraph does indeed maintain its focus on these two elements by offering

specific examples of each.

2. On the following lines, briefly explain how the examples and details that the Myerses supply help to keep the divisions distinct and complete.

The examples and details that Myers and Myers supply help to keep the divisions

distinct and complete because they illustrate how totally different these two kinds of

perception are.

CHALLENGE 12.1 **Considering Purpose in Division and Classification Paragraphs**

COLLABORATION

This chapter features several sample division and classification paragraphs. The names of the authors of these paragraphs, with the appropriate page numbers, are listed on the next page. Working with a partner, take another look at the paragraphs. Then, on the lines next to the names, list the primary purpose and any secondary purposes for each paragraph.

1. William Zinsser, page 148

   Most students will agree that Zinsser's primary purpose is to entertain and his

   secondary purpose is to inform.

   _____

2. Paul Roberts, page 149

   Most students will agree that Roberts's primary purpose is to entertain and his

   secondary purpose is to inform.

   _____

3. Zick Rubin, Letitia Anne Peplau, and Peter Salovey, page 150

   Most students will agree that Rubin, Peplau, and Salovey's primary purpose is to

   inform, and their secondary purpose is to persuade.

   _____

4. Sharon Begley, page 151

   Most students will agree that Begley's primary purpose is to inform and her secondary

   purpose is to entertain.

   _____

FOR FURTHER EXPLORATION

1. Consider one of the following topics:
   - categories of popular music
   - types of television shows
   - kinds of hobbies
   - your city or town
   - ways to waste time
   - groups of students on campus
   - elements of a successful party

   After prewriting on the subject, using one of the strategies you practiced in Chapter 2, identify a specific focus and then write a paragraph of at least five to ten sentences in which you use division and classification to analyze your subject. Use the material in this chapter to guide you.

2. This chapter features several sample paragraphs:

- an analysis that shows that what has traditionally been thought of as different or separate is actually the same (William Zinsser, page 148)
- an explanation of the types of popular leisure time activities (Paul Roberts, page 149)
- an explanation of things that affect our behavior (Zick Rubin, Letitia Anne Peplau, and Peter Salovey, page 150)
- a discussion of the way things evolve, grow, or change (Sharon Begley, page 151)

For this assignment, think of a complex subject from your own background or experiences similar in some way to those discussed in these paragraphs. After prewriting on this topic, identify a focus and then create a paragraph of at least five to ten sentences in which you use division and classification to make your subject clear for your reader. Use the material in this chapter to guide you.

COLLABORATION

3. Exchange your paragraph with a classmate. Evaluate the paragraph you receive, using the division and classification paragraph checklist below. Write your comments on a separate sheet of paper, and then return the paragraph and your assessment to the writer.

4. Using your reader's comments to guide you, revise your paragraph.

▶ DISCOVERING CONNECTIONS

What do you think of when you look at this picture? The scene captured in this picture is from a celebratory event. Based on the details in the picture, how would you classify the type of event being celebrated? Is it a holiday of some kind? Is it someone's birthday? Is it a cultural celebration? What makes you think so? The picture depicts five large masks striking slightly different poses or decorated differently. In the center is a single man. Why do you think the elements in this image are separated the way they are?

For this assignment, consider one of these questions or some other question the picture suggests. Using the information in this chapter to guide you, write a paragraph of at least five to ten sentences in which you employ division and classification to examine your topic in detail. As you create your paragraph, concentrate on key factors such as a logical method of analysis, a consistent presentation, and distinct and complete groupings. ◀

✓ **Division and Classification Paragraph Checklist**

☐ Does the topic sentence define the scope of the discussion and indicate an emphasis on either division or classification?

☐ Is a logical, consistent method of analysis maintained throughout?

☐ Should any details or examples be further subdivided? If so, underline them.

☐ Are the elements used distinct and complete? If you think any of the material needs to be made clearer or more specific, write, "I'd like to know more about _____" in the margin next to it.

☐ In your judgment, what is the best part of this paragraph? Explain.

☐ Which detail or example would be even better if it were expanded? Why?

RECAP **Division and Classification**

New terms in this chapter	Definitions
division and classification	writing techniques used to break down a subject (**division**) or group ideas (**classification**) for analysis so that the subject is easier to grasp
consistent presentation	using the same principle of division or classification for all the parts of a topic under discussion and providing parallel elements of description or analysis for each
distinct and complete groupings	categories for classification or division that are clearly distinguished from others and expressed in full detail

Writing a Division or Classification Paragraph

Indicate your subject and your focus—**division** or **classification**—in a clear **topic sentence**.

↓   ↑

Choose a **logical method of analysis**.

↓   ↑

Keep your **presentation consistent**.

↓   ↑

Make all **categories distinct** and **complete**.

GOING FORWARD...

**CW 12.8
Division and
classification
review**

Q: I'm still concerned about making sense of this complex subject for my reader. How can I be sure that I use division and classification so that I effectively communicate my point to my reader?

A: Using division and classification to make sense of an intricate subject for your reader is simpler than you might think. Just identify the scope and basis of your analysis through a solid topic sentence and establish and follow a method of analysis. As long as you maintain consistency and focus on distinct and complete groupings, you'll be fine.

CHAPTER 13
Argument

Navigating This Chapter

This chapter will explore the basic requirements for writing an effective argument:

- expressing a clear stance on the issue in a topic sentence
- providing sufficient support
- using a tone that is reasonable and convincing
- avoiding errors in logic
- arranging your support in emphatic order

GETTING STARTED . . .

**CW 13.1
Chapter
basics**

Q: I have strong feelings about my subject, so I know I have a good topic for writing. But what's worrying me is presenting it so I can convince somebody else that my point of view is reasonable and worth considering. What's the best way to present my stand on this subject so that I can persuade my reader to consider what I have to say?

**CW 13.2
Learning
how to
argue**

A: When you set out to persuade your reader, you are writing an **argument**, a paper in which you demonstrate your devotion to the support, criticism, or understanding of some issue. The key is to think of what you needed to know to be convinced. If you present that kind of information to your reader, you will be well on your way to success.

Overview: Understanding Persuasion

**CW 13.3
Overview of
persuasion**

As Chapter 5 notes, **argument** differs from the modes presented in the last eight chapters. Argument is not a mode but an aim or **purpose.** With argument, you use a variety of modes to *persuade* your reader to accept a point of view.

A paragraph asserting that television advertisements for beer and other alcoholic beverages should be banned would be argument. So would one maintaining that ownership of pit bulls, hybrid wolf dogs, and other aggressive breeds should be restricted. Once you have mastered writing argument paragraphs, you'll be ready to write multi-paragraph arguments.

Providing a Topic Sentence That Expresses a Clear Stance on the Issue

**CW 13.4
Finding
arguable
topics**

The topic sentence of an argument paragraph should clearly state the **stance** you are taking on the issue. In other words, it should indicate whether you are *in favor of* or *against* the point being raised. For example, imagine you were writing a paragraph about a National Health Care program to provide health insurance for all U.S. citizens. If you were writing to support this initiative, you might write a topic sentence like this:

EXAMPLE   The federal government owes it to its citizens to establish a National Health Care Program.

But if you were writing to oppose a National Health Care program, you might write a topic sentence like this one:

EXAMPLE   A National Health Care program covering all citizens is a luxury that the United States simply can't afford.

**CW 13.5
Expressing a
clear stance**

In both cases, your reader would be aware of the issue and your opinion of it.

Consider the stance set forth by the topic sentence in this paragraph about a controversial aspect of adoption:

> *Adopted children should be able to read through their sealed adoption files and make contact with their biological parents if they choose.* Many adoptees feel that something is missing in their lives. They feel an emotional gap that can only be filled by learning more about their biological parents. Also, adoptees should have the same rights as everyone else to learn about their heritage, race, and ethnicity. Most people consider this kind of knowledge important. If their adoption records remain sealed, how can adoptees gain a full understanding of their own background? However, the most important reason for unsealing adoption records is medical. Researchers have proven that many diseases and medical conditions, such as diabetes and heart disease, tend to run in families. Therefore, without a full medical history of their biological relatives, some adoptees may actually be at medical risk.

In this paragraph, the topic sentence provides a clear direction for the reader. Both the issue and the writer's stance are explicitly stated: Adoptees should have full access to their adoption records. As a result, the reader is prepared for the supporting sentences that follow.

Developing Sufficient Support through Sound Reasons

**CW 13.6
Developing
sufficient
support**

No absolute guideline exists about the amount of information needed to develop a sound argument. Think of a subject about which you are undecided: How much support would you need to see before *you* would accept that position? You would probably require several solid supporting details and examples before you would be convinced. Your reader demands the same of you when you write. As a general rule, include at least three reasons, or *points*, to support your stance.

CW 13.7 Occasions for writing arguments

As you develop your reasons with details and examples, keep in mind the relationship between *fact* and *opinion*. A **fact** is a verifiable truth. That driving on icy roads is dangerous is a fact. There is no room for discussion. An **opinion**, however, is a belief. It may be founded on impressions, experiences, or a person's base of knowledge. Saying that city officials who fail to treat icy roads don't care about the danger is an opinion. The validity of an opinion depends on how well it is supported by facts. Therefore, incorporate facts as often as possible to support your examples.

To help develop your argument, first list points that support your position. Next, list points that someone holding the opposite point of view might raise. The value of the first list is obvious. These are the points that will form the framework for your argument. The second list is also important, however. By addressing some of these points, you may be able to refute them completely or turn them to your advantage.

Imagine that you are against a proposal to establish English as the official national language of the United States, and you plan to write about that. Here are two lists of ideas you've generated about the subject, one against the proposal and one supporting it.

CW 13.8 Accommodating opposing views

Against the proposal

- The United States was founded so all could enjoy freedom, regardless of background.
- When we force people to reject their heritage, we all lose.
- The proposal discriminates against immigrants—it's prejudice.
- Learning a new language is too difficult a burden for many old people.
- English language classes aren't readily available, especially for working people.
- If we become English-speaking only, some people won't be able to work—added to welfare lists.

In favor of the proposal

- It saves money on things like bilingual education and government forms that now have to be printed in several languages.
- If people want to live here, they should learn to speak English.
- The majority rules.
- Some jobs are advertised only for people who can speak another language besides English. Native speakers shouldn't lose out on jobs because they can't speak another language.

CW 13.9 Listing reasons

The points you've developed to oppose the proposal are valid, so you could feel comfortable including any of them in your writing.

In addition, you could also adapt and use a couple of the points from the list in favor of the proposal. Your thought process might go something like this: Yes it's true that printing government forms in multiple languages and providing bilingual education cost taxpayers money. But as the most prosperous nation on earth, we should put people's needs ahead of dollar signs. And, yes, people who become permanent residents of the United States should learn English, but not because a law mandates it. Clearly, knowing the primary language of the United States opens up economic doors, making life easier overall. Rather than punishing people for not knowing English, our government should more aggressively educate newcomers concerning how speaking English will benefit them.

Now here's an argument paragraph that might result from the material on the lists:

> A law making English the official national language of the United States would be a terrible mistake. For one thing, such a law would discriminate against immigrants. The United States was established on the principle of freedom for all, regardless of background, and it was settled and made great by immigrants. It's unfair to make the newest groups coming to the United States face a greater burden than earlier groups of immigrants faced. Certainly, people should learn English because knowing the main language of the country provides many economic and social benefits. But mastering English isn't that easy, especially if the people are older. Also, except in major cities, language classes aren't always readily available, particularly at convenient hours for people who work. In addition, if we become an English-only nation, some immigrants who don't speak English will be unable to get jobs. Rather than working to support themselves, they will be forced to turn to welfare. But most of all, when we force people to abandon their own language, we are also suggesting that they abandon their culture. Our society has evolved as it has because of the positive contributions of so many groups. When we discourage a group from contributing, we all lose.

CW 13.10
Finding support through source information

CW 13.11
Comparing online and traditional sources of information

CW 13.12
Conducting online sources

CW 13.13
Understanding bibliographic options

As you can see, points from the list opposing the proposal to make English the official national language of the United States dominate here. In addition, some points from the list in favor of the proposal have been refuted and added to the other points. The result is an effective argument paragraph.

As Chapter 4 (pages 71–72) indicates, if you use information from another document or individual to support your argument, you must **document** the source of that information. In some of the argument paragraphs you will write, you can acknowledge your sources in a simple, in-text explanation: "According to a recent report in *U.S. News and World Report,* the number of college students selecting computer science as their major has increased for the seventh straight year."

In many cases, especially with longer, more formal assignments, you will need to provide more specific documentation for your sources. You'll need to include such details as the author's name, the title of the work, the publisher, the date of publication, the pages involved, and so on. Always ask which style of formal documentation your instructor prefers. The reference section of your college library will have guidelines for several methods of documentation.

You will probably find that your instructors will want you to use one of two common systems. One is the Modern Language Association (MLA) method, generally called for with assignments in English or other humanities disciplines. The other is the American Psychological Association (APA) method, generally appropriate for assignments in education, the social sciences, and the natural and physical sciences. Chapter 4 (pages 71–72) provides brief examples of both systems.

COMPREHENSION AND PRACTICE

13.1

Considering Topic Sentences and Sufficient Valid Support

1. Read the following paragraph concerning a proposal to require uniforms for public school students:

CW 13.14
Footnote and
endnote
options

A policy that requires public school students to wear uniforms would be a bad idea for several reasons. First of all, no style of clothing looks good on everyone. In their pre-teen and teen years, students are especially sensitive about their appearance, and having to wear clothing that doesn't fit them well will do little to help their fragile self-esteems. In addition, uniforms are expensive, and students would need to have at least two complete sets of uniforms to allow for laundering. Of course, since most students aren't likely to wear their uniforms after school, parents also have to purchase everyday clothes like jeans, shirts, and skirts, adding significantly to the amount they must spend on clothes. During the school year, students may outgrow their uniforms or the clothing may just wear out, increasing the cost for some families. Most important, a policy requiring students to wear uniforms ignores the rights of families to make clothing decisions that are best for them. Certainly schools should be able to restrict clothing that features obscene or objectionable slogans or that exposes too much skin. But making all students dress the same says that individuality is less important than conformity. The world already has too many followers.

What is the connection here between the topic sentence and the rest of the sentences in the paragraph? Use the lines that follow for your answer.

The topic sentence indicates the stance on the subject—that required uniforms for

high school students is a bad idea. The supporting sentences then provide reasons

that such a policy would be a bad idea.

2. Evaluate this paragraph in terms of valid support on a separate sheet of paper. In your view, are there enough reasons to convince a reader that the point of view is reasonable? Should any of the supporting examples be expanded in any way?

3. On a separate sheet of paper, first list three facts, leaving a couple of lines blank beneath each fact. Then, below each fact, write an opinion about that fact. Use the example below as a guide.

EXAMPLE

Fact: The incumbent mayor defeated her opponent by only 150 votes, less than 1 percent of the people who went to the polls.

Opinion: The mayor's narrow victory indicates that voters are fed up with her quarreling with the president of the city council.

FAST FACT It's not just those political types on Sunday morning political discussion shows who enjoy arguing. The World Debating Championships, for instance, involve some 270 teams from forty nations, making it the world's second largest student event.

Using a Reasonable, Convincing Tone

CW 13.15
Using a
reasonable
tone

Another factor that will affect your reader's acceptance of your point of view is your **tone,** the attitude you express about your subject. If your tone is sarcastic, superior, or patronizing, you may alienate a reader who might otherwise be swayed to agree with your point of view. On the other hand, if your tone is sincere and respectful, you'll enhance the chance that your point of view will be favorably received.

One way to make your writing reasonable and convincing is by avoiding **absolute** terms. For instance, it is better to say that people without survival suits *rarely* survive more than a few minutes in the frigid winter waters of the North Atlantic rather than to say they *never* do. Here is a list of more moderate terms that you can substitute for absolute language:

Absolute Word	Moderate Substitute
all	most
always	frequently
every	many
never	rarely

Avoid personally attacking or insulting opponents of your argument (see Argument *ad hominem,* page 163). With an emotionally charged subject like gun control, for example, it's easy to understand how sentences such as these might appear in an early draft:

> Most people who buy handguns do so for personal protection. *However, a person would have to be stupid not to know* that handguns are statistically more likely to be stolen or to cause accidental injury than to be used effectively for protection.

The message in these sentences is valid, but the name-calling is insulting to both the opponents of the writer's position and readers who are merely poorly informed about this issue.

Now, consider this version of the sentences:

CW 13.16
Revising
tone

> Most people who buy handguns do so for personal protection. *However, many people are unaware* that handguns are statistically more likely to be stolen or to cause accidental injury than to be used effectively for protection.

The message is the same in the second version, but the simple change in phrasing eliminates inflammatory name-calling. Instead, the writer is providing information in an objective tone that is much more likely to make poorly informed readers want to learn more about the issue.

Using Sound Logic

CW 13.17
Recognizing
familiar
fallacies

To persuade a reader, an argument must feature logical reasoning leading to a valid conclusion. You can establish such a *line of reasoning* by engaging in one of two reasoning processes: induction or deduction. Although the goal of these two reasoning processes is the same, they come at the subject from opposite directions.

With **induction**, you move from a series of specific instances or pieces of evidence to a general conclusion. Physicians employ inductive reasoning in diagnosing an illness. For example, a dermatologist might conclude that a patient's skin rash is a form of eczema because every other rash like this one that she has examined has proven to be eczema.

An answer reached in this way involves an *inductive leap*. Although this diagnosis is a reasonable conclusion based on the evidence, it isn't the only possible valid explanation. The rash may closely resemble eczema, but it may actually be the result of another condition. The more specific instances backing it up, the more likely the conclusion is sound.

Deduction, in contrast, involves reasoning from a general statement to a specific conclusion. Say, for example, you know that flat, low-lying inland areas are especially vulnerable to tornadoes. You also know that your cousin lives in a flat, low-lying inland area. You could therefore conclude that your cousin's neighborhood is a likely target for a tornado.

Use of sound logic will strengthen your argument. Faulty logic or **logical fallacies,** like those described in the following table will weaken it.

CW 13.18
Revising
logical
fallacies

Avoid Logical Fallacies

Fallacy	Examples of Fallacious Logic	Instead Use Sound Logic
Argument *ad hominem* (Latin for "argument to the man")		
Attacking the person	That editorial writer criticizes the entertainment business for its portrayal of the American family, yet she is divorced herself.	Respond to the opposing positions.
Bandwagon approach		
Urging acceptance because "everybody does it"	Everyone wants the City Council to institute new zoning requirements.	Cite objective, qualified authorities of statistics.
Begging the question		
Assuming as fact what must be proven	NASA's call for increased funding in these hard times is more proof that these scientists care about nothing but their pet programs.	Provide relevant, documented evidence.
Circular reasoning		
Restating your opinion and calling it a reason	That car is the best choice because, compared to the competition, it is superior.	Give real reasons.
Creating a red herring		
Diverting attention to an unimportant point	Senator Hogg says that genetic engineering is too much like playing God, but she isn't even responsible enough to file her campaign finance reports on time.	Provide compelling evidence.

(continued)

Fallacy	Examples of Fallacious Logic	Instead Use Sound Logic
Either/or reasoning Suggesting only two alternatives when many possibilities exist	If we don't institute statewide testing in high schools, we will face another generation of poorly educated students.	Explore all relevant possibilities.
Hasty generalization Making an assumption based on insufficient evidence	I've used that medicine for two days and my cough is still not gone, so it's obvious that the pills aren't working.	Base conclusions on many objective facts.
***Non sequitur* (Latin for "it does not follow")** Coming to an incorrect conclusion in relation to the evidence	Homeless people don't have permanent places to live, so it's obvious that they have no pride.	Think through relationships using logic.
Oversimplification Wrongfully reducing a complex subject	Using solar energy will eliminate all our energy problems.	State all important aspects; admit inconsistencies.
***Post hoc, ergo propter hoc* (Latin for "after this, therefore because of this")** Assuming a cause-effect relationship between two things that occurred by coincidence	The killer had just eaten at a fast-food restaurant, so something in the food must have triggered his aggression.	Check your thinking for irrational statements.

**CW 13.19
Logic in
argumentative
writing**

Find the logical fallacy in this paragraph on banning some material on the Internet:

Censoring the discussion of certain topics on the Internet is wrong for several reasons. First, censorship of any sort is a violation of the First Amendment to the U.S. Constitution, which guarantees U.S. citizens freedom of speech. Banning particular words and subjects from websites violates this right. Second, many proponents of a ban are seeking censorship because the ideas being communicated are offensive to their religious beliefs. However, the United States was established on the principle of the separation of church and state. No religion must be allowed to dictate what is correct or moral for the majority. If we allow these extremists to decide what is acceptable and what isn't, before long we won't have any rights left. Third, and most important, restricting the flow of knowledge of any sort is counterproductive to society at large. Censoring an important means of worldwide communication creates the possibility that ignorance and hatred might prevail over peace and understanding.

You probably identified the seventh sentence, indicating that failing to stop this act of censorship will lead to an elimination of all our rights. This is a case of *either/or reasoning*. True, if a ban is established, we do face a limitation on *one* right, but it will not lead to a complete elimination of the First Amendment, nor will it affect the other freedoms we enjoy in the United States. Leave out this sentence and you improve the paragraph by eliminating this flaw in logic.

Arranging Your Support in Emphatic Order

Most often writers arrange ideas in an argument paragraph in emphatic order. Using *emphatic order* means arranging your details and examples in such a way that each point builds in greater importance. Presented this way, the reasons compel your reader to continue on. (Emphatic order is discussed at length on pages 60–61.) Your initial point should be lively enough to spark and hold your reader's interest and to begin cultivating acceptance of your point of view. Each point should grow increasingly stronger so that your argument builds to a forceful, convincing conclusion.

Consider the order of the reasons in the following paragraph about keeping animals in captivity and forcing them to perform for humans:

> We humans don't have the right to capture animals and force them to perform for our pleasure in circuses, zoos, or aquatic parks. First of all, even under the best of circumstances, the environments in which these animals are kept differ vastly from what they would enjoy in the wild. For example, in their natural environments, animals like killer whales, polar bears, and dolphins cover territories that measure hundreds of miles. In captivity, they are held in compounds that are a fraction of that size. Receiving regular meals doesn't seem like a fair trade for this loss of freedom to roam. In addition, creatures such as elephants, great apes, and other primates are highly social and accustomed to living in large groups. But most animals in captivity live in far smaller groups, depriving them of the wider interaction they would enjoy in the wild. Worst of all, when we force animals to perform for us, we fail to respect their native intelligence, grace, and dignity. Instead, we allow them to be subjected to long hours of training to make them behave in ways that are simply not normal for these highly intelligent animals. That's what people should think when they see an elephant standing on a tiny stool or a dolphin dancing on its tail across a pool.

As you can see, the supporting sentences follow emphatic order. The initial reason—that the environments in zoos, circuses, and aquatic parks are considerably different from and considerably smaller than the ones in the wild—is strong. It is a compelling reason to support the idea that keeping animals in captivity to perform for people's pleasure is wrong. The second point—that these animals are often kept in isolation—is even stronger. Depriving animals accustomed to living in groups the comfort of others seems especially cruel. But the final point—forcing animals to endure training so they will behave in ways that they don't in nature—is strongest of all. Forcing animals to perform in this fashion goes against their nature. Their behaviors are shaped simply for our pleasure. This final point is a suitable conclusion to the paragraph.

Transitional phrases can help guide your readers through your line of reasoning and highlight the emphatic order. The list below gives some of these transitions.

Transitional Expressions for Argument

To Establish Reasons	*To Answer the Opposition*	*To Conclude*
first (second, third, etc.)	some may say	therefore
most important	on the other hand	thus

COMPREHENSION AND PRACTICE 13.2

Considering Tone, Logic, and Order

1. Read the following paragraph about banning beer and alcohol commercials from television:

> Television commercials for beer and other alcoholic beverages should be banned. For one thing, these advertisements exert pressure on viewers, especially young people, to drink. The ads imply that the only way to be cool is to drink. In addition, these commercials misrepresent the effects of drinking. The people portrayed never get into fights, engage in unsafe sexual activities, or get behind the wheel of a car. In real life, such consequences frequently result from drinking. Some people might argue that banning beer and alcohol commercials is a form of censorship, but people interested in these products can still get information in other ways, for example, through print advertisements in newspapers and magazines. Most important, a ban on TV commercials for smoking in 1971 contributed to an overall reduction in the number of people smoking. If a ban on television commercials for beer and other alcoholic beverages were half as successful, perhaps the number of people who develop drinking problems in the United States would be smaller.

How would you describe the tone in this paragraph? What in the paragraph leads you to this conclusion? Use the lines that follow to respond briefly to these questions.

Most students will use words like *serious, thoughtful,* and *respectful* to describe the

tone, and they will refer to an emphasis on facts and the overall calm presentation as

proof.

_____

_____

2. Assess the order of the supporting examples as they are currently presented. On the lines that follow, indicate whether you would leave the examples ranked as they are or if you would have changed the order, briefly explaining your reasoning.

Answers may vary somewhat. Many students will agree with the order, pointing to the

final point—that the number of smokers declined once television commercials for

cigarettes were taken off the air—as evidence of effective emphatic order. Some

students may want to rearrange the order somewhat, however, feeling that the

misrepresentation of the consequences of drinking is the most serious point of all.

3. Turn again to the list of logical fallacies on pages 163–164. Select three of the types of fallacies, and, on a separate sheet of paper, write an additional example sentence for each, using the current example as a guide.

CHALLENGE 13.1   Considering Additional Purposes in Argument Paragraphs

COLLABORATION

This chapter features several sample argument paragraphs. The specific points of these paragraphs, with the appropriate page numbers, are listed below. Because they are argument paragraphs, their primary purpose is obviously to persuade. Working with a partner, take another look at the paragraph. Then, on the lines next to the specific points, list the secondary purposes for each paragraph.

1. Allowing adopted children to view sealed adoption records, page 158

   Most students will agree that the secondary purpose is to inform. Some students may

   also point out that the piece entertains in that it makes its case clearly and holds the

   reader's attention.

2. Objecting to making English the official language of the United States, page 160

   Most students will agree that the secondary purpose is to inform. Some students may

   also point out that the piece entertains in that it makes its case clearly and holds the

   reader's attention.

3. Censoring the discussion of certain topics on the Internet, page 164

   Most students will agree that the secondary purpose is to inform. Some students may

   also point out that with the problematic sentences removed, the paragraph also

   entertains in that it makes its case clearly and holds the reader's attention.

4. Prohibiting the captivity and forced performance of animals, page 165

Most students will agree that the secondary purposes are to inform and to entertain.

FOR FURTHER EXPLORATION

1. Consider the following topics and then choose the one with which you most strongly agree or disagree.

   - Public higher education should be free for all students who qualify academically.
   - Cities and towns should strongly enforce laws against trash dumping and littering.
   - All public places, including parks and beaches, should be smoke-free zones.
   - Foreign language classes should be required for all students in U.S. elementary schools.
   - State governments should institute competency testing for all prospective teachers.
   - Bike riders, in-line skaters, and skateboarders should be required by law to wear helmets.
   - People convicted of drunk driving should be forced to have special license plates indicating their offense.

   Following one of the strategies that you practiced in Chapter 2, prewrite on the subject you have chosen, developing evidence for your stand on the issue. Then write a paragraph of at least five to ten sentences that expresses and supports your point of view.

2. This chapter features several sample paragraphs:

   - Pitting the rights of one individual against the rights of another (page 158)
   - Changing an aspect of life for people living in the United States (page 160)
   - Dealing with possible censorship (page 164)
   - Addressing the rights of animals (page 165)

   For this assignment, consider a topic like one of these. Review the paragraphs if necessary, choose the area you are most interested in exploring, and prewrite on this subject. Once you have identified your stand on the subject, develop supporting examples and details that you rank in emphatic order. Then develop a paragraph of at least five to ten sentences that effectively supports your point of view, using the material in this chapter to direct you.

COLLABORATION

3. Exchange your paragraph with a classmate. Evaluate the paragraph you receive, using the argument paragraph checklist on the next page. Write your

comments on a separate sheet of paper, and then return the paragraph and your assessment to the writer.

4. Using your reader's comments to guide you, revise your paragraph.

▶ DISCOVERING CONNECTIONS

When you look at this picture, showing three Japanese geishas, what comes to mind? Geishas are women who are specially trained to entertain and serve as hostesses, especially for men. Some might argue that the existence of women fulfilling ancient social roles hurts the chances for women in general to be treated as equals in social and business settings. What do you think? The women in the picture are dressed and made up the same way. Do you think this degree of uniformity in society is good or bad? Why?

For this assignment, address one of these questions or another one the picture inspires. Using the information in this chapter to guide you, write a paragraph of at least five to ten sentences in which you take a stand on your subject and persuade your reader. As you develop your paragraph, make sure you supply sufficient support, use an appropriate tone, avoid errors in logic, and arrange your ideas effectively. ◀

✔ Argument Paragraph Checklist

☐ Does the topic sentence clarify the writer's stance on the issue?

☐ Are there sufficient examples and details to support the stance?

☐ Is the tone reasonable, sincere, and serious? Put a ✔ next to any places where you see a problem in tone.

☐ Is the presentation logical? Underline and label any logical fallacies.

☐ Is material effectively arranged in emphatic order or some other method of arrangement? Explain.

☐ In your judgment, what is the best part of this paragraph? Explain.

☐ Which detail or example would be even better if it were expanded? Why?

RECAP Argument

New terms in this chapter	Definitions
argument	writing that seeks to persuade a reader to accept the writer's point of view
stance	the position taken on a subject—the writer's opinion
fact	a verifiable truth

> **EXAMPLE** The city is in the process of tearing down several historic buildings.

opinion	a belief based on impressions, experiences, or a knowledge base. In argument, opinions must be backed up by facts.

> **EXAMPLE** The city should be trying to preserve historic buildings instead of tearing them down.

documentation	the process of acknowledging the source of supporting information taken from another document or individual
tone	the attitude you express about your subject
induction	a system of reasoning that moves from specific examples to a general conclusion
deduction	a system of reasoning that moves from general premises to a specific conclusion
logical fallacies	common errors in reasoning: argument *ad hominem;* bandwagon approach; begging the question; circular reasoning; creating a red herring; either/or reasoning; hasty generalization; *non sequitur;* oversimplification; *post hoc, ergo propter hoc*

Writing an Argument Paragraph

Use the topic sentence to **express a clear stance** on the issue.

↓ ↑

Include **sufficient support.**

↓ ↑

Maintain an **effective tone.**

↓ ↑

Keep your presentation **logical.**

↓ ↑

Consider **emphatic order** to arrange the supporting material.

GOING FORWARD . . .

**CW 13.20
Argument
review**

Q: I've spent a lot of time developing reasons to support my point of view on this subject. What I'm not sure about is whether they will have the kind of impact I want them to have on my reader. How can I make sure that my examples provide effective support?

A: You've done the hard work already. You have identified and expressed a stance on the issue and you have developed some solid supporting examples. To be sure they have the kind of impact on your reader that they have on you, make sure you recognize the relationship between fact and opinion and avoid any errors in logic. At the same time, be sure to employ an appropriate tone and to arrange your supporting examples in emphatic order. Doing these things will give you the best chance of persuading your reader.

PART 3

Moving On to the Essay

CHAPTER 14

Developing an Essay

Navigating This Chapter

In this chapter you will learn what you need to know about writing an essay, including:

- the structure of an essay
- the stages of essay writing: prewriting, composing, and revising
- the importance of the thesis
- the importance of meeting your reader's needs
- the role of the introduction and conclusion

GETTING STARTED...

**CW 14.1
Chapter
basics**

Q: I feel comfortable whenever I have to write a paragraph, but now I have to write a multi-paragraph piece: an **essay.** I really feel intimidated because writing that much seems like an enormous task. What should I do to feel comfortable with writing a much longer paper?

A: First, relax. The process you follow to write an essay is the same one you follow to write a paragraph—prewriting, composing, revising. The difference is *scope.* With a paragraph, you discuss a subject in fairly limited detail. With an essay, you are examining a subject more thoroughly, which calls for more discussion, illustration, and explanation. Actually, once you do relax, you are likely to find you enjoy essay writing because the process liberates you to explore the subjects you choose more thoroughly.

Overview: Understanding the Essay

**CW 14.2
Overview of
the essay**

Up to this point, you have focused on writing paragraphs as a way to develop your skills. But as a college student and as a professional beyond the classroom, you will often be asked to prepare longer pieces of writing. Most college assignments call for multi-paragraph writings, called **essays,** that deal with a subject in greater detail than is possible in a single paragraph. The main difference between a paragraph and an essay is *scope.* A paragraph deals with a subject in a limited way. An essay covers a subject more thoroughly, exploring many facets and angles.

Paragraphs are the building blocks of essays, so what you have already learned about paragraphs will help you write essays. What you have learned about paragraphs is also important for another reason. You follow the same basic process to write an essay that you do when you write a paragraph.

Understanding the Structure of an Essay

An essay consists of three parts: an *introduction,* a *body,* and a *conclusion.*

The Introduction

The **introduction** of an effective essay is usually a single paragraph that indicates the subject and direction of the paper. This paragraph sparks the interest of the reader and compels that reader to continue reading. The most important part of the introduction is the **thesis,** the element that specifies the subject and focus of the entire essay.

The Body

The **body** of an essay is the series of paragraphs that support and illustrate the thesis. How many paragraphs should be provided in the body of an essay depends on the focus and direction of the writing. With an essay of 500 to 700 words, the body will likely consist of four to ten paragraphs, depending on the length of the paragraphs themselves. Regardless of the number of paragraphs, however, each paragraph must contain a clear topic sentence and supporting details, all relating to the thesis.

The minimum number of paragraphs constituting the body of an essay is three. One type of essay featuring a three-paragraph body is called the **five-paragraph essay.** As the name suggests, the five-paragraph essay has five paragraphs total, one introductory paragraph, three body paragraphs, and a concluding paragraph. Each of the three paragraphs of the body discusses one of the three points raised about the topic in the introduction. The five-paragraph essay may prove particularly useful with some timed writing assignments like essay examinations and writing assessments. (See Chapter 16, "Adjusting Your Process: Timed Writing and Summaries," for a more complete discussion of the five-paragraph essay.)

The Conclusion

The **conclusion** of an essay, usually a paragraph, strengthens the overall message expressed by the thesis and the supporting examples and details. The conclusion brings the essay to a logical and appropriate end, summing up the *significance* of the essay. Although most conclusions don't introduce new ideas, sometimes they raise issues that readers may want to pursue.

The following figure shows the structure of a five-paragraph essay:

The Structure of an Essay

```
                              ┌─ Introduction
         Thesis              │
                              │
         ↕                    │
                              │
                              │
         ↕                    │
                              ├─ Body
         ↕                    │
                              │
         ↕                    │
                              │
                              └─ Conclusion
```

Note that the arrows between paragraphs point in both directions. That's because each paragraph should relate both to the thesis and to the paragraphs before and after it.

Examining an Effective Essay

Consider the following essay:

**CW 14.4
Designing
academic
essays**

Making Their Marks: The Popularity of Tattooing and Body Piercing

Many people seem content enough to go through life looking like everybody else. But for others, nothing seems more important than distinguishing how they look from the rest of society. Some set themselves apart by how they dress. Others show their individuality by how they wear their hair. Today, people with an independent streak have found another way to make themselves stand out from the crowd. These people are choosing tattooing or body piercing as their marks or distinctions. These ancient forms of body art are among the most popular trends of the past decade.

The history of decorating the body in these ways goes back thousands of years. Originally, members of a tribe would undergo elaborate tattooing, piercing, or scarring to signify membership in the group. For example, natives of some islands in the South Pacific would tattoo their faces with intricate designs, while ancient tribes in other lands would cut parts of their bodies to leave scars in particular designs.

Tattoos and piercings have been around in more modern times, too. However, until the past 15 years or so, they have been largely associated with bikers and sailors. They held little appeal for the average person. Until recently, tattooing wasn't even legal in many states. The only way for many people to get a tattoo was to find an illegal tattoo parlor or travel to a country where tattooing was legal. Either way, people endured great pain and risked infection just to decorate their skin.

All that has changed today, however. For one thing, tattooing and piercing are legal in many areas throughout the country. Tattoo parlors are now licensed and inspected regularly to make sure they are sanitary. The instruments used are sterilized, in many cases using the same technology that is used to purify dental instruments.

But the biggest change is the clientele who seek tattoos and piercings. It isn't just outlaws looking to get a skull on their biceps. Today bikers and rock stars share the waiting room at the tattoo parlor with teenaged football players, fraternity members, stockbrokers, and other ordinary people looking for something that will mark them as different from the next person.

Nobody knows how long this new interest in tattooing and piercing will last. Right now, though, the number of people with colorful skin decorations and nose, tongue, and belly button jewelry seems to be on the increase. It looks like none of the new tattoo parlors will be closing any time soon.

This writing illustrates all the required elements of an effective essay. Its introduction has a clear thesis: *These ancient forms of body art are among the most popular trends of the past decade.* The thesis is fully supported and explained in the body—four paragraphs that discuss aspects of tattooing and body piercing. The essay then closes with a conclusion that restates the topic and reemphasizes the significance of the points made in the essay.

But how did the essay come to be in this form? The rest of the chapter will show you, walking you step by step through the process of writing an essay.

COMPREHENSION AND PRACTICE 14.1

Explaining the Parts of the Model Essay

1. Briefly explain how the introduction in the essay about tattooing and body piercing prepares the reader for the body to follow.

   The introduction prepares the reader for the body to follow because it states that

   although these forms of body art are not new, they are current ways that people use

   to indicate their individuality. Therefore, the reader is ready for a discussion of the

   different aspects of this trend.

_____

_____

_____

_____

2. For each of the paragraphs in the body, summarize the details that support the thesis.

(2) Tattooing has a long history, including South Pacific tribesmen who tattooed their

faces.

(3) In modern times, tattooing used to be relegated to bikers and sailors. It was illegal

in most states, painful, and potentially infectious.

(4) Tattooing is now legal in many areas. Tattoo parlors are licensed and regulated,

and instruments are carefully sterilized.

(5) The clientele seeking tattooing now include everyday people—teenagers,

housewives, stockbrokers.

3. How does the conclusion sum up the significance of the material presented?

The conclusion points out that it's hard to tell how long the new wave of this old

tradition will remain. It also restates that tattooing and body piercing continue to grow

in popularity.

_____

_____

_____

_____

CW 14.5
Developing
a thesis
statement

Examining the Process of Writing an Essay

ESL Note
See "Writing Essays"
on pages 602–603.

To write an essay, you follow a process that is similar to the one you follow to write a paragraph. When you write an essay, however, you use the stages of *prewriting, composing,* and *revising* to explore the subject in far greater detail.

The first stage of essay writing is prewriting, during which you generate the ideas you'll need to complete your essay. In Chapter 2, "Generating Ideas through Prewriting," you discovered which prewriting technique—or which combination of techniques—you prefer to develop examples and details about a subject. When you are developing an essay, you also prewrite to develop a manageable focus, just as you do when you write a paragraph.

You then develop this focus into your **thesis**, your main point for the essay, expressed in sentence form. Developing a draft thesis is your bridge from prewriting to composing. In this stage, you turn your prewriting ideas into sentences that support, illustrate, or explain the thesis. You then arrange the sentences in paragraphs, including an **introduction** and a **conclusion**, that address the needs of the reader.

With a first draft completed, you **revise**, or refine and polish your draft. When you revise, you first **reassess** its *unity, coherence,* and *use of language.* Then you **redraft** to address any problem spots. Finally, you **edit** to eliminate any remaining errors. Take a look at this figure, which illustrates the process of writing an essay:

The Process of Writing an Essay

As the two-way arrows show, the process of writing an essay often requires you to repeat some steps. In other words, the process is *recursive.*

Imagine, for example, that during the revising stage you find that one or more of the paragraphs need additional detail. You simply return to the prewriting stage to generate new information. You then move to the composing stage to turn the new ideas into correct, reader-centered sentence form. Finally, you would edit this newly generated material to make sure that it is expressed correctly.

Think again of the essay on tattooing and piercing. It was created following the same process. Now let's examine that essay in its various stages.

Prewriting: Generating Ideas and Identifying a Manageable Focus

All writing starts with **prewriting.** Here is a freewriting on *fads and trends,* which contains initial facts and details about tattooing and body piercing:

Ok, what fads and trends are around? Music? Maybe. Different types like Alternative, Retro, Rap? They've all been around for a while, though, so are they really fads or trends? How about clothes? Fashions change so fast. If you spend a lot of money on clothes this year, you are out of style by next year-so annoying! And so expensive. I paid $90 for one pair of shoes last year. How about people getting tattoos? That seems more like it-tattooing and piercing are hot now. Even before it was legal in this state, people got cool tattoos at these illegal tattooing and piercing parties at somebody's house. Nick and Kara went to the next state where tattooing was legal. Three places here in town now. Really safe now-the city health inspector has to check out the places and they have to have special devices like at the dentist to keep the instruments germ free. Piercing-it must hurt a lot, especially depending where you get it. Alikia said it didn't hurt to have her belly button pierced, but she has to be lying. And somebody told me that getting a tattoo on the small of your back hurts the most. How about on your butt? Willy had one of a leprechaun there-now that had to hurt! And tongue rings-ouch! People get piercing and tattoos to make them different from everyone else-body art. My grandmother says that only trashy people get tattoos. She's almost 80, and when she was growing up, only criminals and sailors had tattoos -nobody had piercings. But tattooing goes way back in time-some tribes used to decorate their faces or purposely scar themselves to indicate their membership in a group. Now all kinds of people go-housewives, teenagers, you name it. I should talk to

Urbano about how much it costs—his cousin is a tattoo artist. Today I'll look around at people at the Metro station to see how many of them have piercings, scarrings, or tattoos—I hope nobody sees me staring.

FAST FACT When it comes to generating ideas, master of the horror story Stephen King believes that "[t]here is no Idea Dump, no Story Central, no Island of the Buried Bestsellers." Instead, as you begin your path through the writing process, "two previously unrelated ideas come together and make something new under the sun. Your job isn't to find these ideas but to recognize them when they show up."

As you can see, this freewriting contains a number of interesting details about tattooing and piercing. The writer has highlighted the most promising ideas. From the highlighted material, it's easy to identify a likely focus: tattooing and body piercing as a current popular fad, but with a history.

Developing an Effective Thesis

The bridge between prewriting and composing is developing a draft thesis. Think of the thesis as a signpost in sentence form that lets the reader know what is to come in the rest of the paper. A topic sentence states the main idea of a single paragraph, but a thesis states the main idea of the *entire* essay.

An effective thesis, like an effective topic sentence, is generally composed of two parts: a *subject* and the *writer's attitude about* or *reaction to* that subject. This structure clarifies the purpose of the essay and establishes the reader's expectation about the way the subject will be discussed. For example, if you were writing an essay about the greatest technological advance of the past 50 years, your thesis might look like this:

CW 14.6
Writing thesis statements

EFFECTIVE THESIS

subject ——————— attitude or opinion ———————

The development of the Internet is **the most important technical innovation of the past 50 years.**

CW 14.7
Purpose and thesis statements

This thesis is effective because it features both a subject and an attitude or opinion about the subject. In addition, it indicates that the primary purpose of the piece is to persuade and that the rest of the paper will likely provide examples demonstrating that the Internet was indeed the most significant technological development of the past half century.

One way to remember what a good thesis *is* is to remember what a thesis *isn't*. An effective thesis is **not**

- an **announcement** of your intent, featuring words like *I plan, I intend,* or *This paper concerns,* because these expressions merely repeat what you should make obvious with your thesis.

INEFFECTIVE THESIS I want to talk about how important the development of the Internet has been.

- a **statement of fact,** because a fact is a verifiable truth, leaving no room for discussion or debate:

INEFFECTIVE THESIS | Many people use broadband technology to connect to the Internet.

- a **title**, since a title is not usually a sentence and is generally intended to provide only a broad hint of the subject of your essay:

INEFFECTIVE THESIS | The Internet: The Innovation That Changed the Whole World

COMPREHENSION AND PRACTICE

14.2 Revising Ineffective Theses

Turn each of the following sentences or titles into an effective thesis. Use the example as a guide. Answers will vary. Representative answers are shown.

EXAMPLE | The Shack Where I Grew Up

Although the house where I spent my childhood was a shack, I have many good memories of the days I spent playing there.

1. The metric system is a system of measurement based on units of ten.

Although the metric system is an excellent system of measurement, U.S. citizens continue to resist adopting it.

2. I plan to show that having a good educational experience in kindergarten can have an enormous impact on a child's self-image.

Having a good educational experience in kindergarten can have an enormous impact on a child's self-image.

3. Tabloids like the *National Enquirer* sell millions of copies a week.

People who buy the *National Enquirer* and other tabloids—which sell millions of copies a week—can be classified into four major groups.

4. The Ideal Occupation

One person's idea of an ideal occupation can be another person's idea of daily

torture.

5. I want to show that insurance companies shouldn't be allowed to terminate coverage for people who face extraordinary medical bills.

Insurance companies shouldn't be allowed to terminate coverage for people who face

extraordinary medical bills.

6. Manatees are large aquatic mammals that live within the intercostal waterways of Florida.

Recreational boaters in Florida's intercostal waterways are the single biggest threat to

manatees.

7. I plan to show that taking music lessons can help preschoolers develop a greater ability to learn.

Taking music lessons can help preschoolers develop a greater ability to learn.

8. More and more people are doing their holiday shopping through the Internet.

Holiday shopping on the Internet may someday replace traditional shopping

experiences.

9. Electric Cars: Transportation of the Future

Speed-obsessed American drivers will refuse to drive electric cars until they perform

as well as gas-powered vehicles.

10. I want to show that directors of youth leagues should enact strict rules regarding acceptable behavior for parents at games.

Directors of youth sports leagues should enact strict rules regarding acceptable

behavior of parents at games.

CHALLENGE 14.1 Developing Support for a Thesis

COLLABORATION

The section on developing an effective thesis (page 181) presents the following thesis for an essay:

EXAMPLE The development of the Internet is the most important technical innovation of the past 50 years.

Working with a partner, make a list on a separate sheet of paper of several details and examples that could be used to support this thesis.

Composing

Once you have developed a draft thesis, you move to the **composing** stage, during which you complete a draft of your essay. You've already highlighted the ideas that you initially felt held the most promise for development. Now you should *filter* this material, identifying the information that offers the best support for the thesis you have developed.

With these ideas identified, you need to list them, putting related ideas together. Restated more completely, in correct sentence form, the ideas in these groups will become the basis for the supporting paragraphs of your essay. Therefore, you should also consider the best way to arrange the groups to fulfill the purpose of the essay. This order will serve as a tentative blueprint for your essay.

Here are the most promising ideas about tattooing and piercing from the highlighted material in the freewriting on fads and trends. The thesis indicates that the primary purpose will be to inform—to explain the historical background of tattooing. Therefore, arranging this information in chronological order makes sense.

1. That seems more like it—tattooing and piercing are hot now. People get piercing and tattoos to make them different from everyone else—body art.

2. But tattooing goes way back in time—some tribes used to decorate their faces or purposely scar themselves to indicate their membership in a group.

3. My grandmother says that only trashy people get tattoos. She's almost 80, and when she was growing up, only criminals and sailors had tattoos.
   Even before it was legal in this state, people got cool tattoos at these illegal tattooing and piercing parties at somebody's house.

4. Three places here in town now.
   Really safe now—the city health inspector has to check out the places and they have to have special devices like at the dentist to keep the instruments germ free.

5. Now all kinds of people go—housewives, teenagers, you name it. Nick and Kara went to the next state where tattooing was legal.

Once you have grouped and arranged your best prewriting material, the next step is to express it more completely and clearly, using additional details, examples, and illustrations. As with paragraph writing, should you include any information that you have taken from a specific source, make sure to acknowledge that source. (See pages 71–72 for a more complete discussion of **documentation.**)

As you organize your ideas and write them down, keep your reader's needs in mind so that the essay will be *reader centered.* In other words, your goal is to create an essay that will make sense to somebody else. You know a great deal about most of the subjects you will write about. For this reason, you might incorrectly conclude that your reader has the same background and frame of reference as you do.

The secret to meeting your reader's needs is to think of yourself *before* you learned what you know about the subject. What specific examples and details did you need to understand the subject yourself?

FAST FACT   Don't you just hate it when the word you want is "on the tip of your tongue," but you can't actually say it or get it down on paper? You aren't alone. In fact, it's a phenomenon that's so common that it has a name. And what is that name? Psychologists commonly refer to it as the tip-of-the-tongue phenomenon. Ah, those experts . . .

Creating an Effective Introduction and Conclusion

An essay contains two important paragraphs that perform specialized functions: the introduction and the conclusion. The introduction contains the thesis, engages the reader, and previews the structure of the essay. The conclusion summarizes the point of the essay, restating the significance of the ideas while bringing the paper to a logical and appropriate end.

CW 14.8 Composing introductions

Introduction   You have several techniques available to help you develop an effective introduction. One technique is to use an **anecdote**—a brief, entertaining story that emphasizes the thesis.

Imagine a paper discussing the media's intrusion into the lives of people in the news. The introduction to this paper might include the following story about a victim of the media:

CW 14.9 Your opening paragraph

When my friend Cerene opened the newspaper one morning last year, she saw a story that made her physically sick. There, on page two, was a story about her father's arrest for tax evasion. Included in the story were her name and age. What the story didn't mention was that Cerene's parents had been divorced four years earlier. Her father hadn't contacted her or provided any financial support in all that time. These facts didn't stop the newspaper from dragging her name into the story, even though she had nothing at all to do with her father or his legal troubles. Cerene was perfectly innocent, yet she still had to face the embarrassment of seeing her name published in an unflattering situation. The media shouldn't be able to drag anyone's name into a story that doesn't genuinely involve that person.

Another technique is to use relevant facts or statistics:

EXAMPLE | A recent *USA Today* poll found that 75 percent of all Americans think the media focus too much on the private lives of news makers.

**CW 14.10
Turning
your
introduction
into an
engaging
lead**

To show the reader what direction the essay will take, the next sentence could state that the discussion will focus on examples from politics, business, show business, and sports.

Still another technique is to begin the introduction with a relevant saying or quotation:

EXAMPLE | My grandmother's favorite expression was, "Keep your nose out of other people's business, and they'll keep their noses out of yours."

Another technique is to begin with a **rhetorical question.** This type of question is designed not to be answered, but to provoke thought or discussion:

EXAMPLE | How would you like to suffer a personal loss and then read all the personal details in the paper the next morning?

Placing your thesis as the first or second sentence of your introduction lets your reader know the point of your essay immediately. Placing it toward or at the end of the introduction, however, can arouse interest, drawing your reader into your subject. Regardless of where you place the thesis, keep in mind that your introduction should always suggest the direction the essay will take.

**CW 14.11
Extending
your
conclusion**

Conclusion   The conclusion is the writer's last word on the subject, a final thought or a question for the reader to consider. In general, conclusions don't present new information in detail. The place to develop new thoughts and ideas fully is the body, not the conclusion.

As with an introduction, concluding an essay with an anecdote that embodies the point of the paper is a good technique. Other times a relevant question or quotation will be the best alternative. The technique you ultimately choose should depend upon the particular situation. Whatever technique helps you bring the essay to an effective close is the correct choice for that essay.

Here is an effective conclusion for a paper discussing the media's intrusion into the lives of people in the news:

No one is saying that news reporters shouldn't have the right to publish or broadcast the news. But they do have a responsibility to make sure that the material they broadcast or publish is actually news and not gossip. Everybody has the right to personal privacy, even public figures, and the media should respect this right.

COMPREHENSION AND PRACTICE 14.3

Understanding Techniques for Introductions and Conclusions

1. Of the list of techniques available to use in introductions or conclusions (pages 185–186), which do you find most interesting? Why?

Answers will vary.

_____

_____

CW 14.12 Conclusion confusion

2. On a separate sheet of paper, briefly explain which you think you would find easier to write for an essay, an introduction or a conclusion, and why.

Understanding the Relationship between Topic Sentences and the Thesis   As Chapter 3, "Composing: Creating a Draft," indicated, the main sentence in any paragraph is called the *topic sentence*. An essay is a multi-paragraph writing, so it contains several topic sentences, each of which is directly connected to the thesis.

Here is the thesis from a paper about honesty in the United States:

EXAMPLE

In the United States today, it seems as if people don't care about honesty and lawful behavior any more.

As the thesis indicates, the rest of the essay deals with examples of dishonesty or illegal behavior. The first paragraph of the body, for example, discusses regular violations of drug laws. The next paragraph deals with employee theft, and the next one discusses incompetence and dishonesty in public works projects. The final paragraph in the body discusses the public reaction following the impeachment of the president of the United States several years ago. The conclusion then restates the significance of the thesis—that in all areas of life, society no longer values honesty as it once did.

The figure on page 188 illustrates the relationship between the thesis and the topic sentences of this essay. As the figure shows, each topic sentence deals with some form of dishonesty or unlawful behavior. In terms of the relationship between the thesis and these topic sentences, *dishonesty or unlawful behavior* represents the *common thread,* the element that all the paragraphs share. This thesis indicates that honesty is no longer valued. Each topic sentence directly supports, illustrates, or explains this thesis by presenting a different aspect of dishonesty.

CHALLENGE 14.2   Relating Thesis and Topic Sentences

COLLABORATION

Review the final draft of the essay about tattooing and piercing on pages 176–177. Find the topic sentence of each paragraph. Working with a partner, show the relationship between the thesis, the topic sentences in the body, and the topic sentence in the conclusion. Create a figure like the one that follows on page 188.

The Relationship between Topic Sentences and the Thesis

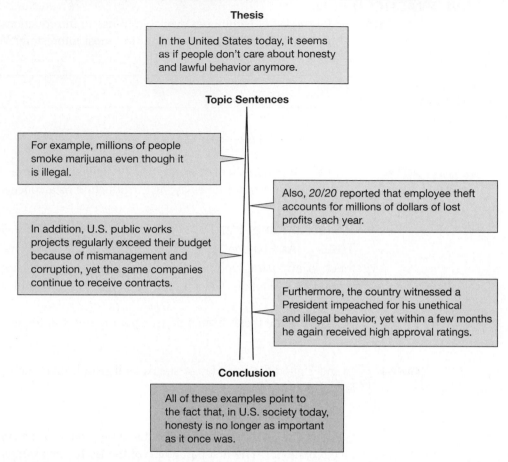

Thesis

In the United States today, it seems as if people don't care about honesty and lawful behavior anymore.

Topic Sentences

For example, millions of people smoke marijuana even though it is illegal.

Also, *20/20* reported that employee theft accounts for millions of dollars of lost profits each year.

In addition, U.S. public works projects regularly exceed their budget because of mismanagement and corruption, yet the same companies continue to receive contracts.

Furthermore, the country witnessed a President impeached for his unethical and illegal behavior, yet within a few months he again received high approval ratings.

Conclusion

All of these examples point to the fact that, in U.S. society today, honesty is no longer as important as it once was.

Developing a Solid First Draft Once you have organized selected details into a list like the one on pages 184–185, then it's time to develop a solid first draft of the essay. Using your list to guide you, you should be able to compose an introduction, body, and conclusion, all expressed in complete sentence form.

Here is the *first draft* of the paper on tattooing and piercing:

Making Their Marks: The Popularity of Tattooing and Body Piercing

(1) Today a number of people are choosing tattooing or body piercing to make them feel different. Right now these forms of body art are really popular.

(2) In modern times, tattoos have usually been associated with bikers and sailors. Until recently, it was illegal. People went to illegal tattoo parlors to get them. They had to put up with pain and possible infection.

(3) The history of decorating the body goes back thousands of years. Natives of some islands in the South Pacific would tattoo their faces with intricate designs. Some of these islands are still experiencing volcanic eruptions. One eruption a few years ago destroyed most of a small town. Some ancient tribes cut other parts of their bodies to leave scars in particular designs.

(4) All that has changed. Tattooing and piercing are legal in many areas throughout the country. Tattoo parlors are licensed and inspected. The instruments used are sterilized.

(5) A big change is who goes for tattoos today. Besides tough guys getting some designs done, everybody goes, too, so that they can all be different.

(6) Nobody knows how long fads like tattooing and piercing will stay in fashion. People still seem to be interested, so it will probably be around for a while.

This first draft contains the basics: a thesis, prewriting ideas expressed in sentence form, and paragraphs arranged into an introduction, body, and conclusion. At this point, however, it is in a limited and rough form. Before it fulfills the promise that it holds, it needs to be reexamined and reworked. In other words, it needs to be revised.

Revising

Once you have completed a draft of your essay, it is a good idea to take a break of a day or so. This way you will bring a rested and refreshed eye to the final stage of the writing process: **revising.** When you revise, you *refine* and then *polish* your draft. You follow the same steps to revise an essay that you follow to revise a paragraph. First, you *reassess* your draft, then you *redraft,* and finally you *edit.*

Reassessing   When you **reassess** a piece of writing, you reexamine the essay for several factors. For example, a successful essay must be

- *unified*—all examples and details must be directly connected
- *coherent*—all the material must have clear transitions and be expressed in standard English and be arranged in a logical order
- *effectively worded*—all ideas must be specific and concise

Revising for Unity   In a successful essay, all the elements work together to support the thesis. When you reassess your draft, examine each component to make sure it is directly connected to your main idea. Sometimes, an entire paragraph is not connected to the thesis. In other cases, individual sentences within a paragraph lack unity. In both cases, the result is the same: The reader is distracted from your main point.

Look again, for example, at paragraph 3 of the draft essay on tattooing and piercing. As the topic sentence indicates, the main point of the paragraph concerns the history of tattooing. In order for the paragraph to be unified, all the sentences must be directly connected to that point. Which material breaks the unity?

The history of decorating the body goes back thousands of years. Natives of some islands in the South Pacific would tattoo their faces with intricate designs. Some of these islands are still experiencing volcanic eruptions. One eruption a few years ago destroyed most of a small town. Some ancient tribes cut other parts of their bodies to leave scars in particular designs.

You probably identified the third and fourth sentences, which concern volcanic eruptions. Because these sentences aren't directly related to tattooing and piercing, they must be eliminated to maintain unity.

Revising for Coherence   An effective essay is one in which one idea flows smoothly on to the next. This quality, called *coherence,* is achieved (1) by providing adequate *transitions* between paragraphs and between sentences and (2) by *organizing* your ideas in a logical order.

Transitions   As Chapter 4, "Refining and Polishing Your Draft," showed, transitions help establish a smooth flow of ideas. Both *synonyms* and *common transitional expressions* help show relationships among your ideas. (See pages 55–56 for lists of transitions.) When you reassess a draft, examine it closely for any gaps or points where the flow between sentences or paragraphs should be improved.

Consider again paragraph 4 from the first draft essay about tattooing and piercing:

> All that has changed. Tattooing and piercing are legal in many areas throughout the country. Tattoo parlors are licensed and inspected. The instruments used are sterilized.

This paragraph from the draft essay contains good information. Right now, however, the paragraph is choppy and doesn't flow smoothly. Part of the reason is that the information itself is not as complete and detailed as it should be. In addition, however, it needs some transitions. Without transitions the paragraph isn't as coherent as it should be.

Now look at the final draft of the same paragraph. Notice how much better this paragraph is, thanks to the additional details (italics) and transitions (boldface):

> All that has changed **today, however. For one thing,** tattooing and piercing are legal in many areas throughout the country. Tattoo parlors are **now** licensed and inspected *regularly to make sure they are sanitary.* The instruments used are sterilized, **in many cases** *using the same technology that is used to purify dental instruments.*

Proper Organization   The second element of coherence is logical order. A successful essay is organized in such a way that the reader can easily follow it. Chapter 4 discussed several methods of establishing order:

1. *Emphatic order*   arranging points according to their importance
2. *Spatial order*   arranging descriptive details on the basis of their physical relationship with each other
3. *Chronological order*   arranging events on the basis of order of occurrence

When you reassess a draft, check the arrangement to make sure it is consistent and logical. If the essay features spatial order, reevaluate the presentation to make sure that the reader is able to visualize the scene. If the essay follows emphatic order, check the presentation to ensure that it sustains the reader's interest and effectively accentuates the thesis. If the writing is arranged in chronological order, look closely at the sequence of events, making sure each event is presented in the order in which it actually occurred. Because the essay discusses tattooing through the years, following chronological order would make great sense. But take a look at paragraphs 2, 3, and 4 of the first draft essay on tattooing and piercing (with the sentences breaking the unity of paragraph 3 removed). Is there a problem with the order of these paragraphs?

> In modern times, tattoos have usually been associated with bikers and sailors. Until recently, it was illegal. People went to illegal tattoo parlors to get them. They had to put up with pain and possible infection.
>
> The history of decorating the body goes back thousands of years. Natives of some islands in the South Pacific would tattoo their faces with intricate designs. Some ancient tribes cut other parts of their bodies to leave scars in particular designs.
>
> All that has changed. Tattooing and piercing are legal in many areas throughout the country. Tattoo parlors are licensed and inspected. The instruments used are sterilized.

You probably noticed that paragraph 2 discusses the present, paragraph 3 discusses the past, and paragraph 4 discusses the present again. As Chapter 4, "Refining and Polishing Your Draft," explains (page 58), writers occasionally use flashbacks to provide necessary background information. But the reader would likely find the information in these paragraphs easier to follow if they were presented from past to present, as this version shows:

> The history of decorating the body goes back thousands of years. Natives of some islands in the South Pacific would tattoo their faces with intricate designs. Some ancient tribes cut other parts of their bodies to leave scars in particular designs.
>
> In modern times, tattoos have usually been associated with bikers and sailors. Until recently, it was illegal. People went to illegal tattoo parlors to get them. They had to put up with pain and possible infection.
>
> All that has changed. Tattooing and piercing are legal in many areas throughout the country. Tattoo parlors are licensed and inspected. The instruments used are sterilized.

Of course, these paragraphs still need some attention before they are suitable for a final draft. Now, at least, the order has been effectively adjusted to make things easier for the reader.

Revising for Effective Language   A successful essay is one in which the language captures the meaning the writer intends. When you reassess a draft, look for any spots in which the language is vague, general, or unclear. Then replace this weak language with specific and concise terms. If they will help to re-create the experience or clarify your point, you should include additional examples or details.

Here is a paragraph from "The Brown Wasps," an essay by writer Loren Eiseley. He discusses what happens when he makes a visit hoping to see a cottonwood tree. He and his father had planted it some sixty years earlier, and he has now discovered that the tree is gone. Which details help the reader visualize and understand the experience presented here?

> I came close to the white picket fence and reluctantly, with great effort, looked down the long vista of the yard. There was nothing there to see. For sixty years that cottonwood had been growing in my mind. Season by season its seeds had been floating farther on the hot prairie winds. We had planted it lovingly there, my father and I, because he had a great hunger for solid and live things growing, and because none of these things had long been ours to protect. We had planted the little sapling and watered it faithfully, and I remembered that I had run out with my small bucket to drench its roots on the day we moved away. And all the years since it had been growing in my mind, a huge tree that somehow stood for my father and the love I bore him.

Chances are that you identified details such as *the white picket fence, the long vista of the yard,* the *seeds floating,* and *the hot prairie winds.* In addition, you probably noticed *the little sapling* that the young Eiseley *watered faithfully* with a *small bucket* that he remembers using to *drench its roots on the day* his family *moved away* from the area. These specific details and examples bring the scene and situation into sharp focus.

Take another look at paragraph 5 from the first draft of the essay on tattooing and piercing:

> A big change is who goes for tattoos today. Besides tough guys getting some designs done, everybody goes, too, so that they can all be different.

As you can see, this paragraph fails to create a clear picture for the reader. In the first sentence, *who goes for tattoos* is awkward and unclear. In the second sentence, *tough guys getting some designs done* doesn't specify who was involved or what was done. Worst of all, *everybody* is an indefinite pronoun, so it is general and nonspecific. In addition, the statement isn't true. As popular as tattooing may seem, a large segment of the population is not tattooed.

Now consider this version:

> But the biggest change is the clientele who seek tattoos and piercings. No longer is it just outlaws looking to get a skull on their biceps. Today bikers and rock stars share the waiting room at the tattoo parlor with teenaged football players, fraternity members, stockbrokers, and other ordinary people looking for something that will mark them as different from the next person.

As you can see, the ineffective *who goes for tattoos* has been replaced by *the clientele who seek tattoos and piercings,* phrasing that is far more specific and effective. In addition, the general phrases *tough guys getting some designs done* has been changed to *outlaws looking to get a skull on their biceps,* and *bikers and rock stars,* phrasing that specifies who is under discussion and what was done. Finally, the indefinite *everybody* is replaced by a list specifying exactly what groups of people are now seeking tattoos. These groups include *teenaged football players, fraternity members, stockbrokers, and other ordinary people.* Changed in this way, the language in this paragraph is clearer and far more specific than the language in the first draft version.

Seeking Help from an Objective Reader   In addition to reassessing your draft yourself, it's always a good idea to get feedback from an objective reader. Choose someone who will respond honestly and intelligently to your work. Your reader will find the following reader assessment checklist useful in responding to your first draft.

✔ **Reader Assessment Checklist**

☐ Do you understand the point I am making? Does my thesis statement clearly state the topic along with my perspective on it? (thesis)

☐ Do I stick to that point all the way through? Does the topic sentence of each paragraph relate to the thesis? (unity)

☐ Are all my ideas and examples clearly connected and easy to follow? (coherence)

☐ Are the words I've used specific and concise? (effective language)

☐ Are my introduction and conclusion effective?

☐ What changes do you think I should make?

Here are a reader's comments in reaction to the first draft essay on tattooing and piercing:

> I learned a lot from your paper—it's good. You have a good thesis, and the paragraphs in the body are all connected to it. The introduction and conclusion are also pretty good. The best feature is the topic. I know lots of people with tattoos, so I was really interested in the ideas you provided. I think a couple of things would make your paper even better. I was a little confused in the beginning with the order of the paragraphs. Maybe you could rearrange a couple so that the history would be easier to follow. And the stuff about the volcanoes doesn't really seem to have much to do with tattoos—maybe you should eliminate it. But my biggest suggestion is that you expand your paper. The stuff you have included is really interesting, and as I read I wanted to know even more.

I think if you expand your discussion, including the introduction and conclusion, and add other examples in the body, your paper would be outstanding.

With these kinds of suggestions, you are prepared to move to the next step: redrafting.

COMPREHENSION AND PRACTICE 14.4

Understanding Effective Revision

1. Of the questions making up the reader assessment checklist on page 193, which do you find easiest to answer? Why?

   Answers will vary.

2. Why is it a good idea to give yourself a break between the composing and revising stages of writing?

   It gives you a little distance, or objectivity, so you can review the material with a fresh

   eye. It also allows you to be rested before looking for errors.

3. How can an objective reader help you improve your essay?

   An objective reader will be honest and will see errors that you may miss.

Redrafting   With the various weaknesses in your essay identified, you are ready to begin **redrafting.** When you redraft, you need to rethink your essay, considering the best way to bring the scene or situation into even better focus. Redrafting involves addressing any problem spots in unity, coherence, logical order, and specific language identified by you or your objective reader.

You also need to **amplify:** to provide additional specific examples and details to support your ideas and fill any gaps. As Chapter 3, "Composing: Creating a Draft" (pages 29–50), indicates, the transitional expressions *for example* and *for instance* are helpful to you and your reader. They remind you to supply a specific supporting example and they cue your reader that a specific illustration will follow.

Editing: Eliminating Errors   The final step in revising an essay is **editing.** The purpose of this part of the revising process is to eliminate any remaining grammatical or spelling errors. Make it a point to be well rested whenever you edit. Fatigue can make it easy to overlook obvious errors.

When you edit, use the following proofreading checklist, which lists several of the most common writing problems, to identify specific weaknesses in your essay. Next to each listing is the abbreviation commonly used to identify this error when it appears in a paper. The inside back cover of this book includes a more complete list of errors and abbreviations.

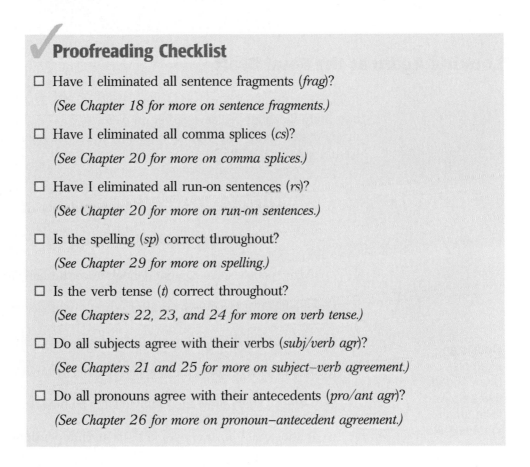

✓ Proofreading Checklist

☐ Have I eliminated all sentence fragments (*frag*)?

(See Chapter 18 for more on sentence fragments.)

☐ Have I eliminated all comma splices (*cs*)?

(See Chapter 20 for more on comma splices.)

☐ Have I eliminated all run-on sentences (*rs*)?

(See Chapter 20 for more on run-on sentences.)

☐ Is the spelling (*sp*) correct throughout?

(See Chapter 29 for more on spelling.)

☐ Is the verb tense (*t*) correct throughout?

(See Chapters 22, 23, and 24 for more on verb tense.)

☐ Do all subjects agree with their verbs (*subj/verb agr*)?

(See Chapters 21 and 25 for more on subject–verb agreement.)

☐ Do all pronouns agree with their antecedents (*pro/ant agr*)?

(See Chapter 26 for more on pronoun–antecedent agreement.)

When it comes to your own essay, you may find that you have no problems with some items on the list. At the same time, your paper may contain weaknesses not covered on the list. Therefore, the best thing to do is adapt the list so that it covers your own particular problem spots. Then use this personal proofreading checklist every time you write, regardless of whether it's an essay, a term paper, or a letter.

Working with a proofreading partner, someone who can look for errors with a fresh perspective, is also a great idea. Also, if you are using a computer, take full advantage of any spell checking or style checking features. Always proofread your paper one more time after using these functions, however, to make sure that all errors have been corrected. Despite all the advances in computer software, a computer still doesn't reason the way a human does. If you write *desert* when you actually mean *dessert,* the computer may not discover this oversight because *desert* is a correctly spelled word.

FAST FACT   One problem with proofreading has to do with *selective perception*. Studies have shown that experienced readers don't actually read every word and so cover somewhere between 180 and 600 words a minute. This is when selective perception comes into play. Because we know how to spell simple or familiar words, we perceive them on the page as we know they *should be* rather than as they actually *are*. The secret to effective proofreading, then, is to *slow down*. Force yourself to read every word, meaning you will read about one word every 1.75 seconds—35 words per minute.

Looking Again at the Final Draft

Remember the final draft of "Making Their Marks: The Popularity of Tattooing and Body Piercing" you saw earlier on pages 176–177? Here it is again, this time in annotated form. The various notations point out how the essay has changed from first to final draft.

Making Their Marks: The Popularity of
Tattooing and Body Piercing

Details and examples have been added. In this amplified form, the introduction provides a more complete direction for the reader. Instead of two sentences, the introduction is now seven.

> Many people seem content enough to go through life looking like everybody else. But for others, nothing seems more important than distinguishing how they look from the rest of society. Some set themselves apart by how they dress. Others show their individuality by how they wear their hair. Today, people with an independent streak have found another way to make themselves stand out from the crowd. These people are choosing tattooing or body piercing as their marks or distinctions. These ancient forms of body art are among the most popular trends of the past decade.

The order of these paragraphs has been adjusted to maintain chronological order.

> The history of decorating the body in these ways goes back thousands of years. Originally, members of a tribe would undergo elaborate tattooing, piercing, or scarring to signify membership in the group. For example, natives of some islands in the South Pacific would

Unrelated sentences have been removed, so the paragraph is now unified.

Additional details
and examples
appear throughout
about the history
of tattooing.

tattoo their faces with intricate designs, while ancient
tribes in other lands would cut parts of their bodies to
leave scars in particular designs.

Additional details
and examples
appear throughout
about the history
of tattooing.
Note the
additional specific
details about the
state of tattooing
until recently.

Tattoos and piercings have been around in more
modern times, too. However, until the past 15 years or
so, they have been largely associated with bikers and
sailors. They held little appeal for the average person.
Until recently, tattooing wasn't even legal in many
states. The only way for many people to get a tattoo
was to find an illegal tattoo parlor or travel to a
country where tattooing was legal. Either way, people
endured great pain and risked infection just to
decorate their skin.

Note the
additional
specifics about
safety measures
as well as the
added transitions.

All that has changed today, however. For one thing,
tattooing and piercing are legal in many areas throughout the country. Tattoo parlors are now licensed and
inspected regularly to make sure they are sanitary. The
instruments used are sterilized, in many cases using the
same technology that is used to purify dental instruments.

The general
language is now
specific, and it is
supported with
several detailed
examples of
people who seek
tattoos.

But the biggest change is the clientele who seek
tattoos and piercings. It isn't just outlaws looking
to get a skull on their biceps. Bikers and rock
stars share the waiting room at the tattoo parlor
with teenaged football players, fraternity members,
stockbrokers, and other ordinary people looking for
something that will mark them as different from the
next person.

Nobody knows how long this new interest in tattooing and piercing will last. Right now, though, the number of people with colorful skin decorations and nose, tongue, and belly button jewelry seems to be on the increase. It looks like none of the new tattoo parlors will be closing any time soon.

> The conclusion is now three sentences rather than two. The details are more specific. As a result, the conclusion brings the essay to a more complete, logical close.

As the notations show, developing this final draft involved making a significant number of changes. The point here is that writing isn't a one-shot process. Often you will find that you need to work through several drafts before your essay is as effective as it could be.

When you compare the first draft of this essay with the final draft, one thing is obvious. Revision works, as the following instructor's comments indicate:

> Congratulations—this revision is excellent. You have improved the paper in so many ways. The new supporting examples make your point about these trends much clearer. Your introduction is much more detailed and effective—it really prepares the reader for the rest of the essay. You've also adjusted the presentation of some of the paragraphs so that they are in chronological order. In each paragraph, you've made sure to include solid examples and plenty of transitions. And your conclusion does a great job of encapsulating the significance of your essay. You should definitely include a clean copy of this essay in your portfolio. You should also submit it to be included in the class anthology that we will be putting together at the end of the course.

CHALLENGE 14.3 Evaluating a First Draft Essay

COLLABORATION

1. Read the following first draft essay on home shopping. Then, working with a partner, answer the questions that follow on a separate sheet of paper.

The Home Shopping Phenomenon

(1) Home shopping has become a popular alternative for busy shoppers.
(2) There are a couple of different home shopping networks. All the shows seem to work the same, a host introduces the product, describes it, and posts the price. Then a phone number is flashed. You can get a good deal on collectibles and sports memorabilia.

(3) The home shopping networks sells designer clothing, including outer-wear and shoes. Occasionally, a fashion designer comes on to discuss the clothing while fashion models walked around displaying them.

(4) Celebrities come on to sell her own brands of fragrances or jewelry. Cheap rings, bracelets, or necklaces can cause allergic reactions. The celebrities chat with the hosts and encourage viewers to buy.

(5) What makes it all especially convenient is that you never have to leave your couch to shop. When you see what you want on the screen, you dial the 1-800 number, give a credit card number, and the item is on it's way to your door. No crowded mall parking lots, no long lines at the registers.

(6) In today's fast-paced world, it's often hard to find time to go out shopping, especially during the holiday season.

    a. Evaluate the introduction and conclusion. In what way would you suggest they be changed?

    b. Which paragraph in this draft supplies the best support for the thesis? Explain why.

    c. Turn again to the reader assessment checklist (page 193) and the proofreading checklist (page 195), and use them to assess and edit this first draft. On a separate sheet of paper, make a list of problem spots and errors that need to be addressed.

2. Imagine that the writer has asked you to write a critique (a short paragraph of around ten sentences) in which you indicate (a) what is good in the essay and (b) what still needs work. On a separate sheet of paper, write that critique.

FOR FURTHER EXPLORATION

1. Consider the following list of topics:

- a complaint you have about some personal, school, work, or national issue or situation
- your stand on a controversial issue in the news today
- the one personal possession that you feel is most valuable to you
- what physical beauty means to you
- how kids' pastimes and hobbies have changed since you were a child
- how to remain calm during a stressful time
- a lesson you learned the hard way

Choose the subject that most interests you. Prewrite on this topic, identifying a focus and highlighting the most promising ideas. Then prepare an essay of at least five paragraphs that explores your subject in detail. Use the material in this chapter, especially the sample essay about tattooing (pages 176–177), to guide you as you develop your essay.

COLLABORATION

2. Exchange your draft essay with a classmate. Using the proofreading checklist (page 195), evaluate the essay you receive. Identify any errors you see in the essay you receive, using the abbreviations presented in the checklist and on the inside back cover of this book. Then return the paper to the writer.

3. Correct any errors your proofreading partner identified in your essay and complete a final draft.

▶ DISCOVERING CONNECTIONS

When you look at this picture of East Indian dancers, what comes to mind? Does the picture make you think of a special occasion—a wedding or a cultural celebration perhaps? Do the elaborate, colorful outfits make you think of fashion in general or what expressions such as "Clothes make the person" mean? How about the faces of the dancers—what kinds of thoughts, feelings, or memories do their expressions evoke in your mind? Where do you think this dance is taking place? What kinds of dances have you participated in or watched? How would your life be different if you suddenly had to relocate to this area of the world?

For this assignment, consider one of these questions or another that the picture inspires. Using the information in this chapter to guide you, create an essay of at least five paragraphs that examines your topic in full detail. Make sure you supply an introduction that includes a clear thesis, plenty of supporting examples and details, and a concluding paragraph that restates the significance of what you have told your reader. ◀

RECAP Developing an Essay

New terms in this chapter	Definitions
essay	a multi-paragraph writing that deals more extensively with a subject than a paragraph does
introduction	a paragraph that opens an essay, providing a clear thesis and engaging the reader
thesis	the sentence in the introduction that specifies the main subject of the essay and the writer's attitude or position on it
body	the series of paragraphs that provide support and illustration for a thesis
conclusion	a paragraph that closes the essay, summarizing the essay's point and bringing it to a logical and appropriate end
five-paragraph essay	an essay form, especially useful with some timed writing situations, which features an introduction presenting three main points, a body containing three paragraphs discussing those three points, and a conclusion restating the significance of these points
anecdote	a brief, entertaining story, often used to make a point
	An anecdote may be used effectively in an introduction or a conclusion.

New terms in this chapter	Definitions
rhetorical question	a question designed not to be answered, but to provoke thought or discussion A rhetorical question may be used effectively in an introduction to engage readers.
amplifying	the process of providing additional, specific details and examples

The Process of Writing an Essay

Prewrite on a **topic.**
Identify a **focus.**
Develop a **thesis.**

Arrange the most promising prewriting ideas in a logical order and turn them into **supporting sentences.**
Develop the supporting sentences into **paragraphs.**
Write paragraphs for an **introduction** and **conclusion.**

Reassess your draft for **unity, coherence** (transitions and organization), and **effective language.**
Redraft to eliminate any weaknesses identified in reassessing.
Edit to eliminate any **grammatical** or **spelling errors.**

GOING FORWARD...

**CW 14.13
Developing
an essay
review**

Q: I know that with an essay I have the chance to discuss a subject more thoroughly, and I do like that. So how do I make sure that the essay I create actually captures my subject in the more complete way I want to?

A: The secret to success in this area is to focus on **providing specific details and examples**—lots of them. Your scope is larger with an essay than it is with a paragraph, so you have many more blanks to fill in. When you back up what you say and spell out exactly what you mean, you enable your reader to see things as you see them.

CHAPTER 15

Examining Types of Essays

▶ **Navigating This Chapter**

In this chapter, you will learn how to use the modes to write:

- narration essays
- description essays
- example essays
- process essays
- definition essays
- comparison and contrast essays
- cause and effect essays
- division and classification essays
- argument essays

GETTING STARTED . . .

CW 15.1
Chapter basics

Q: I'm sure I will be writing essays on a variety of subjects. Will I be able to use what I've learned so far about writing different kinds of paragraphs to help me write essays?

A: Absolutely. Everything you learned about the writing process and the characteristics of the different modes for paragraphs is just as valid for writing essays. Rely on the skills you have developed so far, and you will be able to write effective essays that meet the needs of your reader.

Overview: Understanding How to Use the Modes to Develop Essays

CW 15.2
Overview of essay types

As the previous chapters point out, effective writing fulfills a purpose while communicating the writer's ideas. Chapters 5 through 12 show how to use the various **modes** or organizing strategies to develop paragraphs: *narration, description, example, process, definition, comparison and contrast, cause and effect,* and *division and classification.* Chapter 13 explains that *argument* differs from the modes because it is a **purpose** or aim, not a mode.

Chapter 14 introduces the essay, explaining how this type of writing differs from a paragraph. Probably the most significant difference is in scope. When you write an essay, you deal with a subject in far greater detail than you can with a single paragraph. To write an essay, you actually use a number of modes in combination. This chapter explores ways to use the modes to help you create effective essays.

The Relationship between Your Purpose and the Modes

**CW 15.3
Your
purpose and
the modes**

Understanding the connection between your purpose and the modes is crucial. As Chapter 1, "Ensuring Success in Writing," explains, people write to fulfill one of three purposes: to *inform,* to *entertain,* or to *persuade.* The modes are your means to fulfill the purpose you choose. In most essays, one mode will dominate, with other modes providing additional support.

Open your favorite magazine, and read a few of the articles. Perhaps one article reports recent findings about fat consumption and heart disease. In this case, the writer's primary purpose is to *inform* readers about the data linking diet and heart disease. Another article takes a lighthearted look at the shopping habits of U.S. families. In this case, the writer's primary purpose is to *entertain.* Of course, not all writing that entertains is intended to make you laugh. For example, a story about a small town raising money to send a promising young musician to college might not be funny, but it would entertain you. Finally, the primary purpose of an article asserting that nuclear power plant construction should be halted until safety concerns are addressed would be to *persuade.*

Look closely at the articles, and you will also see the modes in action. For example, the article about the scientific research might feature *cause and effect* as its primary mode to link coronary disease to diet. It might also feature such modes as *example* to develop specific case studies and *definition* to explain the terms used in the article.

The essay about people's shopping habits might have *division and classification* as a primary mode to explain the various ways that people approach shopping. It might also include such modes as *description* to create images of the shoppers in action and *narration* to follow them as a video camera might.

The essay about nuclear power plants might feature *example* as the primary mode to illustrate the dangers at specific nuclear power plants. It might also feature *process* to show how nuclear power plants generate electricity. In addition, it might include *cause and effect* to show how radiation leakage could affect nearby residents' health. Finally, it might include *description* to show in vivid terms the destruction that could result from a nuclear accident.

**CW 15.4
Academic
expectations
across the
disciplines**

Most essay assignments will call for one particular mode to dominate. Remember, though, that you will actually use a combination of modes to fulfill your purpose. The rest of this chapter will examine ways to use the modes to develop essays.

Using Narration to Develop an Essay

**CW 15.5
Using
narration to
develop an
essay**

As Chapter 5 explained, writing that relates a series of events is *narration.* For example, if you were writing a paper about your first day at a new job, narration would be a natural choice. Like narrative paragraphs, **narrative essays** are usually arranged in *chronological order.* In addition, narrative writing is often presented from the *first person point of view* (using *I, me, my*), although it may be written in the *third person* (using *he, she, her, him, they*). In order to be effective, a narrative essay must also be *unified* and include plenty of specific details for support.

Examining a Narrative Essay

Take a look at this narrative essay about the first day at a new job:

Lost and Confused: My First Day in the Hospital Halls

(1) Any change is difficult to handle. Beginning a new job is no different, especially when the new job involves more responsibility than the last one. My first day as a dietary aide at City Hospital was such an ordeal, I don't think I'll ever forget it. <u>By the end of that first workday, I was so frustrated and embarrassed that I never wanted to return.</u>

(2) <u>Here's how it all began.</u> At 6:45 on that first morning, half an hour before my shift officially started, I entered the imposing building and headed to the first floor, where the kitchen and cafeteria are located. In spite of my nervousness, I found my time card and punched in. I then introduced myself to the woman sitting at the desk next to the time clock and asked her where I should go next. She told me to report to Mr. Javits in the kitchen.

(3) <u>Just as I was beginning to think I would make it through the day, I met Mr. Javits, and I became convinced that I wouldn't.</u> First, he looked at me and yelled, "Who the hell are you?" After I explained that I was a new dietary aide, he quickly assigned me to set up and deliver morning meals to the entire cardiac unit. Mr. Javits warned me that any mistake in preparation or delivery of the meals could have serious consequences for the patients. By the time he finished talking, my shirt was soaking wet.

(4) <u>My first round of deliveries was a disaster.</u> The cardiac unit was being renovated, and the painting crew had removed the room numbers. I figured that once I identified one room, I would be able to find the rest easily. The rooms weren't arranged sequentially, however, so I had to personally identify all the patients and go through their menu choices with them. As a result, I fell behind schedule at each room. I began to know what salmon must feel like as they try to swim upstream.

(5) <u>The worst was yet to come.</u> When I returned to the cafeteria with the trays, Mr. Javits was waiting for me. He began yelling and demanding to know where I had been. As I pointed to the notice on the wall announcing the renovation of the cardiac floor, I accidentally bumped Mr. Javits's hand and spilled his cup of coffee over the front of his uniform. At this point, I felt that the end of the day would never come.

(6) <u>The lunch shift was almost as bad as the breakfast shift.</u> This time, Mr. Javits assigned me to the orthopedic area. To distribute the meals, I had to travel the length of the hospital and take two different sets of elevators. By the time I collected the trays and returned them to the cafeteria, I was late again. My shift was scheduled to end at 2:30, and it was almost 3 P.M. Fortunately, Mr. Javits had already left.

(7) After this kind of start, it is hard to believe that I soon became an expert on the hospital. Within a couple of days, I knew my way around the building. After a month, Mr. Javits even put me in charge of training new workers. I also found out that most of my co-workers had had similar experiences on their first day working in the hospital cafeteria. Like me, they had been completely intimidated at the prospect of something new.

CHALLENGE 15.1   Analyzing the Sample Narrative Essay

Refer to the sample narrative essay above to answer each question.

1. Reread the introduction of the essay. Underline the thesis.

2. Underline the topic sentences of paragraphs 2 through 6. In an essay, each topic sentence relates back to the thesis, but it also serves as a building block for its own main idea. Work with a partner to analyze the role of these sentences. On a separate sheet of paper, explain (a) how each topic sentence in the essay is related to the thesis and (b) how each one is developed by its supporting paragraph information.

3. On the same sheet, list transitional expressions that help establish the sequence of events.

FOR FURTHER EXPLORATION

CW 15.6 Writing in the humanities

1. Using the essay on page 204 to guide you, write a narrative essay on your first day at a new job or on one of the following topics:
   a. your biggest social error
   b. the best phone call you've ever received
   c. a school, team, club, or family reunion
   d. a time you were caught in a lie
   e. an encounter with the police
   f. a trip to the "big city"
   g. an experience you witnessed on a bus, train, or plane

CW 15.7 Writing in the sciences

2. Exchange your draft with a partner. Evaluate the essay using the narrative essay checklist on page 206. Write your answers on a separate sheet of paper, and then return the essay and your assessment to the writer.

3. Using your reader's comments to guide you, revise and redraft your narrative essay.

▶ DISCOVERING CONNECTIONS 15.1

What do you think of when you see this picture? This photo shows Red Square in Moscow, Russia. For decades, during a period known as the Cold War, the United States and Russia—then, arguably, the most well-known country making up the U.S.S.R.—were sworn political enemies. Knowing that these countries were once fierce adversaries, what do you think it was like for the first traveler from the United States to set foot in Red Square after the Cold War ended? Now carefully observe the two figures in the right forefront of the image—have you ever taken similar photos while on a trip of some kind? Where did you go? Who were you with? Did you have a good time? Why or why not?   (*continued*)

For this assignment, select one of these questions or some other question that the picture suggests. Using the discussion of narration on the previous pages to guide you, develop an essay of at least five paragraphs in which you use narration to tell your story fully. ◀

✓ Narrative Essay Checklist

☐ Does the introduction set the scene for the sequence of events to follow?

☐ Is a *first person* or *third person* point of view used consistently?

☐ Does the paper follow chronological order? If a flashback has been used, has the switch in time been made clear for the reader?

☐ Is the essay unified, with all supporting ideas and examples related to the main idea? Circle any material that isn't unified.

☐ Are there enough specific details and examples to guide the reader? Put a   next to any spot that you'd like to know more about.

☐ In your judgment, what is the best part of this essay? Explain.

CW 15.8 Practicing first and third person voice

Using Description to Develop an Essay

CW 15.9 Using description to develop an essay

As Chapter 6 showed, writing that uses words to paint a picture of a scene, individual, or experience is *description*. Effective description emphasizes specific sensory details, as it would in an essay about an unusual experience. **Descriptive essays** often combine both *objective* description (observable details and sensations) and *subjective* description (the impressions that the details and sensations create within the writer). In addition, descriptive writing often uses *spatial order* to organize details for the reader.

FAST FACT   Not all people find it easy to provide sensory details when they use description. People who suffer from *anosmia*, for example, would have difficulty, as would those who suffer from *ageusia*. A person who has *anosmia* is unable to detect smells, and a person who has *ageusia* is unable to taste.

Examining a Descriptive Essay

Take a look at this descriptive essay about an unusual experience:

Bright Lights, Loud Music: *Not* Your Average Planetarium Show

(1) If someone invited you to a planetarium show, what would you expect? You are probably thinking of seeing pictures of stars and constellations. You may even be thinking, "Boring!" At first, that's what I thought when two friends invited me to a show at the Hayden Planetarium in New York City, but

I was mistaken. <u>On that night my eyes and ears were exposed to more sensation and stimulation than they had ever been exposed to at one time.</u>

(2) I was on vacation visiting friends who go to school in New York City, and they told me that we were going to the planetarium that evening. I had been to other planetarium shows before, and I had always enjoyed seeing images of the various constellations projected on the inside of a dome. I was a bit surprised, though, that my friends, two of the wildest people I have ever met, had picked such a tame adventure. After all, it was Friday night, and we were in one of the most exciting cities in the world.

(3) When we arrived at the planetarium at 8:30, I began to wonder exactly what was going on. About 300 people, most of them under twenty-five, were just starting to stream through the doors under the sign that said "Genesis Laser Show." Like the other planetariums I had been in before, this one had rows of soft seats that reclined so that people could comfortably look up at the ceiling. I settled into my seat just as the lights began to dim, and a display of the various constellations appeared on the ceiling.

(4) That's when I got my second surprise of the night. The constellations on the ceiling suddenly disappeared, plunging the planetarium into darkness. Then a series of speakers practically exploded with a tune by the rock group Genesis. Suddenly, rows of red, blue, and yellow lasers projected a series of brilliantly colored designs that moved to the beat of the music all across the inside of the domed ceiling.

(5) The music was so loud that I felt as if I were on stage with the group. I could feel each beat of the drum reverberate right through my body. I felt as if I was completely surrounded by the music through all fifteen of the songs.

(6) But what I was hearing was nothing compared to what I was seeing. The designs pulsed and glowed and blinked all across the dome. Even if I tried to close my eyes, the light seemed to break through my eyelids. It was as if those lasers had some magical power to force me to keep looking. It was like being able to look at the sun without having to worry about burning your eyes. The light was brilliantly bright, yet cool and comfortable at the same time.

(7) Finally, after forty-five minutes, the music stopped, the lights came on, and the crowd filed out the double doors into the hot July night. I felt exhausted but exhilarated at the same time. Outside, the bright street lights and the blaring New York City traffic seemed mild compared to what I had just experienced.

(8) An evening that I expected to be merely calm and pleasant turned out to be a true adventure for my ears and eyes. Now every time I hear a song by Genesis on the radio, I immediately think back to one of my favorite vacation memories, a night filled with sound and light.

CHALLENGE 15.2   Analyzing the Sample Descriptive Essay

Refer to the sample descriptive essay above to answer each question.

1. Reread the introduction of the essay. Underline the thesis.

2. Working with a partner, analyze paragraphs 2 through 7 of the essay. On a separate piece of paper, explain how each one develops this thesis. Rate these

six paragraphs according to how effectively they use description: 1 = very effective; 2 = somewhat effective; 3 = not effective.

3. Working with the same partner, bracket each sentence of description in paragraphs 3 through 7. In the margin, write *S* next to each sentence of subjective description; write *O* next to each sentence of objective description.

4. Does the essay use spatial order? On your paper, explain where and how it is used.

FOR FURTHER EXPLORATION

1. Using the sample descriptive essay to guide you, write an essay on an unusual experience of your own or on one of the following topics:
   a. a physical injury or bout with illness
   b. a normally busy place, now deserted
   c. what you see in a painting or photograph or hear in a song
   d. the sensation of being alone
   e. the feeling of speaking in front of a group of strangers
   f. the sensation of riding a roller coaster or some other thrill ride
   g. a distinctive, renowned, or unique restaurant, deli, bakery, or bar

2. Exchange your draft with a partner. Evaluate the essay using the descriptive essay checklist on page 209. Write your answers on a separate sheet of paper, and then return the essay and your assessment to the writer.

3. Using your reader's comments to guide you, complete the final draft of your descriptive essay.

▶DISCOVERING CONNECTIONS 15.2

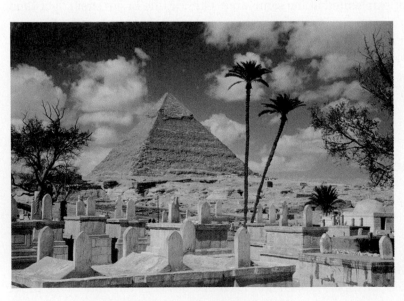

When you look at this photo, what thoughts come to mind? Does the picture make you think of what the scene must have been as thousands of workers labored to build this structure? What do you imagine this scene was like? Egyptian pyramids were burial chambers for pharaohs. Does it make you think of a cemetery or memorial area you have visited? What are the most distinctive markers, monuments, mausoleums, and so on that you have seen there? This pyramid, more than 4,500 years old, is one of several pyramids, plus the Sphinx, located in the Giza plateau outside of Cairo, Egypt. How do you imagine you would feel standing in the midst of these enormous reminders of the ancient world?

For this assignment, address one of these questions or another question that the picture inspires. Using the discussion of description on the previous pages as a guide, develop an essay of at least five paragraphs in which you use description to re-create the scene for your reader. ◀

✔ Descriptive Essay Checklist

☐ Does the introduction engage the reader? Does the thesis prepare you for the event to be described?

☐ Does the essay include effective use of both objective and subjective description?

☐ Are the paragraphs arranged so that the reader can picture the scene being painted? Explain.

☐ Does each paragraph feature a number of specific, concrete sensory details to support the thesis?

☐ In your judgment, what is the best part of this essay? Explain.

☐ Which detail or example would be even better if it were expanded? Why?

Using Example to Develop an Essay

CW 15.10 Using example to develop an essay

As Chapter 7 discussed, *example* uses specific instances to illustrate, clarify, or back up some point you've made. An **example essay** would be a natural choice to discuss various superstitions. When you write an essay that relies heavily on this technique, make sure that the examples you include are *relevant* and *specific*. In addition, *amplify*—provide enough examples to develop your main idea fully. Don't forget to take advantage of the transitional expressions *for instance* and *for example* to alert your reader that a specific example is to follow. Finally, pay close attention to how you arrange the examples you include so that they have the maximum effect on your reader. With many example essays, you may find *emphatic order* particularly useful.

Examining an Example Essay

Consider this five-paragraph example essay about superstitions:

Superstitions: The Irrational Beliefs That Influence Our Behavior

(1) All cultures seem to have some beliefs that can be thought of as superstitions. All over the world, people believe that doing or possessing certain things can bring them good luck or cause them bad luck. The most common

groups of superstitions involve objects that can bring good luck, behaviors that can influence luck, and actions that can cause bad luck.

(2) The belief in good luck charms is one of the best-known superstitions. Many people keep special objects that they believe will somehow keep them safe or provide an extra edge. For some people, the good luck charm is a particular shirt or key chain. For others, the good luck charm is the more traditional rabbit's foot or four-leaf clover.

(3) In addition to lucky objects, many people believe that performing certain rituals can provide good luck. If you've ever watched a professional sporting event, you've probably seen players performing a series of movements. Sometimes a basketball player will take a certain number of bounces—no more, no less—before shooting a foul shot. Some baseball players, while waiting for a pitch, will adjust their equipment, from batting helmet to wristbands to gloves, always in the same order. Regardless of the particular actions, the players perform them because they believe they will bring them good luck.

(4) Other well-known superstitions are those bits of advice to ward off bad luck passed down from generation to generation. For instance, from childhood, people are often told that breaking a mirror will bring seven years' bad luck. Others warn us not to walk under a ladder, not to open an umbrella inside a house, and not to let a black cat cross our paths. Of course, no evidence exists that any of these things cause bad luck, but people often follow these directions, just to be sure.

(5) Exactly why people believe in superstitions is difficult to understand. Maybe it is because life in general is so uncertain. In any case, when you notice people holding a special object, performing some little ritual, or following some old directive, wish them luck. They need it, or at least they think they do.

CHALLENGE 15.3 Analyzing the Sample Example Essay

Refer to the sample example essay above to answer each question.

COLLABORATION

1. Working with a partner, analyze paragraphs 2 through 5 of the essay. On a separate piece of paper, summarize the example each presents to support the thesis that there are several common groups of superstitions.

2. Working with the same partner, analyze each example. On your paper, list the number of the paragraph that you find most effective. Explain why its example is effective.

FOR FURTHER EXPLORATION

1. Using the example essay to guide you, write an essay on superstitions or rituals you follow or have witnessed or on one of the following topics:
   a. proper manners
   b. ways to improve the quality of life in your neighborhood, city, or town

c. college challenges

d. ways to cut costs

e. duties as a pet owner

f. shortcomings in today's high schools

g. driving dangers

2. Exchange your draft with a partner. Evaluate the essay using the example essay checklist below. Write your answers on a separate sheet of paper, and then return the essay and your assessment to the writer.

3. Using your reader's comments to guide you, complete the final draft of your example essay.

▶ DISCOVERING CONNECTIONS 15.3

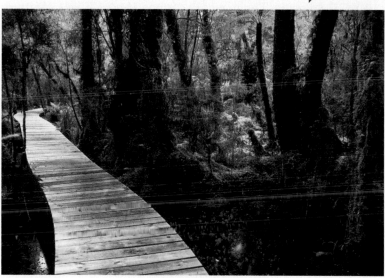

What do you think of when you look at this picture? The path leads into a rain forest—does the image make you consider the many different ways that such areas benefit humanity? Does it make you think of various activities you or somebody else might enjoy by following that path? Or does the picture make you think of the walkway not as an actual trail but as a metaphor for what may lie ahead for you? What different paths could you follow in the next several years?

For this assignment, consider one of these questions or some other question that the picture suggests to you. Using the discussion of example on the previous pages to direct you, create an essay of at least five paragraphs in which you use example to illustrate the possibilities your main idea holds. ◀

CW 15.11 Using narration and description in an essay

✓ Example Essay Checklist

☐ Does the introduction spell out the concept or principle to be illustrated?

☐ Are all the examples directly connected to the thesis? Put a ✓ next to any example that you feel is not relevant.

☐ Are all the examples specific? Put an * next to any example that you feel needs to be made more specific.

☐ Are there enough examples to support the thesis? Write *for example* or *for instance* next to any passage that you think could use another example.

(continued)

□ Are the examples effectively arranged? Make a note next to any example you think should be moved to a different place.

□ In your judgment, what is the best part of this essay? Explain.

□ Which example would be even better if it were expanded? Why?

Using Process to Develop an Essay

**CW 15.12
Using
process to
develop a
essay**

Chapter 8 introduced *process,* the writing technique used to explain how to do something, how something occurs or is done, or how you did something. For instance, an essay explaining how to burn a CD would clearly be a **process essay.** When you are explaining how to do something, you should use the *imperative mood* to address the reader directly. The imperative mood is usually not appropriate for other types of process writing. If you were writing an essay explaining how acid rain affects the environment or an essay detailing how you investigated your family history to create a family tree, you would not address the reader directly. Many process essays are organized in linear order, using transitional words such as *first, next, then, afterward,* and so on. Be sure that each step describes a small and manageable part of the task, and that you warn your reader about any particularly difficult or potentially confusing steps.

Examining a Process Essay

Consider this essay, which explains the process of creating a CD:

**CW 15.13
Composition
patterns:
process
essay**

The Burn That Saves You Money: Creating Your Own CD

(1) At one time, if you wanted to play recorded music, you listened to a vinyl record. Then came eight-track tapes and then cassette tapes. These innovations improved sound quality and made listening more convenient. But the development of the compact disc has taken sound quality and convenience to an even higher level. At the cost of about $18, however, CDs can be expensive, especially if you aren't interested in all the songs. Now there's a solution to this problem. The answer is to create or burn your own CD, a simple process that requires a computer, a CD burner, a blank CD, and a little bit of your time.

(2) To begin the process, decide on the song or songs you want to copy and then put the CD into the CD drive on your computer. Now put a blank CD in the CD burner. Some CD burning programs auto-start, but if yours doesn't, just open the program from the start menu.

(3) The menu that appears when the program begins will ask which type of CD you want to make. Select audio. At this point, you'll be asked about burn speed. Higher speeds generally increase the chances for a faulty CD burn, so you might want to select a low or moderate speed for this first time.

(4) Once you have selected a burn speed you'll be asked to select from three commands: *test, copy,* or *test and copy.* Choosing *test and copy* is the best alternative because it will identify any corrupted material and keep the new disc free from problem audio tracks. At this point, you can also choose to copy

the source material to your hard drive. Having the track on your computer is a good idea, just in case you encounter difficulty and need the backup copy.

(5) When you've completed these steps, a screen, split horizontally into two windows, will appear. In the top window, a list of the tracks of the source CD will appear. The bottom window will be blank. Click and drag the audio tracks you want to copy from the top window to the bottom. Repeat this step for each audio track you want to add to the blank CD.

(6) With all the tracks you want to copy in the lower window, look at the toolbar at the top of the screen. Click on the button with a red circle that says "Create CD." Now just let the computer do the work. Depending on how many audio tracks you are copying, the actual burning will take somewhere between 20 and 60 minutes. When the new CD is complete, the computer will eject it, and you'll have your own personalized CD, with just the songs you want.

(7) The process of burning a CD may seem a little confusing at first, but after one time you'll be turning out CDs like a pro. Your reward for your efforts will be a collection of CDs containing all the songs you want, at a fraction of the cost. How can you lose?

CHALLENGE 15.4 Analyzing the Sample Process Essay

Refer to the sample process essay above to answer each question.

COLLABORATION

1. Working with a partner, find and underline the thesis in the introduction.

2. What are the steps of burning a CD? List them in order on a separate sheet of paper.

3. Find and underline transitional expressions that help establish linear order in the essay.

COLLABORATION

4. With your partner, evaluate each step in the process. Do you need more information about any steps? What questions would you ask the writer to get the information you need?

FOR FURTHER EXPLORATION

1. Using the sample process essay to guide you, write your own essay that tells how to carry out a process such as changing a flat tire. If you prefer, write on one of the following:

   a. how to make a bed

   b. how to write out and record a check

   c. how you conducted a study or experiment

   d. how to teach a child to tie a shoe

   e. how a computer functions

   f. how a thunderstorm, tornado, or tsunami occurs

   g. how to serve a volleyball

2. Exchange your draft with a partner. Evaluate the essay using the process essay checklist below. Write your answers on a separate sheet of paper, and then return the essay and your assessment to the writer.

3. Using your reader's comments to guide you, complete the final draft of your essay.

▶ DISCOVERING CONNECTIONS 15.4

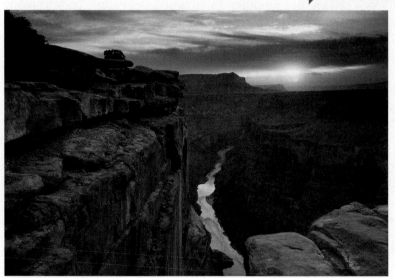

When you look at this picture, taken in the Grand Canyon, what comes to mind? Does the picture make you wonder how such a magnificent place came to be, what forces of nature carved and shaped it? Does the landscape make you think of extreme sports such as rock climbing and riding rapids? What process would you recommend to improve your own or someone else's level of fitness enough to participate in such strenuous activities? Does it make you dream of taking a trip to the Grand Canyon or another U.S. National Park?

For this assignment, consider one of these questions or another that the picture inspires. Using the discussion of process on the previous pages as a guide, create an essay of at least five paragraphs in which you use process to spell out the steps involved in the subject you have chosen. ◀

✓ Process Essay Checklist

☐ Does the introduction identify the procedure or technique to be presented?

☐ Is the reader addressed directly through the imperative mood (*you*)? Is it appropriate for this essay? Why?

☐ Are the steps presented in linear order? Underline any step that is out of order, and then draw an arrow to the spot in the essay where it actually belongs.

☐ Is each step simple and clear? Put a ✓ next to any step that you think should be divided or explained further.

☐ In your judgment, what is the best part of this essay? Explain.

☐ Which detail or example would be even better if it were expanded? Why?

Using Definition to Develop an Essay

CW 15.14 Using definition to develop an essay

Chapter 9 introduced *definition,* the writing technique used to identify the essential characteristics or qualities of an object, location, or individual. An essay setting forth the characteristics of road rage, for example, would use definition. To write a **definition essay,** you need to recognize the *elements of an effective definition:* The term is placed in its appropriate class and then differentiated from the other elements in its class. In general, you should provide a *working definition* in the introduction and then build an *extended definition* throughout the body of the paper. This is done by supplying *clear, specific,* and *detailed* examples and illustrations. At the same time, take into consideration both the *denotation,* the literal meaning of the term, and its *connotations,* additional subjective or emotional impacts it will have on readers. Also, don't be afraid to turn to synonyms, negation, and etymology—a word's origin and historical development—as a way to enhance the definition. In addition, you should present the material you include in an order that enhances understanding.

Examining a Definition Essay

Look at this essay, which defines road rage:

Road Rage: The Anger That Can Kill

(1) You've probably witnessed the behavior yourself. You are in a car someplace and you are stalled in traffic. After a minute or two, someone behind you begins honking the horn, revving the engine, and yelling and swearing out the window. In some cases, the driver gets out of the car and walks up to where the traffic is stalled and begins yelling and gesturing. Sometimes, the behavior escalates until the driver is pounding or kicking the other car and perhaps physically fighting with other drivers. This kind of behavior occurs often enough that it has a name. It's called road rage.

(2) Occasionally becoming annoyed while driving is normal. People aren't always as careful as they should be when they drive. Also, construction, accidents, and rush hour traffic can often slow progress on the roads to a crawl. But when simple annoyance turns into burning anger, that is road rage.

(3) One thing that makes road rage different from normal annoyance is the degree of emotion involved. When road rage hits, it's not as if there has been a gradual build-up. Instead, road rage is more like the sudden eruption of a volcano. At one moment, a person seems calm, and at the next, that person is completely transformed, screaming, gesturing wildly, and sometimes threatening whoever has caused the problem.

(4) When people suffer from road rage, they seem unable to differentiate between minor and major problems. It makes no difference if the delay is caused by a simple breakdown or a serious multi-car crash. The reaction is the same intense, unreasonable anger.

(5) Unfortunately, road rage isn't limited to honking a horn repeatedly or yelling at others. Often, road rage leads to serious violence and sometimes death. News reports frequently include stories of road rage that escalates until someone has been killed. A few years ago, for example, a driver became convinced that another driver had cut him off. He chased the other car at high speed, forced it off the road, and then used a hunting bow to shoot the other driver to death.

(6) Life is full of annoyances, and people need to learn how to deal with them, especially when it comes to driving. But for some people, irritation quickly grows to enormous proportion. When it does, it becomes road rage, and the results are bound to be unpleasant and, sometimes, deadly.

CHALLENGE 15.5 Analyzing the Sample Definition Essay

Refer to the sample definition essay above to answer each question.

1. Find and underline the thesis in the first paragraph. On a separate sheet of paper, write the term that is defined and the writer's working definition of it.

2. Working with a partner, analyze paragraphs 2 through 5. First, underline the topic sentence in each. Then study the way each topic sentence is developed. On your paper, summarize the way each paragraph develops or extends the definition.

3. Why are the supporting paragraphs presented in this order? On your paper, explain why you think the writer organized the paper in this way. Would you change the order? Tell how and explain why.

FOR FURTHER EXPLORATION

1. Using the essay on pages 215–216 to guide you, write an essay on your definition of good manners or on one of the following topics:
   a. humor
   b. a perfect date
   c. a masterpiece of music, art, or literature
   d. a sports, music, dance, computer, or religious fanatic
   e. a good coach
   f. conscience
   g. responsibility

2. Exchange your draft with a partner. Evaluate the essay using the definition essay checklist on page 217. Write your answers on a separate sheet of paper, and then return the essay and your assessment to the writer.

3. Using your reader's comments to guide you, complete the final draft of your definition essay.

▶ **DISCOVERING CONNECTIONS 15.5**

What thoughts come to mind when you look at this picture? How do you feel about the attempts made to beautify the camel? Are the attempts successful? When it comes to an animal, what does beautiful even mean? Or do you focus on the look on the camel's face? If you saw this kind of look on a human's face, what emotion do you think it would indicate? The Bedouin, nomadic tribes who live in the deserts of North Africa and the Middle East, still depend on camels for transportation. They live a lifestyle that some describe as *timeless*. What does timeless mean to you?

For this assignment, consider one of these questions or some other question that the picture suggests to you. Using the discussion of definition on the previous pages to guide you, develop an essay of at least five paragraphs in which you use definition to delineate the special qualities of your chosen topic. ◀

✔ **Definition Essay Checklist**

☐ Does the introduction introduce the term or principle to be defined?

☐ Does the essay begin with a working definition and then develop an extended definition?

☐ Does the extended definition reflect both the denotations and connotations of the term defined and draw on synonyms, negation, or etymology?

☐ Are the supporting details and examples clear and specific? If you find any that are too general or too abstract, suggest a way to clarify or sharpen them.

☐ Are the supporting paragraphs effectively arranged in an appropriate order? Explain.

☐ In your judgment, what is the best part of this essay? Explain.

☐ Which detail or example would be even better if it were expanded? Why?

Using Comparison and Contrast to Develop an Essay

CW 15.15 Using comparison and contrast to develop an essay

As Chapter 10 discussed, the writing technique that focuses on examining alternatives is called *comparison and contrast. Comparison* means examining similarities, and *contrast* means examining differences. For example, an essay evaluating electronic books versus printed texts would call for comparison and contrast. In your college courses, you will often be called on to explain how two people, objects, or phenomena are alike or how they are different. With most comparison and contrast essays, restrict your focus to *two subjects* that have some common ground. In addition, be sure you have an adequately developed *basis of comparison* using at least three points.

To arrange a **comparison and contrast essay**, use either a *block format* or an *alternating format.* For the block format, include a thesis in your introduction, and then present the first point, the second point, the third point, and so on for Subject A. Afterward, examine the first point, the second point, and the third point for Subject B.

For the alternating format, examine the two subjects at the same time. In other words, after the introduction, address the first point for Subject A and Subject B, then the second point for Subject A and Subject B, then the third point for Subject A and Subject B, and so on. This method is helpful for longer papers. It may be hard for a reader to keep all the points for Subject A in mind while reading the second half of such a paper. See page 137 for illustrations of both the block and alternating formats.

FAST FACT   Where can you see comparison and contrast at work on a regular basis? Pick up any copy of *Consumer Reports,* a magazine that has earned its solid reputation by closely examining competing brands of everything from food products to appliances.

CW 15.16 Writing the comparison and contrast essay

Examining a Comparison and Contrast Essay

Here's a five-paragraph comparison and contrast essay that contrasts electronic books and printed books:

E-Books? Will They Replace the Printed Text?

(1) For hundreds of years, when people picked up a book, they could count on one thing. The book would look pretty much like books have looked since the development of the printing press. But consumers now have a new choice: electronic books. The development of E-books makes it possible for people to read on a special computerized reader, about the size of a hardcover book. The text to be read can be downloaded from the Internet or accessed from a CD. The manufacturers promise that this innovation will change the reading habits of readers in the twenty-first century, but I don't agree. When it comes to cost, availability of texts, and convenience, you can't beat an old-fashioned printed book.

(2) One thing that manufacturers of E-book technology don't talk much about is the cost. It's true that E-books themselves, whether online or from a CD, are fairly inexpensive, often costing under $10. The computerized device needed to be able to read the E-books, however, costs between $250 and

$500. The price is expected to decline as the technology improves, but right now, that's a hefty investment to read a book. In contrast, when it comes to traditional books, even a hardcover best seller costs under $30. Paperbacks and discounted hardcover books cost far less. Of course, with an actual book no additional device is needed, either. All you have to do is open the cover and turn the pages.

(3) Another concern for consumers is the availability of titles. At this point, some publishers have just begun creating electronic versions of their books. Experts believe it will be a number of years before the number of available E-book titles comes anywhere close to matching the number of print books. Therefore, even if you were to make the investment in an E-book reader, you might still not have access to electronic versions of all the books you want to read. You would never face such a situation with traditional books. Major traditional booksellers like Barnes and Noble have thousands of titles on hand. If you can't find it on their shelves, you can order it from Internet giant Amazon.com. If a printed book exists, someone can get it for you, and often within a few days.

(4) When it comes to reading, maybe the biggest concern for the average person is convenience. In this category, E-books don't yet measure up well. For example, the screens of many of the systems can be hard to read, and battery life can be a problem. In addition, the devices require careful handling to avoid damaging their sensitive electronics. You don't have any of these concerns with a traditional book, however. What could be easier and more convenient? You don't have to worry about screen brightness or batteries. If you drop it, you just pick it up, dust it off, and resume reading. If you want to read at the beach or in the bathtub, go right ahead. If you spill something on it, just wipe off the page. It's just that simple.

(5) In today's world, computers continue to play an increasingly large role. In most cases, they make our lives better or easier in some way. But when it comes to reading, I don't think the computer has yet been able to improve on what already exists. For now, a traditional printed book is far superior to any electronic version.

CHALLENGE 15.6   Analyzing the Sample Comparison and Contrast Essay

Refer to the sample comparison and contrast essay above to answer each question.

1. In the introduction, what point is made about E-books versus printed books? What does the introduction tell you about the purpose of this essay? Write your answers on a separate sheet of paper.

2. Working with a partner, analyze paragraphs 2 through 4. What basis of comparison is used to examine the two types of books? List the basis of comparison on your paper.

3. Still working with a partner, identify the format used to arrange this essay. On your paper, prepare a diagram like the one on page 137 in Chapter 10 to illustrate the organizational plan.

FOR FURTHER EXPLORATION

1. Using the essay just presented to guide you, write a comparison or contrast essay on selecting a laptop computer versus a traditional model or on one of the following topics:

   a. life in two different countries, cities, towns, or regions

   b. two jobs you've held

   c. two religions

   d. two types of video or board games

   e. the way you react to a situation versus the way one of your parents would react

   f. two musical groups, professional athletes, or political leaders

   g. two forms of exercise or athletic activity

COLLABORATION

2. Exchange your draft with a partner. Evaluate the essay using the comparison and contrast essay checklist on page 221. Write your answers on a separate sheet of paper, and then return the essay and your assessment to the writer.

3. Using your reader's comments to guide you, complete the final draft of your comparison or contrast essay.

▶ DISCOVERING CONNECTIONS 15.6

When you see this picture of Prague, the capital city of the Czech Republic, what ideas come to mind? Does the picture make you think of how the skyline and structures of this area, the Old Town Square section of Prague, compare with the skyline of your own city or town or the area where your campus is located? The dominant structure in the picture, the Tyn Church, was built in 1365, and many of the other buildings visible in the scene are hundreds of years old. If you had a choice, would you prefer to live in a historic home or a place that is ultramodern in design? Why? How do you think people who live in historic cities such as Prague react to their surroundings in comparison to travelers who visit?

For this assignment, focus on one of these questions or another that the picture inspires. Using the discussion of comparison and contrast on the previous pages to guide you, develop an essay of at least five paragraphs in which you use comparison and contrast to evaluate the alternatives your topic presents. ◀

✓**Comparison and Contrast Essay Checklist**

☐ Does the introduction specify the essay's focus and the subjects to be compared or contrasted?

☐ Does the essay concentrate on two subjects?

☐ Is a basis for comparison established and followed? Make sure that each characteristic or element is discussed in detail for each subject. Put a ✓ at any point where an element or characteristic is missing, and write *amplify* above any point that should be discussed in greater detail.

☐ Has the block format or the alternating format been used to arrange the paragraphs? Would the essay be more effective if it were arranged differently, for example, using block format instead of alternating format or vice versa?

☐ In your judgment, what is the best part of this essay? Explain.

☐ Which detail or example would be even better if it were expanded? Why?

Using Cause and Effect to Develop an Essay

Cause and effect, the writing technique you use to focus on what led to something or what happened as a result, is discussed in Chapter 11. Cause is *why* something occurred, and effect is the *outcome* or *consequence* of an occurrence. An extended writing in which you discuss how a new job has changed your life would be a cause and effect essay.

For a **cause and effect essay**, remember that most events or experiences have *more than one* cause and *more than one* effect. Therefore, don't oversimplify. Furthermore, be sure that any cause and effect relationships you suggest aren't actually *coincidence*—events that occur close to the same time by accident. Finally, arrange the various causes or effects you present in a logical order.

Examining a Cause and Effect Essay

Look at this essay about the various consequences of advancing to a more responsible job:

More Than a Promotion

(1) When I was about ten years old, I spent two weeks at my cousin's house just outside of Chicago. One day we went into the city with my aunt to see the department store that she managed. She showed us around the store

and then took us up to her office. I sat quietly watching her make phone calls and instruct her staff on what she wanted done that day. After half an hour, I knew I wanted to do just what she did for a living when I grew up. Six months ago, I got my chance to fulfill my dream when I was made the night and weekend manager at a large drug store. Almost overnight, I went from simply doing my job as a part-time clerk to keeping the ten people I supervise happy and productive. The many changes my promotion has brought about have definitely made me a different person.

(2) <u>One way the promotion has changed my life is financial.</u> When I was a clerk, I worked twenty hours a week at $7 an hour with no benefits. After taxes, my weekly pay was about $115. As a manager, I work at least forty hours a week for a weekly salary of $500, and I have full insurance coverage. Since I've become a manager, I have been able to buy a car and save money on a regular basis. With a little luck, I should be able to afford to move out of my mother's house and into my own apartment in six months or so.

(3) <u>My new responsibilities have also helped build up my self-confidence.</u> At first, I almost didn't take the job because I wasn't sure I could handle the responsibility. My supervisor convinced me to take it by telling me that she wouldn't have recommended me if she didn't feel I was capable. After the first few weeks on the job, I found out something about myself that I had never realized. Not only was I able to handle responsibilities such as motivating other workers, setting work schedules, and doing the payroll, but I was actually good at all these things. Because of these successes, I'm more confident whenever I face a new task.

(4) <u>Taking the promotion has also meant I had to grow up a lot.</u> For one thing, I had to learn to budget my personal time. As a manager, I work almost twice as many hours as I did when I was a clerk. Furthermore, managers often have to attend meetings at night or on weekends and do paperwork at home. No longer do I have time to ride around with my friends. I also can no longer do things like call in sick when I just don't feel like working. A clerk might be able to get away with that, but a manager can't. Managers are paid to be responsible.

(5) <u>I've also had to adjust to a new relationship with the people I supervise.</u> Before, I was one of them, but now I'm their boss. I have to make decisions about such things as who has to work Friday and Saturday nights and who gets extra hours when business is good. I now also have to evaluate them every four months to see who gets merit raises and who doesn't. Some of the people I was friendliest with when I was a clerk barely talk to me now because I won't play favorites when it comes to schedules and raises. I sometimes feel guilty when I have to give someone a bad evaluation for job performance or lack of punctuality. I know that when I was a clerk, I sometimes was lazy and showed up late or left a few minutes early. But I'm a manager now, and I have a responsibility to make sure that my company is getting its money's worth.

(6) I've been a manager for four months now, and I can honestly say that I enjoy the job far more than I ever expected to. I like earning more money, and the idea that people are willing to put their trust in me has made me more confident overall. I also like the fact that I've learned to take responsibility. I know that, overall, this job has helped to make me a better person.

CHALLENGE 15.7   Analyzing the Sample Cause and Effect Essay

Refer to the sample cause and effect essay on pages 221–222 to answer each question.

1. What event is the focus of this cause and effect essay? Does the essay explore the causes for this event or the consequences of it? Write your answers on a separate sheet of paper.

COLLABORATION

2. Working with a partner, analyze paragraphs 2 through 5 of the essay. First, underline the topic sentence of each paragraph. Then, on your paper, write the specific changes that occurred in the writer's life.

COLLABORATION

3. Imagine that the focus of this essay was on causes, not effects. Consider the causes of the promotion—diligence at work, a positive attitude, natural leadership ability, and a supervisor's confidence. Working with your partner, write a cause and effect paragraph that focuses on these causes. (Remember—your thesis should state the effect and reveal that you will explore the causes.)

FOR FURTHER EXPLORATION

1. Using the essay "More Than a Promotion" to guide you, write an essay on the cause(s) or effect(s) of a change in employment, schools, or personal relationships. If you prefer, choose one of the following topics:

   a. parental pressure for better performance in the classroom or on the playing field

   b. your interest in music, art, or sports

   c. a phobia

   d. lack of consumer confidence in a company or product

   e. curiosity about a subject

   f. a belief in a religious, ethnic, sexual, or racial stereotype

   g. prejudice

COLLABORATION

2. Exchange your draft with a partner. Evaluate the essay using the cause and effect essay checklist on page 224. Write your answers on a separate sheet of paper, and then return the essay and your assessment to the writer.

3. Using your reader's comments to guide you, complete the final draft of your cause and effect essay.

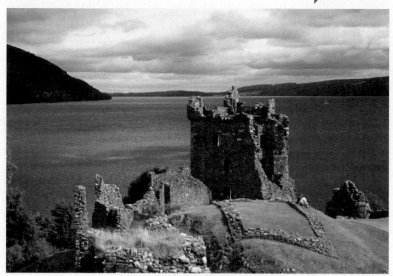

▶DISCOVERING CONNECTIONS 15.7

What do you think of when you see the following picture? Does it make you wonder what might have compelled people to build such a structure to keep others out? What kinds of struggles or hostilities do you think might have led the residents to fortify themselves in this way? What effects do you think facing such a structure might have had on the rest of the population? Ruins like these are popular tourist destinations. Why do you think some people line up to see what other people might just describe as a pile of rubble? The remains of the castle overlook one of Scotland's famous lakes or *lochs*—does the picture make you wonder why some people believe in the existence of the Loch Ness Monster or other creatures of legend?

For this assignment, address one of these questions or some other question that the picture brings to mind. Using the discussion of cause and effect on the previous pages to guide you, develop an essay of at least five paragraphs in which you use cause and effect to study the reasons leading to or the consequences stemming from your subject. ◀

✔ Cause and Effect Essay Checklist

☐ Does the introduction indicate a focus on either cause or effect?

☐ Are the cause and effect relationships supported with enough examples and details to avoid oversimplification? If you feel more specific details are required, write "I'd like to know more about _____" in the margin next to the poorly explored passage.

☐ Does the essay distinguish between direct and related causes and effects? Underline any details that seem like coincidences rather than true causes or effects.

☐ Are the supporting paragraphs effectively arranged in a logical order?

☐ In your judgment, what is the best part of this essay? Explain.

☐ Which detail or example would be better if it were expanded? Why?

Using Division and Classification to Develop an Essay

Chapter 12 discussed the writing technique you use to analyze a complex subject: **division and classification.** *Division* is the separation of a subject into its component parts. *Classification* is the arrangement of the subcategories into groups on

CW 15.20
Using division and classification to develop an essay

the basis of common characteristics or principles. An essay in which you discuss types of televised sports would use both division and classification. When you write a division and classification essay, make sure to choose a *logical method of analysis* so that your reader can understand the basis for your examination. In addition, make sure you keep your *presentation consistent,* with divisions or classifications that are *clearly related.* At the same time, keep your groupings *distinct* and *complete*—that is, distinguished from others and expressed in full detail.

FAST FACT   If you were asked to classify the greatest writers of all time, what choices would you make? When the editors and staff of *The World Almanac and Book of Facts 2001* were asked, these are the choices making up their top ten list: 1. John Steinbeck; 2. William Shakespeare; 3. Pat Conroy; 4. Jane Austen; 5. Charles Dickens; 6. Barbara Kingsolver; 7. Emily Dickinson; 8. Henry James; 9. Emily Bronte; 10. Thomas Hardy.

Examining a Division and Classification Essay

Look at this essay about the various types of televised sports:

CW 15.21
How to write a division and classification essay

Television: The Sports Fan's Paradise

(1) One of the most popular activities in the country is watching sports. Most sports fans would prefer to attend games in person, but cost and other life responsibilities keep most people from attending more than a few games a year. Fortunately, for sports fans, network television and cable outlets make it possible to watch some kind of sporting activity on a daily basis. Most of the sports available on television for fans to enjoy can be grouped in four basic categories.

(2) The first group is probably the type that has been featured on television the longest: major league professional sports. This group includes Major League baseball, NFL football, NBA basketball, and NHL hockey. More recently, WNBA basketball and Major League soccer have also enjoyed wide exposure. Fans love these games because of long-standing rivalries between teams and the opportunity to see a sport's elite players.

(3) Another category that draws fans includes individual sports like golf and tennis. These sports, unlike the major league group, have no organized leagues or seasons. Instead, fans have the chance to see the stars of these sports compete all year long in both national and international competitions.

(4) College sports represent another group of televised sporting events. This category of sports remains among the most watched, especially football and basketball games. The various Bowl Games at the end of the football season and the NCAA March Madness basketball tournament games are among the ratings leaders each year.

(5) The fourth group is one that has grown in popularity over the past ten years. This category might be termed alternative sports. These sports, which once appeared only on such sports cable stations as ESPN and ESPN2, have gradually become more mainstream. Events as the World's Strongest Man contests, bodybuilding events, and Ultimate Frisbee games now often appear for wider audiences to enjoy. The events that have attracted the most attention in this group are various extreme sports featured in competitions like the X-Games. These competitions feature stunt BMX biking and skateboarding events as well as such innovations as street luge.

(6) Certainly, there are other popular sporting events besides those in these categories. NASCAR racing, bowling, Summer and Winter Olympics, and skating competitions all draw big television audiences. But these four categories do include the sports that American fans find most captivating, at least for now. Stay tuned.

CHALLENGE 15.8　Analyzing the Sample Division and Classification Essay

Refer to the sample division and classification essay above to answer each question.

1. Find and underline the thesis statement in the first paragraph. Then, on a separate sheet of paper, list the essay's subject and the classes into which it is divided.

COLLABORATION

2. Find and underline the topic sentences of paragraphs 2 through 5. Working with a partner, analyze these paragraphs. On your paper, name each class of televised sports and describe the characteristics of each type that is discussed.

COLLABORATION

3. Working with a partner, identify another category of televised sports or subdivide one of the existing categories. Then write a paragraph that illustrates or explains this new classification.

FOR FURTHER EXPLORATION

1. Using the essay on televised sports to guide you, write a division and classification essay on types of movies or sitcoms, or on one of the following topics:
   a. styles of clothing in your drawers or closet
   b. types of responsibilities a first-year college student faces
   c. kinds of shoppers you might see during holiday shopping
   d. types of comedy
   e. the structure of a company, organization, or institution
   f. types of lies
   g. styles of teaching or learning

COLLABORATION

2. Exchange your draft with a partner. Evaluate the essay using the division and classification essay checklist on page 227. Write your answers on a separate sheet of paper, and then return the essay and your assessment to the writer.

3. Using your reader's comments to guide you, complete the final draft of your essay.

▶ DISCOVERING CONNECTIONS 15.8

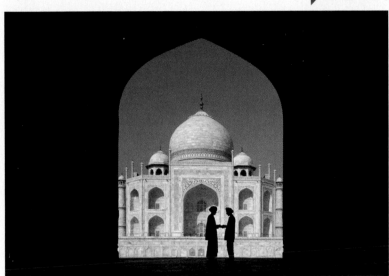

When you look at this picture, what do you notice first? Are your eyes drawn to the mosque in the background or the figures in the foreground? How does the photographer manage to divide your attention this way? Does the photo make you think of religion? How are religions generally divided and classified? In your travels in the United States or abroad, how often have you encountered architecture that represents places of worship? What makes each building distinctly characteristic and representative of one religion versus another?

For this assignment, address one of these questions or another question that the picture brings to mind. Using the discussion of division and classification on the previous pages to guide you, develop an essay of at least five paragraphs in which you use division and classification to zero in on the parts or categories that make up your subject. ◀

✔ Division and Classification Essay Checklist

☐ Does the introduction specify the focus of the discussion and indicate an emphasis on either division or classification?

☐ Are the elements distinct and complete? If you think any divisions or classes need to be subdivided further to make them clearer or more specific, write, "I'd like to know more about _____" in the margin next to them.

☐ Does the essay feature a logical, consistent method of analysis throughout?

☐ Are the supporting paragraphs presented in an effective order?

☐ In your judgment, what is the best part of this essay? Explain.

☐ Which detail or example would be even better if it were expanded? Why?

Writing an Argument Essay

CW 15.22
Using
modes to
write an
argument

As Chapter 13 explained, *argument* isn't a writing technique or a mode. It is writing that uses a combination of modes to persuade. An **argument essay** takes a firm stand on an issue and then attempts to convince readers to agree with that stand. For example, an essay suggesting that child beauty pageants are harmful to participants would be an argument because its purpose would be to convince readers to accept the writer's viewpoint.

When you write an argument essay, it's important to make your stance on the issue clear in the introduction. In the body, supply at least three convincing reasons why readers should agree with you. Back up each reason with sound support. Should you draw any of your supporting information from a document or individual, always acknowledge your source. Also, adopt a reasonable tone; avoid an emotional or condescending view. It's often better to use qualifying terms such as *most, rarely,* and *frequently* rather than absolute ones such as *all, never,* and *always.* In addition, make sure that your argument essay has a logical line of reasoning and that you have avoided the errors in logic known as *logical fallacies.* See the list of logical fallacies on pages 163–164. Finally, be sure to arrange your points in a logical order, such as order of importance.

Examining an Argument Essay

Look at this argument essay about child beauty pageants:

CW 15.23
Writing a
research
essay

The Beast Is the Beauty Contest

(1) On Christmas Day, 1996, six-year-old JonBenet Ramsey was murdered in Boulder, Colorado. Shortly after her tiny body was discovered, the story of her brief life became public, especially details about her involvement in child beauty pageants. Within a few weeks, the spotlight was turned on the pageants themselves. The public quickly learned that at these events, held in nearly every state across the United States, children as young as ten months old don makeup and fancy clothing to compete for crowns and titles. Despite the large number of people who claim that these events are a form of innocent fun and recreation, these reports clearly indicate that children's beauty pageants can have a negative and lasting effect on their young participants.

(2) Proponents of child beauty pageants, including promoters and parents of contestants, compare these events to other childhood pastimes such as Little League or playing "dress-up." They argue that the competitions can help youngsters develop poise and self-confidence. A lucky few, they point out, even earn scholarships or launch careers in acting or modeling. However, these people are ignoring the fact that the lessons these competitions teach are damaging to a child's future.

(3) The first lesson children learn is that personal appearance is everything. The "dressing-up" that they do in these pageants is far from innocent play. Right from the start, they see that the right hairstyle, the most stylish outfit, and the perfect makeup win the prizes. How you look, not who you are, is what is truly important in this world. Unfortunately, this harmful attitude may stay with a child well into adulthood, coloring the way she interacts, forms relationships with others, and values herself.

(4) Those who compare beauty pageants with Little League are also forgetting that beauty, unlike a sport, cannot be developed and improved through practice. If a child's appearance does not conform to society's standards for beauty, then winning the competition is out of the question. Children who fail at these events may learn to feel unattractive, rejected, and worthless before they even have a chance to develop an adult body. Moreover, even those who enjoy success as children may run into trouble when they reach adolescence. When they grow taller or heavier, or when they develop acne, they may no longer meet society's standards for beauty. If they have based their sense of self-worth on their appearance, then these children are in danger of developing disorders such as depression, anorexia, or bulimia.

(5) The most damaging aspect of child beauty pageants, however, is that children learn to display themselves as sex objects before they can possibly understand what sexuality is all about. As news reports have shown, many of the contestants have to appear before adult judges in elaborate makeup, scaled-down versions of provocative dresses, and bathing suits. They also learn to flirt and use their bodies to attract attention. In a world in which sex crimes against children make daily headlines, such practices are deeply disturbing and potentially harmful.

(6) Although it is tempting to argue that child beauty pageants should be banned, that is not a good long-term solution. Instead, parents should think carefully about the lessons and values that children are likely to learn from these events. If parents really considered the consequences of those lessons, then the competitions might die a natural death. Vermont, for example, failed to produce a Miss America candidate a few years ago because the women in that state refused to enter a contest that judges people on looks and other superficial qualities.

(7) If parents do not want their children to grow up thinking that appearance is all that matters, then they should keep their children away from activities that twist and exploit a child's natural desire for attention. Beauty contests are far more likely to make children, like poor JonBenet, the victims of adult desires than to deliver the fame and fortune they seem to promise.

CHALLENGE 15.9 Analyzing the Sample Argument Essay

Refer to the sample argument essay above to answer each question.

1. Find the thesis statement in the first paragraph. Write it on a separate sheet of paper.

2. Working with a partner, analyze the paragraphs in the body of the essay. How many reasons does the writer give to support this thesis? On your paper, list each reason.

3. Analyze the support given for each reason. Which is most convincing to you? Which reason is least convincing? Working together, brainstorm further support for this reason (or develop an alternative reason) and revise or replace this paragraph.

FOR FURTHER EXPLORATION

1. Using the essay on child beauty pageants to guide you, write an argument essay taking a stance on whether beauty contests—for adults or children—are harmful. If you prefer, choose one of the following topics instead, and write an argument essay in which you support or refute it:

   a. Assisted suicide should be legal for terminally ill patients.

   b. Alternative sentencing such as home confinement, boot camps, or extended community service should be used for some lawbreakers.

   c. Athletes proven to have used steroids or illegal supplements should face a lifetime ban from their sport.

   d. College students should have to pass competency examinations in writing, critical thinking, and mathematics before receiving their degrees.

   e. Police should be able to search cars without a warrant if they suspect someone has an illegal weapon.

   f. The media should not be allowed to reveal the names of victims of sexual abuse.

   g. All college students should be required to perform 30 hours of community service as part of their graduation requirements.

COLLABORATION

2. Exchange your draft with a partner. Evaluate the essay using the argument essay checklist on page 231. Write your answers on a separate sheet of paper, and then return the essay and your assessment to the writer.

3. Using your reader's comments to guide you, complete the final draft of your argument essay.

▶ DISCOVERING CONNECTIONS 15.9

What thoughts come to mind when you look at this picture? Although these boys and girls are standing together, do you think they are also segregated in some way? How? Why do you think some people here in the United States want to segregate people on the basis of sex? Where do you stand on this issue? Standing behind the children are a number of adults watching them interact. Does their presence make you consider the problems that sometimes occur at youth sporting activities in the United States? Do you think that before being allowed to watch their children play in these leagues, adults should have to agree to follow a behavior code? The children in this picture appear to be participating in some kind of cultural or arts festival. Does it make you wonder about the amount of attention that U.S. public schools pay to teaching things like music, art, dance, and so on? Is the time devoted adequate or should it be increased?

For this assignment, address one of these questions or some other question that the picture brings to mind. Using the discussion of argument on the previous pages to guide you, develop an essay of at least five paragraphs in which you present and support your stand on the issue you have chosen. ◀

✔ Argument Essay Checklist

☐ Does the introduction clarify the stance on the issue?

☐ Are there at least three reasons, properly documented if necessary, to support the stance?

☐ Is the tone throughout the essay respectful and concerned? Put a ✓ next to any sentence in which the tone seems inappropriate.

☐ Is the presentation logical? Underline any errors in logic.

☐ Does the essay feature qualifying terms rather than absolute ones when appropriate?

☐ Are the supporting paragraphs effectively presented in emphatic order or some other method of arrangement? Explain.

☐ In your judgment, what is the best part of this essay? Explain.

☐ Which detail or example would be even better if it were expanded? Why?

RECAP Examining Types of Essays

New terms in this chapter	Definitions
modes	organizing strategies to develop paragraphs and essays
purpose	your intent or aim when you write
narrative essay	a multi-paragraph writing that relates a sequence of events in story fashion
descriptive essay	a multi-paragraph writing that uses concrete, sensory language to recreate a scene, situation, or individual
example essay	a multi-paragraph writing that uses specific instances to illustrate, clarify, or back up a thesis
process essay	a multi-paragraph writing that spells out how to do something, how something is done, or how you did something *(continued)*

New terms in this chapter	Definitions
definition essay	a multi-paragraph writing that specifies the characteristics or elements of some object, location, or individual
comparison and contrast essay	a multi-paragraph writing that examines similarities and differences between two or more subjects
cause and effect essay	a multi-paragraph writing that considers reasons leading to some situation or condition or the outcomes or consequences of an event or phenomenon
division and classification essay	a multi-paragraph writing that analyzes a complex subject either by separating it into its component parts or by grouping its parts into categories Some division and classification essays use both approaches.
argument essay	a multi-paragraph writing that takes a firm stand on an issue and then attempts to convince readers to agree with that stand

The Relationship between the Purpose of an Essay and the Modes

Determine the *purpose* of the writing task		Choose your *main* mode		Employ *supporting* modes
Topic: What is sexual harassment? **Purpose:** to **inform**	→	Identify the characteristics of sexual harassment using **definition.**	+	Support your definition using **example, cause and effect,** and **comparison and contrast.**

GOING FORWARD . . .

CW 15.24 Examining types of essay review

Q: When I have to write an essay, how will I know which of the organizing strategies—the **modes**—to use?

A: Actually, the answer you are looking for comes from the assignment itself. For example, if the assignment calls for a story from your childhood, then you'll rely primarily on narration. But if the assignment asks for a discussion of the result of some event, then you'll turn to cause and effect. Remember the characteristics of the various organizing strategies, and you'll find it easy to use the right modes to fulfill the different writing tasks you'll face.

CHAPTER 16
Adjusting Your Process: Timed Writing and Summaries

▶ **Navigating This Chapter**

This chapter discusses strategies that will lead you to success whenever you must:

- answer essay questions
- complete a writing assessment
- prepare a summary

GETTING STARTED . . .

**CW 16.1
Chapter
basics**

Q: I feel more confident with writing assignments that I can do outside the classroom—when I can work at home, on my own schedule, and on a subject of my own choice. What I'm concerned about is having to complete a timed writing or summarize an article written by someone else. What can I do to become more comfortable with these kinds of assignments?

A: To become more comfortable with timed writings and summaries, you first need to recognize the nature of the specific task—exactly what you need to do and under what time and length guidelines you need to work. Then it's a simple matter of choosing and applying the strategy—the particular approach—that matches the task.

Overview: Understanding How to Deal with the Pressure of Timed Writing

**CW 16.2
Overview of
timed
writing**

It doesn't make a difference what field you are talking about—sports, business, music, medicine, law, or engineering. With few exceptions, people do their best work when they have time to think through a task, to *plan, concentrate,* and *reexamine* it. As the previous chapters illustrate, taking your time to plan, concentrate, and reexamine helps you produce your best writing.

No matter what field, however, people will face situations in which they have no time to spare. In these situations, they must *adapt* the process they normally follow so that they can perform effectively in less-than-ideal conditions. A journalist, for example, must be prepared to deviate from a planned series of questions if the interview takes an interesting turn and the deadline is looming. An athlete on the field or court must make immediate adjustments if someone misses a shot or commits a foul. An actor must be ready to ad-lib if another actor "drops a page," leaving out crucial dialogue. An EMT must be prepared to treat the victim of an auto accident in the vehicle if the person is trapped. In each of these cases, the situations give these people little choice. If they don't adapt, they won't succeed. It's as simple as that.

With writing, you will also occasionally face circumstances calling for you to adjust the process you follow. For instance, answering an **essay question** and completing a **writing assessment** generally involve tight time constraints. Preparing a **summary** may not always involve a strict time limit, but it does require you to work in a different direction. Instead of developing your own ideas in full detail, you reduce someone else's ideas to their essence.

FAST FACT   Don't panic at the panic you might feel when you see an essay question. Your goal should be to reduce your apprehension, not eliminate it completely. That's because research suggests that a little test anxiety can actually enhance performance.

Answering an Essay Question Effectively

CW 16.3
Writing
essay exams

An **essay question** is a specific writing assignment given as part of an examination. It calls for a clear, concise, multi-paragraph response within a limited period of time. Answering an essay question isn't all that different from completing other writing tasks. Your goal is the same: to work through the writing process and to communicate to your reader what you know about the question.

You may not believe it, but an essay question can be **easier** to answer than multiple-choice or short-answer questions. Nonessay kinds of questions focus on single bits of information, so they end up quizzing you on what you *don't know*. But essay questions test you on what you *do know*, providing you with the opportunity to demonstrate in detail what you understand about the subject.

Developing an effective strategy for writing a successful essay answer involves following three simple steps: **preparation, anticipation,** and **rehearsal.** Consider the figure on page 235.

As the figure shows, the three steps are closely connected. Preparation gives you the foundation for the rest of the process, and anticipation gears you up for rehearsal.

Preparation

CW 16.4
Listing your
current
preparation
strategies

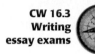

The best way to *prepare* yourself to answer essay questions is to apply yourself in your coursework. Learn the information you will need during an exam by (1) reading actively and (2) taking effective classroom notes.

Active Reading   To get the most out of your assigned reading, read *actively*.

- Read the introduction and conclusion to each chapter for an overview of the material.
- Preview all headings and subheadings in the selection. They highlight main ideas in the chapter.

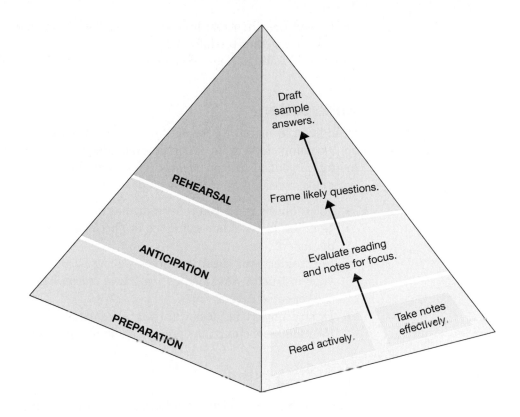

- Read any *charts, boxed areas,* or *lists.* They summarize important information.
- If the book or article you are reading belongs to you, highlight or underline information you judge to be important—*specific* names, dates, distances, conditions, and so on.
- Look for any *definitions* and information presented *in order* (*first, second, third,* and so on). Be alert for *transitional expressions* and words like *important, crucial,* and *vital* that signal important material will follow.
- Write any points that you feel are especially important in the *margin* or in your *notebook.*
- Use the material you have highlighted or underlined to prepare a *summary,* a greatly reduced version of the original, expressed in your own words. A discussion of summary writing appears later in this chapter.

Effective Note-Taking   To take effective notes, follow these guidelines:

- Filter what you hear in class. Concentrate on recording information that is new to you or that you are unsure of.
- Assume that any material your instructor puts on the board is important.
- Listen when your instructor uses words like *important, vital, crucial,* and so on. These words are clues to what the instructor feels you need to know.
- Focus on definitions and material the instructor repeats or presents in sequence (*first, second, third*).
- Keep your notes as neat and orderly as possible, writing on every other line so that you always have room to add information.
- Use abbreviations or your own personal shorthand system.

- Reread your notes an hour or so after the class is over and flesh out, clarify, and tie together the information.
- Write a summary, interpretation, or analysis of the material.

Anticipation

CW 16.5
**Key terms
of various
writing
modes**

In addition to learning your course material, it is wise to think strategically about an upcoming essay exam. Begin by evaluating your notes and readings to identify the topics your instructor might use for essay questions. To *anticipate* these essay questions, consider the following guidelines:

- Focus on the ideas you've identified as important in your reading.
- Note the focus of any questions or checklists your instructor has provided or discussed.
- Reconsider your classroom notes, paying particular attention to material that your instructor described as *important, crucial, vital,* and so on or that he or she repeated several times.
- Discuss important ideas with your classmates. This will help you clarify your own thinking, and it may provide additional perspectives on those ideas.

Rehearsal

Once you have identified the information you feel is likely to be included on the examination, you should *rehearse.* In this context, rehearsal means creating several **practice questions**, the type of queries that might appear on an exam, and then drafting answers.

Drawing Up a Practice Question   Imagine, for instance, that you are studying for an essay exam in your introductory psychology class. Over the past two weeks, you've discussed a great many topics in relation to the sensation of pain. From your notes and reading, you have identified the psychological factors involved in the perception and management of pain as the likely focus of essay questions.

With this focus identified, you create the following practice question, intended to be answered within 20 minutes or so:

> Research in the area of pain management suggests that psychological factors are involved in the perception of pain. What three psychological factors influence pain perception? Be sure to provide a concrete example for each factor. Also, what are three treatments commonly used to manage pain? Again, be sure to provide a concrete example for each treatment and an explanation as to why the treatment works.

On a real exam, you must first identify exactly what the essay question is asking you to do. Even though you have developed the sample question yourself, you should follow the same strategy. That way, each practice session will mirror the process you will follow during an exam.

In this case, the question asks you to supply a total of *six* points, with a specific example of each. *Three* of the points must be psychological factors, and *three* must be common treatments. With this information identified, you are ready to move to the next step: answering a practice question.

Developing a Sample Essay Answer   As indicated above, you have set a time limit of 20 minutes to develop an effective answer, so you need to get to work. Incidentally, with such a tight time constraint, don't expect that your writing will be perfect. Perfection takes hours, not minutes. Instead, plan to do the best writing you can under those circumstances. Concentrate on making your answer *complete* in terms of **content** and *correct* in terms of **form.**

Here are the steps you should follow when answering an essay question. The time estimate is based on the 20 minutes set aside to develop an effective answer:

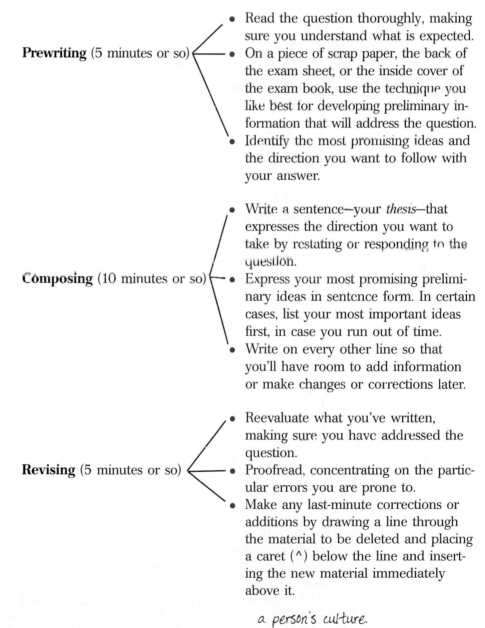

Prewriting (5 minutes or so)
- Read the question thoroughly, making sure you understand what is expected.
- On a piece of scrap paper, the back of the exam sheet, or the inside cover of the exam book, use the technique you like best for developing preliminary information that will address the question.
- Identify the most promising ideas and the direction you want to follow with your answer.

Composing (10 minutes or so)
- Write a sentence—your *thesis*—that expresses the direction you want to take by restating or responding to the question.
- Express your most promising preliminary ideas in sentence form. In certain cases, list your most important ideas first, in case you run out of time.
- Write on every other line so that you'll have room to add information or make changes or corrections later.

Revising (5 minutes or so)
- Reevaluate what you've written, making sure you have addressed the question.
- Proofread, concentrating on the particular errors you are prone to.
- Make any last-minute corrections or additions by drawing a line through the material to be deleted and placing a caret (^) below the line and inserting the new material immediately above it.

                                                                    a person's culture.
EXAMPLE   A second factor that influences pain is ~~different cultures.~~
                                                                    ^

Here again is the essay question:

> Research in the area of pain management suggests that psychological factors are involved in the perception of pain. What three psychological factors influence pain perception? Be sure to provide a concrete example for each factor. Also, what are three treatments commonly used to manage pain? Again, be sure to provide a concrete example for each treatment and an explanation as to why the treatment works.

Now, here are the prewriting ideas you've generated in response to the question:

> OK, 3 psy. factors? 1. anxiety, like worrying about a date making a headache worse 2. culture, your culture tells you how to react, like men not complaining 3. experience with pain, the pain you have from an injury or from having a baby makes you expect to have the same pain or more the second time. Now 3 effective treatments? 1. acupuncture is used to treat things like headaches—works by releasing endorphins 2. medication-pain killers like percodan following surgery work by keeping Substance P from being released—the result is euphoria 3. cognitive therapy, learning new ways to deal with pain. Instead of saying "I can't stand this pain," tell yourself "the pain is only temporary"—works because people feel more in control

As you can see, the prewriting material includes the six points the question calls for. Now you need to express your focus—the *thesis*. In this case, you can simply restate the main idea of the question, that psychological factors play a role in both the perception and treatment of pain:

> Research shows that psychological factors are involved in pain perception and treatment.

At this point, convert your promising prewriting ideas into correct sentences that support or illustrate your thesis. Always take a moment to identify the best order to present the material. The question itself provides a scaffolding, indicating how you should arrange your supporting ideas. For example, the essay question about pain asks first about perception and second about treatment. Therefore, it makes sense to present your points in that order. Once you have completed your answer, take a few moments to reevaluate what you have written. Does it actually answer the question? Finally, proofread and neatly make any last-minute corrections.

Here is the resulting answer, with annotations pointing out the key features.

Clear thesis expressing the main idea

First psychological factor with an example

Second psychological factor with an example

Third psychological factor with an example

First pain treatment with an example

Second pain treatment with an example

Note correction

Note correction

Research shows that psychological factors are involved in pain perception and treatment. (One factor) that will make pain worse is anxiety. For example, if you have a headache and feel anxiety that the headache will prevent you from going on a date, the headache is likely to hurt even more than it originally did. A (second factor) that influences pain is ~~different cultures.~~ _a person's culture_ Different cultures have different rules about how people should react to pain. For example, some cultures believe that men should not complain about pain. A man from this type of culture might feel severe pain but still not see a doctor because he doesn't want to seem unmanly. A (third factor) that is involved in pain perception is past experience. For instance, if a woman has a lot of pain when her first baby is born, she is likely to expect a lot of pain when her second baby is born. This expectation, based on past experience, is likely to make the pain ~~worst~~ _worse_ because you experience what you expect to experience.

Three types of pain treatments are acupuncture, medication, and cognitive therapy. (Acupuncture) involves inserting small needles into the body to lessen pain. For example, if you get migraines, you might go for acupuncture in order to lessen the pain. It is thought that acupuncture works by closing gates and releasing endorphins. (Medication) involves taking drugs to stop the pain. For example, if you have surgery, you might take percodan. It is thought that medications work by blocking

Third pain treatment with an example ——

> the release of Substance P and creating euphoria.
> (Cognitive therapy) involves learning new ways to interpret
> pain. For example, the person with back pain might be
> taught to think, "This pain is only temporary" instead
> of "I can't stand this pain." It is thought that cogni-
> tive therapy lessens pain by increasing the person's sense
> of control.

As you can see, this process led to an effective answer that directly addresses the question. It identifies and illustrates three psychological factors related to pain perception and three methods to treat pain. The points are presented in sentence form and arranged in a logical order. In short, the answer is simple, clear, complete, and correct, exactly what you need to get the best grade possible on your essay examination.

COMPREHENSION AND PRACTICE 16.1

Focusing on Answering Essay Questions

1. On the following lines, explain the advantages you enjoy with essay questions that you don't with multiple-choice or fill-in-the-blank questions.

   With an essay question, you have the opportunity to demonstrate what you know

   about a subject. With multiple-choice or short-answer questions, you might not know

   one fact being asked, even though you know many other related facts.

2. On the lines below, briefly explain what you find most difficult about answering essay questions and why you think you experience this difficulty.

   Answers will vary. Students will likely identify their difficulties as the time pressure and

   anxiety over making errors in form, and they will likely say that their reason is past

   negative experiences.

3. Choose a newspaper or magazine article of about 1,000 words or a passage of that length in one of your textbooks. Actively read the document, following the guidelines for active reading (pages 234–235).

CHALLENGE 16.1 Developing and Answering Essay Questions

1. Imagine that you are preparing for an essay examination in one of your courses. Go through the reading you have done and your relevant classroom notes. On a separate sheet of paper, list the key information that appears in both your reading and your notes.

2. From this list of material, develop three essay questions. Write each question on a separate sheet of paper.

3. Prepare answers of 200 to 300 words for each question. Write each answer immediately under the appropriate question.

COLLABORATION

4. Exchange your questions and answers with a partner. Evaluate the material you receive, using the essay answer checklist below. Return the answer and your assessment to the writer.

5. Correct the problem spots your reader has identified in your answers.

✔ Essay Answer Checklist

☐ Does the essay answer directly address the question being asked? Make a note in the margin next to any point that does not relate to the question.

☐ Should any section of the answer be amplified? Put a ✓ next to the section that needs more explanation.

☐ Are there any mistakes in spelling or usage? Circle any errors.

FAST FACT   A few years ago, Educational Testing Services of Princeton, New Jersey, quietly changed the name of the college admissions test familiar to thousands upon thousands of high school students, teachers, and parents. What was once known as the Scholastic *Aptitude* Test is now the Scholastic **Assessment** Test. What a difference a word makes—or does it? To most people, it's still just the SAT.

Completing a Writing Assessment Effectively

U.S. college students today face a number of challenges that their counterparts a decade ago generally did not. Among these new challenges in an increasing number of institutions are mandated **entrance** and **exit assessments.** Students must complete these tests to be admitted to a particular course or to receive credit for it. In many cases, these evaluations require that a student prepare an effective writing in accordance with specific guidelines on a particular topic, often within a given time period.

To succeed with this kind of writing assessment, you do many of the same things you do when you answer an essay question. Consider these guidelines:

- Be realistic when facing a timed writing assessment. Don't expect to write a perfect paper. Your job is to write an essay that proves your overall competence. In most cases, the resulting writing won't be the best paper you are capable of. That takes much more time than the assessment conditions are likely to allow.

- Make sure you understand exactly what the assessment is asking you to do. That means carefully examining the topic and any information accompanying it before you begin developing ideas. Underline or write down key words and phrases from the assignment that suggest the direction or focus you are expected to take. These words and phrases will guide you as you begin to work through the writing process.
- Pay close attention to time management. Once you know how much time you will have, divide the writing process up accordingly. For instance, if you have 50 minutes total, devote approximately 10 minutes to prewriting and approximately 25 minutes for composing. You will then have at least 10 minutes for the revising stage.
- Make sure that the paper you write is as complete and correct as possible under the circumstances. Doing so means including an introduction with a clear thesis, several body paragraphs supporting that thesis, and a conclusion closing the paper effectively. Make any last-minute corrections or additions neatly the same way you do with answers to essay questions.

Understanding the Five-Paragraph Essay

CW 16.6 Outlining the five-paragraph essay

Because you are working such a tight time line, you may want to consider using a format called the **five-paragraph essay**. With this format, you use the thesis to specify three main points relative to the topic. Then, in the next three paragraphs—the body of the essay—you discuss each subtopic, one per paragraph. Finally, you add a conclusion that restates the thesis and three supporting points.

In the previous chapter, you may have noticed that some of the sample essays followed this format. For example, here again is the essay from pages 209–210 on superstitions, with annotations highlighting the format:

Superstitions: The Irrational Beliefs That

Influence Our Behavior

Thesis —————

(1) All cultures seem to have some common beliefs that can be thought of as superstitions. All over the world, people believe that doing or possessing certain things can bring them good luck or cause them bad luck. The most common groups of superstitions involve objects that can① bring good luck, behaviors② that can influence luck, and actions that can③ cause bad luck.

Three points relative to superstitions

(2) The belief in good luck charms① is one of the best-known superstitions. Many people keep special objects

Discussion of point ①, with examples

that they believe will somehow keep them safe or provide an extra edge. For some people, the good luck charm is a particular shirt or key chain. For others, the good luck charm is the more traditional rabbit's foot or four-leaf clover.

(3) In addition to lucky objects, many people believe that (performing certain rituals) ② can provide good luck. If you've ever watched a professional sporting event, you've probably seen players performing a series of movements. Sometimes a basketball player will take a certain number of bounces–no more, no less–before shooting a foul shot. Some baseball players, while waiting for a pitch, will adjust their equipment, from batting helmet to wristbands to gloves, always in the same order. Regardless of the particular actions, the players perform them because they believe they will bring them good luck.

Discussion of point ②, with examples

(4) Other well-known superstitions are those (bits of advice to ward off bad luck) ③ passed down from generation to generation. For instance, from childhood, people are often told that breaking a mirror will bring seven years' bad luck. Others warn us not to walk under a ladder, not to open an umbrella inside a house, and not to let a black cat cross our paths. Of course, no evidence exists that any of these things cause bad luck, but people often follow these directions, just to be sure.

Discussion of point ③, with examples

(5) Exactly why people believe in superstitions is difficult to understand. Maybe it is because life in

Conclusion with a sentence recapping the three points

general is so uncertain. In any case, when you notice people (holding a special object,) (performing some little ritual,)
or (following some old directive,) wish them luck. They need
it, or at least they think they do.

Examining a Sample Writing Assessment

Writing assessments appear in a variety of forms. One common type presents a brief excerpt. Students are instructed to read the excerpt and then respond to a specific writing assignment related to the passage. Here's an example of this type of assessment:

Exit Assessment

Name _____

Student ID Number _____

Date _____

Read the following passage and then write an essay of 300 to 500 words on one of the options that follow the excerpt. Use the pages attached to this sheet. You have 50 minutes to complete all work. Your essay will be judged on its overall effectiveness. Therefore, try to develop a writing that features

- a clear thesis
- solid supporting examples, effectively arranged
- appropriate, specific language
- correct usage, spelling, and punctuation

Assignment

Consider this excerpt from Isabel Briggs Myers's *Taking Type into Account in Education.*

> Children in all the grades should be given maximum opportunity to learn the things that have meaning and interest for them in terms of their own kind of perception and their own kind of judgment. To the extent that they are given this opportunity, they gain not only in interest but in application and intelligence as well. People of any age, from six to sixty, apply themselves with greater vigor to the task at hand when they are interested. People of any age are more intelligent when they are interested than when they are bored.

Now choose *one* of the following options and develop a writing that responds to it:

Option A: Based on Briggs Myers's statement and your own experiences with school, what specific changes would you suggest to make sure that every school becomes the kind of place where more learning takes place?

Option B: In this passage, Briggs Myers uses the word *interest* several times to emphasize how important this element is to success in learning and in life. Consider the examples Briggs Myers provides along with what you've seen, read, and experienced. Then give your view of the types of interest or curiosity that can lead to success in school and the world beyond.

The guidelines provided indicate that the maximum amount of time available to complete the writing is 50 minutes, so it's important to get to work immediately. When an assessment assignment offers more than one possibility, the first step is to select the option that holds the most appeal. Then spend about 10 minutes doing some prewriting.

Here, for example, is some brainstorming in response to Option B:

Different kinds of curiosity lead people to success

- Curiosity about the world

  kids want to learn about clouds and rain,

  about plants and animals

  about where they come from

  helps them understand their relationship with the rest of

     the world

- Curious about their families

  what about their history

  any famous ancestors?

- Interest in letters and numbers

  in school kids are curious about letters and numbers

  understand them, words and math suddenly make sense-like

     magic

- Curiosity about what jobs involve

  what their parents do for jobs

This writing assessment essay is effective for several reasons. For one thing, the introduction directly addresses the assignment and contains a clear thesis. For another thing, the body contains several supporting ideas expressed in detail. Finally, it has a conclusion that reemphasizes the points made in the essay.

As the annotations indicate, this assessment essay follows the format of the five-paragraph essay presented earlier. If the time available permits, however, always feel free to include more than three points about your subject. Think of three as the minimum number of points you need to present, and you'll be all set.

COMPREHENSION AND PRACTICE 16.2

Focusing on Writing Assessments

1. Regardless of the task involved, what happens to you when a strict deadline for completion is imposed? Use the lines below to explain your reaction.

   Answers will vary. Some students will report that they feel more motivated. Others,

   however, will report that they experience a heightened degree of anxiety and dread

   when they face a strict time deadline for completing a writing task.

2. Take another look at the annotated five-paragraph essay on superstition (pages 246–247). One the lines below, explain how the introduction of the essay prepares the reader for the body to follow.

   The introduction prepares the reader for the discussion to follow because it identifies

   the nature of the discussion that follows: common types of superstitions.

3. On the following lines, briefly explain the relationship between good time management and success with a timed writing assessment.

   Good time management skills lead to success with a writing assessment because

   they enable you to budget time, allowing you to plan, develop, and revise a complete

   piece of writing.

CHALLENGE 16.2   Completing a Writing Assessment

1. Here again is **Option A** of the sample exit assessment provided earlier:

   > Based on Briggs Myers's statement and your own experiences with school, what specific changes would you suggest to make sure that every school becomes the kind of place where more learning takes place?

Now take 50 minutes and complete an assessment essay that responds to this option.

COLLABORATION

2. Exchange your completed assessment essay with a writing partner. Evaluate the essay you receive, using the writing assessment checklist below. Return the essay and your evaluation to the writer.

3. Correct any problem spots your reader has identified.

✔ Writing Assessment Checklist

☐ Does the introduction have a clear thesis that directly addresses the topic or scenario assigned in the assessment? Write a brief note in the margin if you think the introduction is off target.

☐ Do all the paragraphs provide specific support for the thesis? Put a ✓ next to any paragraph that doesn't offer support.

☐ Does the conclusion restate the significance of what has been presented? Write a brief note in the margin next to the introduction if you think the conclusion doesn't bring the assessment to an effective close.

☐ Are there mistakes in spelling or usage? Circle any errors.

FAST FACT   One magazine that operates on the principle that less is more is *Reader's Digest,* which has turned the process of summarizing writings into an art form. And people certainly seem to like it. *The New York Times 2001 Almanac* reported that in 1999 *Reader's Digest* was the third-best-selling American magazine, with a circulation of 12,962,369.

Writing an Effective Summary

As part of your studies, you will often have to take some document, identify the key points in it, and then express them in a greatly reduced form. The resulting writing is called a **summary**. In some fields, a summary is called an *abstract* or *précis.* Depending on the length of the document itself, a summary may be as little as five to ten percent of the original. You therefore need to focus on only the most important or significant points in the original. That way, you will produce a document that expresses the essence of the original.

As with an essay answer and a writing assessment, an effective summary is the product of a series of steps, which are listed on page 250. Follow this process, and you'll find writing a summary much easier:

1. Read the original document *actively.*
   a. Read the title, introduction, headings and subheadings, conclusion, and other features designed to indicate the key points in the writing.
   b. Reread the writing, highlighting key ideas.
      ✓ Note any **signal words** emphasizing importance, for example, *crucial, vital, significant, prominent, extraordinary.* These words generally indicate the value the author has placed on the material.
      ✓ Note any charts, boxed information, or lists as well as specific names, dates, distances, amounts, conditions, and statistics. These elements often represent a brief version of what the writer considers important.

2. Make a list of the key ideas you've identified.
   a. Express these ideas in your own words. Consult a dictionary for any word in the original that is unfamiliar to you so that you express its meaning correctly.
   b. Write these ideas out in complete sentence form.

3. Eliminate the *least* essential ideas from your preliminary list.
   a. Avoid more than one reference to the same point.
   b. Trim or discard lengthy examples and explanations.
   c. Cut any material taken from footnotes.

4. Use the sentences you have written to create a draft summary.
   a. Include enough information so that the summary makes sense for someone who has not read the original.
   b. Present the material in your summary in the same order as the original document.
   c. Unless instructed otherwise, don't include your own opinion of the original.
   d. Provide transition wherever it is needed so that your draft seems like a coherent paragraph and not just a list of sentences.

5. Revise your draft summary.
   a. Make sure that the summary makes sense independent of the original.
   b. Make sure you have supplied sufficient transition.
   c. Make sure you have eliminated any of your own commentary of the original.
   d. Make sure you have eliminated any errors.

Examining the Summarizing Process of Preparing a Summary

Here is a passage from E. D. Hirsch's *Cultural Literacy: What Every American Needs to Know.* Creating an effective summary begins with the identification of the most essential information in the original, as the highlighted sections indicate:

My son assures me that his pupils are not ignorant. They know a great deal. Like every other human group, they share a tremendous amount of knowledge among themselves, much of it learned in school. The trouble is that, from the standpoint of their literacy and their ability to communicate with others in our culture, what they know is ephemeral and narrowly confined to their own generation. Many young people strikingly lack the information that writers of American books and newspapers have traditionally taken for granted among their readers from all generations. For reasons explained in this book, our children's lack of intergenerational information is a serious problem for the nation. The decline of literacy and the decline of shared knowledge are closely related, interdependent facts.

The evidence for the decline of shared knowledge is not just anecdotal. In 1978 NAEP [The National Assessment of Educational Progress] issued a report which analyzed a large quantity of data showing that our children's knowledge of American civics had dropped significantly between 1969 and 1976. The performance of thirteen-year-olds had dropped an alarming 11 percentage points. That the drop has continued since 1976 was confirmed by preliminary results from an NAEP study conducted in late 1985. It was undertaken both because of concern about declining knowledge and because of the growing evidence of a causal connection between the drop in shared information and in literacy. The Foundations of Literacy project is measuring some of the specific information about history and literature that American seventeen-year-olds possess.

Although the full report will not be published until 1987, the preliminary field tests are disturbing. If these samplings hold up, and there is no reason to think they will not, then the results we will be reading in 1987 will show that two-thirds of our seventeen-year-olds do not know that the Civil War occurred between 1850 and 1900. Three-quarters do not know what *reconstruction*

means. Half do not know the meaning of *Brown decision* and cannot identify

either Stalin or Churchill. Three-quarters are unfamiliar with the names of

standard American and British authors. Moreover, our seventeen-year-olds

have little sense of geography or the relative chronology of major events.

Reports of youthful ignorance can no longer be considered merely im-

pressionistic.

This passage doesn't have any title, headings, or subheadings, but as the highlighting shows, it does contain a number of specific names, situations, conditions, and classifications. In addition, a number of points are introduced by or related to signal words such as *serious, significantly, alarming,* and *disturbing.* Altogether, roughly half of the original has been identified as essential to some degree.

Once the list has been trimmed so that it contains only the most essential ideas, they are expressed in correct sentence form and combined to create the summary:

E. D. Hirsch states that today's American high school students generally lack information that American writers believe everyone knows. For example, reports from the National Assessment of Educational Progress show significant declines in students' knowledge of American civics, which supports this view. Also disturbing are the preliminary results of the Foundations of Literacy study. They indicate that two-thirds of those tested didn't know when the Civil War occurred. In addition, large proportions couldn't define *reconstruction,* explain the *Brown decision,* or identify prominent historical figures such as Churchill and Stalin.

This summary is eighty-eight words long, one-quarter the length of the original passage, so it more than fulfills the requirement that it be one-third or less than the original. Even more important, the summary effectively captures and communicates the meaning of the original.

COMPREHENSION AND PRACTICE 16.3

Focusing on Summarizing

1. On the following lines, briefly explain how reading actively can help you begin the process of developing a summary.

When you read actively, you identify the key ideas in a piece of writing through an

examination of the introduction, headings and subheadings, conclusion, signal words,

and any charts, boxed information, lists, and specific names, dates, distances, and so

on. From these key ideas, you develop your summary.

2. In your view, why is providing transition important in preparing a summary? Use the following lines for your answer.

Most students will acknowledge that including transition is important in a summary

because it provides a bridge between the bits of key information that now lack the

supporting details and examples that may have provided a more obvious connection

between these elements in the original.

3. In general, which do you find more difficult, identifying essential information in a document or expressing that information? On a separate sheet of paper, identify the task you find harder and explain why.

CHALLENGE 16.3 Developing an Effective Summary

1. Make a copy of a passage of approximately 500 words from a newspaper, magazine, or book. Following the guidelines presented, create a summary on a separate sheet of paper that is one-third the length of the original.

COLLABORATION

2. Exchange the passage you used as well as your draft summary with a writing partner. Read the passage you receive, and then on a separate sheet of paper evaluate your partner's summary, using the summary checklist below. Return the passage and draft summary, along with your notes, to your reader.

3. Using your partner's comments to guide you, revise your summary.

CW 16.7
Tips for
writing
essay exams

✓ Summary Checklist

☐ Is the main point of the summary clear? Write a brief note in the margin near the beginning of the summary if you think the main point should be stated more directly.

☐ Is there any portion that you think could be reduced or eliminated without making the summary less effective? Put a ✓ next to any section that could be trimmed or cut.

☐ Is there sufficient transition throughout? Put a ✓ next to any spot that could use some transition.

QUICK STUDY | Student Example

This chapter focuses on three common applications of writing. Two involve dealing with the pressure of time. The third involves condensing something without losing the essence of the original. Here is a paragraph on a related subject—an experience when a shortage of time led to a serious mistake:

One day last month, I almost got killed as a result of trying to beat the clock. I had come home from school at 3 P.M. to do some reading for one of my classes before heading to work at the supermarket for 5:30. I sat in my big comfortable living room chair to read, and unfortunately I quickly fell asleep. When I awoke, it was 5:13, which gave me only 17 minutes for a trip that usually took at least 20. I ran to my car, started it up, and raced down the road much faster than the 35 mph posted for the route. But my luck ran out when I reached an intersection a couple of miles from the store. Suddenly, a truck started to cross the road in front of me. I jammed on my brakes, swerved to the right, and went across the sidewalk and into a vacant lot behind it, where I finally came to a stop in a huge cloud of dust. For the next 30 seconds or so, I sat there shaking as I thought about how close I came to hitting that truck broadside. From that day on, no matter how late I am, I just take it slow. The next time I might not be so fortunate.

First complete the following activities in response to this paragraph:

1. On the following lines, explain how the details in the body of this paragraph help to support the main idea expressed in the topic sentence.

   The topic sentence specifies that the paragraph concerns a close call on the roads.

   The specific details and examples in the supporting sentences illustrate how

   dangerous the situation was.

2. On a separate sheet of paper, evaluate this paragraph. Identify what you see as the strongest point and explain why. Also, if you think some area should be developed more fully, indicate and explain that as well.

3. Using the material in this chapter to guide you, provide a brief summary (two-sentence maximum) on the lines that follow of the experience discussed in this paragraph. Answers will vary somewhat. A sample example is given.

   The writer fell asleep at home after returning from school and was in danger of being

   late for work. The writer was speeding to make up time and narrowly avoided a

   collision with a truck, ending up driving across the sidewalk and into a vacant lot.

Now explore the topic in writing. You can respond, as the paragraph above does, to an instance when you had to deal with the pressure of time, or you can respond to one of these other topics related to the focus of this chapter:

- a plea to change the way testing is done in schools
- the best tip you have for improving time management
- what you would keep if you had to eliminate 90 percent of your possessions
- something in your life or in the world at large that would be better if it were greatly reduced or condensed

1. Prewrite on the subject you have chosen, identifying a focus and several key ideas, and then complete a draft paragraph of at least five to ten sentences.

2. Exchange your draft with a classmate. Evaluate the paragraph you receive. If you discover any weaknesses in content or form, make a note in the margin and then return the paper to the writer.

3. Consider the comments and corrections your reader has made and create a final draft of your paragraph.

RECAP Adjusting Your Process: Timed Writing and Summaries

New terms in this chapter	Definitions
essay question	a specific writing assignment given as part of an examination that calls for a clear, concise, multi-paragraph response within a limited period of time.
writing assessment	a writing assignment, often administered with strict time limits, required to qualify for or complete a course or level of education
summary	a greatly reduced version of a document that effectively captures and communicates the essence of the original. sometimes called an *abstract* or *précis*
practice question	an essay question that a student creates to rehearse for an exam Formulate practice questions by identifying key topics in readings and notes.
five-paragraph essay	a format that involves an introductory paragraph introducing three aspects of a subject, a three-paragraph body discussing each of these aspects, and a conclusion recapping these points
signal words	language that emphasizes importance: *crucial, vital, significant, prominent, extraordinary*

The Process of Preparing for an Essay Exam

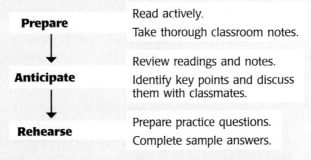

Prepare   Read actively.
Take thorough classroom notes.

Anticipate   Review readings and notes.
Identify key points and discuss them with classmates.

Rehearse   Prepare practice questions.
Complete sample answers.

(continued)

Points to Consider When Completing a Writing Assessment

Recognize the difficulties of writing under time.

Identify exactly what is being asked.

Divide up the stages of the writing process on the basis of the time available.

Consider using the five-paragraph essay format.

Make your writing as clear and complete as possible.

The Process of Creating a Summary

1. **Actively read the original document.**
   Note title, the introduction, any headings, and conclusion.
   Reread, highlighting key ideas.
   - Note signal words.
   - Note charts, boxed information, and lists.
   - Note statistics and specific names, dates, amounts, and distances.

2. **List the key ideas.**
   Express them in your own words.
   Write them in sentences.

3. **Edit the list to reflect only the most essential information.**
   Eliminate multiple references.
   Cut lengthy examples and supplemental information.

4. **Use the sentences you have written to create a draft summary.**
   Make the summary coherent and complete.
   Don't include your own opinion.
   Add necessary transition.

5. **Revise the draft.**
   Does it make sense independent of the original?
   Is there enough transition?
   Is it free from any commentary?
   Are there any remaining errors?

GOING FORWARD . . .

CW 16.8 Timed writing review

Q: It definitely feels different—so much more intense—when I write a summary or complete a timed writing compared to writing a paragraph or essay outside of class. Is there anything special I can do to deal with the pressure I feel?

A: It feels different when you tackle these kinds of assignments because it *is* different. The pressure you feel is not your imagination. But pressure doesn't have to paralyze you. What you need to do is recognize that you won't be able to do your best possible work under these circumstances—few people can. Instead, set your sights on doing the best work you are capable of doing *under these circumstances*. Your work won't be as polished as it would be if you completed the work under a less strict time line, but that doesn't mean it won't be good.

PART 4

Developing Sentence Sense

CHAPTER 17
The Sentence

Navigating This Chapter

In this chapter, you will discover how to identify and use:

- action verbs, linking verbs, helping verbs, verb phrases, and compound verbs
- simple subjects, complete subjects, and compound subjects

GETTING STARTED

CW 17.1
Chapter basics

Q: I've completed some prewriting on my subject and developed a focus for my paper. Now I have to turn my prewriting ideas into complete sentences. How do I make sure that I communicate my focus and supporting ideas in proper sentence form?

A: To make sure that you express your focus and your good supporting ideas in complete sentence form, you need to check for the basic components of a sentence in each unit you write. That means you need to make sure that each verb has a subject and that the resulting unit expresses a complete thought.

Overview: Understanding Sentence Basics

ESL Note
See "Sentence Basics" on pages 589–590 and "Word Order" on pages 591–592.

CW 17.2
Overview of sentence basics

Learning to recognize and construct complete sentences is crucial to your success as a writer. For a group of words to be a **sentence**, it must contain a *subject* and *verb* and express a complete thought. The verb represents the action or condition presented. The subject is the doer of the action or the person, place, thing, or idea that is being described. Keep in mind that many of the sentences you write will have more than one subject–verb unit. But to qualify as a sentence, a group of words must have at least one subject–verb unit that makes independent sense.

Understanding Verbs

CW 17.3
Understanding verbs

By definition, a **verb** is a word that shows action or a link between the subject and another word that renames or describes it. In most English sentences, the subject precedes the verb. However, when you're identifying the components in the sentence, look for the verb before you look for the subject. Without a verb, there would be no subject.

A verb that describes what the subject did, does, or might do is called an **action verb:**

CW 17.4
Action verbs

EXAMPLE | Sally *sang* six songs at the party last night.

We *enjoyed* her performance.

Not all verbs are action verbs. A **linking verb** links the subject and a word that identifies or describes it, indicating a state of being. Take a look at these common linking verbs and the examples that follow:

CW 17.5
Linking verbs

Common Linking Verbs

forms of *to be* (am, is, was, were, will be, might have been, etc.)	feel become appear	look seem taste, smell

EXAMPLE | In high school, Sun Yee *was* a member of the Student Council.

Gregory *seems* happy with his choice.

Was is a linking verb because it connects *Sun Yee* with a word that identifies her: *member.* The linking verb *seems* links *Gregory* with the descriptive word *happy.*

To identify the verb in a sentence, try asking yourself *what word describes action or shows a connection between two things?*

Sometimes the verb in a sentence is composed of more than one word. These verbs may be either verb phrases or compound verbs. A **verb phrase** is a *main verb* plus a *helping verb,* as the italicized words in the following examples show:

EXAMPLE |

helping   main
verb   verb
Rosa *is managing* the office.

helping main
verb   verb
They *had bought* several sweaters last month.

Study the list of common helping verbs shown here:

Common Helping Verbs

am	being	do	have	must	were
are	can	does	is	shall	will
be	could	had	may	should	would
been	did	has	might	was	

CW 17.6
Verb
phrases

A **compound verb** consists of two or more verbs connected by *and* or *or*, which share the same subject. Look at the italicized verbs in the following examples:

EXAMPLE

During the rainstorm, the house lights *blinked* and *flickered.*

Uncle Tony *was, is,* and always *will be* a Red Sox fan.

FAST FACT   It isn't a verb but a form of a verb called a *verbal*—in this case, an *infinitive*—that makes one of the single most famous and recognizable sentences in all of literature so memorable. This infinitive, repeated twice in a row, in both positive and negative form, is spoken by Hamlet in Act III, Scene I, line 56, of William Shakespeare's magnificent tragedy of the same name: "To be, or not to be—that is the question. . . ."

COMPREHENSION AND PRACTICE

17.1

CW 17.7
Identifying
verbs

Identifying Verbs

Underline the verbs in the following sentences. In the space above each, label the verb *A* (action) or *L* (linking). Remember—some verbs may be phrases or compound; check to be sure you have underlined the whole verb. Use the example to guide you.

EXAMPLE

                                                          A
Attitudes toward technology in education <u>have changed</u> in recent years.

                                                                      A
(1) Since the beginning of the twentieth century, many women <u>have</u>
                                                                      L
<u>fought</u> for equal rights. (2) Because of their efforts, life for today's women <u>is</u>
clearly better than in any other time in American history. (3) In the early
                                          A
1900s, for example, Margaret Sanger <u>took</u> a stand on birth control. (4) During
                              A
this time, Sanger bravely <u>challenged</u> vice laws concerning birth control. (5) She
   A
<u>took</u> the extraordinary step of distributing information about contraception. (6)
                         A   A
In addition, she <u>researched</u> and <u>wrote</u> *Family Limitation,* a book dealing with
this controversial subject. (7) An educational tool for family planning like this
              L
one <u>was</u> not available to the general public before this. (8) Sanger actually
   A
<u>served</u> time in jail because of her activism. (9) The availability of safe, legal
                               L
birth control today <u>is</u> the result of her crusade for reform. (10) Women today
   A
<u>enjoy</u> greater freedom and a better quality of life because of Sanger's efforts.

COMPREHENSION AND PRACTICE

Using Verbs in Your Writing

CW 17.8 More practice with identifying verbs

17.2 Choose ten of the following verbs, verb phrases, and compound verbs. Use them to write ten sentences on a separate sheet of paper.

1. pass and dribble	has found	records	opens
2. scurries	decays	celebrated	protested
3. had called	are discussing	jogs	have thought
4. have moved	study or fail	mix	triumphed

CHALLENGE 17.1   Identifying and Evaluating Verbs in an Essay

1. Choose a selection from Part Seven that you would like to read. As you read, identify verbs that the author has used in ten sentences.

2. On a separate piece of paper, copy these sentences, and label the verb(s) in each: *action* or *linking*. Also label any *verb phrases* or *compound verbs*.

COLLABORATION

3. Share the sentences with your classmates. On the paper you receive, indicate which of the action verbs that you have identified are the most effective and why.

Recognizing Subjects

CW 17.9 Recognizing subjects and verbs

In addition to a verb, the second component required for a group of words to be a sentence is a **subject.** In a sentence, the subject is the word that performs the verb's action or condition. It is either a **noun,** a word that names a person, place, thing, or idea, or a **pronoun,** a word that substitutes for a noun. Finding a subject is easy. First, find the verb, and then ask yourself *who or what is doing what is being discussed?* The word that answers the question is the subject.

What are the verbs and the subjects in the sentences below?

EXAMPLE

The sales representative asked several preliminary questions.

The bus will be late because of the accident downtown.

In the first example, the verb is *asked.* Now ask *who or what asked several preliminary questions?* The subject is *sales representative.* In the second example, the verb is *will be.* Ask *who or what will be late because of the accident downtown?* The subject is *bus.*

Most sentences have both a simple subject and a complete subject. The **simple subject** is an individual word that identifies who or what is doing the action or being discussed. The **complete subject** is that simple subject plus any words or phrases that describe or modify it. A **modifier** is a word or a group of words that describe a noun or pronoun, telling *which one* or *what kind.*

In the sentences below, both the verbs and complete subjects are identified. Find the simple subject of each sentence.

EXAMPLE

┌────────────── complete subject ──────────────┐ ┌────── verb ──────┐
Inexpensive wireless phones with Internet capability have recently *been intro-*

┌──┐
duced.

┌──────────complete subject──────────┐ ┌verb┐
An apartment in those complexes offers an affordable option for working families.

In the first sentence, the simple subject is *phones.* In the second sentence, it is *apartment.*

Being able to identify the simple subject is important because the verb must *agree with* or match the simple subject. Modifiers in the complete subject can mislead you into selecting the wrong verb form, especially if the words are in a **prepositional phrase.** For more about subject–verb agreement see Chapter 21. A prepositional phrase begins with a *preposition* and ends with a noun or pronoun called the *object of the preposition.* The preposition *relates* that noun or pronoun to another word in the sentence, often by indicating location, direction, or time. Here is a list of common prepositions:

Common Prepositions

about	behind	during	on	to
above	below	except	onto	toward
across	beneath	for	out	under
after	beside	from	outside	underneath
against	besides	in	over	unlike
along	between	inside	past	until
among	beyond	into	since	up
around	but (except)	like	than	upon
as	by	near	through	with
at	despite	of	throughout	within
before	down	off	till	without

Consider again the examples above, this time with the prepositional phrases italicized:

EXAMPLE

┌── prepositional phrase ──┐
Inexpensive wireless phones *with Internet capability* have recently been introduced.

┌prepositional phrase┐
An apartment *in those complexes* offers an affordable option for working families.

In the first sentence, the preposition is *with,* and the object of the preposition is the singular word *capability.* In the second, the preposition is *in,* and the object of the preposition is the plural word *complexes.* Writers sometimes make the mistake of making the verb agree with the object of the preposition rather than with the simple subject. Remember—*an object cannot be a subject.* Therefore, be careful to identify the simple subject.

Sometimes a **compound subject** answers the question *who or what is doing the action or being discussed?* Compound subjects consist of two or more nouns or pronouns, usually connected by *and* or *or.* These subjects may cause confusion for writers, who must decide whether the subject is singular or plural.

EXAMPLE

Dana or Rebekka answers the phone in the office after 5 P.M.

Squirrels, birds, and opossums live in the trees and shrubs behind the cafeteria.

In the first sentence, the verb is *answers,* and the answer to the question *who or what answers?* is the compound subject, *Dana or Rebekka. Or* implies a choice. Only one person answers the phone, so the verb is singular. In the second sentence, the verb is *live,* and the answer to the question *who or what live?* is the compound subject, *squirrels, birds, and opossums. And* implies addition, making the subject plural. All these animals live in the trees and shrubs, so the verb is plural.

As Chapter 8, "Process," explains, with the **imperative mood** or **command,** the subject is *understood* rather than explicitly stated. When you write, "Place your shoes in plastic bags before packing them in your suitcase," the subject isn't actually expressed. Yet, it is obvious that you are saying, "**You** place your shoes in plastic bags before packing them in your suitcase." In other words, the subject is *understood* to be **you.**

FAST FACT The shortest complete sentence in English is two letters long: the command, "Go!" The shortest declarative sentence is three letters long: "I am."

COMPREHENSION AND PRACTICE

17.3

CW 17.10 **Identifying subjects**

Distinguishing between the Simple and the Complete Subject

Underline the complete subject, and circle the simple subject in the sentences below. Remember—the simple subject is the specific noun or pronoun that is doing the action or being discussed. Use the example as a guide.

EXAMPLE

The (crowd) in the streets waited impatiently for the beginning of the fireworks display.

(1) Sports (championships) on television attract huge viewing audiences. (2) The NCAA Final Four Basketball (tournament) in March is one good example. (3) Tennis (fans) can cheer for their favorite players in the popular Wimbledon tournament during July. (4) The glitzy (Super Bowl) with its hours of pregame shows attracts the most armchair quarterbacks all year. (5) However, the traditional (favorite) of many couch potato fans is still October's World Series.

COMPREHENSION AND PRACTICE

Identifying the Principal Parts of Compound Subjects

17.4 Each sentence in the following paragraph has a compound subject. Underline these compound subjects and then circle the principal parts—the simple subjects—making up the compound sentence, as the example shows.

EXAMPLE

Ceiling (fans) and window (fans) can help cool a room and avoid the high cost of air conditioning.

(1) My (brothers) and (sisters,) our (friends,) and (I) used to treat the Greene Schoolyard in our old neighborhood as our personal playground. (2) My best friend (Benni) and (I) would have a jump rope contest near the front door of the school every afternoon. (3) My sister (Linna) or (another) of the older girls would be the contest judge. (4) Around back, my older brothers (Ronnie) and (Ramon) had drawn a big chalked square on the brick wall for speed ball games. (5) During speed ball, a form of baseball, the older (boys) and a (few) of the girls would pitch a rubber ball against the square. (6) A chalk (mark) on the ball or a (smudge) in the square was evidence of a strike. (7) Late (summer) and early (spring) marked football and soccer season. (8) The narrow (lawn) at the side of the building and the dirt (yard) behind it were perfect fields for these sports. (9) Every afternoon after school, my brother (James) and (one) of the other big kids would divide up the rest of us into two teams. (10) The (lawn,) the dirt (yard,) and the (rest) of the schoolyard are all gone now, with two big additions to the school filling space.

CHALLENGE 17.2 **Using Compound Subjects in Your Writing**

1. On the next page is a list of compound subjects. Choose ten of these subjects, and on a separate piece of paper, write a sentence using each one. Add modifiers if you wish.

heat and humidity	a shovel and rake
swimming or sailing	soccer and football
red meat, eggs, and cheese	travel and tourism
hardcovers and paperbacks	Macintosh and Gateway
wind and rain	my father and mother
winning or losing	breakfast and lunch

2. Exchange sentences with a partner. Underline the verbs in each sentence; then return the draft to its writer. Check your sentences to be sure each has a correct verb. If not, revise your sentences to be sure they are correct and complete.

CHAPTER QUICK CHECK Sentence Basics

CW 17.11 Sentence- level editing

In each sentence in the following passage, identify all subjects and verbs. Underline each complete subject, and then circle each simple subject. With any compound subjects, circle each of the simple subjects within it. Double underline all verbs, verb phrases, and compound verbs. Put an X in front of any sentence in the imperative mood. Use the example to guide you.

EXAMPLE

The (lawyer) with her briefcase and her client with a small notebook had been stopped and searched by the police officer at the door.

(1) Because of a recent technological development, a complete (book) can be produced in less than an hour. (2) (Experts) in this field refer to this innovation as Print on Demand and believe strongly in its future. (3) With this technology, (books) and other (documents) are digitized and stored in electronic form. (4) Individual (customers) and small (businesses) can then select books and print them up right in the bookstore. (5) As a result of this development, the (problem) of out-of-print books should be greatly reduced or completely eliminated. (6) In electronic form, a (book) will never go out of print or be out of stock. (7) Major (publishers) of commercial and academic books can now publish smaller batches of books and save money as a result. X (8) Think of the possibilities. (9) For instance, without a contract, (novelists,) short story (writers,) and (poets) have few publishing opportunities. (10) With Print on Demand, these (people) can fulfill their publishing dreams and distribute their work themselves.

QUICK STUDY   Student Example

This chapter examines the components necessary to present something in complete form. Here is a paragraph on a related subject—two concepts, characteristics, or people that in your view belong together:

Confidence is an important personal quality, but it should always be accompanied by common sense. For example, no matter how confident people feel before an exam, they would be foolish not to study or at least review the material before the test. The same thing is true for athletic activities. It's one thing to be confident about swimming a long distance in a pool or completing a difficult climb on a climbing wall. At the same time, it would be silly not to recognize that swimming in the open water and climbing an actual cliff are much more dangerous. Police officers, fire fighters, and others in high-risk occupations depend on a mixture of confidence and common sense. Confidence enables them to act quickly and decisively, but common sense helps to keep them from ignoring their training and taking a step that could put them or somebody else in unnecessary danger. In every aspect of life, then, the secret is to maintain a balance between confidence and common sense.

First complete the following activities in response to this paragraph:

1. On the following lines, briefly explain how the topic sentence prepares the reader for the discussion in this paragraph.

   The topic sentence states that confidence must be tempered with common sense,

   and then the supporting sentences provide illustrations of why.

2. In your view, which sentence provides the strongest support for the topic sentence? On a separate sheet of paper, write the sentence, underlining all verbs and circling all subjects, using the material in this chapter to guide you. Then explain why you think this sentence offers the strongest support.

3. Do you agree with the order of the examples in this paragraph or would you recommend a different arrangement? Use the lines on the next page to explain your reasoning.

Answers may vary. Most students will agree with the arrangement of the examples,

but some may suggest moving one or more of the examples because they feel the

overall impact would be improved.

Now explore the topic in writing. As the paragraph above does, you can discuss two ideas or people that in your view shouldn't be separated, or choose one of these other topics related to the focus of this chapter:

- what you feel is necessary to feel complete as a person
- the elements necessary for a group or team to function effectively
- a conversation you misunderstood because something was left out or not made clear
- an action you wish you had taken in response to some problem you faced

1. Prewrite on the subject you have chosen, identifying a focus and several key ideas, and then complete a draft paragraph of at least five to ten sentences.

2. Exchange your draft with a classmate. Evaluate the paragraph you receive. If you discover any problems spots, especially in terms of complete sentences, make a note in the margin and then return the paper to the writer.

3. Consider the comments and corrections your reader has made and create a final draft of your paragraph.

SUMMARY EXERCISE Sentence Basics

In each sentence in the following passage, identify all subjects and verbs. Underline each complete subject, and then circle each simple subject. With any compound subjects, circle each of the simple subjects within it. Double underline all verbs, verb phrases, and compound verbs. Put an X in front of any sentence in the imperative mood.

(1) Honor students are not always the smartest students in class. (2) They probably organize, plan, and prepare the most effectively, however.

(3) Organized students purchase necessary tools for their classes. (4) The items and equipment at the top of their shopping list might include an assignment notebook and calendar, highlight markers, and folders. (5) A pocket dictionary and computer disks are other useful tools.

(6) Successful students with job or family commitments have scheduled manageable study time in advance. (7) They have analyzed their time needs

for study and balanced their schedules. (8) Study schedules must be flexible and realistic. (9) Emergencies can happen and may interrupt work on assignments. (10) A list of assignments and due dates is an excellent planning tool. (11) Less serious students do the fun, easy assignments first. (12) Successful students, however, complete the assignments in a logical order. (13) They tackle challenges a step at a time.

(14) Preparation also leads to good grades. (15) One good study technique is called prereading. (16) Smart students preview the textbook materials before the lecture. (17) Introductions, chapter highlights, and review sections often emphasize key points. (18) Successful students read assignments on time, take good class notes, and anticipate test questions. (19) This preparation before the day of a test repays them with good scores as well as better learning.

(20) Good grades are within your reach. (21) Make effective study habits your number one priority.

FOR FURTHER EXPLORATION

1. Consider one of the following topics:

   - the use of cameras in the courtroom
   - the importance of thinking young
   - the behavior of tourists
   - an experience you wish you could live over
   - a rule or law you would like to see changed

   Prewrite on the subject, using one of the strategies you practiced in Chapter 2, and work your way through the rest of the writing process. Then complete a draft essay of at least 500 words on this subject.

COLLABORATION

2. Exchange your draft with a classmate. Check the draft you receive for weaknesses, especially errors in subject–verb usage. Mark any word groups in which a subject or a verb is missing, using the material in this chapter as a guide, and then return the draft to the writer.

3. Revise your essay, correcting any errors in subject–verb usage or other problems discovered by your reader.

RECAP The Sentence

New terms in this chapter	Definitions
sentence	a series of words containing a subject and verb and expressing a complete thought
verb	a word or words that describe the action or the condition of the subject
action verb	a word or words expressing action completed by the subject **EXAMPLE** Marcel *held* the door for his sister.
linking verb	a word or words connecting the subject with other words that identify or describe it The most common linking verbs are the forms of *to be.* **EXAMPLE** Katherine *is* an excellent athlete.
verb phrase	a main verb plus one or more helping verbs **EXAMPLE** Karen *has been taking* dancing lessons for five years.
compound verb	two or more verbs connected by a conjunction and relating to the same subject **EXAMPLE** Shannon *cooked* and *served* the meal.
subject	the noun or pronoun that is the doer of the action or the focus of the verb Find the subject by answering the question *who or what is doing the action or being discussed?* **EXAMPLE** *Paul* enjoyed the party.
noun	a word that names a person, place, or thing **EXAMPLE** The *river* overflowed its banks.
pronoun	a word that substitutes for a noun **EXAMPLE** *He* loves to tell ghost stories.
simple subject	the noun or pronoun that answers the question *who or what is doing the action or being discussed?*
complete subject	the simple subject plus any words or phrases that describe or modify it **EXAMPLE** The *books on that shelf* are best-sellers.

(continued)

New terms in this chapter	Definitions
modifier	a word or group of words that tell you *which* or *what kind* when used with a noun or pronoun
	EXAMPLE *My older, wiser* sister gave me *some good* advice.
prepositional phrase	a group of words beginning with a preposition and ending with a noun or pronoun that is the object of the preposition
	The subject of a sentence can *never* be in a prepositional phrase.
	EXAMPLE The clothes *on the floor* are dirty.
subject–verb agreement	a state in which the subject and verb agree in number
compound subject	two or more nouns or pronouns connected by a conjunction and acting as the subject for the same verb
	EXAMPLE Our wonderful *friends* and our dear *neighbors* collected money to help us after the fire.

The Basic Elements of a Sentence

Subject ———— **Verb**

↓

Expression of a Complete Thought

GOING FORWARD...

CW 17.12 Grammer and style: an editing checklist

Q: The ideas I've developed are good—I feel confident about that. So isn't that enough—is it really so important that they be expressed in complete sentences?

A: Yes—if you want your reader to appreciate your good ideas, you have to present them in a way that your reader can fully comprehend them. That means complete sentences. There is no other way to ensure that your reader will understand your ideas the way you do.

CHAPTER 18
Fragments

Navigating This Chapter

In this chapter, you will learn how to avoid and correct fragments created by:

- omitting a subject or a verb
- mistaking a phrase for a sentence
- mistaking a subordinate clause for a sentence
- mistaking an appositive for a sentence

GETTING STARTED...

**CW 18.1
Chapter
basics**

Q: I know a sentence fragment is a serious writing error, but I'm not sure why. What is it about a fragment that makes it such a big deal?

A: Think of the name of the error—*fragment*. A fragment is a piece of something larger. A sentence fragment is a big deal because it is only a portion of a sentence, which makes it *incomplete communication*.

Overview: Recognizing and Writing Complete Sentences

**CW 18.2
Overview of
writing
complete
sentences**

To communicate your full meaning to your reader, you must make sure you express your good ideas in correct sentence form. That means you must avoid **sentence fragments,** units in which one of the elements required for a complete sentence is missing. In other words, sentence fragments lack a verb or a subject or fail to communicate a complete thought to the reader. Sentence fragments are serious errors. Because they do not convey complete ideas, fragments can leave readers unclear about your intended meaning.

Correcting Fragments with Missing Subjects or Verbs

ESL Note
See "Sentence Basics"
on pages 589–590.

**CW 18.3
Recognizing
sentence
fragments**

Fragments occur for several reasons. One common cause is the lack of a verb or subject. As the previous chapter shows, to be a sentence, a group of words must contain a verb and subject. When you are checking your own sentences, first identify the verb. If you cannot find an action or linking verb, the group of words is a fragment. Look at the following group of words:

FRAGMENT   The use of acupuncture to treat rheumatoid arthritis.

**CW 18.4
Sentence
fragments:
an example**

There is no verb here, only a noun and its modifiers, so this group of words is a fragment. To change it to a sentence, add a verb and complete the thought.

REVISED   The use of acupuncture to treat rheumatoid arthritis *shows* the growing influence of alternative medicine.

Sometimes a group of words has a subject and a word or group of words that seems to be a verb but in fact cannot function as a verb. These words, called **verbals,** are verb forms that can't communicate a complete action or meaning. Consider the italicized verbals in the following groups of words:

FRAGMENT   The front-end manager *looking* for volunteers for an overtime shift.

Daisy *spoken* to Clarise an hour before the accident.

Eddie *to run* the Chicago Marathon again.

All three groups of words are fragments because they contain verbals, not verbs. To make them into sentences, substitute true verbs for the verbals, as these versions show:

SENTENCES   The front-end manager *looked* for volunteers for an overtime shift.

or

The front-end manager *is looking* for volunteers for an overtime shift.

SENTENCES   Daisy *spoke* to Clarise an hour before the accident.

or

Daisy *had spoken* to Clarise an hour before the accident.

SENTENCES   Eddie *ran* the Chicago Marathon again.

or

Eddie *will run* the Chicago Marathon again.

See Part Five, "Understanding Subjects and Verbs," for more on using verbs correctly.

Even if a group of words has a verb, it's not a sentence unless it also has a subject. As the previous chapter showed, the subject is the word or group of words that answers the question *who or what is doing the action or being discussed?* If no word answers the question, then there is no subject, and the group of words is a fragment.

Consider the following group of words:

FRAGMENT Told Sally's boss about Sally's excellent computer skills.

This group of words is not a sentence. There is a verb—*told*—but if you ask *who or what told*, there is no answer.

To correct this fragment, simply add a subject:

┌──── subject ────┐
SENTENCE *Professor Tessier* told Sally's boss about Sally's excellent computer skills.

FAST FACT On occasion, experienced writers use what can be called an *intentional fragment,* a group of words that is deliberately expressed as an incomplete sentence, to create some effect. Perhaps the longest and best-known intentional fragment appears in James Joyce's extraordinary novel *Ulysses.* The final section of the book, which records Molly Bloom's thoughts as she lies in bed, is a 46-page fragment, beginning and ending with the same word, "Yes."

COMPREHENSION AND PRACTICE

Correcting Fragments with Missing or Incomplete Verbs

18.1 The following groups of words are fragments because they contain verbals, not verbs. Correct each fragment by (1) crossing out the misused word and writing an appropriate verb above it or (2) adding a verb. There is more than one way to correct each fragment. Use the example to guide you. Answers may vary. Likely answers are given.

CW 18.5 Correcting fragments

pressed
EXAMPLE The dry cleaner ~~pressing~~ my good white shirt.

baked
(1) My aunt Julia ~~baking~~ the most delicious sweets. (2) The whole family
gathered
~~to gather~~ at her home every Sunday evening for dessert. (3) She ~~serving~~ hot
served
ate   visited
apple pie, rich chocolate cake, or creamy pudding. (4) We ~~eating~~ and ~~visiting~~
was
for a couple of hours. (5) This tradition ~~being~~ our family's favorite weekend

activity.

COMPREHENSION AND PRACTICE

Correcting Fragments with Missing Subjects or Verbs

CW 18.6
Correcting fragments

18.2 The following groups of words are fragments because they lack a subject, a verb, or a helping verb. On the lines provided, write an appropriate subject or verb, and complete the thought. Label your added portions *S* or *V*. Use the example as a guide. Answers may vary. Likely answers are given.

EXAMPLE   Wildflowers _____*bloomed*_____ by the roadside.

CW 18.7
Identifying fragments and complete sentences

1. _____S_____
   _____The victim_____ picked the robber from a police lineup.

2. Shirley _____V_____
   _____*began*_____ running after the bus.

3. _____S_____
   _____Wine_____ is a good gift to give if you don't know the recipient very well.

4. The cookbook _____V_____
   _____*includes*_____ the complete recipe in Spanish.

5. The chocolate roses _____V_____
   _____*were*_____ melting in the hot midday sun.

COMPREHENSION AND PRACTICE

Identifying and Correcting Fragments with Missing Subjects and Verbs

CW 18.8
Correcting verbals

18.3 The following passage contains several fragments that lack either a subject or a verb. Underline each fragment, and then correct each by adding a subject or a verb above the appropriate spot and a ^ below it. Use the example to guide you.

EXAMPLE

The food in the cooler had
^ H̶a̶d̶ to be thrown out because of contamination.

(1) A few weeks ago, I visited a wonderful place, a newly opened butterfly sanctuary. (2) The sanctuary itself $\underset{\wedge}{\overset{is}{\text{}}}$ a large closed area within a larger building.

(3) In this area, flowering plants are arranged in a number of small garden settings. (4) R̶u̶n̶ ̶a̶c̶r̶o̶s̶s̶ $\underset{\wedge}{\overset{\text{Several paths crisscross}}{\text{}}}$ the sanctuary, allowing people easy access to the entire area. (5) The butterflies $\underset{\wedge}{\overset{\text{live}}{\text{}}}$ in a completely safe environment, with no predators of any kind. (6) As a result, they are able to fly around and feed freely. (7) C̶a̶n̶ $\underset{\wedge}{\overset{\text{Visitors can}}{\text{}}}$ walk right up to brightly colored butterflies for a close look at their delicate features and distinct wing patterns. (8) Sometimes, butterflies land on people's clothing. (9) Above the exit, a sign asks people to check themselves to avoid

CW 18.9
More on
sentence
fragments

The beautiful scene within that sanctuary

accidentally taking butterflies out the door upon leaving. (10) ~~Will~~ remain with
                                                                 ^

me for a long time.

CHALLENGE 18.1 **Writing Supporting Sentences for a Paragraph**

COLLABORATION

Working with a partner, compose a paragraph of at least five sentences to support one of the topic sentences listed below.

1. Knowledge of a second language is important in today's global economy.

2. Reading a book is more satisfying than watching a movie based on that book.

Exchange your sentences with another writing team. Check the paper you receive for fragments. Write *frag* in the margin beside each fragment you find. Return the paper to its writers. Make any corrections needed to your paper.

Correcting Phrase Fragments

CW 18.10
Correcting
phrase
fragments

A *phrase* is a group of two or more related words that lacks a subject–verb unit. As the previous chapter indicated, two common types of phrases are *verb phrases* (page 259) and *prepositional phrases* (pages 262–263). When a phrase is left to stand alone, it is a **phrase fragment**.

Look at the following groups of words:

FRAGMENT Will soon be sleeping.

Inside the house.

The first example is a verb phrase, and the second is a prepositional phrase. They both lack a subject–verb combination, so both are fragments.

To correct phrases that are incorrectly used as sentences, you need to supply the missing elements, as these versions show:

— subject —

SENTENCE *My grandfather* will soon be sleeping.

subject verb

Daryl left his jacket inside the house.

**COMPREHENSION
AND PRACTICE
18.4**

Identifying and Correcting Phrase Fragments

The following passage contains several fragments resulting from phrases used incorrectly as sentences. Underline these fragments. Then, on a separate piece of paper, rewrite the paragraph, turning the fragments into sentences. Use the example to guide you. Answers will vary.

EXAMPLE	Under the porch.

The frightened kitten hid under the porch.

(1) Being a musician demands a lot of dedication. (2) Have to practice hours daily. (3) Some musicians keep an unusual schedule. (4) Until the early morning hours. (5) Then they sleep until the afternoon. (6) Family life becomes difficult. (7) With this work schedule. (8) Sometimes musicians face weeks without employment. (9) Through all this, musicians keep playing. (10) Have a need to bring the joy of music to their audiences.

COMPREHENSION AND PRACTICE

Rewriting Phrases as Sentences

18.5 On a separate sheet of paper, turn the following verb phrases and prepositional phrases into sentences by adding subjects or verbs or both and completing the thoughts. Use the example as a guide. Answers will vary.

EXAMPLE	over the lake

The sun dawning over the lake was beautiful.

1. throughout the neighborhood

2. inside my room

3. were laughing

4. on the subway

5. have been warned

6. behind the warehouse

7. will leave soon

8. through the back door

9. are playing

10. was canceled

Correcting Subordinate Clause Fragments

Even if a group of words contains a subject and a verb, it is still a fragment if it does not express a complete thought. For example, a **subordinate clause fragment** contains a subject and a verb, but it cannot stand on its own. Its function is to explain or describe another portion of the sentence. It is called *subordinate* because it depends on a **main clause,** the primary subject–verb unit of the sentence, to make complete sense.

Look at these subordinate clause fragments:

FRAGMENT

⌐subject⌐ ⌐— verb —⌐
After the *EMTs arrived.*

⌐ subject —⌐ ⌐verb⌐
That *Michaela saw* outside the bus station.

Both examples have subjects and verbs, but neither one expresses a complete thought. Each leaves the reader waiting for more information.

To correct this type of fragment, you have a couple of choices. You could add or delete words so that the clause makes sense on its own:

SENTENCE

The EMTs arrived within minutes of receiving the emergency call.

Michaela saw Theo outside the bus station.

In the first sentence, *after* has been deleted, and *within minutes of receiving the emergency call* has been added. In the second sentence, *That* has been deleted, and *Theo* has been added. Both groups of words are now sentences. Furthermore, the meaning of both groups of words has changed considerably.

You can also choose to correct this type of fragment by adding a main clause to the subordinate clause. Together, they should express a complete thought:

SENTENCE

After the EMTs arrived, *they began treating the injured people immediately.*

The car that Michaela saw outside the bus station *was broken down.*

These changes make the meaning of the original clauses clearer and more specific. They do not alter the meaning as the preceding corrections do.

FAST FACT The nature of conversation helps to explain why some fragments occur in writing. In spoken discussion, when one person asks, "Why didn't you call?" the other person generally doesn't repeat the words just expressed in the question. Instead, the second person gives just the answer, something like, "Because I lost your number." It works in conversation because both people are present. But writing isn't talking. You need both parts of the discourse to make a complete sentence, and when people forget to do so, a fragment results.

COMPREHENSION **Identifying Subordinate Clause Fragments**
AND PRACTICE

18.6 The following passage contains several subordinate clause fragments. Underline these fragments, as the example shows.

EXAMPLE <u>Even though the new movie had received poor reviews.</u> The crowd waiting to see it was huge.

(1) In the near future, your pockets or purse may no longer jingle the same way. (2) <u>Because the penny may soon disappear from use.</u> (3) <u>Although not everyone agrees with their stance.</u> (4) Some merchants and retail groups are asking the government to eliminate this coin. (5) In their view, the penny no longer serves a useful purpose. (6) <u>That it had served over its long history.</u> (7) These critics complain about the nuisance factor of dealing with all those pennies. (8) <u>Unless the purchase is for an even amount of money.</u> (9) Every cash transaction involves the use of several pennies. (10) According to people pushing to eliminate the penny, a better plan is to round off all final prices to denominations ending in 5 or 10.

COMPREHENSION **Rewriting Subordinate Clauses as Sentences**
AND PRACTICE

18.7 On a separate sheet of paper, turn the following subordinate clauses into sentences by adding a main clause. Check your work for correct use of capitals and punctuation. Use the example to guide you. Answers will vary.

EXAMPLE even though the class had ended

The students continued their discussion, even though the class had ended.

1. who plans to ride to the game on the team bus

2. whenever a false alarm is sounded

3. which hung on a chain around her neck

4. until I get a haircut

5. so that I can improve my keyboarding skills

6. unless management agrees to give them a raise

7. although it won two Academy Awards

8. in order that my wife and I could both attend the concert

9. because the neighborhood parents petitioned the school department

10. since it wasn't my fault

COMPREHENSION AND PRACTICE

18.8

Identifying and Correcting Subordinate Clause Fragments

The following passage contains several subordinate clause fragments. Underline these fragments. Then, on a separate piece of paper, rewrite the paragraph, turning the fragments into sentences. Use the example as a guide.

EXAMPLE

Who has a quick temper.

My boss, who has a quick temper, should learn how to relax.

(1) Sweetgrass basket making is a historic craft. (2) Which dates back to the late 1600s in this country. (3) When slaves from West Africa were brought to South Carolina. (4) They brought their skills in cultivating rice. (5) Their knowledge was essential to plantation owners. (6) Because these Europeans had little experience with growing rice. (7) To winnow the rice, slave women made durable, pliable household baskets. (8) The women chose the plentiful sweetgrass to work with. (9) Although more and more coastal farmers started to cultivate rice. (10) The craft of sweetgrass basket making stayed locally in and around Charleston, South Carolina, among the descendants of these slaves.

CHALLENGE 18.2   Analyzing and Completing Sentences

COLLABORATION

To make sure each sentence you revised in Comprehension and Practice 18.8 expresses a complete thought, ask a partner to read your completed revision aloud, pausing for a few seconds after the period at the end of each sentence. Note any groups of words you hear that can't stand on their own. Turn these groups of words into complete sentences. Repeat this process for your partner.

Correcting Appositive Fragments

An **appositive** is a word or group of words that renames or explains another noun or pronoun. Some appositives contain subjects and verbs, but like subordinate clauses, appositives don't express complete thoughts on their own.

Look at the following appositives:

FRAGMENT

The spot where my *car had broken* down.

A talent *she* usually *kept* hidden.

Both groups of words have subjects and verbs, but both are fragments because they don't express complete thoughts.

To eliminate this kind of fragment, you can change and adjust the order of the words to express a complete thought:

SENTENCE

My *car had broken* down at that spot.

She usually *kept* that talent hidden.

Alternatively, you can join the fragment with a main clause so that it expresses a complete thought:

SENTENCE

Fortunately, a car dealership was on the corner, the spot where my car had broken down. (*The appositive now focuses on* corner.)

Tami entertained the crowd by singing, a talent she usually kept hidden. (*The appositive now modifies* singing.)

COMPREHENSION AND PRACTICE

18.9

Identifying and Correcting Appositive Fragments

The following passage contains several appositive fragments. Underline these fragments. Then, on a separate piece of paper, turn those fragments into complete sentences. Use the example to guide you.

EXAMPLE

A task that frustrates him.

Tim had to balance his checkbook, a task that frustrates him.

(1) Last year, I worked during the summer as a nanny. (2) <u>The best temporary job I ever had</u>. (3) My duties included dressing, feeding, and entertaining two children. (4) <u>The nicest, most well-behaved kids I have ever known</u>. (5) They enjoyed the zoo, the beach, and the park. (6) <u>Only a few of the places I took them</u>. (7) They were always excited, no matter what we did. (8) They especially liked the school playground. (9) <u>A place that was always nearly deserted in the summer</u>. (10) I was sorry to see that summer end.

COMPREHENSION AND PRACTICE

Rewriting Appositives Correctly as Sentences

18.10 On a separate sheet of paper, turn each of the following appositives into a sentence by adding a main clause containing a word for the appositive to rename or explain. Use the example to guide you. Answers will vary.

EXAMPLE

a park on the outskirts of the city

Evergreen Acres, a park on the outskirts of the city, is the best place to view the comet.

1. the quietest person in the office

2. the minister who led the protest

3. an inexpensive, plastic toy

4. the most influential musician of the decade

5. a dangerous intersection for pedestrians

6. the welcoming smell of fresh-brewed coffee

7. the person who always cheers me up

8. a color that I love

9. the best seat in the auditorium

10. a required course in my major

CHALLENGE 18.3 **Working with Subordinate Clauses and Appositives**

1. Read one or more of the essays in Part Seven. Find at least three subordinate clauses and at least two appositives. On a separate piece of paper, write the sentences that contain these elements.

2. Exchange your sentences with a classmate and then discuss with your partner or group how they contribute to the ideas in the sentences that contain them.

CHAPTER QUICK CHECK Fragments

Underline the fragments in the following passage. Then, on a separate sheet of paper, revise the passage by correcting the fragments, using the techniques you practiced in this chapter. Remember that fragments can be corrected in a variety of ways.

(1) One of the best-known U.S. monuments, the Vietnam Veterans' Memorial, has had a controversial history. (2) After the government announced their plans for a memorial to honor Vietnam combat casualties. (3) A number of architects submitted designs for consideration. (4) By a blue ribbon selection committee. (5) Chose a design by a young Asian-American woman, Maya Lin. (6) Lin's plans called for a wedge-shaped black, polished-granite wall. (7) With the names of the war dead inscribed in rows across its surface. (8) Although some people immediately praised Lin's design. (9) One critic described it as a "black scar in the earth." (10) Despite this rocky beginning, the Memorial among the most visited of all the historical sites in Washington, D.C.

QUICK STUDY Student Example

This chapter focuses on the problems that result from incomplete information. Here is a paragraph on a related subject—something that didn't make sense until it was viewed from a different perspective:

Until I began my job as a server at a restaurant. I never understood the importance of learning how to work well with others. When I was a little kid. I always preferred to play and do things by myself, so I never enjoyed doing any group work in school. It didn't make any difference whether my group was solving a math problem, working on an art project, or completing a research assignment. I always secretly felt that I could have done the work faster and more effectively on my own. But now that I am part of a team at the restaurant, I know how important working as a team is. For example, the other servers and I depend on the hostess to manage the flow of diners, and she depends on us to be fast, efficient, and courteous. The kitchen staff depends on us to record the orders accurately, and we depend on them to prepare each order correctly and get them out quickly to keep the customers satisfied. If anybody on the team messes up. The mistake affects all of us. Unhappy customers don't leave good tips, and sometimes they don't come back. Because of the experiences I have at this job. I finally appreciate the value of working as a team.

First complete the following activities in response to this paragraph:

1. Several brief passages in this paragraph are highlighted. Evaluate these sections for sentence fragments. On a separate sheet of paper, turn any fragments into correct sentences, using the material in this chapter to help you correct them.

2. On the following lines, briefly explain how the sentences in the body of the paragraph connect and support the main idea of the paragraph.

   The sentences in the body connect with and support the main idea of the paragraph

   because they offer illustrations of the importance of learning to work as a team.

   _____

3. The paragraph relies largely on comparison and contrast to tell this story. In your view, which of the two periods contrasted is stronger and more effective, the discussion of the past or the discussion of the present? On the lines below, identify and briefly explain your choice.

   Answers will vary, but most students will probably choose the later period, feeling that

   these examples are more complete and detailed than those concerning the earlier

   period.

Now explore the topic in writing. You could discuss some idea or concept that you didn't understand until you viewed it as part of larger issue like the paragraph above does. You might also choose one of these subjects related to the subject matter of this chapter:

- how a group you are or were a part of changed when someone else joined it
- how some aspect of life would be different if a part or element of it were removed
- a situation in which something small or seemingly insignificant became a major disruption
- what did or could happen if someone acts without fully understanding the consequences

COLLABORATION

1. Exchange your draft with a classmate. Evaluate the paragraph you receive. If you discover any problem spots, especially sentence fragments, make a note in the margin and then return the paper to the writer.

2. Consider the comments and corrections your reader has made and create a final draft of your paragraph.

SUMMARY EXERCISE Fragments

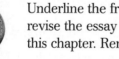

CW 18.11 More practice with identifying fragments

Underline the fragments in the following essay. Then, on a separate piece of paper, revise the essay by correcting the fragments, using the techniques you practiced in this chapter. Remember that fragments can be corrected in a variety of ways.

(1) One of the major stars of the world of cooking is Chef Emeril Lagasse. (2) Referred to by his many fans simply by his first name. (3) Emeril has enjoyed an enormously successful career in the arenas of world-class restaurants and television.

(4) Emeril's success had simple beginnings. (5) Born in Fall River, Massachussetts, an old New England mill town. (6) As a youngster, he worked in a Portuguese bakery. (7) An ideal place to learn to make bread and pastries. (8) Also worked in the kitchen of the St. John's Club, a small ethnic restaurant in Fall River, mastering many aspects of food preparation.

(9) He studied culinary arts at Diman Regional Vocational Technical High School in Fall River. (10) Although he was offered a college music scholarship.

(11) Emeril chose to study culinary arts at Johnson and Wales University in Providence, Rhode Island.

(12) After graduating and traveling to France to learn the secrets of French cuisine. (13) Emeril returned to the United States to work in major restaurants in Philadelphia, Boston, New York, and then New Orleans. (14) He made his mark in New Orleans, over the years opening three restaurants there. (15) Several other restaurants in Las Vegas and Orlando. (16) With his trademark exclamation, "Bam!" Emeril has also captivated television audiences with his two Food Network shows, *The Essence of Emeril* and *Emeril Live.* (17) Which are broadcast into approximately 70 million households each day.

(18) From his first work in a small Fall River bakery. (19) Emeril has seen his career grow to almost unbelievable levels. (20) Along the way, he has inspired much interest in cooking throughout the United States.

FOR FURTHER EXPLORATION

1. Consider one of the following topics:
   - the habits or behavior of sloppy people
   - the story behind a private or family joke
   - a famous vacation destination
   - your favorite place to study or read
   - a chore or task at home or work that you find particularly frustrating

   Prewrite on the subject, using one of the strategies you practiced in Chapter 2, and work your way through the rest of the writing process. Then complete a draft essay of at least 500 words on this subject.

2. Exchange your draft with a classmate. Check the draft you receive for weaknesses, especially sentence fragments, using the material in this chapter as a guide. Underline any fragments and then return the draft to the writer.

3. Revise your essay, correcting any fragments or other problems discovered by your reader.

RECAP Fragments

New terms in this chapter	Definitions
sentence fragment	a group of words that fails to express a complete thought because it lacks a subject, a verb, or other needed words

> **EXAMPLE** Although they tried not to laugh [not a complete thought]

verbal	a verb form that is used as another part of speech and therefore doesn't communicate a complete action or meaning

A verbal cannot substitute for a verb in a sentence.

> **EXAMPLE** *Running* down the stairs

phrase fragment	a group of two or more related words that lacks a subject–verb combination, used incorrectly as a sentence

> **Verb phrase** Are looking

> **Prepositional phrase** About time

subordinate clause fragment	a group of words that contains a subject and a verb but does not express a complete thought

A subordinate clause must be joined to a main clause to express a complete thought.

> **EXAMPLE** That had struck the coast

main clause	the primary subject–verb unit of a sentence

> **EXAMPLE** *The hurricane* that had struck the coast *was not expected.*

appositive	a word or group of words that renames or explains a noun or pronoun next to it

An appositive must be connected to a main clause to express a complete thought.

> **EXAMPLE** A retired police officer

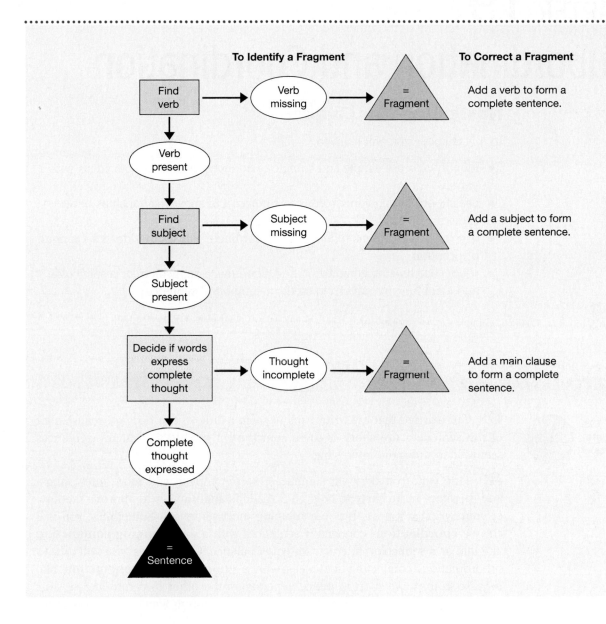

To Identify a Fragment — To Correct a Fragment

Find verb → Verb missing → = Fragment — Add a verb to form a complete sentence.

Verb present

Find subject → Subject missing → = Fragment — Add a subject to form a complete sentence.

Subject present

Decide if words express complete thought → Thought incomplete → = Fragment — Add a main clause to form a complete sentence.

Complete thought expressed

= Sentence

GOING FORWARD...

**CW 18.12
Review of
sentence
fragments**

Q: What's the best way to avoid fragments in my writing?

A: Making sure your writing is free from sentence fragments is easier than you might think. The answer is to focus on what makes a sentence a sentence. Check to make sure that each unit you write contains a subject and verb and expresses a complete thought. Do this every time, and you will keep your writing fragment-free.

CHAPTER 19
Subordination and Coordination

▶ **Navigating This Chapter**

In this chapter, you will learn to:

- identify and use simple and complex sentences to express your ideas with variety
- use subordinating conjunctions to connect and show relationships between clauses
- use relative pronouns to introduce subordinate clauses that describe a noun or pronoun
- use a coordinating conjunction and a comma, a semicolon, or a semicolon and a conjunctive adverb to create a compound sentence

---

GETTING STARTED...

CW 19.1
Chapter
basics

Q: I'm worried that my writing might seem a little stiff or boring because a lot of my sentences are short. Is there something I can do so that my sentences seem fuller and more interesting?

A: One way to make your sentences more complete and more interesting—and therefore more likely to hold your reader's attention—is to improve the flow of your writing. You do this by combining short sentences. Sometimes, you will choose **coordination**—connecting sentences with a **coordinating conjunction** like *and* or a semicolon to create an equal balance. Other times, you will turn to subordination—connecting sentences with a **subordinating conjunction** like *because* so that one short sentence depends on the other to communicate your full meaning. Both methods will help keep your writing lively and highly readable.

Overview: Combining Clauses for Sentence Complexity

CW 19.2
Overview of
combining
clauses

When you write, you must express your ideas in complete sentence form. As the previous two chapters emphasize, this means that you must make sure each unit contains a subject and verb expressing a complete thought. When a group of words contains a single subject–verb unit expressing a complete thought, the structure is called a *simple sentence*. If you used only simple sentences, however, your writing style would be pretty boring. You can emphasize some ideas by using **subordination**, which means combining an idea in a main clause with an idea in a **subordinate clause.** The subordinate clause depends on the main clause to make sense. Alternatively, you can join ideas through **coordination**, in which two main clauses (or simple sentences) are linked by a semicolon or by a coordinating conjunction and comma.

Using Subordination

To use **subordination** effectively, you need to understand the difference between a simple sentence and a complex sentence. A **simple sentence** consists of only one subject–verb unit or *clause*, as this example shows:

SIMPLE SENTENCE   The *reporter* on the scene *detailed* the degree of damage.

As a writer, you will also rely on **complex sentences**, which combine a main, or independent, clause, and a **subordinate**, or dependent, **clause.** Subordinate clauses are introduced by either **subordinating conjunctions** or **relative pronouns:**

Common Subordinating Conjunctions

after	before	since	when
although	even though	so that	whenever
as	if	than	where
as if	in order that	though	wherever
as soon as	once	unless	whether
because	rather than	until	while

Relative Pronouns

that	who
what	whom
which	whose

If you join a simple sentence and a subordinate clause in a complex sentence, the simple sentence becomes the **main clause**, as this example shows:

main clause ——— subordinate clause —

COMPLEX SENTENCE   *The reporter on the scene detailed the degree of damage* where the explosion had occurred.

In a complex sentence, you may also place the subordinate clause before the main clause. In this case, a comma is needed before the conjunction. No matter where it is placed, the main clause of a complex sentence contains the most important idea.

Subordinating conjunctions do more than connect clauses. They also indicate the *relationship* between the two clauses in terms of time, purpose, result, condition, or cause. Study the following complex sentences:

main clause ——— subordinate clause ———

EXAMPLE   My car insurance increased $500 this year *because* I received a speeding ticket.

┌─────── subordinate clause ───────┐┌──── main clause ────┐

EXAMPLE | *If* Linda concentrates on her studies, she could earn a scholarship.

In the first sentence, *because* indicates that the first occurrence—the increase in insurance rates—is the result of the second occurrence. In the second, *if* suggests under what condition Linda will earn a scholarship.

Relative pronouns are used to introduce subordinate clauses that either *describe* a noun or *specify* a noun or pronoun in the sentence. Look at the following sentences, with the subordinate clauses italicized:

EXAMPLE | Any person *who provides encouragement and emotional support* is a true friend.

Food *that is low in fat* is better for a healthy heart.

In the first sentence, the relative pronoun *who* introduces the subordinate clause specifying what kind of person qualifies as a true friend. In the second, the relative pronoun *that* indicates which type of food is heart healthy.

COMPREHENSION AND PRACTICE
19.1 Identifying Subordinate Clauses

The following sentences are complex, containing both a main and a subordinate clause. Underline the subordinate clause in each sentence, and circle the subordinating conjunction or relative pronoun that introduces it, as the example shows.

EXAMPLE | Caring for a young child (who) is sick can be a stressful job for any parent.

(1) Today, people have easy access to newspapers from around the world (because) electronic versions of these papers are available on the Web. (2) Even small hometown newspapers (that) are delivered to doors every morning can be read on a computer. (3) (Once) an Internet browser is opened, it is easy to find a particular newspaper. (4) (If) the Web address is already known, users simply have to enter the address and hit Return. (5) The newspaper Web site (that) has been requested will quickly appear. (6) A search engine like Google or Yahoo can find a newspaper (when) the specific Web address isn't known. (7) (After) a line for the home page of the paper appears, users simply have to click on that line. (8) Within seconds, the electronic version of the newspaper fills

the screen, (which) contains some top stories as well as links to other parts of the paper. (9) (Because) a link to the newspaper's archives is often provided, readers can also review stories from previous editions of the paper. (10) The pages (that) are prepared by the nation's large newspapers are also regularly updated, giving readers the most current news possible.

COMPREHENSION AND PRACTICE	Combining Simple Sentences to Create Complex Sentences

19.2 The following paragraph is composed of simple sentences. On a separate piece of paper, rewrite it, joining ideas to create complex sentences. Use subordinating conjunctions and relative pronouns to introduce subordinate clauses. (Refer to the lists on page 289.) Be sure that the ideas you want to emphasize are in the main clauses of your new sentences. You may decide to leave some simple sentences just as they are for variety. Be sure you use punctuation and capitals correctly.

(1) I have made taking a walk a top priority in my daily routine. (2) I walk two miles in the park. (3) The park is near my apartment. (4) My walk is important to me for many reasons. (5) First, the exercise helps me deal with stressful situations. (6) These may come up at work. (7) I have many responsibilities, including preparing the work schedule for all workers. (8) Some mornings it is cold or raining. (9) I refuse to give up the most important hour of my day. (10) All in all, my morning walk is an invigorating way to start my day.

CHALLENGE 19.1   Evaluating Your Use of Subordination

COLLABORATION

Exchange the paragraph you revised in Comprehension and Practice 19.2 with a partner. Compare your versions, and discuss why you made the changes that you did. Did you leave any sentences as simple sentences? Did you emphasize the important ideas by making them the main clauses of the complex sentences? Choose the sentences in each version that you both agree are most effective. Then write a final version of the paragraph, and read it to your class.

Using Coordination

CW 19.4
Using coordination

Another way to join related ideas is to use **coordination**. This is a technique for connecting two or more sentences to give each one equal emphasis. The resulting sentence is called a **compound sentence**.

Achieving Coordination by Using Coordinating Conjunctions

The most common way to create a compound sentence is to connect simple sentences with a **coordinating conjunction** and a comma. Writers may also use coordination to join complex sentences to simple ones or to join complex sentences to one another. The parts of a compound sentence are called **independent clauses** because each part is essentially a simple sentence and can stand on its own. Coordination cannot be used to join clauses that could not function on their own as complete sentences.

The coordinating conjunction in a complex sentence shows the relationship between the equally important ideas that it joins. Here is a list of the coordinating conjunctions.

Coordinating Conjunctions

and	for	or
but	nor	so

Using coordination can help you eliminate choppiness from your writing. Consider these two pairs of sentences:

CHOPPY   The heavy rain flooded the streets. Lightning started two small fires.

The toddler started to fall from the top step. A woman coming up the stairs managed to steady him.

As they are now, these two sets of sentences sound choppy. Now consider the same pairs of sentences when a conjunction and comma are used to join each pair of sentences:

COMBINED   The heavy rain flooded the streets, *and* lightning started two small fires.

The toddler started to fall from the top step, *but* a woman coming up the stairs managed to steady him.

These compound sentences are more fluid than the sets of simple sentences. The coordinating conjunctions clearly show how the two ideas within each subject–verb pair are related.

FAST FACT   U.S. President Abraham Lincoln made good use of subordination and coordination in his famous Gettysburg Address. The final sentence of the speech is a whopping 82 words long, which is nearly a third of the length of the entire address.

COMPREHENSION
AND PRACTICE
19.3

Developing Skills with Coordination

Join each pair of simple sentences in the paragraph below with a comma and a coordinating conjunction to create one compound sentence. Insert the new material in the space above, using the example to guide you. Answers will vary. Sample answers are given.

, and the

EXAMPLE   The doors opened. ~~The~~ lines inched slowly ahead.

, and she

(1) Last Monday, Marisol walked to the Transit Office. ~~She~~ bought a pass

, but then

for a full week's transportation. (2) She paid for the pass with a check. ~~Then~~

she forgot to put her checkbook back in her backpack. (3) With her new pass

, and she

in hand, she took the bus to school for a full morning of classes. ~~She~~ didn't

think about her checkbook until lunch. (4) At that point, Marisol had to act

, or she

fast. ~~She~~ faced the loss of all the money in her account. (5) She immediately

, and luckily

called the Transit Office. ~~Luckily,~~ the head clerk had put her checkbook aside

for her.

COMPREHENSION
AND PRACTICE
19.4

Using Coordination

Fill in the blanks, adding a clause that is related to the existing clause before or after the coordinating conjunction. Use the example as a guide. Answers will vary. Sample answers are given.

EXAMPLE   The basketball game was tied, **so** ———————————

the coach left the starting five on the court.

1. The restaurant that I wanted to go to was closed, **so** ————————

   we tried the new Thai restaurant next door.

2. *The Thai restaurant was not open,* ———————————————

   nor was the coffee shop open down the street.

3. Our stomachs were growling, **so** ———————————————

   we decided to take the bus to another restaurant across town.

4. The wait at the bus stop was long, **but** _____

we bought hot pretzels to snack on.
_____

5. It's a good thing the pretzel vendor came by, _____

or I would have fainted from hunger.

Achieving Coordination by Using Semicolons

Another way to achieve coordination is to use a *semicolon* (;) to connect independent clauses. A semicolon, which has the same power to connect as a coordinating conjunction with a comma, makes the connection more direct. You will learn more about the use of semicolons in Chapter 31, "Other Punctuation and Capitalization."

Consider the two versions of the following sentence:

EXAMPLE   The day had been long and hot, *and* all I wanted to do was take a shower.

The day had been long and hot; all I wanted to do was take a shower.

In the first version, the coordinating conjunction *and* joins the two clauses, *adding* the second thought. In the second version, the semicolon joins the two ideas directly, emphasizing the close relationship between them. Semicolons are used to join sentences that have such a clear, obvious connection.

In addition to using a semicolon alone, you can add a twist to this technique by including a **conjunctive adverb** after the semicolon. Take a look at the following list of conjunctive adverbs:

Common Conjunctive Adverbs

also	however	similarly
besides	instead	still
consequently	meanwhile	then
finally	moreover	therefore
furthermore	nevertheless	thus

Conjunctive adverbs *suggest a relationship* between two thoughts, as the following compound sentences show:

EXAMPLE   In-line skating is great exercise; *furthermore*, it's great fun.

I had planned to get to work early; *however*, two accidents on the highway delayed me for 45 minutes.

Neither *furthermore* nor *however* is used to connect the sentences. The semicolon does that. Note that this technique requires two punctuation marks: a semicolon *before* the conjunctive adverb and a comma *after* it.

FAST FACT   And you thought the semicolon was just a strange-looking mark of punctuation. The 1870–73 Texas Supreme Court was given the derogatory name of Semicolon Court by contemporary lawyers in the Lone Star State. The Court earned this title because the justices ruled that a semicolon in one article of state election law made the general election of 1873 unconstitutional and invalid. The ruling was never enforced, however, and the government that came into power removed the three judges that made up the Semicolon Court.

COMPREHENSION AND PRACTICE

Achieving Coordination by Using Semicolons

19.5 As you read the sentences in the paragraph below, decide which ones are closely related in meaning. On a separate sheet of paper, create a new version of the passage, using a semicolon to join these closely related sentences. Use the example to guide you.

EXAMPLE   Janet had always considered Michelle a courageous, ethical person. Michelle's
                                                                        ;
actions that morning only reinforced her belief.   ^

(1) Getting contact lenses was one of the best decisions I ever made. (2) My vision is so much better now. (3) I am also much happier with my appearance. (4) I have had to wear glasses since the tenth grade. (5) No high school student wants to look at the world through thick lenses. (6) At the end of the year, I asked my parents to get me contact lenses. (7) Unfortunately, they simply couldn't afford to buy them for me. (8) I decided at that point to save up myself. (9) All together, it took my two months of overtime to pay for the examination, fitting, and lenses. (10) It was time and money well spent.

COMPREHENSION AND PRACTICE

Combining Sentences Using Conjunctive Adverbs and Semicolons

19.6 Complete each sentence by adding a conjunctive adverb and an independent clause after the semicolon. Use the list of conjunctive adverbs on page 294. Don't forget a comma after the conjunctive adverb. Use the example as a guide. Answers will vary. Representative answers are given.

EXAMPLE   The waiting room at the clinic was crowded; _____
       however, I decided to stay until the doctor was available.

1. Washington, D.C.'s Metro system is clean and efficient; _____

   therefore, visitors to the nation's capital enjoy using it.

2. The wheels on the subway cars are made of special material that reduces

   noise; _consequently, you can hear announcements made in the stations._

   _____

3. Last year a record number of visitors used the system; _____

   nevertheless, the cars never looked dirty or littered.

4. The New York subway system is quite different; _____

   instead, it is noisy and dirty.

5. New Yorkers often choose the bus over the subway; _____

   however, it remains one of the country's busiest systems.

COMPREHENSION AND PRACTICE

19.7

CW 19.5
Using coordination and subordination

Using Coordination and Subordination

The paragraph below contains simple sentences. Decide where it can be improved through coordination and subordination. Then rewrite the new version on a separate piece of paper. Use all the methods you have practiced in this chapter to create compound and complex sentences. You may decide to leave some sentences as they are. Use the example as a guide.

EXAMPLE

Many people try to avoid taking Statistics I. It is a difficult course.

Many people try to avoid taking statistics I because it is a difficult course.

   (1) Asthma is a chronic, dangerous lung condition. (2) It can be treated. (3) The causes of asthma are increasing. (4) More and more people suffer from asthma every year. (5) Asthma attacks can be triggered by air pollution, dust, a cold, and even exercise. (6) During an asthma attack, bronchial tubes in the lungs get irritated and constrict. (7) Patients cough, wheeze, and struggle to breathe as a result. (8) Asthma sufferers can lead normal lives. (9) They need proper medication and medical supervision. (10) They also need to understand and avoid the conditions that trigger their asthma attacks.

CHALLENGE 19.3   Evaluating Your Sentence Combining Techniques

COLLABORATION

Share the paragraph you revised in Comprehension and Practice 19.7 with a partner, and compare the choices you each made to combine ideas. In your discussion, answer the following questions:

**CW 19.6
Practicing
sentence
combining**

- What options did you use for achieving coordination?
- Where did you use subordination?
- Why did you make the changes that you did?
- Where is your revision different from your partner's?
- Which ideas did you leave expressed as simple sentences? Why?

CHAPTER QUICK CHECK Subordination and Coordination

**CW 19.7
More practice
with
subordination
and
coordination**

The writing below is composed of simple sentences. On a separate sheet of paper, revise it by combining sentences to emphasize ideas, to show connections among ideas, and to make the writing smooth. Use the methods you have practiced in this chapter to create complex or compound sentences. In some cases, you may decide to leave a particular sentence as it is. Answers will vary.

(1) Memory is a fascinating subject. (2) Scientists continue to study different aspects of this mental capability. (3) One area of continued focus is the connection between aging and a weakening of memory processes. (4) The ability to remember seems to diminish with age. (5) This point may be true to some extent. (6) People of all ages sometimes forget where they have parked their cars or left their keys. (7) Current research points to lack of attention rather than some problem in the brain as the cause of some memory lapses. (8) The desire to suppress traumatic recollections accounts for others. (9) In their recollections, trauma victims often innocently include untrue or inaccurate details or events. (10) Courts are now having to rethink their attitudes about the accuracy of eyewitness reports of crimes.

QUICK STUDY   Student Example

This chapter focuses on creating relationships between elements. Here is a paragraph on a related subject—the meaning or importance of being independent:

My most important personal goal is to become more financially independent. I had my daughter. I had to move out of my mother's place and apply for financial assistance from the state. Now I live in a subsidized apartment. I receive health care and vouchers for food. I truly appreciate all this help. I hate the way I have to live. I want to have a job so that I can rent my own place and take care of all the expenses for both of us. I want to be the one who pays the bills. I want to be the one in charge. That's the main reason I'm here taking courses. Without a college degree, I'll never be able to develop financial independence. I hope to get into the Radiologic Technology Program. I can become an X-ray and ultrasound technician. With a job in this field, I can finally achieve my goal and be self-supporting.

First complete the following activities in response to this paragraph:

1. Take a look at the brief highlighted passages in this paragraph. Consider how the passages might benefit from coordination or subordination. Then, on a separate sheet of paper, improve the sentences through coordination or subordination to improve the sentences. Use the material in this chapter to guide you.

2. In your view, which of the details in the paragraph offer the strongest support for the topic sentence? On the following lines, identify the example and explain your choice.

   Answers will vary. Likely selections will include the details explaining the writer's current

   living situation (sentences 2–5), the details spelling out the writer's goals (sentences 13

   and 14), and the details concerning the writer's attitude about the situation (sentences

   6–10), each of which offers strong support for the topic sentence.

3. If you were going to make any suggestions for developing this paragraph more fully, what area or areas would you identify and why? Use the lines below for your answer.

   Answers will vary, although many students will want to know more about the identified

   career choice and how it will lead to financial independence.

Now explore this general idea in writing. As the paragraph above does, you could examine the importance of or ways to develop independence. You might also choose one of these subjects:

- the most important relationship you have known or experienced
- what it means to be genuinely equal
- guidelines for being an effective supervisor or superior
- an experience during which working together with someone did not work out as planned

1. Exchange your draft with a classmate. Evaluate the paragraph you receive. If you discover any weaknesses, especially any spots where subordination or coordination would improve the flow of the writing, make a note in the margin and then return the paper to the writer.

2. Consider the comments and corrections your reader has made and create a final draft of your paragraph.

SUMMARY EXERCISE Subordination and Coordination

The writing below is composed of simple sentences. On a separate piece of paper, revise it by combining sentences to emphasize ideas, to show connections among ideas, and to make the writing smooth. Use the methods you have practiced in this chapter to create complex or compound sentences. In some cases, you may decide to leave a particular sentence as it is. Answers will vary.

(1) Important documents in our nation's history are housed in the National Archives in Washington, D.C. (2) Many of the documents are old and fragile. (3) They are carefully protected from further deterioration. (4) Many people see these documents. (5) They are impressed both by their importance and by the care taken to preserve them for the future.

(6) The Constitution, signed by representatives of twelve of the original states in 1787, is housed in the Archives. (7) It is only four pages long. (8) The Constitution contains the foundation of our democratic system. (9) Visitors can see two pages of this famous document. (10) They are housed in bronze and glass cases. (11) The cases are filled with helium gas to preserve the old parchment.

(12) The Archives also displays the Declaration of Independence and the Bill of Rights. (13) The Declaration of Independence, written primarily by Thomas Jefferson, was adopted on July 4, 1776. (14) The Bill of Rights was ratified more than two hundred years ago. (15) Citizens, judges, and scholars still discuss it today. (16) This document speaks about freedom of the press, freedom of religion, freedom of speech, and the right to bear arms. (17) These are still controversial issues today.

(18) All of these documents are stored every night in a special vault. (19) The bronze and glass cases are lowered electronically to the bottom of a vault. (20) It is twenty-two feet below the ground.

FOR FURTHER EXPLORATION

1. Consider one of the following topics:
   - the most effective advertisement—radio, Internet, television, or print—you've been exposed to
   - problems with the U.S. criminal justice system
   - your dreams for the future

- the worst thing you ever experienced or witnessed in elementary school
- what, if anything, should be done to restrict objectionable material on television

Prewrite on the subject, using one of the strategies you practiced in Chapter 2, and work your way through the rest of the writing process. Then complete a draft essay of at least 500 words on this subject.

COLLABORATION

2. Exchange your draft with a classmate. Check the draft you receive for any problems, especially spots where coordination and subordination would improve the writing, using the material in this chapter as a guide. Put a checkmark next to any problem you identify, with a note in the margin explaining your reasoning. Then return the draft to the writer.

3. Revise your essay, correcting any fragments or other problems discovered by your reader.

RECAP Subordination and Coordination

New terms in this chapter	Definitions
subordination	a way to combine unequal ideas, giving emphasis to one and making the other dependent upon the former
simple sentence	a sentence consisting of a subject and a verb and their modifiers
	EXAMPLE A mouse had eaten a hole in the bag of popcorn.
complex sentence	a sentence consisting of a main clause and a subordinate clause
subordinate clause	a subject–verb unit that doesn't express a complete thought; also called a *dependent clause*
	EXAMPLE Subordinate clauses are introduced by *subordinating conjunctions* or *relative pronouns*.
subordinating conjunction	one of a group of connecting words used at the beginning of a subordinate clause to join it to an independent clause: *after, although, as, as if, as soon as, because, before, even though, if, in order that, once, rather than, since, so that, than, though, unless, until, when, whenever, wherever, whether, while* The subordinating conjunction expresses the relationship between the two clauses.
	EXAMPLE The downtown flooded *because* we had torrential rains.
relative pronoun	one of a group of words used to introduce subordinate clauses that describe or specify a noun or pronoun in a main clause: *that, what, which, who, whom, whose*
	EXAMPLE An author *whose* work I admire is Jamaica Kincaid.

New terms in this chapter	Definitions
main clause	a subject–verb unit that can stand on its own but is combined with another subject–verb unit A main clause is an *independent clause.*
coordination	the combining of independent clauses of equal importance into *compound sentences* to eliminate choppiness and repetition
compound sentence	a sentence containing two or more independent clauses joined by a connector: (1) a *coordinating conjunction* and a comma, (2) a *semicolon*, or (3) a semicolon plus a *conjunctive adverb*
coordinating conjunction	one of a set of joining words used to connect words or ideas of equal rank: *and, but, for, nor, or, so*, and *yet*
independent clause	a clause with a subject and a verb that can stand alone as a sentence A compound sentence consists of two or more independent clauses joined by a connector. **EXAMPLE** *Spring is on the way*, and *the temperature is rising.*
conjunctive adverb	one of a group of words used with a connector to link ideas by showing how they are related: *also, besides, consequently, finally, furthermore, however, instead, meanwhile, moreover, nevertheless, similarly, still, then, therefore*, and *thus* A conjunctive adverb cannot connect simple sentences itself but does emphasize the connection provided by semicolons. A conjunctive adverb requires a comma after it when used with a semicolon connecting simple sentences. **EXAMPLE** Cheetahs are an endangered species; *however,* many cheetahs were born at zoos last year.

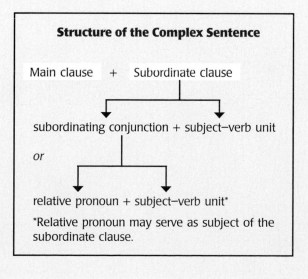

Structure of the Complex Sentence

Main clause   +   Subordinate clause

subordinating conjunction + subject–verb unit

or

relative pronoun + subject–verb unit*

*Relative pronoun may serve as subject of the subordinate clause.

(continued)

Structure of the Complex Sentence

Independent clause + [comma and coordinating conjunction *or* semicolon *or* semicolon, conjunctive adverb, and comma] + Independent clause

GOING FORWARD...

CW 19.9
Verb-tense
consistency

Q: I can see how coordination and subordination work. I'm just not always sure when I should use one instead of the other to combine sentences. Is there any way for me to know whether coordination or subordination is the right choice?

A: Which method of combination to use depends on the effect you are trying to create. When you want to eliminate choppiness between short sentences that have about the *same significance*, coordination is the answer. But when you want to improve flow between short sentences that have *different degrees of importance*—or you want to give one short sentence more significance than another—subordination is the way to go.

CHAPTER 20

Comma Splices and Run-on Sentences

Navigating This Chapter

In this chapter, you will learn how to recognize and avoid comma splices and run-on sentences. You will practice correcting these errors by using:

- a coordinating conjunction and a comma
- a subordinating conjunction
- a semicolon (or a semicolon and a conjunctive adverb)
- a period

GETTING STARTED ...

**CW 20.1
Chapter
basics**

Q: I know I have good ideas on my subject, so I'm happy about that. What has me a little concerned is that I might be just running one idea into the next instead of expressing them in correct sentences. Am I right to be worried about this?

A: You are right to be concerned—you just can't simply run your good ideas together and achieve the kind of communication you want to. When you run one idea into another, you make one of two sentence errors, either a *comma splice* or a *run-on sentence*. Both are serious mistakes because they tell your reader that you aren't sure where one of your idea ends and the next begins.

Overview: Understanding Comma Splices and Run-on Sentences

**CW 20.2
Overview of
comma
splices and
run-on
sentences**

Two of the most common and most serious sentence errors are the **comma splice** and the **run-on sentence.** A comma splice is an error in which sentences are incorrectly connected by a comma, a mark of punctuation that *can't* connect. A run-on sentence is an error in which two sentences are run together without proper punctuation or an appropriate connector. Both errors are serious because they distract readers from the point you are making. To avoid these two sentence errors, you must first recognize and then correct them in your writing.

Identifying Comma Splices and Run-on Sentences

ESL Note
See "Sentence Basics" on pages 589–590 and "Punctuation and Capitalization" on pages 600–601.

The first step in correcting comma splices and run-on sentences is to identify them. Start by locating the subjects and verbs in your sentences. Then check if you have joined two subject–verb units with only a comma. If so, you have a comma splice. *Commas cannot connect independent clauses.* Commas indicate a pause, or they separate elements within a sentence, but they can't connect.

Take a look at this example:

COMMA SPLICE | ⌐ subject ¬ ⌐ verb ¬   ⌐ subject ¬ ⌐verb¬
The *flashlight flickered* out, the *batteries were* obviously dead.

CW 20.3
Recognizing
comma
splices

Each unit contains a subject and verb, and each could stand alone as a simple sentence. But a comma can't connect, so the result is a comma splice.

To check for run-on sentences, follow the same method. First, locate the subjects and verbs in your sentences. Then check to see whether you have joined two subject–verb units without any *connector* or *separator*. If so, you have created a run-on sentence.

Read out loud the following example, which has a / where one unit ends and the next begins:

RUN-ON SENTENCE | subject verb   subject ⌐—— verb ——¬
My car *horn is* broken again / *I have replaced* it twice already.

CW 20.4
Recognizing
run-on
sentences

As you can see, this example consists of two subject–verb units, each of which could stand on its own. Nothing either connects or separates these units. Instead, the first unit just *runs into* the second, which is why this type of error is called a run-on sentence, or simply a run-on.

Incidentally, one reason comma splices occur is that the ways that commas function are often misunderstood. Therefore, one way to avoid making comma splices is to understand what commas do. When you write, you use commas in the following ways:

- To indicate the pause between clauses connected by conjunctions

EXAMPLE | The door was closed, but it wasn't locked.

- To separate items in a series

EXAMPLE | We looked for the missing ring around the apartment in the backyard, and in the car.

- To set off introductory material

EXAMPLE | With the additional memory, the computer performed much faster.

- To set off elements that interrupt sentence flow

EXAMPLE | Showing up early on your first day, for instance, is a great way to impress a new boss.

- To set off direct quotations

EXAMPLE "I'm just not interested in that class," Vincente explained.

- To fulfill several other purposes, including

> setting off the salutation of a personal letter (Dear Zelda,)
>
> setting off the parts of dates from the rest of the sentence (March 31, 1982, was the day Jacqueline was born.)
>
> setting off parts of addresses (His last permanent address was 44 Bogle Street, East Ridge, NM 34268.)
>
> indicating thousands within numbers (3,211 or 3,211,000)
>
> setting off a name when you address someone directly (I want you to know, Marilyn, that you have made a tremendous impact on this office.)

CW 20.5 Sentence construction and sentence errors

If you use commas for these purposes only, you decrease your chances of making a comma splice. For a more complete discussion and additional examples of proper comma use, see Chapter 30, "Commas."

COMPREHENSION AND PRACTICE

Identifying Comma Splices and Run-on Sentences

20.1 The paragraph below contains several comma splices and run-on sentences. To identify them, first underline every subject and verb. Then note where one idea ends and the next begins and put a / between these units. If the subject–verb units are joined by only a comma, put *CS* for comma splice in front of it. If there is no connector or separator, put *RS* for run-on sentence in front of it. Use the example to guide you.

EXAMPLE *RS*The <u>city</u> should <u>lower</u> the speed limit on Plymouth Avenue/the <u>area</u> <u>is</u> very congested.

CS (1) Over the past few years, youth sports leagues in the United States have been the focus of much attention,/the behavior of adult fans and parents is the primary reason for this concern. RS(2) News reports across the country have recorded numerous incidents involving parents yelling and interrupting games and practices/these confrontations sometimes have even led to physical violence. CS(3) In one infamous incident, a parent physically attacked a coach,/the coach died as a result. RS(4) Clearly, some reform is necessary /some people have suggested banning any adult spectators as a solution to the problem. CS(5) The purpose of these leagues <u>is</u> to give children the chance to have fun,/adults need to let the kids play without any interference.

COMPREHENSION AND PRACTICE 20.2 **Recognizing Comma Splices and Run-ons**

The following paragraph contains several comma splices and run-on sentences. Put an * in front of any comma splice or run-on, and insert a / where one sentence should end and the next should begin. Use the example to guide you.

EXAMPLE

*Jennifer didn't show up for class again today,/this is the fifth time she has been absent this month.

(1) *In national politics, money talks/a candidate can't expect to win today without enormous financial backing. (2) It isn't unusual for a congressional campaign to cost each candidate several million dollars or more. (3) *People simply can't afford to run a campaign alone,/they must count on donations. (4) Incumbents have a great advantage over challengers in terms of fundraising. (5) *Incumbents already have contacts,/businesses are therefore more willing to donate to them. (6) *With a little luck, the donations will pay off/the incumbents will act on behalf of those businesses once they are re-elected. (7) *Challengers have no power and no influence,/they have difficulty getting corporate support. (8) *Of course, there are exceptions/misconduct or criminal charges against an incumbent will often shift popular and financial support to a challenger. (9) *Our campaign finance system is not productive or fair/we need to reform the laws that govern it. (10) We should have a system that enables us to elect the best candidate, not the one with the biggest campaign chest.

CHALLENGE 20.1   **Checking for Comma Splices and Run-ons in Your Writing**

Take a paragraph or essay that you are working on, and exchange it with a partner. Underline the subjects and verbs in each sentence of the paper you receive. Then put a / between any clauses you see that can stand alone. If you discover any comma splices or run-ons, mark these errors. Return the draft to your partner. Save your own draft for later use.

Correcting Comma Splices and Run-ons by Using Coordinating Conjunctions

CW 20.6
Using coordinating conjunctions

One way to correct comma splices and run-on sentences is to use a coordinating conjunction such as *and, but*, and *or* between independent clauses. (See page 292 for a complete listing of coordinating conjunctions.) Besides providing connection, these conjunctions help you eliminate choppiness and repetition.

Consider these examples, with corrections added:

COMMA SPLICE | The clock is more than 100 years old, ^*yet* it keeps perfect time.

RUN-ON | Karen does volunteer work at an extended-care facility ^*, and* she also has a weekend job.

In the first sentence, *yet* provides the connection and shows opposition between ideas. In the second, a comma plus *and* now link the two clauses; *and* suggests addition of ideas. The sentences now flow better, and, more important, they are now correct. By the way, as the examples above show, always include a comma *before* a conjunction used to connect simple sentences.

FAST FACT   Among English words, *and* ranks as the third most commonly used word. This little word is versatile, too, serving as a means of correcting comma splices and run-on sentences, and it links individual words, phrases, and clauses. Depending on the items being connected, *and* can also provide a comic connection, as it does in these actual street locations identified by State Farm Insurance: the intersection of Grinn *and* Barret in West Chester, Ohio; the intersection of Ho *and* Hum in Carefree, Arizona; the intersection of Antonio *and* Banderas in Santa Margarita, California; and the intersection of Hickory *and* Dickory *and* Dock in Harahan, Louisiana.

COMPREHENSION AND PRACTICE

20.3

Using Coordinating Conjunctions to Connect Clauses

Each numbered item in the following paragraph is either a run-on sentence or a comma splice. If the item is a run-on, put a / between the independent clauses. Then above the /, add a comma and the coordinating conjunction (*and, or, but, for, nor, so*, or *yet*) that best connects the thoughts in the independent clauses. If the item is a comma splice, simply insert a / and the correct coordinating conjunction between the clauses. Use the examples to guide you. Answers may vary.

EXAMPLE

, but

I had completed my art project on time/I forgot to bring it.

and

Annie has black hair,/it and curls naturally.

but

(1) Finally, Martin Luther King Day is celebrated in all 50 states,/it certainly took a while.

, and

(2) For a time, it was a federal holiday/most states celebrated it.

, and

(3) A few states, however, did not observe it,/schools, businesses, and government offices in those states remained open.

, so

(4) Many individuals in these states were outraged about this/they stayed home from work and kept their children out of school in protest.

for

(5) A special day in Dr. King's honor is well deserved,/he gave his life to improve civil rights for all of us.

COMPREHENSION AND PRACTICE 20.4

Using Coordinating Conjunctions to Correct Comma Splices and Run-on Sentences

The following paragraph contains several comma splices and run-on sentences. Put an * in front of any comma splice or run-on sentence. Then put a / between independent clauses. Choose an appropriate coordinating conjunction from the list below and insert it above where one sentence should end and the next should begin. Don't forget to add a comma if it isn't already there. Use the example to guide you.

and	nor
but	so
for	yet
or	

EXAMPLE

, yet

*The officer was clearly lying/the judge allowed his testimony.

Representative answers are given. Actual answers may vary somewhat.

*(1) A new bakery and coffee shop in my neighborhood has been open for

, but

only three weeks/already business seems excellent.

, and

*(2) The shop is called The Stafford Road Stop/it sells a wide variety of bagels, muffins, doughnuts, and other pastries.

*(3) The shop is located right across the street from a Metro

                                                        so
stop,/ many of the patrons stop by on their way into the downtown area.

(4) The shop itself is bright and clean, with a large display case and ten small

tables, each with two chairs in front of it.*(5) A counter with stools is against
                        , so
the front wall/patrons can enjoy their food while looking at the busy street

scene outside.*(6) The staff doesn't hesitate to ask customers about their fa-
                    , and
vorite selections,/they don't hesitate to inquire about the need for new prod-

ucts.*(7) According to the owner, Ms. Liliana Godek, they will have your fa-
                    , or
vorite baked goods on hand/they will add them to the menu.*(8) She also
                    and
prides herself on her coffee,/patrons can choose from several types, including

at least two types of decaffeinated coffee. (9) The quality of all her products is

excellent, yet the prices are reasonable. (10) All in all, the Stafford Road Stop

gives every sign of becoming a success story.

CHALLENGE 20.2 Working with Coordinating Conjunctions

Consider again the list of coordinating conjunctions in Comprehension and
Practice 20.4. Then, working with a partner, write two sentences on a separate
sheet of paper for each conjunction and use the conjunction to connect the simple sentences. When you are done, explain in a few sentences which conjunction
you found most useful and why.

Correcting Comma Splices and Run-ons by Using Subordinating Conjunctions

**CW 20.7
Using
subordinating
conjunctions**

Another way to eliminate comma splices and run-on sentences is to add a subordinating conjunction such as *after, because, if,* and *unless* to connect clauses. (See
page 289 for a complete listing of subordinating conjunctions.) As Chapter 19,
"Subordination and Coordination," showed, subordinating conjunctions indicate a
relationship between the ideas they connect. Consider the following examples:

COMMA SPLICE

Because oil
~~Oil~~ from the leaking barge fouled the water for over 20 square miles, more

than 1,000 birds were killed.

RUN-ON

                                                            even though
On Wednesday afternoon, the needed items were still not here they promised
                                                           ^
to deliver them by Tuesday.

In the first example, *because* joins two ideas related by cause and effect: The death of the birds *resulted from* an oil spill. In the second example, *even though* links the ideas and also indicates the relationship between them: Items were not delivered *despite the fact that* they had been promised.

COMPREHENSION AND PRACTICE 20.5

Using Subordinating Conjunctions to Correct Comma Splices and Run-on Sentences

Each numbered item in the following paragraph is either a run-on sentence or a comma splice. First, put a / between the independent clauses. Then add one of the subordinating conjunctions listed below to show a relationship between the clauses. In some cases, more than one correct answer is possible. With a comma splice, you'll need to add only the subordinating conjunction, but with a run-on sentence, you'll need to add a comma as well as the conjunctive adverb. Use the example as a guide.

after	before
although	since
because	when

EXAMPLE

Before the
~~The~~ police arrived,/traffic was backed up for three miles.
^

(1) *Before* I started work/I never saw the importance of knowing a second lan-
^   ,
guage. (2) Having bilingual workers is important,/*because* the needs of all customers
can be met. (3) *When* I thought about it/learning a second language seemed like a
^   ,
great idea for me. (4) I am training to be a paralegal,/*Although* I will have to deal with
^
people from a wide variety of backgrounds. (5) I know more than one lan-
,   *Since*
guage/a law office will be more interested in hiring me.
                    ^

COMPREHENSION AND PRACTICE 20.6

Correcting Comma Splices and Run-on Sentences by Using Subordinating Conjunctions

In the following paragraph, find the comma splices and run-ons, and put an * in front of each one. Then choose an appropriate subordinating conjunction (*because, since, even though, when, although,* or *so that*), and insert it in the proper place above the line to make the sentence correct. Make sure to add a comma if it is needed. Use the example to guide you.

EXAMPLE

> *because*
> *They were late leaving the campground ^ they had to wait for Gil and Sheila.

(1)*Some people are counted as unemployed or underemployed by the government, *although* ^ they actually have an income. (2) They are part of the "underground economy." (3)*Most people in this situation work for cash only *so that* ^ they can hide their income from government agencies. (4)*In most cases, they charge substantially less *because* ^ their salary is tax free. (5) Sometimes these workers are amateurs just picking up a little extra cash on the weekends or nights. (6)*They don't want to declare their earnings, *since* ^ the extra income might raise their overall tax burden. (7)*Sometimes trained specialists and union artisans join the underground economy *when* ^ they are between jobs or laid off. (8) Many members of the underground economy have no other means of support. (9)*They work below the minimum wage *because* ^ they would have no employment otherwise. (10)*The underground economy continues to thrive, *even though* ^ the government has tried to control it.

CHALLENGE 20.3 Working with Subordinating Conjunctions

For Comprehension and Practice 20.5, you corrected comma splices and run-on sentences by using subordinating conjunctions to connect the subject–verb units. Working with a partner, choose three of these sentences, and, on a separate sheet of paper, substitute different subordinating conjunctions. Then discuss how these new conjunctions change the meaning of the sentences.

Correcting Comma Splices and Run-ons by Using Semicolons

A semicolon (;) has the same power to connect simple sentences that conjunctions have. Using a semicolon to provide the link between sentences enables you also to emphasize the connection between the units, adding another dimension to your meaning, as these examples, with corrections, show:

COMMA SPLICE The new store features specialty paper products; their greeting cards are all

printed on recycled paper.

RUN-ON The guest speaker waited for questions from the class; nobody said a word.

In the first example, the clause about the nature of the store is now properly joined to the clause explaining one of the products. In the second example, the clause explaining the speaker's expectation is connected by a semicolon to the clause describing the class's lack of response.

To clarify the relationship between the clauses, you can use a conjunctive adverb (*also, furthermore, instead, however, moreover, then, therefore*, etc.) with a semicolon. (See page 294 for a complete list of conjunctive adverbs.) Consider these examples:

EXAMPLE The suit was expensive; *however*, it was very well made.

After playing for five minutes, the band suddenly left the stage; *meanwhile*, two technicians began to check the sound system.

In each example, the semicolon joins the ideas, and the conjunctive adverb clarifies why the ideas are linked. Notice that a comma is needed after each of these conjunctive adverbs.

FAST FACT A case of mistaken identity can explain some comma splices and run-on sentences. Because it indicates something contrary, people often assume that *however* is a conjunction, like *but*. It isn't, though—it's a *conjunctive adverb*. You can tell because *however* can be moved to several spots in a clause without changing the meaning. For example:

- The front parking lot is full. *However*, the three lots behind the building are empty.

- The front parking lot is full. The three lots behind the building, *however*, are empty.

- The front parking lot is full. The three lots behind the building are empty, *however*.

COMPREHENSION AND PRACTICE 20.7

Working with Semicolons to Correct Comma Splices and Run-on Sentences

Each numbered item in the following paragraph is either a comma splice or a run-on sentence. First, put a / between the independent clauses. Then insert a semicolon, alone or with an appropriate conjunctive adverb, to connect the clauses. If you add a conjunctive adverb, write it followed by a comma above the point where the first clause ends and the second begins. (A complete list of conjunctive adverbs appears on page 294.) Use the examples to guide you.

EXAMPLE

;

At first, the puppy wouldn't come out from behind the chair/Caitlyn eventually
^
coaxed it out with a doggie biscuit.

or

; *however,*

At first, the puppy wouldn't come out from behind the chair/Caitlyn eventually
^
coaxed it out with a doggie biscuit.

Representative conjunctive adverbs are given. Actual answers may vary somewhat.

; moreover,

(1) The city is sponsoring its first Summer Arts Festival/the goal is to have
^
such a festival to mark the beginning of each season. (2) The Summer Arts

; however,

Festival will take place under a large tent in Wachusetts Park/ the other three
^
festivals will be held in the Historical Center Annex downtown. (3) Visual and

; furthermore,

performance artists in the surrounding area have been invited to take part/
^
vendors selling everything from ethnic food to specialty clothing to craft items
will set up booths. (4) The city's tourist board has hired a company specializ-

; nevertheless,

ing in such events to coordinate the festival/various city officials have re-
^
mained closely involved in the planning. (5) Everyone involved is hoping for a

; however,

big success at this first festival/the city has stated its determination to provide
^
support for a one-year cycle regardless of attendance at the initial event.

COMPREHENSION AND PRACTICE

20.8

Using Semicolons to Correct Comma Splices and Run-on Sentences

The following paragraph contains several comma splices and run-on sentences.
Put an * in front of any comma splice or run-on sentence. Then insert a semicolon, with or without a conjunctive adverb. If you use a conjunctive adverb, insert it above where one sentence should end and the next should begin, and put
a comma after it. Use the examples to guide you. Answers may vary.

EXAMPLE

;

The injury to her ankle was severe/ she was in great pain.

or

; *consequently,*

The injury to her ankle was severe/ she was in great pain.

(1) Jasmine earns money for college by delivering the morning newspaper. (2)*An adult can make a pretty good paycheck this way ; the person just has to be willing to get out of bed at 5 A.M. every day. (3)*Her route covers ten miles outside the city ; she delivers a total of 200 papers on weekdays and 100 on Sundays. (4)*Jasmine never complains ; however, her job is far from easy. (5)*She spends the first hour folding papers and putting them in plastic bags ; these steps are vital in order to keep the papers dry. (6) She then piles the papers into the passenger's seat in her car and begins driving. (7)*The process of delivering the papers is a little dangerous ; therefore, she puts her emergency blinkers on and drives slowly along her route. (8)*Her delivery method is interesting ; she grabs a paper from the seat and throws it completely over the car and into the subscriber's yard. (9) By 6:30, she has finished her entire route. (10)*She then stops at the bakery at the end of her route for coffee ; she is too tired to read the paper, though.

COMPREHENSION AND PRACTICE 20.9

Using Semicolons with Conjunctive Adverbs to Correct Comma Splices and Run-on Sentences

The following passage contains a number of comma splices and run-on sentences. Correct them by using a semicolon and one of the conjunctive adverbs listed below, as the example illustrates.

also	meanwhile	then
consequently	moreover	therefore
furthermore	nevertheless	thus

EXAMPLE The heavy rains destroyed the old earthen dam ; therefore, the mayor was forced to declare a state of emergency.

Answers in terms of conjunctive adverbs are representative. In some cases, more than one answer is acceptable.

(1) Advances in photography have made it possible for the average person to record the world in a professional way. (2) Digital cameras, many costing

less than $300, capture sharp, precise images and record them on a photo

storage card the images can be transferred to a computer and turned into
     ; then
∧

prints. (3) Through various easy-to-use computer programs, the pictures can

be manipulated or enhanced; furthermore in their electronic form, digital pic-

tures can be e-mailed. (4) With a few easy steps, a person can use these im-

ages to illustrate Web pages they can be combined with music and text to cre-
     ; moreover,
                  ∧

ate an inviting and informative Web site. (5) With digital photography, no film

is wasted on out-of-focus pictures nobody has to spend additional money to
     ; also,
          ∧

develop a roll of film. (6) The advances have been just as dramatic in the area

of video recording. (7) Today's video cameras are light, compact, and

powerful, they capture events with great clarity. (8) The color display available
  ; nevertheless,
  ∧

on most models makes it easy to see exactly what the lens is recording the
                     ; therefore,
                     ∧

operator is able to make any adjustments with ease. (9) The cost of these com-

pact video cameras has continued to drop many vacationers and even people
     ; consequently,
               ∧

on the street carry them.

CHALLENGE 20.4   Working with Semicolons and Conjunctive Adverbs

COLLABORATION

For Comprehension and Practice 20.7 (pages 312–313), you made some choices about how to connect clauses in a paragraph by using either a semicolon or a semicolon and a conjunctive adverb. Now, working with a partner, compare your two versions of the passage. Discuss why you made your choices. If, after your discussion, you prefer another way of joining some of your sentences, make those changes.

Correcting Comma Splices and Run-ons by Using Periods

Another way to correct comma splices and run-on sentences is to use a period between the subject–verb units to create separate sentences. This option isn't a good idea if the simple sentences are short because it may make your writing seem choppy. If the sentences are longer, however, separating them may be a good choice, as these examples show:

COMMA SPLICE   Larry's plan is to earn his two-year degree in Business Administration and

. He

Marketing, ~~he~~ then will enroll at the university to earn his undergraduate de-

gree.

RUN-ON   Serena and Venus Williams have brought genuine excitement back to women's

. Their

tennis ~~their~~ matches, especially the ones against each other, have been ratings

blockbusters.

You could certainly eliminate these errors by using a conjunction and a comma or a semicolon. The sentences that would result would be a bit long, however, and long sentences can be difficult to follow. Therefore, using a period to create separate simple sentences is a better choice. When you use this option to correct run-on sentences and comma splices, remember to capitalize the first word of the second sentence.

COMPREHENSION AND PRACTICE

20.10

Using a Period to Separate the Units

In this paragraph, using a period to separate the independent clauses is probably the best option because the clauses are long. Put a / between the clauses, and then insert a period to eliminate the run-on sentence or comma splice. Start the first word of a new sentence with a capital letter. Use the example to guide you.

EXAMPLE   By noontime on opening day, the line leading into the stadium was already a

. Inside,

quarter of a mile long/~~inside,~~ 10,000 people had already taken their seats,

waiting for the first ball to be thrown out.

(1) The recent hurricane changed the entire landscape at Horseneck

. Fortunately,

Beach, ~~fortunately,~~ only a few of the houses along the edge of the beach suf-

fered from the effects of severe erosion. (2) The most severely damaged house

was owned by Mr. Lionel Partridge, one of the oldest residents of the commu-

. The

nity, ~~the~~ storm ripped off the front of the house, sending all his belongings into

the churning ocean. (3) The contour of the beach itself showed the most dra-

. The

matic change of all, ~~the~~ dunes separating the beach from the road were completely flattened. (4) Foundations of several homes destroyed by earlier hurri-

. They

canes were visible again/~~they~~ had been buried for more than 25 years.

. The

(5) Even with the changes, Horseneck Beach is still beautiful, ~~the~~ whole experi-

ence should remind everyone of the tremendous power of nature.

COMPREHENSION AND PRACTICE

Working with a Period to Separate the Units

20.11 The following paragraph contains several comma splices and run-on sentences. Put an * in front of any comma splice or run-on sentence. Then put a / between the independent clauses. Insert a period where the first sentence should end, and then start the word that begins the second sentence with a capital letter. Use the example to guide you.

. The

EXAMPLE *The landscapers spent the afternoon digging up the dead sod/~~the~~ grass had

been completely destroyed by grubs.

. Even

(1) *Max's first experience with a credit card was not a good one, ~~even~~ at

age twenty-one, he wasn't ready for the responsibility. (2) Five years ago, he

filled out an application for a credit card at his favorite clothing store. (3) *A

. His

week later, the card came in the mail/~~his~~ troubles began at that point. (4) *His

. He

original plan was to buy one item a week, ~~he~~ would then pay off the entire bill

at the end of the month. (5) *For the first two months, he had no trouble keep-

. As

ing up with the payments/~~as~~ a result, Max decided to buy more things.

(6) However, his bill for the third month was more than $800, and he had put

. For

aside only $200. (7) *Max panicked and didn't pay the bill, ~~for~~ the next two

months he received the same bill, plus a finance charge. (8) *A few weeks later,

. It

Max received a letter from the credit department of the store, ~~it~~ instructed him

to call the department. (9) He was scared and ashamed, so he also ignored

that letter. (10) *Shortly after that, Max received a letter threatening him with

. After

legal action/~~after~~ that warning, he began to make payments again, and he cut

up his credit card.

CHALLENGE 20.5 Correcting Comma Splices and Run-ons in Your Writing

Return to the work you completed for Challenge 20.1 (page 307). Using the methods you have learned in this chapter, correct any comma splices and run-ons that your partner marked. Then reassess your writing. Do your ideas flow more smoothly? Are the relationships among the ideas clear?

CHAPTER QUICK CHECK Comma Splices and Run-on Sentences

CW 20.8
Correcting
comma
splices and
run-ons

The following passage contains a number of comma splices and run-on sentences. First, identify these errors by putting an ***** in front of each one. Then, using the various techniques discussed in this chapter, correct the errors. In some cases, more than one solution is possible. Answers may vary. Sample answers are shown.

(1) Among the most persistent urban myths circulating on the Internet are those involving scientific or medical matters. *(2) One group of myths involves great suffering and sometimes painful death for people, _{after} they have been exposed to exotic poisons or flesh-eating bacteria. *(3) The twists in the stories involve how they contracted the afflictions_; these people allegedly were infected from contact with everyday items like vending machines and pay phones. *(4) Everybody is exposed to such common objects_{, so} the stories seem vaguely possible. *(5) Some of the myths involve rare, deadly insects or spiders_{. The} the bite of these creatures in public restrooms, fast-food restaurants, and convenience stores, causes paralysis or death. *(6) Of course, these insects or creatures either don't actually exist or don't pose a threat to humans_{; nevertheless,} people still believe in them. *(7) In one persistent myth, a pet owner flushes a baby alligator down a toilet in a big city like New York or Chicago_{, and} the alligator eventually grows to gargantuan size in the sewer system below. *(8) In some myths, the U.S. government or some sinister force adds a dangerous drug or compound to prepared foods_{, and} in some cases a particular brand is actually named. (9) This kind of hoax can cause widespread damage to an innocent manufacturer by weakening consumer confidence in their product. *(10) The nature of the Internet guarantees the fast spread of any new rumors_{; consequently,} millions of people hear and pass on the latest hoax in a matter of minutes.

QUICK STUDY   Student Example

This chapter discusses the importance of recognizing the logical limits, the beginnings and ends, of the ideas you express. Consider this paragraph on a related topic, an experience that marked the end of a period or stage of life:

> September 11, 2001, was a day that eliminated any sense that we could ever truly be safe and secure. On that morning, I walked into work in New York City at approximately 9:05 A.M. As usual, I picked up the phone to call my boyfriend back at home in New Jersey to let him know that I had arrived safely. Each time I dialed the number, however, I got a busy signal. I felt that familiar stirring in the pit of my stomach that always indicates that something is wrong. Just as I was about to lift the receiver to try dialing again, I looked up and saw my friend standing in the doorway she looked horror-stricken. "We're being attacked. They're flying planes into the World Trade Center Towers," she blurted out. My heart froze, my older brother worked on the seventy-seventh floor of Tower One. Immediately, I called my sister-in-law in Brooklyn to see if she had any news the line was busy. My heart began to pound, and my hands began to shake. I dialed again and again until, at last, my sister-in-law picked up to tell me she hadn't been able to reach my brother. For the next several hours, I just dialed every number I could think of, my parents, my brothers, my sisters, my boyfriend, hoping for some news. I finally made it home from Manhattan more than twelve hours later. As soon as I walked in the door, my boyfriend grabbed hold of me and told me that my brother was OK. At that moment, all I felt was relief, from that point on my life hasn't been the same. Never again will I ever have the sense of safety and security I felt before I learned about the World Trade Center attacks.

First complete the following activities in response to this paragraph:

1. Several sentences in this paragraph are highlighted. Evaluate these sections for problems with comma splices and run-on sentences. Put a / where one sentence should end and the next one begin. Then, on a separate sheet of paper, correct the errors, using one of the methods outlined in this chapter to eliminate them.

2. Of all the details included in this paragraph, which do you think is the strongest? Why? Use the following lines for your answer.

Answers will vary, although most students will probably identify the details about first

learning of the attacks on the World Trade Center. Other possibilities include the details

about the repeated frantic phone calls and about her brother's ultimate safe escape.

3. This paragraph includes a direct quotation:

"We're being attacked. They're flying planes into the World Trade Center

Towers," she blurted out.

Do you agree with this choice or would the paragraph have been better if it instead included a paraphrase of the quotation like this:

She told me that somebody was flying planes into the World Trade Towers.

On the following lines, indicate your choice and briefly explain your reasoning.

Most students will agree that the direct quotation is the better choice because it

captures the emotion and terror of the moment.

Now explore the topic in writing. Like the paragraph above, you could discuss an experience that marked the end of some period in your life or the beginning of another. Or you might also choose one of these subjects related to the subject matter of this chapter:

- a place or thing from your childhood to which you still feel a strong connection
- the difficulties of beginning something new
- a time when you accidentally missed a signal or failed to make a connection
- the key limits that parents should impose on their children

COLLABORATION

1. Exchange your draft with a classmate. Evaluate the paragraph you receive. If you discover any errors, especially comma splices or run-on sentences, make a note in the margin and then return the paper to the writer.

2. Consider the comments and corrections your reader has made and create a final draft of your paragraph.

SUMMARY EXERCISE Comma Splices and Run-on Sentences

The following passage contains a number of comma splices and run-on sentences. First, identify these errors by putting an * in front of each one. Then, using the various techniques discussed in this chapter, correct the errors. In some cases, more than one solution is possible. Answers may vary. Sample answers are shown.

(1) In the neighborhood where I grew up, there was an old, abandoned house. (2)*According to all the kids in the neighborhood, it was haunted I didn't believe them. (3)*At age eleven, I finally explored that house with my two best friends, I have always regretted this adventure.

(4)*The house was located across the street from our school it seemed to call to us every time we passed it. (5)*Jack and Nickie wanted to break in, I kept talking them out of it. (6)*Finally, I could resist no longer we made our plans to enter the haunted house on the following Saturday night.

(7)*At eight o'clock that evening, we met in my backyard I had told my mother we were going to play basketball under the lights at nearby Pulaski Park. (8) We often played at night, so she wasn't suspicious. (9)*We left my yard quickly and headed off to the house we were all set for the big break-in.

(10) We had spent a few days planning our caper, so we had come well prepared. (11)*Nickie brought a hammer and a crowbar Jack took his father's big flashlight. (12)*I brought a screwdriver and a pair of pliers we wanted to be prepared for every possibility.

(13)*Twenty minutes later, we reached the house it was pitch dark and very quiet. (14)*We went around back and entered through the cellar door the lock was badly rusted, so we only had to pry a little with the crowbar. (15)*Once inside, we crept down the stairs to the dirt cellar it was dark and clammy. (16)*Jack shined his light around the cellar, everything was covered with dust and cobwebs. (17)*We never made it upstairs, the floorboards squeaked, and we ran out at lightning speed.

(18) *We ran two blocks before stopping <ins>. None</ins> none of us had ever been so scared in our whole lives. (19) We all headed home and agreed not to tell any-one else. (20) *I've kept the secret <ins>; however,</ins> I don't know if Nickie or Jack ever told.

FOR FURTHER EXPLORATION

1. Consider one of the following topics:

   - how to maintain a healthful diet
   - a childhood experience in the principal's or school nurse's office
   - the responsibilities and dangers of credit cards
   - the one environmental or social issue that never receives the attention it de-serves
   - the advantages—or consequences—of being popular

   Prewrite on the subject, using one of the strategies you practiced in Chapter 2, and work your way through the rest of the writing process. Then complete a draft essay of at least 500 words on this subject.

2. Exchange your draft with a classmate. Check the draft you receive for weak-nesses, looking in particular for comma splices and run-on sentences. Mark these errors with CS (for comma splice) and RS (for run-on sentence), using the material in this chapter as a guide, and then return the draft to the writer.

3. Revise your essay, correcting any comma splices and run-on sentences or other problems discovered by your reader.

RECAP Comma Splices and Run-on Sentences

New terms in this chapter	Definitions
comma splice	an error in which sentences are incorrectly connected by a comma
	EXAMPLE The storm dumped four inches of rain across the region, / several cities and towns suffered heavy flooding.
run-on sentence	an error in which two sentences are run together with no punctuation or connectors
	EXAMPLE James forgot his wallet at home / he didn't realize it until he arrived at the register.

To Identify Comma Splices and Run-on Sentences

1. Identify all subject–verb units.

2. Establish whether the clauses can stand alone.

Four Ways to Correct Comma Splices and Run-on Sentences

1. subject–verb unit + *comma and coordinating conjunction* + subject–verb unit

2. subject–verb unit + *subordinating conjunction* + subject–verb unit

    or

    subordinating conjunction + subject–verb unit and *comma* + subject–verb unit

3. subject–verb unit + *semicolon* + subject–verb unit

    or

    subject–verb unit + *semicolon, conjunctive adverb, and comma* + subject–verb unit

4. subject–verb unit + *period* + subject–verb unit (begin with capital)

GOING FORWARD...

**CW 20.11
Run-ons,
comma
splices, and
more**

Q: What's the best way for me to make sure I have correct sentences and not comma splices or run-on sentences?

A: To avoid these errors, evaluate each sentence that you write. If this unit of ideas expresses a single point, you are all set. But if it expresses more than one idea, ask yourself this simple sentence: Do I want to connect these two ideas or keep them separate? If you want to connect them, then use a conjunction with a comma in front of it or a semicolon. If you want to separate them, put a period— or an exclamation point or question mark—between the two points you have made. That's all there is to it.

PART 5

Understanding Subjects and Verbs

CHAPTER 21
Subject–Verb Agreement

Navigating This Chapter

In this chapter, you will learn how to recognize and avoid the following difficulties with subject–verb agreement:

- problems when the subject follows the verb
- problems when words come between subjects and verbs
- problems with indefinite pronouns
- problems from other causes, including compound subjects; collective nouns; singular nouns ending in -s; and words referring to measurements, money, time, and weight

GETTING STARTED . . .

CW 21.1
Chapter basics

Q: When I go over what I've written, I'm not always sure that my subjects and verbs fit together. What should I do to make sure that my subjects and verbs always match up?

A: First, the good news is that, for the most part, errors involving **subject–verb agreement** occur in only the present tense. This means your job is easier than you might think. First, isolate each verb and its subject. Once you've done this, double-check the verb ending, making sure you've used a singular form for a singular subject and a plural form for a plural subject. It's as easy as that.

Overview: Understanding Subject–Verb Agreement

CW 21.2
Understanding subject–verb agreement

When two parties, either companies or individuals, plan a joint enterprise, they draw up an **agreement,** a document outlining the details of their relationship. That way, both parties know the roles they will play to ensure that everything runs smoothly. In writing, agreement means essentially the same thing. Each subject must agree in **number** with its verb in order for your sentences to run smoothly. As the term suggests, number refers to the **quantity** or **amount** the word indicates, either *singular,* meaning one, or *plural,* meaning more than one. Singular subjects call for singular verb forms, and plural subjects call for plural verb forms. Maintaining subject–verb agreement is essential because subjects and verbs communicate the basic meaning of your sentences.

Avoiding Agreement Errors When the Subject Follows the Verb

ESL Note
See "Sentence Basics" on pages 589–590 and "Agreement" on pages 592–594.

The secret to avoiding errors in **subject–verb agreement** is to identify the subject. To do this, as Chapter 17, "The Sentence," shows, ask yourself *who or what is doing the action or being discussed?* The answer to that question is the subject.

In the majority of the sentences you write, the subject comes before the verb, as these examples show:

EXAMPLE

┌──────subject──────┐ ┌─verb─┐
Volunteer relief workers provide a valuable service at the scenes of fires, accidents, and natural disasters.

CW 21.3
Avoiding errors in subject–verb agreement

┌subject┐┌verb┐
The *Internet puts* the world at a person's fingertips.

But not all sentences follow this pattern. In some sentences, the subject appears after the verb. One type of sentence in which the subject follows the verb is a question:

EXAMPLE

┌verb┐┌──────subject──────┐ ┌verb┐
Do division supervisors attend weekly planning meetings?

verb subject┌──verb──┐
Is ESPN planning to broadcast the X-Games again?

CW 21.4
Recognizing subject–verb agreement problems

In the first sentence, *supervisors* is the subject; in the second, *ESPN* is the subject. Note, however, that in each case, part of the verb precedes the subject: *do* in the first sentence and *is* in the second.

Sentences beginning with *there* or *here* also feature subjects that follow the verb. *There* and *here* are adverbs, and only a noun or pronoun can be the subject of a sentence. So in sentences beginning with *there* or *here*, the actual subject follows the verb, as these examples show:

EXAMPLE

┌verb┐   ┌subject┐
There *are* several new *signs* near the new highway exit.

┌─verb─┐   ┌─subject─┐
Here *comes* the guest *speaker* on the subject of health care reform.

CW 21.5
Issues in subject–verb agreement

In the first sentence, *signs* is the subject, even though it follows the verb *are*. In the second sentence, the subject is *speaker*, even though it follows the verb *comes*.

FAST FACT   In typical sentences that begin with *there* or *here*, what do these words mean? Nothing. Used to open sentences in this way, *there* and *here* are called **expletives.** They simply serve to start a sentence. To strengthen your writing, use words that MEAN something. In other words, avoid using *there* and *here* to begin your sentences.

COMPREHENSION AND PRACTICE

21.1

CW 21.6
Maintaining
subject–verb
agreement

Identifying Subjects That Follow the Verb

For each sentence in the following passage, identify the verbs and subjects, circling the verbs and underlining the subjects. Use the following example as a guide.

EXAMPLE   Here (is) the missing <u>notebook</u>.

(1) Decades after their introduction, there (are) still many game <u>shows</u> on television. (2) There (is) <u>nothing</u> challenging about some of them, for instance *Wheel of Fortune*. (3) Then there (is) *<u>Jeopardy!</u>* (4) (Is) there a harder game <u>show</u> anywhere? (5) (Don't) the <u>producers</u> of *Jeopardy!* (have) any mercy for the poor contestants?

COMPREHENSION AND PRACTICE

21.2

Maintaining Agreement When Subjects Follow the Verb

Each of the sentences in the following paragraph contains a pair of verbs in parentheses. First, find and underline the subject with which the verb must agree. Then circle the verb that agrees with that subject, using the example to guide you.

EXAMPLE   (Has/(Have)) <u>Mary Beth</u> and <u>Joe</u> rented their apartment yet?

(1) (Doesn't/(Don't)) <u>people</u> know how easy it is to register as a bone marrow donor? (2) According to recent news articles, there ((is)/are) a <u>shortage</u> of bone marrow donors. (3) It's too bad, because here ((is)/are) a wonderful <u>opportunity</u> to help save someone's life, and people are missing out on it because of misconceptions about the procedure itself. (4) First, there ((is)/are) a blood <u>test</u>. (5) ((Is)/Are) there a simpler <u>form</u> of testing available? (6) Once a blood sample is taken, there (is/(are)) some sophisticated <u>tests</u> done at a special lab, and the results are entered into a special bone-marrow-donor registry. (7) Here ((is)/are) the <u>point</u> at which everyone waits for a match between someone in need of a transplant and a potential donor. (8) Once a match is identified and the donor is notified, there (is/(are)) a few simple <u>steps</u> during which

marrow is extracted from the donor's hip. (9) For the donor, the good news is that there (is/are) very little <u>discomfort</u>. (10) (Does/Do) people have to know any more than this to get involved?

CHALLENGE 21.1 Examining Subjects and Verbs in Your Writing

1. Comprehension and Practice 21.1 discusses two television game shows, *Wheel of Fortune* and *Jeopardy!* What is your favorite game show? Why do you like it? Write a paragraph of at least five to ten sentences on this subject, using present tense verbs only.

COLLABORATION

2. Exchange your paragraph with a partner. On the paper you receive, identify the subjects and verbs by underlining the subjects and circling the verbs. Put a ✓ next to any sentence that contains an error in subject–verb agreement. When you are finished, return the paragraph to your partner, and check the work your partner did on your paragraph.

Avoiding Agreement Errors When Words Come between the Subject and Verb

CW 21.7 Practicing subject–verb agreement

Often, problems with subject–verb agreement occur because of the words you use *between* subjects and verbs. Don't be fooled by the noun closest to the verb, which may not actually be the subject. Instead, be sure that you identify the person or thing that is performing the action or that is being discussed.

In some cases, what comes between a subject and verb is a *prepositional phrase.* As Chapter 17, "The Sentence," explains, a prepositional phrase begins with a preposition and ends with a noun or pronoun. Common prepositions include *about, against, around, behind, beneath, by, down, during, inside, out, through, to, up, within,* and *without.* Here is an example of a sentence with a prepositional phrase coming between the subject and the verb:

                   prepositional
       subject┐ ┌— phrase —┐ ┌verb

EXAMPLE   The spare tire *under the tools* was flat.

In this sentence, the verb *was* agrees with the singular subject *tire,* not with the noun closest to it, the plural object of the preposition, *tools.*

Other times, a subject and its verb are separated by a *subordinate clause.* As Chapter 19, "Subordination and Coordination," explains, a subordinate clause is a subject and verb unit introduced by a subordinating conjunction or relative pronoun. Common subordinating conjunctions include *after, although, because, if, since, unless, until, when, whether,* and *while.* Common relative pronouns include *that, which, who,* and *whose.* Here is a sentence in which the subject and verb are separated by a subordinate clause:

EXAMPLE

┌─subject─┐ ┌──────────── subordinate clause ────────────┐ ┌verb┐

Students *who have computer network experience* enjoy great job prospects.

In this sentence, the verb agrees in number with the actual subject, *students,* not with the word closest to the verb, *experience.*

COMPREHENSION AND PRACTICE 21.3

Identifying Subjects Separated from Verbs by Other Words

For each sentence in the following passage, identify the verbs and subjects, circling the verbs and underlining the subjects. This task will be easier if you cross out any words that come between subject and verb, as the example shows.

EXAMPLE

On some days, the <u>crowd</u> ~~in the cafeteria lining up for lunch~~ (reaches) the back of the building.

(1) <u>Advertisements</u> ~~on the Internet, especially on Web pages and search engines,~~ (continue) to generate controversy. (2) For one thing, some <u>people</u> ~~using the Web, especially those using it for work,~~ (find) the advertisements annoying. (3) The most distracting <u>ones,</u> ~~according to these users,~~ (pop up) in the middle of the screen. (4) Other <u>critics</u> ~~of the practice~~ (dislike) the lack of government regulation over the advertisements. (5) Yet many other <u>people</u> ~~using the 'Net for pleasure or work simply~~ (pay) little attention to the ads.

COMPREHENSION AND PRACTICE 21.4

Maintaining Agreement with Subjects Separated from Verbs by Other Words

Each of the sentences in the following passage contains a pair of verbs in parentheses. First, find and underline the subject with which the verb must agree. Then circle the verb that agrees with the subject you have underlined, as the example shows.

EXAMPLE

The <u>burners</u> on the stove, which are now covered with drips of paint from the ceiling, (needs/(need)) to be replaced soon.

(1) A good general <u>contractor</u> who can perform a wide variety of tasks ((remains)/remain) a rare individual. (2) Too often, <u>people</u> needing work done

(enters/enter) the process with uncertainty and trepidation. (3) Stories about unscrupulous contractors doing inferior work (does/do) nothing to reassure them. (4) But my friend Lou Ledoux, the owner of South-End-Boys Contracting, the company he started after doing carpentry work part time for years, (qualifies/qualify) as that rare individual. (5) Lou, who does any kind of work, from new construction to general repairs, (does/do) no advertising. (6) Nevertheless, his schedule, particularly during the good-weather months, (remains/remain) full. (7) That's because people, especially those operating on a strict budget, (needs/need) a contractor who is skilled, dependable, and honest. (8) Nobody who has seen the quality of one of his finished projects (has/have) any doubts about Lou's ability. (9) In terms of dependability, the needs of his clients to see the work completed according to schedule (represents/represent) Lou's top priority. (10) But Lou's calm demeanor regardless of any complications (impresses/impress) people most of all.

Avoiding Agreement Errors with Indefinite Pronouns

Another potential difficulty with subject–verb agreement involves indefinite pronouns. *Indefinite pronouns* are used to refer to general rather than specific people and things, for instance, the indefinite *somebody* rather than the specific *Bill*, the indefinite *anything* rather than the specific *a burrito*. See pages 411 and 417–418 in Chapter 26, "Pronouns: Understanding Case, Clear Pronoun–Antecedent Agreement, and Nonsexist Pronoun Usage," for a further discussion and a complete list of indefinite pronouns.

Some indefinite pronouns are singular, some are plural, and some are singular or plural depending on how you use them. Of these words, *another, anybody, anyone, anything, each, either, everybody, everyone, everything, much, neither, nobody, no one, nothing, one, somebody, someone,* and *something* are singular and call for singular verb forms:

EXAMPLE

singular
┌singular┐┌verb form
Nobody wants to deal with stress on a daily basis.

singular
┌singular┐┌verb form
Someone has to find the owner of that puppy.

Both, few, many, and *several* are always plural and call for plural verb forms:

EXAMPLE

plural ┌verb form
plural
Both of the apartments *look* well maintained.

┌plural
Many of the more than one hundred people attending the presentation now
┌plural verb form
want to participate in the training program.

All, any, more, most, none, and *some* are either singular or plural depending on the word they refer to in the sentence. With one of these pronouns, check the word it refers to. If that word is singular, choose a singular form of the verb; if it is plural, choose a plural form of the verb, as these examples show:

EXAMPLE

┌─singular─┐   singular
┌verb form┐
All her *enthusiasm* suddenly *disappears* at the thought of rehearsing.

plural
┌plural┐┌verb form
All their *books* *are* missing.

COMPREHENSION AND PRACTICE

Maintaining Agreement with Indefinite Pronouns

21.5 Underline the verbs in the following sentences. Then fill in the blank in each sentence with an appropriate indefinite pronoun from the list below. In some cases, you may need to use the same pronoun more than once.

anyone   everyone   no one   none   some

EXAMPLE Of the new medications available to combat asthma, _____*some*_____ have proven

to be especially effective.

(1) _____Everyone_____ likes to save money. (2) Now, _____no one_____ has to

pay high long-distance fees, thanks to the Internet. (3) With the right Internet

service provider and computer hardware, _____anyone_____ can route long-

distance calling through the Internet. (4) Because of occasional problems in

sound quality, _____some_____ view this innovation as a waste of time.

(5) But according to a recent article on the subject, _____none_____ of the

small business owners currently paying $500 or more a month in standard

long-distance fees seem to agree.

COMPREHENSION AND PRACTICE

Identifying Correct Agreement with Indefinite Pronouns

21.6 For each sentence in the following passage, identify the subject by underlining it. Then circle the verb that agrees with that subject from the pair of verbs in parentheses. Use the example to guide you.

EXAMPLE | <u>Nobody</u> in the office (**has**/have) a personal parking space.

(1) <u>Springfield</u>, like most medium-sized cities, (**has**/have) several major neighborhoods. (2) The east end of the city is called "the Flint," and <u>nobody</u> (**seems**/seem) to know where the name came from. (3) <u>Many</u> of the people living in the Flint (traces/**trace**) their heritage to Canada. (4) <u>Everyone</u> who lives in the south end of the city (refer/**refers**) to this neighborhood as "Maplewood." (5) <u>Some</u> of the larger homes in this part of the city (displays/**display**) the elegance of the Victorian Age. (6) The neighborhood in the center of the city is called "Below the Hill," and <u>many</u> of the young professionals working in the city (lives/**live**) here. (7) This part of the city is undergoing a rejuvenation, and <u>everyone</u> (**has**/have) been rushing to buy and restore the brownstone buildings that line the streets. (8) "The Highlands" and "the Lowlands" in the hilly north end of the city are the other two neighborhoods, and <u>everybody</u> in the city (**enjoys**/enjoy) the beauty of these two areas. (9) <u>Both</u> (has/**have**) tree-lined streets and large homes with big yards. (10) <u>Each</u> also (**features**/feature) a clear view of the Springfield River.

CHALLENGE 21.2 **Writing Sentences Using Indefinite Pronouns That Can Be Either Singular or Plural**

COLLABORATION

Here again is the list of indefinite pronouns that are either singular or plural depending on what they refer to:

all	any	more
most	none	some

Working with a partner, write two sentences for each, one in which the word refers to a singular word and one in which the word refers to a plural word.

Avoiding Agreement Errors from Other Causes

The following situations can also create confusion as you make decisions about subject–verb agreement.

When the Subject Is Compound

As Chapter 17, "The Sentence," indicates, not all subjects are individual words. Many are *compound subjects:* more than one noun or pronoun connected in most cases by *and* or *or.* Compound subjects connected by *and* are almost always plural. The exceptions are subjects that are commonly thought of as one, such as *pork and beans, peanut butter and jelly, peace and quiet, ham and eggs,* and *rock and roll.*

EXAMPLE A *headache* and a *bruise* on her arm *were* the only indications that Margarita had been in an accident.

If the two subjects are singular and connected by *or,* use a singular form of the verb:

EXAMPLE A *doughnut* or a *muffin is* not going to help anyone on a diet.

But if the subjects are both plural, use a plural form of the verb:

EXAMPLE *Doughnuts* or *muffins are* not going to help anyone on a diet.

When the compound subject consists of one singular word and one plural word connected by *or,* make the verb agree with the subject closest to it:

EXAMPLE The *supervisor* or the *workers are* responsible for the decreased level of production.

Workers is closer to the verb, so the correct choice is the form that agrees with *workers.*

When the Subject Is a Collective Noun or Is Introduced by a Cue Word

Collective nouns are words that name *groups* of items or people. Common collective nouns include *audience, class, committee, faculty, flock, herd, jury, swarm,* and *team.* (See Chapter 25, "Nouns: Working Effectively with Words That Name," for more on collective nouns.) Collective nouns are singular, so they call for singular verb forms:

EXAMPLE This year's *team has won* twenty-five games so far.

In some cases, certain words, called *cue words,* help you to identify whether a subject is singular or plural. Common singular cue words include *a, an, another, each, either, every, neither,* and *one.* A subject introduced by one of these words will be singular and call for a singular verb form:

EXAMPLE   ┌singular┐   singular ┌verb form
Neither sales representative *recalls* the meeting.

Common plural cue words include *all, both, few, many, several,* and *some.* Subjects introduced by these words call for a plural verb form:

EXAMPLE   ┌plural   plural ┌verb form
Few great novels ever *make* good movies.

When the Subject Is a Singular Word Ending in -*s*, a Word Referring to an Amount, or a Word That Has the Same Singular and Plural Form

Certain words that end in -*s* may look plural, but they are actually singular and call for singular verb forms. Common words in this category include *economics, ethics, mathematics, measles, mumps, news, physics,* and *politics.*

EXAMPLE   ┌singular┐ ┌singular verb form
Physics appears to be growing in popularity in schools across the nation.

Nouns used to refer to measurements, money, time, and weight can also cause some confusion in terms of subject–verb agreement. These words may seem plural, but because they are used to refer to the entire amount as one unit, they are actually singular and call for singular verb forms:

EXAMPLE   ┌───singular───┐ ┌singular verb form
Fifty dollars is much more than any ticket is worth.

Finally, with certain words such as *antelope, deer, fish,* and *species,* use either a singular or plural form of the verb depending on whether you mean one or more than one:

EXAMPLE   singular ┐┌─singular verb form─┐
That *moose has broken* out of its holding area.

┌plural┐ ┌singular verb form
Those *moose look* so peaceful as they stand together.

FAST FACT   The word "news" is actually an *acronym,* a word that draws its name from the initials of the words it refers to. For example, *scuba* is an acronym for *self-contained underwater breathing apparatus.* And what is *news* an acronym for? It gets its name from the four directions from which information appears and is gathered: *north, east, west,* and *south.*

COMPREHENSION AND PRACTICE

Maintaining Agreement with Compound Subjects

21.7 Each of the sentences in the following passage includes a pair of verbs in parentheses. First underline the compound subject, and then circle the verb that agrees with that subject. Use the example to guide you.

EXAMPLE

Even after working all afternoon, David and Bobbie still (has/*have*) not been able to start the car.

(1) In today's modern world, eye specialists and patients looking to improve their eyesight (has/*have*) a number of alternatives available. (2) For those still interested in glasses, ultra-thin lenses and smaller shapes (has/*have*) replaced coke-bottle lenses and clunky frames. (3) Today, style and comfort (*do*/does) not have to be sacrificed, thanks to the advent of low-cost designer frames. (4) In addition, bifocals or trifocals (has/*have*) been replaced in many cases with an innovative type of lens that allows the wearer to see clearly regardless of the distance. (5) For those wanting to do without glasses altogether, daily-wear contact lenses or extended-care contact lenses (remains/*remain*) the most common options. (6) Colored lenses and patterned lenses (is/*are*) among the variations of contacts available to the daring and style-conscious wearer. (7) Bifocal contacts and contacts that reshape the lens (is/*are*) recent innovations in this field. (8) Also, conventional surgery or laser surgery (*enables*/enable) people with vision problems to go without glasses or contacts. (9) Of course, any surgery has risks, so with this type of procedure, either the eye specialist or a specially trained technician thoroughly (*explains*/explain) to the patient what will occur. (10) The improved vision and freedom from vision aids of any type (makes/*make*) these surgical alternatives an increasingly popular choice among the young and physically active.

COMPREHENSION AND PRACTICE 21.8

Maintaining Agreement with Collective Nouns, with Singular Words Ending in -s, and with Words Referring to Amounts

Each of the following sentences contains the infinitive of a verb (*to* + a simple form of the verb—*to speak*) in parentheses. Identify the subject of the verb by underlining it, and then write the proper *present tense* form of the verb on the line provided. Remember—the story is told in the present, so use present tense forms only. Use the example as a guide.

EXAMPLE The <u>audience</u> (to be) _____ is _____ clearly enjoying the concert.

(1) The <u>committee</u> in charge of selecting the Youth Center's Volunteer of the Year (to have) _____ has _____ an important job. (2) A nominating <u>team</u> of five committee members first (to select) _____ selects _____ five semifinalists from the many nominations. (3) In most years, 50 to 100 <u>nominations</u> (to be) _____ are _____ not unusual. (4) The <u>ethics</u> of the situation (to require) _____ requires _____ careful, objective scrutiny of the nominations. (5) That's because <u>politics</u> often (to play) _____ plays _____ a part in the nominating process, with companies and organizations lobbying for the opportunity to highlight the activities of one of their employees to thousands of people across the state. (6) <u>Economics</u> (to do) _____ does _____ not come into play, however, because no monetary reward is attached to the award. (7) After the initial selections are made, two <u>hours</u> (to pass) _____ passes _____ while the team ranks the candidates in ten categories on a 1–5 scale. (8) Ultimately, simple <u>mathematics</u> (to determine) _____ determines _____ the winner, with the nominee holding the highest composite score being unanimously named Volunteer of the Year. (9) Despite efforts to keep the results secret until the annual recognition banquet, <u>news</u> often (to spread) _____ spreads _____ among the rest of the committee. (10) On the night of the recognition banquet, as the <u>audience</u> (to applaud) _____ applauds _____ for the winner, the committee sits back and enjoys what their hard work has brought about.

CHALLENGE 21.3 Revising to Achieve Subject–Verb Agreement

COLLABORATION

Working with a partner, help the writer of the following Letter to the Editor revise to eliminate the errors in subject–verb agreement. Cross out the wrong verb form and write the correct one above it. Some sentences are correct as they are.

Dear Editor:

(1) Right now, few members of the City Council ~~appears~~ *appear* to be taking the city's traffic problems seriously. (2) Thirty minutes ~~are~~ *is* clearly an unreasonable amount of time to spend stuck in downtown traffic. (3) Under the worst circumstances, drivers should be able to complete this two-mile drive in half *OK* that time. (4) The streets blocked off to make the pedestrian mall five years ago ~~represents~~ *represent* the main impediment to improving the flow of traffic. (5) As a result, anyone who travels on the downtown streets ~~have~~ *has* to take a series of narrow one-way streets in order to get around the mall. (6) When buses or a tractor trailer ~~enter~~ *enters* the area, traffic slows down even more than usual. (7) Even the blue-ribbon committee that originally lobbied in favor of the pedestrian mall to bring more consumers downtown ~~want~~ *wants* it removed. (8) Of course, eliminating the pedestrian mall will cost money, and so most members of the council ~~seems~~ *seem* hesitant to vote in favor of the change. (9) But each of our elected officials ~~have~~ *has* a responsibility to act in the best interest of the citizens. (10) There ~~is~~ *are* many voters who are watching carefully and will make sure that the councilors who won't act will be out of a job.

CHAPTER QUICK CHECK Mastering Subject–Verb Agreement

**CW 21.8
Making
subjects and
verbs agree**

The following passage contains the various kinds of errors in subject–verb agreement discussed in this chapter. Consider again the ways to correct these errors illustrated in this chapter. Then identify errors in agreement, crossing them out and writing the correct verb form above the incorrect one, as the example shows:

EXAMPLE Several of my friends from my old neighborhood still ~~plays~~ ^{play} basketball together two nights a week in the City League.

(1) Speed and convenience ~~seems~~ ^{seem} to be what most customers are looking for when they go grocery shopping. (2) Because everyone, especially those who have demanding work schedules, ~~want~~ ^{wants} to spend less time in line, more and more retailers are experimenting with an innovation. (3) Under this new system, a customer with fewer than 20 items ~~go~~ ^{goes} to a self-service area. (4) In this area, there ~~is~~ ^{are} 15 stations, each with a computer screen and a small platform containing an electronic scanner. (5) The steps involved in the process ~~requires~~ ^{require} no special training. (6) All the instructions ~~appears~~ ^{appear} on the computer screen. (7) The UPC code, printed on all items, ~~are~~ ^{is} the key to the process. (8) This series of vertical bars and numbers ~~indicate~~ ^{indicates} the name and price of the item. (9) The customer runs the UPC code of each item in front of the scanner, and an electronic tone and visual image on the screen ~~tells~~ ^{tell} the customer that the sale has been recorded. (10) A team of three workers ~~monitor~~ ^{monitors} the 15 checkout stations, ready to address any problems customers encounter.

QUICK STUDY   Student Example

**CW 21.9
Practicing
subject–verb
agreement**

This chapter focuses on choosing elements to go together. Take a look at the following paragraph on a related subject—a good strategy to persuade people:

One of the best ways to convince someone to accept your ideas are to discuss your point of view calmly and rationally. People don't always react when someone yell and scream about an issue. This lack of response don't necessarily mean that they agree, however. Some people may not respond because they are trying to avoid an ugly scene, and others may just be uncomfortable or afraid to be around an angry person. But when you discuss a subject rationally, people usually listen. In many cases, people will be more inclined to sign your petition, go along with your plans for the weekend, or reconsider their stand on an issue because of your calm, positive approach to the subject. Today, there is too many people who try to persuade others by being loud and obnoxious. In my view, a respectful tone and positive attitude represents the best strategy to win people over to your side.

First complete the following activities in response to this paragraph:

1. Several sentences in this paragraph are highlighted. Evaluate these sections for errors in subject–verb agreement. On a separate sheet of paper, rewrite sentences containing errors, using the material in this chapter to help you correct them.

2. In your view, does the topic sentence of this paragraph prepare the reader for the discussion that follows in the body of the paragraph? What leads you to this conclusion? Use the following lines for your answer.

   Most students will agree that the topic sentence does prepare the reader for the

   discussion to follow. The topic sentence suggests a way to persuade people to accept

   a point of view, and the supporting sentences illustrate reasons why people fail and

   succeed to do so.

3. This paragraph, which deals with how to persuade people, is itself a piece of persuasive writing: an **argument** paragraph. (See pages 157–171 for more on argument.) But how successful is the paragraph in convincing you that this approach is a good way to convince others? On a separate sheet of paper, explain your reaction to the paragraph, identifying what you see as its strengths and its weaknesses.

Now explore the topic in writing. You could focus, as the paragraph above does, on some strategy or technique to improve personal communications or relationships. Or you might choose one of these subjects related to the subject matter of this chapter:

- a time that you experienced or witnessed a disagreement
- a complaint you have about a product or service that didn't live up to its guarantee
- why compromising can often be so hard
- what people need in order to be compatible

COLLABORATION

1. Exchange your draft with a classmate. Evaluate the paragraph you receive. If you discover any problem spots, especially errors in subject–verb agreement, make a note in the margin and then return the paper to the writer.

2. Consider the comments and corrections your reader has made and create a final draft of your paragraph.

SUMMARY EXERCISE Mastering Subject–Verb Agreement

**CW 21.10
More
practice with
subject–verb
agreement**

The following passage contains the various kinds of errors in subject–verb agreement discussed in this chapter. Consider again the ways to correct these errors illustrated in this chapter. Then identify errors in agreement, crossing them out and writing the correct verb form above the incorrect one.

(1) There ~~is~~ *are* many choices available for the person looking for a laptop computer. (2) Thanks to price cuts by most major manufacturers, anybody wanting the option of a portable computer now ~~have~~ *has* that possibility. (3) This new class of laptops ~~appear~~ *appears* to consist of the first portables with broad consumer appeal.

(4) Attractive laptop computers with huge amounts of memory now ~~costs~~ *cost* far less than ever before. (5) Only a few years ago, $3,000 ~~were~~ *was* considered a bargain-basement price for a basic portable computer. (6) Right now, a laptop with ten times as much memory and many more built-in features, including wireless capability, ~~run~~ *runs* under $2,000.

(7) In the past two years alone, there ~~has~~ *have* been improvements almost beyond belief. (8) Today, for example, five pounds ~~are~~ *is* considered heavy for these powerhouse portables. (9) A tiny keyboard or awkward pointer was a negative feature of many of the older portable computers. (10) Today, however, everybody trying the new generation of laptops ~~give~~ *gives* positive marks to these features.

(11) Either a brighter active-matrix color screen or the many built-in features ~~is~~ *are* also cited by consumers as factors that cause them to consider purchasing a laptop. (12) In addition, there ~~have~~ *has* been great interest in the DVD

drives and extended-life batteries available to consumers. (13) All these features ~~has~~ been applauded by prospective buyers. [have]

(14) According to consumer responses, here ~~are~~ the most popular improvement: speed. [is] (15) Everyone trying these new laptops ~~remark~~ on this improvement, especially with complex tasks. [remarks] (16) Many of these laptops ~~features~~ the newest generation of Pentium chips. [feature] (17) Now some of the most complex functions ~~takes~~ only a few seconds. [take]

(18) ~~Does~~ manufacturers expect these innovations in laptops to lead most people to abandon their desktop computers? [Do] (19) Nobody ~~seem~~ to know for sure. [seems] (20) But with prices for portable computers so low, a real choice between desktop computers and this new generation of laptops ~~exist~~ for the first time. [exists]

FOR FURTHER EXPLORATION

1. Consider one of the following topics:

   - the appeal of a particular computer or online game
   - the reason people gossip or the consequences that can result when they do
   - bad behavior on the streets and highways
   - an occasion when you said exactly the wrong thing
   - the difference between being friendly and flirting

   Prewrite on the subject, using one of the strategies you practiced in Chapter 2, and work your way through the rest of the writing process. Then complete a draft essay of at least 500 words on this subject.

COLLABORATION

2. Exchange your draft with a classmate. Check the draft you receive for weaknesses, paying particular attention to subject–verb agreement. Circle any subjects and verbs that don't agree, using the material in this chapter as a guide, and then return the draft to the writer.

3. Revise your essay, correcting any errors in subject–verb agreement or other problems discovered by your reader.

RECAP Subject–Verb Agreement

New terms in this chapter	Definitions
subject–verb agreement	a state in which the subject and verb agree in number Use a singular form of a verb with a singular subject. Use a plural form of a verb with a plural subject.

Ways to Maintain Agreement

When the **subject follows the verb**

in a question ⟶ *Does she know* the directions to the party?

in a sentence beginning with *there* or *here* ⟶ There *are* six *days* left in the term.

Identify the verb and ask "who or what?" to find the subject.

When the **subject and verb are separated** by other words

prepositional phrases ⟶ The *baby* across the hall *cries* all night.

subordinate clauses ⟶ The substitute *teacher*, because she is strict, *controls* the class.

Identify the verb and ask "who or what?" to find the subject.

When the **subject is compound**

with *and* the subject is usually plural ⟶ *Marcus and Simon are* friends.

unless the compound is considered one ⟶ *Rock and roll is* here to stay.

with *or* the subject can be singular ⟶ *Red or blue is* my favorite color.

with *or* the subject can be plural ⟶ *Pancakes or waffles are* good for breakfast.

Find the conjunction and determine what is being connected.

When the **subject is an indefinite pronoun**

singular ⟶ *Everyone is* late today.

plural ⟶ *Both* of my grandparents *are* immigrants.

Use singular verbs with singular pronouns and plural verbs with plural pronouns.

When the **subject is a collective noun or singular noun ending in -s**

collective noun ⟶ The *jury returns* today.

singular noun ending in -s ⟶ The *news follows* my favorite comedy.

If the subject is a unit, use a singular verb.

(continued)

Singular Indefinite Pronouns

another	each	everything	nobody	somebody
anybody	either	neither	nothing	someone
anyone	everybody	no one	one	something
anything	everyone			

Plural Indefinite Pronouns

both	few	many	several

Indefinite Pronouns Affected by the Words That Follow Them

all	more	none
any	most	some

GOING FORWARD...

Q: I understand the importance of making subjects and verbs agree. My big concern is catching the errors in agreement before I hand in my paper. Is there a technique that can help me find and fix these kinds of mistakes while I am working on my draft?

A: One technique that will help you catch mistakes in subject–verb agreement is to read your writing *out loud*—or have someone read it out loud to you. Slow down when you come to a subject and verb. This one little step can help you avoid big problems with subject–verb agreement.

CHAPTER 22

Basic Tenses for Regular Verbs

Navigating This Chapter

In this chapter, you will discover how to use the following for regular verbs:

- the present tense to describe a fact, an action, or a situation that is happening now or that happens habitually
- the future tense to describe an action or situation that hasn't occurred yet
- the past tense to describe an action or situation that has already occurred
- the past participle and perfect tenses to describe an action or situation that was either completed in the past or will be completed in the future

GETTING STARTED . . .

CW 22.1 Chapter basics

Q: One aspect of writing that I have trouble with is working with verbs, especially choosing the right verb ending. I often mix them up, adding a *-d* or an *-ed* to the end of a verb or putting *will* in front of one for no good reason. Why is it so confusing to work with verbs?

A: Working with verbs in English can sometimes be confusing because of the various verb tenses. But the frustration is worth it. Having various verb tenses to work with is actually a plus for you as a writer. These specialized forms make it possible for you to write about events that have already occurred, events that will occur, and so on. In other words, they enable you to capture just the right time period for each situation.

Overview: Understanding Tense

ESL Note
See "Agreement" on pages 592–594.

CW 22.2 Understanding tense

To a writer, no words hold more importance than verbs. As Chapter 17, "The Sentence," demonstrates, verbs convey action or link elements in a statement. Through verbs, you communicate about people, events, concepts, or possibilities. Verbs also indicate the period of time involved, whether it is *past, present,* or *future.* This time element is called **verb tense.** You indicate a change in verb tense by changing the form. Most verbs in English are **regular,** meaning that you convert their present form to past and future tenses in consistent ways.

Using the Simple Present, Simple Future, and Simple Past Tenses

CW 22.3
Understanding the present tense

The **present tense** signifies a fact, action, or situation that is happening *at the moment* or that happens habitually. For regular verbs, the simple present tense is the basic form of the verb, the one you would use in the simplest "I" statement: I laugh, I jump.

What makes the present tense a little confusing is that its form changes depending on the subject. If the subject is *singular,* meaning *one* person or thing, then the verb ends in *-s* or *-es.* If the subject is plural (or the singular *I*), the verb has no *-s.*

EXAMPLE   All day long, that dog *digs* holes in the yard.

Most children *enjoy* a magic show.

The subject in the first example is singular (*dog*), so the verb ends in *-s: digs.* In the second example, the plural subject *children* calls for a verb without an *-s* ending: *enjoy.* The exceptions to this guideline are the pronouns *I* and *you.* Even though *I* is singular, you don't add an *-s* to the present tense verb when *I* is the subject:

EXAMPLE   I *play* basketball every weekend.

You also don't add an *-s* to a present tense verb when *you* is the subject, even when it is singular:

EXAMPLE   You always *clean* your apartment on Saturday.

CW 22.4
Understanding the future tense

The simple **future tense** conveys an action or relationship *that hasn't occurred yet.* For regular verbs, the future tense for both singular and plural subjects is formed by adding *will* to the basic form of the verb. No *-s* or *-es* is necessary.

EXAMPLE   The actors *will prepare* for the play. The director *will coach* them.

CW 22.5
Understanding the past tense

The simple **past tense** indicates an action or situation *that has already occurred.* For regular verbs, the simple past tense is formed by adding *-ed* to the basic verb form. If the verb ends in *-e,* only a *-d* is added. For some regular verbs that end in *-y,* or with a single consonant preceded by a single vowel, forming the past tense requires a little more work. You must either change the last letter or add a letter before you add the *-d* or *-ed* ending. Chapter 29, "Spelling: Focusing on Correctness," discusses ways to treat these verbs. Again, the simple past tense is the same for both singular and plural subjects.

EXAMPLE   Osvaldo *answered* many questions in botany class.

Several dozen applicants *responded* to our ad for an assistant manager.

How to Form Simple Tenses for Regular Verbs (Example verb–*call*)

	Simple Present Tense (Use the basic form of the verb, adding *-s* or *-es* for singular subjects except *I* and *you*.)	**Simple Past Tense** (Use the basic form of the verb plus *-d* or *-ed*.)	**Simple Future Tense** (Use the basic form of the verb plus *will*.)
Basic or "I" form	I *call* friends in the evening.	I *called* friends last night.	I *will call* friends tomorrow evening.
Singular	Ami *calls* friends in the evening.	Ami *called* friends last night.	Ami *will call* friends tomorrow evening.
Plural	Joe and Estella *call* friends in the evening.	Joe and Estella *called* friends last night.	Joe and Estella *will call* friends tomorrow evening.

CW 22.6
Understanding verbs and other parts of speech

For more on the use of present tense verbs, see Chapter 21, "Subject–Verb Agreement."

FAST FACT Khmer, the native language of Cambodia, has no past or future tense. Writers and speakers use other words to mark changes in the time under discussion.

COMPREHENSION AND PRACTICE

Working with Future Tense Verbs

22.1 Complete the following sentences by adding a completing thought containing a future tense verb. Use the example to guide you.

CW 22.7
Using *will* to indicate the future

Answers will vary. Representative answers are given.

EXAMPLE When the warm weather arrives, *the campus will look beautiful*.

1. At the end of this century, ⎯⎯⎯⎯⎯⎯⎯⎯⎯⎯⎯

   we will look back at an era of enormous technological growth.

2. When the election results are finally tabulated, ⎯⎯⎯⎯⎯⎯⎯⎯

   we will measure the success of our campaign strategy.

3. After Albert shaves his moustache and cuts his hair, ⎯⎯⎯⎯⎯⎯

   his family will not recognize him.

4. As soon as the semester is over, ⎯⎯⎯⎯⎯⎯⎯⎯⎯⎯⎯

   Professor Hall will return to Paris.

5. The proposed increase in property taxes _____

   will fund the city hall addition.
   _____

6. Once the jury reaches a verdict, _____

   the newspapers will have a field day.
   _____

7. A new manufacturing plant is opening up in town, so _____

   new shops and restaurants will open up, too.
   _____

8. If you learn to speak a second language, _____

   you will expand both your horizons and your job skills.
   _____

9. Soon, high-speed trains _____

   will connect the two capital cities.
   _____

10. When the parade is over, the city's public works department _____

    will clean the streets along the parade route.
    _____

COMPREHENSION AND PRACTICE

22.2

CW 22.8
Using the
past tense

Working with Past Tense Verbs

The italicized verbs in the sentences below are in the present tense. Change them to the past tense by adding *-d* or *-ed*. Cross out the present tense verb, and write the revised verb in the space above as the example shows.

EXAMPLE   During the first few classes, the instructor ~~tries~~ *tried* to make the class comfortable with the subject matter.

(1) My friend Andrea ~~*works*~~ *worked* with stained glass. (2) She ~~*constructs*~~ *constructed* small items such as holiday ornaments. (3) She also ~~*creates*~~ *created* larger items. (4) For example, she ~~*designs*~~ *designed* wall displays. (5) My favorite ~~*shows*~~ *showed* an open door leading into a cozy room, as a way to say "Welcome."

COMPREHENSION AND PRACTICE

22.3

Using Past Tense Verbs to Complete Sentences

Use the following list of basic verbs to complete the paragraph below. Make all verbs past tense by adding *-d* or *-ed*.

purchase	line	wash	measure	redecorate
brush	fold	pick	start	place

(1) Last weekend, my friend Kathy ____redecorated____ the living room in her apartment by wallpapering. (2) First, she ____measured____ the walls to find out how much wallpaper to buy. (3) Then she ____purchased____ the paper, along with a kit containing several wallpapering tools. (4) She also ____picked____ up two containers of premixed wallpaper paste. (5) She then ____washed____ down the walls to make sure the surface was clean. (6) Once the walls dried, she ____started____ to hang the wallpaper. (7) After cutting a strip of paper to the correct length, she ____brushed____ paste onto the back of the paper. (8) Next, she ____folded____ the strip of paper in half and carried it from the table to the wall. (9) She unfolded the paper and ____placed____ its top edge against the ceiling. (10) She then ____lined____ up the right side of the paper against the guideline she had drawn to ensure that the paper was straight.

Using the Perfect Tenses

CW 22.9 Using the perfect tense

Writers use another verb form called the **past participle** to form additional tenses: past perfect, present perfect, and future perfect. All of the **perfect tenses** are formed by adding a helping verb to the past participle of a verb. For regular verbs, the past participle is the same as the simple past tense: the basic verb form plus *-d* or *-ed*.

This chapter discusses perfect tense verbs that use *has, have,* or *had* as helping verbs. Chapter 24, "Passive Voice, Additional Tenses, and Maintaining Consistency in Tense," will discuss progressive tense verbs that use *am, is, was,* and *were* as helping verbs.

To form the perfect tenses for regular verbs, use the helping verbs shown below:

Perfect Tense	=	*Helping Verb*	+	*Past Participle*	*Example*
Past perfect		had		walked	I *had walked.*
Present perfect		has, have		walked	I *have walked.*
Future perfect		will have		walked	I *will have walked.*

Perfect tense verbs cover time in a slightly different way than simple past, present, and future tenses do.

- The *past perfect tense* expresses action completed in the past before some other past action or event. (Jim *had bought* Nikki's birthday gift before they broke up.)
- The *present perfect tense* expresses action completed at some indefinite period in the past, or action that began in the past and is still going on. (Jim *has bought* me a birthday gift every year since 1988.)

- The *future perfect tense* refers to actions that will be completed in the future before some other future event or action. Note that this tense requires the word *will* before the helping verb. (By August, Jim *will have bought* all his Christmas gifts.)

Study the time line below, which shows the relationship of all the tenses discussed in this chapter.

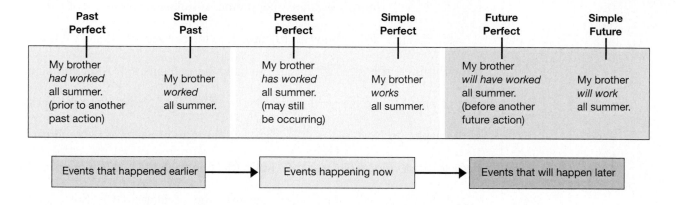

Past Perfect	**Simple Past**	**Present Perfect**	**Simple Perfect**	**Future Perfect**	**Simple Future**
My brother *had worked* all summer. (prior to another past action)	My brother *worked* all summer.	My brother *has worked* all summer. (may still be occurring)	My brother *works* all summer.	My brother *will have worked* all summer. (before another future action)	My brother *will work* all summer.

Events that happened earlier	→	Events happening now	→	Events that will happen later

FAST FACT   When you change the form of a word to indicate time or condition, as you do with verbs in English, the words are said to be *inflected*. If you feel bad about having to deal with inflection with verbs, just be thankful we don't speak Old English, one of the ancestor languages of modern English, anymore. According to scholars, Old English, which was spoken from around A.D. 450 to 1100, was heavily inflected, meaning that nearly all types of words were changed depending on the time, person, case, mood, or number being discussed.

COMPREHENSION AND PRACTICE

Working with the Perfect Tenses

22.4   On another sheet of paper, rewrite the following sentences, changing the present tense verb to either the present perfect, past perfect, or future perfect form. In some cases, more than one tense can be used. Use the example to guide you.

EXAMPLE   Josh earns all of his tuition money.

Josh will have earned all of his tuition money. (Future perfect)

1. The blue jay eats the blueberries on the ground below the bush.

2. The pie chills in the refrigerator at least two hours before dinner.

3. Bryan asks his friend for help with algebra.

4. The meteorologist forecasts a stormy weekend.

5. Dan states his preferences for vacation before anyone else.

6. The class turns in a teacher evaluation.

7. The secretary sorts the papers on the manager's desk.

8. I revise my essay one more time before submitting it.

9. The artist sketches the scene for an oil painting.

10. The baseball team practices every day for six weeks.

COMPREHENSION AND PRACTICE

Using Perfect Tenses to Complete Sentences

22.5 Each of the sentences in the following paragraph contains a past participle that is missing a helping verb, Write the correct helping verb in the space provided to form a complete verb in the perfect tense. Then label these verbs in the space above the line. Use *PaP* for past perfect tense, *PP* for present perfect tense, and *FP* for future perfect tense. Remember that the future perfect tense requires the word *will* along with the helping verb. Use the example to guide you.

EXAMPLE

PaP

My daughter was delighted that the groundhog _____*had*_____ failed to see his shadow this year.

(1) When mid-September comes to the northeastern United States, the hot

PP

days of summer _____*have*_____ passed for good. (2) The heat that several

PaP

weeks earlier _____*had*_____ felt so oppressive is now just a memory.

PaP

(3) The lawns that _____*had*_____ suffered from the combination of intense

PP

sun and low rainfall _____*have*_____ become lush again, at least for another

PP

few weeks. (4) In the most northern areas, the first frost _____*has*_____ even

occurred, which for some plants indicates the end of one cycle of their lives.

PP

(5) By this point, the woods _____*have*_____ also entered another phase.

PP

(6) They _____*have*_____ begun the beautiful show that year after year

amazes locals and draws thousands of tourists. (7) Throughout the region, the

PP

various shades of dark green seen in the spring and summer _____*have*_____

largely disappeared. (8) In their place, brilliant shades of red, orange, and yel-

PP

low _____*have*_____ appeared. (9) Unfortunately, by the time winter arrives,

FP

the explosion of color _____*will have*_____ disappeared, with the once-colorful

leaves lying in dull heaps under the trees.

CHALLENGE 22.1   **Writing with the Perfect Tenses**

1. Using the paragraph in Comprehension and Practice 22.5 as a model, write a paragraph of at least five to ten sentences about the signs of spring in your part of the country. Use at least one perfect tense verb in each sentence.

COLLABORATION

2. Exchange your writing with a partner. On the paper you receive, underline the perfect tense verbs and label them, using the abbreviations you used in Comprehension and Practice 22.5. Then return the paragraph to the writer. Check to see whether all the labels are accurate. Which perfect tense did you choose most often? Which perfect tense did your partner choose most often? With the class, discuss how the topic affected your choices.

CHAPTER QUICK CHECK   Working with Basic Verb Tenses

CW 22.10
Identifying
correct verb
forms

For each italicized verb in the following passage, identify the tense, using the labels listed below.

Pr = present tense   *F* = future tense   *PP* = present perfect tense
Pa = past tense   *PaP* = past perfect tense   *FP* = future perfect tense

(1) Quincy Jones *ranks* [Pr] as one of the true giants in American popular music. (2) Born in 1933 on Chicago's South Side and raised in Seattle, Jones *knew* [Pa] from age 11 that he *loved* [Pa] music. (3) During his more than 50 year career in music, "Q," as he *is* [Pr] known to his friends, *has affected* [PP] popular music to a profound degree. (4) Early in his career Jones *had worked* [PaP] with such musical giants as Dizzy Gillespie, Count Basie, Duke Ellington, Frank Sinatra, and Sarah Vaughan. (5) As a producer, arranger, and conductor, Jones *has put* [PP] his mark on the work of a number of rock and roll artists, including Ray Charles, Diana Ross, and Stevie Wonder. (6) In the 1970s, he *suffered* [Pa] two brain aneurysms that *left* [Pa] him with a metal plate in his head, but he *refused* [Pa] to let them slow him down. (7) In fact, in 1982, Jones *stepped* [Pa] back into the spotlight as the producer of pop star Michael Jackson's *Thriller*, one of the best-selling recordings of all time, and more recently, he *has worked* [PP] with a number of Rap artists, including Ice-T. (8) In addition to his work in the music studio, Jones *has enjoyed* [PP] great success in a number of other areas. (9) For instance, in 1961, Jones

became the vice-president of Mercury Records, the first African American to serve in such a capacity, and he *is* co-founder of *Vibe* magazine. (10) His induction into the American Academy of Arts & Sciences *is* a fitting acknowledgment for someone who certainly *will continue* to influence popular music.

QUICK STUDY | **Student Example**

CW 22.11
More on
verb tenses

This chapter discusses the aspect of writing that deals with time. Consider the following paragraph on a related subject—how passing of time affects people:

Time definitely *appears* to flow at different speeds depending on what is going on in life. When you are waiting for something to begin, the clock seems to be just barely moving. For example, when children are waiting for a birthday party or the end of school, the hours *become* days. The same thing is true when teenagers *have planned* a special date or parents and grandparents are waiting for the birth of a child. But the opposite is often true once the special event *has concluded.* The long-awaited party, vacation, or date *has flashed* by, and in the blink of an eye, the tiny infant *has become* a toddler. The same people who *wanted* time to speed by now wish they could make the clock stop so they can enjoy the experience. Yet, if another special event is a few weeks off, they *will want* the hands of the clock to start spinning forward again. Of course, all this concern about speeding up or slowing down time is silly because time *runs* at the same speed no matter how much people *desire* to control it

First complete the following activities in response to this paragraph:

1. Several of the verbs in this paragraph are italicized. Identify the tense of each verb above it, using the material in this chapter to guide you. Then, on a separate sheet of paper, briefly explain why you think these forms of verbs have been used rather than other tenses.

2. On the following lines, briefly explain how the concluding sentence relates to the main idea expressed in the topic sentence and brings the paragraph to a logical close.

The topic sentence discusses how time appears to speed up or slow down depending

on circumstances, and the sentences in the body offer examples of this fluid nature.

The concluding sentence then reiterates the main point while noting that the

fluctuation is an illusion and so brings the paper to a logical close.

3. The organizing strategy of example plays a big role in this paragraph. In your view, which of the examples supplied does the best job of supporting and illustrating the main point of this paragraph? What about the example makes it particularly effective? Use the lines that follow for your answer.

Answers will vary, although many students will choose the example about childhood

because of their own experiences.

Now explore the topic in writing. As the paragraph on page 353 does, you could concentrate on how the passing of time affects you. You might focus on one of these topics related to the subject matter of this chapter:

- time that you spent on something that you now wish you hadn't
- the hardest part about managing personal time
- a moment that is frozen in time for you
- the best time of life

COLLABORATION

1. Exchange your draft with a classmate. Evaluate the paragraph you receive. If you discover any problem spots, especially in the use of simple and perfect verb tenses, circle the errors and then return the paper to the writer.

2. Consider the comments and corrections your reader has made and create a final draft of your paragraph.

SUMMARY EXERCISE Working with Basic Verb Tenses

CW 22.12
Maintaining
tense
consistency

For each italicized verb in the following passage, identify the tense, using the labels listed below.

Pr = present tense   *F* = future tense   *PP* = present perfect tense
Pa = past tense   *PaP* = past perfect tense   *FP* = future perfect tense

(1) Recent research on the human brain *offers* [Pr] us a number of interesting findings about the "wiring" of this fascinating organ. (2) Scientists are now theorizing that, before your birth, your brain *programmed* [Pa] itself. (3) It *dedicated* [Pa] large numbers of nerve cells to performing basic functions. (4) However, it *reserved* [Pa] even more nerve cells for specialized functions that help you learn about the world. (5) These findings *add* [Pr] great significance to the way that we *treat* [Pr] children. (6) We now believe that a child's neurons *will thrive* [F] with appropriate stimulation. (7) Without direct stimulation and use, however, these nerve cells *will wither* [F] away.

(8) This research *will encourage* [F] parents and teachers to change some of our old views about learning. (9) For one thing, the findings *suggest* [Pr] that there are certain peak periods of opportunity for learning. (10) They *indicate* [Pr] that children will make the greatest strides in learning mathematics between birth and four years. (11) The same thing *appears* [Pr] to be true for learning music. (12) Parents who *had played* [PaP] simple number games and *had introduced* [PaP] their children to music during this period *saw* [Pa] impressive results.

(13) The findings also *urge* [Pr] us to examine how we *have treated* [PP] language. (14) Children *learn* [Pr] language most easily from birth to age ten. (15) The first few years of life *matter* [Pr] most. (16) It now *appears* [Pr] likely that those infants and toddlers who master language quickly *have heard* [PP] more words than other children. (17) In addition, children who *have listened* [PP] to many words before they reach age two *will have developed* [FP] large vocabularies by the time they reach adulthood.

(18) If these preliminary findings *prove* [Pr] to be true, parents and schools *will want* [F] to make some serious adjustments. (19) For one thing, teachers *will expect* [F] parents to be much more involved at home, since a great deal of

valuable learning time occurs before children attend public school. (20) In

addition, schools *will arrange* to offer instruction in a second language much

earlier, perhaps as early as the first few grades.

FOR FURTHER EXPLORATION

1. Consider one of the following topics:

   - the reluctance of many people to take personal responsibility
   - the story behind or associated with a special memento or keepsake
   - the causes or consequences of pollution
   - the impact of the entertainment industry on average people
   - what should not be shown on commercial television and why

   Prewrite on the subject, using one of the strategies you practiced in Chapter 2, and work your way through the rest of the writing process. Then complete a draft essay of at least 500 words on this subject.

COLLABORATION

2. Exchange your draft with a classmate. Check the draft you receive for weaknesses, paying particular attention to the use of simple and perfect verb tenses. Circle any errors, using the material in this chapter as a guide, and then return the draft to the writer.

3. Revise your essay, correcting any errors in verb use or other problems discovered by your reader.

RECAP Basic Tenses for Regular Verbs

New terms in this chapter	Definitions
verb tense	the form of a verb that tells when the action or situation occurs, either in the present, future, or past
present tense	the basic form of the verb signifying a fact, action, or situation that is occurring now or habitually Many singular present tense verbs end in *-s* or *-es*.
	Example My son *cleans* our apartment on the weekend.
	Example We *ignore* the dust during the week.
future tense	the form of the verb signifying a future action or state of being; the basic verb plus *will*
	Example This weekend he *will wash* the kitchen floor.

New terms in this chapter	Definitions
past tense	the form of the verb signifying an action or state of being that has already occurred; the basic form of the verb plus -d or -ed **Example** He *shopped* for groceries on Saturday.
past participle	for regular verbs, a form created by adding -d or -ed to the basic form Use the past participle with a helping verb to form the perfect tenses. **Example** Martha *had ended* the relationship months ago.
perfect tenses	verb tenses formed by adding some form of *to have* to the past participle of another verb Perfect tenses express actions that are complete with reference to another indicated time. **Example** We *have shared* the work this way for a few months. **Example** I *had finished* the rest of the chores earlier. **Example** We *will have succeeded* in sharing responsibilities.

Forming the Basic Tenses for Regular Verbs

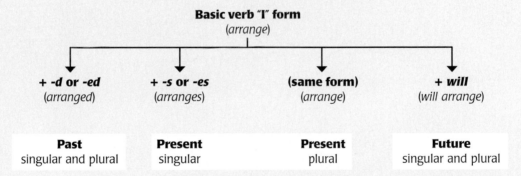

Basic verb "I" form
(*arrange*)

+ -d or -ed (*arranged*)	**+ -s or -es** (*arranges*)	**(same form)** (*arrange*)	**+ will** (*will arrange*)
Past singular and plural	**Present** singular	**Present** plural	**Future** singular and plural

Forming the Perfect Tenses for Regular Verbs

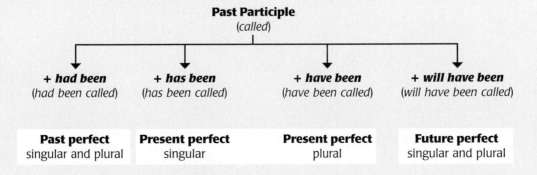

Past Participle
(*called*)

+ had been (*had been called*)	**+ has been** (*has been called*)	**+ have been** (*have been called*)	**+ will have been** (*will have been called*)
Past perfect singular and plural	**Present perfect** singular	**Present perfect** plural	**Future perfect** singular and plural

GOING FORWARD . . .

Q: Is there any technique or strategy that can help me avoid making mistakes with verb tense when I am working on a draft?

A: The best way to make sure that you use the correct form of a verb is to stop periodically as you compose a draft. If you check for any incorrect switches in verb tense each time you stop, you'll avoid a lot of frustration with this aspect of writing.

CHAPTER 23

Irregular Verbs and Frequently Confused Verbs

Navigating This Chapter

In this chapter, you will learn how to:

- form the present, past, and past participle forms of common irregular verbs
- work effectively with forms of *to be*
- choose correctly between *can* and *could* and between *will* and *would*

GETTING STARTED ...

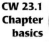

CW 23.1
Chapter basics

Q: The regular verbs, the ones that follow the rules, don't give me much trouble. The ones that I have a hard time with are the **irregular** verbs, the ones that don't follow the rules. I keep mixing them up, plus a few others like *can* and *could* and *will* and *would.* Why is it so hard to keep them straight?

A: It's no surprise that irregular verbs and verb pairs like *can* and *could* and *will* and *would* cause you the most trouble. In general, people keep groups of things straight by recognizing consistencies and patterns running through the entire group. But as a group, irregular verbs don't follow predictable patterns as they change tense, and that's what makes working with them so frustrating.

Overview: Understanding Irregular Verbs and Other Verb Problems

CW 23.2
Overview of irregular verbs

Chapter 22, "Basic Tenses for Regular Verbs," illustrated how to form the basic tenses of regular verbs. As that chapter pointed out, making the past and past participle forms for regular verbs is easy and predictable. You simply add either -*d* or -*ed* to the end of the basic verb form: *create—created, talk—talked.* The problem, of course, is that all verbs don't form their past or past participle forms in predictable ways. These **irregular verbs** hold the most potential to confuse writers. The verb *to be* is perhaps the most troublesome of these irregular verbs because it has so many forms. Other verbs that give writers trouble are the confusing pairs *can* and *could* and *will* and *would.*

Identifying Irregular Verbs

CW 23.3
Using irregular verbs

The verbs in the following list are all irregular. As you learned in Chapter 22, "Basic Tenses for Regular Verbs," the past participle form (column three below) is used with a helping verb to form a perfect or progressive tense verb.

Irregular Verb Forms

Present Tense	Past Tense	Past Participle (+ a helping verb)
am/is/are	was/were	been
arise	arose	arisen
awaken	awoke, awaked	awoke, awaked
become	became	become
begin	began	begun
bend	bent	bent
bind	bound	bound
bite	bit	bitten, bit
bleed	bled	bled
blow	blew	blown
break	broke	broken
bring	brought	brought
build	built	built
burn	burned, burnt	burned, burnt
burst	burst	burst
buy	bought	bought
catch	caught	caught
choose	chose	chosen
cling	clung	clung
come	came	come
cost	cost	cost
creep	crept	crept
cut	cut	cut
deal	dealt	dealt
dig	dug	dug
dive	dived, dove	dived
do/does	did	done
draw	drew	drawn
dream	dreamed, dreamt	dreamed, dreamt
drink	drank	drunk
drive	drove	driven
eat	ate	eaten
fall	fell	fallen
feed	fed	fed
feel	felt	felt
fight	fought	fought
find	found	found

CW 23.4
Resources
on verbs
and verbals

Present Tense	Past Tense	Past Participle (+ a helping verb)
flee	fled	fled
fling	flung	flung
fly	flew	flown
forbid	forbade, forbad	forbidden
forget	forgot	forgotten, forgot
freeze	froze	frozen
get	got	got, gotten
give	gave	given
go/goes	went	gone
grind	ground	ground
grow	grew	grown
hang	hung	hung
hang (execute)	hanged	hanged
have/has	had	had
hear	heard	heard
hide	hid	hidden, hid
hold	held	held
hurt	hurt	hurt
keep	kept	kept
kneel	knelt, kneeled	knelt, kneeled
knit	knit, knitted	knit, knitted
know	knew	known
lay	laid	laid
lead	led	led
leap	leaped, leapt	leaped, leapt
leave	left	left
lend	lent	lent
let	let	let
lie	lay	lain
light	lighted, lit	lighted, lit
lose	lost	lost
make	made	made
mean	meant	meant
meet	met	met
mistake	mistook	mistaken
pay	paid	paid
plead	pleaded, pled	pleaded, pled
prove	proved	proved, proven
put	put	put
quit	quit	quit
raise	raised	raised
read	read	read
ride	rode	ridden

(continued)

CW 23.5
Using
irregular
verbs
incorrectly

Present Tense	Past Tense	Past Participle (+ a helping verb)
ring	rang	rung
rise	rose	risen
run	ran	run
say	said	said
see	saw	seen
seek	sought	sought
sell	sold	sold
send	sent	sent
set	set	set
sew	sewed	sewn, sewed
shake	shook	shaken
shine	shone, shined	shone, shined
shine (polish)	shined	shined
shoot	shot	shot
show	showed	shown, showed
shrink	shrank, shrunk	shrunk, shrunken
shut	shut	shut
sing	sang	sung
sit	sat	sat
sleep	slept	slept
slide	slid	slid
sling	slung	slung
slink	slunk, slinked	slunk, slinked
sow	sowed	sown, sowed
speak	spoke	spoken
speed	sped, speeded	sped, speeded
spend	spent	spent
spit	spit, spat	spit, spat
spring	sprang, sprung	sprung
stand	stood	stood
steal	stole	stolen
stick	stuck	stuck
sting	stung	stung
stink	stank, stunk	stunk
stride	strode	stridden
strike	struck	struck, stricken
string	strung	strung
strive	strived, strove	striven, strived
swear	swore	sworn
sweat	sweat, sweated	sweat, sweated
swell	swelled	swelled, swollen
swim	swam	swum
swing	swung	swung
take	took	taken
teach	taught	taught
tear	tore	torn

Present Tense	Past Tense	Past Participle (+ a helping verb)
tell	told	told
think	thought	thought
throw	threw	thrown
understand	understood	understood
wake	woke, waked	woken, waked, woke
wear	wore	worn
weave	wove, weaved	woven, weaved
weep	wept	wept
win	won	won
wind	wound	wound
wring	wrung	wrung
write	wrote	written

As the table shows, the past and past participle forms of irregular verbs are often different. Consider these examples:

EXAMPLE

The windows in the building *shook* each time the furnace started up.

The front picture window *had shaken* so much that it actually cracked.

Because of their unpredictability, irregular verbs in all their forms must be memorized. As you learn the irregular verb forms, keep two things in mind: (1) You *don't* use a helping verb with the past tense, and (2) You *must* use a helping verb with the past participle.

FAST FACT One way we learn things is to group them on the basis of some similarity and then memorize the pattern. This method generally works well, but don't count on having just one group when you need to form the past and past participle forms of irregular verbs ending in -ng. With *sing*, for example, the past is *sang* and the past participle is *sung*. The pattern is the same for *ring* (*rang* and *rung*) and *cling* (*clung* and *clung*). But with *fling*, the *a* disappears, and the past and past participle is *flung*. The same is true for *sting* (*stung* and *stung*), *swing* (*swung* and *swung*), and *wring* (*wrung* and *wrung*). For *spring*, the past participle is *sprung*, but the past can be either *sprang* or *sprung*. That brings us to *bring*. It stands alone, with its past and past participle both *brought*.

COMPREHENSION AND PRACTICE

Forming Perfect Tenses for Irregular Verbs

23.1 In the following paragraph, fill in the blanks with the past participle form of the verb in parentheses to form a perfect tense verb. Remember to provide the appropriate helping verb (*have, has,* or *had*) for each past participle. Then label these verbs in the space above the line. Use *PaP* for past perfect tense, *PP* for present perfect tense, and *FP* for future perfect tense. Use the example to guide you.

EXAMPLE	It looks as though Caryl's eye (swell) _____ $\overset{PP}{\text{has swollen}}$ _____ shut.

(1) When I asked my friend Jarod how he (cut) _____ $\overset{PaP}{\text{had cut}}$ _____ his forehead, he began to laugh. (2) Then Jarod told me that he (fall) _____ $\overset{PaP}{\text{had fallen}}$ _____ while in-line skating, but he hadn't hurt himself. (3) Feeling very proud of himself for having avoided any injury, he stood up, but he (forget) _____ $\overset{PaP}{\text{had forgotten}}$ _____ to tighten the binding on his left skate boot. (4) He fell again, and when he wiped his forehead and saw red on his fingers, he realized he (hurt) _____ $\overset{PaP}{\text{had hurt}}$ _____ himself. (5) He said that his friends (make) _____ $\overset{PP}{\text{have made}}$ _____ him captain of the Olympic klutz team, but he vows he (prove) _____ $\overset{FP}{\text{will have proven}}$ _____ them wrong by the end of the skating season.

COMPREHENSION AND PRACTICE

Using Irregular Verbs in Your Writing

23.2 On a separate sheet of paper, write three related sentences for each of the irregular verbs listed below: one each for the present tense, the past tense, and the past participle forms. Remember—the past participle requires a helping verb to form a perfect tense verb. Use the example to guide you.

EXAMPLE	Kathy and John always <u>hear</u> the noise from the Fourth of July fireworks.
	Last night, they also <u>heard</u> the oohs and ahhs of the crowd.
	In previous years, Kathy and John <u>have heard</u> the band as well as the fireworks.

1. keep	3. sleep	5. freeze	7. write	9. raise
2. bite	4. shake	6. speak	8. become	10. stand

COMPREHENSION AND PRACTICE

Using Irregular Verbs Correctly

23.3 The following narrative takes place in the past. Each sentence contains a present tense verb in parentheses. Write the correct past form of this verb on the line that follows. Use the form that the context calls for; include a helping verb if necessary. In some cases, more than one correct answer is possible. Use the example to guide you. Answers may vary.

EXAMPLE When I was growing up, I always (do) _____*did*_____ my assigned chores as quickly as I could.

(1) Recently I (spend) _____spent_____ a most memorable evening when several friends and I attended a production by Blue Man Group. (2) Our seats were in the front row, and what I (see) _____saw_____ and (hear) _____heard_____ that night still amazes me. (3) We saw everything the Blue Men (do) _____did_____ up close, from drumming on huge PVC pipes to splashing fluorescent paint across the stage to burying part of the audience in tissue paper. (4) The theater program explained that Blue Man Group (begin) _____began_____ as a kind of musical and theatrical "happening" in New York City in 1987. (5) Eventually, the concept of the Blue Men emerged: three performers who (wear) _____wore_____ deep blue makeup and interacted on stage with everyday items like breakfast cereal, tissue paper, and, of course, television, to great comic effect. (6) From that point on, the original Blue Men, Matt Goldman, Phil Stanton, and Chris Wink, (know) _____knew_____ they had a hit on their hands, both in terms of the stage show and the hard driving music backing the action on stage. (7) They (bring) _____brought_____ such energy and fun to their performance that word rapidly spread about the production. (8) In fact, the original shows (become) _____became_____ so popular that Blue Man troupes were established in several other cities, including Boston and Las Vegas. (9) They received some national attention when they (make) _____made_____ a series of television advertisements for Pentium Processors. (10) The Grammy nomination Blue Man Group received in 2001 for their original music (prove) _____proved_____ that they are more than just three pretty, blue faces.

CHALLENGE 23.1   **Revising the Tense of a Paragraph**

Ten verbs are listed below. On a separate sheet of paper, use at least five of these verbs in the present tense to write a paragraph of at least five to ten sentences. Exchange your work with a partner, and rewrite the paragraph you receive, changing the tense of each verb to either the past or past perfect form. Consult the list of irregular verbs (pages 360–363) as necessary.

feed	eat
give	sit
make	grind
see	bring
break	forget

Working with Forms of *To Be*

**CW 22.6
Working
with forms
of *to be***

The most irregular of the irregular verbs is the verb **to be.** For example, it is the only verb that uses different forms for different persons in the past tense. However, memorizing the various forms of *to be* is not that difficult because many do *not* change when the subject changes.

Look at the table below, which shows the most common forms of the verb *to be:*

Common Forms of the Verb *To Be*

When the subject is . . .	the present tense is . . .	the past tense is . . .	the future tense is . . .	the past participle is . . .
I	am	was	will be	been
he, she, *or* it	is	was	will be	been
we, you, *or* they	are	were	will be	been

As you can see, *will be* and *been* are used with *all* subjects, although different helping verbs are needed for *been.*

To simplify your understanding of *to be,* concentrate on those forms that *do* change, as this version of the same table shows:

When the subject is …	the present tense is …	the past tense is …	Examples
I	am	was	I *am* tired tonight. I *was* more energetic yesterday.
he, she, *or* it	is	was	He *is* late for his dental appointment. She *was* early for her guitar lesson.
we, you, *or* they	are	were	You *are* the best friend I've ever had. They *were* childhood sweethearts before they were married.

If you keep these forms straight, you'll have far fewer problems using *to be*. In addition, keep in mind two rules when you are using forms of *to be*.

1. Never use *been* without *has, have,* or *had:*

EXAMPLE

have been
For some time, we ~~been~~ looking for a house.

had been
Just a year earlier, that superstar comedian ~~been~~ a complete unknown.

2. Never use *be* by itself as the verb in a sentence:

EXAMPLE

are
We ~~be~~ proud of your achievement.

are
You ~~be~~ the reason for this celebration.

Although you may hear violations of these rules in informal speech, such usages are not acceptable for the writing you will do in college and the workplace.

COMPREHENSION AND PRACTICE

23.4

Working with Forms of *To Be*

In the following paragraph, complete each sentence by writing the correct form of the verb *to be* in the space provided. Use the tables on page 366 and above for help with the most irregular forms of *to be*. Use the example as a guide.

EXAMPLE

Annette ____will be____ thirty on her next birthday.

(1) Today, one way to get a brighter smile ____is____ to use a chemical whitener. (2) Some observers of trends in business believe that these whiteners ____are____ among the fastest growing personal care products

in this decade. (3) These analysts note that many people _____are_____ embarrassed by stains on their teeth but don't want to pay $300 to have a dentist bleach them. (4) Unfortunately, until now, there _____was_____ no alternative. (5) Now, however, an over-the-counter product _____is_____ finally available for the general public.

COMPREHENSION AND PRACTICE

Correcting Errors in the Forms of *To Be*

23.5 In the following paragraph, correct the errors in the use of *be* and *been*. Cross out the error, and write the verb correctly above it as the example shows.

EXAMPLE
        is
Mary ~~be~~ the most experienced worker in the office.

    (1) With all the injuries suffered in professional boxing each year, it ~~be~~ *(is)* hard to understand why we allow the sport to continue. (2) Nevertheless, boxing is still legal, and it ~~been~~ *(is)* causing permanent damage to hundreds of people every year. (3) The brutality of boxing ~~been~~ *(is)* no longer reserved for men only, either. (4) A few years ago, the first professional bouts between female boxers ~~been~~ *(were)* broadcast. (5) Regardless of the sex of the combatants, the impact of a punch ~~be~~ *(is)* unbelievably damaging. (6) Fighters ~~be~~ *(are)* often lifted off their feet when they ~~been~~ *(are)* hit. (7) The physical state of former heavyweight champion Muhammad Ali ~~was~~ *(is)* the greatest argument that boxing should be banned. (8) At the beginning of his career, Ali ~~been~~ *(was)* among the most articulate people in the world of sports. (9) Now he ~~be~~ *(is)* barely able to speak. (10) Ours ~~are~~ *(is)* a civilized society, so why do we allow this brutality to continue?

COMPREHENSION AND PRACTICE

Working with Forms of *To Be*

23.6 Change the verbs in the following paragraph to the past tense. Cross out the present tense verb, and write the past tense form above it. Use the example to guide you.

> was
EXAMPLE | Marcy ~~is~~ the right person to run the business.

> was
(1) In the city, a group of volunteers ~~is~~ organized to clean up the water-
> were
front area. (2) These workers ~~are~~ organized by the local chapter of the Sierra
> was
Club. (3) The hope of the organizing committee ~~is~~ to attract fifty volunteers.
> were
(4) Many spots ~~are~~ in terrible shape. (5) After years of neglect, the three-mile
> was
stretch of beach near Reflecting Lake ~~is~~ full of litter like old tires and beer cans.
> was   was
(6) The worst area ~~is~~ the spot near the abandoned Kerr Mill. (7) This section ~~is~~

the hardest to reach because of a city barrier to keep people out. (8) Neverthe-
> was
less, the area ~~is~~ a frequent party spot for teenagers in the city. (9) Class slivers
> were
from hundreds of windows broken by vandals ~~are~~ everywhere on the pave-
> were
ment around the old mill building. (10) However, the volunteers ~~are~~ so dedi-
> was
cated that the area ~~is~~ soon clean and attractive enough for family picnics.

CHALLENGE 23.2 Explaining Problem Verbs

Identify the form of *to be* that you think is most difficult to use, and write a paragraph of at least five to ten sentences in which you explain why you find this
form confusing. Include brief sentences illustrating how you use the form incorrectly, and then show what you must do to use it correctly.

Choosing between *Can* and *Could* and between *Will* and *Would*

Beginning writers often have trouble choosing between **can** and **could** as helping
verbs. These two verbs both mean *to be able to*. *Can* is used to indicate the present
tense, and *could* is used to indicate the past tense:

EXAMPLE | At this moment, no one in the conference *can beat* our relay team.

Last season, no one in the conference *could beat* our relay team.

Sometimes *could* is also used to indicate a *possibility* or *hope* of doing something:

EXAMPLE Our competitors wish they *could beat* our relay team.

Beginning writers also have trouble deciding between the helping verbs **will** and **would.** Although both verbs are used to indicate the future, each links the future with a different period of time.

Look at the following versions of the same sentence, with the verbs italicized:

EXAMPLE
present
┌ tense ┐
Carlos *thinks* that he *will major* in computer programming.

past
┌ tense ┐
Carlos *thought* that he *would major* in computer programming.

The first sentence says that *right now* Carlos intends to focus on computer programming in the future. The second sentence indicates that *at an earlier time,* he had intended to study computer programming.

In some instances, *would* is also used to indicate a *hope* or *possibility* rather than a certainty, as this sentence shows:

EXAMPLE Many people *would* be able to save if they budgeted carefully.

FAST FACT *Can* means to be physically or mentally able. *May* means to be allowed or permitted to do something. A common error is to make a request using *can* when *may* is the logical choice. For example, as long as mobility isn't a problem for you, asking *"Can* I go out the open front door?" would be incorrect because you are certainly able to move through the doorway. The correct phrasing, because you are asking if doing so is all right, is *"May* I go out the open front door?"

COMPREHENSION AND PRACTICE Choosing between *Can* and *Could* and between *Will* and *Would*

23.7 In each sentence in the following paragraph, circle the correct verb in parentheses as the example shows.

EXAMPLE If he didn't work, Arnie (will, (would)) take an evening class.

(1) From personal experience, I know that being able to speak a second language ((can,) could) make a real difference in your chances to get a job. (2) If you are able to converse with people who don't speak English, you ((will,))

would) be a great candidate for a number of jobs that involve customer contact. (3) Before I learned to speak Spanish, I saw advertisements for several good jobs that I knew I (can, could) never get because I didn't speak Spanish. (4) Instead of feeling sorry for myself, I decided I (will, would) work harder in my conversational Spanish class. (5) Thanks to that class, I (can, could) now apply for those good jobs with confidence.

COMPREHENSION AND PRACTICE

Correcting Errors in the Use of *Can* and *Could* and *Will* and *Would*

23.8 The following passage contains a number of errors in the use of *can* and *could* and *will* and *would*. Correct the errors by crossing out the incorrect word and writing the correct word above it. If a sentence is correct as written, write *OK* above it. Use the example as a guide.

EXAMPLE

will

I don't know if I ~~would~~ be available to begin work on Monday.

will

(1) Soon, physicians ~~would~~ have a new weapon in their battle to help burn

OK

victims. (2) The Food and Drug Administration (FDA) recently approved an artificial skin that can be used in grafting procedures. (3) Up until now, pa-

could

tients ~~can~~ expect attempts at skin grafting to fail more often than not.

(4) When a person is severely burned, in many cases only the outer layer of

will

skin ~~would~~ grow back. (5) If the skin graft cannot attach itself to healthy tissue,

will

the procedure ~~would~~ fail. (6) So, before the artificial skin became available, the

could

best that burn patients ~~can~~ hope for was to minimize the number of failures.

would

(7) Each time a graft failed, the surgeon ~~will~~ harvest a new graft and begin the

procedure again. (8) Now, however, it appears that the new artificial skin

will   *OK*

~~would~~ dramatically improve the success rate for grafting. (9) The new material, which eventually breaks down to be absorbed by the body, will provide an anchor for the skin graft. (10) Now that the FDA has approved the use of this

will

artificial skin, doctors ~~would~~ soon begin using it in their surgical procedures.

CHALLENGE 23.3 Analyzing Correct *Can/Could* and *Will/Would* Choices

Imagine you have been asked to explain the difference between *can* and *could* and between *will* and *would* to a group of middle school students. Working with a partner, write a paragraph of at least five to ten sentences that explains the differences, making sure to provide examples of correct and incorrect usage for each word.

CHAPTER QUICK CHECK Eliminating Problems with Irregular Verbs and *Can* and *Could* and *Will* and *Would*

Proofread the following sentences, and revise any errors you find in the use of irregular verbs *can* and *could* or *will* and *would*. Cross out the incorrect word or words, and write a correct version above it, as the example shows. If a sentence is correct as written, write *OK* above it. In some cases, more than one answer is possible.

EXAMPLE

> *had drunk*
> The fifteen-year-old driver ~~had drank~~ an entire six-pack of beer before he stole my car and crashed it.

(1) Thanks to the wonders of modern technology, the old-fashioned treasure hunt ~~be~~ *is* now a brand new game. (2) This modern variation of an old activity is called *Geocaching, Geo* for geography and *cache* for something hidden, and it ~~has grew~~ *has grown* in popularity in the past couple of years. *OK* (3) Right now, across the world, thousands of "stashes," generally plastic containers filled with inexpensive trinkets, have been hidden and are waiting to be discovered. (4) The sport was created by a man in Oregon who ~~think~~ *thought* of a way to use the formerly classified radio signals from a network of government navigational satellites to explore for "buried treasure." (5) To participate in Geocaching, participants need a computer, a compass, and a hand-held Global Positioning System, or GPS. (6) Participants first ~~went~~ *go* to geocaching.com, a Web site listing the longitude and latitude of caches in a particular area. (7) Players then ~~took~~ *take* these coordinates and enter them into the GPS unit. (8) The GPS device taps into the satellite system, which ~~sent~~ *sends* players to within 35 feet of the stash. (9) Once participants have this information, they ~~could~~ *can* use hints provided on the Web site to do some old-fashioned detective work and find where in that

35-foot radius the stash is hidden. (10) Once participants ~~found~~ [find] a particular

stash, they often remove one object, replace it with another, record their suc-

cess on the Web site, and start some research for their next adventure.

QUICK STUDY | Student Example

This chapter focuses on elements that don't always match normal standards. Take a look at this paragraph on a related subject, someone you know or have met who doesn't conform:

When I hear the word *nonconformist,* the first person I think of is Billy

Hardy, a kid who ~~gone~~ [went] to my high school. Billy always ~~find~~ [found] a way to stand out

from everyone else. For example, one time during senior year, he ~~shown~~ [showed] up

with his hair dyed several different colors. A couple of weeks later, after

everybody was used to this style, he arranged it in dread locks. A week after

that he shaved his head, which ~~lead~~ [led] to a suspension because the vice principal

said he looked like a skinhead. It was a ridiculous move because Billy was ac-

tually a very mellow, accepting person with friends from every group in the

school. He just laughed about the suspension and enjoyed the three days off

from school. Also, even though he could play sports better than most kids in

gym class, he ~~will~~ [would] not go out for the athletic teams because he ~~think~~ [thought] that kind

of competition was a waste of time. Instead, he would ~~rode~~ [ride] his mountain bike

out to the state reservation and go hiking by himself. In addition, he was prob-

ably the smartest kid I have ever met, but he rejected pressure from teachers

and administrators to take his studies more seriously. For instance, when he

had ~~took~~ [taken] the SATs, he earned the highest score in the school, but he wouldn't

even go to the award ceremony for the top scorers. He said that high SAT

scores didn't mean he was better than anyone else. I have never ~~meet~~ [met] anyone

as original as Billy Hardy, and I doubt I ever ~~would~~ [will].

First complete the following activities in response to this paragraph:

1. Several of the irregular verbs in this paragraph are highlighted. Above the verb, write the version of the verb that you think should be used. Then check your answers against the lists supplied in this chapter to see if you have chosen properly.

2. In this paragraph, the organizing strategy of definition plays a significant role. On the lines below, briefly explain how the examples and details in the body of the paragraph contribute to the definition of *nonconformist*.

   The examples regarding hair style, athletics, and academic achievement all add to the

   definition because all are instances of behavior that doesn't conform to what many

   high school students do.

3. The paragraph features three main supporting ideas, one concerning appearance, one about sports, and one about academic performance. Do you agree with the current arrangement or would you have set up the examples differently? On a separate sheet of paper, discuss your opinion of the order of the supporting material, explaining your reasoning.

Now explore the topic in writing. Like the paragraph on page 373, you could discuss someone who qualifies as a nonconformist, or you might focus on one of these subjects related to the subject matter of this chapter:

- an item that isn't up to date or doesn't match what most people have but that you still use or rely on
- why conformity can sometimes be a problem
- an occasion at work, school, or home when what you expected to happen or to experience was radically different from normal
- how to fight the pressure to be just like everyone else

COLLABORATION

1. Exchange your draft with a classmate. Evaluate the paragraph you receive. If you discover any errors, especially in the use of irregular verbs, make a note in the margin and then return the paper to the writer.

2. Consider the comments and corrections your reader has made and create a final draft of your paragraph.

SUMMARY EXERCISE Eliminating Problems with Irregular Verbs and *Can* and *Could* and *Will* and *Would*

Proofread the following sentences, and revise any errors you find in the use of irregular verbs *can* and *could* or *will* and *would*. Cross out the incorrect word or words, and write a correct version above it. If a sentence is correct as written, write *OK* above it. In some cases, more than one answer is possible. Some answers may vary.

(1) Today, you ~~could~~ ^{can} buy a greeting card for just about any occasion or person. (2) As might be expected, there ~~be~~ ^{are} plenty of cards for standard events such as birthdays, weddings, and so on. ^{OK} (3) What is surprising is the range of holidays, occasions, and special needs and concerns addressed through greeting cards.

^{OK} (4) If you have had no luck in buying the perfect birthday present for someone, you can find a card that apologizes for your failure. (5) You can also ~~bought~~ ^{buy} birthday cards for every variety of relative you can imagine. (6) For example, if you want to get a card created specifically for great-grandmothers or stepsons, you ~~could~~ ^{can} find one.

(7) In addition to the cards commemorating traditional events, such as Thanksgiving, Christmas, Hanukkah, and Valentine's Day, you ~~would~~ ^{will} find cards for special occasions, such as St. Patrick's Day and Halloween. ^{OK} (8) The list continues to grow, too. (9) For example, cards celebrating Kwanzaa recently ^ been added to stores across the nation. ^{have}

^{OK} (10) If your boss just gave birth, you don't need to worry. (11) There ~~be~~ ^{are} cards to mark the occasion. (12) You can ~~chosen~~ ^{choose} between pink ones for girls and blue ones for boys. ^{OK} (13) Do you need a card to apologize to your old friend for not writing sooner? (14) Just check the racks, and you ~~could~~ ^{can} find one.

(15) These cards ~~isn't~~ ^{aren't} just for family and close friends, either. (16) They ~~came~~ ^{come} in different levels of familiarity. (17) For example, if you need a sympathy card for someone you barely ~~known~~ ^{know}, one is available. (18) There even ~~been~~ ^{are} greeting cards for ex-spouses and ex-in-laws.

(19) Whether you like humor, sentimentality, or inspirational messages, you ~~would~~ ^{will} discover a greeting card that suits you. ^{OK} (20) Just head to the nearest card store, and plan to spend some enjoyable time reading over the possibilities.

FOR FURTHER EXPLORATION

1. Consider one of the following topics:

   - the difficulty of getting in or staying in shape
   - misconceptions about life in a big city or a small town
   - why rude behavior seems to be increasing
   - a time when you watched a classmate or teammate be treated unfairly
   - what you think children need to grow up happy and confident

   Prewrite on the subject, using one of the strategies you practiced in Chapter 2, and work your way through the rest of the writing process. Then complete a draft essay of at least 500 words on this subject.

COLLABORATION

2. Exchange your draft with a classmate. Check the draft you receive for weaknesses, checking in particular for errors in irregular verb use. Circle any incorrect verbs and write the correct version above it, using the material in this chapter as a guide, and then return the draft to the writer.

3. Revise your essay, correcting any errors in irregular verb use or other problems discovered by your reader.

RECAP Irregular Verbs and Frequently Confused Verbs

New terms in this chapter	Definitions
irregular verbs	verbs that do not form their past tense and past participle in typical ways

Strategies for Learning Irregular Verb Forms: Grouping by Pattern			
	Present	**Past**	**Past Participle**
All tenses use the same form	let	let	let
	burst	burst	burst
Past tense and past participle use the same form	feel	felt	felt
	mean	meant	meant
In each tense, one letter changes	ring	rang	rung
	drink	drank	drunk
In past tense, one letter changes; in past participle, one letter is added	throw	threw	thrown
	blow	blew	blown

to be	the most challenging irregular verb for writers

Always use *has, have,* or *had* with *been*.
Never use *be* alone as a verb.
Follow the chart below for tenses of *to be*.

Common Forms of the Verb *To Be*

When the subject is . . .	the present tense is . . .	the past tense is . . .	the future tense is . . .	the past participle is . . .
I	am	was	will be	been
he, she, *or* it	is	was	will be	been
we, you, *or* they	are	were	will be	been

Verb pairs often confused

can/could	helping verbs that mean *to be able to*

Use *can* to show present tense.

> **EXAMPLE**   Jose *can* win the contest.

Use *could* to show past tense, or the possibility or hope of being able to do something.

> **EXAMPLE**   If I *could* sing, I'd join the chorus immediately.

will/would	helping verbs that indicate the future

Use *will* to point to the future from the *present*.

> **EXAMPLE**   Howard promises he *will* return before midnight.

Use *would* to point to the future from the *past* and to indicate a hope or possibility.

> **EXAMPLE**   Howard promised he *would* return before midnight.

GOING FORWARD . . .

CW 23.8 Review of irregular verbs

Q: I know I can't rely on the rules to show me how to form the different tenses for irregular verbs, so is there some strategy that can help me keep them all straight?

A: Probably the best way to keep irregular verb forms straight is to go through the list of irregular verbs in this chapter. Highlight the ones you didn't even realize were irregular and the ones that you frequently confuse and make your own list of problem verbs. Add the forms of *can* and *could* and *will* and *would* to the list and then memorize the list. It's not an easy or foolproof method, but it will definitely improve your chances of selecting the proper verb form.

CHAPTER 24

Passive Voice, Additional Tenses, and Maintaining Consistency in Tense

▶ Navigating This Chapter

In this chapter, you will learn how to:

- form the passive and active voices and learn when each is appropriate
- form and use the progressive and perfect progressive tenses correctly
- maintain consistency in verb tense

GETTING STARTED . . .

**CW 24.1
Chapter
basics**

Q: There's just so much to keep track of with verbs. What's *voice?* Are there other verb tenses to worry about? And is being consistent in the use of verb tense in a piece of writing that important?

A: You are right—when it comes to verb use, there is probably more to keep straight than with any other aspect of writing. Keep in mind, however, that this complexity works to your advantage. *Voice,* for example, involves presenting the subject of a sentence so that it either does the action or is acted upon or discussed. This flexibility enables you to discuss ideas from different vantage points. Yes, there are other tenses—the progressive and perfect progressive tenses—and they enable you to discuss something developing or happening over time. And, yes, consistency of any kind keeps things simple, so consistency in tense enables your reader to follow the time relationships you present.

Overview: Understanding Additional Elements of Verb Use

**CW 24.2
Understanding
additional
verb use**

To work effectively with verbs, you need to do more than master such essentials as basic and perfect tenses for regular and irregular verbs. As a writer, you also need to consider the differences between active and passive voice. In addition, you need to learn to deal with the progressive and perfect progressive tenses. And finally, you need to understand the importance of being consistent with verb tense in a piece of writing.

Forming the Passive and Active Voice

CW 24.3
The active and passive voice

When you combine the past participle form of a verb with a form of *to be,* such as *am, is, was,* or *were,* you are using the **passive voice.** In a sentence with a passive voice verb, the subject *receives* the action:

PASSIVE

⎡ subject ⎤ ⎡—verb—⎤
Madeleine was told the good news about her promotion by the manager of the production team.

⎡—— subject ——⎤ ⎡—— verb ——⎤
Several *improvements were made* in the customer service area by David.

CW 24.4
Forming the passive voice

In general, the passive voice is considered less forceful than the active voice. Also, it can sound awkward (The game *was won* by us). With a verb in the **active voice,** the subject *performs* the action and is the *focus* of the sentence.

ACTIVE

⎡—subject—⎤ ⎡—verb—⎤
The *manager* of the production team *told* Madeleine the good news about her promotion.

subject verb
David made several improvements in the customer service area.

CW 24.5
Forming the active voice

Using a string of passive verbs in your writing tends to weaken it. The active voice generally makes your language sound more direct, powerful, and concise. In addition, because it indicates the doer of the action, the active voice also establishes responsibility for that action. Therefore, the passive voice should be used sparingly. However, it is useful for expressing actions in which the actor is unknown or for emphasizing the receiver of an action.

EFFECTIVE PASSIVE VOICE

⎡subject⎤ ⎡—— verb ——⎤
The stolen *necklace was returned;* no questions were asked.

FAST FACT   Here are a couple of points to consider about passive voice: (a) Writers sometimes hide behind passive voice, using it to avoid identifying who did, initiated, or should be held accountable for what is under discussion. For example: A serious error in accounting was made last month, resulting in a $50,000 budget deficit. (b) Legal and governmental documents often feature passive voice. Interesting, isn't it?

COMPREHENSION AND PRACTICE

Identifying Passive and Active Voice

24.1

CW 24.6
More on the active and passive voice

Underline the simple subjects and verbs in the following sentences. Watch for compound subjects and verbs and compound sentences. Label active voice verbs with an *A* and passive voice verbs with a *P.* Remember—if the subject receives the action, the sentence is in the passive voice. Use the example to guide you.

EXAMPLE During the police chase, several <u>shots</u> <u>were fired</u>.[P]

(1) Last month, my <u>roommate Trey and I</u> <u>held</u>[A] a yard sale to get rid of our unwanted things. (2) During the week before the sale, the <u>items</u> for sale <u>were</u>[P] all <u>identified</u>. (3) <u>We</u> <u>spent</u>[A] several nights deciding on prices and putting little tags on each item. (4) <u>We</u> also <u>placed</u>[A] a small ad in the community newsletter, and <u>we</u> <u>posted</u>[A] signs throughout the neighborhood. (5) By 9 A.M. on the Saturday of our sale, our <u>treasures</u> <u>were piled</u>[P] on tables in front of the apartment house. (6) <u>People</u> <u>started</u>[A] arriving by 10. (7) For the next two hours, every <u>item</u> <u>was handled</u>[P], but not one <u>thing</u> <u>was bought</u>[P]. (8) At 2 P.M., <u>Trey and I</u> <u>called</u>[A] off our sale. (9) Then <u>everything</u> <u>was carried</u>[P] upstairs where <u>it</u> <u>was</u>[P] originally <u>found</u>. (10) Finally, by 7 P.M. the <u>apartment</u> <u>was straightened</u>[P] out, and <u>we</u> <u>began</u>[A] to laugh about our short careers as entrepreneurs.

COMPREHENSION AND PRACTICE

Using Passive Voice

24.2 In the paragraph below, fill in the blanks with the passive forms of the verbs in parentheses. Use the example to guide you.

EXAMPLE The championship game (to televise) _was televised_.

CW 24.7 Using passive voice

(1) Recently, a bicycle path (to complete) _was completed_ along the edge of the Allen River, right near downtown. (2) The path (to intend) _was intended_ to beautify the old abandoned railroad route. (3) The tracks (to tear) _were torn_ up and smooth asphalt (to lay) _was laid_ over the track bed. (4) The path (to design) _was designed_ to be wide enough for four bicyclists. (5) In addition, all the lighting along the path (to repair) _was repaired_ so that the path could be used late at night. (6) On the first weekend, a local television camera crew (to send) _was sent_ to film the opening day crowd. (7) The officials who attended were delighted when

they noted that helmets (to wear) _____were worn_____ by most of the cyclists.

(8) The first weekly amateur bike race (to conduct) _____was conducted_____ at 5 P.M.

(9) Prizes (to supply) _____were supplied_____ by several local businesses. (10) When

the day ended, police estimated that the new path (to enjoy) _____was enjoyed_____

by more than 150 bicyclists.

CHALLENGE 24.1   Analyzing the Effect of Active and Passive Voice

COLLABORATION

With a partner, rewrite the paragraph from Comprehension and Practice 24.1 on pages 379–380 in two ways. In one version, use every verb in the active voice; in the other, make every verb passive. Use a separate sheet of paper for your paragraphs. Evaluate both versions of the paragraph, and then answer the following questions. Discuss your answers with the rest of the class.

CW 24.8
Switching
from active
to passive
voice

1. Who or what is the subject in each sentence?

2. Who or what should be emphasized in each sentence?

3. Which version of each sentence do you think is most effective? Why?

Using the Progressive and Perfect Progressive Tenses

CW 24.9
Using
progressive
and perfect
progressive
tenses

In addition to using the basic tenses, you also need to master the progressive and perfect progressive tenses.

The Progressive Tenses

The simple and perfect tenses that you learned about in Chapter 22, "Basic Tenses for Regular Verbs," and Chapter 23, "Irregular Verbs and Frequently Confused Verbs," also have **progressive** forms to indicate ongoing action. For the simple past, present, and future, progressive tenses are formed by adding a form of *to be* to the **present participle** (the *-ing* form) of a verb.

Progressive Tense	= *Form of To Be* +	*Present Participle*	*Example*
Present progressive	am, are, is	going	I *am going.*
Past progressive	was, were	going	I *was going.*
Future progressive	will be	going	I *will be going.*

- The *present progressive tense* indicates something that is currently ongoing. (I *am taking* piano lessons.)
- The *past progressive tense* indicates something that was ongoing in the past. (She *was serving* an internship while she attended the university.)
- The *future progressive tense* indicates something that will be ongoing in the future. (They *will be showing* slides continuously throughout the open house.)

The Perfect Progressive Tenses

You form the **perfect progressive tenses** by using the *-ing* form of a verb with *have been, has been, had been,* or *will have been.*

Perfect Progressive Tense	= Helping Verb	+ Present Participle	Example
Present perfect progressive	has been, have been	studying	She *has been studying.*
Past perfect progressive	had been	studying	She *had been studying.*
Future perfect progressive	will have been	studying	She *will have been studying.*

- The *present perfect progressive tense* indicates an action that began in the past but that is still ongoing. (Our membership *has been growing* steadily for five years.)
- The *past perfect progressive tense* indicates an action that had been happening in the past but that stopped before the present. (Until 1996, our membership *had been growing.*)
- The *future perfect progressive tense* indicates an action that will be ongoing in the future but that will end before something else begins. (By 2008 our membership *will have been growing* for six straight years.)

Remember—all of these tenses allow you to express actions in time with great precision. It is much more important to learn how to use them than it is to be able to name them or even identify them. When you do the exercises below, refer back to this section if you get confused about the correct tense.

COMPREHENSION AND PRACTICE

24.3   **Recognizing the Progressive and Perfect Progressive Tenses**

In the sentences below, underline the progressive and perfect progressive tense verbs. Then, in the space above the line, label those verbs, as the example shows. Use the following abbreviations to label the verbs.

PPr = present progressive   *PPPr* = present perfect progressive

PaPr = past progressive   *PaPPr* = past perfect progressive

FPr = future progressive   *FPPr* = future perfect progressive

EXAMPLE

PPPr
Lately, I <u>have been spending</u> all my spare time surfing the Internet.

PPr
(1) As a result of my government class, I <u>am becoming</u> a news junkie.

PaPPr
(2) In the first week of this class, we <u>had been discussing</u> current affairs.

PaPr

(3) One morning, the instructor was lecturing on the role played by the media

PaPPr

in all news events. (4) I had already been considering a subscription to

Newsweek, so I decided to follow through. (5) Within a couple weeks, I was

PaPr

also scanning two or three newspapers online every day. (6) The more I do,

PPPr

the more I have been noticing the different ways print reporters present the

PPPr

news. (7) My television viewing habits have been changing, too. (8) Now in-

PPr

stead of watching sitcoms or some prime-time dramas, I find that I am turning

PPPr

on CNN every night. (9) In addition, I have been watching other all-news sta-

FPPr

tions like MSNBC, Fox News, and CNBC. (10) I will soon be declaring a major,

and my new interest in the news is leading me to consider history, govern-

ment, and pre-law.

COMPREHENSION AND PRACTICE

Using the Present Progressive Tense

24.4   For each sentence below, change the present tense verb in parentheses to a progressive tense verb. Write the correct verb form in the blank space as the example shows.

EXAMPLE   My sister (watches) ___*is watching*___ *Nightline* now.

(1) Right now at work, I (take) ___am taking___ a safety course. (2) The instructor (try) ___is trying___ hard to make the class interesting, and I think she (succeed) ___is succeeding___. (3) At this point, we (evaluate) ___are evaluating___ our work environment to make sure our building is as safe as possible. (4) In fact, two of my co-workers (create) ___are creating___ a crisis management plan. (5) In particular, they (concentrate) ___are concentrating___ on ensuring that everyone in the building knows exactly where to go in the case of fire. (6) Also, the course (cover) ___is covering___ basic first aid techniques. (7) For example, we (learn) ___are learning___ how to recognize things like shock, complications from diabetes, and allergic reactions. (8) In addition, we (review) ___are reviewing___ how

to help someone who (choke) _____is choking_____ by using the Heimlich maneuver. (9) Most important of all, everybody (learn) _____is learning_____ how to perform CPR. (10) So far, all the people on my crew feel that we (gain) _____are gaining_____ a truly valuable education.

COMPREHENSION AND PRACTICE

Using the Perfect Progressive Tense

24.5 Choose at least five verbs from the following list. Then, on a separate sheet of paper, write a paragraph in which you use perfect progressive tense forms (a form of *to have* plus the present participle) of the verbs you have selected. Use the example as a guide.

to ask	to answer
to complain	to reassure
to think	to observe
to speak	to laugh
to look	to find

EXAMPLE | to think

I had been thinking about dropping out before I spoke to Dennis.

CHALLENGE 24.2 **Working with Verb Tenses in Your Writing**

1. Choose two verbs from the list of irregular verbs on pages 360–363 and two regular verbs. Write three sentences for each, using verbs in the progressive and perfect progressive tenses.

COLLABORATION

2. Exchange your writing with a partner. On the paper you receive, underline the verbs and label them either progressive (*P*) or perfect progressive (*PP*). Then return the sentences to the writer.

Maintaining Consistency in Tense

ESL Note
See "Agreement" on pages 592–594.

CW 24.10 Maintaining consistency in tense

In addition to choosing the correct tense for your sentence context, you must use that tense *consistently*. To maintain **consistency in tense,** use a logical pattern for your verb choices, and avoid switching carelessly from one tense to another. Actions or situations occurring now call for the present tense. If they happened earlier, the past tense is needed, and if they have not yet happened, then the future tense is called for.

It's important to use a consistent time frame within a paragraph and especially within a sentence. To write about past events, use the past tense; don't switch, without good reason, to the present or the future. Use present tense verbs to write about events occurring now.

PAST TENSE	The pitcher ~~stands~~ *stood* on the mound and *stared* at the batter.
PRESENT TENSE	The pitcher *stands* on the mound and ~~stared~~ *stares* at the batter.

The tense you choose will depend upon the context of your writing. You must make the choice that is most logical to help readers understand the thoughts or events you are writing about.

FAST FACT   The way we speak helps to explain a number of errors in writing because we sometimes transfer a habit from one method of communication to another. Incorrect switches in verb tense may fall into this category. Look at this familiar way of telling a story: "I walked over to the counter and sat down. All of a sudden, this man gets up and starts screaming at the cashier." In speech, the switch from past tense in the first sentence to present tense in the second can be explained as an attempt to make the scene seem more alive or real. On paper, however, these kinds of switches aren't acceptable.

COMPREHENSION AND PRACTICE

Maintaining Consistency in Tense

24.6 Fill in the blanks in the following sentences with the correct form of the verb in parentheses to maintain consistency in verb tense. Use the example as a guide.

EXAMPLE | Once the police arrived, a crowd (to start) _____*started*_____ to gather.

(1) When I first started doing my work in college, the main thing that (to hold) _____*held*_____ me back was my lack of self-esteem. (2) When it came to studying, I was so sure I couldn't do the work that I (to do) _____*did*_____ not even bother. (3) For the first few weeks, I (to fail) _____*failed*_____ every quiz and examination I took. (4) As a result, I (to become) _____*became*_____ more convinced that I had no ability. (5) My lack of confidence (to begin) _____*began*_____ to influence other aspects of my life. (6) I (to think) _____*thought*_____ that nobody liked me. (7) Of course, because I didn't bother with anybody, nobody (to bother) _____*bothered*_____ with me either, so I became more convinced that I had no worth. (8) I was just about ready to drop

out when my business instructor (to talk) _____talked_____ to me and said that

I could do the work. (9) Her words (to shock) _____shocked_____ me. (10) I (to

decide) _____decided_____ that if she thought I could do it, I would give college

one more try.

COMPREHENSION AND PRACTICE

Keeping Verb Tense Consistent

24.7 Several sentences in the following passage suffer from inconsistency in verb tense. Cross out each error, and write the correct verb form above it. Use the example as a guide.

CW 24.11 Using verb forms

EXAMPLE   As I walked along Main Street, suddenly I ~~see~~ *saw* my friend Kelly with somebody I didn't recognize.

(1) One of the most unusual places I've seen is Clarkin Caverns. (2) Even though we ~~go~~ *went* there almost nine years ago, I still remember what a strange and wonderful place it is. (3) The last time I ~~am~~ *was* there, I first ~~have~~ *had* to go into a small ticket center. (4) Once there were enough people to make up a group, a guide ~~walks~~ *walked* us to an extra large elevator, which quickly ~~lowers~~ *lowered* us about sixty feet beneath the surface of the earth. (5) When I stepped out of the elevator, I ~~am~~ *was* amazed at what I saw. (6) All around me were beautiful rock formations, and as the group ~~walks~~ *walked* around, the guide talked about the cavern. (7) She ~~explains~~ *explained* the differences between *stalactites,* which "grow" down from the roof of the cavern, and *stalagmites,* which "grow" up from the ground. (8) As we walked, I ~~keep~~ *kept* looking all around, because I was afraid a bat was going to fly down and get caught in my hair. (9) At the end of the tour, our guide ~~puts~~ *put* out the lights for a minute so we ~~can~~ *could* experience total darkness. (10) It ~~is~~ *was* so dark that I ~~can't~~ *couldn't* even see my hands in front of me; never had a place felt peaceful and spooky at the same time.

COMPREHENSION AND PRACTICE

Evaluating Tenses for Effectiveness

24.8 In each sentence below, fill in the blanks with a form of the verb in parentheses, using a consistent tense. Then, on a separate sheet of paper, copy the paragraph over, using verbs in a different tense to fill in the blanks. Reread both versions, and write a brief paragraph in which you explain which tense you feel is most effective and why. Use the example as a guide.

EXAMPLE

The young boy (to kick) _____*kicked*_____ an empty can into the vacant lot.

or

The young boy (to kick) _____*kicks*_____ an empty can into the vacant lot.

(1) My old computer (to be) _____is (was)_____ such a piece of junk. (2) Every day I (to switch) _____switch (switched)_____ it on and (to hope) _____hope (hoped)_____ for the best. (3) On some days, the screen (to light) _____lights (lit)_____ right up. (4) On other days, however, it (to remain) _____remains (remained)_____ blank, with no sign of life. (5) Every time this (to happen) _____happens (happened)_____, I (to unplug) _____unplug (unplugged)_____ the unit for a couple of minutes. (6) I (to check) _____check (checked)_____ all the connections before plugging it in again. (7) This process (to be) _____is (was)_____ usually enough to get the computer to start up. (8) Once started, however, the computer (to crash) _____crashes (crashed)_____ frequently. (9) As a result, I sometimes (to lose) _____lose (lost)_____ some documents. (10) That computer often (to cost) _____costs (cost)_____ me as much time as it (to save) _____saves (saved)_____ me.

CHALLENGE 24.3   **Analyzing the Effect of Inconsistent Tense**

COLLABORATION

Reread the paragraph in Comprehension and Practice 24.7 in its original (uncorrected) form. Then, working with a partner, write a brief paragraph in which you explain what effect inconsistent verb tense has on the reader's ability to understand the point of the writing.

CHAPTER QUICK CHECK Mastering Voice, Progressive and Perfect Progressive Tenses, and Consistency in Verb Tense

The following passage contains a number of the errors and weaknesses in verb use outlined in this chapter. Using the various examples throughout the chapter to guide you, identify problems with voice, tense, and consistency. Cross out the incorrect form, and write the correct form above it, as the example shows. In some cases, more than one correct answer is possible.

EXAMPLE

entered
After Karen and Eddie ~~enter~~ the plane, they quickly stored their carry-on luggage and took their seats.

(1) Car-sharing programs, an idea popular for some time in Europe and
beginning
Canada, is ~~begun~~ to catch on in such U.S. cities as San Francisco, Boston,
will be
Seattle, and Portland, Oregon. (2) Soon, organizers ~~had been~~ establishing car-sharing groups in several other major U.S. cities, including Boulder, Colorado, and Honolulu, Hawaii. (3) These kinds of programs benefit both
operate
the individuals involved and the cities in which they ~~operated~~. (4) After all,
are
when several people ~~will be~~ sharing rather than owning cars exclusively,
participants pay a yearly
fewer cars clog busy city streets. (5) To join a group, ~~a yearly fee is paid by~~
fee
~~participants~~ in the range of $200 to $500. (6) In return, members ~~were~~ able
are
to use cars owned by the organization for a nominal fee, perhaps $1.50 to
covers
$2.00 an hour. (7) The yearly fee ~~covered~~ registration, insurance, and maintenance costs, so members are generally responsible only for a small mileage
are
charge, if anything. (8) When they ~~had been~~ going to need a car, members call or log into the organization's Web site and make a reservation. (9) ~~Then~~
Users then pick up a car
~~a car is picked up by the users~~ at one of several lots around the city. (10)
return
When users are done with the car, they simply ~~returned~~ it to the same site, turn in the keys, and head for home, free from the headaches that car owners face.

QUICK STUDY | **Student Example**

This chapter discusses different aspects of action and consistency. Take a look at the following paragraph on a related subject—how someone you observed reacted to an awkward or unpleasant situation:

> The thing I remember on my first trip to an airport was how gracefully
>   Act
> the woman behind the airline counter reacted to some irate customers. The
>   Act
> weather that morning was terrible, and no planes could take off for a few
> hours because of the thick fog. My own flight wasn't supposed to leave until
>   Act   Act
> 2 P.M., so I just sat at the gate and hoped the weather would improve by
>   Act
> then. From nine to noon, customer after customer went up to the attendant to
> ask about the status of their flights. No matter how agitated or angry the people
>   Pass
> were, all their questions were answered by the woman calmly and politely.
> She told them that the entire airport was fogged in and promised to do her
> best to reschedule them once the weather improved. The worst customer was
> a man about 40 years old, dressed in shorts and a brightly flowered shirt.
>   PP Act
> This obnoxious man had been complaining loudly to everyone around
>   Pass
> him. When the counter was reached by him, he began yelling at the attendant
>   PP Act
> and pounding on the counter. He said he had been planning this trip for a
> year and demanded that she immediately put him, his wife, and their two
> children on a plane so they could catch their connecting flight to Disney
>   P Act
> World. His wife and kids just stood there. They were staring at the floor,
> obviously totally embarrassed by this unnecessary scene. Now whenever I
>   P Act
> am thinking of yelling at someone, I think of how ridiculous that man looked
> and try to react as coolly and calmly as that attendant did.

First complete the following activities in response to this paragraph:

1. A number of subjects and verbs in this paragraph are highlighted. Using the material in this chapter to guide you, label any highlighted progressive (P) and perfect progressive verbs (PP). Also, identify any highlighted active (Act) and passive (Pass) voice verbs, and then, on a separate sheet of paper, change

the sentences containing awkward passive voice verbs so that they will be in the active voice, as the examples in the chapter illustrate.

2. On the following lines, briefly explain the main point as expressed in the topic sentence and describe how the information in the body of the paragraph supports this main idea.

The main point expressed in this topic sentence is that someone treated angry

customers with respect during the writer's first visit to an airport. The supporting

sentences support this point by providing examples of how this employee dealt with

rudeness.

3. Go back through the paragraph and circle all verbs that are in the active voice. How do these active voice verbs affect the impact of the paragraph? Use the lines below for your answer.

Most students will agree that the active voice verbs add a sense of liveliness to the

writing that the passive voice can't provide.

Now explore the topic in writing. As the paragraph on page 389 does, you could concentrate on how the passing of time affects you. You might also focus on one of these topics related to the subject matter of this chapter:

- a time when you regret not taking action
- something that you wish was progressing more quickly
- a gift that keeps on giving
- actions people can take to improve their lives

1. Exchange your draft with a classmate. Evaluate the paragraph you receive. If you discover any problem spots, especially concerning voice, tense, and consistency, circle the errors and then return the paper to the writer.

2. Consider the comments and corrections your reader has made and create a final draft of your paragraph.

SUMMARY EXERCISE Mastering Voice, Progressive and Perfect Progressive Tenses, and Consistency in Verb Tense

CW 24.12 Comparing the passive and active voice

The following passage contains a number of the errors in verb use outlined in this chapter. Using the various examples throughout the chapter to guide you, identify errors in voice, tense, and consistency. Cross out the incorrect form, and write the correct form above it. In some cases, more than one correct answer is possible. Some answers may vary. Representative answers are given.

(1) I often wish I ~~spend~~ [had spent] more time reading as a child. (2) If ~~more reading~~ [I had done] ~~has been done by me~~ [more reading], I wouldn't now feel so embarrassed and frustrated every time I ~~sat~~ [sit] down to read.

(3) When I ~~start~~ [started] elementary school, I missed almost half of first grade because of illness. (4) While all my classmates ~~are~~ [were] learning the basics of reading, I was at home in bed. (5) In spite of this, at the end of the year, I ~~am~~ [was] promoted anyway, and my difficulties began.

(6) I never misbehaved in class, so ~~breaks were always given to me by my teachers~~ [my teachers always gave me breaks]. (7) When I read aloud, if I ~~hesitate~~ [hesitated] over a word, my teacher would say it for me. (8) As a result, I ~~become~~ [became] very good at pretending to be able to read.

(9) Although I ~~was fall~~ [fell] further behind each year, I ~~keep~~ [kept] getting promoted. (10) When ~~courses were failed by me~~ [I failed courses], I went to summer school. (11) Even though I attended summer classes, I ~~am~~ [was] still not learning anything.

(12) In my senior year of high school, I ~~have earned~~ [earned] straight D's for the first term, except for English, which I ~~will be failing~~ [failed]. (13) Because she ~~is~~ [was] concerned about me, my English teacher arranged for me to take a reading test. (14) When ~~the test was finished by me~~ [I finished the test], I discovered that I ~~am~~ [was] not even reading on the sixth-grade level. (15) My teacher ~~gets~~ [got] me a special reading tutor, and after working hard the rest of the year, I ~~am~~ [was] able to read well enough to graduate with my class.

(16) However, when I ~~am thinking~~ [thought] about college, all my shame and frustration returned. (17) I failed the college's reading placement test, and ~~a remedial reading course had to be taken by me~~ [I had to take a remedial reading course]. (18) I ~~will be~~ [was] determined not to lose this chance to make something of myself, so I ~~work~~ [worked] as hard as I could. (19) I'm proud to say that by the end of that course, I ~~am~~ [was] reading better than any of the other students in the class. (20) However, I still ~~felt~~ [feel] insecure about my ability, and I ~~was~~ [am] planning to keep working to change my attitude.

FOR FURTHER EXPLORATION

1. Consider one of the following topics:

   - an effective way to deal with a demanding or difficult person
   - the hottest, coldest, or most uncomfortable day you can ever remember
   - the easiest academic subject
   - the most important personal quality
   - a situation or event that was a significant learning experience for you or someone you know

   Prewrite on the subject, using one of the strategies you practiced in Chapter 2, and work your way through the rest of the writing process. Then complete a draft essay of at least 500 words on this subject.

2. Exchange your draft with a classmate. Check the draft you receive for weaknesses, paying particular attention to voice, tense, and consistency. Circle any errors, using the material in this chapter as a guide, and then return the draft to the writer.

3. Revise your essay, correcting any errors in verb use or other problems discovered by your reader.

RECAP Passive Voice, Additional Tenses, and Maintaining Consistency in Tense

New terms in this chapter	Definitions
passive voice	a characteristic of sentences in which the subject receives the action of the verb
	EXAMPLE Her bicycle was stolen.
active voice	a characteristic of sentences in which the subject does or is responsible for the action
	EXAMPLE A photographer took a picture of the scene.
progressive tenses	forms of a verb created by combining some form of *to be* with the present participle of another verb
	Progressive forms express ongoing actions or situations.
	EXAMPLE Karen and Brendan *are talking* about buying a house.
	EXAMPLE Louis *was reading* in the library.
	EXAMPLE Laura *will be wallpapering* her room soon.

New terms in this chapter	Definitions
present participle	formed by adding *-ing* to the basic form of regular and irregular verbs

> **EXAMPLE**   play*ing;* ris*ing*

perfect progressive tenses	forms of a verb created by combining some form of *to have* with the present participle of another verb

Perfect progressive forms express actions or situations that occur over a period of time.

> **EXAMPLE**   Karen and Brendan *have been talking* about buying a house.

> **EXAMPLE**   Louis *had been reading* in the library.

> **EXAMPLE**   By 0 P.M., Laura *will have been wallpapering* her room for five hours.

consistency in tense	refers to a logical pattern for the verbs within a sentence, paragraph, or essay

Consistency requires avoiding careless mixing of verb tenses and maintaining a unified time frame within a piece of writing.

> **INCONSISTENT**   I *answer* all the questions that were asked.

> **CONSISTENT**   I *answered* all the questions that were asked.

Forming the Progressive Tenses

(continued)

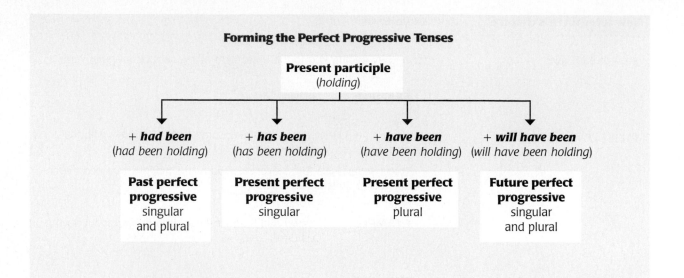

GOING FORWARD...

Q: I can see that it's important to choose the right voice and to be consistent with verb tense, including the progressive and perfect progressive tenses. I'm just not sure I am making the right decisions. Are there any techniques or hints that will help me here?

A: Here are some strategies that will help. In terms of voice, make the active voice your first choice. Use the passive voice only for those occasions when you don't know the doer of the action or you need to focus on the receiver. To use the progressive and perfect progressive tenses, always take a moment to see if you are talking about something while it is happening during a time period. If so, choose the progressive and perfect progressive tenses. Finally, stick with the tense you start with, unless you can explain why you need to change it. Just stopping to question whether you are using the right tense is often enough to keep you from incorrectly switching tenses.

PART 6

Keeping Your Writing Correct

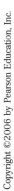

CHAPTER 25

Nouns: Working Effectively with Words That Name

▶ **Navigating This Chapter**

In this chapter, you will learn how to:

- turn a singular noun into a plural one
- recognize singular nouns that end in *-s*
- use collective nouns effectively
- use cue words to identify the number of a noun

GETTING STARTED...

**CW 25.1
Chapter
basics**

Q: When I write, I seem to rely a lot on words that name people, places, and things—nouns. Why do these words play such a big role in my writing?

A: Nouns show up so frequently because of the significance the people and things they name play in your writing. For that reason alone, it makes sense to concentrate on using them effectively and correctly.

Overview: Understanding Nouns

**CW 25.2
Understanding
nouns**

To understand and keep straight all the elements and aspects of the world around us, we name them. The words we use to do so are **nouns.** Nouns are classified into two groups. Those that name a nonspecific person or thing—*a police officer, a continent, a short story*—are called **common nouns.** Those that name a particular person or thing—*Officer Donna Boyd, Asia, "Everyday Use"*—are called **proper nouns** and are always introduced by a capital letter. More important, nouns have two forms. Those that name individual people or things are *singular,* and those that name several are *plural.* Mastering this aspect of noun use is crucial to your success as a writer, because it holds potential for error.

Reviewing the Function and Form of Nouns

**CW 25.3
The function
and form of
nouns**

Nouns are the most versatile part of speech in English. Although writers don't generally think about all of them when they write, nouns can perform six different functions in a sentence:

- Nouns can serve as a **subject** of a sentence, as this example shows:

EXAMPLE | Many small *farms* have gone out of business in the past decade.

    subject

- Nouns can also serve as a **predicate nominative,** the word that answers "Who or What?" *after* a linking verb (such as *is* or *was*), as this example shows:

EXAMPLE | Kevin was the *goalie* for the varsity soccer team.

predicate nominative

- In addition, nouns can serve as a **direct object,** the word that answers "Whom or What?" *after* an action verb, as this example shows:

EXAMPLE | Karen mailed the *letter* at the campus mail center.

direct object

- Nouns can serve as an **indirect object** as well, the word that answers "To Whom or For Whom?" or "To What or For What?" *after* an action verb, as this example shows:

EXAMPLE | The pharmacist gave the *customer* a brochure explaining the drug's side effects.

indirect object

- Nouns can also serve as the **object of a preposition,** the word that follows a preposition and completes a **prepositional phrase,** as this example shows:

EXAMPLE | The coat in the *closet* originally cost $200.

object of the preposition

- Finally, nouns can serve as an **appositive,** a word that helps explain or illustrate another noun, as this example shows:

EXAMPLE | The child clutched her favorite *toy,* a small stuffed *kitten.*

appositive

Regardless of a noun's function, you must select the proper form—singular or plural—for each situation. Fortunately, changing nouns from singular to plural is generally easy. To make most nouns plural, simply add *-s* to the singular form:

Singular	*Plural*
cup	cup**s**
decision	decision**s**
flower	flower**s**

Some nouns form their plurals in other ways. For example, most words that end in -*ch*, -*sh*, -*x*, and -*s* form their plurals by adding -*es*:

Singular	*Plural*
brush	brush**es**
mix	mix**es**
pass	pass**es**
watch	watch**es**

CW 25.4
Using singular and plural nouns

For words that end in a -*y* preceded by a consonant, form the plural by changing the -*y* to -*i* and adding -*es*:

Singular	*Plural*
candy	cand**ies**
enemy	enem**ies**
eulogy	eulog**ies**
mystery	myster**ies**

Certain words that end in -*f* or -*fe* form their plurals by changing the ending to -*ves*:

Singular	*Plural*
half	hal**ves**
leaf	lea**ves**
shelf	shel**ves**
wife	wi**ves**

Combined or *hyphenated* words form their plurals by adding -*s* to the main word:

Singular	*Plural*
attorney-at-law	attorney**s**-at-law
brother-in-law	brother**s**-in-law
maid of honor	maid**s** of honor
runner-up	runner**s**-up

Some common words form their plurals by changing letters within the word:

Singular	*Plural*
foot	f**ee**t
man	m**e**n
mouse	m**i**ce
tooth	t**ee**th

Some words have the same singular and plural forms:

Singular	*Plural*
deer	**deer**
rice	**rice**
sheep	**sheep**
species	**species**

FAST FACT Besides being names for garments that cover the lower part of the body and that have separate coverings for both legs, what do the nouns *pants* and *trousers* and *slacks* have in common? They are all *plural* words for a *singular* item of clothing.

In addition, some words that end in *-o* form their plural by adding *-s: sopranos* and *pros.* Other words that end in *-o* form their plural by adding *-es: tomatoes* and *heroes.* Some words from foreign languages form their plurals in keeping with their original language: *analysis/analyses* and *crisis/crises.*

If you have a question about the plural form of a noun, a dictionary should be your first stop. It gives the plural ending after the singular form if the noun forms its plural in an irregular way.

COMPREHENSION AND PRACTICE

Identifying the Function of Nouns

25.1 In each of the following sentences, a noun is underlined. Using the discussion of the function of nouns on page 397 to guide you, write the function of each underlined noun above it, as the example shows:

EXAMPLE
predicate nominative
The manager of the club was once a professional <u>musician</u> herself.

(1) Rock guitarist Carlos Santana has enjoyed a remarkable <u>career</u> [*direct object*] in music that has now spanned five decades. (2) Santana first came into national <u>prominence</u> [*object of the preposition*] at the original Woodstock music festival with his captivating performance before the half million fans in attendance. (3) From that point, his <u>infusion</u> [*subject*] of Latin and Afro-Cuban flavors into a rock rhythm caught the ears of America. (4) *Santana,* his 1969 debut <u>album</u> [*appositive*], and *Abraxas,* his 1970 multiple platinum follow-up album, produced several hit songs. (5) Some of these songs, including "Evil Ways," "Black Magic Woman," and *"Oye Como Va,"* are still favorite <u>selections</u> [*predicate nominative*] on radio stations across the country. (6) Throughout the <u>years</u> [*object of the preposition*] that followed, Santana continued recording and performing, using the opportunity to remind the world of the need for peace, tolerance, and compassion. (7) In 1998, Santana's <u>accomplishments</u> [*subject*] were recognized by his peers when he was inducted into the Rock and Roll Hall of Fame. (8) In 1999, Santana's star rose once again with *Supernatural,* his 36th <u>album</u> [*appositive*]. (9) *Supernatural* earned the <u>guitarist</u> [*indirect object*] nine Grammys and to date has sold well in

excess of 10 million copies. (10) With this album, on which he collaborated with contemporary artists like Wyclef Jean, Rob Thomas, and Lauryn Hill, Santana is a household <u>name</u> once more.

predicate nominative

**COMPREHENSION
AND PRACTICE**

Making Nouns Plural

25.2 In the paragraph below, change the italicized singular nouns to their plural forms. Cross out each singular noun, and write the plural noun above it. Review the rules above. Use the example to guide you.

EXAMPLE | As we drove through the city, we saw the ~~church~~ and the ~~museum~~.

churches *museums*

(1) The bus tour I took last spring introduced me to Midwestern architecture, from *skyscraper* and *cathedral* to *university* and *barn*. (2) After *year* of reading *magazine* and *book* about architecture, I finally decided to take a first-hand look at some *treasure* of Americana. (3) Our group, which filled two *bus,* was a chatty, friendly group of *individual* from a variety of *country*. (4) Our first stop was Chicago, where we toured famous *building*: the Sears Tower, the Hancock Observatory, and Water Tower Place. (5) The view from the Observatory was breathtaking: sparkling *roof,* swimming *pool* like gems atop *skyscraper,* bustling *street,* and a vast expanse of Lake Michigan spread out before us. (6) After several brief walking *tour* in the city, we were off for the country, munching *sandwich* and swapping *story* about the history we had learned. (7) Our *guide* pointed out interesting *style* of *barn* and *silo* and explained the *influence* that produced them as we glided past big, prosperous *farm*. (8) In *community* along the Mississippi River, quaint little *church* and *house* on *stilt* enchanted us. (9) We even toured several Victorian *mansion* and the *home* of two former U.S. *president*. (10) Inspired by my adventure, I am preparing slide *show* and *article* about the *structure* I saw and the *theory* and *history* behind them.

skyscrapers cathedrals universities barns years magazines books treasures buses individuals countries buildings roofs pools skyscrapers streets tours sandwiches stories guides styles barns silos influences farms communities churches houses stilts mansions homes presidents shows articles structures theories histories

CHALLENGE 25.1   Recognizing the Function of Nouns

COLLABORATION

Choose two consecutive paragraphs from one of the reading selections in Part Seven, "Connecting: Responding to Reading." Then, working with a partner, make a list on a separate sheet of paper of each noun in the passage and the function it is serving.

Considering Singular Nouns Ending in *-s*, Collective Nouns, and Cue Words

**CW 25.5
Working
with
collective
nouns and
cue words**

Although most nouns are made plural by adding *-s*, not all nouns that end in *-s* are plural. Words that fall in this category include the following:

Singular Words That End in *-s*

economics   mathematics   mumps   physics   statistics
ethics   measles   news   politics

Because these words end in *-s*, it's easy to choose the incorrect verb form when one of these nouns is the subject. Remember—these words are singular and therefore call for singular verb forms. See Chapter 21, "Subject–Verb Agreement," for more information.

Collective nouns are words that stand for *groups* of items or individuals. Here is a list of common collective nouns:

Common Collective Nouns

audience	faculty	group	populace
class	family	herd	school
committee	flock	jury	team
congregation	government	office	tribe

Even though they represent a number of people or things, collective nouns are singular in form. In most cases, a collective noun used as a subject requires a singular form of the verb, as the following sentences illustrate:

EXAMPLE

The *jury wants* to see a copy of the trial transcript.

The *faculty looks* forward to meeting the incoming students.

You should also become familiar with the following **cue words.** When they precede the subject, they alert you that it is singular and therefore calls for a singular verb.

ESL Note
See "Articles" on pages 597–598.

Common Singular Cue Words

a, an	every
another	neither
each	one
either	

EXAMPLE   *Every* student *needs* a notebook to use as a journal.

Either book *is* a good choice as a gift.

Also be aware of the following words. When they precede the subject, they cue you that it is plural and therefore calls for a plural verb.

Common Plural Cue Words

all	many
both	several
few	some

EXAMPLE   *Many* children *are* actually afraid of clowns.

Several stray cats *live* in my neighborhood.

COMPREHENSION AND PRACTICE **Working with Collective Nouns and Cue Words**

25.3   Underline the collective noun or cue word in each sentence below. Decide whether the subject is singular or plural. Then circle the correct verb. Use the example as a guide.

EXAMPLE   Each class (has, have) its unique demands on my time and energy.

(1) A group that (seems, seem) to be diminishing day by day is people who read newspapers. (2) From all appearances, the average family today (is, are) far less interested in print journalism than the family of thirty years ago. (3) As a result, the audience that a reporter reaches with a story today (has, have) lessened—in some cases by more than 25 percent. (4) The jury (is, are) still out as to why readership has dropped off so drastically. (5) Several recent studies (has, have) indicated that people prefer to get their news from television. (6) Some critics (maintains, maintain) that newspapers' continuing emphasis on sensationalism has turned many people away. (7) The government (has, have) recently funded a major study, but the results won't be available for several months. (8) Meanwhile, a blue ribbon committee of editors and publishers (has, have) decided to conduct a separate study. (9) At

this point, each member of the committee ((feels) feel) that if action isn't taken,

the number of newspapers published will continue to plummet. (10) One con-

cern shared by both the industry and the government ((is) are) the indication

that the populace overall ((is) are) reading less than it did a decade ago.

FAST FACT   If you've ever wondered where new words come from, read the news. Every time something is invented, discovered, or developed, we have to name it. Consider the situation in which a woman agrees to carry the fertilized embryo resulting from the egg and sperm of another couple. What should this activity be called? For the time being, physicians and other professionals have offered these names: *gestational carriers, gestational surrogacy,* and *gestational care.*

COMPREHENSION AND PRACTICE

25.4

CW 25.6
Using
collective
nouns and
cue words

Using Collective Nouns and Verbs Correctly

Complete the following sentences by adding a present tense verb with modifiers. Underline the collective noun or cue word in the first part of the sentence to help you choose the correct present tense verb. Use the example to guide you.
Answers will vary. Representative answers are shown.

EXAMPLE   The herd of cows _____ *heads for the barn like clockwork at 5 P.M.*

1. Every time we try to eat outdoors, a swarm of wasps _____

   descends on our feast.

2. Each month, the congregation at that church _____

   collects food and clothing for a shelter for homeless people.

3. Few chairs in the waiting room _____

   are comfortable enough to sit on.

4. Neither winner of the tri-state lottery _____

   seems to mind sharing the fortune.

5. Many students enrolled in this college _____

   hold part-time jobs and take care of families as well.

6. The audience at the opening night performance of most plays usually _____

   notices a few glitches in the production.

7. By next year, the <u>team</u> of twenty scientists _____

hopes to identify a reason for the change in water quality. _____

8. Many <u>art</u> museums throughout the country _____

offer reduced-price admission for college students. _____

9. Every year, the activities <u>committee</u> at the neighborhood center _____

arranges for tax advice for senior citizens. _____

10. Another <u>sign</u> encouraging government officials _____

is the slow but steady reduction in the unemployment rate. _____

CHALLENGE 25.2   Writing Sentences Using Singular Words Ending in –s and Cue Words

1. On a separate sheet of paper, write a sentence for each of the following words in which the word is the subject of a present tense verb. Review the examples in Chapter 21, "Subject–Verb Agreement," if you need further guidance:

economics	audience	government	statistics	jury
mathematics	committee	news	politics	audience

COLLABORATION

2. Exchange your list of sentences with a partner. Check the sentences you receive to make sure the words have been used correctly and then return the sentences to the writer.

CHAPTER QUICK CHECK Working with Nouns

Each sentence in the following passage contains an error in noun or cue word use. First review the discussion of the number of nouns, collective nouns, and cue words. Then correct each error by crossing out the incorrect word and writing the correct form above it, as the example shows.

EXAMPLE   It took me over an hour to install the new ~~shelfs~~. *shelves*

(1) ~~Storys~~ Stories of computer hackers appear frequently in the news because of

the ingenious ways that these computer whizzes manipulate computer pro-

grams and networks. (2) Often, the articles discuss such actions as illegal

~~entrys~~ entries into classified government networks, the release of computer viruses,

or the theft of credit card numbers. (3) But ~~each~~ many or more hackers argue that they are

being unfairly accused of such crimes. (4) They say that the problem isn't
with hackers but with a group of computer vandals and ~~thiefs~~ thieves called *crackers*.
(5) True hackers aren't interested in using computers to create serious ~~worrys~~ worries
or problems for others. (6) Even when a few ~~hacker~~ hackers break into some network, they do so for the thrill of doing it, not to cause trouble. (7) With crackers, however, the ~~motivationes~~ motivations are quite different. (8) Some crackers use their
considerable computer ~~abilitys~~ abilities to break into a network and corrupt or de-
stroy files, often costing the affected organizations thousands and thousands
of dollars. (9) Others intentionally commit illegal acts such as pirating software, making free long-distance calls, or obtaining supposedly "secure" information on individuals and ~~companys~~ companies. (10) Hackers, who take pride in their
knowledge and ~~skilles~~ skills, object to being lumped together with a group that mis-
uses their expertise.

QUICK STUDY Student Example

This chapter focuses on the means of identification and naming things. Consider
the following paragraph that focuses on a related subject, the name that would be
perfect for a new model of an item, in this case, a new brand of sneakers designed
for the basketball court:

A great brand name for a newly designed pair of sneakers for basketball
would be "Showtime." This title is perfect because of the way basketball is
played today at all levels in the United States. Coaches used to teach their
players fundamentals like passing, ball-handling, setting up a play, and playing
tight defense. But that's not the way it is any more. Now basketball isn't so
much about being part of a team but about being an individual player. The
goal for most players now seems to become a star, the flashier the better.
ESPN and network broadcasts show the performances of top NBA players,

the A heroes OP of basketball. But these broadcasts have given S fans the IO wrong DO idea

about the OP way the S game should be played. Of course, S kids are the most

impressionable PN fans of all. Naturally, they imitate the outrageous DO shots and

trash-talking DO style they've seen instead of concentrating on learning how to

pass or to wait for the best OP shot. They want to play the way that their heroes

play on television. As a result, basketball today has become as much a show as

a game, so that makes "Showtime" the ideal name for a new brand of basket-

ball sneakers.

First complete the following activities in response to this paragraph:

1. Four sentences in the previous paragraph are highlighted. First, circle all the nouns in these sentences. Then, using the material on page 397 to guide you, list above each noun the function it is serving, either *subject* (S), *direct object* (DO), *indirect object* (IO), *object of the preposition* (OP), *predicate nominative* (PN), or *appositive* (A).

2. Writing of any type is effective when it communicates a clear message to a reader. In your view, what role do the various nouns in this paragraph play in helping an audience understand the point being made? Use the lines below for your answer.

   Students will agree that the nouns help the audience understand the point of the

   paragraph because they name the *specific* ideas under discussion.

   _____

3. Assess the final sentence of the paragraph. Then, on the lines below, briefly explain whether you think it serves as an effective concluding sentence and why.

   Answers may vary, but even if they don't agree with the original premise that the

   newer style game is deficient by comparison, most students will agree that the final

   sentence serves as an effective conclusion because it sums up the significance of

   the point made in the body of the paragraph.

Now explore the topic in writing. You could discuss the name you would give a new model or version of car or some other product and why, as the paragraph above does. You might also concentrate on one of these subjects related to the subject matter of this chapter:

- a place you wish you had never visited
- a cue or hint that you missed or misunderstood, leading to a social disaster
- an idea, belief, or concept that many people find difficult to understand
- the story behind a first name or nickname, either your own or someone you know

COLLABORATION

1. Exchange your draft with a classmate. Evaluate the paragraph you receive. If you discover any errors, especially with forms of irregular and collective nouns as well as singular nouns ending in −s, circle them and write the correct form above the incorrect ones, and then return the paper to the writer.

2. Consider the comments and corrections your reader has made and create a final draft of your paragraph.

SUMMARY EXERCISE Working with Nouns

Each sentence in the following passage contains an error in noun or cue word use. First review the discussion of the number of nouns, collective nouns, and cue words. Then correct each error by crossing out the incorrect word and writing the correct form above it. In some cases, other correct versions are possible.
Answers may vary.

(1) Because of advances in technology, ~~every~~ [many/some] educators feel that cursive writing is fast becoming a thing of the past. (2) At one time, good penmanship was considered one of the most important ~~signes~~ [signs] of professionalism. (3) Even today, many people still view handwriting styles as ~~indicationes~~ [indications] of individuality and maturity. (4) Now, however, with ~~many~~ [an] emphasis on using computers for writing, the art of handwriting is losing its status.

(5) At one time, ~~all~~ [every] student was taught handwriting as a separate subject in school. (6) In ~~each~~ [many/some] cases, handwriting teachers were chosen because their own writing was considered excellent. (7) Students learned cursive by first practicing different strokes and ~~ovales~~ [ovals] that they copied from handwriting books. (8) Once these ~~beginneres~~ [beginners] had mastered the various shapes, they would begin work on actual letters and numbers. (9) The ~~childs~~ [children] were then graded on the precision and accuracy of their handwriting.

(10) In ~~every~~ [many] schools today, however, nobody seems concerned about handwriting instruction. (11) According to a recent article, a typical elementary

~~classes~~ [class] spends very little time on handwriting. (12) Apparently, the various other educational ~~crisies~~ [crises] that must be handled in the classroom take priority over handwriting.

(13) Not everyone is concerned that those ~~dayes~~ [days] are a thing of the past in some regions. (14) In fact, many people see this change as one of the many ~~journeyes~~ [journeys] students must follow to become part of the electronic age. (15) In some elementary schools today, as soon as children learn the alphabet, a team of teachers ~~show~~ [shows] them how to use a word processor. (16) They quickly learn to write all their ~~storys~~ [stories] electronically, using a keyboard. (17) Some proponents of the change say that in the future the only ~~scenarioes~~ [scenario] that will call for handwriting will be taking notes in class, completing written tests, or writing signatures.

(18) Cursive writing of one sort or another has been around for ~~centurys~~ [centuries], so no one should seriously expect it to disappear. (19) In fact, good ~~argumentes~~ [arguments] can be made to ensure that it doesn't. (20) Probably the best solution is to teach students handwriting and word processing so that they can take advantage of both ~~wayes~~ [ways] of recording their ideas.

FOR FURTHER EXPLORATION

1. Consider one of the following topics:
   - a cultural or family tradition that you know well
   - the influence of fate in life
   - a situation made worse by hypocrisy
   - how you would prepare if you knew a catastrophic storm were going to hit your community in 12 hours
   - what you would urge your college administration to improve the level of, education or quality of life on campus

   Prewrite on the subject, using one of the strategies you practiced in Chapter 2, and work your way through the rest of the writing process. Then complete a draft essay of at least 500 words on this subject.

COLLABORATION

2. Exchange your draft with a classmate. Check the draft you receive for weaknesses, checking in particular for problems with irregular and collective nouns as well as singular nouns ending in *-s*. Circle any incorrect forms, using the material in this chapter to guide you, and write the correct form above the incorrect ones. Then return the paper to the writer.

3. Revise your essay, correcting any errors in irregular verb use or other problems discovered by your reader.

RECAP Nouns: Working Effectively with Words That Name

New terms in this chapter	Definitions
noun	a word that names a person, place, thing, or idea
	Form plural nouns by adding *-s* or following spelling guidelines.
proper noun	a noun introduced by a capital letter that names a specific person or thing
predicate nominative	a word that answers "Who or What?" *after* a linking verb
direct object	a word that answers "Whom or What?" *after* an action verb
indirect object	a word that answers "To Whom or For Whom?" or "To What or For What?" *after* an action verb
appositive	a word that helps to explain or illustrate another noun
collective noun	a noun that stands for a group of items or individuals
	Collective nouns are singular in form, and generally call for the singular form of the verb.
	Example The *team* is about to win the tournament.
cue word	a word such as *another* or *both* that indicates the number of a noun

GOING FORWARD...

Q: Because I use so many of them, I'm concerned about making errors with nouns. What can I do to make sure I use these words correctly?

A: The good news is that, for the most part, working with nouns is fairly straightforward. The *number* of the word—whether it is singular or plural—is probably the most frequent problem. As long as you make sure to use the correct plural form and to recognize any cue words that signal number, you should be fine.

CHAPTER 26

Pronouns: Understanding Case, Clear Pronoun–Antecedent Agreement, and Nonsexist Pronoun Usage

▶ **Navigating This Chapter**

In this chapter, you will learn how to:

- recognize the types of pronouns
- understand the cases of personal pronouns
- identify number and gender with indefinite pronouns
- ensure that pronouns and antecedents agree in number and gender

GETTING STARTED . . .

CW 26.1
Chapter
basics

Q: When I write, I often use pronouns, but I'm not always sure I am using the correct ones. Why does working with pronouns seem so confusing?

A: You probably find working with pronouns confusing because of some complications involved in their use. For instance, some pronouns—the personal pronouns—have different forms depending on whether they will serve as a subject or as an object or will indicate possession. Also, *number* can be an issue with some pronouns, especially indefinite pronouns, because some are singular, some are plural, and some can be either.

Overview: Choosing the Correct Pronoun

ESL Note
See "Agreement" on pages 592–594.

CW 26.2
Overview of
correct
pronoun
choice

Pronouns are the words that substitute for nouns. Think of pronouns as a kind of verbal shorthand. They enable you to use a brief, easily recognizable alternative for a noun rather than repeating that noun several times. Thus, they add variety to your language. There are several types, including **personal pronouns, indefinite pronouns, demonstrative pronouns, reflexive/intensive pronouns, relative pronouns,** and **interrogative pronouns.** To work effectively with pronouns, you need to attend to several concerns. You must consider the form, or *case,* of personal pronouns and the *number* and *gender* with indefinite pronouns. You also need to make sure that the pronouns and the words they refer to, called **antecedents,** match or *agree.* Otherwise, the people, places, things, and ideas being referred to won't be clear for your reader.

Examining Pronoun Types

Because we use pronouns as alternatives to nouns, pronouns appear frequently in writing. They can be grouped in several classes:

- **personal pronouns,** which refer to *specific* people, places, things, and ideas

I, me, my, mine	we, us, our, ours
you, your, yours	she, he, her, him, hers, his
it, its, their, theirs	

- **indefinite pronouns,** which refer to *general* persons and things

all	each	little	nobody	others
another	either	many	none	several
any	everybody	more	no one	some
anybody	everyone	most	nothing	somebody
anyone	everything	much	one	someone
anything	few	neither	other	something
both				

- **demonstrative pronouns,** which point out *particular* people or things referred to

this	that
these	those

- **reflexive/intensive pronouns,** which add emphasis to antecedents

myself	ourselves
yourself	yourselves
himself, herself, itself	themselves
oneself	

- **relative pronouns,** which introduce dependent clauses, called *relative clauses,* within a sentence

who	which
whom	that
whose	

- **interrogative pronouns,** which begin questions

Who . . . ?	Whom . . . ?	Whose . . . ?
Whoever . . . ?	Whomever . . . ?	Which . . . ?
Whichever . . . ?	What . . . ?	Whatever . . . ?

For the most part, working with pronouns is fairly straightforward. But two issues can make working with some pronouns potentially confusing. The first is **case,** the particular one of three *forms* of a personal pronoun called for in a specific situation. The second is the **number** of the *antecedent,* that is, whether the word the pronoun refers to is singular or plural.

Understanding and Applying Pronoun Case

CW 26.6
Pronoun
case

Among the pronouns that you use most often as a writer are the **personal pronouns,** which point out *particular* people, places, things, and ideas. As the table shows, personal pronouns have three separate forms, or *cases: subjective, objective,* and *possessive.*

Personal Pronouns

	Subjective	**Objective**	**Possessive**
First person	I, we	me, us	my, mine, our, ours
Second person	you	you	your, yours
Third person	she, he, it, they	her, him, it, them	her, hers, his, its, their, theirs

Use the *subjective* case pronouns as *subjects* of sentences.

EXAMPLE   *We* were stuck in traffic for over an hour.

They sat in front of the fireplace.

Use the objective case pronouns as *objects;* objects receive the action of the verb (as *direct objects*) or are governed by a preposition (as *objects of prepositions*). See pages 262–263 for a discussion of prepositional phrases.

direct object ┐

EXAMPLE   In the final inning, the pitcher threw four straight *balls.*

preposition ┐┌ object of the preposition
All the trees *around them* looked the same to the lost children.

Use possessive pronouns to show ownership.

EXAMPLE   *Your* class has been canceled for today.

Her friends were planning a surprise birthday party.

FAST FACT   The pronoun *you* always takes a plural verb, even when it is being used as a singular word.

You need to keep a few points in mind when using personal pronouns.

- *An objective pronoun can never serve as a subject.*

The exceptions are *you* and *it,* which can serve as either subjects or objects. *Her, him, me, us,* and *them* are never subjects. Be careful when you are writing sentences with compound subjects linked by *and* or *or.* Make sure that each word in the compound subject could be used alone with the verb in the sentence.

EXAMPLE

she
Muriel, Billy, and ~~her~~ are taking a drawing course together.

I
Either the hostess or ~~me~~ will seat the guests at the reception.

- *A subjective pronoun can never serve as an object.*

Errors in the use of objective case also tend to occur in compound objects. Again, try using each element in the compound object alone to see if it can serve as an object.

EXAMPLE

him
The boss had to make a choice between *Joe* and ~~he.~~

her
My mother could not remember whether Grandpa taught *my uncle* or ~~her~~ to drive first.

Finally, do not confuse the possessive pronoun *its* with the contraction for *it is* (*it's*). *Its* needs no apostrophe because the word is already possessive. To avoid this error, try inserting *it is* whenever you want to use *its*. If *it is* fits, use *it is* or the contraction *it's*. If *it is* doesn't fit, use the possessive form, *its*.

EXAMPLE

It's
~~Its~~ too late to go to the movies now.

its
The owl flew to ~~it's~~ nest.

COMPREHENSION AND PRACTICE

26.1

CW 26.7
Using
pronouns

Identifying Pronoun Case

In the following passage, underline all personal objective pronouns. Write an *S* above subjective pronouns, an *O* above objective pronouns, and a *P* above possessive pronouns, as the example shows. Use the table of personal pronouns on page 412 for guidance.

EXAMPLE

$\overset{S}{I}$ wanted to show $\overset{O}{\underline{him}}$ how important $\overset{S}{he}$ was in $\overset{P}{\underline{my}}$ life.

(1) Every Monday when $\overset{S}{\underline{we}}$ were in elementary school, $\overset{P}{\underline{my}}$ sister and $\overset{S}{I}$ used to go to the municipal library downtown. (2) $\overset{S}{\underline{It}}$ was almost three miles from $\overset{P}{\underline{our}}$ apartment, and $\overset{P}{\underline{our}}$ parents didn't want $\overset{O}{\underline{us}}$ to walk all that way. (3) So after school, Laura and $\overset{S}{\underline{I}}$ would go to the bus stop a block away and wait for the downtown bus to pick $\overset{O}{\underline{us}}$ up. (4) Because $\overset{S}{\underline{we}}$ were so young, riding the bus was an adventure for $\overset{O}{\underline{us}}$. (5) $\overset{S}{\underline{We}}$ were always a little nervous until the driver

gave us back our bus passes with new holes punched in them. (6) When we finally reached the library, she and I would go right to the shelves to look for books to take home. (7) It was a challenge to see which one of us could find books that would impress the head librarian more. (8) Adventure stories were my favorite, so I always ended up with a pile of them. (9) My sister wasn't as lucky because the library didn't have as many of her favorites—science fiction—in its collection. (10) As we were leaving, the head librarian would always say, in his formal, bass tone, "Be careful going home, girls, and take care of the books because they belong to all of us."

COMPREHENSION AND PRACTICE

Using Personal Pronouns and Identifying Pronoun Case

26.2 Fill in each blank in the following paragraph with an appropriate personal pronoun. Then label the pronoun you have supplied with an *S* for subjective, an *O* for objective, or a *P* for possessive case. Use the example as a guide.

EXAMPLE
Children need to learn a great deal more about _____ *our* _____ world than children did twenty-five years ago.

(1) After a decline in _____ *their* _____ numbers stemming back thirty years or more, bald eagles are making a major comeback throughout North America. (2) During the 1960s, _____ *they* _____ were affected by both industrial pollution and toxic pesticides like DDT. (3) At that time, _____ *we* _____ didn't have a full understanding of the effect of these compounds on the environment. (4) However, as we later learned, these poisons worked _____ *their* _____ way through the food chain, becoming more concentrated in each species. (5) Eagles were especially hard hit; the concentrated chemicals made it impossible for _____ *them* _____ to produce the calcium needed for eggshells. (6) In essence, _____ *our* _____ industrial society was making reproduction impossible for eagles. (7) In the 1970s, _____ *our* _____ government acted to preserve the bald eagle by

declaring _____O_____ an endangered species and banning DDT.
                    it

(8) _____P_____ decisions proved to be the correct ones. (9) Across the
        Its

United States today, the number of nesting pairs of bald eagles is some-

where between 4,000 and 5,000, and _____P_____ species designation
                                          their

has been changed from endangered to threatened. (10) Now it appears that

_____S_____ won't bear responsibility for the extinction of one of
     we

nature's most majestic creatures.

COMPREHENSION AND PRACTICE

Avoiding Usage Errors with Personal Pronouns

26.3 Each sentence in the following paragraph contains an error in personal pronoun use. Cross out the incorrect pronoun, and write the correct form above it. Use the example as a guide.

EXAMPLE
                 she
Traci and ~~her~~ were able to settle their differences.

                       me
(1) Between you and ~~I~~, computer dating service are not the best way to

meet other single people. (2) My friend Brendan said that his cousins Greg
               he
and Mike and ~~him~~ all tried different services and were all disappointed. (3) For
           they
one thing, ~~them~~ had to pay $50 just to register for the services. (4) In addition,

Greg explained that the questionnaire he filled out was too general to give an
              him   him
accurate picture of ~~he~~. (5) Also, the dating services didn't provide ~~he~~ and Mike
                                  them
enough information about prospective dating partners. (6) For ~~they~~, the dates

felt more like blind dates than arranged meetings between compatible people.
                                                   he
(7) Mike agreed, because the woman that the dating consultant and ~~him~~ chose

on the basis of her profile just didn't appeal to him. (8) On the night of their
                        he
date, it was obvious right away that ~~him~~ and his date had nothing in common.
                                       her
(9) After about an hour, the woman asked Mike to take ~~she~~ home. (10) Before
                            she   he
he dropped her off, however, ~~her~~ and ~~him~~ agreed that computer dating ser-

vices are not for them.

CHALLENGE 26.1 Evaluating Your Use of Personal Pronouns

1. Take a look at some of the writings you have already created. Copy several sentences in which you have used personal pronouns. Make sure your sentences include at least one subjective pronoun, one objective pronoun, and one possessive pronoun. If necessary, write new sentences.

COLLABORATION

2. Exchange the sentences with a partner, and check for any pronoun errors. When you get your sentences back, revise any in which your reader found an error.

Maintaining Agreement in Number

CW 26.8 Maintaining agreement in number

A pronoun must agree with its antecedent in *number:* Both must be singular, or both must be plural. Use singular pronouns to refer to singular antecedents and plural pronouns to refer to plural antecedents.

EXAMPLE

singular ⌐antecedent   singular ⌐pronoun
Rachael dropped *her* book bag to the floor with a crash.

plural ⌐antecedent   plural ⌐pronoun
The *students* in health class volunteered *their* time to run the blood drive.

CW 26.9 Recognizing pronoun reference problems

The use of *collective nouns* such as *class, herd, jury,* and *team* can cause confusion in pronoun–antecedent agreement. Remember that collective nouns represent groups of people or things but are generally considered singular, so they call for singular pronouns (see page 401).

EXAMPLE

singular ⌐antecedent¬   singular ⌐pronoun
Last night, the Ordinance *Committee* closed *its* meeting, in violation of the Open Meetings Act.

COMPREHENSION AND PRACTICE

26.4

CW 26.10 Correcting pronoun–antecedent agreement

Maintaining Pronoun–Antecedent Agreement

Each of the following sentences contains a pair of pronouns in parentheses. For each sentence, underline the antecedent, and circle the correct pronoun. Use the example as a guide.

EXAMPLE

Five children had misplaced (his or her, (their)) books.

(1) Last week, several employees of P. A. Cummings International Airport were hospitalized after experiencing nausea and tingling in (his or her, (their)) arms. (2) When an airport official was first contacted by the media, ((she), they)

refused to comment. (3) Instead, the <u>official</u> scheduled a news conference for the next morning, saying (she, they) would respond to questions at that time. (4) In the meantime, state environmental <u>officials</u> studied the airline terminal to see if (he, they) could discover the cause of the illness. (5) The officials first tested the <u>air</u> to see if (it, they) contained carbon monoxide. (6) After that test proved negative, the <u>chemicals</u> used to clean the carpet were checked to see if (it, they) could have caused the illness. (7) The officials discovered that maintenance <u>workers</u> had used too much cleaning solution when (he, they) cleaned one portion of carpeting on the previous evening. (8) The excess solvent dried to a powder behind the ticket counter, and when the <u>employees</u> walked across that area, (his, their) shoes released the chemical. (9) The employees then breathed in the <u>powder</u>, and (it, they) made them ill. (10) At the news conference, the <u>director</u> of the airport announced that (she, they) would have the carpet in that terminal replaced immediately.

**CW 26.11
A guide to
pronoun
reference**

CHALLENGE 26.2   Maintaining Agreement with Collective Nouns

COLLABORATION

Below is a list of collective nouns. Working with a partner, write a sentence using each collective noun as an antecedent with an appropriate pronoun. Write your sentences on a separate sheet of paper. Underline both the collective noun and its replacement pronoun.

association	committee	crowd	gang	mob
club	company	family	group	union

EXAMPLE

The <u>union</u> has ordered a strike if <u>it</u> can't get management to authorize a wage increase.

Maintaining Agreement with Indefinite Pronouns

Indefinite pronouns refer to someone or something general. For instance, the pronoun *somebody* could refer to one of any number of people, and the indefinite pronoun *anything* could refer to one of any number of items or events. The following indefinite pronouns are always singular:

Singular Indefinite Pronouns

another	each	everything	nobody	other
anybody	either	little	no one	somebody
anyone	everybody	much	nothing	someone
anything	everyone	neither	one	something

Singular indefinite pronouns call for singular verbs. In addition, they must be referred to by singular pronouns (*he, him, his, she, her, hers, it, its*).

EXAMPLE *Everyone* standing in line to pay a fine *looks* unhappy.

Anyone who wants to compete in the drama festival must memorize *his* or *her* lines by Friday.

The following indefinite pronouns are always plural:

Plural Indefinite Pronouns

both	others
few	several
many	

EXAMPLE *Several* of the students *have* started a rowing club.

The officials gave high scores to *both* dancers for *their* originality.

Some indefinite pronouns are either singular or plural, depending on the word to which they refer:

Indefinite Pronouns Affected by the Words That Follow Them

all	more	none
any	most	some

When you encounter one of these pronouns, check the word to which it refers. If that word is singular, choose a singular form of the verb, and if it is plural, choose a plural form of the verb.

EXAMPLE

plural ⌐antecedent   plural ⌐ verb ⌐
Some of the *shirts* on sale *were* damaged.

singular ⌐antecedent   singular ⌐ verb
All of the *soil* at that construction site *is* contaminated with chemicals.

When an indefinite pronoun is the antecedent for another pronoun, maintaining agreement can be tricky. To avoid making an error in pronoun–antecedent agreement in this situation, first isolate the two pronouns and then check to see if they are both singular or both plural. If they don't match up, you can either change one of the pronouns or replace the indefinite pronoun with a definite noun so that the pronoun and its antecedent agree, as these examples show:

SINGULAR ANTECEDENT
Anyone needing more information about financial aid should bring ~~*their*~~ *his or her* questions to the Financial Aid Office.

or

PLURAL ANTECEDENT
Students ~~*Anyone*~~ needing more information about financial aid should bring *their* questions to the Financial Aid Office.

PLURAL ANTECEDENT
Few of the parents understood the relief that ~~*his or her*~~ *their* children felt when the test was postponed.

or

SINGULAR ANTECEDENT
Each ~~*Few*~~ of the parents understood the relief that *his* or *her* children felt when the test was postponed.

COMPREHENSION AND PRACTICE 26.5

Selecting Indefinite Pronouns for Correct Agreement

In each of the following sentences, underline the verb that must match the missing word. Then fill in the blank in each sentence with an appropriate indefinite pronoun from the list below. You may use the same pronoun more than once. Use the example to guide you. Answers may vary.

CW 26.12 Using indefinite pronouns

few	everyone	some
somebody	all	many
nobody	no one	none

EXAMPLE   ___Many___ of the delegates <u>have</u> never before <u>attended</u> a political convention.

(1) ___Everyone___ <u>hopes</u> that he or she will do the right thing when faced with a crisis. (2) For example, ___all___ of us <u>like</u> to believe we would rush into a burning building to save the people inside. (3) ___No one/Nobody___ <u>wants</u> to think she or he would stand there frozen with fear. (4) But the truth is that ___no one/nobody___ <u>knows</u> for certain how he or she would react. (5) It is true that, faced with such a situation, ___some___ <u>are</u> able to run right through the flames. (6) Not ___everyone___ <u>is</u> able to

play the role of a hero, however. (7) _____Many_____ of us experience a kind of paralysis in crisis situations. (8) A _____few_____ even become sick or pass out. (9) Faced with the same crisis, _____none_____ of us is likely to react in exactly the same way. (10) Even _____somebody_____ who is a leader in everyday situations may not be able to take charge in a crisis.

COMPREHENSION AND PRACTICE 26.6

Maintaining Agreement with Indefinite Pronouns

Circle the indefinite pronouns in each of the following sentences, and then fill in the blanks with a pronoun that agrees with this antecedent. Use the example to guide you.

EXAMPLE (Few) of the people sitting in the waiting room had already filled out ___their___ applications.

(1) Sometimes it's easy to get the impression that (nobody) wants to get involved in helping ___his or her___ neighbors. (2) News accounts regularly appear, for example, relating how (someone) took advantage of ___his or her___ power or money to make life difficult for other people. (3) As a result, (many) begin to change ___their___ attitudes, becoming increasingly cynical. (4) After a while, people in general begin to doubt whether (anyone) is actually willing to reach out and help in ___his or her___ city. (5) However, a restaurant owner in my town has proved that not (everyone) is apathetic about what happens in ___his or her___ neighborhood. (6) This restaurant owner serves holiday dinners for free to (all) in the surrounding area who otherwise couldn't afford to pay for ___their___ meals. (7) (Several) of the city's most prominent citizens sacrifice time with ___their___ families to serve people who are experiencing hard times. (8) (Most) of the employees of the restaurant also volunteer ___their___ time to serve the meals. (9) (Many) even contribute ___their___ tips from the prior week to pay for gift packages of clothing

and blankets for those seeking a meal. (10) What's especially noteworthy is

that (none) of the people serving the meals earns a dime for ___their___

work, yet they volunteer year after year.

Copyright ©2006 by Pearson Education, Inc.

COMPREHENSION AND PRACTICE

Correcting Errors in Agreement with Indefinite Pronouns

26.7 Each sentence in the following passage contains an error in agreement with an indefinite pronoun. Cross out each error, and then write the correct pronoun above it. Change the verb if necessary. More than one answer may be possible, as the example shows:

EXAMPLE

                                       his or her
Anybody could improve ~~their~~ grades by working harder.

   or

Most students
~~Anybody~~ could improve their grades by working harder.

(1) An interview is uncomfortable enough for a job seeker without the in-
                                       him or her
terviewer trying to give ~~them~~ a hard time. (2) On my last two interviews,
                                       his or her
everybody in the office seemed to do ~~their~~ best to put me on edge. (3)
                                                       his or her
Obviously, no one in these places remembered what ~~their~~ first interview was

like. (4) For example, at a firm looking for a receptionist, several supervisors
                                       their
asked me for an evaluation of ~~her~~ desktop publishing software. (5) Some of
                                       they do
my friends work as receptionists, and ~~he does~~ not even do any writing, let

alone desktop publishing. (6) I later learned that many managers at that com-
                                                       they are
pany ask such questions to test the poise of the people ~~he is~~ interviewing. At
                                                       her or his
the other firm, somebody asked me if I would mind doing ~~their~~ personal er-

rands on my lunch hour. (8) Even worse, someone else asked if I would be
                       him or her
willing to give ~~them~~ a back rub. (9) That subject was clearly a matter of sexual
                                                       his or her
harassment, but no one in the room even raised ~~their~~ eyebrows at the ques-

tion. (10) I wish that someone at a decent company would just offer me a job
           his or her
in ~~their~~ office so I wouldn't have to do any more interviewing.

CHALLENGE 26.3 Maintaining Agreement with Indefinite Pronouns in Your Writing

COLLABORATION

As you now know, the indefinite pronouns *all, any, more, most, none,* and *some* are either singular or plural depending on the word following them. Working with a partner, write two sentences for each of these indefinite pronouns, using each one first as a singular antecedent and then as a plural antecedent.

Maintaining Agreement with Demonstrative and Reflexive or Intensive Pronouns

CW 26.13
Maintaining agreement with demonstrative pronouns

You may occasionally experience difficulties in maintaining pronoun–antecedent agreement with **demonstrative pronouns**, which point out a particular person or thing.

Demonstrative Pronouns

Singular	*Plural*
this	these
that	those

As the list indicates, two demonstrative pronouns are singular (*this* and *that*), and two are plural (*these* and *those*). *This* and *these* point out things that are near or point to things in the future. *That* and *those* point out things that are farther away or point to things in the past.

When you use a demonstrative pronoun to begin a sentence in a paragraph or essay, you may be referring to the antecedent in the previous sentence. In these cases, check for any errors in pronoun–antecedent agreement by identifying that antecedent. If the antecedent is singular, use *this* or *that;* if it is plural, use *these* or *those.*

EXAMPLE
┌——————antecedent——————┐
There have been *four major accidents* near the park entrance.

Those have
~~That has~~ caused the city to install warning signs.

EXAMPLE
The Civic Improvement League is donating $15,000 to establish an
┌——————antecedent——————┐   *This*
urban entrepreneur's scholarship at the college. ~~These~~ will be given to students

majoring in marketing or accounting.

Often writers add a clarifying word to the demonstrative pronoun to make the reference more precise. In this case, the demonstrative pronoun then becomes a *demonstrative adjective,* as in the following versions of the sentences that appear above:

EXAMPLE

antecedent¬   demonstrative   clarifying
                               adjective ¬┌ word

There have been four major *accidents* near the park entrance. *Those crashes*

have caused the city to install warning signs.

The Civic Improvement League is donating $15,000 to establish an urban

┌antecedent¬ demonstrative adjective¬ ┌clarifying word

entrepreneur's *scholarship* at the college. *This award* will be given to students

majoring in marketing or accounting.

Another potential problem in maintaining pronoun–antecedent agreement in-volves the use of **reflexive** or **intensive pronouns,** which are used to emphasize the words to which they refer.

**CW 26.14
Maintaining
agreement
with
reflexive or
intensive
pronouns**

Reflexive or Intensive Pronoun Forms

myself	oneself
yourself	ourselves
himself, herself	yourselves
itself	themselves

You should never use reflexive or intensive pronouns in a sentence unless you have included the word to which the pronoun refers. These pronouns may not be used as subjects.

REFLEXIVE   The capsized sailboat righted *itself.* [*To direct verb's action back to subject*]

INTENSIVE   The president *himself* will testify. [*To emphasize*]

If these pronouns are used incorrectly as subjects, replace the reflexive or inten-sive form with a personal pronoun that suits the situation.

I

EXAMPLE   Connie and ~~myself~~ did most of the work on that presentation.

**COMPREHENSION
AND PRACTICE
26.8**

Maintaining Agreement with Demonstrative Pronouns

Each sentence in the following passage contains an error in pronoun–antecedent agreement involving demonstrative pronouns. In each sentence, cross out the incorrect demonstrative pronoun, and above it write one that matches the antecedent. If necessary, turn the demonstrative pronoun into a demonstrative adjective and add a clarifying word. Use the example to guide you.

EXAMPLE During a storm, a huge tree fell across the power lines, and ~~these~~ caused a major power outage.

this OR this incident

(1) Yesterday, the Red Cross held a blood drive on campus, and ~~these~~ proved to be a big success. *that OR that event* (2) At most drives the Red Cross runs, around thirty to forty people donate, and ~~those~~ is considered good. *that OR that response* (3) At this drive, however, more than a hundred donors showed up, and ~~these~~ was beyond any- *that OR that number* one's hope. (4) Many participants were donating for the first time, and in the beginning ~~these~~ complicated work a little for the officials. *those OR those people* (5) Some new- comers were visibly nervous, and ~~these~~ seemed to affect the mood of others *those OR those participants* waiting in line. (6) To help settle everyone down, the Red Cross workers spoke directly with ~~that~~ appearing especially anxious. *those OR those people* (7) They explained the steps involved, while stressing the simplicity and safety of ~~that~~. *those steps OR those* (8) After the first few newcomers donated blood without a problem, ~~that~~ people behind them in line *those* began to relax. (9) ~~Those~~ made all the difference, and the time passed more *That development OR That* quickly and pleasantly for everyone involved. (10) ~~Those~~ was such a success *That day OR That* that the Red Cross plans to schedule another drive for the end of the semester.

COMPREHENSION AND PRACTICE

Using Reflexive and Intensive Pronoun Forms Correctly

26.9 Fill in the blanks in the following sentences with an appropriate reflexive or inten- sive pronoun form from the list on page 423. Use the example as a guide.

EXAMPLE After waiting at the register for five minutes, the woman finally decided to

check the price ___*herself*___.

1. I will be picking you up at the airport ___myself___.

2. The participants ___themselves___ criticized the organizers of the natural

healing seminar most harshly.

3. At the end of this semester, perhaps you will decide to major in business

___yourself___.

4. After several hours, the storm finally blew _____itself_____ out.

5. Rather than wait for the city crew to arrive, we cleaned up the field _____ourselves_____.

6. The exhausted horse still managed to force _____itself_____ up the steep slope.

7. Instead of consulting a map, Lenna decided to try to figure out a route _____herself_____.

8. When Susie and Brian didn't arrive, we enjoyed the dessert all by _____ourselves_____.

9. Jeremy's ankle _____itself_____ wasn't broken, but all the ligaments were sprained.

10. When you face a stressful situation, you must force _____yourself_____ to remain focused on the task.

Maintaining Agreement with *That, Who,* and *Which* Clauses

Clauses introduced by a **relative pronoun**, *that, who,* or *which,* may also create problems with pronoun–antecedent agreement. If the antecedent that the clause describes is singular, then the verb in the clause must be singular. If the antecedent of the clause is plural, then the verb must also be plural.

EXAMPLE

singular
antecedent *sells*
The *store that* ~~sell~~ baked goods at half price is always crowded.

plural antecedent   *allow*
The *special parking stickers, which* ~~allow~~ a student to park in the campus garage, may be purchased in the bookstore.

COMPREHENSION AND PRACTICE 26.10 Maintaining Agreement with *That, Who,* and *Which* Clauses

The italicized clauses in the following paragraph contain errors in agreement. Circle the antecedent, and then correct the error by crossing out the incorrect verb and writing the correct one above it. Use the example to guide you.

EXAMPLE

was
The (firefighter) *who* ~~were~~ *involved in the rescue* received a citation for bravery.

were
(1) Most (people) *who* ~~was~~ *questioned in a recent survey* felt that their memories weren't as sharp as they'd like. (2) These (respondents), *who* ~~was~~ *between*

the ages of forty-five and sixty-five, felt that their memories had weakened. (3)

For example, their (ability) to match a name with a face, *which a few years ear-*

was
lier ~~were~~ strong, seemed now far less reliable. (4) Also, the (details) of meetings

were
or public gatherings *that in the past ~~was~~ easy to keep straight,* now seemed

were
fuzzier. (5) To these people, these (memory lapses), *which ~~was~~ really upsetting,*

seemed to be signs of old age. (6) Like many of the beliefs about aging, how-

are
ever, (some of the issues) *that ~~is~~ associated with growing older* are more stereo-

type than fact. (7) According to many experts consulted, the (kinds) of mem-

were
ory problems *that ~~was~~ reported* aren't necessarily related to age. (8) Genuine

involve
memory (deficits), *which ~~involves~~ serious and sometimes permanent loss of recog-*

nition of otherwise familiar people and places, affect many segments of society.

experiences
(9) In fact, (anyone) *who ~~experience~~ a sudden memory loss,* regardless of age,

should see a doctor immediately. (10) True memory (problems), *which fortu-*

are
nately ~~is~~ not common, could be a symptom of serious neurological problems

or drug interactions.

COMPREHENSION AND PRACTICE 26.11

Identifying and Correcting Agreement Problems with *That, Who,* and *Which* Clauses

The following passage contains several errors in agreement with *that, who,* and *which* clauses. Cross out any incorrect verb, and write the correct verb above it. If a sentence does not contain an error, write *OK* above it. Use the example as a guide.

EXAMPLE

ride
Because of the crowd, many people who usually ~~rides~~ the 8 A.M. crosstown

bus had to wait for the 8:30 bus.

was
(1) I attended a great workshop that ~~were~~ held at school the other day. (2)

works
A counselor who ~~work~~ in the counseling center on campus presented the

OK
workshop. (3) The program, which was called "How to Build an Effective

Personal Relationship," attracted about twenty participants, both male and

have
female. (4) She first discussed several common misconceptions that people ~~has~~

about love. (5) For example, "love conquers all," a concept which ~~are~~ ^{is} believed

by many people, isn't always true. ^{OK} (6) In some cases, a person can have so

many problems that love alone isn't enough to maintain a relationship. (7)

^{OK} She also disproved the naive idea that there is only one right person in the

world for each of us. (8) Then she showed how people who ~~thinks~~ ^{think} the right

partner will be the salvation for all their problems in life are setting themselves

up for disappointment. (9) All of us who ~~was~~ ^{were} participating in the session were

impressed because we had all had fantasies like those she described. (10) I'm

looking forward to the follow-up session, which ~~are~~ ^{is} scheduled for next Friday.

Keeping the Relationship between Pronoun and Antecedent Clear

**CW 26.15
Maintaining
pronoun–
antecedent
agreement**

To help your reader understand your meaning, you must also make the relationship between the pronoun and the antecedent clear. Look at this sentence:

AMBIGUOUS | *Ed* and *Bill* had a fight, and *he* broke *his* nose.

The problem with this sentence is obvious. It does not make clear who did what to whom. The simplest way to correct this type of error is to restate the sentence completely to eliminate the ambiguity, as this version shows:

REVISED | During their fight, *Ed* broke *Bill's* nose.

**COMPREHENSION
AND PRACTICE
26.12**

**CW 26.16
Pronoun
and
pronoun–
antecedent
agreement**

Identifying the Pronoun–Antecedent Relationship

In each of the following sentences, a pronoun is italicized. Circle the antecedent for each of these pronouns, and draw an arrow from the pronoun to the antecedent, as the example shows. Remember—the antecedent to the pronoun may be in a different sentence.

EXAMPLE | The (lock) on the suitcase was broken, so I asked my uncle to fix *it*.

(1) Although (voice mail) has become very popular over the past few years, many (people) don't like *it*. (2) *They* prefer the human touch that voice mail can't supply. (3) When (people) have a question, all *they* want to do is talk to an

actual person. (4) But many voice-mail (systems) force callers to follow a complicated series of commands, and *they* also often include a dizzying array of options. (5) With some voice-mail systems, if (callers) hit the wrong buttons, *they* can be disconnected and have to call back. (6) Even if (people) manage to reach the proper extension, *they* may not be out of the voice-mail loop yet. (7) If the (individual) at that extension is away or using the system to screen calls, *he or she* will not answer the call personally. (8) A (recording) will instruct the caller to leave a message, and then *it* will indicate which buttons to press to approve the message. (9) If the caller pushes the wrong buttons, some (systems) delete the message, and then *they* ask the caller to go through the entire process again. (10) For the average person, such (a system) often increases the frustration *it* is meant to eliminate.

COMPREHENSION AND PRACTICE	Correcting Unclear or Ambiguous Pronoun References

26.13 Each sentence below contains an unclear or ambiguous relationship between a pronoun and an antecedent. Circle the unclear or ambiguous pronoun. On another sheet of paper, revise the sentence to clarify the relationship. There may be more than one way to correct each sentence. Use the example to guide you.
Sentence revisions will vary.

EXAMPLE | When the vase she threw hit the window, (it) shattered.

The window shattered when the vase she threw hit it.

or

When the vase she threw hit the window, the window shattered.

(1) Last week's accident downtown involving a bus and a tanker truck caused major structural damage to a highway overpass, and (it) is still being investigated. (2) Heavy rain was falling and the truck was reportedly exceeding the speed limit, and (that) may have contributed to the accident. (3) Also that stretch of Whipple Avenue bends sharply and there are no stop signs along the way, and (that) didn't help the situation either. (4) When the tanker collided

with the bus, (it) burst into flames. (5) The bus then hit a curb, and the driver couldn't handle (it). (6) The bus wasn't carrying passengers at the time, and it was an older model, so (that) may have made the bus less stable. (7) The bus also hit a light pole, and (it) was badly damaged. (8) The cab and the tanker broke apart, and then (it) slammed into the side of the overpass. (9) Traffic was snarled and a crowd gathered on the sidewalk, and (that) created problems at rush hour. (10) The pavement under the overpass is badly gouged and the concrete over the entrance of the overpass is crumbling, and (that) is expected to be repaired within a month.

CHALLENGE 26.4   Writing with Clear Pronoun–Antecedent Agreement

Working with a partner, write a sentence to precede each of the sentences provided below. Make sure to include an antecedent that matches the pronoun that begins the second sentence. If necessary, add a clarifying word to those pronouns. Study the example first. Answers will vary. Sample answers are given.

> *Yesterday, Diane reminded me of the time the two of us locked ourselves out of the office.*
>
>   *story*
> That still makes me laugh.
>   ^

1. Margaret regrets what she did after witnessing a car crash yesterday.

   She left the scene of the accident before the police arrived.

2. A fire broke out in Mario's kitchen last month.

   It caused the restaurant to be closed for an entire week.

3. The doors and hallways in this building are very narrow.

         entries
   These should be modified to make access easier for disabled people.
       ^

4. Tim and Ellen couldn't agree on what to do last Saturday night.

They finally decided to rent a movie.

5. My family just gave me a large amount of money for my twenty-first birthday.

gift
That means I won't have to take out a loan to attend classes next semester.
      ^

6. Representatives from several government agencies set up temporary headquarters

in town hall this afternoon.

They will be available to answer questions for the next two days.

7. A small supermarket recently opened in the abandoned store in the strip mall

downtown.

It should make life easier for the people living in that area.

8. The company finally agreed to install new air filters throughout the building.

That agreement was the solution everyone was hoping for.

9. Television networks are now offering fewer dramatic mini-series.

It indicates that people are no longer interested in them.

10. The furniture was delivered by noon.

That development left us with the rest of the afternoon to straighten every-

thing out.

Avoiding Problems with Gender in Pronoun–Antecedent Agreement

CW 26.17 Using appropriate language

Gender refers to whether a word is masculine or feminine. Making sure that pronouns agree in gender is usually much easier than making them agree in number. In English, inanimate objects and ideas don't have masculine or feminine forms as they do in languages such as Spanish and French.

With personal pronouns, identifying gender is easy. *I, me, we, you,* and *your* can be either feminine or masculine. Likewise, the plural pronouns *they, them, their,* and *themselves* apply to both genders. The personal pronoun *it* refers to objects only. In fact, you need to worry about gender only with third person pronouns: *she, her, hers, he, him,* and *his.* To correct errors in agreement with any of these words, change the pronoun so that it matches the gender of the word to which it refers:

EXAMPLE

Mother Teresa devoted ~~his~~ her life to helping the poor in India.

As the man turned to leave, a ticket fell out of ~~her~~ his coat.

When you use pronouns, you should also eliminate any accidental *sexism* in your writing. **Sexist language,** as the National Organization for Women (NOW) and the National Council of Teachers of English (NCTE) have been pointing out since the 1970s, is language that inappropriately designates gender. The word *foreman,* for instance, suggests that only a man can direct a group of workers.

Words have tremendous power. When you use words like *chairman, salesman,* or *mailman,* you send out the message that only males should conduct meetings, sell things, or deliver mail. The proper way to deal with these words is to make them gender-neutral, that is, with references to neither sex: *supervisor, chairperson, salesperson,* and *mail carrier.*

You must also be concerned with sexism when you use singular indefinite pronouns such as *anybody, someone,* or *everybody.* These words can be either masculine or feminine. It was once acceptable to use *he, him, himself,* and *his* to represent both sexes when referring to a singular indefinite pronoun. Today, however, this usage is considered sexist, so you should either use pronouns of both genders or rewrite the sentence to make both your pronoun and your antecedent plural.

If you choose the first option, you can connect a feminine and a masculine pronoun with *or* to refer to the indefinite pronoun: *he or she, him or her,* and *his or her,* rather than *he, him,* and *his.* Reverse the pairs if you prefer: *she or he, her or him, her or his.*

EXAMPLE

Everybody should be prepared to do *her or his* best.

The other option is to make both pronoun and antecedent plural. This method is generally a better choice. It eliminates sexism and eliminates the possibility of making an error in gender agreement, as this version shows:

EXAMPLE

People should be prepared to do *their* best.

FAST FACT   One of the strangest stories concerning sexist language originated in a small town in New England. At a meeting of the town council, one official proposed renaming those familiar black discs in the middle of any town and city street across the nation from manhole cover to personhole cover.

COMPREHENSION AND PRACTICE

26.14

CW 26.18 Ensuring nonsexist language

Avoiding Problems with Gender in Pronoun–Antecedent Agreement

In the following passage, identify errors in pronoun gender and uses of sexist language. Cross out each error you find, and write the correction above it in the space provided between the lines. More than one correct answer may be possible. Use the example as a guide. Answers may vary.

EXAMPLE

~~Anyone who rides a motorcycle~~ *People who ride motorcycles* should wear his ~~helmet~~ *their helmets*, even on short trips.

or

Anyone who rides a motorcycle should wear ~~his~~ *her or his* helmet, even on short trips.

(1) My ambition is to finish school and begin a career in the business world. (2) My first step will be sales because ~~a good salesman~~ *good sales representatives* can earn a great salary and help ~~her~~ *their* company at the same time. (3) Of course, to be effective, ~~a salesman has~~ *sales representatives have* to develop contacts in the firms with which ~~he deals~~ *they deal*. (4) To do this, ~~a salesman has~~ *sales representatives have* to make regular rounds and get to know as many people as possible in the companies ~~she visits~~ *they visit*. (5) For example, when ~~a salesman visits~~ *sales representatives visit* a company, ~~he~~ *they* should first visit the ~~foreman~~ *supervisor* to find out what ~~her~~ *his or her* needs are.

(6) Succeeding as part of the sales force is just the first step in my career plans. (7) Eventually, I hope to work my way up to chief executive officer, or even ~~chairman~~ *chairperson* of the board of directors. (8) ~~An effective chairman~~ *Effective chairpeople* can make money for ~~herself~~ *themselves* and ~~his~~ *their* corporation by ensuring that the managers are doing a good job. (9) Everybody has ~~her~~ *his or her* own management strategies, but I feel the best strategy is to make sure that people are treated fairly and paid according to their efforts. (10) With these kinds of simple ideas, anybody should be able to make ~~his~~ *his or her* mark in the business world.

COMPREHENSION AND PRACTICE

Avoiding Sexist Language

26.15

CW 26.19
Avoiding
sexist
language

Below is a list of sexist words. In the spaces provided, write a neutral, nonsexist alternative for each one. Make sure you don't substitute another equally sexist word in its place. For instance, don't replace *stewardess* with *steward.* Instead, use *flight attendant.* Then, on a separate sheet of paper, compose a sentence using each of your substitutions.

fireman _____firefighter_____   actor _____performer_____

congressman __congressperson__   anchor woman __anchorperson__

mankind _____humankind_____   businessman __businessperson__

weatherman __weather forecaster__   policewoman __police officer__
_____[or meteorologist]_____

CHALLENGE 26.5 **Evaluating Sexist Language and Nonsexist Alternatives**

COLLABORATION

Make a list of the sexist words you have read or used in your own writing. Working with a partner, discuss your lists. Develop a nonsexist version for each word on your list. Then, still working with a partner, compose a brief paragraph in which you discuss the ways that sexist language may affect people.

CHAPTER QUICK CHECK **Working with Pronouns**

Proofread the following essay for problems with pronoun–antecedent agreement; agreement with *who, that,* and *which* clauses; and sexist language. Eliminate the problems by crossing out the incorrect word and writing a more effective choice above it. If a sentence is correct as written, write *OK* above it. In some cases, more than one solution is possible. Use the example to guide you.

EXAMPLE

The DVD player was out of stock, so I asked for a rain check in order to pur-

                                          it
chase it at the same price when ~~they~~ came in.

                                                        is
(1) A recent development, which ~~are~~ called face-recognition technology, is

being hailed as a way to track and identify criminals. (2) With face-recognition

                                                              them
systems, computers record images of faces and then converts ~~it~~ into another

         These images
form. (3) ~~That~~ can come from a variety of sources, including pictures taken of

large groups of people at sports stadiums or busy city streets. (4) The face-

                              each person OR the people
recognition programs then isolate ~~each person~~ in the picture and carefully

create an individual blueprint or map of ~~their~~ faces. (5) To do so, the software [his or her face OR their faces]

focuses on ~~somebody's~~ unique features, such as ~~their~~ cheekbones, jaw shape [somebody's OR people's] [his or her OR their]

and line, and eye shape, size, and location to each other. (6) The system con-

verts this information into a computer code and stores ~~them~~ in a database. (7) [it]

In the case of a crime, law enforcement officials can use the system to match [OK]

these images to others taken by surveillance cameras in stores, banks, govern-

ment buildings, and airports. (8) ~~Spokesmen~~ for face-recognition companies [Spokespeople]

claim that these systems are nearly foolproof. (9) Some civil liberties organiza-

tions disagree, however, citing independent testing that ~~show~~ these systems to [shows]

be only 60 to 70 percent accurate. (10) In addition, these groups warn of po-

tential legal fallout, because ~~no one~~ in the pictures taken in public areas ~~has~~ [no one OR no individuals] [has given OR have given]

permission for ~~their~~ images to be used and stored. [his or her OR their]

QUICK STUDY | Student Example

This chapter concerns matters of making reference, showing ownership, or substitut-
ing one thing for another. Take a look at the following paragraph on a related subject. What comes to mind when you think back to some place or event in your life?

Whenever I drive by the elementary school I attended, I think of my Aunt
Amelia. Aunt Mil, as everyone in my family called her, was actually my
mother's aunt, and she never married or had kids of her own. When my sisters and I were little, my mother had to be at work for 7 A.M., so she couldn't
get us ready for school. To help my mother, Aunt Mil would come to our
apartment at 6:30 every school morning, just before my mother left for work.
Mom would wake us up, kiss us, and head for work, warning us to behave for
Aunt Mil. In front of my mother, Aunt Mil would always sound tough, but as
soon as my mother was outside, Aunt Mil would start spoiling us. On many
days, (she) would let (us) pick what (we) wanted to have for breakfast, even if (it) [Aunt Mil] [writer and sisters] [writer and sisters] [the selection]

_{writer and sisters} _{writer and sisters}
meant cooking (us) pancakes or French toast. After making (us) promise not to

_{writer and sisters} _{Aunt Mil} _{writer and sisters} _{writer and sisters}
tell (our) mother, (she) would also give (us) a couple of dollars to buy candy on (our)

_{writer and sisters}
way home from school. Whenever (our) mother had to work overtime, Aunt

_{writer, mother, and sisters}
Mil would come back to (our) apartment in the afternoon and start supper for

_{writer, mother, and sisters}
(us). She followed this routine with us until I started high school. By this time,

she was almost 80, and her diabetes had become so severe that she could

barely walk. When I was in my junior year, she had a stroke and died, and I

miss her to this day. Every time I see my old school, I think of Aunt Mil and

smile.

First complete the following activities in response to this paragraph:

1. Three of the sentences in this paragraph are highlighted. Circle all the pronouns. Then above each pronoun, write its antecedent, using the material in this chapter to guide you.

2. As Chapter 4 notes (pages 54–56), providing transition is crucial in keeping your writing coherent, and using pronouns is one of the means of providing transition. On a separate sheet of paper, explain how the pronouns in this paper make it easy for readers to follow the story and see the connection between ideas.

3. On the following lines, briefly explain which example in the paragraph provides the best evidence that Aunt Mil was a memorable individual and why you feel this way.

Answers may vary. Many students will refer to the examples about Aunt Mil's

willingness to come to their home every school morning or to make the kids the

breakfast of their choice because they show how generous and caring she was.

Others will note her return on many afternoons to prepare supper for the family or her

dollars for them to spend on candy.

Now explore the topic in writing. As the paragraph above does, you could discuss a person, place, or thing that is connected in some way to a specific locale or event. You might also focus on one of these topics related to the subject matter of this chapter:

- a word or phrase that you use with someone close to you that others don't necessarily understand the same way

- a situation that could change drastically depending on the circumstances
- something you own about which you feel great pride
- a time at work or school during which you behaved differently because a substitute was in charge

COLLABORATION

1. Exchange your draft with a classmate. Evaluate the paragraph you receive. If you discover any problems spots, especially in the use of pronouns, circle the errors, write the correct form above the incorrect one, and then return the paper to the writer.

2. Consider the comments and corrections your reader has made and create a final draft of your paragraph.

SUMMARY EXERCISE Working with Pronouns

Proofread the following essay for problems with pronoun–antecedent agreement; agreement in *who, that,* and *which* clauses; and sexist language. Eliminate the problems by crossing out the incorrect word and writing a more effective choice above it. If a sentence is correct as written, write *OK* above it. In some cases, more than one solution is possible. Some answers may vary.

(1) I am godmother to my brother's five-year-old twins, a boy and a girl,
                                                         them
and I recently went to the toy store to buy ~~him or her~~ birthday presents. (2)
    OK
Unfortunately, the expedition turned out to be a depressing experience. (3) I
                                                   he or she
discovered that a person can find plenty of toys, but ~~they~~ will find that most of

them are unbelievably expensive or inappropriate for young children.
       OK   OK
(4) First, I went to the game aisle. (5) With the exception of Candyland,

Cootie, and a few other simple games, which the twins already owned, all the

board games were too complicated or too expensive. (6) There were plenty of

computer game cartridges, but I couldn't afford to buy the game unit
    itself   OK
~~themselves~~. (7) Also, the one game cartridge that seemed as if it would be suit-
                                                 sales representatives
able for children their age was almost $80. (8) One of the ~~salesmen~~ said that
                                     game   it was
she had just reordered that particular ~~cartridge~~ because ~~they were~~ so popular.
    OK
(9) My niece and nephew also wanted some action figures. (10) Anybody
        his or her
who has ~~their~~ own children or has ever baby-sat knows how much kids enjoy
                    OK
pretending. (11) James and Jenna are no different. (12) Both of them enjoy

playing ~~his or her~~ *their* own special roles and pretending to have super powers. (13) However, their favorite characters, which ~~changes~~ *change* colors when dunked in water, cost over $35 each. (14) That *overpricing* amazed me.

(15) *OK* Even more amazing and sickening was the number of realistic-looking guns and war toys in the store. (16) Why would ~~anyone~~ *people* want to spend a lot of money so their children could pretend to kill each other? (17) The huge arsenal I observed, however, made it seem as if ~~almost everybody wants~~ *most people want* to buy their children a toy machine gun.

(18) *OK* By the time I finished shopping, I was much sadder and poorer than I had been on the way in. (19) My godchildren loved ~~his or her~~ *their* cards and toys, and that helped me feel better. (20) However, after spending an afternoon seeing what kinds of toys are out there, I'm glad I don't have to make ~~that~~ *those* choices for my own children yet.

FOR FURTHER EXPLORATION

1. Consider one of the following topics:
   - the advantages—or disadvantages—of fame
   - a time when you witnessed someone you know act in an uncharacteristic way
   - the most unusual room you have ever been in
   - why you think people sometimes give up when they still have a chance of achieving a goal
   - the relationship between knowledge and fear

   Prewrite on the subject, using one of the strategies you practiced in Chapter 2, and work your way through the rest of the writing process. Then complete a draft essay of at least 500 words on this subject.

2. Exchange your draft with a classmate. Check the draft you receive for weaknesses, paying particular attention to the use of pronouns. Circle any errors, using the material in this chapter as a guide, and then return the draft to the writer.

3. Revise your essay, correcting any errors in verb use or other problems discovered by your reader.

RECAP Pronouns: Understanding Case, Clear Pronoun–Antecedent Agreement, and Nonsexist Pronoun Usage

New terms in this chapter	Definitions
pronoun	a word used in place of a noun

> **Example** Georgie picked up a *rock* and threw *it* at the abandoned house.

antecedent	the word or words to which a pronoun refers

Singular antecedents call for singular pronouns; plural antecedents call for plural pronouns.

> **Example** The little *girl* dropped *her* hat.

Indefinite pronoun antecedents must agree with their pronouns.

> **Example** *Everyone* who has a coupon will receive 25 percent off *her or his* purchase.

personal pronoun	a pronoun that specifies a particular person, place, thing, or idea

Personal pronouns have three separate forms, or cases, to show person.

Personal Pronouns

	Case		
	Subjective	**Objective**	**Possessive**
First person	I, we	me, us	my, mine, our, ours
Second person	you	you	your, yours
Third person	she, he, it, they	her, him, it, them	her, hers, his, its, their, theirs

indefinite pronoun	a pronoun used to refer to someone or something in general

Singular Indefinite Pronouns

another	each	everything	nobody	other
anybody	either	little	no one	somebody
anyone	everybody	much	nothing	someone
anything	everyone	neither	one	something

Plural Indefinite Pronouns

both	others
few	several
many	

Indefinite Pronouns Affected by the Words That Follow Them

all	more	none
any	most	some

demonstrative pronoun	singular: *this, that* plural: *these, those* If a demonstrative pronoun begins a sentence, find the antecedent in the preceding sentence. A demonstrative pronoun placed next to a noun is then called a *demonstrative adjective.* **Example**　Some clothes in *that* box are damaged. *Those* should be mended.
reflexive/intensive pronoun	a combination of a personal pronoun with *-self* or *-selves: myself, yourself, himself, herself, itself, ourselves, yourselves, themselves.* Reflexive or intensive pronouns are used for emphasis (Ginny *herself* paid for the repair) or to direct the action of the verb back to the subject (Peter threw *himself* across the saddle).
relative pronoun	*that, who, which, whom, whose* A relative pronoun introduces a clause that describes an antecedent; the verb in the clause must agree with the antecedent. **Example**　The *attorney* who *is* addressing my class this morning graduated from this college.
interrogative pronoun	What . . .? Whatever . . .? Which . . .? Whichever . . .? Who . . .? Whoever . . .? Whom . . .? Whomever . . .? Whose . . .? An interrogative pronoun introduces a question. **Example**　*What* is the problem?
gender	refers to whether a word is masculine or feminine Pronouns must match the gender of their antecedents.
sexist language	language that inappropriately excludes one gender Try using plural antecedents and pronouns instead. **Example**　*All bicyclists* using the municipal bike path must wear *their* helmets.

GOING FORWARD...

Q: Are there any strategies I can follow to make sure I always choose the right form of a pronoun?

A: Choosing the right pronoun for each situation, as this chapter shows, is a matter of understanding the features of the types of pronouns. For instance, when it comes to subjects and objects, you need to focus on just the personal pronouns because they are the ones that have separate subject and object forms. And number isn't an issue with most pronouns because which ones are singular and which ones are plural is usually obvious. Keep these characteristics about pronouns straight and you'll find it easier to work with them.

CHAPTER 27

Adjectives, Adverbs, and Other Modifiers: Using Describing and Modifying Words Effectively

▶ **Navigating This Chapter**

In this chapter, you will learn how to:

- use the positive, comparative, and superlative forms for adjectives and adverbs
- distinguish between commonly confused adjectives and adverbs
- avoid dangling and misplaced modifiers
- avoid double negatives

**CW 27.1
Chapter
basics**

Q: When I am thinking of what I want to write, the ideas always seem vivid and bright. But when I actually write them down, they sometimes seem vague or lifeless. What can I do to make sure that my ideas are just as interesting and full of life on paper as they are in my mind?

A: Adjective and adverbs are the answers you are looking for. These words *modify* or describe other words. When you use adjectives and adverbs correctly and effectively, they make the words they are modifying—and your writing in general—clearer and more specific.

Overview: Understanding the Roles of Adjectives and Adverbs

**CW 27.2
Overview of
adjectives
and adverbs**

Nouns and pronouns name people and things, and verbs show the action or situations in which those people and things are involved. But writing that relies on nouns and verbs alone would be ineffective. It wouldn't be clear, precise, or colorful enough to communicate your ideas to your reader. To make your writing effective, you need to include **modifiers,** words that **describe** or **limit** other words in a sentence. **Adjectives** are words that modify nouns or pronouns, and **adverbs** are words that modify verbs, adjectives, and other adverbs. Both adjectives and adverbs are useful for making comparisons and expressing negation. If you look back at the paragraphs and essays you have written so far, you'll discover that you've used many adjectives and adverbs. You'll also see that they inject life into your writing, so it's important to master their use.

Understanding Adjectives and Adverbs

CW 27.3
Understanding
positive forms
of adjectives

Adjectives and adverbs have three forms: positive, comparative, and superlative. The **positive form** of an adjective describes a noun or pronoun without making a comparison. It tells the reader *how many, what kind,* or *which one.*

EXAMPLE The *small* dog is *fierce.*

CW 27.4
Understanding
positive forms
of adverbs

In this sentence, the adjective *small* tells *which* dog and the adjective *fierce* describes *what kind* of dog.

The positive form of an adverb describes a verb, an adjective, or another adverb without making a comparison. It tells the reader *how, when,* or *to what extent.*

EXAMPLE *Finally,* the child spoke *quietly* to the nurse.

In this sentence, the adverb *finally* tells *when,* and the adverb *quietly* describes *how* the child spoke.

> **FAST FACT** *A, an,* and *the* are a subgroup of adjectives called *articles, A* and *an* are the *indefinite* articles, referring to a nonspecific person or thing (a professor, an apple) and *the* is the *definite* article, referring to a particular person or thing (the professor, the apple). And they are busy little words. For example, *an* is the forty-third most commonly used English word, and *a* is the fourth most frequently used. And *the?* It's number one—the word that appears most frequently in English.

COMPREHENSION
AND PRACTICE

27.1

Identifying Adjectives and Adverbs

In the passage below, circle the positive form of the adjectives and underline the positive form of the adverbs. Use the example to guide you.

EXAMPLE Chika <u>often</u> organizes (athletic) activities for the children in her neighborhood.

CW 27.5
Recognizing
adjectives
and adverbs

(1) Last Saturday, my friends and I went for a (quick) lunch at the Granite Café, a (new) deli near the college. (2) The restaurant is located in a building that was <u>once</u> the office of the Mill City Granite Works. (3) The building itself is constructed of (massive) slabs of granite that were <u>actually</u> quarried at the Mill City Granite Works. (4) The (deep) cavity left when the quarry closed 50 years ago <u>gradually</u> filled with water, so the building is all that is left of this

once highly (successful) business. (5) The city was planning to knock down the (run-down) building before the café owners bought and rehabilitated it. (6) The owners, Lynette and her brother Kevin, think that the (historical) significance of the building would probably help attract customers. (7) At noontime on Saturday, Marcel, Shelly, Kathryn, and I first picked a (large) table near the window. (8) Then we examined the (extensive) menu to decide on our meals. (9) We quickly chose from the (full) array of sandwiches and (homemade) soups. (10) The (final) bill for the four of us was $20, which was a (real) bargain.

Creating Comparative and Superlative Forms of Adjectives and Adverbs

CW 27.6
Adjective or adverb?

The **comparative form** of an adjective or an adverb is used to compare *two* things.

ADJECTIVE | This new word processing program is *more complex* than the one I used last year.

ADVERB | The nursery school students play *longer* than the first graders.

CW 27.7
Form and function of adjectives

In the first sentence, the adjective *more complex* compares one computer program with another. In the second sentence, the adverb *longer* compares the extent to which two groups of children play.

The **superlative form** of an adjective or an adverb is used to compare *more than two* things.

ADJECTIVE | This store has the *lowest* prices for name-brand clothes as well as household appliances.

ADVERB | Of all the young women in the chorus, Eleanor was the one who danced *most gracefully*.

CW 27.8
More on adjectives

In the first sentence, the adjective *lowest* compares the prices of many stores. In the second sentence, the adverb *most gracefully* compares the style of many dancers.

For adjectives and adverbs of one syllable, create the comparative by adding -*er*, and create the superlative by adding -*est* to the end of the positive form of the word.

Positive	*Comparative*	*Superlative*
dark	dark**er**	dark**est**
high	high**er**	high**est**
far	farth**er**	farth**est**
hard	hard**er**	hard**est**

CW 27.9
Four aspects
of adverbs

For adjectives and adverbs of more than two syllables, place *more* in front of the word for the comparative or *most* in front of the word for the superlative.

Positive	*Comparative*	*Superlative*
ridiculous	**more** ridiculous	**most** ridiculous
intelligent	**more** intelligent	**most** intelligent
remarkably	**more** remarkably	**most** remarkably
unfortunately	**more** unfortunately	**most** unfortunately

If the adjective or adverb is *two* syllables, which of these two methods should you use? The answer depends on the word. Some two-syllable words take an *-er* or *-est* ending:

Positive	*Comparative*	*Superlative*
early	earl**ier**	earl**iest**
angry	angr**ier**	angr**iest**
lazy	laz**ier**	laz**iest**
funny	funn**ier**	funn**iest**

Other two-syllable words require that you use *more* or *most* before them:

Positive	*Comparative*	*Superlative*
private	**more** private	**most** private
slowly	**more** slowly	**most** slowly
careful	**more** careful	**most** careful
safely	**more** safely	**most** safely

CW 27.10
More on
adverbs

To avoid errors, look up two-syllable adjectives and adverbs in the dictionary. In addition to definitions, a dictionary gives the correct spelling for adjectives and adverbs that form their comparative and superlative forms by adding *-er* or *-est*. If no *-er* or *-est* forms are listed, then use *more* and *most*.

Regardless of the number of syllables, never use both *more* and *-er* or *most* and *-est* with the same adjective or adverb. Expressions like *more faster* and *most completest* are always wrong.

Some adjectives and adverbs form their comparative and superlative forms in irregular ways:

Positive	*Comparative*	*Superlative*
bad (adjective)	worse	worst
badly (adverb)	worse	worst
good (adjective)	better	best
well (adverb)	better	best
little	less	least
much	more	most

As you can see, two pairs of words on this list share the same comparative and superlative forms. However, these similar words have different functions. *Bad* and *good* are adjectives used to identify *what kind* of people, places, ideas, or things a writer is discussing. *Well* and *badly* are adverbs used to explain *how* something was done.

COMPREHENSION AND PRACTICE

Using Comparative and Superlative Forms Correctly

27.2 Each sentence in the following paragraph contains an incorrect positive, comparative, or superlative adjective or adverb. Cross out the incorrect form, and write the correct form above it, as the example shows.

> EXAMPLE   Secretariat was the ~~most fast~~ *fastest* racehorse I had ever seen.

CW 27.11
Understanding the comparative forms

CW 27.12
Understanding the superlative forms

(1) My friend Laura wants to be a singer, and she already sings ~~more well~~ *better* than most professionals. (2) She has the ~~most sweet~~ *sweetest* voice I've ever heard. (3) She even does a great job with the National Anthem, which most singers claim is the ~~more~~ *most* difficult song around. (4) Her sound is like Whitney Houston's, except Laura's voice is ~~more deep~~ *deeper*. (5) Laura is so talented that she tried out for a local talent show when she had the flu, had the ~~worse~~ *worst* audition of her life, and still won a place in the show. (6) A local agent who manages Laura says that her abilities are improving ~~quicklier~~ *more quickly* than those of his other singers. (7) Even though it's ~~most~~ *more* difficult now than it was ten years ago for an unknown singer to get a record contract, Laura has been sending "demo" CDs all over the country. (8) She figures that at ~~worse~~ *worst*, all the record companies will turn her down, and she will have wasted a few dollars. (9) Meanwhile, she is attending college, which has made her parents ~~more happy~~ *happier* than they were when she announced that she wanted to be a professional singer. (10) Right now the ~~more~~ *most* frustrating thing of all for Laura is finding time both to study and to rehearse.

Working with Confusing Pairs of Adjectives and Adverbs

ESL Note
See "Word Order" on pages 591–592.

**CW 27.13
Deciding
between
well & good,
bad & badly**

Some words have both adjective and adverb forms. Choosing the right form can be confusing for writers. The list below contains the most commonly confused pairs of adjectives and adverbs:

Adjective	*Adverb*
awful	awfully
bad	badly
good	well
poor	poorly
quick	quickly
quiet	quietly
real	really

Deciding between *good* and *well* and between *bad* and *badly* probably causes the most headaches for writers. *Good* and *bad* describe a person or thing, whereas *well* and *badly* describe how something is done. In other words, you can say that a person is a *good* singer or a *bad* singer, but you must say that this individual sings *well* or sings *badly*.

Consider the following examples:

EXAMPLE

Shannon is a *good* chef.

Elie cooks *well*.

In the first sentence, the adjective *good* tells *what kind* of chef Shannon is. In the second, *well* acts as an adverb, describing *how* Elie cooks.

**COMPREHENSION
AND PRACTICE**

27.3

Working with Confusing Adjective and Adverb Pairs

In the sentences below, underline the correct adjective or adverb from the choices given in parentheses. Use the example to guide you.

EXAMPLE

Once again, the Orlando Magic played (poor, <u>poorly</u>) last night.

**CW 27.14
Using
adjectives
and adverbs**

(1) To do my best schoolwork, no matter what the subject, I need a (<u>quiet</u>, quietly) place. (2) When I am in the back of the library or in my room, I can concentrate (good, <u>well</u>). (3) It's (awful, <u>awfully</u>) hard to arrange to be alone sometimes, but it is worth the effort. (4) When I'm around other people, I find it (real, <u>really</u>) difficult to stay focused. (5) Somebody will start talking about a

movie or game, and I am (quick, <u>quickly</u>) part of the conversation. (6) Instead

of concentrating on my statistics or sociology, I end up wasting time in a point-

less discussion, and as a result I do (bad, <u>badly</u>) on my next quiz or exam. (7) I

especially do (poor, <u>poorly</u>) when I try to write a paper with others around.

(8) Again, I find what my friends are doing (awful, <u>awfully</u>) distracting, and the

resulting paper shows it. (9) To make sure I become as (<u>good</u>, well) a writer as

possible, I make it a point to write all my drafts when and where I am sure to

be alone. (10) Since I changed my work habits, I have noticed a (<u>real</u>, really)

improvement in the quality of my performance in all my classes.

COMPREHENSION AND PRACTICE 27.4 Correcting Errors in the Use of Confusing Adjectives and Adverbs

The following sentences contain some errors in the use of adjectives and adverbs. Cross out the incorrect form, and then write the correct one above it. If a sentence is correct as written, write *OK* above it. Use the example to guide you.

EXAMPLE

quickly
The dog ran out from between the two cars so ~~quick~~ that the driver couldn't avoid hitting it.

(1) For years, I needed eyeglasses ~~bad~~ *badly*, but I didn't know it. (2) In grade

school, I performed ~~poor~~ *poorly* on any test that required me to read the blackboard.

(3) At first, my teachers thought I was being lazy and that I could do ~~good~~ *better OR well* if I

paid more attention in class. (4) Then my third-grade teacher sent me for a vi-

sion test, and the doctor said I was ~~awful~~ *awfully* nearsighted. (5) I was ~~real~~ *really* afraid I'd

have to wear glasses like my grandfather's, with ugly frames. (6) As it turned

out, my glasses didn't look so ~~badly~~ *bad*, and the difference they made in my life

was unbelievable. (7) Until I got glasses, I was used to sitting ~~quiet~~ *quietly* in the back

of the room, participating only when forced to. (8) After I got my glasses, all

that changed ~~quick~~ *quickly*. (9) When I could see every word on the board well, all I *OK*

wanted to do was make up for lost time. (10) Although I still received a few

~~poorly~~ *poor* test scores, school became a ~~more happy~~ *happier* experience for me.

CHALLENGE 27.1 Using Confusing Pairs of Adjectives and Adverbs in Your Writing

COLLABORATION

Write topic sentences for three paragraphs. Include in each sentence an adjective or adverb from the list of confusing pairs on page 445. Then, working with a partner, develop one of the sentences into a paragraph. Include adjectives and adverbs to make your writing colorful and precise.

Avoiding Dangling and Misplaced Modifiers

ESL Note
See "Word Order" on pages 591–592.

As you saw in Chapter 24, "Passive Voice, Additional Tenses, and Maintaining Consistency in Tense," the present participle, or *-ing* form of a verb, can be combined with a helping verb to form a verb in the progressive tense. Without a helping verb, this form can't act as the verb in a sentence. When it describes another word or phrase, it is called a **participle**, as these examples show:

EXAMPLE

Yelling angrily, Dion left the room.

The teacher tried to quiet the *laughing* children.

CW 27.15
Understanding the *-ing* form as a modifier

In the first sentence, the participle *Yelling* is describing the proper noun *Dion*. In the second sentence, the participle *laughing* is describing the noun *children*.

Using participles can help you combine ideas and eliminate choppiness in your writing. Consider these sentences, none of which uses participles.

EXAMPLE

The telephone service workers had coffee in the small restaurant. They took a break from work.

The teenaged girl behind the counter polished the glass pastry cabinets. She whistled softly.

CW 27.16
Misplaced dangling modifier

Although the sentences in each example are correct, they are choppy. By changing one of the sentences to a dependent clause beginning with a participle and making a few other changes in wording, you can combine these sentences:

EXAMPLE

Taking a break from work, the telephone service *workers* had coffee in the small restaurant.

Whistling softly, the teenaged *girl* behind the counter polished the glass pastry cabinets.

In the first example, the participle and the words that follow it, *Taking a break from work*, now describe *workers*. In the second example, the participle and the words that follow it, *Whistling softly*, now describe *girl*.

When you use a participle, be sure to place it near the word it describes in a sentence. Otherwise, your readers may not understand what word it is describing. Consider these examples:

FAULTY | *Hanging from the ceiling,* Jacob saw the new lamp.

Looking for her dress, the cat suddenly jumped onto Janet's back.

The participle in the first sentence is *Hanging.* Right now, however, the sentence suggests that it is *Jacob* and not the new lamp that is *hanging* from the ceiling. This type of error, which occurs when a modifier is placed near a word that it does not modify rather than near the word it does, is called a **misplaced modifier.** The participle in the second sentence is *Looking.* At this point, the sentence indicates that *Janet's cat* was *looking* for a dress. This type of error, which occurs when a modifier has no word that it can logically modify, is called a **dangling modifier.**

Avoiding these types of errors is simple. Always check any sentence in which you have included a participle to make sure the modifier is describing the correct word. If there is an error, you can correct it by putting the participle next to the word it modifies or by changing the wording of the sentence:

CORRECTED | *Hanging* from the ceiling, the new lamp caught Jacob's eye.

or

Jacob stared at the new lamp *hanging* from the ceiling.

CORRECTED | *Looking for her dress,* Janet suddenly felt her cat jump onto her back.

or

As Janet was looking for her dress, her cat suddenly jumped onto her back.

Not all misplaced modifiers involve participles. Any modifier, whether it is an individual word or a group of words, is a misplaced modifier if it suggests a relationship between words when no such relationship does or could exist. Consider these examples:

MISPLACED | *As a young child,* my great-grandfather often took my sister to the park.

The new sales representative sold the portable stereo to the woman *with the built-in compact disc player.*

CW 27.17
Dangling
modifiers

The modifiers in these two sentences are obviously misplaced because the resulting sentences just don't make sense. A person can't be a young child and a great-grandfather at the same time. And people don't have stereo components in their bodies.

Avoid these kinds of misplaced modifiers by restating parts of the sentence or rearranging the order of the sentence so that the modifiers are next to the words they modify, as these corrected versions show:

CORRECTED   As a young child, my sister often went to the park with my great-grandfather.

The new sales representative sold the portable stereo with the built-in compact disc player to the woman.

COMPREHENSION AND PRACTICE

Identifying Participles

27.5   Each sentence in the following paragraph contains a participle. Underline the participle and the word it describes. Draw a line connecting the two elements, as the example shows.

EXAMPLE   Staring at the map, Gracie tried to determine where she was.

(1) Entering a convenience store downtown last week, my brother Joe knew something was wrong. (2) Trying to figure out what the problem was, he looked around the store. (3) Picking up a few items and talking, two older women walked from the back of the store. (4) Waiting for them to finish their shopping, Joe looked around the rest of the store. (5) Standing behind the counter, the clerk seemed particularly nervous. (6) Turning around, Joe saw a figure all in black, with sunglasses and a baseball hat pulled low. (7) Quickly striding toward the register, this man appeared to reach for something under his jacket. (8) Pretending he couldn't find what he wanted, Joe inched toward the door. (9) Driving by the store at that moment, a police car caught his attention. (10) Responding to Joe's yells for help, the officers headed into the store in time to stop the robbery.

COMPREHENSION AND PRACTICE

Working with Participles

27.6   Sentences 1–10 on the next page contain an underlined participle that acts either as a verb or a modifier. Label the word with a *V* or an *M* to indicate its function. For words labeled *V*, find and underline the helping verb. For words labeled *M*, find and underline the word being described. Study the examples first.

EXAMPLE   By the time Henry reached the finish line, he <u>was gasping</u>.^V

^M
Swirling around the room, the <u>dancer</u> was dressed in red.

^M
1. <u>Laughing</u> uncontrollably, <u>Janine</u> finally had to sit down.

^M
2. A group <u>protesting</u> capital punishment demonstrated outside the prison.

^V
3. The bus <u>is leaving</u> right now.

^V
4. The pipe <u>had been leaking</u> for several weeks before anyone noticed.

^M
5. <u>Staring</u> straight into the camera, the <u>reporter</u> smiled and began her report.

^M
6. <u>Smiling</u>, the <u>president</u> accepted the gift and sat down.

^M
7. The <u>man walking</u> on the treadmill was at least seventy-five years old.

^V
8. Renee <u>was cooking</u> a gourmet dinner.

^M
9. The <u>woman changing</u> the tire was covered with grease.

^M
10. <u>Waving</u> happily, the <u>child</u> stepped out of the bus.

COMPREHENSION AND PRACTICE
27.7

CW 27.18
Recognizing misplaced modifiers

Identifying and Correcting Dangling and Misplaced Modifiers

Each of the following sentences contains a dangling or misplaced modifier. First, underline the dangling or misplaced modifier. Then, on a separate piece of paper, restate or rearrange each sentence so that the modifiers are describing the correct words. More than one correct answer is possible. Use the example as a guide.

EXAMPLE   <u>Flying around the lamp</u>, the child was fascinated by the moth.

CORRECTED   <u>Flying around the lamp</u>, the moth fascinated the child.

or

The child was fascinated by the moth <u>flying around the lamp</u>.

CW 27.19
Correcting errors with modifiers

(1) Expecting nothing but a normal day, the discovery Jennifer made one late spring afternoon changed her outlook for the summer. (2) She had been applying for a job for a month requiring computer skills. (3) Having taken a

course in computer applications, spreadsheets and *PowerPoint* presentations were among her areas of expertise. (4) Sending out applications to several companies downtown, her hopes were that one of these places would come through for her. (5) But the hopes seemed distant after three weeks looking for a good job. (6) Everything changed when lying under her refrigerator, Jennifer found a letter that she had dropped the previous day. (7) When she read the letter, she broke into a smile, informing her that she had been offered a job for the summer. (8) Shaking, the phone seemed to move as she called to accept the job. (9) As a prospective employee, her supervisor, Ms. Tally, told Jennifer about the various duties involved. (10) Hanging up the phone, her smile of happiness grew even broader.

**CW 27.20
More practice
with
correcting
errors with
modifiers**

CHALLENGE 27.2 Using Participles to Combine Sentences

COLLABORATION

Working with a partner, combine the following simple sentences to eliminate choppiness by changing one of the sentences into a participle. All of these modifiers should be phrases rather than single words. Study the example first.

EXAMPLE The puppy was waiting for its supper. It was wagging its tail.
Wagging its tail, the puppy was waiting for its supper.

1. Caroline was walking around the park. She was trying to get some exercise.

   Trying to get some exercise, Caroline was walking around the park. OR, Walking

   around the park, Caroline was trying to get some exercise.

2. Reggie was reading a novel. He was sitting on the couch.

   Sitting on the couch, Reggie was reading a novel. OR Reading a novel, Reggie was

   sitting on the couch.

3. The strikers were marching in front of the factory. They were carrying signs.

   Carrying signs, the strikers were marching in front of the factory. OR Marching in front

   of the factory, the strikers were carrying signs.

   _____

   _____

4. The truck was fleeing from two police cars. It was traveling the wrong way on the highway.

   Traveling the wrong way on the highway, the truck was fleeing from two police cars.

   OR Fleeing from two police cars, the truck was traveling the wrong way on the

   highway.

   _____

5. The little boy was playing hide and seek. He was hiding from his friends.

   Hiding from his friends, the little boy was playing hide and seek. OR Playing hide and

   seek, the little boy was hiding from his friends.

   _____

   _____

6. Jeremy and Jackie enjoyed the reflection of the stars on the water. They sat on a bench overlooking the harbor.

   Enjoying the reflection of the stars on the water, Jeremy and Jackie sat on a bench

   overlooking the harbor. OR Sitting on a bench overlooking the harbor, Jeremy and

   Jackie enjoyed the reflection of the stars on the water.

   _____

7. The skateboarders took advantage of the empty streets on the holiday afternoon. They practiced in front of City Hall Plaza.

   Taking advantage of the empty streets on the holiday afternoon, the skateboarders

   practice in front of City Hall Plaza. OR Practicing in front of City Hall Plaza, the

   skateboarders took advantage of the empty streets on the holiday afternoon.

   _____

8. The crowd at the comedy club laughed uncontrollably at the comedian. They were formerly reserved but came alive when she began her routine.

Laughing uncontrollably at the comedian, the formerly reserved crowd at the comedy

club came alive when she began her routine. OR Leaving their reserve behind and

coming alive when the comedian began her routine, the crowd at the comedy club

laughed uncontrollably.

9. Leslie opened the trunk and pulled out the tire. He got to work changing the flat.

Opening the trunk and pulling out the tire, Leslie got to work changing the flat. OR

Getting to work changing the flat, Leslie opened the trunk and pulled out the tire.

10. The scholarship winner waved in acknowledgment. She smiled at her grand-mother.

Waving in acknowledgment, the scholarship winner smiled at her grandmother. OR

Smiling at her grandmother, the scholarship winner waved in acknowledgment.

Avoiding Double Negatives

Expressing negation can also cause problems for writers. *No, never, nowhere, no-body, nothing, no one,* and *none* are all used to express the idea of *no.* Adverbs like *scarcely, hardly,* and *barely,* as well as *not,* the adverb used to create *contractions* (such as *did + not = didn't*), also express negation.

When two of these negative words are used in the same sentence, they form what is called a **double negative.** Double negatives are never acceptable in college or professional writing. To avoid double negatives in your writing, check your sentences to make sure you have only one negative in each.

Correcting a double negative is easy: Simply eliminate one of the negative words or change it to a positive form. Note the negatives in the examples on the following page as well as the methods used to correct the errors.

EXAMPLE

Although my feet are very narrow, I have ~~not~~ had no trouble finding reasonable work shoes.

or

Although my feet are very narrow, I have not had ~~no~~ ^any^ trouble finding reasonable work shoes.

EXAMPLE

The firefighters couldn~~'t~~ do nothing to stop the forest fire.

or

The firefighters couldn't do ~~nothing~~ ^anything^ to stop the forest fire.

As corrected, each of these sentences expresses the point originally intended, but now each does so with a single negative.

FAST FACT It wasn't always wrong to use a double negative. In fact double negatives can be seen in writings from the earlier days of modern English, including in the plays of Shakespeare. But some eighteenth-century English grammarians, intent on making English express the same kind of logic as mathematics, applied the mathematical rule that two negatives make a positive to language. Eventually, this application came to be the acceptable form, and the double negative came to be considered the nonstandard or illiterate form.

COMPREHENSION AND PRACTICE   Avoiding Double Negatives

27.8 In the following paragraph, circle the correct words in parentheses, avoiding double negatives. Use the material above and the following example as a guide.

EXAMPLE

Madeleine and David don't plan to travel ((anywhere), nowhere) special this summer.

(1) Even though I don't know ((anything), nothing) about professional sports, I enjoy going to see a professional baseball game once in a while. (2) In fact, I never turn down ((any), no) invitation to see the Mud Hens. (3) This minor league team has not had ((any), no) problem attracting crowds since they opened their new stadium five years ago. (4) The design of the stadium is a major factor, since the place has (any, (no)) obstructed-view seats. (5) I have

never heard (anybody, nobody) who has attended a game there say a negative thing about the place. (6) In addition, the food services provider doesn't have (any, no) items for sale that cost more than $3, and they often publish discount food tickets in the paper. (7) As a result, even big families don't have (any, no) problem enjoying a few snacks during the game. (8) On game nights, when my cousin can't get (anybody, nobody) from work to drive him to the park, I drive and he buys me a ticket. (9) At most games, the crowd is large, and you can't find (any, no) empty seats behind home plate. (10) Unfortunately, it seems as if every time I go to a game, the team has (any, no) luck and ends up losing.

COMPREHENSION AND PRACTICE

Identifying and Correcting Double Negatives

27.9 Some of the sentences in the paragraph below contain double negatives. Put an *
in front of any sentence containing a double negative, and then rewrite the sentence on a separate sheet of paper. More than one correct version is possible. Use the example as a guide.

EXAMPLE

*She wouldn't never leave town without contacting me first.

She would never leave town without contacting me first.

or

She wouldn't leave town without contacting me first.

(1) Bad habits are a plague not only for the offenders but also for the victims of the offending behavior. (2)*For instance, many people who swear in public probably don't intend to offend nobody. (3)*However, even if these people don't mean nothing by it, their bad habit can frighten, anger, or depress listeners. (4) Another bad habit many people share is not listening fully to those who are talking to them. (5)*These offenders engage you in conversation, ask you a question, and then do not pay no attention as you try to answer. (6)*There is not hardly anything more frustrating than trying to

communicate with someone whose mind has moved on to other things. (7) The worst habit of all is gossiping about others. (8)*Gossiping is particularly unfair because the people being discussed are not around to say nothing to defend themselves. (9)*They never have no chance to confront the people talking about them. (10)*Unfortunately, I am guilty of all these bad habits myself, so I don't have the right to lecture nobody else.

CHALLENGE 27.3 Building an Argument for Using Standard English

COLLABORATION

Although some people use double negatives in casual speech, these errors aren't acceptable in college or professional writing. Imagine you have been asked to address a class of sixth graders on the subject of using proper language in writing and speaking. Working with a partner, list on a separate sheet of paper at least four reasons you would give to explain why double negatives and other nonstandard forms (*ain't, we be*, and so on) are unacceptable. Still working together, turn your list into a paragraph that could be handed out to the sixth grade students as a guide.

CHAPTER QUICK CHECK Working with Adjectives and Adverbs

The following passage contains errors involving double negatives, incorrect forms of adjectives and adverbs, and misplaced modifiers. Cross out each error and write the correct form above it. For misplaced modifiers, you may need to insert new words or cross out an entire clause and rewrite it. Also, there may be more than one way to correct the double negatives. Use the example to guide you.

EXAMPLE   Greg's new digital phone is ~~more~~ smaller than Krystall's.

                           most compelling
(1) One of the ~~compellingist~~ literary voices of the current age is Jamaica Kincaid. (2) Best known for her beautiful coming-of-age novel *Annie John*, pub-
                   Kincaid was born on the Caribbean island of Antigua
lished in 1983, ~~the Caribbean island of Antigua is where Kincaid was born~~. (3) Not experiencing ~~no~~ happiness or fulfillment while growing up, she de-
                                        in the Caribbean
cided to abandon Antigua and head to the United States. (4) She left her home at age 17 ~~in the Caribbean~~, and she traveled to New York City where she became an *au pair*, a live-in babysitter. (5) After attending colleges in New York
                                          a
and New Hampshire but not earning ~~no~~ degree, she began her professional

By this time, she

writing career. (6) ~~She~~ had also changed her name from Elaine Potter

Richardson ~~by this time~~ to Jamaica Kincaid. (7) During the mid-1970s, Kincaid

well

was writing so ~~good~~ that she began to attract attention for her work in several

periodicals, particularly the *New Yorker*. (8) After viewing her writing, the pub-

quickly

lisher ~~quick~~ invited her to join the staff of this influential publication, and she

remained associated with the periodical for twenty years. (9) Kincaid is con-

superb

sidered to be one of the most ~~superbest~~ post-colonial writers, artists whose

writing concerns countries formerly under the control of the British Empire.

(10) In works like *Annie John, Lucy*, and *The Autobiography of My Mother*,

really

Kincaid explores a number of ~~real~~ intense and sensitive themes, including

alienation, isolation, and mother-daughter relationships.

QUICK STUDY   Student Example

This chapter focuses on ways of enhancing, labeling, or ranking ideas, individuals, actions, and so on. Consider this paragraph on a related subject, something that at this point you don't do well and would like to do better:

One thing that I wish is that I didn't swim so bad. I first learned to swim at

the YMCA during a school vacation when I was in the fifth grade. During that

week, the instructor taught us how to float and do a few basic strokes and

kicks. By the end of the week, I was able to stay afloat and paddle around a little.

But I'm embarrassed to say that fifteen years later I still swim poor. I hate not

being a more competenter swimmer because it has kept me from doing things

that I'd really like to try. For example, last year a bunch of my friends went on

a trip to do some snorkeling. Worrying that they would think I was afraid of the

water, an excuse about having other plans was all I could think of. Now the

same group is planning to try windsurfing, and I would really like to go along

on the trip, but I just don't have no confidence when I am in the water. If I could only find a class for adults that would teach swimming basics, I know that I could overcome this fear. I don't want to be competitive swimmer. I just want to be in water over my head without feeling like I'm about to drown.

First complete the following activities in response to this paragraph:

1. Five of the sentences in the previous paragraph are highlighted. Evaluate these sentences for mistakes in the use of adjectives and adverbs, dangling or misplaced modifiers, and double negatives, using the material in this chapter as a guide. Circle any errors and then, on a separate sheet of paper, rewrite the sentences to eliminate the mistakes.

2. On the lines below, briefly explain how the order in which this paragraph is arranged help to make it easier for a reader to understand the point being made.

Most students will agree that the order is chronological, and it helps the reader

understand the point because it emphasizes the cumulative effect that being unable

to swim well has had.

3. The paragraph discusses several reactions the writer experienced, including feeling fearful, embarrassed, and unconfident. Choose one of these sensations and then, on a separate sheet of paper, write a brief paragraph in which you explain what experiencing it feels like.

Now explore the topic in writing. As the paragraph above does, you could focus on something that you don't do especially well but that you would like to do better. Or you might turn your attention to one of these topics related to the subject matter of this chapter:

- something—a room or apartment, a car, an outfit, and so on—that you completely transformed
- a time when you discovered that something didn't match the description you had been given
- the best—or worst—movie, concert, artistic or athletic performance you've ever seen
- how to enhance or improve your social life

COLLABORATION

1. Exchange your draft with a classmate. Evaluate the paragraph you receive. Look for any problems, especially with the use of adjectives and adverbs, including misplaced and dangling modifiers and double negatives. Circle any errors, write corrected versions above them, and then return the paper to the writer.

2. Consider the comments and corrections your reader has made and create a final draft of your paragraph.

SUMMARY EXERCISE Working with Adjectives and Adverbs

The following passage contains errors involving double negatives, incorrect forms of adjectives and adverbs, and misplaced modifiers. Cross out each error, and write the correct form above it. For misplaced modifiers, you may need to insert new words or cross out an entire clause and rewrite it. Also, there may be more than one way to correct the double negatives.

(1) I didn't ~~never~~ think my life would improve when a 24-hour supermarket opened in my neighborhood, but I was in for a pleasant surprise. (2) I have
  a
never been ~~no~~ believer that bigger always means ~~more~~ better. (3) Also, the
                                                      awfully
idea of grocery shopping at midnight seemed ~~awful~~ strange to me, but I decided to give it a try.
            really
(4) I was ~~real~~ surprised to see how few people had the same idea. (5)
                                                      small
When I drove into the parking lot at midnight, I saw a ~~smallest~~ number of
        a small crowd inspected
cars. (6) Cluttering the aisles, the produce section ~~had a small crowd~~. (7) They
                          ^   ^
were thumping melons, inspecting heads of lettuce, and picking apples just as
                                            brightest
they would if the sun were shining its ~~most bright~~.
        quickly
(8) I ~~quick~~ discovered the appeal of shopping at night. (9) First of all, there
were   simpler
~~weren't~~ hardly any customers at midnight, so it was ~~more simple~~ to maneuver
                                          any
in the aisles. (10) Also, I didn't have to fight ~~no~~ crowds, so I felt ~~more~~ freer to
examine the selection of items at my leisure.
                    calmer   quietly
(11) The store seemed ~~calmest~~, too. (12) Speaking more ~~quiet~~ than they
                                          were
do during the day, ~~I found~~ the workers more pleasanter. (13) Even the check-
            awfully   loudest
out area was ~~awful~~ still. (14) The most ~~loud sound~~ was the beep of the computer scanners.
                        was [OR wasn't a]
(15) Best of all, there ~~wasn't~~ no long wait in line to check out and pay for
my groceries. (16) Normally, I am squeezed in between people who apparently
~~don't~~ have no limits on their grocery budgets. (17) Imagine my delight when I
                          quickly
found I could check out ~~quick~~, without the normal ten-minute wait in line.

(18) Leaving the parking lot, I felt that this shopping trip was a positive experience. (19) I liked going about my shopping ~~quiet~~ ^{quietly} and ~~calm~~ ^{calmly}, without being bothered by other shoppers. (20) The only problem was that the next day I was ~~more~~ sleepier than usual.

FOR FURTHER EXPLORATION

1. Consider one of the following topics:

   - the effects of reforms in public assistance
   - the best way to spend a first date
   - the ideal place to live
   - how to stretch a dollar
   - the most disorganized or sloppy person you know

   Prewrite on the subject, using one of the strategies you practiced in Chapter 2, and work your way through the rest of the writing process. Then complete a draft essay of at least 500 words on this subject.

COLLABORATION

2. Exchange your draft with a classmate. Check the draft you receive for weaknesses, checking in particular for errors in the use of adjectives and adverbs, including misplaced and dangling modifiers and double negatives. Circle any mistakes and, using the material in this chapter to guide you, indicate the correct version above the error. Return the paper to the writer.

3. Revise your essay, correcting any errors in irregular verb use or other problems discovered by your reader.

RECAP Adjectives, Adverbs, and Other Modifiers: Using Describing and Modifying Words Effectively

New terms in this chapter	Definitions
modifier	a word that describes or limits other words in a sentence
adjective	a word that describes a noun or pronoun An adjective answers the question *which one, how many*, or *what kind?*
adverb	a word that describes a verb, adjective, or another adverb An adverb tells *how, when, where, to what extent*, or *how much*.

New terms in this chapter	Definitions
positive form	the form of an adjective or adverb that describes a noun or pronoun without making a comparison
	EXAMPLE tall, poorly
comparative form	the form of an adjective or adverb used to compare two things
	EXAMPLE **more** handsome, loveli**er**
superlative form	the form of an adjective or adverb used to compare more than two things
	EXAMPLE **most** remarkable, slow**est**
participle	a verb form that functions as an adjective in a sentence
	EXAMPLE *Singing sweetly*, the nightingale darted from tree to tree.
	Use participles when combining sentences and eliminate choppiness.
misplaced modifier	a modifier placed near a word that it does not modify
	Place a participle near the word or words it describes in a sentence.
dangling modifier	a modifier with no word that it can logically modify
double negative	an incorrect construction using two negative words in the same unit of ideas
	EXAMPLE *Nobody* should bring ~~*nothing*~~ anything flammable.
	Negative words include *no, not, never, nowhere, nobody, nothing, no one, none, scarcely, hardly, barely*.

Guidelines for Adjective and Adverb Forms

Type of word	Positive	Comparative	Superlative
One-syllable word	brave	positive form + *-er* brav**er**	positive form + *-est* brav**est**
Words of three or more syllables	enjoyable	*more* + positive form **more** enjoyable	*most* + positive form **most** enjoyable
Some two-syllable words	funny	change *-y* to *-i* + *-er* funn**ier**	change *-y* to *-i* + *-est* funn**iest**
Other two-syllable words	famous	*more* + positive form **more** famous	*most* + positive form **most** famous

(continued)

Commonly Confused Adjectives and Adverbs

Positive	Comparative	Superlative
bad (adjective)	worse	worst
badly (adverb)	worse	worst
good (adjective)	better	best
well (adverb)	better	best
little	less	least
much	more	most

GOING FORWARD...

**CW 27.21
Using
modifiers
correctly**

Q: What can I do to make sure that I don't make any mistakes when I use adjectives and adverbs?

A: To avoid errors in their use, you need to be aware of the most likely problems. These problems include using the wrong form when making comparisons, placing a modifier in the wrong position in a sentence, and using two negatives (such as *no, never,* and *not*) in the same clause.

CHAPTER **28**

Parallelism: Presenting Related Items in a Similar Form

Navigating This Chapter

In this chapter, you will discover how to maintain parallelism:

- with words in a series
- with phrases
- with words linked by correlative conjunctions such as *either/or*

GETTING STARTED . . .

CW 28.1 Chapter basics

Q: I seem to get tripped up when I am presenting ideas in pairs or a series. When I'm done, the sentence sometimes sounds funny, as if the ideas I put together don't fit with each other. What am I doing wrong?

A: The name for what you sometimes struggle with is **parallelism**, the technique used to make related ideas flow together. For ideas to be parallel, they must follow the same basic form. When one item ends in *-ing,* for example, but one or more of the others don't, the whole unit won't sound right. That's because all the items aren't set up the same way—they aren't parallel.

Overview: Balancing Ideas in Your Writing

CW 28.2 Overview of balancing your ideas

Multiple births are often newsworthy events. You have probably seen a video clip or a picture in the newspaper of triplets or quadruplets, all dressed in identical clothes. When it comes to compiling a series of items in your writing, this is the image you should keep in mind. That's because you must also "dress" or present any related ideas so that they look the same—in other words, so they are parallel. Maintaining **parallelism** means presenting any series of ideas, whether the items are individual words or groups of words, in the same form. Faulty parallelism is a serious problem because the reader focuses on the items that don't match rather than on the good ideas being presented. Therefore it's important to spend some time mastering this aspect of writing.

Maintaining Parallelism with Words in a Series

**CW 28.3
Maintaining
parallelism
with words
in a series**

When you use words in a series, all the words should have the same grammatical structure. Generally, coordinating conjunctions (*and, but, for, nor, or, so,* and *yet*) are used to join the words. To maintain parallelism, keep two things in mind:

1. *Connect only similar parts of speech.* Join nouns with nouns, verbs with verbs, adjectives with adjectives, and so forth. Do not connect a verb with an adjective, a noun with an adverb, and so forth.

2. *Do not connect individual words in a series to phrases or clauses.* Keep the structure of the series, as well as the number of words in it, parallel.

EXAMPLE | Steve Martin is an actor, a comedian, and ~~he writes plays~~. *a playwright*

**CW 28.4
Achieving
parallelism**

The weather this summer has been hot, rainy, and ~~a steam bath~~. *steamy*

FAST FACT   Rhyme is a form of parallel structure. But don't count on being able to employ this particular variation of parallelism with *month, orange, purple,* or *silver,* because no English words rhyme with them.

**COMPREHENSION
AND PRACTICE**

Using Parallel Words in a Series

28.1   Complete each statement with a word that maintains the parallel structure of the sentence. Use the example as a guide.

EXAMPLE | The antique painting was dusty, scratched, and ___*faded*___.

**CW 28.5
Maintaining
parallelism**

(1) How can you tell whether someone is telling the truth or a _____lie_____? (2) This question has stymied everyone, including parents, spouses, and __criminal investigators__, as long as there has been a civilized society. (3) Existing polygraph tests measure truthfulness on the basis of such signs of anxiety as increased perspiration and __heart rate__. (4) But polygraph results are not considered reliable because not everyone reacts to tragedy, adversity, or __stress__ in the same way. (5) Some people react by shaking, sweating, and __crying__, while others simply become seemingly emotionless. (6) Also, complicating the issue is that outright lies, denial, and __exaggeration__ are all

types of dishonesty, but people don't judge them all the same way. (7) Now new brain research may make it possible to tell if a person's statement is trust-worthy or ___dishonest___. (8) To find out whether brain activity will signal when someone is being truthful or ___devious___, neuroscience researchers used an MRI to measure brain activity of eighteen volunteers. (9) The volunteers were given a specific playing card—for example, the jack of hearts or the ___ace of clubs___—and told to lie when a computer correctly identified the card. (10) The MRI results showed different levels of brain activity depending on whether the person was telling the truth or ___lying___.

COMPREHENSION AND PRACTICE

28.2

CW 28.6 More practice maintaining parallelism

EXAMPLE

Maintaining Parallel Structure with Words in a Series

Each sentence in the following passage contains an error in parallelism. Cross out the errors, and, when necessary, write the correct version above the faulty one. In some cases, you can correct the sentence by simply eliminating words. In some cases, more than one correct answer is possible. Use the example as a guide.

                                                                    become irritable
Every time I try to stop smoking, I gain weight, get headaches, or ~~irritability takes over~~.

                                                                     ambition
(1) You need a good education and ~~to be ambitious~~ to get a decent job to-day. (2) A few decades ago, people could find employment as long as they
                                                          learn
were willing to work hard and ~~learning~~ on the job. (3) Plenty of jobs existed
                                                                             having
that didn't involve working with complex equipment or ~~to have~~ a specialized math or science background. (4) Even if people had weak writing skills or
lacked
~~lacking~~ strong reading skills, they could still find regular work. (5) Now, how-ever, even a high school diploma or ~~having~~ a G.E.D. doesn't automatically land you a job. (6) I know from experience that employers in the twenty-first century want employees who are intelligent, enthusiastic, and ~~they want them to be~~ well educated. (7) After my military service, I missed out on a number of good jobs because the employers said I lacked technical experience or post-

secondary education ~~was needed by me~~. (8) After a year of looking for a desirable job, I became discouraged, angry, and ~~I was~~ depressed. (9) Now I am in college, working in the computer lab and ~~computer science is being studied by me~~. _{studying computer science} (10) As a result, I will have some specific knowledge, confidence, and ~~I will also have~~ experience to offer an employer.

Maintaining Parallelism with Phrases

CW 28.7
Maintaining parallelism to phrases

Phrases connected by *and* and *or* must also follow parallel structure. A phrase is a group of words that acts as a single word. Common types of phrases include prepositional phrases, *-ing* phrases, and *to + verb* phrases. It's correct to connect prepositional phrases with other prepositional phrases or *to + verb* phrases with other *to + verb* phrases. To correct errors that join nonparallel phrases, all you have to do is change the incorrect phrase to match the others, as these examples show:

EXAMPLE

The explosion affected people living *near the house, around the neighborhood,* and the ~~*entire city was involved*~~. *throughout the entire city*

When she's not in art class, she is busy *sketching animals, painting nature scenes, or* ~~*to draw portraits*~~. *drawing portraits*

My grandmother always loved *to knit sweaters and* ~~*decorating*~~ *handkerchiefs*. *to decorate*

COMPREHENSION AND PRACTICE
28.3

CW 28.8
Identifying parallel structures

Using Parallel Structure with Phrases

Circle the coordinating conjunctions in each of the sentences below. Then underline the phrases that the conjunctions connect. If the connected phrases are not expressed in parallel form, change one so that it matches those to which it is connected. More than one correct answer may be possible. Use the example as a guide.

EXAMPLE

The car crashed <u>through the fence, across the yard,</u> (and) ~~it went~~ <u>into the pool</u>.

(1) Until I was ten years old, I was frequently in trouble for <u>breaking windows, beating up other kids,</u> (and) ~~to bother~~ <u>old people in my neighborhood</u>. _{bothering} (2) I had a terrible attitude, whether I was <u>at school, on the street</u> (or) ~~I was~~ home, ^{at} until I joined the Agnes Kidd Memorial Boys (and) Girls Club. (3) The staff at

the Club taught me to respect others, to help those less able, ~~and~~ ~~respecting~~ [to respect]

other people's property. (4) Within a month, I became a different person at

home, around the neighborhood, ~~and~~ ~~to spend time with~~ in school. (5) I had

been having trouble with math ~~and~~ ~~reading was troublesome for me~~, ~~so~~ I [reading]

spent time with a tutor from the after-school program at the Club. (6) Because

of the staff's influence, I began to become more attentive to my younger sis-

ters ~~and~~ ~~doing my chores~~ without being reminded. (7) Before long I was [to do my chores]

bringing home good report cards, making new friends, ~~and~~ ~~I was feeling more~~

confident. (8) I am determined to repay the staff for their help with my atti-

tude ~~and~~ ~~they helped me~~ with school. (9) To do so, I intend to study hard in

college ~~and~~ ~~earn~~ my degree in elementary education with a minor in physical [to earn]

education. (10) Then I can begin working with children in a community center

~~or~~ ~~maybe to get a job~~ in an elementary school.

COMPREHENSION AND PRACTICE

Keeping Phrases Parallel

28.4 The sentences in the following passage contain errors in parallelism of phrases. Cross out these errors, and then provide correct versions above the faulty ones if necessary. In some cases, you can correct the sentence simply by eliminating words. More than one correct answer may be possible with some sentences. Use the example to guide you.

EXAMPLE   Elaine looked for her lost credit card under the bed, behind the bureau, and

~~she~~ even ~~looked~~ in her old pocketbook.

(1) Yesterday, a guest speaker in my American history class gave an out-

standing lecture on racist attitudes, unfair stereotypes, and ~~on~~ race relations.

(2) When my professor first announced that Dr. George Henry from City

University would be showing a film, giving a speech, and ~~he would then an-~~ [answering]

~~swer~~ questions, I was annoyed. (3) In high school and ~~when I had presenta-~~

~~tions~~ in other college classes, I had never gained much from such performances. (4) In particular, I usually found the video presentations hard to follow because of the small monitor size and ~~the sound conditions was poor~~ ^{poor sound conditions}.

(5) However, when the class began, I quickly discovered that whether he was discussing the video, asking questions, or ^{relating} ~~he related~~ a personal experience, Dr. Henry had my complete attention. (6) For example, he handed out a questionnaire delving into our racial fears and ^{exposing} ~~to expose~~ our hidden racist outlooks.

(7) He urged us to read the questions carefully, to answer honestly, and he ~~told us~~ to consider the implications of our answers. (8) As I read over my answers, I began to realize that many educators, ^{businesspeople} ~~people in the business world~~, and politicians hold racist feelings without even being aware of them. (9) After his lecture, Dr. Henry led a discussion on ways to improve race relations, eliminate stereotypes, and ^{overcome} ~~overcoming~~ our unconscious racist feelings. (10) I left that classroom with a different perspective on racism and ^{on guest speakers.} ~~my attitude about guest speakers was new~~.

CHALLENGE 28.1   Analyzing Effective Use of Parallel Structure

Here is a brief passage from *Night,* Elie Weisel's powerful memoir of his experiences in Nazi death camps. Working with a partner, underline any parallel words or phrases. Circle the conjunctions. Find the most effective use of parallel structure, and explain to the class why it is effective.

All around me death was moving in, silently, without violence. It would seize upon some sleeping being, enter into him, (and) consume him bit by bit. Next to me, there was someone trying to wake up his neighbor, his brother, perhaps, (or) a friend. In vain. Discouraged in the attempt, the man lay down in his turn, next to the corpse, (and) slept too. Who was there to wake him up?

FAST FACT   If you want an example of what correct parallelism can add to a piece of writing, look no further than the Declaration of Independence. As this passage shows, the strong repetition of *that* clauses hammers home the essence of the philosophy upon which our country was founded: "We hold these truths to be self-evident, that all men are created equal, that they are endowed by their Creator with certain unalienable Rights, that among these are Life, Liberty, and the pursuit of Happiness. That to secure these rights, Governments are instituted among Men, deriving their just powers from the consent of the governed. That whenever any Form of Government becomes destructive to these ends, it is the Right of the People to alter or abolish it. . . ."

Maintaining Parallelism When Using Correlative Conjunctions

**CW 28.9
Maintaining
parallelism
with
correlative
conjunctions**

You must also be careful to maintain parallelism when you use the following word pairs, called **correlative conjunctions,** to connect items:

both/and	not only/but also
either/or	whether/or
neither/nor	

These pairs indicate two possibilities, alternatives, conditions, and so on. The words or phrases that these pairs connect must be parallel. To eliminate faulty parallelism in this kind of construction, make the second item match the first, as these examples show:

EXAMPLE   I tried to sneak into the club *by both trying the back door* and *~~I showed~~ the* ^*by showing*^ *guard a fake ID.*

The salesclerk was *neither polite nor ~~did she work efficiently~~* ^*efficient*^.

**COMPREHENSION
AND PRACTICE
28.5**

Maintaining Parallelism with Units Connected by Correlative Conjunctions

Complete the following sentences by filling in the blanks with words or phrases that complete the thought and maintain sentence parallelism. Use the example as a guide. Answers will vary. Representative answers are shown.

EXAMPLE   By the time I get to the shower in the morning, either all the hot water is used up or ___all the towels are missing___.

1. The fire at my neighbor's apartment last Christmas was terrifying not only for my friend but also ___for all the people on the block___.

2. The fire started when one of her house guests either dropped a cigarette on a

   chair or _____ fell asleep while smoking _____.

3. Regardless of the cause, the damage was heavy, not only to the apartment it-

   self but also _____ to her belongings _____.

4. When I looked out the window on the night of the fire, the roof was not only

   smoking but also _____ emitting bright orange flames _____.

5. At first I couldn't tell whether the smoke was coming from her apartment or

   _____ from the apartment next to hers _____.

6. By the time the fire department arrived, both the front door and

   _____ the side entrance _____ were engulfed in flames.

7. Whether she was suffering from smoke inhalation or

   _____ shock _____, my neighbor was hospitalized for three days.

8. Neither my family nor _____ I _____ could sleep until we

   knew that she and her guests were all right.

9. Fortunately, my neighbor was able to collect insurance money and

   _____ replace her belongings destroyed in the fire _____.

10. Since then, she doesn't allow smoking in her apartment, so anyone wanting to

    goes down the stairs and out
    smoke either steps out on the balcony or _____
    on the street
    _____.

COMPREHENSION AND PRACTICE 28.6

CW 28.10 Parellelism and coherence

Using Parallelism Correctly in Your Writing

One element in each of the following groups is not parallel. Cross out the nonparallel element, and revise it to make it parallel. Then, on a separate sheet of paper, write a sentence using each item.

1. both a midterm and ~~we must write~~ three papers

2. either a situation comedy or ~~to watch~~ a talk show

   past the gym
3. near the cafeteria, ~~the gym,~~ and beside the administration building

   dribble
4. ~~dribbling,~~ pass, and shoot

5. not only interesting but ~~it was~~ funny, too

6. whether it is during the summer or the winter ~~is when it occurs~~

      using the Internet
7. playing video games, ~~the Internet is used~~, and watching DVDs

8. across the street and ~~she went~~ up the stairs

   knowing
9. ~~to know~~ the answer but being afraid to volunteer in class

               who made
10. both the person ~~making~~ the complaint and the person who was accused

CHALLENGE 28.2   Analyzing Parallelism in Literature

1. Read the following excerpt, which makes great use of parallelism, from John Steinbeck's *The Grapes of Wrath*. This powerful epic novel details the struggle of the Joads, a family who traveled west during the Great Depression in a vain search for work, security, and dignity. In this passage, Steinbeck describes one source of anguish for starving families like the Joads. They were forced to stand idly by while agribusinesses bent on controlling prices destroyed surplus food.

   The people come with nets to fish for potatoes in the river, and the guards hold them back; they come in rattling cars to get the dumped oranges, but the kerosene is sprayed. And they stand still and watch the potatoes float by, listen to the screaming pigs being killed in a ditch and covered with quick-lime, watch the mountains of oranges slop down to a putrefying ooze; and in the eyes of the people there is failure; and in the eyes of the hungry there is a growing wrath. In the souls of the people the grapes of wrath are filling and growing heavy, growing heavy for the vintage.

2. Working with a partner, identify and underline the parallel elements you find in this passage.

3. Discuss ways in which the parallel structure helps you understand the point Steinbeck is making.

CHAPTER QUICK CHECK   Maintaining Parallelism

CW 28.11
More
practice
identifying
parallel
structure

Check the sentences in the following passage for the types of errors in parallelism described in this chapter. Cross out each incorrect form, and write any correction in the space above it. In some cases, more than one correct answer is possible. If a sentence is correct as written, write *OK* above it. Use the example as a guide.

EXAMPLE   The homeless woman who won the $20 million Big Game Lottery has been interviewed by newspaper reporters, radio personalities, and ~~she has been seen talking to~~ all the major national television news anchors.

(1) Some engineers are beginning to experiment with a surprising material for building new structures and ~~to renovate~~ ^{renovating} old ones: cardboard. (2) Of course, cardboard has been around for a long time, but until recently almost everyone thought it wouldn't be any good as a primary structural component in houses and ~~to be used in~~ other buildings. (3) They think of how easy it is to tear up a cardboard gift box or ~~poking~~ ^{(to) poke} a hole in a cardboard shipping container, and they rule out other uses for this product. (4) As they see it, cardboard is too weak, flimsy, and ~~it is~~ insubstantial to be used for serious building projects. (5) But structural engineers have discovered that when it is properly prepared and treated, cardboard can be both durable and ~~it is also~~ surprisingly strong. (6) ^{OK} Cardboard is, after all, made from recycled paper, which means that it is actually composed of processed wood. (7) When it has been tightly compressed, coated with water-resistant chemicals, and ~~it has been~~ manufactured for different lengths and widths, cardboard has proven to be both strong and resilient. (8) In fact, some structural engineers in England demonstrated the strength of cardboard by designing and ~~they built~~ ^{building} a cardboard bridge that they then drove a car across. (9) In addition, engineers recently constructed a school building that, except for the concrete foundation, ~~they used~~ glass windows, and roof framing, is largely made of treated cardboard. (10) The school building stands as proof that whether the cardboard is a small gift box or a large shipping container ~~is made from cardboard~~, it may have another life that most of us have never considered.

QUICK STUDY | **Student Example**

This chapter deals with similarities and differences in related elements. Consider the following paragraph on a related subject, how family life today differs from life years ago:

Family life today differs greatly from family life forty or fifty years ago in terms of size, family make-up, and how the family spends time together. Forty or fifty years ago, families seemed larger, many times having three or more children. Sometimes other relatives like grandparents, there were cousins, too, or aunts and uncles lived in the same household. Today, households seem smaller. Extended family members generally live on their own, either in their own homes or they live in apartments or assisted living centers. Most families today also have fewer children. In my neighborhood, for example, most of the families have two or three children, and in my high school class only two kids had more than two siblings. Another difference is that forty or fifty years ago, many families had two parents living in the same house, and usually only one of those parents worked outside the home. Today, single-parent families are more common, and in families with two parents living is the same home, both often have jobs. Forty or fifty years ago, families used to spend their time together differently, too. If they had a television, it was probably one set that the entire household had to share, which often meant they watched shows together. Today, many families have two or more televisions, often with full cable, so different family members can watch television without spending time together or to be in the same room with each other. If they also have computer game systems and Internet access, family members spend time using this technology rather than interacting with each other. I am happy I am living in today's modern world, but I also have to admit that today's families don't enjoy the same degree of togetherness that families forty or fifty years ago did.

First complete the following activities in response to this paragraph:

1. Four of the sentences in this paragraph are highlighted. Evaluate these sentences for errors in parallelism, using the material in this chapter to guide you. Circle the errors and then, on a separate sheet of paper, rewrite the sentences correctly.

2. The organizing strategy of comparison and contrast plays a significant role in this paragraph. (See pages 128–137 for more on comparison and contrast.) On the lines that follow, briefly explain how using comparison and contrast makes the subject easier for the reader to understand.

   This organizing strategy makes it easier for the reader to understand because the

   arrangement presents examples of the past head-to-head with examples from the

   present.

   _____

   _____

3. What do you think of the way the examples are arranged in this paragraph? Do you agree with the current order, or would you suggest rearranging them? Use the following lines to identify your standpoint and your reasoning.

   Answers will vary. Many students will agree with the order as it is, arguing that a

   movement from the size of families to the make-up of families to the way that families

   spend time holds the reader's interest. Others, however, will feel that how families

   spend time together is less significant than family size or make-up and should

   therefore be presented in a less emphatic place in the paragraph.

Now explore the topic in writing. As the paragraph above does, you could concentrate on some issue associated with family relations or family life. You might also focus on one of these topics related to the subject matter of this chapter:

- what you think (or *know* from experience) it is like to be a twin or triplet
- a group you know or are part of that is like a family
- the person in your family that you most resemble in terms of personality, physical appearance, and so on
- a time you heard something—a rumor about a friend, an offer for a product, and so one—that just didn't sound right

COLLABORATION

1. Exchange your draft with a classmate. Evaluate the paragraph you receive. If you discover any problem spots, especially with parallelism, circle the errors and then return the paper to the writer.

2. Consider the comments and corrections your reader has made and create a final draft of your paragraph.

SUMMARY EXERCISE Maintaining Parallelism

Check the sentences in the following passage for the types of errors in parallelism described in this chapter. Cross out each incorrect form, and write your correction in the space above. In some cases, more than one correct answer is possible. If a sentence is correct as written, write *OK* above it. Answers may vary.

OK

(1) Alcohol abuse is one of the most misunderstood problems in the world. (2) Even though researchers have shown that alcoholism is a disease,

laziness

many people still think that it's a sign of a defect, weakness, or ~~the person is lazy~~. (3) As a result, many individuals suffering from this disease are more

to seek

likely to hide the problem than ~~seeking~~ treatment.

(4) In the United States, drinking is treated as sexy, glamorous, and ~~you can look~~ macho. (5) For example, television commercials for alcohol show beautiful bars filled with attractive models, sports stars, or ~~some are~~ celebri-

OK

ties, all having fun. (6) People are encouraged to think that they can be like those glamorous, famous people if they drink.

(7) However, for many, drinking is neither glamorous nor ~~it is not~~ special; instead, their genetic makeup means that drinking is as dangerous for them as

playing

~~to play~~ Russian roulette. (8) Without even being aware of it, they become de-

they change   OK

pendent on alcohol, and their patterns of living ~~can change, too~~. (9) As time

^   ^

passes, they need to drink more and more alcohol to function. (10) Without al-

minds

cohol, both their bodies and their ~~mental state of being~~ go through excruciat-ing symptoms of withdrawal.

OK

(11) Alcoholism is a disease of denial, and many individuals suffering from it are unable to admit they have a problem. (12) In some cases, they lose their families, their jobs, their friends, and their self-respect ~~is gone~~ before they finally

admit that they are addicted. (13) Unfortunately, some alcoholics choose to die

rather than ~~acknowledging~~ that they have a problem. *to acknowledge*

OK

(14) Those who do accept that they are addicted can begin recovery with a

treatment program. (15) They can go into a detoxification center, ~~they might go~~

~~to~~ a public treatment center, or a private substance abuse clinic. (16) With pro-

fessional care, they undergo withdrawal from alcohol and also ~~receiving~~ coun- *receive*

seling to understand why they feel the need to drink. (17) For recovering alco-

holics, Alcoholics Anonymous provides a support group; they can draw

strength from others who have admitted they are alcoholics, are taking steps to

overcome their addiction, and ~~put~~ their lives back together. *are putting*

(18) Most of us think of addiction as a problem with drugs such as co-

caine, heroin, or amphetamines ~~are making a comeback~~. (19) However, the

^

most common addicts do not stick needles in their arms or ~~are swallowing~~

in their mouths

pills; they abuse alcohol. (20) If more of us were aware that alcohol abuse af-

^   *sex,*

fects people without regard for age, race, ~~people of both sexes~~, or religion,

then perhaps fewer would start down that road to alcohol addiction.

FOR FURTHER EXPLORATION

1. Consider one of the following topics:

   - what the expression *The American Dream* means to you
   - the greatest invention of all time
   - something about you that most people would find surprising
   - the different types of people you see at a sporting event or concert
   - the worst kind of dishonesty

   Prewrite on the subject, using one of the strategies you practiced in Chapter 2, and work your way through the rest of the writing process. Then complete a draft essay of at least 500 words on this subject.

2. Exchange your draft with a classmate. Check the draft you receive for weaknesses, checking in particular for any errors in parallelism. Circle any errors, using the material in this chapter as a guide, and then return the draft to the writer.

3. Revise your essay, correcting any errors in verb use or other problems discovered by your reader.

RECAP Parallelism: Presenting Related Items in a Similar Form

New terms in this chapter	Definition
parallelism	a way of creating structural balance in writing by expressing similar or related ideas in similar form

Individual words that are connected by a conjunction should be parallel.

> **EXAMPLE**   That car is *old* and *rusty*.

Phrases that are connected by a conjunction should be parallel.

> **EXAMPLE**   She looked *in the closet* and *under the bed.*

Words that follow pairs of correlative conjunctions should be parallel.

> **EXAMPLE**   *Neither* the police *nor* the insurance adjuster could identify the cause of the accident.

correlative conjunction	conjunctions used in pairs (like *both/and* and *either/or*) to connect items

Parallelism means balancing words.

pens	pencils

and, or

Parallelism means balancing phrases.

a package of pens was purchasing pens to use a pen	a box of pencils was selling pencils to break a pencil

and, or

Parallelism means balancing items with connecting pairs.

neither sleet **either** signal agreement **both** newer **not only** attractive **whether** in the house	**nor** hail **or** indicate disagreement **and** shinier **but also** intelligent **or** at the park

GOING FORWARD

Q: How can I be sure to present related ideas in a form that will sound right, *be* right, and flow in the best way for my reader?

A: Maintaining correct parallelism is actually simpler than it may seem at first glance. The key is to focus on conjunctions because they are the words that form connections. Check any items connected by conjunctions, especially by *and, or,* and *but,* and then use the first item in the series as a pattern for the others.

CHAPTER 29
Spelling: Focusing on Correctness

Navigating This Chapter

In this chapter, you will learn how to:

- spell plural forms correctly
- add prefixes and suffixes
- decide whether to double the final consonant of a word before adding *-ing* or *-ed*
- spell words with *ie* or *ei* combinations
- choose correctly among *-sede, -ceed,* and *-cede,* and other endings that sound alike
- deal with commonly confused words
- master the most commonly misspelled words

GETTING STARTED ...

CW 29.1 Chapter basics

Q: No matter how hard I try to learn the rules, I still seem to have trouble with spelling. Why is the spelling of English so hard to master?

A: Mastering the spelling of American English is difficult for a number of reasons, many related to the history of the language. English has been drawn from a number of other languages, so exceptions to the spelling rules are common. It's these exceptions to the rules—not the rules themselves—that give people the most difficulty.

Overview: Understanding the Importance of Correct Spelling

ESL Note
See "Spelling" on page 598.

CW 29.2 Overview of correct spelling

CW 29.3 Fixing spelling errors

Any experienced writer will tell you the same thing: spelling *always* counts. For one thing, errors in spelling are often the most obvious flaws in writing, especially if the reader is someone who finds spelling easy. Make no mistake about it—some people simply don't have much difficulty with spelling, so for them spelling errors almost jump off the page. For others, however, the story is quite different. These people find spelling words correctly or noticing misspellings to be an enormous and frustrating task.

There are valid reasons why they do. For example, not all English words are spelled as they sound. Other words with different meanings sound the same. Some words conform to spelling rules, while others deviate from them. But as complicated as it is, those who find spelling difficult shouldn't expect much sympathy. Readers *always* expect correct spelling, and any misspelled words can spoil the effect of an otherwise excellent paper.

The good news is that a number of techniques can help you become a better speller. Besides learning basic spelling rules, you can review commonly confused words and maintain a personal dictionary of words that you have trouble spelling.

Basic Rules for Forming Plurals

CW 29.4
Recognizing
spelling
problems

As Chapter 25, "Nouns: Working Effectively with Words That Name," illustrated, the most basic rule for forming plurals is to add *-s* to the singular forms:

book   book**s**   computer   computer**s**   banana   banana**s**

However, there are numerous exceptions to this basic rule, as the following guidelines show.

Nouns that end in *-ch, -sh, -x,* and *-s*   For nouns that end in *-ch, -sh, -x,* and *-s,* form the plural by adding an *-es:*

porch   porch**es**   fox   fox**es**   lash   lash**es**

CW 29.5
Common
words that
sound alike

Nouns that end in *-y*   The plural for most nouns ending in *-y* depends on the letter preceding the *-y.* If that letter is a vowel (*a, e, i, o, u*), simply add *-s:*

delay   delay**s**   key   key**s**   tray   tray**s**

If the letter before the *-y* is a consonant, change the *-y* to *-i* and add *-es:*

worry   worr**ies**   duty   dut**ies**   sky   sk**ies**

Nouns that end in *-o*   For nouns that end in *-o,* look at the preceding letter to decide whether to add *-s* or *-es.* If the letter preceding the final *-o* is a *vowel,* simply add *-s:*

radio   radio**s**   stereo   stereo**s**   trio   trio**s**

If the letter before the *-o* is a *consonant,* you usually add an *-es:*

potato   potato**es**   echo   echo**es**   veto   veto**es**

Exceptions   Nouns referring to music, such as *altos, falsettos, solos,* and *sopranos,* do not obey this rule. In addition, with a few nouns ending in *-o* preceded by a consonant, you may add either *-s* or *-es:*

cargo   cargo**s** *or* cargo**es**   motto   motto**s** *or* motto**es**
zero   zero**s** *or* zero**es**

Words that end in *-f* or *-fe*   Learn which plurals end in *-fs* or *-fes* and which ones must change to *-ves.* Some nouns that end in *-f* or *-fe* form plurals with a simple *-s:*

safe   safe**s**   belief   belief**s**   chief   chief**s**

For others, however, you must change the *-f* to *-ves:*

thief   thie**ves**   knife   kni**ves**   wife   wi**ves**

For some nouns, two forms are acceptable:

scarf   scarf**s** *or* scar**ves**   hoof   hoof**s** *or* hoo**ves**
dwarf   dwarf**s** *or* dwar**ves**

If you are in doubt about how to form the plural for one of these words, use a dictionary to find the proper spelling.

**CW 29.6
Understanding
word
division
problems**

Nouns with Latin endings   Make nouns with Latin endings plural in keeping with the original language:

alumnus   alumn**i**   crisis   cris**es**

For some of these nouns, however, it is also acceptable to add *-s* or *-es* to form the plural:

appendix   appendi**xes** *or* append**ices**

memorandum   memorand**a** *or* memorand**ums**

index   inde**xes** *or* indi**ces**

Hyphenated or combined nouns   For hyphenated and combined nouns, form the plural by adding *-s* to the main word:

sister**s**-in-law   leftover**s**   attorney**s** general

**CW 29.7
Understanding
abbreviations**

Irregular plurals   With some common words, form the plural by *changing letters within the word or adding letters to the end:*

man   m**en**   foot   f**ee**t   louse   l**i**ce   child   child**ren**

Nouns with the same singular and plural forms   A few common words have the same form whether they are singular or plural:

one deer   several deer   one sheep   many sheep
one species   five species

**CW 29.8
Using
numbers in
writing**

Nonword plurals and words discussed as words   For abbreviations, figures, numbers, letters, words discussed as words, and acronyms, form the plural by adding either an *-s* or *-'s* (apostrophe + *-s*). Use the *-'s* with all lowercase letters, with the capital letters *A, I, U,* or any other time when adding the *-s* alone might confuse the reader:

one A   four A**'s**   one i   several i**'s**   one the   many the**'s**

COMPREHENSION AND PRACTICE

Identifying the Correct Plural Form of Words

29.1 In each blank, write the plural form of the word in parentheses, as the example shows. Use the guidelines above for help.

EXAMPLE | Oak (leaf) _____*leaves*_____ remain on the trees through the fall and into the winter.

(1) We love to ride our bikes along the bike (path) _____paths_____ that run alongside the (highway) _____highways_____ in surrounding (county) _____counties_____. (2) We all wake up very early, pack our (lunch) _____lunches_____ and (bottle) _____bottles_____ of water, and hit the trail. (3) After a few miles, we are in the countryside where (farm) _____farms_____ line the (roadside) _____roadsides_____. (4) All the (quality) _____qualities_____ of these calm places begin to work their magic, draining away (stress) _____stresses_____ that have built up all week. (5) We love the leisurely way that (field) _____fields_____, rustic barns with weather-beaten exteriors, household gardens with their rows of staked-up (tomato) _____tomatoes_____, and little rural (church) _____churches_____ rise up to meet us and then slip past. (6) We often spot (deer) _____deer_____, (fox) _____foxes_____, (rabbit) _____rabbits_____, and assorted other wildlife. (7) Occasionally, wild (turkey) _____turkeys_____ break from the long grass beside the path and fly helter-skelter into the dazzling sunlight. (8) In the distance, the (roof) _____roofs_____ of townhouses and office buildings glint. (9) This kind of peace, far from office (memorandum) _____memoranda/memorandum_____, and all the (stimulus) _____stimuli_____ that add stress to our lives, is good for the soul. (10) We return home in the evening tired but happy and ready to face our (responsibility) _____responsibilities_____.

COMPREHENSION AND PRACTICE

29.2

CW 29.9
Spelling
plurals

Providing the Correct Plural Form of Words

Following the guidelines on pages 480–481, provide the plural of each italicized word in the following passage. Cross out the singular form, and write the plural above it, as the example shows.

EXAMPLE

The ~~hero~~ *heroes* were two ~~man~~ *men* who tackled the purse snatcher.

(1) Winter seems to bring with it a variety of *illness* (illnesses), and this past winter was one of the worst *season* (seasons) in a long time for *family* (families) with young *child* (children). (2) I am a single parent of two *son* (sons), both under five *year* (years) old and both with *allergy* (allergies). (3) Last month, both *boy* (boys) had *bout* (bouts) with *cold* (colds) or *infection* (infections). (4) It was hard for me to see my two *baby* (babies) suffer. (5) There were many *night* (nights) when I was still counting *sheep* (sheep) at 2 or 3 A.M. (6) One morning, after staying up with them most of the night, I awoke with *pain* (pains) in my chest. (7) It felt as though ten *knife* (knives) were cutting into my *lung* (lungs). (8) "Why us?" I thought. "How many *crisis* (crises) do we have to endure?" (9) Finally, I called one of my *sister-in-law* (sisters-in-law) and asked her to take me to the clinic. (10) The doctor diagnosed double pneumonia, which kept me out of *class* (classes) for two *week* (weeks). (11) I've never been one to fantasize about *superhero* (superheroes), but there were certainly *time* (times) last winter when I dreamed of being rescued.

CHALLENGE 29.1   Working with Plural Nouns

1. On a separate sheet of paper, choose five of the following singular nouns and make them plural. Then write a present tense sentence for each, as this example shows:

EXAMPLE

leaf
The **leaves** begin to fall during late September.

attorney-at-law	deer
play	birch
echo	wife
analysis	duty
glass	handkerchief

Words	Definitions	Examples
its	possessive form of *it*	The kitten kept dunking *its* nose in the milk.
it's	contraction for *it is* and *it has*	*It's* funny to see the kitten with a milk mask.
knew	understood [past tense]	The senator *knew* her constituents well.
new	recent, unused, fresh	She felt that it was time for someone *new* to take a turn.
know	to understand [present tense]	You *know* what the problem is.
no	negative, the opposite of *yes*	The problem is that we get *no* direction from Jerry.
now	at this point	The question *now* is what are we going to do about it?
lay	to put down, spread out	Once you *lay* the chair on its side, disconnect the arms.
lie	to rest or recline	Then *lie* down on the floor and find the seam running up the back of the chair.
lead	to go first, direct [present tense]	Parents should always *lead* their children by example.
	soft metal; graphite [rhymes with *bed*]	The responsibilities of parenthood sometimes feel like a *lead* weight.
led	went first, directed [past tense]	When they are grown, you'll be glad you *led* them well.
loose	not tight, unfastened	*Loose* clothing is better for exercise.
lose	to misplace, fail, not win	If you *lose* the game, don't *lose* your sense of humor.
of	stemming from, connected with or to	Peter is fond *of* late night TV.
off	away from, no longer on	On his day *off,* he sleeps late.
passed	went by [past tense of *pass*]	An ambulance suddenly appeared and *passed* us.
past	time gone by, former time	From *past* experience, I knew that it was heading to Parklane Hospital.
personal	individual, private	The shoplifter had a history of *personal* problems.
personnel	employees, staff	When the security *personnel* took her to the manager's office, she began cursing and kicking.

Words	Definitions	Examples
precede	to come before	One goal of this intervention program is to identify what *precedes* an incident of child abuse.
proceed	to go on	After they study the causes, they *proceed* through the formal process of filing an official complaint.
principal	(*noun*) the head of a school;	In high school, Giselle wanted to get back at the *principal* by ordering ten pizzas in his name.
	(*adjective*) primary, chief	My *principal* objection to this plan was that it was dishonest.
principle	a rule of conduct; a basic truth	One of my *principles* is to be honest.
quiet	still; silent	After Ioanie finished yelling, the room was completely *quiet*.
quite	very; completely	Her friends were *quite* surprised that their party had disturbed her.
than	conjunction, used in comparisons	From a distance, people think John is older *than* his older brother Billy.
then	next, at that time	*Then* they take a closer look and see that Billy has wrinkles and gray hair.
their	the possessive form of *they*	The reporters were ordered to reveal the names of *their* sources to the judge.
there	refers to direction or location	Immediately, the lawyers who were *there* objected.
they're	contraction for *they are*	The reporters will be going to jail because *they're* not going to follow the judge's orders.
threw	tossed, hurled [past tense]	The supervisor accidentally *threw* out the envelope containing the day's receipts for the store.
through	in one side and out the other, from beginning to end	We had to go *through* twenty bags of trash before we found the envelope.
to	in the direction of, toward	Susan and Lai stopped at a gas station for directions *to* the hotel.
	also used to form an infinitive	They needed *to* fill the tank anyway.
too	also, excessively	They bought some snacks for the evening, *too*.
two	more than one, less than three	They had stopped just *two* blocks away from the hotel. *(continued)*

Words	Definitions	Examples
waist	middle part of the body	He constantly worries that his *waist* is getting bigger.
waste	use up needlessly; leftover material	If he'd eat less junk food, he wouldn't *waste* so much time worrying.
weak	not strong, feeble	No matter how much I study, my memory still seems *weak*.
week	seven days	Even after a *week* of study, I still don't know those math theorems.
weather	atmospheric conditions	The *weather* has been unusually mild.
whether	indicating an alternative or question	Scientists are now trying to determine *whether* these warmer temperatures are due to global warming.
were	past tense plural of *are*	My mother and I *were* hoping to drive to Washington, D.C., in April.
we're	contraction for *we are* or *we were*	*We're* going to go in September instead.
where	indicates or raises a question about direction or location	The neighborhood *where* my uncle lives is near the National Zoo.
who	used as a subject	It took us several minutes to discover *who* had started the fight on the floor.
whom	used as an object	Once we cleared the room, we decided which shoes belonged to *whom*.
who's	contraction for *who is* or *who has*	I'm not sure *who's* supposed to drive.
whose	possessive form of *who*	I don't know *whose* car we will use, either.
your	possessive form of *you*	Sometimes knowing all the rules governing *your* job is not enough.
you're	contraction for *you are*	Once *you're* on the job by yourself, rules don't help much.

COMPREHENSION AND PRACTICE 29.7

Identifying the Correct Word from Pairs of Commonly Confused Words

In each sentence in the following passage, circle the correct word from the pair in parentheses. Use the example to guide you.

EXAMPLE   A job can have a profound (affect, (effect)) on your whole life.

(1) If I had to (choose, chose) the strangest experience in my (passed, past), it would be the summer I worked third shift at the aluminum barrel factory. (2) When the interviewer asked me if I was willing to work from 11 P.M. (to, too) 7 A.M., I thought it was a great idea. (3) I figured I could (lead, led) a beachcomber's life by day and (than, then) go nightclubbing with my friends before my shift started. (4) My brother tried to tell me that the job would be (know, no) picnic, but I ignored him and took it. (5) After the first two days, I realized that I had planned on everything (accept, except) sleep. (6) Instead of going to the beach when I came home from work, I'd wash up and (than, then) crawl into bed. (7) I always had a tough time drifting (of, off) to sleep because there was no (quiet, quite) around my house during the day. (8) I could (hear, here) every laugh and conversation and was aware of the beautiful summer (weather, whether) slipping by. (9) (Their, There) were few days when I could wake up in time to go to the beach. (10) My (principal, principle) goal became making it through each week. (11) (Its, It's) no exaggeration to say that was the worst summer I ever suffered (threw, through).

COMPREHENSION AND PRACTICE

Identifying Errors with Commonly Confused Words

29.8 Each sentence in the following paragraph contains an error with one of the words from the list of commonly confused words. Cross out the incorrect words and write the correct ones above them, as the example shows.

EXAMPLE

principal
His ~~principle~~ objection to the job offer was that it involved a two-hour-a-day commute.

(1) I suffered my first serious injury a month ago when I stepped in a
hole
~~whole~~ in the sidewalk. (2) From the moment my right foot touched the edge of
knew
the broken sidewalk, I somehow ~~new~~ I was about to hurt myself. (3) I even
already
tried to shift the weight from that foot, but unfortunately I was ~~all ready~~ in the

middle of my stride. (4) As I came down on the side of my foot with all my

weight, I could almost ~~here~~ *hear* the tissue tearing. (5) The pain was overpowering,

and I had to sit down in order to remain ~~conscience~~ *conscious*. (6) ~~Than~~ *Then* I took a look at

my ankle and became sick to my stomach. (7) It was swollen to at least three

times ~~it's~~ *its* normal size. (8) In addition, my entire right leg felt as heavy as a bar

of ~~led~~ *lead*. (9) Fortunately, ~~their~~ *there* was a pay phone about five steps away, so I called

my brother for a ride to the hospital. (10) The doctor said it is generally better

to ~~brake~~ *break* an ankle than to tear several ligaments as I had.

CHALLENGE 29.2 Using Commonly Confused Words Correctly

1. The sentences in Comprehension and Practice 29.8 contain ten incorrectly used words. Take each of these incorrectly used words and write a sentence in which you use the word correctly.

COLLABORATION

2. Exchange the sentences you have written with a writing partner. In the sentences you receive, make sure that the words are now used correctly. Note any problem spots and return the sentences to the writer.

FAST FACT   Dyslexia is a condition that causes those affected to see some letters reversed, making reading and writing difficult. This disorder is less common among those speaking languages such as Italian, which look like they sound, than those speaking English, which so often doesn't sound like it looks.

Learning the Most Commonly Misspelled Words

**CW 29.15
The most
commonly
misspelled
words**

In addition to remembering the various spelling rules and their exceptions, you should also keep your own personal spelling dictionary. Make a list, *in alphabetical order,* of words you misspell in your day-to-day writing. Keep this list with your dictionary for handy reference when you write.

A computer file is the best place to maintain your list. You can easily insert new words in alphabetical order and print out a new copy. If you hand write your list, leave two or three lines between words. When you discover a misspelled word in one of your papers, add it on an extra line.

Look through the list of commonly misspelled words that follow and mark the ones that you misspell. Include these words in your personal spelling dictionary.

Commonly Misspelled Words

A

absence	acquired	all right	answer	assented
academic	acre	although	Antarctic	association
acceptance	across	aluminum	anxious	athlete
accident	actual	always	apologize	attacked
accidentally	actually	amateur	apparatus	attempt
accommodate	address	among	apparent	attendance
accompany	administration	amount	appreciate	attorney
accomplish	advertise	analysis	approach	authority
accumulate	again	analyze	approval	auxiliary
accurate	agreeable	angel	argument	available
accustom	aisle	angle	arrival	awful
ache	alcohol	angry	article	awkward
achieve	a lot	anonymous	ascended	
acquaintance				

B

bachelor	bathe	believe	boundaries	bureau
balance	beautiful	benefit	breath	bury
bargain	because	biscuits	breathe	business
basically	beginning	bookkeeping	brilliant	
bath	belief	bottom	Britain	

C

cafeteria	cereal	cocoa	committee	cooperate
calendar	certain	collect	company	cooperation
campaign	change	colonel	comparative	corporation
cannot	characteristic	color	competent	correspondence
careful	cheap	colossal	competitive	courteous
careless	chief	column	conceivable	courtesy
catastrophe	children	comedy	condition	criticize
category	church	comfortable	consistent	curriculum
ceiling	cigarette	commitment	continuous	
cemetery	circuit	committed	convenience	

D

daily	definitely	diameter	discuss	dominate
daughter	definition	diary	disease	doubt
dealt	dependent	different	disgust	dozen
debt	describe	direction	distance	drowned
deceased	description	disappointment	distinction	duplicate
decision	despair	disastrous	distinguish	
defense	despise	discipline	dominant	

(continued)

E

earliest	emergency	environment	essential	exhausted
efficiency	emphasis	equip	exaggerated	existence
efficient	emphasize	equipment	excellent	experience
eligible	employee	equipped	excessive	extraordinary
embarrass	envelop	especially	excitable	extremely
embarrassment	envelope			

F

fallacy	February	fiery	fourth	fulfill
familiar	feminine	foreign	freight	further
fascinate	fictitious	forty	frequent	futile
fatigue				

G

garden	genuine	gracious	guarantee	guest
gauge	ghost	grammar	guardian	guidance
general	government	grateful	guess	gymnasium
generally				

H

handicapped	height	humor	hygiene	hypocrite
handkerchief	hoping	humorous	hypocrisy	

I

illiterate	incidentally	inevitable	intelligence	irresistible
imaginative	incredible	infinite	interest	irreverent
immediately	independent	inquiry	interfere	island
immigrant	indictment	instead	interpret	isle
important				

J

jealousy	jewelry	judgment

K

kitchen	knowledge	knuckles

L

language	leave	lengthen	library	literature
later	legitimate	lesson	license	livelihood
latter	leisure	letter	lieutenant	lounge
laugh	length	liable	lightning	luxury

M

machinery	marriage	mathematics	medicine	miniature
maintain	marry	measure	medieval	minimum
maintenance	marvelous	mechanical	merchandise	minute

(continued)

M *(continued)*

miscellaneous	missile	moderate	mortgage	mustache
mischief	misspell	month	mountain	mutual
mischievous	mistake	morning	muscle	mysterious

N

naturally	necessity	nickel	noticeable	nuisance
necessary	negotiate	niece		

O

obedience	occurrence	omit	opportunity	organization
obstacle	official	opinion	oppose	original
occasion	often	opponent	optimism	ought
occurred				

P

pamphlet	perceive	phase	practically	probably
parallel	percentage	phenomenon	precisely	procedure
paralyze	perform	physical	preferred	professor
parentheses	performance	physician	prejudice	protein
participant	permanent	picnic	preparation	psychology
particularly	permitted	piece	presence	publicity
pastime	perseverance	pleasant	pressure	pursuing
patience	personality	politics	primitive	pursuit
peasant	perspiration	possess	priority	
peculiar	persuade	possibility	privilege	

Q

qualified	quantity	quarter	question	questionnaire
quality				

R

readily	recognize	relevant	renewal	resistance
realize	recommendation	relieve	repeat	responsibility
really	reference	remember	repetition	restaurant
reasonably	referring	remembrance	requirement	rhythm
receipt	regretting	reminisce	reservoir	ridiculous
receive	reign	removal	residence	
recipient				

S

salary	sensible	sophisticated	stature	stretch
sandwich	separate	sophomore	statute	subsidize
scenery	sergeant	souvenir	stomach	substantial
schedule	severely	specimen	straight	substitute
scissors	similar	statistics	strategy	subtle
secretary	solemn	statue	strength	sufficient

(continued)

S *(continued)*

summarize	surprise	surprising	susceptible	suspicion
superior				

T

technique	thorough	tournament	transferring	tremendous
temperament	thoroughly	tragedy	travel	truly
temperature	through	traitor	traveled	Tuesday
tendency	tomorrow	transfer	treasure	typical
theory	tongue			

U

unanimous	urgent	useful	utensil

V

vacancy	valuable	vein	villain	visibility
vacuum	vane	vicinity	violence	visitor
vain	vegetable			

W

warrant	Wednesday	weird	writing	written

Y

yesterday

Z

zealous

COMPREHENSION AND PRACTICE

Identifying and Correcting Commonly Misspelled Words

29.9 Each sentence in the following passage contains a misspelled version of a word from the list of commonly misspelled words. Cross out the misspelled word and write the correct version above the incorrect one as the example shows:

EXAMPLE
    balance
Their bank ~~balence~~ had already dropped below $100.

    (1) Today, it seems as if there's more and more corruption in the
government
~~goverment~~. (2) The newspapers are filled with stories of public officials who

                          judgment
have shown incredible lapses in ~~judgement~~ leading to their arrests. (3) For ex-

ample, a year ago our own mayor was accused of giving a big contract to one

        acquaintances   occasion
of his ~~acquaintances~~. (4) On another ~~occassion~~, a state police officer was caught

selling drugs he had confiscated. (5) Last ~~Wenesday~~ ^{Wednesday}, a high-ranking official in the Defense Department was accused of demanding kickbacks from the companies that supply military hardware. (6) With the ~~posibility~~ ^{possibility} of being caught so strong, you'd think that public officials would not be tempted. (7) Sometimes, you wonder how much ~~inteligence~~ ^{intelligence} these individuals possess. (8) Personally, I'm ~~discusted~~ ^{disgusted} with the whole situation. (9) I think that public officials convicted of a crime against the people they are representing should ~~definately~~ ^{definitely} be imprisoned. (10) It should be a maximum security prison, too, so they have to face the ~~embarasment~~ ^{embarrassment} of being known as common criminals.

CHALLENGE 29.3 Developing a Personal Dictionary and Using It to Correct Spelling in Your Writing

CW 29.17 More practice with identifying misspelled words

Begin your own personal proofreading dictionary by scanning the list of commonly misspelled words on pages 497–500 and highlighting the ones you have trouble with. Make a separate list of just these words, in alphabetical order. Then review two or three assignments that you have recently written in this or other classes. Proofread for spelling errors, following the spelling guidelines in this chapter. Add any misspelled words you find in these writings to your own personal spelling dictionary.

CHAPTER QUICK CHECK Spelling Skills

CW 29.18 The Merriam-Webster Dictionary online

The following passage contains numerous misspelled words. Using the various rules and examples in the chapter to guide you, find and cross out errors. Write the correct version above the incorrect one, as the example shows:

EXAMPLE

The best ~~advise~~ *advice* I've ever heard is to treat everyone the way you want to be treated.

(1) The story of Rubin "Hurricane" Carter is an almost ~~unbeleivable~~ ^{unbelievable} tale of injustice. (2) Carter spent 20 years in a maximum security prison, half of it in solitary confinement, for a triple murder that he hadn't ~~commited~~ ^{committed}. (3) In 1966, this contender for the ~~middlewieght~~ ^{middleweight} boxing crown was arrested and charged with a triple homicide in Paterson, New Jersey. (4) Despite his

unwavering assertion of innocence, Carter was convicted and ~~than~~ [then] sentenced

to three life terms, just narrowly escaping the electric chair. (5) But by the mid-

1970s, the state's two key witnesses against Carter admitted that ~~there~~ [their] testi-

mony was false. (6) This fact, along with the publication of Carter's autobiog-

raphy and the hit song about the case by folk rocker Bob Dylan, enabled the

world to ~~here~~ [hear] about Carter's situation. (7) Finally, after two retrials, a judge in

1988 declared that Carter's original conviction had been based on shoddy

evidence and ~~predjudice~~ [prejudice], and Carter once again tasted freedom. (8) ~~Threw~~ [Through] the

release a few years ago of *Hurricane,* a major motion picture starring Denzel

Washington as Carter, another generation learned the story of this sad inci-

dent in the American justice system. (9) Now in his sixties, Carter works on

the behalf of the wrongfully accused and has ~~travelled~~ [traveled] the country lecturing

on hope and tolerance. (10) Despite his years of false imprisonment, he re-

fuses to give in to anger and bitterness, just as he refused to allow the system

to ~~brake~~ [break] his spirit.

QUICK STUDY | Student Example

This chapter focuses on rules and their exceptions, on matters of correctness and incorrectness. Take a look at the following paragraph that focuses on a related subject, an exception to some rule or guideline:

Nothing is more important to me (then) [than] telling the truth, yet I think there

are times when (its) [it's] (exceptable) [acceptable] to tell someone a lie. For example, if someone

asks what I think about a new hairstyle or outfit, and it doesn't look great,

what's the sense in telling the truth? It's too late to change anything, and my

negative opinion certainly won't help the person feel any better. In this

situation, it's kinder to make a general or neutral statement like, "It's really

different," or, "It's OK," even if it isn't exactly the truth. I also (beleive) [believe] it's

sometimes (alright) [all right] to lie by withholding information, as long as the result is not

embarrassing

dangerous or hurtful to anyone. For instance, if I know an (embarassing) story

acquaintance   friend   quiet

about an (aquaintance), and a (freind) asks me about it, I keep (quite) unless I have

a reason to talk about the incident. Most of the time, the truth is none of

anyone else's business and it would just needlessly damage the other person's

truly

reputation. I (truely) think that honesty is the best policy, but when the truth

could do more harm than good, it shouldn't be the only policy.

First complete the following activities in response to this paragraph:

1. Four sentences in the previous paragraphs are highlighted. Evaluate these sentences for misspelled and incorrectly used words. Circle each error and write the correctly spelled version above it.

2. The second sentence contains a rhetorical question, a question that, as Chapter 14 explains, is designed not to be answered but to provoke discussion or thought. Do you think the same idea would be more effective—or less—if it were phrased in statement form instead? Why? Use the lines below for your answer.

Most students will express the idea that the same idea would be less effective as a

statement, noting that the question implies how obvious it is to the writer that telling

this kind of lie is a better solution than hurting someone's feelings. Some will argue for

the statement form, feeling that some readers might feel the question is an invitation

for the reader to disagree.

3. Asserting, as this paragraph does, that lying is acceptable is a controversial stand. On a separate sheet of paper, assess the supporting examples in the paragraph, explaining whether in your view they offer sufficient support to accept the premise that dishonesty can sometimes be justified and why you feel this way.

Now explore the topic in writing. As the paragraph above does, you could discuss an acceptable reason to ignore a rule or guideline. You might also concentrate on one of these subjects related to the subject matter of this chapter:

- the traffic law you find most difficult to follow
- someone you know who enjoys breaking the rules
- the best way to correct a misunderstanding between friends or family
- the one rule that everyone needs to follow

COLLABORATION

1. Exchange your draft with a classmate. Evaluate the paragraph you receive. If you discover any weaknesses, especially spelling errors or incorrectly used words, circle them and write correctly spelled versions above the incorrect ones. Then return the paper to the writer.

2. Consider the comments and corrections your reader has made and create a final draft of your paragraph.

SUMMARY EXERCISE Spelling Skills

The following passage contains numerous misspelled words. Using the various rules and examples in the chapter to guide you, find and cross out errors. Write the correct version above the incorrect one.

(1) Peer pressure is one of the strongest forces people have to face in their
lives
lifes. (2) Being excepted is important to most people. (3) When people go
accepted

experience
against peer pressure, though, they can find it a very lonely expereince.

misbehave
(4) Many times students missbehave in school because of peer pressure.

noticeable
(5) The influence of this force is particularly noticable in middle and high

school classes. (6) If a group of kids in the hallway is making trouble, for ex-
quiet
ample, quite kids will sometimes join in because they don't want the other

kids to think they are different. (7) By themselves, these quiet kids would
there
never make any fuss, but if their is a group, peer pressure takes over.

generally
(8) Kids generaly have their first experiences with sex, alcohol, or drugs

should've OR should have
because of peer pressure. (9) Even though they know they should of refused,

some young people have been pressured into doing things they weren't ready
using
for. (10) If kids are at a party and someone is drinking or useing drugs, many

kids find it hard to resist trying. (11) They feel that if they don't, the other kids
weird
will think they are wierd or childish.

affects
(12) Peer pressure effects people after high school, too. (13) For example,
where
if people are in class in a college wear hardly anyone asks or answers ques-

tions, they may find themselves acting like their classmates. (14) Most people
friends
don't want to look like a show-off or teacher's pet in front of their freinds. (15)

If most people in a department don't like the boss, the others may hesitate to
volunteer   occurrence
volunter for any extra work. (16) With this kind of occurence, most people will

simply go along with the group because they want to fit in so badly.

(17) Although peer pressure is a strong force, it is one that must be ~~resist-ted~~. (*resisted*) (18) People have to learn to do what is correct for them, even if it means they won't win everyone's ~~approvel~~. (*approval*) (19) When they ~~procede~~ (*proceed*) in this way, they will find that others respect them for who they are. (20) Once people begin behaving in a way that is most authentic for them, they won't ~~waist~~ (*waste*) so much time worrying what others think.

FOR FURTHER EXPLORATION

1. Consider one of the following topics:

   - your first visit to a hospital as a patient or a visitor
   - the appropriateness of vigilante justice
   - an issue or concern with organ donation
   - what in your life causes you to waste the most time
   - a work of literature—a poem, a short story, a novel, a play—that caused you to change your thinking on a subject

   Prewrite on the subject, using one of the strategies you practiced in Chapter 2, and work your way through the rest of the writing process. Then complete a draft essay of at least 500 words on this subject.

2. Exchange your draft with a classmate. Check the draft you receive for problems, in particular errors in spelling. Circle any incorrectly spelled or misused words, using the material in this chapter to guide you, and write the correct form above the incorrect ones. Then return the paper to the writer.

3. Revise your essay, correcting any errors in irregular verb use or other problems discovered by your reader.

RECAP Spelling: Focusing on Correctness

New terms in this chapter	Definitions
prefix	letter or letters added to the beginning of a word that change its meaning: *un-, dis-, semi-, re-, il-*
	Examples **un**able, **il**legible
suffix	letter or letters added to the end of a word that change its meaning: *-ness, -able, -ous, -ly, -er, -ed, -ing*
	Examples sad**ness**, slow**ly**

(continued)

Spelling Guidelines for Adding Prefixes and Suffixes
(Check the dictionary for exceptions to these general guidelines.)

To add a prefix	prefix + word (no spelling change) dis + approve = **dis**approve
To add -ly or -ness	word + -ly or -ness (usually no spelling change) clear + ly = clear**ly**
	Change -y to -i before adding -ly or -ness silly + ness = sill**iness**
To add -ed	Change -y to -i before adding -ed carry + ed = carr**ied**
To add a suffix that begins with a vowel	Drop -e at the end of a word before adding suffix cope + ing = co**ping**

	Double the final consonant if
	• the word has one syllable
	  stop + ed = stop**ped**
	• the final consonant is preceded by a single vowel
	  hot + est = hot**test**
	• the accent is on the last syllable of a word with two or more syllables
	  admit + ing = admit**ting**

To add a suffix that begins with a consonant	Keep -e at the end of a word hope + ful = hope**ful**

GOING FORWARD...

Q: So if I can't rely just on the rules to help me become better at spelling, what can I do to become a better speller?

A: There's no substitute for making yourself familiar with the spelling rules—that's the first step. But to continue to improve as a speller, keep a list of the words that *in particular* give you trouble. Every time you write, use this list to check your draft. Before long, you will find that your spelling is getting better and that you notice errors more easily.

CHAPTER 30
Commas

Navigating This Chapter

In this chapter, you will learn how to use a comma to:

- indicate a pause between two clauses connected by a conjunction
- separate items in a series
- indicate a brief break between introductory material and the main part of the sentence
- set off words, phrases, and clauses that interrupt the flow of a sentence
- set off a direct quotation from the rest of a sentence
- set off elements in certain letter parts, dates, addresses, and numerals
- set off nouns of direct address

GETTING STARTED . . .

CW 30.1 Chapter basics

Q: The mark of punctuation that I feel least confident using is the comma. I'm never really sure if I've used enough or too many of them. Why is working with commas so confusing?

A: If you are concerned about comma use, join the crowd. Even experienced writers have difficulty with—and disagreements about—comma use. One reason that comma use can be confusing is what the mark represents: a pause. When people speak, they pause for a number of reasons—to take a breath, to call attention to a point, to figure out what to say next, and so on. But in writing, not all those pauses would call for commas. If one thought is over, for example, the pause would actually be a *full stop,* which would be a period—or a question mark or exclamation point. And sometimes no mark of pause is needed because no distinct slowing is actually needed or called for.

Overview: Understanding Comma Use

ESL Note
See "Punctuation and Capitalization" on pages 600–601.

CW 30.2 Overview of understanding comma use

With speech, you frequently pause within thoughts to emphasize or clarify some point. With writing, you use the same technique. When you want to signal these pauses within a sentence, the mark of punctuation you will use most often is a **comma.** Your reader depends on these pauses to gain the full meaning of what you've written, so mastering the use of commas is important to your success as a writer.

Using a Comma between Clauses Connected by Conjunctions

CW 30.3
Using a
comma
between
clauses

A comma is used to indicate a pause between clauses connected by a conjunction or a pair of conjunctions.

COMPOUND SENTENCE

coordinating conjunction
The movie was good, *but* the book was better.

COMPOUND SENTENCE

correlative conjunction   correlative conjunction
Either the wind blew the campfire *out, or* the ranger put it out.

COMPLEX SENTENCE

subordinating conjunction
Even though the office was warm, everyone put in a full day's work.

[*Use a comma when the subordinate clause comes first.*]

COMPREHENSION AND PRACTICE

30.1

CW 30.4
Commas
and the
commotions
they cause

Working with Commas and Conjunctions

Add a comma, a conjunction, and another clause to complete the following sentences. Review Chapter 19, "Subordination and Coordination," to remember rules for creating complex and compound sentences and to find lists of subordinating and coordinating conjunctions. Use the example to guide you. Answers will vary. Representative answers are given.

EXAMPLE

When Jerry misplaced his calculator, he had to buy a new one.

1. Many people do not want to serve as jurors, but
   _____

   jury duty is part of every citizen's responsibility.

2. Serving on a jury can disrupt a person's life

   , and it may also cause financial hardship
   _____

3. Although some people give pretty lame excuses,
   _____

   prospective jurors are often able to delay serving for a variety of reasons.

4. Being part of the judicial system is interesting

   , and some people find it an invaluable experience.
   _____

5. The juror's day at court starts at 8:30 A.M.

   , and it may sometimes last until 5:00 P.M.
   _____

6. Before the trial begins,
   _____

   all the jurors are sworn in.

7. Then, the presentations by the lawyers begin

, and the jurors usually listen carefully. _____

8. In my state, most jurors serve for only a day

, but some trials take much longer. _____

9. Jurors may serve for up to a month for trials of capital crimes

, so they may be put up in a hotel. _____

10. Although it is not usually necessary, _____

jurors are sometimes sequestered.

Using Commas to Separate Items in a Series

Commas are used to separate three or more items in a series. When only two items are connected by *and, or,* or *but,* no comma is needed.

WORDS IN SERIES   Jacqueline spends her summer days *swimming, sailing, sunbathing,* or *sleeping.*

PHRASES IN SERIES   *In the fall, in the winter,* and *in the spring,* however, her schoolwork leaves her little time for these activities.

FAST FACT During the 1980s, the style sheet of a major American corporation instructed its workers not to use the comma before *and* or *or* in a series such as "computers, printers and software," which amounted to one fewer keystroke. When asked for a reason, company officials argued that not including this comma would save time.

COMPREHENSION AND PRACTICE   Using Commas in a Series

30.2 Fill in the blanks in the following sentences, supplying the items to complete each series. Place commas where necessary. Use the example as guidance.
Answers will vary. Comma placements are shown.

EXAMPLE   The ____*city*____ and ____*county*____ cooperate on a recycling program that requires people to separate ____*plastic,*____ ____*paper,*____ and ____*glass*____ from the rest of their trash.

(1) I work full-time on the third shift, so my workday begins at 11 P.M., when other people are _____ or _____. (2) The plant where I work makes plastic items such as _____, _____, and _____. (3) The machines I work with generate a great deal of _____ and _____, so I dress lightly and wear ear plugs. (4) In addition to running my machines, I supervise two other workers to make sure they _____ and _____. (5) The factory has a series of small windows near the ceiling, and if I look up from my machine, I can see _____, _____, and _____. (6) After three hours, I take my first break, during which I _____, _____, or _____. (7) When my break is over, I _____ and _____. (8) Before I know it, it's supper time, so I _____, _____, or _____. (9) During the rest of the shift, I have time to complete my paperwork, including _____ and _____. (10) At 7 A.M., I head home to bed while everybody else is _____, _____, or _____.

Using a Comma to Set Off Introductory Material

**CW 30.5
Using a
comma
to set off
introductory
material**

Often the main portion of a sentence is introduced by a word, phrase, or clause that indicates a time, place, or condition. If this introductory material consists of *four or more words* or contains a *verbal,* separate it from the rest of the sentence by a comma. (See page 272 for a discussion of verbals.)

EXAMPLE   *Within the pile of shredded paper,* the mouse nursed three babies.

Yelling and splashing frantically, Courtney drifted away from shore.

Occasionally, you will use a word or brief phrase to introduce a sentence. Use a comma to set off such an introductory element if it helps to emphasize or clarify the main point of the sentence.

EXAMPLE | *In fact,* the substitute teacher had never even been in the school before.

Soon after, the meeting was interrupted by strange noises.

COMPREHENSION AND PRACTICE

Using Commas after Introductory Phrases and Clauses

30.3 If the introductory phrase in each of the sentences in the following paragraph needs a comma, insert it. If a comma appears where it is not necessary, cross it out. Use the example to direct you.

EXAMPLE | At the major intersection near the entrance of the school, an accident was slowing/ down traffic.

(1) After hatching on Florida beaches and crawling off into the surf, tiny loggerhead turtle hatchlings begin a journey that will take them across the Atlantic Ocean and back again. (2) Over/ a period of several years, the baby loggerheads will travel thousands of miles as they swim and ride the warm currents of the Atlantic, feeding and growing. (3) For a number of years, no one has been sure of exactly how they managed to navigate such an enormous trip while avoiding the colder waters that would kill them. (4) However, a recent study suggests that the answer lies in the innate ability of these creatures to react to natural magnetic fields marking a section of the ocean waters. (5) Called the Atlantic Gyre, this area is an oceanwide current of warm water that moves in a clockwise fashion, eastward across the Atlantic, along the coasts of Spain and Africa, and back westward to the east coast of the United States. (6) The turtles/ apparently/ follow a series of magnetic markers that keep them within the warmer waters that they need to survive. (7) For the study/ that led to these findings, loggerhead hatchlings were placed in a specially designed saltwater tank. (8) To simulate particular magnetic fields, researchers equipped the tank with special copper coils. (9) Then/ they outfitted

the turtles with a device that would record the direction that the hatchlings were swimming. (10) As the scientists changed magnetic fields⌃the baby turtles responded by swimming in a direction that would keep them within the safe warm-water zone in the open ocean.

Using Commas to Set off Elements That Interrupt Sentence Flow

CW 30.6 Using commas to set off interruptive elements

Sometimes you use commas within a sentence to surround a word, phrase, or clause that interrupts the flow of the sentence. For instance, when a word adds emphasis, provides transition, or renames or illustrates another word in the sentence, use commas to set it off:

EXAMPLE   Our next car, *however,* ran like a top.

The crow, *for example,* is a highly intelligent bird.

We had skybox seats, *the best in the stadium,* for the game.

Also use commas to set off *nonrestrictive elements,* clauses or phrases that could be left out of the sentence without changing its basic meaning. Nonrestrictive clauses and phrases add extra but nonessential information:

┌────── nonrestrictive clause ──────┐

EXAMPLE   This year's spring weather on Cape Cod, *which is usually calm and warm,* was cool and blustery.

If you were to leave *which is usually calm and warm* out of the sentence, the reader would still understand the main point. The clause is *nonrestrictive.*

Some clauses and phrases are *restrictive,* meaning that your reader needs them to identify or restrict the meaning of the word they modify. Therefore, you don't set them off with commas, as this example shows:

┌────── nonrestrictive clause ──────┐

EXAMPLE   All students *driving vehicles with handicapped plates* may park in the first row of Parking Lot C.

Leave the italicized phrase out of this sentence, and you send the wrong message. Without these words, the sentence says that *all* students may park in a lot that is actually reserved for disabled students only. Therefore, *driving vehicles with handicapped plates* is restrictive, and no commas are used.

COMPREHENSION AND PRACTICE

Using Commas around Elements That Interrupt Sentence Flow

30.4 Read the sentences in the following paragraph. If a comma is needed in a sentence, write it in the blanks provided. If no comma is needed, put an **X** in the blank. Study the example first.

EXAMPLE

My asthma __,__ which usually doesn't cause me much trouble __,__ has been flaring up recently.

(1) Sometimes parents __X__ who are old enough to know better __X__ can go overboard in protecting their children. (2) A newspaper article about two children __,__ which I read in the dentist's office __,__ tells an incredible story about parental overprotection. (3) The mother of a three-year-old daughter __,__ according to the story __,__ obtained a restraining order to keep a three-year-old boy away from her child. (4) She said that her daughter __,__ who attends preschool with the boy __,__ is afraid to play in the park because of the boy's aggression. (5) Why didn't the judge __,__ who should temper justice with common sense __,__ tell the parents to straighten out the difficulties between their children by themselves? (6) I wonder whether that little girl __,__ with a mother like hers __,__ will ever learn to solve problems on her own.

COMPREHENSION AND PRACTICE

Considering Comma Use with Elements That Interrupt Sentence Flow

30.5 In the following sentences, insert commas where you think they are needed to set off words from the rest of the sentence. Put *OK* above any sentence that doesn't require additional commas. Use the example as a guide.

EXAMPLE

Joie began singing lessons with her neighbor, a former professional, only to discover that she really didn't enjoy studying voice.

(1) Although some people believe otherwise, I don't believe that *fate*, a predetermined path that people are forced to follow, controls people's lives. (2) I believe that all people, regardless of their stature in the world, have free will

and are not simply stepping in footsteps that some universal power has placed there for them. (3) Consider, for example, the careers people pursue or the individuals they associate with. (4) As I see it, people make specific choices in terms of what they will do with their lives and who their friends will be. (5) Although their personal skills, abilities, and interests will help to shape their choices, the people themselves, not some universal force, will make the final decision. (6) Rather than being born to become something, people become successful in a field, which could be anything from teaching to computers to medicine, by adapting their gifts and talents to suit it. (7) With personal relationships, especially with the people we marry or live with, destiny plays no role. (8) For example, the idea that everyone has a predetermined soul mate, a person waiting to share another's every idea and dream, just isn't realistic. (9) If fate determines our lives, then that means that horrible tragedies, events that cause enormous pain, happen by design. (10) I know that such terrible things do occur, but I refuse to believe that some all-powerful force, which can see and control everything that happens, would make people endure such sorrow on purpose.

Using Commas to Set Off Direct Quotations

CW 30.7 Using commas to set off direct quotations

As a writer, you will sometimes want to *quote,* to write down word for word what other people say. When you do so, you let your reader know that the words are a *direct quote* by enclosing the passage in quotation marks (" "). (See Chapter 4, "Refining and Polishing Your Draft," for a discussion of the inclusion of direct quotations in a paper.) You then use a comma to set the direct quote off from the *attribution,* the part that identifies the speaker.

Note the placement of the comma in these three formats incorporating a direct quotation.

1. When the quote is at the beginning of a sentence, insert a comma within the closing quotation mark:

EXAMPLE *"My wallet—it's not in my pocketbook,"* Katlyn said, with an edge of panic in her voice.

2. When the quote is at the end of a sentence, place a comma before the opening quotation mark:

EXAMPLE   She said quietly, *"I can't find it anywhere."*

3. When the quote is interrupted in the middle by the attribution, insert a comma within the closing quotation mark of the first portion and a second before the opening quotation mark of the second portion:

EXAMPLE   *"And I'm sure I had it,"* she cried, *"when we left the mall."*

Recognizing Other Situations in Which Commas Are Needed

CW 30.9
Recognizing
comma
problems

In addition to these uses of commas, remember to use a comma

- to set off the salutation of a personal letter (not a business letter): *Dear Monique,*
- to set off the parts of dates from the rest of the sentence: *August 25, 2002,* was a crucial day for my family.
- to set off parts of addresses in a sentence: His last permanent address was *756 Craft Street, Tampa, FL 34268.*
- to indicate thousands within numbers: *9,870* or *9,000,000*
- to set off a name when you address someone directly: I'm telling you, *John,* that you need to save for retirement.

FAST FACT   The comma may be the hardest working of the marks of punctuation, but at least the U.S. Postal Service has tried to give it a little rest. In order to make it easier for their Optical Character Recognition (OCR) system to sort mail, postal officials have suggested that all punctuation be omitted in addresses on envelopes. This step eliminates the comma that customarily appears between city and state. It's actually a good thing that the Postal Service made the request because computer databases create the labeling for much bulk mail, and in some computer language systems, commas have a meaning entirely different from the pause humans intend. These databases use commas as a *delimiter*—a sign that tells the computer to leave a space or start a new document or some other command—making it an addressing no-no.

COMPREHENSION AND PRACTICE   **Using Commas with Quotation Marks**

30.6   In the following paragraph, underline each attribution, and insert commas and quotation marks where needed to separate the attribution from the exact words of the speaker. Use the example as a guide.

EXAMPLE   Then the <u>announcer said</u>"I'm afraid I have some bad news to report."
                                              ^   ^

(1) Things aren't the way they used to be," my Great-Aunt Dot complained the other day. (2) She said, "I don't mean to complain, but you young people don't seem to have done much to make this world a better place. (3) When I was young," she continued, "my generation worked to improve things around us." (4) She stopped for a minute, shook her head, and said, "Maybe I'm not being fair." (5) Aunt Dot then asked me outright, "What do you think of your generation?"

(6) When I could see that her concern was genuine, I smiled at her and answered, "Well, I think my generation is doing all right." (7) I paused for a minute to think and said, "People my age *do* care about the world around them." (8) Aunt Dot seemed unconvinced, so I asked, "What about the park clean-up program, the recycling drive, and the March for Justice, all sponsored by high-school and college students? (9) As she nodded in agreement, I added, "Of course, I think your generation did much more, with your dedication to Civil Rights and work to eliminate poverty." (10) She smiled, and I added, "We will just have to try harder to emulate your generation."

COMPREHENSION AND PRACTICE

Using Commas

30.7 Help this job applicant make a positive impression with this cover letter. Proofread and insert commas where they are needed. If a numbered item needs no commas, write *OK* above it.

325 Whipple Street
East Franklin, MA 02652
December 1, 2006

Ms. Mary Hayes
Director of Human Resources
East Franklin Y.M.C.A.
49 Richmond Street
East Franklin, MA 02650

Dear Ms. Hayes:

(1) I am writing to apply for the part-time position as Assistant to the Director of Youth Services, which you have advertised in the *East Franklin*

Gazette. (2) Having spent the past three summers as a youth counselor in the "Kids at Work" summer job program here in East Franklin͵ I have the experi-ence͵ enthusiasm͵ and qualifications your position requires.

(3) I have just completed my first year at Bristol Community College͵ where I am majoring in criminal justice. (4) After I receive my degree͵ I plan to work full time with young people͵ either through a social agency or the State Police Outreach Center.

(5) As a counselor for "Kids at Work"͵ I was in charge of twenty teenagers between the ages of fourteen and eighteen. (6) In fact͵ this position called for both responsibility and leadership. (7) During my first two summers on the job͵ for example͵ I arranged work schedules͵ supervised work activities͵ and taught a job skills seminar. (8) The seminar was so successful that my director made it a permanent part of the summer program. (9) For the past two summers͵ I've also served as senior counselor͵ which means I was in charge of training all new counselors.

(10) All in all͵ my experiences have prepared me well for the position of Assistant to the Director of Youth Services͵ and I look forward to meeting with you to discuss my qualifications in greater detail. (11) Please schedule me for an interview at your convenience. (12) Thank you.

(13) Sincerely͵

Cosette J. Valjean

Cosette J. Valjean

CHALLENGE 30.1   Analyzing Comma Functions in Literature

CW 30.10 Using commas

COLLABORATION

Read the following passage from Harper Lee's Pulitzer prize-winning novel *To Kill a Mockingbird.* In this passage, narrator Jean Louise Finch discusses the town's Halloween celebration.

Notice the various ways Lee has used commas in the passage. After you have finished reading the paragraph, discuss with a partner what function each of the commas serves. In the first sentence, for instance, the two commas set off a word that interrupts the flow of the sentence.

I soon learned, however, that my services would be required on stage that evening. Mrs. Grace Merriweather had composed an original pageant entitled *Maycomb County: Ad Astra Per Aspera,* and I was to be a ham. She thought it would be adorable if some of the children were costumed to represent the county's agricultural products: . . . Agnes Boone would make a lovely butter-bean, another child would be a peanut, and on down the line, until Mrs. Merriweather's imagination and the supply of children were exhausted.

Our only duties, as far as I could gather from our two rehearsals, were to enter from stage left as Mrs. Merriweather (not only the author, but the narrator) identified us. When she called out, "Pork," that was my cue. Then the assembled company would sing, "Maycomb County, Maycomb County, we will aye be true to thee," as the grand finale, and Mrs. Merriweather would mount the stage with the state flag.

CHAPTER QUICK CHECK Comma Use

CW 30.11 Identifying correct comma usage

Add commas where they are needed in the sentences below. Review the functions of commas to help you as you proofread. Use the example to guide you.

EXAMPLE

The open house at the hospital, sponsored by the new physical therapy center, will begin at 9 A.M. on Saturday, November 24.

(1) If it's true that we tend to overlook the value of things that are right in front of us, then there is no better illustration than our lack of attention to estuaries. (2) An estuary is a partially enclosed wetland area where fresh water from rivers, streams, and other tributaries flows into the ocean, mixing fresh and salt water. (3) Here in the United States, San Francisco Bay, Boston Harbor, Tampa Bay, and Puget Sound are all examples of estuarine areas. (4) No one would argue that estuaries are beautiful areas, noted for appealing to tourists as well as homeowners, but they serve an even more vital role in terms of the environment. (5) As water flows through an estuary, for example, the marsh filters out pollutants and sediments, leaving the fresh and salt water cleaner. (6) In addition, the marsh land and various plants help to soak up and divert flood waters, prevent erosion, and protect property along the shore from damage. (7) Most important of all, estuaries provide the perfect habitat for an

enormous range of sea life, including migratory birds‸aquatic plants, crabs, lobsters‸shellfish, and reptiles. (8) Estuaries are generally protected from tides and ocean waves by sandbars, barrier islands, or reefs‸so they are ideal areas for reproduction. (9) In fact, some 75 percent of the commercial fish catch of the continental United States‸which is worth some $2 billion‸is dependent on estuaries. (10) When this fragile ecosystem is destroyed by filling or dredging‸the results can include such severe consequences as widespread fish kills and unsafe drinking water.

QUICK STUDY   Student Example

CW 30.12
The comma

This chapter concerns matters related to pausing between things, keeping them separate, or setting them off for emphasis. Now consider the following paragraph that concerns an associated topic, the most meaningful quote or proverb you know:

The most meaningful quotation I have ever heard is this one: "A child's life is like a piece of paper on which every passerby leaves a mark." My middle-school English teacher wrote it on the board on the first day of class‸and I have never forgotten it because I think it is so true. Children can be easily influenced by what they hear and see around them. They believe that what adults in positions of authority‸like parents or grandparents‸teachers‸members of the clergy‸and so on do or tell them is correct. For instance‸if children see adults treating each other with respect or hear those adults tell them they are smart‸talented‸and beautiful‸they accept it as true. But when children witness those same adults behaving badly‸mistreating others‸expressing prejudices‸drinking excessively‸or using illegal drugs‸they think that's normal and acceptable‸too. Even worse‸when adults call children stupid‸ugly‸or worthless‸telling them that they will never amount to anything‸children will believe them. If adults just took a moment to consider this proverb‸fewer children would grow up believing terrible things about themselves and others.

First complete the following activities in response to this paragraph:

1. The paragraph above contains no commas. Using the material in this chapter to guide you, insert commas where they are needed.

2. On the lines below, briefly explain how the concluding sentence emphasizes the connection between the topic sentence and the supporting sentences.

The concluding sentence emphasizes the connection between the topic sentence and

the supporting sentences because it reiterates the idea that adults have the power to

influence the thinking of children they come into contact with and so must be careful

about what they say and do.

3. The supporting sentences in this paragraph present positive effects that adults can have on children and then present negative ones. On a separate sheet of paper, evaluate this order. Identify whether you agree with the current arrangement or would suggest presenting the negative effects before the positive ones. In either case, explain your reasoning.

Now explore the topic in writing. As the paragraph above does, you could discuss a saying or proverb and why you think it's important. You might also focus on one of these topics related to the subject matter of this chapter:

- a pause or break you took that you now wish you hadn't
- a public figure who deserves to be set off from others
- a time when you had to deal with the separation from a person or place important to you
- examples of interruptions students typically face as they try to study for a test, complete a project, or finish a paper

COLLABORATION

1. Exchange your draft with a classmate. Evaluate the paragraph you receive. Look for problem spots, especially in comma use. Indicate any point where a comma is needed and cross out any unnecessary commas, and then return the paper to the writer.

2. Consider the comments and corrections your reader has made and create a final draft of your paragraph.

SUMMARY EXERCISE Comma Use

CW 30.13
More
practice
with comma
usage

Add commas where they are needed in the sentences below. Review the functions of commas to help you as you proofread.

(1) From what I have observed, most people spend too much time chasing

after the wrong things in life. (2) The things that are truly valuable, such as good health, love, friendship, family, and spirituality, are right there in front of us. (3) Unfortunately most of us don't see the obvious.

(4) Instead of noticing these marvelous gifts, we tend to concentrate on other aspects of life. (5) Some of us focus on such pursuits as making money, buying fancy cars or clothes, and gaining status. (6) In so many cases, people spend their whole lives driving themselves toward these goals.

(7) However, when they near the end of their lives, people sometimes begin to realize that material possessions are not fulfilling. (8) They've had the fancy cars, for instance, or the beautiful homes. (9) What they discover, though, is that they still feel empty. (10) When they realize how unfulfilled they are, they focus on the truly important things. (11) After years of ignoring their families, for example, they may desperately try to make up for lost time. (12) If they are lucky, they can still rebuild those bridges.

(13) In many cases, however, people don't have enough time left to attend to everything they've ignored. (14) If they haven't maintained their health, for instance, they may be saddled in old age with problems like ulcers, diabetes, heart disease, or cancer. (15) If they had acted earlier, perhaps they could have avoided or at least controlled these conditions. (16) Now, after years of ignoring warning signs, they often must face permanent consequences.

(17) The answer, of course, is to reassess what we value most right now. (18) After all, at the end of life, nobody says, "I wish I had devoted more time to work." (19) The truly important things, the ones on which we should focus, are in front of us at all times. (20) Whenever I hear someone say, "The best things in life are free," I just nod my head and smile.

FOR FURTHER EXPLORATION

CW 30.14
Using
commas

1. Consider one of the following topics:

   - your favorite place from your childhood
   - what personal beauty truly is or should be
   - ways that creativity appears in day-to-day living
   - why some parents behave so badly at youth sporting events
   - a time you witnessed the behavior of or had to deal with a bully

   Prewrite on the subject, using one of the strategies you practiced in Chapter 2, and work your way through the rest of the writing process. Then complete a draft essay of at least 500 words on this subject.

COLLABORATION

2. Exchange your draft with a classmate. Check the draft you receive for weaknesses, especially with the use of commas. Using the material in this chapter as a guide, put a ✓ where a comma is needed and cross out any unnecessary commas. Then return the draft to the writer.

3. Revise your essay, correcting any errors with comma use or other problems discovered by your reader.

RECAP Commas

New term in this chapter	Definition
comma	a punctuation mark that indicates a pause within a sentence

Comma Functions

To indicate a pause between two clauses connected by a conjunction

EXAMPLE   She picked up the pen, but then she put it down again.

To separate items in a series

EXAMPLE   Accounting, marketing, and management are all areas that interest me.

To separate an introductory phrase of four or more words from the rest of the sentence

EXAMPLE   Until the end of the race, I'll keep my fingers crossed.

To set off words, phrases, or clauses that interrupt the flow of a sentence

EXAMPLE   The people in the front of the line, those who had camped out all night on the sidewalk, bought the first tickets.

To set a direct quotation off from the rest of a sentence

EXAMPLE   "This course has been wonderful," said Lee-Ann.

To set off the salutation in a personal letter

    EXAMPLE   Dear Latisha,

To set off parts of dates and addresses and names of direct address

    EXAMPLE   Will you join us, Tim, on July 14, 2006, at Flying Y Ranch, Casper, Wyoming?

To indicate thousands within numbers

    EXAMPLE   6,950 or 1,000,000

GOING FORWARD...

**CW 30.15
Quiz on
comma
usage**

Q: Sometimes when I write, I use too many commas, and other times I don't use enough. How can I make sure I'm putting commas just where they are needed?

A: One technique to strengthen your understanding of the seven basic ways that commas generally function is to write seven brief sentences of your own, each sentence showing one use of the comma. List these sentences on a separate sheet of paper and keep it next to your computer or in your writing notebook for fast reference.

CHAPTER 31

Other Punctuation and Capitalization

▶ **Navigating This Chapter**

In this chapter, you will learn how to use:

- periods, question marks, and exclamation points to indicate the end of a sentence
- quotation marks to indicate a person's exact words
- apostrophes to indicate ownership or to take the place of letters left out when contractions are formed
- colons to signal important information
- semicolons to emphasize a connection between independent clauses
- parentheses and dashes to signal additional information
- capitalization to emphasize words

GETTING STARTED . . .

**CW 31.1
Chapter
basics**

Q: Sometimes I'm not sure which mark of punctuation fits in a particular situation. I also often struggle with capitalization. I don't capitalize words I should, and other times I capitalize words that don't need it. Why do these two aspects of writing seem so confusing?

A: Dealing with punctuation and capitalization can seem confusing because each writing situation requires you to make multiple decisions regarding their use. The good news is that these two aspects of writing are governed by rules, and the rules are fairly straightforward.

Overview: Maintaining Correctness and Clarity through Punctuation and Capitalization

ESL Note
See "Punctuation and
Capitalization" on
pages 600–601.

**CW 31.2
Understanding
end
punctuation**

When people use the expression "nuts and bolts," they generally mean the various bits and pieces that hold things together. In writing, think of *punctuation* and *capitalization* as the nuts and bolts, the elements that hold writing together. **Punctuation** involves the use of the various symbols that guide your reader through your writing. **Capitalization** involves the use of an uppercase letter at the beginning of a word to make it stand out or clarify its meaning. Like the nuts and bolts that hold the massive girders of a bridge together, these elements of writing play a vital role in communicating your ideas to your reader. Therefore, it's important that you master their usage.

Using Periods, Question Marks, and Exclamation Points

CW 31.3
Brief
overview of
punctuation

To indicate the end of a sentence, use one of three marks of end punctuation. Use a **period** to indicate a stop at the end of a sentence that makes a statement:

EXAMPLE | The old man sitting under the tree is my uncle.

Use a **question mark** when a sentence expresses a question directly:

EXAMPLE | Where did you park the car?

Use an **exclamation point** when a sentence expresses strong excitement or emotion:

EXAMPLE | Watch out for that hot pipe!

Be careful not to overuse exclamation points. Use them only when you need to demonstrate profound excitement or emotion, not merely to spice up your writing.

COMPREHENSION
AND PRACTICE

Selecting the Correct End Punctuation

31.1 The sentences in the following passage all lack end punctuation. In the space provided, write the correct mark of end punctuation for each sentence, as the example shows.

EXAMPLE | The technician reported that the computer system wouldn't be repaired for

two weeks___.

CW 31.4
More help
with end
punctuation

(1) Giant dinosaurs may have ruled the earth 100 million years ago, but a

recent discovery indicates that even the giants among these giants may have

had something to fear___ (2) According to paleontologists, that something was

Sarcosuchus imperator, a cousin of the modern-day crocodile that was 40 feet long and weighted a whopping 10 tons<u>! OR .</u> (3) The first evidence of this massive creature, a six-foot skull, was found in a desert area of Niger, West Africa, in 1964 by a team of French scientists<u> . </u> (4) Subsequent digs in 1997 and 2000 yielded additional skulls and enough other fossilized remains to create a skeleton that is nearly 50 percent complete<u> . </u> (5) How fearsome was Sarcosuchus<u> ? </u> (6) For one thing, its jaws contained more than 100 teeth, including large numbers that could tear flesh and crush bone<u> . </u>. (7) This mighty predator had other adaptations that made it especially suited for its life as a river dweller<u> . </u> (8) For instance, it had a huge bulbous growth at the end of its snout, which experts believe enhanced its ability to breathe and smell, and its eyes tilted upward<u> . </u> (9) As this huge crocodile quietly lurked beneath the surface, almost completely hidden, even the largest dinosaurs of its time would easily be fast food<u> . </u> (10) Imagine what a good Hollywood director could do with that lunchtime scene<u>! OR .</u>

Using Quotation Marks

CW 31.5
Quotation
marks and
direct
quotations

When you record a person's words exactly as they were said, the resulting material is called a **direct quotation**. Direct quotations must be enclosed in **quotation marks**:

EXAMPLE   The smiling clerk said, "Thank you. Come again."

Notice that the first word of a direct quotation is capitalized and that the end punctuation is placed within the closing quotation mark. Notice also that a comma sets the direct quotation off from the *attribution,* the words that identify the speaker. You can also place the direct quotation before the attribution:

EXAMPLE   "Thank you. Come again," the smiling clerk said.

CW 31.6
Using
quotation
marks

Notice that a comma is still needed to separate the direct quotation from the attribution. In this case, the comma is placed *within* the closing quotation mark. Punctuation of direct quotations is discussed further in Chapter 30, "Commas." In writing, an exchange of direct quotations between two speakers is called a **dialogue.** Start a new paragraph each time you switch speakers so that readers can keep track of who is talking.

EXAMPLE   "Marguerite, you know I can't stand the smell of tuna fish," said Brian.
"But you know it's my favorite food. How could I give it up?" she replied.

When you restate or explain what someone has said, the resulting expression is called an **indirect quotation.** No quotation marks are needed because indirect quotations do not represent a person's exact words.

EXAMPLE   Then the clerk behind the counter thanked us and said that she hoped we'd come again.

The company president said that profits for the third quarter were far lower than she had anticipated.

Quotation marks are also used to set off titles of short documents such as magazine or newspaper articles, book chapters, songs, short stories, and poems:

EXAMPLE   Leon read the fourth chapter, "Your Child's Brain," aloud to Joyce.

Listening to "Unchained Melody" always makes me cry.

COMPREHENSION AND PRACTICE

Distinguishing between Direct and Indirect Quotations

31.2   Some of the sentences below contain indirect quotations, and others contain direct quotations. Insert quotation marks in the space above the direct quotations, as the example shows.

EXAMPLE   "Please check to make sure that you've locked the door," my grandmother said as we left her apartment.

CW 31.7 Quoting and paraphrasing

(1) "The secret to success in life is self-confidence," said the speaker at the motivational seminar I attended recently. (2) As I sat in the audience, I asked myself if I had the kind of self-confidence she described. (3) I thought of how often my best friend had told me that I should believe in myself as much as others do. (4) The last time he said this, I finally said, "I think you're wrong." (5) I said, "Real confidence isn't necessarily what people see on the surface." (6) He told me he agreed, but he still felt that I didn't see myself in the positive way that others saw me. (7) The speaker at the seminar emphasized this same point when she said, "It's all a matter of recognizing your strengths and

weaknesses." (8) She added, "Once you can do that, you can overcome your

fears." (9) After the presentation I went up to the podium and told her she had

helped me change my view of myself. (10) "My friend has told me the same

thing," I said, "and hearing what you had to say made me realize how correct he

was."

COMPREHENSION AND PRACTICE 31.3

CW 31.8
Understanding quotation marks

Converting and Punctuating Direct and Indirect Quotations

Some of the sentences below contain indirect quotations, and others contain direct quotations. On a separate sheet of paper, rewrite each indirect quotation as a direct quotation, and rewrite each direct quotation as an indirect quotation. Use the examples to guide you.

EXAMPLE

Lauren explained that she found the hours too long and the work too confusing.

"I just find the hours too long and the work too confusing," Lauren explained. [*Indirect to direct*]

EXAMPLE

"I don't know why, but I love broccoli," said Brendan.

Brendan said that he doesn't know why, but he loves broccoli. [*Direct to indirect*]

(1) When I walked into the emergency room on the day I cut my head while running, the attendant behind the counter asked me to explain what had happened. (2) I felt myself blush as I said, "I ran into the side of a building." (3) He looked up from the desk and asked me to repeat what I had said. (4) I told him again that I had run into a building.
(5) "How could that happen?" he asked.
(6) "A piece of the building was jutting out, and I didn't see it," I explained.
(7) "Are you kidding me?" he asked, beginning to laugh. (8) I told him that I was serious and that I'd appreciate it if he would lower his voice. (9) "I'm sorry," he said, as he tried to stop laughing. (10) When he finally asked a doctor to examine me, he graciously refrained from laughing as he told her why I needed help.

CHALLENGE 31.1 Writing Dialogue

COLLABORATION

On a separate sheet of paper, write a recent exchange between yourself and a friend or family member in dialogue form. Make all sentences direct quotations, and remember to begin a new paragraph every time the speaker changes.

CW 31.9
Working
with sources

Exchange your work with a partner. On the paper you receive, circle any errors you find in the use of end punctuation or quotation marks. Return the paper to the writer. Correct any errors that your partner circled in your paper.

Using Apostrophes

CW 31.10
Understanding
apostrophes

Writers use **apostrophes** (') to show possession and form contractions. Make singular nouns possessive by adding an apostrophe and -*s,* even if the noun ends in -*s:*

EXAMPLE | artist**'s** easel; girl**'s** wallet; business**'s** assets

If the possessive form sounds awkward to you, change it to a prepositional phrase. Rather than writing *Jonas's response,* write *the response of Jonas.*
Make most plural nouns possessive by adding only an apostrophe:

EXAMPLE | artist**s'** easels; girl**s'** wallets; leopard**s'** spots

For plural words that *don't* end in -*s,* form the plural by adding an apostrophe and -*s:*

EXAMPLE | men**'s** shirts; people**'s** attitudes; children**'s** toys

Pronouns such as *your* and *its* are already possessive, so they don't require an apostrophe. To make indefinite pronouns—such as *anybody, everybody, anyone, everyone,* and *nobody*—possessive, add an apostrophe and an -*s:*

EXAMPLE | everyone**'s** fault; anybody**'s** attention

To make compound subjects possessive, determine whether you are discussing one item that is possessed jointly or separate items owned by each subject. If the subjects jointly possess something, put an apostrophe and an -*s* after the last subject. If each subject possesses his or her own item, then add an apostrophe and an -*s* to each subject:

EXAMPLE | Lenny and Lila**'s** house [*One item jointly owned*]

Lenny**'s** and Lila**'s** paychecks [*Two items separately owned*]

For compound words like *maid of honor* and *father-in-law,* form the possessive by adding an apostrophe and an -*s* to the end of the word. Do the same for names of businesses and corporations that are compound:

> **EXAMPLE**   brother-in-law**'s** car; Lord & Taylor**'s** sale

CW 31.11
Recognizing
apostrophe
problems

Apostrophes are also used to form *contractions,* words that you create by combining two words. The apostrophe takes the place of the letters left out when the words are combined.

Here is a list of common contractions:

Common Contractions

aren**'t** are not	he**'s** he is, he has	should**'ve** should have
can**'t** cannot	I**'d** I would	that**'s** that is
couldn**'t** could not	I**'ll** I will	they**'ll** they will
didn**'t** did not	I**'m** I am	they**'re** they are
doesn**'t** does not	isn**'t** is not	who**'s** who is, who has
don**'t** do not	it**'ll** it will	won**'t** will not
hadn**'t** had not	it**'s** it is, it has	you**'d** you would
hasn**'t** has not	she**'d** she would	you**'ll** you will
haven**'t** have not	she**'ll** she will	you**'re** you are
he**'d** he would	she**'s** she is, she has	
he**'ll** he will	shouldn**'t** should not	

Notice that the letters in a contraction follow the same order as they do in the original two words. The exception is *won't,* the contraction for *will not.*

When you write, be sure to distinguish between *it's,* the contraction for *it is* and *it has,* and *its,* the possessive pronoun, which requires no apostrophe.

COMPREHENSION
AND PRACTICE
31.4

CW 31.12
Using
apostrophes

Using Apostrophes

Each sentence below contains a number of italicized words. Some need an apostrophe to show possession; others can be combined into contractions. Write the appropriate contraction or possessive form above each italicized section, as the example illustrates.

> **EXAMPLE**   *We will* reach *Frannys* house in about twenty-five minutes.
>   *We'll*   *Franny's*

(1) *It is* [It's] hard to believe that the local commuter rail station *has not* [hasn't] been replaced yet. (2) *Did not* [Didn't] the *mayors* [mayor's] task force recommend five years ago that the station be knocked down and rebuilt? (3) *I am* [I'm] surprised that the public safety *commissioners* [commissioner's] office has not condemned the structure. (4) After all, the building and the parking lot look as if they *have not* [haven't] been maintained for ten years, and *that is* [that's] a shame. (5) The other stations along the line *are not* [aren't] any older, and *they are* [they're] regularly cleaned and painted. (6) Why *has not* [hasn't] the same

> _Troy's_
>
> attention been given to _Troys_ station? (7) Certainly the number of people us-
>
> _system's_   _hasn't_
>
> ing the commuter rail _systems_ Fast Trax trains from this station _has not_ less-
>
> _it's_
>
> ened. (8) In fact, _it is_ just the opposite, with 10 percent more city residents de-
>
> _they'll_   _don't_
>
> ciding that _they will_ ride these trains from this station. (9) I _do not_ think I am
>
> _haven't_
>
> overreacting when I say that city officials _have not_ done everything they
>
> _should've_   _Isn't_   _city's_
>
> _should have._ (10) _Is not_ our well-being the _citys_ first responsibility?

COMPREHENSION AND PRACTICE

Correcting Errors in the Use of Apostrophes

31.5 The following passage contains errors resulting from missing or misused apostrophes. Rewrite incorrect words, inserting an apostrophe wherever one is needed, and eliminating unnecessary apostrophes. Use the example as a guide.

EXAMPLE

                      brother's   _its_

After he smashed up his brothers car, Matt knew it's resale value would take a dive.

> _can't_
>
> (1) You cant beat the companionship a dog gives, but you must be willing
>
> _you've_   _its_
>
> to invest a little time. (2) First of all, youve got to make sure that it gets all it's
>
> _dog's_
>
> shots. (3) You must also make sure that the dogs other needs are met. (4) For
>
> _don't_   _You'll_
>
> example, dont buy just any dog food. (5) Youll find that your dog is healthier
>
> and has more energy if you buy food that contains the right mix of vitamins
>
> _it's_
>
> and minerals. (6) In addition, whether its you, a friend, or another family
>
> member, somebody has to make sure that your pet gets exercise every day. (7)
>
> _you're_
>
> Also, unless the dog is a purebred that youre planning to mate, you should
>
> have it spayed or neutered so that nobody ends up with a bunch of unwanted
>
> _puppies_   _you're_
>
> puppie's. (8) If youre patient, you can train your dog to follow your commands
>
> _won't_
>
> very quickly. (9) That way, you wont have to worry that your dog will misbe-
>
> _you'll_
>
> have. (10) If you follow these steps, youll be able to count on a number of
>
> _years_
>
> year's of companionship from a loving animal.

COMPREHENSION   **Using Apostrophes in Your Writing**
AND PRACTICE

31.6   Use apostrophes to create contractions or phrases with possessive nouns from each of the following items. Then, on a separate sheet of paper, write a sentence that includes each word you create, as the example shows.

EXAMPLE   the notebook of Bernard _____ *Bernard's notebook* _____

After a long search, I found Bernard's notebook under the couch.

1. do not _____ *don't* _____

2. the house of that family _____ *that family's house* _____

3. I would _____ *I'd* _____

4. the answer of the professor _____ *the professor's answer* _____

5. it is _____ *it's* _____

6. the sweater of Ray _____ *Ray's sweater* _____

7. should have _____ *should've* _____

8. the schedule of Nick _____ *Nick's schedule* _____

9. she will _____ *she'll* _____

10. the music of today _____ *today's music* _____

CHALLENGE 31.2   Using *Its* and *It's* in Your Writing

COLLABORATION

As you can see from the list of common contractions on page 530, contractions of *it has* and *it is* are written as *it's*. For this Challenge, write ten sentences, five in which you use *its* and five in which you use *it's*. Then recopy the sentences, eliminating all apostrophes, and exchange your sentences with a partner. On the paper you receive, insert apostrophes where they are needed, and return the paper to the writer. Check to see whether you and your partner agree on the changes made to each of your papers.

Using Other Marks of Punctuation

CW 31.13
Understanding
colons

Colons

A **colon** calls attention to what comes next. It is used to introduce a formal statement such as an explanation or announcement or a long or formal quotation. It is also used to introduce a list, often in combination with the words *as follows* or *the following*. Study the following examples:

EXAMPLE

Now it was clear why Grandfather had been behaving so strangely: He had suffered a small stroke.

So far, I've test-driven four cars: a Toyota Corolla, a Dodge Neon, a Saturn Ion, and a Ford Focus.

In the first example, the colon introduces an explanation. If the explanation is a full sentence, it should begin with a capital letter. In the second example, the colon introduces a list.

Do not use a colon for a list that follows a verb or a preposition.

EXAMPLE

You must bring two pencils, a calculator, and a good eraser.

Colons have other functions, too:

- Use a colon after the salutation of a formal letter (*Dear Ms. Newman:*).
- Use a colon to separate hours and minutes (*10:45*), biblical chapter and verse (*John 4:11*), and the city of publication and the publishing company in bibliographic citations and footnotes (*New York: Longman*).

COMPREHENSION AND PRACTICE

Using Colons

31.7 Insert colons where they are needed in the space above the following sentences. If a sentence is correct, write *OK* above it. Use the example to guide you.

EXAMPLE

My goal was simple : write a play, sell it to Broadway and Hollywood, and become filthy rich.

CW 31.14
The colon

(1) Today, I had a 3:30 P.M. appointment with Dr. Smits to ask her permission to enroll in her advanced computer applications course. (2) I had not completed the course prerequisites : CPR 101, Introduction to Computers, and CPR 102, Networking. (3) However, I did have something that I thought might encourage her to add me to her class : three years' experience working with computers at my job. (4) My plan was simple : explain what systems and software I had used and ask her to substitute my experience for the prerequisites. (5) I arrived early so that I could do the one thing that I hadn't done : organize

my presentation. (6) By 325, I was well organized, but I was also feeling nervous. (7) If she refused, I would have to do something I considered ridiculous take courses that duplicated all the experience I already had. (8) When she arrived, she quietly listened to my story and quickly gave her answer yes.

OK

(9) Thanks to her willingness to credit my work experience, I can start out at the proper level and fill those two spots in my curriculum with other courses that will help me grow as a professional.

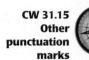

CW 31.15
Other
punctuation
marks

Semicolons

A **semicolon,** as you saw in Chapters 19, "Subordination and Coordination," and Chapter 20, "Comma Splices and Run-On Sentences," has the same power to connect as *and* preceded by a comma. But when you use the semicolon alone, you are saying that the connection between the clauses is so strong that no word is needed to signal it:

EXAMPLE

By ten o'clock, Elaine's car had already been stuck in the snow three times; she just wanted to turn around and read for home.

The semicolon connects the two thoughts and emphasizes the connection between Elaine's experience and her wish to quit.

As Chapter 19, "Subordination and Coordination," also showed, using a conjunctive adverb with a semicolon is another way to connect clauses. Conjunctive adverbs, which include words such as *however, finally,* and *therefore,* can suggest a relationship between sentences. A conjunctive adverb alone can't connect, though, so you must use a semicolon *before* the conjunctive adverb to connect the sentences:

EXAMPLE

David has had plenty of experience as a pipe fitter; *however,* he hasn't done much welding.

The semicolon connects the two sentences, and the conjunctive adverb *however* stresses that David's experience as a pipe fitter doesn't include welding.

COMPREHENSION
AND PRACTICE
31.8

CW 31.16
Understanding
semicolons

Using Semicolons

Many of the sentences in the following paragraph are missing semicolons. In the space above these sentences, insert semicolons where they are needed. Some sentences are correct. Just mark these sentences *OK*. Use the example first to direct you.

EXAMPLE
Cliff couldn't have been involved in the incident ; he was out of town on that day.

**CW 31.17
Using
semicolons**

(1) Last year, my friend Lani's life was thrown into turmoil ; she discovered that she had been adopted. (2) This knowledge upset her greatly ; she felt more confused and insecure than she had ever felt before. (3) After twenty years, she suddenly discovered that she had other biological parents ; she couldn't understand why her mom and dad hadn't told her before now. (4) For the first time in her life, Lani felt anger and resentment toward her mother and father ; she felt that she could no longer trust them. (5) Lani's adoptive parents didn't help the situation much ; OK they just acted as if nothing had changed. (6) Furthermore, the discovery made her troubled relationship with her brother, her adoptive parents' biological child, much worse. (7) Lani had always felt that she and her brother were very different ; now she understood why she felt that way. (8) This feeling was replaced by insecurity ; Lani feared that her parents loved her brother more than her. (9) After a year of counseling, Lani has adjusted ; she has finally accepted that she was adopted. (10) She understands that her parents had good intentions ; they simply didn't consider the possible consequences.

**CW 31.18
More help
with
semicolons**

Parentheses and Dashes

Parentheses enclose information added to a sentence but not vital to it. Added dates, asides, and explanations may be enclosed in parentheses.

EXAMPLE
The people in the car (all wearing seatbelts) escaped injury.

Hypothermia (dangerously low body temperature) threatens the elderly during these cold stretches.

**CW 31.19
Understanding
parentheses**

In the first example, the parentheses enclose added information that the reader doesn't actually need to understand the sentence. In the second example, the parentheses enclose the definition of a specialized term.

Dashes are used to set off information that deserves special attention.

EXAMPLE

The murderer turns out to be—but I don't want to spoil the ending for you.

As the winners were announced—the crowd had been waiting more than an hour for this moment—a loud cheer filled the auditorium.

In the first example, the dash indicates an abrupt change in thought and sentence structure. In the second, the dashes set off information that emphasizes the importance of the main idea. Dashes and parentheses are sometimes interchangeable. However, dashes indicate a stronger interruption. Neither mark should be used frequently, or it will lose its effectiveness.

COMPREHENSION AND PRACTICE

31.9

CW 31.20
Understanding dashes

Using Parentheses and Dashes

Some sentences in the following passage need either parentheses or dashes. Correct the sentences by inserting the proper marks of punctuation. In some cases, more than one correct answer is possible. Write *OK* above any sentence that is correctly punctuated. Study the example first. Answers may vary.

EXAMPLE

In the back of the arcade (the one on Main Street, not the one on Plymouth Avenue) police found the missing boy.

(1) Working as an aide in two hospitals St. Jude's and United has proven to me that I want to become a nurse. (2) In the two years that I've worked at these hospitals, I have gotten to know some of the most dedicated people I've ever met. (3) These are people who put their patients before everything even themselves. (4) I've seen some of them stay an hour beyond their shift because a patient took a sudden turn for the worse. (5) In the cardiac intensive care units at St. Jude's there is one for adults and another for infants I've seen nurses going out of their way to reassure patients and their families. (6) The nurses don't mind because they feel comforting people is an important part of their job. (7) I've even seen them trying to calm the emergency medical technicians EMTs who have had to transport a badly injured person. (8) When you consider the hours and the stress, the pay isn't great around $25,000 a

year, but there are other things to be gained. (9) When you can see that
you've made someone feel better, you can walk away with a good feeling.
(10) Sometimes not as often as you might think you can even help to save lives.

Understanding Capitalization

Capitalization, the practice of using initial capital letters to distinguish words, is governed by basic guidelines for standard use.

- Always capitalize the first word of any sentence:

EXAMPLE | The bike was the first thing the thieves took.

- Always capitalize the personal pronoun *I:*

EXAMPLE | As far as **I** am concerned, Eileen is the only one of my childhood friends who ever understood me.

- Capitalize *proper names* of individuals or things, including holidays, countries, states, historical periods or events, buildings, monuments, months (but not seasons), days of the week, planets, races, religions, and nationalities:

Marge **H**ill	**A**rgentina	**L**incoln **M**emorial	**V**alentine's **D**ay
Renaissance	**M**ay (but **s**pring)	**C**ivil **W**ar	**M**onday
Venus	**I**slam	**C**hinese	**B**aptist
Maine (**ME**)			

- Capitalize words designating family relationships when these words are part of, or a substitute for, a specific name:

EXAMPLE | When I was in elementary school, **A**unt Mary always went with my parents to parent/teacher night.

- Capitalize the first letter of a formal title such as *Doctor, Senator,* or *Mayor* when the title is used with a name:

EXAMPLE | We expect **M**ayor Cummings to call a news conference soon.

- Capitalize words like *Street, Avenue,* and *Boulevard* when these words are part of a specific address:

EXAMPLE   50 Earle **S**treet

- Capitalize geographical regions in the United States and other parts of the world, but not directions:

EXAMPLE   After being stationed in the **F**ar **E**ast for three years, I settled in the **M**idwest on the **e**ast side of the **M**ississippi.

- Capitalize the names of languages and the main words of *specifically* named courses:

EXAMPLE   Introduction to **P**hysics; **E**cology of **N**orth **A**merica; **W**riting 101; **S**panish; **S**wahili

- Capitalize the names of languages, whether or not they refer to specific academic subjects:

EXAMPLE   **C**hinese; **K**hmer; **P**ortuguese

- Capitalize the main words in the titles of books, magazines, newspapers, television shows, songs, articles, poems, movies, and so on. Do not capitalize a preposition or conjunction of fewer than five letters or *a, an,* or *the* unless it is the first word in the title.

EXAMPLE   *The Invisible Man; Rolling Stone; Of Mice and Men;* "**A** Rose for Emily"

- Capitalize the names of specific brands, companies, clubs, associations, and so on:

EXAMPLE   **M**azda **P**rotege; **G**eneral **E**lectric; **N**ational **O**rganization for **W**omen

- Capitalize *acronyms,* words formed from the first letters of several words:

EXAMPLE   **MADD** (**M**others **A**gainst **D**runk **D**riving)

AIDS (**A**cquired **I**mmune **D**eficiency **S**yndrome)

- Capitalize the first words at the beginning of a letter, known as the *salutation,* and the first word of the ending, called the *complimentary close:*

Common Salutations	***Common Complimentary Closes***
Dear Dr. Lannon:	Sincerely,
Dear Kurtis,	Very truly yours,
Dear Sir or Madam:	Respectfully,

FAST FACT   The dot that you put over a lowercase *i* actually has a name. It is called a **tittle.**

COMPREHENSION AND PRACTICE

31.10   Circle the correct letter—capital or lowercase—from each set in parentheses. Refer to the guidelines above if you are in doubt. Use the example to direct you.

Working with Capital and Lowercase Letters

EXAMPLE   (F/f)or any florist, the busiest days of the (Y/y)ear are (V/v)alentine's (D/d)ay and (M/m)other's (D/d)ay.

CW 31.22 Using capitalization

(1) (P/p)rofessor (G/g)odwin, my instructor for (I/i)ntroduction to (B/b)usiness, always stresses the importance of making a good appearance on the job. (2) (O/o)n the first day of (C/c)lass, (P/p)rofessor (G/g)odwin said, "(I/i)f you want (P/p)eople to take you seriously, you must dress as if you belong on the cover of (B/b)usinessweek." (3) (H/h)e urged us to go down to (S/s)outh (M/m)ain (S/s)treet and (W/w)est 53rd (S/s)treet, where (R/r)etail stores like (E/e)ddie (B/b)auer and (M/m)arshall (F/f)ield's and the (C/c)orporate offices for (T/t)imex and (J/j)ohn (H/h)ancock are located. (4) (T/t)here, he said, we would see (M/m)anagers and (E/e)xecutives dressed in (C/c)onservative (B/b)usiness suits. (5) (N/n)one of these (B/b)usinesspeople is dressed in (L/l)evi's (J/j)eans or (N/n)ike (S/s)neakers because all of them know the importance of dressing well on the job.

COMPREHENSION AND PRACTICE

31.11   Decide which words in the following business letter should be capitalized. Cross out the incorrect lowercase letter, and write the capital above it. Each line or sentence is numbered for you.

Correcting Errors in Capitalization

CW 31.23
More help
with
capitalization

                   B   V   W

(1) 49 buena vista way

     S C   I

(2) st. charles, il 60174

     M

(3) march 31, 2006

     D   C   C   D

(4) director, consumer complaint division

     M   C   C

(5) megahertz computer company

            B   S

(6) 25 blythe street

     S   A

(7) springfield, ak 67583

     D   D

(8) dear director:

       A   I   M

(9) a month ago, i purchased one of your megahertz 5000 personal com-

                                           S   I

puters, model number 328. (10) since then i have taken it to your authorized

 S C   M

st. charles service center, microcomputers and more, five times for repairs.

          A

(11) although the costs were covered by my warranty, i feel that the number

                                                  I   I

of repairs required has been excessive. (12) i have therefore decided that i

want to return the computer for a full refund.

      W   I   M E   I

(13) when i returned to mr. electronics, the store from which i had originally

                      M   M T   L

purchased my megahertz 5000, ms. tamara lacey, who manages the electron-

ics department, told me that your company will not authorize a refund be-

                                                I   M L

cause the case of the computer had been opened. (14) i explained to ms. lacey

that the case had been opened by a service technician authorized by

 M   S

megahertz. (15) she insisted that since the computer was no longer in its origi-

nal condition, your company would not give me a full refund.

      I   M L

(16) i sincerely hope that ms. lacey is mistaken and that you will authorize my

        I   M   I

refund. (17) i originally decided to purchase a megahertz 5000 because i had

                   M   C   C

read that the megahertz computer company was particularly sensitive to the

                                  A

needs of its customers. (18) as the enclosed copy of my original sales slip

                                                              P

shows, my total purchase price, including tax, was $1,453.55. (19) please con-

tact me if you need additional information.

         S

    (20) sincerely,

         S   H A

    (21) steven h. amster

CHALLENGE 31.3 Revising for Correct Capitalization

1. As you revise your writing, check to be sure you have capitalized correctly. To practice focusing on this aspect of revising, select two paragraphs that you have drafted, and exchange them with a partner.

CW 31.24 More help with capitalization

2. Using the guidelines on pages 537–539, check the paragraphs you receive to make sure the words are correctly capitalized. Circle any problems you notice, and return the paragraphs to the writer.

3. Correct any errors your reader has identified.

CHAPTER QUICK CHECK Punctuation and Capitalization

CW 31.25 More information on all punctuation marks

The following passage contains numerous errors in the use of end punctuation, quotation marks, apostrophes, colons, semicolons, dashes, parentheses, and lower-case and capital letters. Consult the examples throughout the chapter. Then correct all errors by inserting needed punctuation or by writing corrected words in the space above, as the example shows.

EXAMPLE

Until last year, my neighbor Pete, who served in ~~vietnam~~ *Vietnam*, didn't realize he had been exposed to ~~agent orange~~ *Agent Orange* during his tour of duty there.

(1) One of the most important steps for job-seekers is to make sure their resumes are widely circulated and reviewed? (2) Thanks to the Internet, people have another way to ensure that the maximum number of employers review work credentials on-line resume-posting services. (3) When resumes are posted on the Web, an individuals qualifications can be quickly examined with a few clicks of a computer mouse. (4) The leading global careers site several million hits monthly is Monster.com, which traces its origins to a site called The Monster Board, created in 1994 by Jeff Taylor. (5) In 1999, the Monster Board merged with Online Career Center, and the resulting company eventually became Monster Jobs, which is now based in maynard, massachusetts. (6) Taylor, who is CEO Chief Executive Officer of the company, came up with the concept for the site while he was an undergraduate at the University of Massachusetts, in Amherst, Massachusetts. (7) In 1999, Taylor gambled on the

power of conventional advertising when Monster.com spent $4 million to pur-
chase three 30-second commercials during the super bowl. (8) As a result,
Monster began to draw huge numbers of visitors to its site, and Taylor didnt
make the mistake that other Internet companies had made after an advertising
blitz. (9) As Taylor later started a speech, We're the only Internet site that advertised on the Super Bowl that didn't crash because of added traffic. (10) In
2001, not content to leave anything undone, Taylor finished up something he
had left behind eight years earlier the requirements for his college degree.

QUICK STUDY | Student Example

This chapter discusses signals for beginnings and endings, possessing and condensing, and emphasizing or minimizing. Consider this paragraph on a related
subject, the personal possessions you would keep if you had to reduce your belongings to what you could fit in a single shoebox:

What would I save if I could keep only one shoebox full of personal belongings Most of what I would keep might seem odd to some people First of
all, I would keep a coin bank in the shape of a chevrolet corvette, which used
to sit on my grandfathers workbench My grandmother gave it to me after my
Grandfathers funeral It would take up almost a quarter of the box, but how
could I not keep it Every time I look at it, it reminds me of him In addition, I
would keep my Godchilds many drawings from when she was in Nursery
School They show the two of us doing things together like going to the playground and to the Beach If I fold them up carefully, I'd still have almost half
the box available I would fill the rest of the box up with several things One
would be a stack of about 100 photos from my childhood showing everything
from vacations at disneyworld and yellowstone national park to birthday parties to graduations Then, in the space I had left, I would stick the ticket stubs
and wristbands I have saved from all the concerts and sporting events I have

ever attended, especially from the first time I saw the chicago cubs play The

things I would keep have no monetary value, but I consider them the most

valuable things I own because of the memories they hold

First complete the following activities in response to this paragraph:

1. The sentences in the previous paragraph have no end punctuation. In addition, there are errors in capitalization and apostrophe use. Insert the proper end punctuation and correct any errors in capitalization and apostrophe use.

2. How does the topic sentence of this paragraph prepare the reader for the discussion that follows in the body and the statement expressed in the closing sentence? Use the lines below for your answer.

The topic sentence prepares the reader for the discussion in the body because it

identifies—in question form—the idea that the writer will focus on valuable personal

items, an idea reiterated in the closing sentence.

3. On a separate sheet of paper, assess the order of presentation of the supporting examples, explain why you think the writer arranged them in this way, and state whether you agree with it and why or why not.

Now explore the topic in writing. As the paragraph above does, you could discuss what you would keep if you had to reduce your belongings to a precious few. Or you might turn your attention to one of these topics related to the subject matter of this chapter:

- something about your personality that you wish you could de-emphasize
- a question to which you wish you knew the answer
- the characteristic or feature that distinguishes a family member or friend from the ordinary person
- the most surprising announcement you have ever heard

COLLABORATION

1. Exchange your draft with a classmate. Evaluate the paragraph you receive. Look for any problems, especially in terms of punctuation and capitalization. Circle any errors, write corrected versions above them, and then return the paper to the writer.

2. Consider the comments and corrections your reader has made and create a final draft of your paragraph.

SUMMARY EXERCISE Punctuation and Capitalization

The following passage contains numerous errors in the use of end punctuation, quotation marks, apostrophes, colons, semicolons, dashes, parentheses, and lowercase and capital letters. Consult the examples throughout the chapter. Then correct all errors by inserting needed punctuation or by writing corrected words in the space above.

There are acceptable alternative answers for some items.

(1) For almost forty years 1905–1945 franklin and eleanor roosevelt forged one of the most remarkable partnerships in the History of the united states. (2) It began with marriage, moved on to public service, and ended with contributions to political life and social reform that transformed our nations indeed the worlds history. (3) The marriage of the wealthy, outgoing roosevelt to his shy fifth Cousin, eleanor, led first to the births of their children elliot, james, john, fdr, jr., and anna. (4) eleanor put her ambition for Public Service on hold to raise the children meanwhile, the young roosevelt proved himself an able and progressive leader to the new york democrats.

(5) In 1921, the family suffered a staggering blow while they were vacationing at their summer home on campobello island in new brunswick, canada, roosevelt was stricken with polio. (6) This was a terrible shock roosevelt had always been strong, active, and very able physically but the couple neither bent nor broke. (7) Eleanor who later encouraged her husband to return to Politics now became both a physical and psychological support. (8) Although confined to a wheelchair for the rest of his life, FDR went on to become a master politician and one of the worlds most revered leaders.

(9) Roosevelt was elected governor of new york in 1929 he became president of the united states in 1932. (10) For three consecutive terms from 1932–1945, he led the Country through two of the most traumatic upheavals of the century the great depression and world war ii. (11) the Roosevelt team proved equal to the challenge of these catastrophic events they conceived and

implemented inventive programs and projects such as the ^N^new ^D^deal, the ^W^works ^P^progress ^A^administration, the ^T^tennessee ^V^valley ^A^authority, and the ^C^civilian ^C^conservation ^C^corps.

(12) When the ^J^japanese attacked ^P^pearl ^H^harbor, Roosevelt responded for an outraged nation, calling ^D^december 7, 1941, ^"^ a day that will live in infamy, ^"^ a saying that is now a part of history. (13) Through the war years, he worked closely with ^P^prime ^M^minister ^W^winston ^C^churchill of ^G^great ^B^britain. (14) ^T^these two men personally determined military strategy for the ^A^allies in the ^W^west.

(15) During all these years, Eleanor was a tireless worker for social causes, such as ^c^Civil ^r^Rights for ^A^african ^A^americans and women. (16) She set a standard for public involvement and accomplishment that is still unmatched. (17) Her workday began at 6:00 A.M. and ended after midnight. (18) She not only conducted press conferences and had her own ^r^Radio ^p^Program, but she also wrote the daily newspaper column, ^"^ ^M^my ^D^day. ^"^ (19) Friends and enemies alike wondered, ^"^ Was there an end to this woman's energy ?^"^ (20) Eleanor's ^,^ tireless work and travel, public speaking and leadership, and selfless advocacy of the underdog made her well known to the world and beloved to millions.

(21) FDR, exhausted and in terrible health, died in 1945, months before the ^W^War ended. (22) Eleanor went on to serve as a ^U.S.^u.s. delegate to the ^U^united ^N^nations and helped draft the ^U.N.^u.n. ^D^declaration of ^H^human ^R^rights. (23) ^I^in addition, she wrote two books :^T^this I ^R^remember and ^T^the ^A^autobiography of ^E^eleanor ^R^roosevelt. (24) When she died in 1962, ^E^eleanor ^R^roosevelt was, as one ^b^Biographer has said ^"^ the most admired person in the world. ^"^ (25) The lives of these two remarkable people had ended, but this verse is an appropriate epitaph. ^"^ They are not dead who live in lives they leave behind. In those whom they have blessed, they live a life again. ^"^

FOR FURTHER EXPLORATION

1. Consider one of the following topics:

   - the qualities a natural leader possesses
   - a competition or contest you won—or one you lost
   - two situations in which you would speak, dress, or behave differently
   - the importance of understanding one's cultural, ethnic, or religious background
   - something you have in common with someone in your family or a friend whom you don't especially like

   Prewrite on the subject, using one of the strategies you practiced in Chapter 2, and work your way through the rest of the writing process. Then complete a draft essay of at least 500 words on this subject.

COLLABORATION

2. Exchange your draft with a classmate. Check the draft you receive for weaknesses, checking in particular for errors in punctuation and capitalization. Circle any mistakes, using the material in this chapter to guide you, and return the paper to the writer.

3. Revise your essay, correcting any errors in punctuation and capitalization or other problems discovered by your reader.

RECAP Other Punctuation and Capitalization

New terms in this chapter	Definitions
punctuation	a system of symbols that signals starts, stops, and pauses in writing
capitalization	the practice of emphasizing words by beginning them with capital letters
period (.)	an end mark used to indicate the end of a statement
	EXAMPLE I have a dream**.**
question mark (?)	an end mark used to indicate the end of a question
	EXAMPLE Have we met before**?**
exclamation point (!)	an end mark used to indicate the end of an exclamation and to show great feeling
	EXAMPLE Stop**!** That area is mined**!**
direct quotation	a record of someone's exact words
	EXAMPLE Peter said, "If you'll wait, I'll go with you."

New terms in this chapter	Definitions
quotation marks (" ")	marks used to set off someone's exact words
dialogue	an exchange of direct quotations between two or more people Mark shifts in speakers with new paragraphs. **EXAMPLE** "I said I wanted to go home at ten," said Joe. "Yes, but you didn't specify A.M. or P.M.," said Dianne.
indirect quotation	a restatement of someone else's words **EXAMPLE** Peter asked me to wait and said he'd go with me
apostrophe (')	a mark used in a noun to show ownership or possession or in a contraction to signify letters left out To show possession: add **'s** to singular nouns a child's book add **'** to plural nouns the students' answers add **'s** to plural nouns that don't end in **-s** women's concerns To form contractions: add **'s** to show letters omitted in the contraction haven't
colon (:)	a mark that indicates a pause in a sentence and that introduces a quotation, formal statement, or list Begin full sentences following colons with a capital letter. **EXAMPLE** The news was good**:** The test results were negative.
semicolon (;)	a connecting mark that separates related independent clauses but emphasizes the connection between them **EXAMPLE** Shelley is dramatic**;** her twin sister is quite shy.
parentheses	marks that enclose non-vital information within a sentence **EXAMPLE** The movie **(**which she saw with her sister**)** made Mavis cry.
dashes	marks that set off information to create emphasis **EXAMPLE** Vincent Van Gogh**—**who mutilated his ear**—**was a genius.

(continued)

Guidelines for Capitalization

The first word in a sentence

| **EXAMPLE** | **A** light bulb burned out in the kitchen. |

The personal pronoun *I* and the proper names of people, things, and places

| **EXAMPLE** | **S**ean and **I** are going to **T**ulsa on **F**riday. |

Words that designate family relationships when they are part of, or a substitute for, a specific name

| **EXAMPLE** | **U**ncle Rod always calls to check on **G**randma. |

Formal titles used with a person's name

| **EXAMPLE** | **D**r. Warner has been selected for the award. |

Words that are part of a specific address or specific section of a country

| **EXAMPLE** | Our plant in the **S**outhwest is located at 1411 **L**incoln **W**ay in **T**ucson. |

Main words in specific academic subjects, languages, and titles

| **EXAMPLE** | In my **I**ntroduction to **E**nvironment class, we are reading Rachel Carson's ***S**ilent **S**pring*. |

Brand names, company and association names, and letters of acronyms

| **EXAMPLE** | My sister works for **AT**&**T**. |

First letters of the salutation and complimentary close of a letter

| **EXAMPLE** | **D**ear Paul, **Y**ours truly, |

GOING FORWARD...

Q: There's so much to keep straight about punctuation and capitalization. What's the best way for me to develop greater skill with them?

A: True, when it comes to punctuation and capitalization, there is a good deal to remember. Knowing which to choose is easier than you might think, however, because the various marks of punctuation are distinct from each other. The same is true for capitalization. Whether a word should be capitalized of not depends on where the word appears in the sentence and what class of word—proper or common—it is.

PART 7

Connecting: Responding to Reading

Navigating This Section

In this section of the text, you can explore:

- a variety of modes that writers use to fulfill their purpose
- additional subjects for writing
- strategies writers use to express their ideas and experiences

Overview: Responding to Reading

**CW VII.1
Exploring
literature
online**

Reading **actively** and responding to what other authors have written is another way to ensure your success as a writer. When you read actively, you respond to the ideas other authors have developed and discover the strategies they have used to express those ideas. This part of the text includes writings by both professional authors and students. After each selection, you will find questions to help you think about and respond to the ideas in the readings. Additional assignments will help you explore the connections between those ideas and your own experiences. The questions will also encourage you to use the various modes in your own writing.

Taking Notes

You have already learned that writing effectively has many benefits. In the same way, the more you practice reading actively, the more you will profit from what you read. As a way to improve your reading skills, your instructor may ask you to record in a journal your responses, questions, and comments about what you read. You should also *annotate* or make notes in the margins of the pages you are reading or highlight sections for later reference. You might also collect responses in a computer file or on an audiocassette tape. Whatever method or methods you use, cultivate the habit of taking notes. Your notes will help you prepare for discussions with your classmates and explore ideas for your own writing assignments.

Active Reading Strategies

**CW VII.2
Active
reader**

Sometimes it is difficult to know what questions to ask and what notes to take. The five guidelines below apply to any reading assignment. They will provide direction and help you focus your responses to the readings.

Review them before you begin to read each selection, and be sure to record your responses as you read.

1. **Establish the context**

   What's going on? Who is involved? When did it happen? Where? How? Why? These are the questions that news stories generally answer in their opening sentences to establish the *context* for readers. As you read, use these kinds of questions to identify details and examples that establish the context of the reading.

2. **Explore the modes**

As you learned in Chapters 5 through 15, writers use modes, or organizing strategies, to communicate their ideas to readers. These are narration, description, example, process, definition, comparison and contrast, cause and effect, and division and classification. To construct an argument, writers use a combination of these modes. As you read, first determine the author's purpose for writing. Is it to inform, to entertain, or to persuade? What is the dominant mode the author uses to fulfill this purpose? What other modes does the author use, and how are they combined?

3. **Explore the main ideas**

As you read, highlight or record in your journal parts of the reading that state the author's thesis. Do the same for evidence that supports that idea. Finally, highlight or record the author's conclusions about the subject.

Try to identify the main ideas or topic sentences of the paragraphs. Can you trace a common thread, the element that all the paragraphs have in common? Are there sentences or paragraphs that confuse you or sections that you don't understand? Make note of these to discuss with your classmates. Next, identify supporting information that helps you understand the writer's points. What details catch your eye? Why are these effective?

4. **Respond to the ideas**

What do you think of the essay? Why do you think the way you do? Do you agree with the ideas the author has expressed? Are you familiar with the context or the ideas in the reading? Does the author present an experience or view of the world that is new to you? Your answers to these questions will help you greatly in understanding the writing. As you talk or write about the piece, you will also be making sense of it. Remember as you read that a good piece of writing touches the reader. When you read, explore what the writer has done to make this happen.

**CW VII.3
Active
reading
strategies**

5. **Read again**

Active reading can be challenging and rewarding. Effective readers usually read a piece of writing more than once. You'll no doubt discover some elements or aspects in a second reading that you missed in the first. Regardless of what they are, these elements helped to make that writing successful. It is worth your effort to analyze them so that you will be able to use a similar approach in your own writing.

Active Reading Illustrated

Here is a brief excerpt from "The Future of TV Sports Is Glowing," by Ted Rose. This article explores and explains how technological innovations are changing the way televised sports are presented. The annotations illustrate the way active reading can help you uncover the writer's meaning and the various techniques that enabled the writer to communicate that meaning:

Modes: Main purpose—to inform

Main Ideas: Topic sentence

Context: Who

Context: What

The task presented many technical challenges, but [Stan] Honey was most concerned about how computers would locate the puck on the ice. Under normal conditions, baseballs and golf balls travel pre-dictable—thus, mathematical—trajectories. Not so a hockey puck. Instead, surrounded by dozens of wooden sticks and metal skates wielded by aggressive hockey players, a puck can carom in any direction.

Modes: Process

Supporting ideas

Modes: Comparison and contrast

Modes: Cause and effect

Context: Why

Working with a team of 12 engineers, Honey designed a special puck that emitted bursts of infrared energy, and a system of sensors to be placed around the arena to detect those emissions. With this sensor data, a computer could identify the puck's location. That, along with information from broadcast cameras themselves, produced the desired result: the TV-viewing fan could find the puck on the ice because a blue glow would illuminate it. When a player fired a puck at a high speed (usually more than 50 miles per hour), a red tail would follow in the wake. (*Brill's Content*, May 1999, 64–65)

Main Ideas: Topic sentence

Modes: Process and cause and effect

Context: Who

Context: What

Context: How

Supporting ideas

Context: How

Modes: description

Response: Pretty cool! Just another way computers are changing the world. Lots of people wouldn't watch hockey on TV before because it was too hard to follow the puck. This innovation has changed that for sure.

As the annotations illustrate, active reading helps you isolate a number of elements of the writing. For instance, it helps you focus on the *context: what* was involved (the development of a hockey puck that would be easier to see on a television screen), *who* was involved (Stan Honey and a team of twelve engineers), and *how* they did it (they built a puck that emits signals and installed sensors throughout the ice rink).

Active reading also enables you to note the various *modes* (*comparison and contrast, process, cause and effect,* and *description*), as well as the *main ideas* (the *topic sentences* and the *supporting sentences*). And the *response* to the reading helps you focus on the significance or meaning of the passage to a more complete degree. When you understand how a writer communicates ideas to a reader, you are better able to communicate your own ideas to your reader. That's why active reading is so important.

5:00 A.M.: Writing as Ritual

Judith Ortiz Cofer

•••

Franklin Professor of English and Creative Writing at the University of Georgia, Judith Ortiz Cofer has won awards and international recognition for her writing, which includes a novel, essays, short stories, and several volumes of poetry. In this selection from The Latin Deli, *a book of prose and poetry, she writes about how she discovered the time she needed to create. In what ways does setting aside time to do something make that activity more important?*

1   **A**n act of will that changed my life from that of a frustrated artist, waiting to have a room of my own and an independent income before getting down to business, to that of a working writer: I decided to get up two hours before my usual time, to set my alarm for 5:00 A.M.

2   When people ask me how I started writing, I find myself describing the urgent need that I felt to work with language as a search; I did not know for a long time what I was looking for. Although I married at nineteen, had a child at twenty-one—all the while going through college and graduate school *and* working part-time—it was not enough. There was something missing in my life that I came close to only when I turned to my writing, when I took a break from my thesis research to write a poem or an idea for a story on the flip side of an index card. It wasn't until I traced this feeling to its source that I discovered both the cause and the answer to my frustration: I needed to write. I showed my first efforts to a woman, a "literary" colleague, who encouraged me to mail them out. One poem was accepted for publication, and I was hooked. This bit of success is really the point where my problem began.

3   Once I finished graduate school, I had no reason to stay at the library that extra hour to write poems. It was 1978. My daughter was five years old and in school during the day while I traveled the county, teaching freshman composition on three different campuses. Afternoons I spent taking her to her ballet, tap, and every other socializing lesson her little heart desired. I composed my lectures on Florida's I-95, and that was all the thinking time I had. Does this sound like the typical superwoman's lament? To me it meant being in a constant state of mild anxiety which I could not really discuss with others. What was I to say to them? I need an hour to start a poem. Will someone please stop the world from spinning so fast?

4   I did not have the privilege of attending a writers' workshop as a beginning writer. I came to writing instinctively, as a dowser finds an underground well. I did not know that I would eventually make a career out of writing books and giving readings of my work. The only models I knew were the unattainable ones: the first famous poet I met was Richard Eberhart, so exalted and venerable that he might as well have been the Pope. All I knew at that time was that at twenty-six years of age I felt spiritually deprived, although I had all the things my women friends found sufficiently fulfilling in a "woman's life" plus more; I was also teaching, which is the only vocation I always knew I had. But I had found poetry, or it had found me, and it was demanding its place in my life.

5   After trying to stay up late at night for a couple of weeks and discovering that there was not enough of me left after a full day of giving to others, I relented and

did this odious thing: I set my alarm for five. The first day I shut it off because I could: I had placed it within arm's reach. The second day I set two clocks, one on my night table, as usual, and one out in the hallway. I had to jump out of bed and run to silence it before my family was awakened and the effort nullified. This is when my morning writing ritual that I follow to this day began. I get up at five and put on a pot of coffee. Then I sit in my rocking chair and read what I did the previous day until the coffee is ready. I take fifteen minutes to drink two cups of coffee while my computer warms up—not that it needs to—I just like to see it glowing in the room where I sit in semidarkness, its screen prompting "ready": ready whenever you are. When I'm ready, I write.

6   Since that first morning in 1978 when I rose in the dark to find myself in a room of my own—with two hours belonging only to me ahead of me, two prime hours when my mind was still filtering my dreams—I have not made or accepted too many excuses for not writing. This apparently ordinary choice, to get up early and to work every day, forced me to come to terms with the discipline of art. I wrote my poems in this manner for nearly ten years before my first book was published. When I decided to give my storytelling impulse full rein and write a novel, I divided my two hours: the first hour for poetry, the second for fiction; two pages minimum per day. Well or badly, I wrote two pages a day for three and one-half years. This is how my novel, *The Line of the Sun,* was finished. If I had waited to have the time, I would still be waiting to write my novel.

7   My life has changed considerably since those early days when I was trying to be everything to everyone. My daughter is eighteen and in college, not a ballerina, Rockette, or horsewoman but a disciplined student and a self-assured young person. Thus I do not regret the endless hours of sitting in tiny chairs at the Rock-Ette Academy of Dance or of breathing the saturated air at the stables as I waited for her. She got out of her activities something like what I got out of getting up in the dark to work: the feeling that you are in control, on the saddle, on your toes. Empowerment is what the emerging artist needs to win for herself. And the initial sense of urgency to create can easily be dissipated because it entails making the one choice many people, especially women, in our society with its emphasis on the "acceptable" priorities, feel selfish about making: taking the time to create, stealing it from yourself if it's the only way.

EXPLORING THE READING THROUGH DISCUSSION

1. Why does Judith Ortiz Cofer begin to write poetry?

2. What is the problem to which Cofer refers at the end of the second paragraph? How does she solve her dilemma?

3. List the steps in Cofer's writing ritual.

4. What does Cofer create as a result of following her ritual? Did she gain anything else?

5. Cofer uses colons several times in her essay. Find those sentences that include colons. Why do you think she chose to use this punctuation mark when she did? Refer to Chapter 31, "Other Punctuation and Capitalization," as you explore this question.

DEVELOPING VOCABULARY

List any words in this selection that are new to you. Write your understanding of each word from the context. Then look up each word in the dictionary, and write the definition that you think best fits the meaning in this writing.

_____

_____

_____

_____

DISCOVERING CONNECTIONS THROUGH WRITING

CW VII.4 Basic guidelines for reading literature

1. Describe the steps you follow in your own writing ritual, if you have one. Include details to answer your readers' questions about when, where, and why you follow this process.

2. Do you take time to engage in an activity that makes you feel that you "are in control, on the saddle, on your toes"? Describe what you do and what the positive results are.

3. It took Cofer nearly ten years to write her first book of poetry and three and one-half years to finish her first novel. Do you have a long-term goal? Explain what your goal is and what steps you are taking to reach it.

Fish Cheeks

Amy Tan

Amy Tan is an acclaimed writer who has explored the relationships between immigrant Chinese mothers and their daughters. Her first novel, The Joy Luck Club *(1989), is based on some of her own experiences. As you read this essay, first published in* Seventeen *magazine, try to understand the feelings of a little girl living in two cultures. How can feeling different from others affect your social interactions?*

1   I fell in love with the minister's son the winter I turned fourteen. He was not Chinese, but as white as Mary in the manger. For Christmas I prayed for this blond-haired boy, Robert, and a slim new American nose.

2   When I found out that my parents had invited the minister's family over for Christmas Eve dinner, I cried. What would Robert think of our shabby Chinese Christmas? What would he think of our noisy Chinese relatives who lacked proper American manners? What terrible disappointment would he feel upon seeing not a roasted turkey and sweet potatoes but Chinese food?

3   On Christmas Eve I saw that my mother had outdone herself in creating a strange menu. She was pulling black veins out of the backs of fleshy prawns. The kitchen was littered with appalling mounds of raw food: A slimy rock cod with

bulging eyes that pleaded not be thrown into a pan of hot oil. Tofu, which looked like stacked wedges of rubbery white sponges. A bowl soaking dried fungus back to life. A plate of squid, their backs crisscrossed with knife markings so they resembled bicycle tires.

4   And then they arrived—the minister's family and all my relatives in a clamor of doorbells and rumpled Christmas packages. Robert grunted hello, and I pretended he was not worthy of existence.

5   Dinner threw me deeper into despair. My relatives licked the ends of their chopsticks and reached across the table, dipping them into the dozen or so plates of food. Robert and his family waited patiently for platters to be passed to them. My relatives murmured with pleasure when my mother brought out the whole steamed fish. Robert grimaced. Then my father poked his chopsticks just below the fish eye and plucked out the soft meat. "Amy, your favorite," he said, offering me the tender fish cheek. I wanted to disappear.

6   At the end of the meal my father leaned back and belched loudly, thanking my mother for her fine cooking. "It's a polite Chinese custom to show you are satisfied," explained my father to our astonished guests. Robert was looking down at his plate with a reddened face. The minister managed to muster up a quiet burp. I was stunned into silence for the rest of the night.

7   After everyone had gone, my mother said to me, "You want to be the same as American girls on the outside." She handed me an early gift. It was a miniskirt in beige tweed. "But inside you must always be Chinese. You must be proud you are different. Your only shame is to have shame."

8   And even though I didn't agree with her then, I knew that she understood how much I had suffered during the evening's dinner. It wasn't until many years later—long after I had gotten over my crush on Robert—that I was able to fully appreciate her lesson and the true purpose behind our particular menu. For Christmas Eve that year, she had chosen all my favorite foods.

EXPLORING THE READING THROUGH DISCUSSION

1. What is the lesson that the author appreciates after "many years"? Why doesn't she agree with her mother at the time?

2. Compare the responses of the two families to the dinner. How did the narrator feel? Why?

3. What sensory details does Tan use to describe the Christmas Eve menu? Can you find examples of both objective and subjective description in this essay?

4. What transitional expressions are included in the essay?

5. Do you think "Fish Cheeks" is a good title for this story? Explain why.

DEVELOPING VOCABULARY

List any words in this selection that are new to you. Write your understanding of each word from the context. Then look up each word in the dictionary, and write the definition that you think best fits the meaning in this writing.

DISCOVERING CONNECTIONS THROUGH WRITING

**CW VII.5
Writing
about
literature**

1. The narrator's mother tells her, "You must be proud you are different. Your only shame is to have shame." Do you agree? Write about a situation you know or an experience you have had that supports her belief.

2. Have you participated in a traditional event or shared a special occasion with friends of another religion or culture as Robert and his family do? How did you feel? What did you learn? Provide plenty of concrete examples in your essay.

3. Write a narrative about a holiday celebration you remember well. In your essay, be sure to use effective description to put your readers at the scene.

Intimacy and Independence

Deborah Tannen

Deborah Tannen is University Professor of Linguistics at Georgetown University as well as a well-known media commentator. As you read this excerpt from her book You Just Don't Understand, *ask yourself this question: How can spoken communication sometimes complicate the lives of couples?*

1   *Intimacy* is key in a world of connection where individuals negotiate complex networks of friendship, minimize differences, try to reach consensus, and avoid the appearance of superiority, which would highlight differences. In a world of status, *independence* is key, because a primary means of establishing status is to tell others what to do, and taking orders is a marker of low status. Though all humans need both intimacy and independence, women tend to focus on the first and men on the second. It is as if their lifeblood ran in different directions.

2   These differences can give women and men differing views of the same situation, as they did in the case of a couple I will call Linda and Josh. When Josh's old high-school chum called him at work and announced he'd be in town on business the following month, Josh invited him to stay for the weekend. That evening he informed Linda that they were going to have a houseguest, and that he and his chum would go out together the first night to shoot the breeze like old times. Linda was upset. She was going to be away on business the week before, and the Friday night when Josh would be out with his chum would be her first night home. But what upset her the most was that Josh had made these plans on his own and informed her of them, rather than discussing them with her before extending the invitation.

3   Linda would never make plans, for a weekend or an evening, without first checking with Josh. She can't understand why he doesn't show her the same courtesy and consideration that she shows him. But when she protests, Josh says, "I can't say to my friend, 'I have to ask my wife for permission'!"

4   To Josh, checking with his wife means seeking permission, which implies that he is not independent, not free to act on his own. It would make him feel like a child or an underling. To Linda, checking with her husband has nothing to do with permission. She assumes that spouses discuss their plans with each other because their lives are intertwined, so the actions of one have consequences for the other. Not only does Linda not mind telling someone, "I have to check with Josh"; quite the contrary—she likes it. It makes her feel good to know and show that she is involved with someone, that her life is bound up with someone else's.

5   Linda and Josh both felt more upset by this incident, and others like it, than seemed warranted, because it cut to the core of their primary concerns. Linda was hurt because she sensed a failure of closeness in their relationship: He didn't care about her as much as she cared about him. And he was hurt because he felt she was trying to control him and limit his freedom.

6   A similar conflict exists between Louise and Howie, another couple, about spending money. Louise would never buy anything costing more than a hundred dollars without discussing it with Howie, but he goes out and buys whatever he wants and feels they can afford, like a table saw or a new power mower. Louise is disturbed, not because she disapproves of the purchases, but because she feels he is acting as if she were not in the picture.

7   Many women feel it is natural to consult with their partners at every turn, while many men automatically make more decisions without consulting their partners. This may reflect a broad difference in conceptions of decision making. Women expect decisions to be discussed first and made by consensus. They appreciate the discussion itself as evidence of involvement and communication. But many men feel oppressed by lengthy discussions about what they see as minor decisions, and they feel hemmed in if they can't just act without talking first. When women try to initiate a freewheeling discussion by asking, "What do you think?" men often think they are being asked to decide.

8   Communication is a continual balancing act, juggling the conflicting needs for intimacy and independence. To survive in the world, we have to act in concert with others, but to survive as ourselves, rather than simply as cogs in a wheel, we have to act alone. In some ways, all people are the same: We all eat and sleep and drink and laugh and cough, and often we eat, and laugh at, the same things. But in some ways, each person is different, and individuals' differing wants and preferences may conflict with each other. Offered the same menu, people make different choices. And if there is cake for dessert, there is a chance one person may get a larger piece than another—and an even greater chance that one will *think* the other's piece is larger, whether it is or not.

EXPLORING THE READING THROUGH DISCUSSION

1. Tannen writes that "humans need both intimacy and independence." Do you agree? Why? Give examples.

2. How are the worlds of "connection" and "status" different? In which world would you rather live? Explain.

3. "Communication is a continual balancing act." Explain your understanding of this statement.

4. According to the author, how do men and women differ in the way they make decisions? Do you agree with Tannen?

5. What examples does the author provide to help readers understand the terms *intimacy* and *independence?*

DEVELOPING VOCABULARY

List any words in this selection that are new to you. Write your understanding of each word from the context. Then look up each word in the dictionary, and write the definition that you think best fits the meaning in this writing.

_____

_____

_____

_____

DISCOVERING CONNECTIONS THROUGH WRITING

CW VII.6 More on writing about literature I

1. Help Josh and Linda or Louise and Howie solve their communication problems. Write your advice, explaining how they can juggle their "conflicting needs for intimacy and independence."

2. Define the terms *masculine* and *feminine.* Provide examples, as Tannen does, to help readers understand what you mean by these terms.

3. Do you think men and women view the same situations in different ways, as Tannen suggests? Tell a story about a situation that supports this statement or about a situation that contradicts Tannen's opinion.

Nightwatch

Paul Fletcher

In this essay, originally published in 1990, teacher and writer Paul Fletcher writes about a minor car accident that led to more harm than a broken fender. As you read, see if you can discover the facts of what happened one night in a small town. Can the preconceived ideas we have about others affect our behavior?

1   It is a quiet spring night. In the oak-paneled living room of one of the gussied-up old houses that line Main Street, my daughter, Rosemary, and her boyfriend, Dan, are watching TV. A fire burns in the nicely detailed fireplace.

2   *Crash. Tinkle, tinkle, bang!*

3   Dan leaps up.

4   "Damn! If that's my car. . . ."

5   He throws open the front door and runs out, with Rosemary at his heels.

6   The driver's side of Dan's station wagon is, as they might have said years ago in this old seacoast town, "stove in." Dan and Rosemary are just in time to see a Mustang take off.

7   Then, unaccountably, the car comes to a halt; it slowly backs into a driveway and stands there, idling. In the moonlight, one can just make out the head and shoulders of the driver, a young woman.

8   By now, several neighbors are out on the street, under the bare horsechestnut trees. Against the old Colonial church, the shadows of the trees look like the ghosts of slaves. In the half-light, their bony arms seem to be warding off an overseer's whip.

9   From the back of the historic house on the corner, a young black man emerges. He is followed by another, and another, and yet another, until there are five young black men standing across the street from the driveway where the young woman sits in the Mustang.

10   The great tower of the old church, which has watched over the town since the days of the slave trade, chimes one.

11   A police car, its blue lights flashing, pulls up, and a young officer approaches the young woman in the car. She appears to be dazed. She is blonde, well dressed, in the preppie fashion—apparently a student at the local college.

12   "I didn't do any damage," she moans, more to herself or her absent parents than to anyone else.

13   Dan shakes his head as he looks at the large strip of chrome from his station wagon protruding from her front-wheel sprockets.

14   Under the great church tower, there in the moonlight, everyone seems to be frozen in time: the young woman; the police officer, joined now by a backup; the neighbors; the five young black men—all members, it turns out, of the college's basketball team. One of them seems to know the woman, and he steps toward her, to try to calm her.

15   "Take it easy," he seems to say, though his voice is muffled by those of the by-standers.

16   It appears that the young woman is intoxicated. One of the police officers tries to conduct a sobriety test, and she stands there flailing her slender arms as she tries to connect with the tip of her nose.

17   "Be cool," encourages the young man.

18   "Get away from her!" barks the officer. His even features turn distorted with rage.

19   "Get away from her!" he repeats.

20   "I'm only trying to help."

21   Now everything speeds up, and it seems that the policeman has struck the youth.

22   "That'll teach you," he says.

23   Did he jab the young man in the kidneys? Despite the bright, brittle moon-light, it's too dark to see.

24   Murmurs of protest emanate from the onlookers. The police officers hustle the young man into one of the patrol cars.

25   The church clock watches.

26   Gradually, the distorted mien of the angry policeman reverts to normal. He strides over to Dan.

27   "You wouldn't mind signing this report, would you, sir?" he says. "Just to witness that this young man was disorderly—don't want any stuff about police brutality."

28   Dan refuses. "I saw you manhandle that young man. He was only trying to quiet the girl."

29   The patrol car with the young woman and the young man drives off. Rosemary turns to go back into the house with Dan. She looks up at the church tower, which looms over the peaceful skyline of our old town, as it has always done, since the time when black people here were traded and transported.

EXPLORING THE READING THROUGH DISCUSSION

1. Describe the neighborhood where this story takes place. Do you think the setting is important? Why?

2. Why is the police officer whose face is "distorted with rage" so angry?

3. Do you agree with Dan's decision to refuse to sign the report? Why?

4. Why do you think the author called his story "Nightwatch"? Who or what is watching?

5. What point of view does Fletcher use to write his narrative essay? Do you agree with his choice? Explain.

DEVELOPING VOCABULARY

List any words in this selection that are new to you. Write your understanding of each word from the context. Then look up each word in the dictionary, and write the definition that you think best fits the meaning in this writing.

_____

_____

_____

_____

DISCOVERING CONNECTIONS THROUGH WRITING

**CW VII.7
More on
writing
about
literature II**

1. Have you ever seen an incident in which a person was treated unfairly because of his or her race, religion, ethnicity, or sexual orientation? Write about what happened, using effective description to create a vivid sense of the scene. Provide details that will clarify the causes and effects of the behavior.

2. Fletcher writes about the early history of the seacoast town in which this story takes place. Write about the history of your own community. How has it changed? How does the city or town commemorate its roots?

3. Describe an accident that you have witnessed or been involved in. Be sure to include descriptive details to help readers visualize the scene as you saw it.

Hit and Run

Susan Messer

···

In this essay, first published in the Chicago Reader, *Susan Messer tells the story of her usual mid-day exercise routine that becomes a frightening experience. As you read, consider if you would have acted the same way the author did. Can you recall a time when you wish you had spoken up when you saw something wrong but you were afraid to do so?*

1   I'm out running. My standard route, two–three miles around town. The noon hour. It's a warm fall day, so I'm wearing my usual warm-weather running outfit. Electric-green baggy shorts—of a sweatshirt material with a drawstring waist—and a raggedy old T-shirt. My route goes within a few blocks of the big high school with the golden bricks, the red tile roof, the arched windows, and the broad Frank Lloyd Wright–type eaves. Wright lived here during the formative years of his career, trying his ideas out this way and that, so Oak Parkers have the good fortune to find his influence all around us in the prairie-style architecture he spawned: pared-back horizontal lines, broad porches, bands of windows, wide Japanese-looking eves, flattish roofs.

2   But it's not a museum we live in. It's a real place, filled with living, breathing people at every stage of life. And when I'm out running near the high school during lunch time, some of these people are living full tilt while I attempt to dodge the action: teenagers drag racing down the streets, hanging out car windows, shouting to friends, squealing tires, no stops at stop signs. Thrill seekers.

3   It's a clear sunny day, and I'm sailing, sailing east toward home, down Superior Street, a straight-away that runs halfway through town. A dark-colored Mercedes comes up behind and passes me. It's got two high school boys in it, and the driver's got his side window open, arm extended, and he's waving a big Styrofoam cup. At the same time, a van comes up the street toward me, heading west. The Mercedes kid and the van driver must be either friends or enemies because when the two vehicles approach each other, the Mercedes kid tosses the Styrofoam cup up in a big arc. The cup bounces off the van, falls in the street, and the two drivers keep right on going, disappearing around various corners. The big cup just lies there, rolling back and forth in the breeze, some gloppy ice cream drink beside it.

4   I don't want to interrupt my run, but still. There's the cup in the street, and I'm the only one around. And I don't like litter. I grew up in the era of the anti-litterbug campaign (these high school kids apparently did not), and I can get strident, soap-boxy, on the subject: "What do they think? The world is their garbage can?"

5   I usually don't speak up about such things though because I'm afraid. My husband, in contrast, is not so afraid. Once, years ago, in a parking lot, he reprimanded a nun—A NUN—who we saw toss something, a cup or a napkin or a paper bag, as she got out of a car. She was young, and she wore the short veil of a nun on her head. And she was with several other women dressed similarly.

6   "Excuse me," my husband called. "I think you dropped something." And he stood there pointing down at her litter on the blacktop until she came back and picked it up.

7   So I'm looking at the lonely Styrofoam cup as it rolls back and forth in the breeze, muttering under my breath about the decline of Western civilization, when to my surprise, Mr. Mercedes pulls around the corner again, heading my way. I pick up the cup and stand in the middle of the street, electric-green shorts like a target, waving the cup around just as he was a few minutes ago.

8   My idea is that when he pulls up beside me, I'll do like my husband did. "Excuse me," I'll say. "I think you dropped something." Then, I'll simply ask him to throw the cup away in a garbage can. But it doesn't work out that way because instead of slowing down to see what I want, he speeds up. As he flies by me, I toss the cup at him, and it arcs right in through the open window, hitting him on the thick dark arm of his sunglasses. *Clunk.*

9   He slams on the brakes, his face a mask of rage.

10   "What are you doing?" he yells.

11   "Don't throw your stuff in the street."

12   "Don't throw things at me!" He says it as if we've got a long-term relationship, and this is a problem that's come up between us countless times.

13   "Just don't throw your stuff in the street." And then I start to get scared. This could be the moment when a modern-day kid pulls out his automatic weapon. But he doesn't. He just steps on the gas, leaving me in a cloud of dust.

14   I'm shaking. And the best thing I can do is run toward home, watch my back, in case my new enemy circles around again.

15   Within a few blocks of my house, I hear the sirens. They sound like they're all around me. A police car flies by, lights flashing, siren screaming, and it blocks off the entry way to my street. I'm already picturing the courtroom: *It was just a Styrofoam cup, your honor. Just an impulsive moment. We all make mistakes.*

16   Now I'm at my intersection, and I see my house just within reach, two doors up from the corner. I glide past the police car that's blocking the way, and the police officer doesn't even look at me. His eyes are focused farther up the block, and I look that way too, where the fire engines are stopped, and a small knot of neighbors are gathered on a lawn. Gradually, the knot loosens. The police get back into their car, the firefighters into their trucks, and the neighbors disperse: It was a false alarm in my neighbor's security system. And within moments, I'm safe in my house, the door closed behind me, trying to catch my breath.

EXPLORING THE READING THROUGH DISCUSSION

1. Who hits and runs in this essay? Do you agree with those actions? Explain.

2. In the concluding paragraph, the author writes that she is "safe in [her] house, the door closed behind [her]." Why is she afraid?

3. What sensory details does the author use to help put readers on the scene with her?

4. Where does the author introduce a flashback? How would her story be different without this section?

5. Find examples of sentence fragments in the essay. Do these confuse readers or do they add to the effectiveness of the story? Explain.

DEVELOPING VOCABULARY

List any words in this selection that are new to you. Write your understanding of each word from the context. Then look up each word in the dictionary, and write the definition that you think best fits the meaning in this writing.

_____

_____

_____

_____

DISCOVERING CONNECTIONS THROUGH WRITING

**CW VII.8
More on
writing
about
literature III**

1. The author writes that her neighborhood is "a real place, filled with living, breathing people at every stage of life." Describe your own neighborhood and some of the people who live in it. Be sure to use both subjective and objective description in your writing.

2. With the help of your college or public library staff or by searching the Web, find out what you can about Frank Lloyd Wright, the man who is mentioned in the introduction. Compare what you learn with how he and his work are described in the essay.

3. The author "grew up in the era of the anti-litterbug campaign." Is this campaign over? Write to state your view on the seriousness of littering.

Words, Good or Bad, Can Echo through a Lifetime

Bob Greene

Language can change lives. That belief is the main point of Bob Greene's article, first published as a column in the Chicago Tribune. _He writes about the power of both spoken and written words to affect people's lives, often not deliberately. How important has someone's praise or criticism been to your own success?_

1   "**A**re you too stupid to do anything right?"

2   The words—spoken by a woman to a little boy who evidently was her son— were spoken because he had walked away from her. Chastised—these words were said at a volume high enough that all the strangers in the vicinity could hear—the boy, his face blank, his eyes downcast, returned quietly to the woman's side.

3   Not a big moment. Perhaps—not anything that could qualify as abuse or neglect or any of the other unhappy words that have become a part of our national lexicon. Yet small moments sometimes last for a very long time. Small moments sometimes last for eternity.

4   And a few words—words that mean little at the time to the people responsible for them—can have enormous power. "Are you too stupid to do anything right?" Words like that can echo.

5   So can words of the other kind.

6   What makes me think about this is a story I heard recently from a man named Malcolm Dalkoff. He's 48; for the last 24 years he has been a professional writer, most of these years spent in the advertising industry. Here is what he told me:

7   As a boy in Rock Island, Ill., he was terribly insecure and shy. He was quiet, he was scared, he mostly stayed by himself. He had few friends, and no sense of self-confidence.

8   In October of 1965, his English teacher at Rock Island High School—her name was Ruth Brauch—gave the class an assignment. The students had been reading "To Kill a Mockingbird," by Harper Lee. Mrs. Brauch assigned the class members to write a chapter that would follow the last chapter of the novel. Their own chapter.

9   Malcolm Dalkoff wrote his chapter and turned it in. Today, he cannot recall feeling anything special about the act of writing that chapter, or what grade Mrs. Brauch gave him.

10   What he does remember—what he will never forget—are the four words his teacher wrote in the margins of the paper:

11   "This is good writing."

12   Four words. And they changed his life.

13   "Up until I read those words, I had no idea of who I was or what I was going to be," he said. "After reading her note I went home and wrote a short story, something I had always dreamed of doing but never really believed I could do."

14   Over the rest of that year in school, he wrote many short stories, always bringing them to school for Mrs. Brauch to look at and evaluate. She was encouraging: she was tough; she was honest. "She was just what I needed," Dalkoff said.

15   He was named co-editor of his high school paper: his confidence grew, his horizons broadened, he started off on a successful and fulfilling life. He is convinced that none of this would have happened had that woman not written those four words in the margin of his paper.

16   At his 30th high school reunion in Rock Island, the teachers did not attend—just the returning students, now men and women in middle age. But Dalkoff, back home for reunion weekend, went to Mrs. Brauch's house; she was now retired.

17   And he told her. He told her what her four words had done for him. He told her that because she had given him the confidence to believe that he might be worth something, the confidence to try to be a writer, he had been able to pass that confidence on to the woman who would become his wife, who became a writer herself. He told Mrs. Brauch about a woman who worked in his office—a woman who was working in the evenings toward a high school equivalency diploma—who had come to him for help. She respected him because he was a writer, he said—that is why the woman trying to get her diploma at night turned to him for advice and assistance.

18   Mrs. Brauch was especially moved by that story—the story of helping the young woman. "I think we both realized at that moment that Mrs. Brauch cast an incredibly long shadow," he said.

19   When Dalkoff came to Mrs. Brauch's house, he brought as a gift some books he had especially enjoyed over the years.

20   She said to him, "You shouldn't have."

21   He thought to himself: She's right. It should have been castles.

22   "Are you too stupid to do anything right?"

23   "This is good writing."

24   So few words. And they can last forever. They can change everything.

EXPLORING THE READING THROUGH DISCUSSION

1. The author recalls the story of a man who is convinced that he would not have the life he enjoys if a teacher had "not written those four words in the margin of his paper." Do you agree with him about the power of words?

2. What do you imagine are the effects of the words that the little boy hears?

3. In what ways did Mrs. Brauch "cast a long shadow"?

4. Find examples of the author's use of dashes in his essay. Why do you think he selects this punctuation? What other choices could he have made?

5. Do you think the author's final brief paragraphs provide an effective conclusion? Explain.

DEVELOPING VOCABULARY

List any words in this selection that are new to you. Write your understanding of each word from the context. Then look up each word in the dictionary, and write the definition that you think best fits the meaning in this writing.

_____

_____

_____

_____

DISCOVERING CONNECTIONS THROUGH WRITING

**CW VII.9
More on
writing
about
literature IV**

1. What words have influenced you? Write to explain what effects those words have had.

2. "Small moments sometimes last for eternity." In your experience, what small moment have you later found to be important? Write to tell the story of your experience.

3. A good teacher is defined in this essay as one who is encouraging, tough, and honest. Write to define a good teacher, a good parent, or a good coach. When you write, focus on three characteristics of that person to help your reader understand your definition.

Remote Control—
How to Raise a Media Skeptic

Susan Douglas

* *

Susan Douglas teaches in the Department of Communication Studies at the University of Michigan. She is a media critic, scholar, and author of many articles and several books, including the acclaimed Where the Girls Are: Growing Up Female with the Mass Media. *As you read this selection, explore your own thoughts about the influence of television, especially on children. Do you believe it's important for children to understand how television attempts to sway opinion?*

1   "**M**ommy, Mommy, come here, now! Hurry, you're gonna miss it. It's Barbie's High-Steppin' Pony, and its legs really move! Hurreeeeey!"

2   "No!" I bark, as I'm wiping the dog barf up from the carpet, stirring the onions again so they don't burn, and slamming the phone down on a caller from Citibank who wants to know how I'm doin' today. It is 5:56 P.M., and I'm in no mood. "I don't come for commercials, and besides, the horse doesn't really move—they just make it look that way."

3   "Oh yeah?" demands my daughter, sounding like a federal prosecutor. "It can too. It's not like those old ones where you told me they faked it—this one really does move."

4   So now I have to go see and, indeed, the sucker takes batteries, and the stupid horse moves—sort of. "See, Mommy, the commercials don't always lie."

5   Moments like this prompt me to wonder whether I'm a weak-kneed, lazy slug, or, dare I say it, a hypocrite. See, I teach media studies, and, even worse, I go around the country lecturing about the importance of media literacy. One of my talking points is how network children's programming is, ideologically, a toxic waste dump. Yet here I am, just like millions of parents during that portion of the day rightly known as hell hour—dinnertime—shoving my kid in front of Nickelodeon so my husband and I can get dinner on the table while we whisper sweet nothings like "It's your turn to take her to Brownies tomorrow" and "Oh, shit, I forgot to tell you that your mother called three days ago with an urgent message."

6   We let her watch Nickelodeon, but I still pop in to ridicule Kool-Aid commercials or to ask her why Clarissa's parents (on *Clarissa Explains It All*) are so dopey. I am trying to have it both ways: to let television distract her, which I desperately need, and to help her see through its lies and banalities. I am very good at rationalizing this approach, but I also think it isn't a bad compromise for overworked parents who believe Barbie is the anti-Christ yet still need to wash out grotty lunch boxes and zap leftovers at the end of the day.

7   It's best to be honest up front: My house is not media proofed. I am not one of those virtuous, haloed parents who has banished the box from the home. I actually believe that there are interesting, fun shows for my daughter to watch on TV. (And I'm not about to give up *ER*).

8   But I'm also convinced that knowing about television, and growing up with it, provides my daughter with a form of cultural literacy that she will need, that will tie her to her friends and her generation and help her understand her place in the world. So instead of killing my TV, I've tried to show my daughter basic bullshit-detecting techniques. Don't think your choices are either no TV or a zombified

kid. Studies show that the simple act of intervening—of talking to your child about what's on television and why it's on there—is one of the most important factors in helping children understand and distance themselves from some of the box's more repugnant imagery.

9   I recommend the quick surgical strike, between throwing the laundry in and picking up the Legos. Watch a few commercials with them and point out that commercials lie about the toys they show, making them look much better than they are in real life. Count how many male and female characters there are in a particular show or commercial and talk about what we see boys doing and what we see girls doing. Why, you might ask, do we always see girls playing with makeup kits and boys playing with little Johnny Exocet missiles? Real-life dads change diapers, push strollers, and feed kids, but you never see boys doing this with dolls on commercials. Ask where the Asian and African-American kids are. Point out how most of the parents in shows geared to kids are much more stupid than real-life parents. (By the way, children report that TV shows encourage them to talk back to their folks.) Tell them that all those cereals advertised with cartoon characters and rap music (like Cocoa Puffs and Trix) will put giant black holes in their teeth that only a dentist with a drill the size of the space shuttle can fix.

10   One of the best words to use when you're watching TV with your kids is *stupid*, as in "Aren't Barbie's feet—the way she's always forced to walk on her tiptoes—really stupid?" or "Isn't it stupid that Lassie is smarter than the mom on this show?" (My favorite Barbie exercise: Put your kitchen timer on for a minute and make your daughter walk around on her tiptoes just like Barbie: she'll get the point real fast.) *Cool*—a word that never seems to go out of style—is also helpful, as in "Isn't it cool that on *Legends of the Hidden Temple* (a game show on Nickelodeon) the girls are as strong and as fast as the boys?" Pointing out what's good on TV is important too.

11   See, I think complete media-proofing is impossible, because the shallow, consumerist, anti-intellectual values of the mass media permeate our culture. And we parents shouldn't beat ourselves up for failing to quarantine our kids. But we can inoculate them—which means exposing them to the virus and showing them how to build up a few antibodies. So don't feel so guilty about letting them watch TV. Instead, have fun teaching them how to talk back to it rather than to you.

EXPLORING THE READING THROUGH DISCUSSION

1. What are Susan Douglas's objections to what is on television? Do you agree with her? Why does she allow her daughter to watch TV?

2. Douglas says she is "trying to have it both ways." Do you think her compromise solution works?

3. Douglas says that television provides her daughter with "a form of cultural literacy." Explain your understanding of that term.

4. Who do you think is the audience Douglas directs her writing to? What is her purpose for writing? What details in the writing lead you to this conclusion?

5. The author uses several voices and types of language in her writing. Find examples of language that let you hear Douglas the professor and media critic and examples of language that let you hear Douglas the busy wife and parent. Is the effect of this confusing? Interesting? Convincing?

DEVELOPING VOCABULARY

List any words in this selection that are new to you. Write your understanding of each word from the context. Then look up each word in the dictionary, and write the definition that you think best fits the meaning in this writing.

_____

_____

_____

_____

DISCOVERING CONNECTIONS THROUGH WRITING

1. "Pointing out what's good on TV is important too," states Douglas. Using specific examples, write about what you think is good on TV.

2. Watch several children's programs on network television, as well as the commercials aired before, during, and after, and take notes of what you see. What would you want to point out to a child to help him or her see through any "lies and banalities"?

3. Susan Douglas suggests that television programs don't portray us as we are in real life. Do you agree with her? Write an essay in which you take a stand and argue that television does or does not reflect people as you know them to be.

My Paradise

Naihsin Weng (student)

....

If you have ever left familiar surroundings for a new home, you might understand why everyday memories are so important to this student author. As you read, try to discover the details that help you imagine her home as she remembers it. Why do you think places from our past leave us such strong memories?

1   **W**hen I was twelve years old, living in Taiwan, my father bought a new apartment, which was close to our original apartment, only five minutes away. So my parents decided to move all our belongings by ourselves little by little. I was coming and going frequently, by riding my beloved pink bicycle with a basket in the front which was full of my treasures. At that time, I felt very excited because I was going to live in a brand-new apartment. Moving to a new apartment was so fresh to a twelve-year-old girl. I did not even feel sad about leaving my original house. Maybe that was because my parents still kept it, so I could go back any time. From then on, we started to call the original place "old house," and call our new apartment "new house."

2   After living in our new house for a month, I started to miss our old house. The simple reason was just that I could not find friends to play with me in our new

building. So I needed to run back to my old house and play with my neighbors there. The neighbor kids were around my age. We were all innocent and friendly because of good education. Our parents were all teachers and colleagues in a high school. The school had several dormitories for teachers on the block. So we had all lived there and were like a big family.

3   Time did not make it easy to stay on course. After six months, I enrolled in the middle school. Homework occupied my playing time and made me say goodbye to my childhood. Later, I became a high school student, and then I was accepted as a student at the university. In those years, I hardly went back to the old house. There were several times I just passed in a rush. I noticed that something had changed, but I just let it go at that. The winter of 1999 I decided to study in the United States, so I went back to the old house and stayed there the whole afternoon to memorize my "home."

4   I opened the main door and heard some noises. The door was not easy to open and close because of its age. I touched some flakes of red paint that were peeling on the door, and the memories started to bring back my childhood.

5   It had been a Chinese New Year's Eve when my father decided to paint the door red, because red symbolized luck. I was a little girl and squatted beside my father. The red was bright, like a rose in full bloom. I told my father that it was beautiful, and my father was very proud of his painting because of my praise. From then on, I knew I was his little princess. My words could make him happy like walking in the clouds.

6   Being a princess, I had some privileges. I could play with other kids without finishing homework. I usually went to the high school with my neighbors. We played basketball, football, and volleyball until the sun was gone and the sky was black. There were always thousands of games we could play in such a large open space. One time we even roasted sweet potatoes on the playground and caught the fish in the school ponds for our BBQ. At that time, our parents were warned about our "bad" behaviors by the police at school. In our small world, we did not realize that we were doing something wrong. We just felt the whole school was like a paradise where we could play anything we wanted.

7   There was a shortcut from the old house to the high school. That was the way my father passed every day. At five-ten in the afternoon. I usually sat on a set of stone steps that were in the middle of the shortcut and waited for my father to come home. When he showed up at the head of the road. I would run as if I were flying, shouting "Pa-Pa," and jumping energetically into his arms.

8   One afternoon, I finished a homework assignment that involved making a swan by using thick paper. I was supposed to wipe oil on the bottom of the swan, so that it could float on the water. Unfortunately, I totally forgot this step. I put my white swan on the surface of water. But soon my swan could not float, and it sank like the *Titanic*. My white swan became a gray one.

9   Then I cried and ran out to the stone steps. I sat there and waited for my father to save my poor swan. A second seemed to be a year. I stretched my neck many times looking for my father's shadow. I knew it was not five-ten yet, but I just hoped that a miracle would happen, which could bring my father here. I even counted the stone steps in three different languages, but my father still did not show up. Maybe because of my crying, I was so tired that I fell asleep on the stone steps. When I woke up, I was in the warm arms of my father. I forgot my sad story of the swan but just held my father tight, as he was my hero.

10   Standing on the playground and overlooking the dormitories, I tried to memorize every scene so that I could bring them to America. The laughter of my friends seemed to whisper in the wind. Most of them still lived there, but they were not at home. They might be studying in different cities now. I did not know if they missed me as now I missed them. Did they remember the taste of hot potatoes on the playground? Did all of them know that I was going to the other side of this earth? Now our worlds were not small any more, but had they found their own paradises yet?

11   I kept walking down and came to the shortcut. The stone steps looked so narrow. I could not imagine how I could sleep there. I looked at the head of the road, and tears came to my eyes. My father was still a teacher here. Will he feel sad when he walks on this road and I am on the other side of the earth? Will he expect a miracle to bring his little princess here?

12   Last September hundreds of powerful earthquakes happened in my country, Taiwan. I went back to my home this January and checked out both the old and new houses. I am glad that my beloved homes still look like the images that I have in my mind. All in all, home is my paradise that nothing can change.

EXPLORING THE READING THROUGH DISCUSSION

1. What do you think the author means when she writes, "I touched some flakes of red paint that were peeling on the door, and the memories started to bring back my childhood"? Have you ever had a similar experience based on a sight or sound or smell?

2. What memories does Naihsin Weng describe? Which description do you think is the most effective? Why?

3. Find examples of objective description and subjective description in this essay.

4. The author's father is a central figure in her memories of her home and childhood. What details in the essay help you get to know him?

5. The author writes about several periods of time in her essay. Identify them. What clues does she include to help readers understand what time in her life she is describing?

DEVELOPING VOCABULARY

List any words in this selection that are new to you. Write your understanding of each word from the context. Then look up each word in the dictionary, and write the definition that you think best fits the meaning in this writing.

_____

_____

_____

_____

DISCOVERING CONNECTIONS THROUGH WRITING

1. Return to a favorite place that you remember from your childhood. Does what you see "still look like the images that [you] have in [your] mind"? What has changed? Compare your memory with the present reality.

2. Naihsin Weng concludes that "home is my paradise that nothing can change." Do you think she is referring only to the geographic location of her home or also to other aspects of her home? Write your definition of "home." Be sure to include both the denotation, or literal meaning of the word, and its connotations, all the associations that come with the word.

3. Have you moved from one home to another? Did you, as did Naihsin Weng, "[try] to memorize every scene" before moving on? Write to tell the story of your moving experience.

Pride

Stephanie Jezak (student)

This student author writes to define "pride," a quality that she believes is very important for everyone to have. Stephanie Jezak's pride is from her sense of achievement in making and reaching her goals. What do you think helps people develop pride and self-respect?

1   Pride is one of the most important things people can have in their lives. Without it, people would have a hard time feeling good about themselves. Pride is an inner feeling of achievement or satisfaction. There are many different things that allow a person to feel self respect. There are a few decisions that I am personally very proud of myself for making.

2   My decision to come back to school was nerve wracking. I was nervous because I hadn't been in a school setting in about six years. After I graduated from high school I took a few classes at B.C.C., but I soon realized I wasn't ready. I was much more interested in going out at night and sleeping in late, and just having fun as most teenagers are. Finally after some encouragement from my boyfriend, and two and a half years at my awful job, I decided it was time. Although very often it's difficult to juggle work and school, I know this will prove to be one of the best decisions I've ever made. The day I graduate will surely be one of my proudest moments because I will have attained one of the most important things in my life, an education.

3   Another decision I am very proud of is my choice to eat a vegetarian diet. This was very important at first. I used to eat meat every day until the day I decided to quit. I had a couple of reasons for becoming a vegetarian; they were based both on health reasons and the treatment of animals. First of all, vegetarian diets are likely to lessen the risk of different types of cancer, and heart disease. And second, I have always sympathized with animals, and since I was young I always wanted to try a meat free diet. It was difficult at that time, however, because my parents bought and prepared all of my meals. Now that I am older I can make decisions

on what food I want to put into my body, and hopefully spare the lives of some animals. I have followed a vegetarian diet for two years now, and I am proud to have made this lifestyle change.

4   My decision to exercise is probably the one that I struggle with the most on a day to day basis. All of my other big decisions are sort of habit now. I do it without thinking much about it (go to school, avoid meat). Exercise, however, I have to force myself to do. I can think of a million bad reasons why I shouldn't or don't have to exercise, but there's always a million more good reasons to do it. When I finish doing my work out I feel this tremendous sense of pride that comes only from this particular activity. I also feel a great sense of relief that I'm done and can relax. I've only been exercising now for about three months, but I think it's something I will increasingly be proud of.

5   Finally, the decision that I have made that I am most proud of is my choice to quit smoking. I continue to make this choice every morning when I wake up. I started smoking when I was sixteen because all of my friends did. I tried many times for many years to quit. Finally at the age of twenty-five I have been smoke free for about eight months. Starting smoking was one of the worst decisions I have ever made, but quitting is certainly one of the best.

EXPLORING THE READING THROUGH DISCUSSION

1. Do you agree with the author about the importance of pride? What is the relationship between pride and self-respect?

2. What are the challenges the author, Stephanie Jezak, has to face to stick with her decisions? Do these difficulties increase her sense of pride?

3. The author is most proud of her decision to quit smoking. What do you think is the decision she should take the most pride in making? Why?

4. What techniques does the author use to provide coherence in her essay?

5. If you could give the author some feedback about her conclusion, what would you suggest?

DEVELOPING VOCABULARY

List any words in this selection that are new to you. Write your understanding of each word from the context. Then look up each word in the dictionary, and write the definition that you think best fits the meaning in this writing.

_____

_____

_____

_____

DISCOVERING CONNECTIONS THROUGH WRITING

1. What are you proud of doing or what decisions are you proud of making? Write about what has given you "an inner feeling of achievement or satisfaction" as Stephanie Jezak has done.

2. Have you ever stopped a bad habit such as smoking? Write to explain the process you followed to succeed.

3. Is it possible to have too much pride? Write to explain what can happen as a result. Be sure to give examples so that your reader understands what excessive pride can do.

Exposed Toes

Diane Riva (student)

Are your old basketball shoes, the ones with the holes, your favorites? Maybe you couldn't spend a day without your floppy slippers? As you read student author Diane Riva's essay about shoes, try to discover the special connection she has to these everyday items. Why do you think people form attachments to personal objects?

1   The shoes scattered throughout the house belong to me. I will find a pair under the dining room table, a pair in the parlor, one or two pairs in the kitchen, and even a few in my bedroom. In my childhood memories, I can still hear my mother asking me to pick up my wayward shoes. Some habits are hard to break, and leaving my shoes wherever my feet release them is one I am still trying to overcome. When I look at my shoes, I see endless memories. They are part of my personality, and if they could talk, what colorful tales they would tell.

2   I own three pairs of black sneakers; they are my proud work shoes, and we spend the most time together. There are times when my feet melt when I enter them. My work as a bartender has enabled my sneakers to taste Guinness Irish stout, fine Russian vodkas, assorted hot coffee drinks, or whatever else I am rushing around the bar to make. They are the constant recipients of the overfilled glass of alcohol.

3   My black, tattered sneakers with tiny knots in the shoelaces have heard hours of endless stories from lonely travelers stopping in the hotel lounge, guests pouring out tales of love, heartache, job stress, divorce, battles won, battles lost, and hundreds of irritating jokes. At the end of my shift, if we are fortunate and it has rained, I give the bottoms of my hard-working sneakers a bath in a fresh puddle. It feels good to wash away work. When my feet arrive home, my sneakers are usually slipped off and left in the parlor to slumber. This is where they will quietly remain until I torture them for another eight hours of work.

4   Along with my sneakers, I own a pair of boat shoes. The tops are a reddish brown, the same color as an Irish Setter, and the soles are made of rubber. I have had these shoes for over six years, and still they do not age as I do. When I occasionally wear my boat shoes, I don't like the way they look on my wide feet, but they feel so good. They know me the least but struggle to be in my world. I will

probably have these shoes for the rest of my life. They are like memories of past boyfriends: hard to get rid of.

5   When I open my closet door, my dress shoes lie dead in dusty boxes. About every four months, I will remove a pair and struggle into them. When I wear these high-heeled shoes, it is usually for a wedding, a Christmas party, or a night on the town. When I add one or two inches to my height, I end up having this pretty feeling, and my legs have a tendency to like the way they look. The sound of a high-heeled shoe on a polished marble floor at a posh restaurant, I will admit, has a certain appeal to me. I gather it is my whole look, from the top of my perfectly set hair to the ends of my smothered toes, that gives me this feeling of attractiveness.

6   But how I look forward to removing these falsely overstated dress shoes and returning them to their dusty coffins. Funny how these shoes never lounge around the house; they are always returned to their boxes. I would not want to insult the everyday, comfortable shoe with the high society heel.

7   Among my most treasured shoes is a pair of sandals. They can be worn throughout all the seasons, with or without socks. My huaraches are from Tiajuana, and on a hot day many years ago, I handpicked them myself from among many of their twins. The soles are made from black, recycled tires, and the upper portion consists of thick, tan leather strips that entwine to form an interesting open-toe design. They call my name constantly, but unfortunately, they are the most inappropriate shoe for all occasions. As I picked up my paycheck from work one cold November day, my boss commented on my unusual footwear for this time of year. He could not help but notice my well-worn extra-wide huaraches and my thick woolen socks, so he stated that it seemed an unsuitable time of year for sandals. I tried to explain the comfort zone of these broken-in shoes, but he just looked at me with confusion. I don't think that he could relate to the love–hate affair that women have with their shoes. I have had the pleasure of spoiling my feet with these huaraches for over eight years. Each spring they take a trip to the cobbler for their yearly checkup. I think the cobbler looks forward to this annual visit and admires the workmanship in these weary old sandals.

8   I must admit my shoes of choice were given to me by my parents, and I wear these constantly. Nothing has to be tied; they have no straps, no buckles, no leather between the toes, no heels. They are never too tight and always fit perfectly—my natural feet. Whenever possible, my feet are out of confinement, barefoot and happy. I love for my feet to touch and feel all the materials of life. They can be tickled, washed, counted, and colored. They hold all of my memories. They were on my honeymoon; they were at my daughter's birth; they feel spring and the ocean first; they have been bitten, cut, and bruised. I never have to look for them, they are always where I left them, and they never have to be put away.

9   As I search throughout my house and pick up my wayward shoes before my mother arrives for a visit. I look down at the bundle of leather and laces in my arms, and days of my past shout out to me. I know why these shoes are scattered about. They are my memories, and I do not want to put them away.

EXPLORING THE READING THROUGH DISCUSSION

1. What is the main point the author wants to make about her shoes? On what basis does she categorize them?

2. What details help you picture the author's shoes and understand how she feels about them?

3. What are Riva's "shoes of choice"? Why are these her favorites?

4. How do the introduction and the conclusion contribute to the effectiveness of this essay?

5. In what order does the author arrange the types of shoes? Do you think this order is effective? Why?

DEVELOPING VOCABULARY

List any words in this selection that are new to you. Write your understanding of each word from the context. Then look up each word in the dictionary, and write the definition that you think best fits the meaning in this writing.

_____

_____

_____

_____

DISCOVERING CONNECTIONS THROUGH WRITING

1. Describe a favorite article of clothing that brings back fond memories or makes you feel good when you wear it. Help your reader understand your feelings by describing the clothing and explaining why it is special to you.

2. As Riva does with shoes, classify another type of clothing or accessory that you own, such as hats, T-shirts, or earrings. Be sure to follow a consistent method of classification.

3. The author writes about struggling into pairs of high-heeled dress shoes. Write an essay in which you support the thesis that being fashionable doesn't always mean being comfortable.

Childhood—Then and Now

Jane Patenaude (student)

....

Has anyone ever told you that "Life isn't the same as it used to be"? As you read this student's comparison/contrast essay, see if you agree with her about how life for children has changed. Do you think that kids have truly changed, or is it a matter of personal perception?

1   **A**s a child I had the freedom to roam most of North Fairhaven. Of course North Fairhaven to me was about four square blocks. Mom always knew where to find me, with friends or at the playground behind Oxford school. It seems to me

that children today don't have the same type of childhood. I can't imagine a parent of today allowing a child to roam neighborhood streets as we did forty years ago. It appears to me that today's children of elementary school age have every minute of their lives filled with activities. They are kept busy with schoolwork, soccer, or other activities. When do they have time to play?

2   For children growing up in the fifties our imaginations were the main source of our entertainment. Most families didn't have a television, so our entertainment came from other sources, such as dolls and balls. Barbie was just a doll then, not a collectible. We changed her outfits and created stories about her, Skipper, and Ken. We played board games, such as Clue and Parcheesi. I remember a Monopoly game that went on a whole summer. In the winter, it seemed to snow more then; we built forts of snow and had snowball fights. Our parents would have to beg us to come inside, even though our lips were turning blue from the cold.

3   Summer months were filled with riding bikes, running through the sprinkler in the back yard, riding on the swings and merry-go-round at the playground, and playing baseball. There were enough of us in the neighborhood to form teams and play Wiffle Ball in the street. Not many cars cruised down our side street to interrupt our game. Bike riding was a favorite pastime. One of my husband's childhood memories is of riding his bike out to Tinkham Pond in East Fairhaven. At a distance of about eight miles, it was an easy ride from the center of town, passing farms and wooded areas. Today this bike ride would entail crossing Route 6 as well as Route 240, a major highway, and two busy shopping centers, not a pleasant ride. To ride out that way today is still nice, but you would most likely transport the bikes to that part of town, then go for a bike ride, especially if you're riding with children. And it is unlikely any parents would let their children head that way on their own.

4   Today children have so much to keep them entertained. Electronic games, television, and videos occupy their time inside the house. Their parents spend a lot of time taxi-ing their children between activities such as soccer, T-ball, art classes, gymnastics, dance classes, and baseball. Kids today have so many diversions; it seems they have little freedom. Some adult is always there watching them or coaching them. I'm sure our parents were just as watchful, but they watched at a distance, checking on us by looking out the back window. They always knew where we were. It just wasn't obvious.

5   Just last summer I was at the beach with a friend. I asked where her eight-year-old son was. I couldn't believe it when she told me he was in the house watching a video. It was a beautiful day, and he was spending it inside watching a video he had seen at least five times. This kid actually has his own battery-operated car that he drives to the beach at the end of his street. As a kid the first thing I did after opening my eyes on a summer day was to look outside to see if the sun was out. I couldn't wait to go outside. And it was a huge treat if we could go to the beach for the day. The closest I came to having a car was one my mom fashioned out of sand with soda cans for headlights.

6   The family that lives across the street has three children, a son in elementary school, another son in middle school, and a daughter in high school. Each school has a different start time. Their mom takes three separate trips to deliver them to school. Two of these schools are within walking distance. Don't kids walk anymore?

7   I feel fortunate to have grown up in such an innocent time, a time when one income was enough to support a family. When I wasn't in school, I was playing in my back yard or at a neighbor's house. It bothers me to see the children at a

nearby child care center playing outside in a penned-in area with adults watching over them, looking more like guards than teachers. While I'm sure there is good and bad in each generation, I'm just glad my childhood was when it was.

EXPLORING THE READING THROUGH DISCUSSION

1. According to the author, what are the main differences between children of her generation and children today? Do you agree?

2. The author states that children are "kept [so] busy with school work, soccer, or other activities," that they don't have time to play. If asked, how do you think she would define "play"? Would you agree with her definition?

3. What are some of Jane Patenaude's reasons for suggesting that the type of childhood she had isn't possible today?

4. The author uses many proper and brand names in her essay. List as many of them as you can. Why do you think she includes these?

5. Is a block format or alternating format used in this comparison and contrast essay? Do you think this was a good choice? Explain.

DEVELOPING VOCABULARY

List any words in this selection that are new to you. Write your understanding of each word from the context. Then look up each word in the dictionary, and write the definition that you think best fits the meaning in this writing.

_____

_____

_____

_____

DISCOVERING CONNECTIONS THROUGH WRITING

1. The author writes about using her imagination as a source of entertainment. What do you think imagination is, and how do you use it? Write to explain your understanding of this term.

2. Do you agree that today's children "seem [to] have little freedom" and that our present time is a less innocent time in which to grow up? Write an essay in which you present the causes of this phenomenon. As you explore this topic, be sure to present enough details to help readers understand the complexity of this situation.

3. Ask a friend or relative who was a child in the 1950s to describe his or her childhood playtime experiences. Are they the same as Jane Patenaude's? Why? Using the mode of comparison and contrast, write about the differences or similarities.

Fear Not

Greg Andree (student)

. . . .

Before this student author took a long walk across a dance floor, he considered what fear is and how it can affect us. As you read, ask yourself whether you have experienced each of the fears Greg Andree describes. What is it about some situations that can make us so afraid?

1   I looked across the dance floor; one of the most attractive women I had ever seen sat talking with some friends. She glanced toward me, but I turned away. Was she really looking at me? Why not? I'm a handsome guy. In fact, my mom tells me that all the time. I took a quick look back at her; she was still looking in my direction.

2   Why wouldn't she be looking at me? But she might just be looking at my friend who was sitting near me, or for that matter, she might just be trying to see what time it was (a clock hung just above my head). I could have misinterpreted a look at a clock for a glance in my direction.

3   What was keeping me from just getting up, walking over to her, and asking her to dance? Well, besides the fear of rejection from her and the dread of humiliation in front of her friends and mine, nothing at all.

4   I remember that as a kid I often sat alone in my basement doing my homework. It was the only place in the house I could go to be alone—well, besides the bathroom. If you spent too much time in there, though, people began to talk.

5   As daylight turned to dusk and then to darkness, the basement's shadows seemed to take on a life of their own; sounds that might have been ordinary before now sounded strange and menacing. I decided that this was no longer the ideal place for me to be alone with my thoughts. I got up and started walking slowly toward the steps that led to my family and the safety of their number. I wanted to run but refused to give the monster the satisfaction of knowing that it drove me from my own basement. I had to be brave and fight the panic that was welling up inside me. By the time I reached the stairs, I could feel its hot breath on my neck. I was sure that the creature was about to attack and drag me down into his hidden lair. Before it could, I ran, taking the stairs two at a time. If I could only reach the top, I would be safe.

6   Looking back now, it seems silly, but to a nine-year-old it was life or death. It's the same as when a thirteen-year-old, afraid of not fitting in, does everything within his power to belong. The worst thing in the world to a young teenager is the "problem" of being unique, having special talents or interests that are outside the margins of acceptability to the "popular" kids in school.

7   An example of this, from a boy's perspective, is that you're accepted if you excel in sports but are hopelessly doomed to exile if you are talented in music or art. As we get older, we realize these talents are gifts, not curses, and are grateful for our uniqueness, although knowing this now didn't make it easier then.

8   Now, as a college student, I have other fears. What if I fail in the career I've chosen, if I don't fulfill my dreams? How will I support myself, my family? Someday, if I do prosper in my career, will I look back at my college years and laugh at fears that now seem so enormous? What will my fears be then? Old age, senility, death? I don't really know.

9   What I do know is that no matter who we are or what our station in life is, we all have fears. Some are reasonable and keep us safe from the dangers that surround us constantly, and others are unreasonable and ridiculous, or seem so to those of us who don't share them. Some make us strive to do better; others keep us from attempting the things we would really like to do. If there's a fear holding you back from accomplishing your dreams, you have two choices: Either find a way to overcome it, or cower in its shadow and learn to live with what could have been.

10   But enough of all that. I was in the middle of one of my adventures. Now, where was I? Never mind, I remember. . . .

11   What should I do? Just sit there and not take the chance, or seize the day as Robin Williams would have said in the movie *Dead Poets Society?* Which is best, to have loved and lost, or, in this case, tried and failed, or to have never tried at all? Finally, I thought of the advice Kevin Kline had given to a young pirate in Gilbert and Sullivan's *Pirates of Penzance:* "Always follow the dictates of your heart, my boy, and chance the consequences."

12   With this in mind, I got to my feet and made my way across the room to where she and her friends were sitting. I stood just a few feet from her. Doing my best Christian Slater imitation, I looked into her eyes and said, "Excuse me, Miss, would you care to dance?" She seemed to think it over for a moment, then took my hand and nodded her approval. "You do understand you'll be dancing with me, right?" I said. She laughed and said that she understood that I was included in the bargain.

13   As we danced, she leaned in close to me, her face inches from mine, and I felt her warm breath caress my cheek. She looked into my eyes and said, "Do you know what time it is? I really couldn't see the clock that well from where I was sitting."

EXPLORING THE READING THROUGH DISCUSSION

1. What types of fear does the writer describe? In what order does he present these? Which fear do you think is the worst?

2. What did the author learn about what he feared as he grew older?

3. Some fears "are reasonable and keep us safe from the dangers that surround us constantly, and others are unreasonable and ridiculous." What examples can you think of to support this statement?

4. What is the thesis of this essay? Why do you think the author placed it where he did?

5. The author's story begins and ends at a dance. Where does the author shift from the chronological order of his narrative? How does he help readers understand that they are reading a flashback?

DEVELOPING VOCABULARY

List any words in this selection that are new to you. Write your understanding of each word from the context. Then look up each word in the dictionary, and write the definition that you think best fits the meaning in this writing.

_____

_____

_____

_____

DISCOVERING CONNECTIONS THROUGH WRITING

1. Write about a time you were afraid. Help readers understand not only what happened but also how the fear affected you. Did it hold you back or make you find a way to overcome it?

2. "If I only had known then what I know now." Have you ever had this thought? Write to explain why.

3. Andree quotes a line he heard in a film version of a Gilbert and Sullivan play: "Always follow the dictates of your heart, my boy, and chance the consequences." Do you agree with this advice? Provide specific examples to help your readers understand why you think the way you do.

Two Peas in a Pod

Erica Nardi

....

In this personal essay, the student author writes to share what it feels like to lose her best friend in an accident. As you read, see if you can discover what strategies Erica Nardi uses to help readers understand her strong, personal feelings. Have you ever faced a loss that has changed you?

1   There is a time in everyone's life when something terrible happens without any word of warning. Death is one of the hardest things that people have to deal with throughout life. The death of a good friend, family member, classmate, or even a pet can have a great effect on anyone. Some are affected so much, it changes their lives forever. In my case, I have experienced what it feels like to lose a good friend, and to me, that was the most difficult incident I have ever had to deal with.

2   I knew Stacey since I was eight years old. We met at one of our brothers' baseball games that we had both been dragged along to. When we first met, we really hit it off. We started playing together on a regular basis and soon enough, Stacey and I were best friends. Up until 6th grade, Stacey and I were inseparable. We did everything together; our parents even used to call us "two peas in a pod." I knew Stacey like the back of my hand; I could finish her sentences as she could finish mine, I could tell when she was upset even when she had a big smile on her face.

3   Once we got in middle school though, Stacey and I started to grow apart. Our brothers did not play baseball anymore and even in school, I never saw her. We started hanging out with different people and had completely different groups of friends. I did not see much of Stacey up until our junior year in high school when she was in my history class. Before long, Stacey and I picked up right where we left off.

4   Every day before 1st period we would meet up at Stacey's locker to walk to class together. Stacey and I did not really do any of our work in history; we just

sat in the back of the room laughing and talking about life. We passed notes and reminisced about funny things that happened in our pasts. As the year went on, Stacey and I just got closer and closer. I really looked forward to history so I could talk to Stacey.

5   June 2nd started as any ordinary day. I was running a little bit late to school, so instead of going to Stacey's locker, I went straight to class. Stacey was never one to be absent or ever be late, so seeing her empty desk beside me was surprising. Along with the rest of the class, I knew something was not right as soon as I looked at my teacher's face. He stood in front of the class, looking down at a piece of paper he held in his hands, searching for words to say. His face was red and his eyes were glued to the paper.

6   There was a long pause before he started off with, "Last night there was a serious accident involving one of our students . . ." I knew right away that it was Stacey. A great sickness came over me. I felt as if someone had thrown a brick at my stomach and all feelings just left my body, leaving me motionless. I did not hear anything my teacher said after that, as I tried to make sense of it in my head. A ton of questions ran through my head as I felt my face start to burn. I wondered if I was ever going to see Stacey again. I looked over at the cold empty seat next to me and I felt the tears start pouring down my face.

7   I left school early that day, for I could not bear listening to all the talk about Stacey. Later that day, I found out Stacey had been coming home from her boyfriend's house and, hurrying home for her 10 o'clock curfew, she hit a tree going 70 miles per hour. The impact instantly killed Stacey, leaving her and her big SUV unrecognizable. I felt a great deal of resentment towards myself. I never got to say any last words to Stacey, and now she will never realize how much she ever meant to me. The saying "you never realize what you have until it's gone," had a completely new meaning to me after that.

8   Stacey was a great person. She was friendly with everyone and she had a great sense of humor. She was one of those people that you could laugh for hours with over something that happened 3 weeks ago. Losing her was like losing a huge part of me. She was the one person that understood everything about me, and who I could talk to about anything. Although I had a lot of other friends other than Stacey, she had been the one that I felt truly cared about me just like I cared about her. I knew she was there for me if I ever needed her, and the same went for me. I still have yet to find a friend like Stacey.

9   For the rest of the school year I walked by Stacey's locker before going to history, almost in hopes she would be there. Going to class almost felt pointless, considering the only reason I liked it before was because Stacey was there. As I sat in class, I avoided looking to my right to see her lifeless seat where she should be. It did not feel right to me to continue having our normal lecture classes without Stacey there. Needless to say, history class was not much fun after that. I found my mind could not focus on schoolwork at all for the remainder of the year.

10   The loss of Stacey changed me as a person greatly. I take life a lot more seriously and I realize now that some things happen in life that you just cannot prevent. It made me stronger as a person and I live each day to its fullest because I will never know when it could be my last. I will always look at Stacey as my best friend and wonder why she had to go at such a young age. I will never forget Stacey, and the memories of her will remain in my heart forever.

EXPLORING THE READING THROUGH DISCUSSION

1. If you could speak with the author, what would you say to her after reading her essay?

2. Who does the author resent after Stacey's death? Why?

3. Where does the author use sensory details in her essay? Do you think the description is effective? Explain.

4. The essay spans approximately eight years, from when the friends first met to junior year of high school. Which specific periods of time does the author amplify the most? Which time is summarized?

5. What are the effects of Stacey's death on the author?

DEVELOPING VOCABULARY

List any words in this selection that are new to you. Write your understanding of each word from the context. Then look up each word in the dictionary, and write the definition that you think best fits the meaning in this writing.

_____

_____

_____

_____

DISCOVERING CONNECTIONS THROUGH WRITING

1. "You never realize what you have until it is gone." Write about an experience you have had that proves this statement.

2. Do you have a best friend? Describe him or her so that readers can understand why your friend is special to you.

3. What are the laws concerning teenage drivers in your state? In your opinion, should stricter limits be imposed?

R-E-S-P-E-C-T

Josh Trepanier (student)

Are people becoming increasingly more rude? Are parents shirking their duties to teach good manners? Or is etiquette less important in our fast-paced world? As you read this student's essay, explore your response to these and other questions that are raised. Why do you think people in general are not more considerate of others?

1   **C**an you remember a time when men held doors for women and elders, and took off their hats when they were inside? Do you recall the days when youngsters wouldn't dare talk back to their parents or grandparents out of sheer respect? People who do remember those instances must be appalled at the lack of manners in today's society. It is becoming increasingly difficult to find people who still use the simple words *please* and *thank you* on a daily basis. Even "polite society" is no longer very polite. The general level of respect people have for other people has declined rapidly in the past few decades and it will continue to decrease until we teach ourselves and our children otherwise.

2   Who is to blame for the current decline in manners? The place where kids are most disrespectful is usually the place where they learn to be that way—at home. Children are refusing to obey parents more and more every day. Eight years ago, I could have never worn my hat at the dinner table; my mom would have thrown a fit. Nowadays, youngsters sit down to supper with their hats on, while playing hand-held video games, and parents don't blink an eye. Some kids are even allowed to use profane language in front of their parents. Such casual attitudes about disrespect are at the root of the growing problem America is having with unmannered youth. If impoliteness around the household continues to go unnoticed, the rude children will someday turn into rude adults, continuing the current trend of disrespectfulness. Of course, the media have also contributed to the growing problem by portraying the rudeness of our youth in a comical light in many modern family sitcoms.

3   Another way Americans show this loss of manners is in how they treat their elders. The number of senior citizens in nursing homes is on the rise, and I'm sure many of them could be just as well taken care of at home. However, some people don't have the patience and respect they once had for their parents, and a nursing home is becoming an easy alternative for rising numbers of elderly people across the country. Elders are also shown less and less respect on the roads. Older people who drive a little slower than the fast-paced younger drivers are harassed by the honking horns, flashing lights, and hand gestures of more youthful drivers. I'm sure the senior citizens of today are wondering why they don't get the same kind of respect they showed their elders. It is too bad that there isn't a single good reason to give them for the loss of manners Americans seem to suffer from.

4   Teachers across the United States experience the bad etiquette of students on a daily basis. For the most part, it is the high school teachers who see the biggest change in their pupils' attitudes. Teens are no longer afraid to talk back to teachers, which would have resulted in a few whacks from a ruler years ago. Maybe if we give the teachers their rulers back, kids might be a little more careful of what they say during school. The problem is that the instructors hear the disrespectful adolescents and let them get away with being totally ignorant. I suppose it's true that they aren't paid to babysit, but by allowing rude behavior to go unchastised for so long, teachers have only made their own jobs more irritating. The students will continue to use little or no manners in school until somebody puts an end to the everyday lack of respect they are allowed to show their teachers.

5   Basically, the problem America is now facing is one of neglect. We can no longer afford to ignore our children's bad manners. Had we put a stop to these lax attitudes about manners when they first showed up in kids, the problem most

likely wouldn't have become as extreme as it is. We, as a nation, need to recognize and rectify the problems that exist due to the rudeness and disrespectfulness of our youth. Although chivalry may be a thing of the past, I think it's time for courtesy and respect to make a comeback in our society.

EXPLORING THE READING THROUGH DISCUSSION

1. How many words with similar meanings to the title, "R-E-S-P-E-C-T," can you identify in the essay? Do the words have different connotations?

2. Did you recognize anyone you know in any of the examples included in the essay? Do you also consider these behaviors to be bad manners?

3. What are some causes for the decline in manners that the author observes?

4. Do the examples of bad manners that the author includes in his writing differ in significance or importance? Are those differences reflected in the organization of the paragraphs?

5. Identify the topic sentences in each paragraph. Besides using topic sentences, what other methods does the author use to achieve coherence in his essay?

DEVELOPING VOCABULARY

List any words in this selection that are new to you. Write your understanding of each word from the context. Then look up each word in the dictionary, and write the definition that you think best fits the meaning in this writing.

_____

_____

_____

_____

DISCOVERING CONNECTIONS THROUGH WRITING

1. Do you agree with the author's thesis? Use plenty of specific examples to support your opinion.

2. Should teachers be stricter concerning student manners in the classroom? If you were a teacher, what specific behaviors do you think you would not allow?

3. The author writes that "*chivalry* may be a thing of the past." What is your understanding of that word? Should chivalry be forgotten? Would you like to see it come back? Be sure to provide reasons to support your argument.

Home Schooling

Lori Ann Moyer (student)

....

Where students go to school, who teaches them, what subjects they study and at what level are some of the topics that Lori Ann Moyer discusses in her essay. As you read, explore in what ways her children's education is different from or similar to your own experience. Do you think it is a good idea for parents to also be their children's teachers?

1   **W**ould you be interested in working a forty-hour job and collecting no paycheck at the end of the week? To top it off, would you like your job duties to include those of teacher, nurse, lunch lady, and tutor? What would make such a job worthwhile, causing me to invest eight years of my life in it? After all, I do have some dreams and goals that can materialize quicker with a second income! This occupation would have to offer me something worthwhile in exchange for all the sacrifices, and it does. Home schooling has provided beneficial options for educating my daughters.

2   Although it is a demanding job, home schooling has provided flexibility concerning the hours and days of the week I conduct classes. I am not limited to operating my school between the hours 8:00 A.M. and 2:30 P.M. Monday through Friday. However, I use this flexibility as an exception, not the rule. When my younger daughter, Alisha, was experiencing stomach pain and needed medical tests, it was easy to schedule appointments and make up for work she missed. After being diagnosed with a hiatal hernia and acid reflux, she had flare ups from time to time which required visits with the specialist. Accordingly, there were bouts with pain causing her discomfort. What a blessing it was being able to school her at home around these circumstances! However, would it be wise to take advantage of such an option only under negative circumstances? I have occasionally used this freedom for spontaneous surprises. One particular time this past winter, it was snowing during regular school hours. Snow comes and goes, but math sticks around forever. Since you are only a kid once, I let them go outside and act their ages. Then there was the time an unexpected opportunity arose for the girls to get a tour of the New Bedford Police Station from Lieutenant Spirlett; we seized the opportunity! In addition, there have been breakfast outings and overnight trips. Since I can designate whichever days I choose to allow vacation time, my husband and I take advantage of cheaper motel rates and less crowded attractions by traveling off-season. As a result of positively motivated flexibility, good memories have been created in our home schooling experience.

3   Another option is being able to coordinate curriculum for each subject based on each daughter's needs. My older daughter, Ashley, is strong in spelling, and she reached a point where her current curriculum was not going to challenge her. I switched to one that met her need for a workout and it was academically rewarding. Also, I am not limited to make each daughter use only her grade level curriculum. Alisha's abilities require challenges that go beyond her grade level. At a certain point, I allowed her to participate in Ashley's history and science classes, which are two grade levels ahead. She had no problems maintaining a good grade and her need was met. Furthermore, changes can be made if testing indicates a curriculum is not covering enough concepts within its scope. When Ashley was in

third grade, she scored a grade equivalency of 7.9 in mathematical problem solving on the Stanford Achievement Test but only a 3.8 in procedures. I switched to a curriculum that introduced procedures at a faster rate. The following year she scored a 9.6 grade equivalency in problem solving and a 10.6 grade equivalency in procedures.

4   Most beneficial is the freedom to adjust the amount of class time spent on each subject. Although some subjects need to be done every day, I can choose the amount of time that is spent on each one. For example, I can reduce the amount of class time in a course the girls are more proficient in and transfer it to another that needs the extra attention. In Ashley's case, I can spend less time on spelling and more on Algebra. I believe this strategy will keep the weaknesses in check and avoid them snowballing into major problems. Likewise, time can be adjusted to allow me to flow with a lesson the girls are hooked into, which enables me to take advantage of their attention and interest. An instance of this occurred last spring when the girls were learning about ionic bonding in science class. I had them cut circles out of construction paper to represent atoms and then use modeling clay to create the nuclei and electrons. Afterwards, they used these atom models to create step by step diagrams illustrating how common table salt is formed. The diagrams explained the transfer of a sodium atom's valence electron from its outermost shell to that of a chlorine atoms' outermost shell, resulting in an ionic bond. This project required extra class time, but the girls enjoyed it and attained understanding of the ionic bonding process. On the other hand, if there is surplus time after all the basics are accomplished, it can be used on some "extras". Educational computer programs such as Jumpstart Typing and Latin Word Roots make a profitable and enjoyable alternative.

5   To sum it up, I have invested my time, energy, and money into home schooling because the options have produced dividends. The Stanford Achievement test taken in April of 2003 showed the following results: Ashley scored in the 88th percentile for her complete battery with PHS (Post High School) grade equivalent, and Alisha scored in the 97th percentile for her complete battery with a PHS grade equivalent. Without doubt, the scores indicated a good academic yield, and as a teacher I rejoice over them. However, as a mother I celebrate the achievement of a strong, solid, loving relationship with my daughters. Home schooling has contributed to both successes, and I will never regret the sacrifices that I have made to answer its call in my life.

EXPLORING THE READING THROUGH DISCUSSION

1. If you have, or plan to have, children, would you consider home schooling? Why or why not?

2. The author, Lori Ann Moyer, includes information about her children's standardized test scores in her essay. Why? What other ways does she measure their success?

3. In the conclusion, the author says that she "will never regret the sacrifices" that she has made as a parent of a home-schooled child. What are these sacrifices?

4. What is the most important benefit of home schooling, according to the author? Do you agree?

5. Does the author use emphatic, spatial, or chronological order to organize her essay?

DEVELOPING VOCABULARY

List any words in this selection that are new to you. Write your understanding of each word from the context. Then look up each word in the dictionary, and write the definition that you think best fits the meaning in this writing.

_____

_____

_____

_____

DISCOVERING CONNECTIONS THROUGH WRITING

1. As a parent, the author asserts that "home schooling has provided beneficial options" for her daughters. From your own experience, what are the benefits of attending school with your peers? Write to support a thesis that takes the opposite point of view of Ms. Moyer's.

2. If you could "adjust the amount of class time spent on [a] subject" which subject would you focus on the most? Write to explain why you would do so.

3. What do you think is the ideal school schedule? Would more or less time be spent in the classroom? When would students and teachers have vacations? How much time would be assigned for homework? Describe your ideal school schedule. Let readers know how your schedule would help students learn.

Appendix A

Tips for ESL Writers

As someone who can speak and write in a language—perhaps two or three—other than English, you should consider yourself truly fortunate. The knowledge of more than one language gives you a genuine advantage in a multicultural country and in a world where all major corporations are multinational.

But mastering writing in English no doubt feels frustrating at times. When you write in English, you must think about the many possible ways that English differs from your native language. For example, a sentence with an unusual word order will confuse your readers, so keep in mind the ways your language and English differ in sentence structure and word order. In addition, you must correct the common problems you have with English grammar so that you communicate clearly. The rules for capitalization, articles, spelling, and punctuation can also be very confusing. However, they help to make your writing correct, and correct standard English is more easily understood. Most important of all, you must think about the logic of paragraphs and essays written in English, which might be very different from the logical forms of composition in your language group and culture. If your goal is communication, you must learn to use the patterns that English speakers use to understand each other. The following guidelines will help you achieve this goal.

Sentence Basics

- Make sure each sentence has a subject and a verb. If a group of words does not have both, it does not express a complete idea. *See Chapter 17, "The Sentence," and Chapter 18, "Fragments."*

FAULTY | ⌐verb⌐ *Thought* of a good idea. [*Subject missing*]

REVISED | ⌐subject—verb⌐ *You thought* of a good idea. [*A statement*]

In writing, the subject can be an implied *you* only if you are making a command. *See the section "Recognizing Subjects" on pages 261–263 in Chapter 17.*

EXAMPLE | ⌐subject—verb⌐ [*You*] *Think* of a good idea! [*A command*]

- Make sure that *is* and *are* verbs are linked to a subject. The words *it* and *there* and words describing a location can sometimes substitute in the normal location of a subject at the beginning of a sentence. In such cases, the actual subject comes after the verb. (Usually, in English, the subject comes *before* the verb.) *See the section "Avoiding Agreement Errors When the Subject Follows the Verb" on page 327 in Chapter 21, "Subject–Verb Agreement," and the section "Working with Forms of* To Be*" on pages 366–367 in Chapter 23, "Irregular Verbs and Frequently Confused Verbs."*

FAULTY

⌐verb
Is a good place to eat near here. [*Subject unclear*]

REVISED

⌐substitute verb ⌐subject
There is a good *place* to eat near here. [There *signals subject* after *verb*]

or

⌐location⌐verb ⌐subject
Near here is a good *place* to eat.

- In English sentences, the word *there* with some form of the verb *to be* is commonly followed by a noun or pronoun, which serves as the subject. The noun or pronoun may have modifiers, or it may be followed by a word or phrase that specifies a place.

EXAMPLE

⌐ noun ⌐ ⌐ modifier ⌐
There will be a new *student entering class today.*

⌐pronoun⌐place
There is *no one here.*

⌐noun⌐ ⌐ place ⌐
There are three *cars in the lot.*

- The word *it* with the verb *to be* is commonly followed by an adjective, an adjective with a modifier, an identification, or an expression of time, weather, or distance.

EXAMPLE

adjective⌐
It is *hot.*

adjective⌐ ⌐ modifier ⌐
It is *hot outside and inside.*

⌐ identification ⌐
What is this? It is *my English book.*

⌐ time ⌐
It is *eleven o'clock on Wednesday morning.*

⌐ weather ⌐
It is *cold and rainy.*

⌐ distance ⌐
It is *twenty miles from school to home.*

The word *there* is not used in these expressions.

FAULTY

There is long. *There* has been a long time.

REVISED

It is long. *It* has been a long time.

Word Order

- In most English sentences, the subject comes first, followed by the verb.

FAULTY

REVISED The *idea is* good.

- Adjectives, even a string of adjectives, usually come *before* nouns. *See Chapter 27, "Adjectives, Adverbs, and Other Modifiers: Using Describing and Modifying Words Effectively," for more information about adjectives.*

FAULTY

REVISED The *tall, thin, handsome man* is talking.

- Groups of words that modify a noun, however, usually come immediately *after* the noun if they begin with a relative pronoun: *who, whom, whose, which, that,* and so forth.

FAULTY

REVISED The *man who won the award* is talking.

- In some cases, modifiers with an *-ed* or *-ing* verb form must go after a noun they identify if they add essential identifying information to the sentence. However, they can appear either immediately before or immediately after a noun about which they add extra information. Study the following examples, in which the *-ing* modifier is necessary to tell *which man. See the section "Avoiding Dangling and Misplaced Modifiers" on pages 447–449 in Chapter 27.*

FAULTY

REVISED The *man sitting next to you* is blind.

Now compare the revised sentence above with the example below, in which the modifier adds extra information.

EXAMPLE

- If the modifier is necessary to identify the noun, you don't use commas to separate it from the noun. If the modifier adds information about the noun, but the sentence makes sense without it, then set the modifier off with commas. *See the section "Using Commas to Set Off Elements That Interrupt Sentence Flow" on page 512 in Chapter 30, "Commas."*

<pre>
          ┌─noun─┐┌─modifier
</pre>
EXAMPLE   My *friend Frank* works hard.

The modifier is needed to identify which friend, *my friend Frank,* not *my friend Tom,* so no commas are needed.

<pre>
          ┌─noun─┐ ┌───────modifier───────┐
</pre>
EXAMPLE   *Frank, who lives next door,* works hard.

The modifier provides extra information that isn't necessary for the sentence to make sense, so it needs commas.

- Adverbs usually are placed after *to be* verbs (*is/are/was/were*) but before other one-word verbs. *See the section "Understanding Adjectives and Adverbs" on page 441 in Chapter 27.*

<pre>
          verb┐┌─adverb
</pre>
EXAMPLE   They *are often* late.

<pre>
          ┌─adverb─┐┌─verb─┐
</pre>
Birds *usually arrive* in the spring.

- Adverbs often go between verbs that have two parts (verb phrases).

<pre>
          helping
          verb ┐adverb┐┌─verb─┐
</pre>
EXAMPLE   They *have often arrived* late.

- Pronouns that rename the subject in the same sentence are usually unnecessary and confusing—even when a long modifier separates the subject from the verb. The order of the words in a sentence makes the idea clear.

<pre>
          subject┐┌──────modifier──────subject┐┌verb┐
</pre>
FAULTY   The *place* where they studied *it was* old.

<pre>
          subject┐┌──────modifier──────┐┌verb┐
</pre>
REVISED   The *place* where they studied *was* old.

Agreement

- Make the subject and verb agree in number. Be especially careful about collective nouns, such as *family* and *class,* and words that specify uncountable things, such as *sugar* and *water. See the section "Considering Singular Nouns Ending in -s, Collective Nouns, and Cue Words" on pages 401–402 in Chapter 25, "Nouns: Working Effectively with Words That Name."*

- You can count *fingers*, *books*, or *students*, so they are called *count* words. You cannot count *freedom*, *advice*, or *machinery*, so they are called *noncount* words. Noncount words always take a singular verb and a singular pronoun reference.

FAULTY

> noncount plural
> noun ⌐⌐ verb ⌐
> *Sugar make* the recipe better.

> plural
> pronoun plural
> reference⌐⌐ verb
> *They are* tasty.

REVISED

> noncount singular
> noun ⌐⌐ verb
> *Sugar makes* the recipe better.

> singular
> pronoun singular
> reference⌐⌐ verb
> *It is* tasty.

- Some words are count with one meaning and noncount with another meaning.

EXAMPLE

Three *chickens are* in the yard. [*Countable animals*]

Chicken is good with white wine. [*Noncountable meat*]

Three pieces of *chicken is* enough. [*Quantity of noncountable meat*]

- As the last example shows, some aspects of noncount words can be measured. You can count the number of *lumps* of sugar, *cups* of milk, *tablespoons* of flour, or *gallons* of water, but you cannot say *ten sugars, three milks, two flours,* and *four waters* as a complete grammatical form. Even though you can number *quantities* like *two pounds, six quarts, three minutes, five dollars,* and *ten gallons,* the "*of* phrase" with the noncount word makes a singular subject, which makes the verb singular (*two pounds of butter is*). You must use a *singular verb* with any quantity of noncount items. *See the sections "Using the Simple Present, Simple Future, and Simple Past Tenses" on pages 346–347 in Chapter 22, "Basic Tenses for Regular Verbs," and "Maintaining Agreement with Indefinite Pronouns" on pages 417–419 in Chapter 26, "Pronouns: Understanding Case, Clear Pronoun–Antecedent Agreement, and Nonsexist Pronoun Usage."*

EXAMPLE

> count
> ⌐noun
> Twelve *cups are* necessary because we have twelve guests. [*12 items*]

> noncount
> ⌐quantity⌐ + ⌐ noun
> Two cups of *water is* enough. [*A measurement of a noncount noun*]

> noncount   count
> noun ⌐   noun ⌐
> Ten *dollars is* enough. [*Amount*]   Ten dollar *bills are* enough. [*Number*]

> noncount   count
> noun ⌐   noun ⌐
> My *luggage is* heavy. [*Amount*]   My two *bags are* heavy. [*Number*]

FAULTY

> noncount
> ⌐quantity⌐ + ⌐ noun ⌐
> Ten gallons of *gasoline are* all I need.

REVISED

> noncount
> ⌐quantity⌐ + ⌐ noun ⌐
> Ten gallons of *gasoline is* all I need.

- Adjectives are *always* singular.

FAULTY | the *talls* men; the *six-year-olds* children

REVISED | the *tall* men, the *six-year-old* children

- Adjectives that end in *-ing* are active, while adjectives that end in *-ed* are passive. *See the section "Forming the Passive and Active Voice" on page 379 in Chapter 24, "Passive Voice, Additional Tenses, and Maintaining Consistency in Tense."*

EXAMPLE | I am *boring*.

This adjective is formed from the active verb. It shows the effect that I have on others—I make them feel bored.

EXAMPLE | I am *bored*.

This adjective is derived from the passive verb. It shows the effect something has on me—something makes me feel bored.

- A single phrase or clause subject takes a singular verb.

FAULTY | ┌─────phrase as subject─────┐ ┌verb   ┌─────clause as subject─────┐ ┌verb
Understanding the rules are hard. *That they must be followed are* clear.

REVISED | ┌─────phrase as subject─────┐ ┌verb   ┌─────clause as subject─────┐ ┌verb
Understanding the rules is hard. *That they must be followed is* clear.

- Verbs presented in a series with commas should agree in tense and form. *See Chapter 28, "Parallelism: Presenting Related Ideas in a Similar Form."*

FAULTY | The child *was running, jumped,* and *has skipped*. [*Mixed tense forms*]

REVISED | The child *ran, jumped,* and *skipped*. [*All past tense forms*]

- Use the present or present perfect tense, not the future tense, in a subordinate time or *if* clause, whose main clause is future tense. *See the section "Maintaining Consistency in Tense" on pages 384–385 in Chapter 24 for more on keeping the voice of tense consistent.*

FAULTY | ┌────────subordinate clause────────┐ ┌─main clause─┐
After I will do my homework, I will go out.

REVISED | ┌────────subordinate clause────────┐ ┌─main clause─┐
After I have done my homework, I will go out.

Confusing Verb Forms

Don't omit the -s in the third person singular, present tense verb forms. *See the section "Using the Simple Present, Simple Future, and Simple Past Tenses" on pages 346–347 in Chapter 22.*

FAULTY   He *come* here every day.

REVISED   He *comes* here every day.

- Memorize the irregular verbs. *See the section "Identifying Irregular Verbs" on pages 360–366 in Chapter 23.* Some verb pairs such as the following can be confusing, but remembering which takes an object and which does not will help you tell the difference. The verbs *shine/shone, lie, sit,* and *rise* never have an object; the verbs *shine/shined, lay, set,* and *raise* always have an object:

No Object	*Object*
His shoes shone.	He shined *his shoes.*
She lay in the sun.	She laid *her books* on the floor.
She sat in the chair.	She set *the table* for four.
The sun rises every morning.	They raised *the flag.*

- Use complete passive verb forms; combine a form of *to be* with the past participle of another verb. *See the section "Forming the Passive and Active Voice" on pages 379–381 in Chapter 24.*

FAULTY   His work finished.

REVISED   His work *was* finished. [*Add form of* to be]

  or

  He finished his work. [*Transform to active voice*]

- Use -*'s* to make contractions using *is* and *has,* but shorten *has* only when it is a helping verb. To sound more formal, avoid contractions like *she's.* Write *she is* instead.

FAULTY   She's some money.

REVISED   She has some money.

INFORMAL   She's ready to help.

FORMAL   She is ready to help.

- Verbs describing a completed mental process (*believe, consider, forget, know, remember, think, understand*), a consistent preference (*drink, swim, eat*), a state of being (*am, appear, have, seem, remember, forget, love*), or a perception (*feel, hear, see, taste*) can never be progressive. If the verb refers to an incomplete process, it can be progressive. *See the section "Using the Progressive and Perfect Progressive Tenses" on pages 381–382 in Chapter 24.*

EXAMPLE   I *consider* my choice good. [*An already completed decision*]

I *am considering* going. [*A decision-making process not yet complete*]

I *think* he should be president. [*A completed intellectual position*]

I *am thinking* about what to do this summer. [*An incomplete thought process*]

I *drink* coffee. [*A consistent preference*]

I *am drinking* coffee. [*An incomplete action*]

FAULTY   I *am seeing* you. I *am liking* you, but I *am loving* cheeseburgers.

REVISED   I *see* you. I *like* you, but I *love* cheeseburgers.

- *Do* and *make* do not mean the same thing in English. *Do* often refers to action that is mechanical or specific. *Make* often refers to action that is creative or general: The teacher *makes* up the exercise (creative), but the student *does* the exercise (mechanical). However, there is no clear rule explaining the difference. You will just have to memorize their usage.

Mostly Mechanical or Specific	*Mostly Creative or General*
do the dishes	make the bed
do the homework	make an impression
do the laundry	make progress
do your hair	make up your mind
do (brush) your teeth	make (cook) a meal
do (write) a paper	make (build) a house
do the right thing	make mistakes
do someone a favor	make a speech
do good deeds	make a living
do away with	make arrangements

FAULTY   I have to *make the homework* before I can *do a speech*.

REVISED   I have to *do the homework* before I can *make a speech*.

- *Tell* and *say* do not mean the same thing in English:

tell time	say a prayer
tell a story or a joke	say hello
tell me	say that we should go
tell the difference	say, "Let's go!"

FAULTY say me; tell hello; say a joke

REVISED tell me; say hello; tell a joke

Articles

Articles (*a, an,* and *the*) can be very confusing in English, so you must pay special attention to them.

- Use *a* before words that begin with consonant sounds and *an* before words that begin with vowel sounds.

1. *A* and *an* mean the same as *one* or *each:* I want *an* ice cream cone. [*Just one*]

2. *A* and *an* go with an unidentified member of a class: *A* small dog came toward her, *a* bone in its mouth. [*Some unknown dog, some unknown bone*]

3. *A* and *an* go with a representative member of a class: You can tell by the way he talks that he is *a* politician.

4. *A* and *an* go with a noun that places an idea in a larger class: The car is *a* four-wheeled vehicle.

See the section "Considering Singular Nouns Ending in -s, Collective Nouns, and Cue Words" on pages 401–402 in Chapter 25.

- *The* serves many functions:

1. *The* modifies known people, objects, or ideas: *the* mother of *the* bride, *the* head of *the* household in which he stayed, *the* Copernican theory

2. *The* goes with superlatives: *the* best, *the* least

3. *The* goes with rank: *the* first book, *the* third child with this problem

4. *The* goes with *of* phrases: the way of *the* world

5. *The* goes with adjective phrases or clauses that limit or identify the noun: *the* topic being discussed.

6. *The* refers to a class as a whole: *The* giraffe is an African animal.

7. *The* goes with the names of familiar objects (*the* store) and the names of newspapers (*The Wall Street Journal*), but not the names of most magazines (*Time*).

8. *The* goes with the names of historical periods (*the* French Revolution), legislative acts (*the* Missouri Compromise), political parties (*the* Democratic Party),

branches of government (*the* executive branch), official titles (*the* President), government bodies (*the* Navy), and organizations (*the* Girl Scouts).

9. *The* goes with rivers (but not lakes), canals, oceans, channels, gulfs, peninsulas, swamps, groups of islands, mountain ranges, hotels, libraries, museums, and geographic regions: *the* Panama Canal, *the* Mississippi River, Lake Superior, *the* Okefenokee Swamp, *the* Hilton, *the* Smithsonian, *the* South.

FAULTY	According to *New York Times,* the Lake Victoria is one of most beautiful lakes in world.
REVISED	According to *the New York Times,* Lake Victoria is one of *the* most beautiful lakes in *the* world.

Spelling

- Follow these steps to avoid common spelling errors:

1. Don't leave *h* out of *wh* words: *which,* not *wich*

2. Don't add an *e* to words that start with *s: stupid,* not *estupid*

3. Don't confuse words that sound alike in English—homonyms—but have different meanings and different spellings:

his/he's (he is)	which/witch	there/their
whether/weather	here/hear	through/threw
advice/advise (noun/verb)	too/to/two	though/thought

4. Don't confuse grammatical functions because of familiar sound combinations: *whose* or *who's* (*who is*), not *who his*

5. Don't confuse words that sound similar using your native language's pronunciation patterns but have different meanings and different sounds in English:

this (singular)/these (plural)	chair/share
read/lead	boat/vote
heat/hit	

See Chapter 29, "Spelling: Focusing on Correctness."

Other Common Grammar Problems

Double Negatives

- Never use a double negative; it is not acceptable in English. As in mathematics, two negatives equal a positive. *See the section "Avoiding Double Negatives" on page 453–454 in Chapter 27.*

FAULTY	$\overline{(-) \quad + \quad (-) = (+)}$ I do*n't* have *no* money. [*Meaning becomes positive*]
REVISED	$\overline{(-) \quad + \quad (+) = (-)}$ I do*n't* have *any* money. [*Meaning remains negative*]

Confusing Words

Some key words are confusing:

- *Too* and *very* don't share the same meaning. *Very* is an intensifier that means *extremely* or *excessively*. It emphasizes quantity. *Too* is often negative and critical. It is sometimes attached to a word that goes with an infinitive (*to* + verb) to emphasize negative effects.

EXAMPLE   It is *very* cold, but we can walk to the restaurant. [Very = *intensely*]

It is *too* cold to walk, so we should take a taxi. [Too = *negative*]

FAULTY   He is *very* fat to play on the soccer team.

REVISED   He is *too* fat to play on the soccer team. [*He cannot play soccer because he is quite overweight.*]

- *Hard* can be an adjective or an adverb, but *hardly* is always an adverb meaning *barely, almost none,* or *almost not at all.*

EXAMPLE   adjective⌐⌐noun⌐
He learned a *hard* lesson. [*A difficult lesson*]

⌐verb⌐ ⌐adverb
He worked *hard.* [*With great effort*]

⌐adverb⌐⌐verb⌐
He *hardly* worked. [*Barely, almost not at all*]

⌐adverb⌐ ⌐noun⌐
Hardly anyone watches black-and-white television. [*Almost no one*]

- *A few* (count) and *a little* (noncount) mean *some,* while *few* and *little* mean *almost none.* The difference is between a positive attitude and a negative attitude.

EXAMPLE   I have *a little* money, so I can lend you some. [*Some, so positive*]

I have *little* money, so I can't lend you any. [*Almost none, so negative*]

A *few* students came, so we were pleased. [*Some, so positive*]

Few students came, so we were disappointed. [*Almost none, so negative*]

- *Some* and *any* both mean an indefinite amount. However, *some* is used in positive statements, while *any* is used in negative statements.

EXAMPLE   I have *some* money. [*Positive*]

I do*n't* have *any* money. [*Negative*]

- Usually, *well* is an adverb, whereas *good* is an adjective. However, *well* can sometimes be an adjective referring to health. *See the section "Working with Confusing Pairs of Adjectives and Adverbs" on page 445 in Chapter 27.*

EXAMPLE

noun¬ ┌adjective
The *boy* is *good.* [*Well-behaved*]

verb¬┌adverb
He doesn't feel *well.* [*Poor health*]

noun¬ ┌adjective
The *boy* is *well.* [*Healthy, not sick*]

Prepositions

Prepositions can be very confusing. *See the section "Recognizing Subjects" on pages 261–263 in Chapter 17.*

- Use *on* when one thing touches the surface of another and *in* when one thing encloses another: *on* the desk (on top), *in* the desk (inside a drawer). Also, use *on* if you must step up to board (get *on* a motorcycle/bus/train/large ship), but use *in* if you must step down (get *in* a small boat/car).
- *Since* goes with a specific initial time (*since* 3 P.M.; *since* July 3); *for* goes with duration, a length or period of time (*for* two hours; *for* ten days).

Punctuation and Capitalization

English rules for punctuation differ greatly from those in other languages.

- All sentences have an ending punctuation mark. Statements end with a period (.). Exclamations end with an exclamation mark (!). Questions end with a question mark (?). Statements, exclamations, and questions end with only one mark. Avoid multiple punctuation marks at the end of sentences. *See the section "Using Periods, Question Marks, and Exclamation Points" on page 525–526 in Chapter 31, "Other Punctuation and Capitalization."*
- Do not use commas to connect complete ideas or statements that can stand alone. Instead, use a period and a capital letter, a semicolon, or a comma and a coordinating conjunction. *See Chapter 20, "Comma Splices and Run-On Sentences."*

FAULTY

We finished class, then we got a pizza, later we went to a movie.
[*Comma splice*]

REVISED

We finished class. Then we got a pizza. Later we went to a movie.
[*Separate sentences*]

or

We finished class; then we got a pizza; later we went to a movie.
[*Clauses joined with semicolons*]

or

We finished class, then got a pizza, and later went to a movie.
[*Simple sentence with compound verb*]

- Commas go before and after a modifying word, phrase, or clause that adds extra information. This means that the sentence can stand alone without the added information. Modifying words, phrases, or clauses that are necessary for identification take no commas. In other words, if the material is crucial to the meaning of the sentence, then do not use commas. *See the section "Using Commas to Set Off Elements That Interrupt Sentence Flow" on page 512 in Chapter 30.*

EXAMPLE Never eat beef *that is undercooked.*

Without the modifier, the sentence meaning is changed and incorrect; use no commas.

EXAMPLE Supermarkets, *which we take for granted,* did not even exist a hundred years ago.

Without the modifier, the sentence retains its basic meaning; use commas.
- Semicolons are used to connect independent clauses. They may also be used to separate longer groups of words or lists that already contain commas.

EXAMPLE Cats are lazy; dogs jump around.

Turn in your uniforms on Friday, May 24; Monday, May 27; or Wednesday, May 29.

- English rules for capitalization differ greatly from those in other languages. *See the section "Understanding Capitalization" on pages 537–539 in Chapter 31 for the English rules.*

Writing Paragraphs

Indentation Don't use a dash (—) to signal the beginning of a new paragraph. Instead, indent the first line of the paragraph to identify your change of subject or focus. *See the section "Recognizing the Structure of a Paragraph" on pages 30–31 in Chapter 3, "Composing: Creating a Draft."*

Unity Every sentence in a paragraph should be connected to the same topic, or main idea. In other words, the material should be unified. *See the section*

"Maintaining Unity" on pages 52–53 in Chapter 4, *"Refining and Polishing Your Draft."* If you change direction in the middle of the paragraph to talk about another idea, even if it is related, your teachers may call it a *digression*. Digressions are allowed in some languages, but not in English. One way to avoid digression is to have a plan for organizing your examples. For example, move from most common to least common, or from the familiar to the unfamiliar, or from the least important to the most important.

EXAMPLE

most common traveler's problem in airports

next most common problem

not usual, but still a problem

an important study habit for final exams

a more important study habit for final exams

the most important study habit for final exams

Finally, avoid digressions by keeping sentences short and tightly connected. Don't try to put too many unrelated ideas in one sentence or paragraph.

FAULTY   The writer warned us about the problem, he said it was very dangerous, he gave us convincing statistics. [*Three separate ideas; comma splice*]

REVISED   The writer used convincing statistics to warn about the dangerous problem. [*Ideas are combined and connected.*]

Writing Essays

Think about Audience Expectations Be businesslike: Go directly to your main idea. Don't try to tell your readers everything. Choose and limit your focus as much as possible. This narrowing of the topic may be much more extreme than you are used to in your language or culture.

Strive for Clarity Most North American readers like everything important to be explained; they don't like to guess what something means. Thus, you must keep your writing clear and simple. At the same time, be as specific as possible with your ideas. Your readers will want facts, details, and examples, so provide as many as you can. In other words, **amplify.**

Don't try to be too formal, but don't rely too heavily on the pronoun *you*. Doing so will make your writing less specific and clear. Say *who* you mean: the student, the tourist, the opposition. Finally, when you revise your sentences, eliminate extra words and imprecise expressions.

FAULTY | the group of people who lead the university and decide on policy

REVISED | the board of governors

Reinforce Your Point with a "Close" Never just stop writing. Always conclude with a few final words about your topic. This conclusion can repeat your main idea, but it should also show the significance of what you have said. Try to say how or why your topic idea is important and worth paying attention to.

Revise to Correct Errors Proofread before you turn in your paper. When you proofread, watch for the common mistakes discussed above. If possible, have a native speaker in one of your classes or a writing lab look at it before you turn it in. *See Chapter 4, "Refining and Polishing Your Draft," Chapter 14, "Developing an Essay," and Chapter 15, "Examining Types of Essays," for guidelines on how to develop and write an essay.*

Appendix B

Exploring the Dictionary

CW B.1
Pronunciation
guides in
dictionaries

Several chapters of this textbook have suggested that you refer to the dictionary to find information or to check the accuracy of your spelling. The dictionary is a tool writers use to verify the spelling of a word or to learn the meaning of an unfamiliar word. This reference tool can also provide other valuable information if you know what is available and where it is located. This appendix will help you learn how to explore the dictionary to gather all the information that is available to you.

Using the Dictionary

Good dictionaries are user friendly. They usually begin with a guide to using the dictionary, sometimes called a usage guide. The guide will probably include a pronunciation key, which uses symbols and phonetic spelling. Phonetic spelling shows the way the word sounds when pronounced correctly. It is necessary because the same letters can be pronounced different ways in English. For example, the double *o* is pronounced differently in *good* and *food*.

The usage guide also lists abbreviations that the dictionary's editors have used, along with the words they stand for. In addition, it may explain what each element of an entry means. Sometimes, you can find a pronunciation key and a list of abbreviations and symbols used in a dictionary on the inside cover. You can always refer to the usage guide to help you find the information you need when you are using the dictionary.

A Sample Dictionary Entry

To help you discover what information is included in a dictionary, take a look at the entry for the word *knowledge* as it appears in *Webster's New World College Dictionary*.

> **knowl·edge** (näl´ ij) **n.** [ME *knoweleche,* acknowledgement, confession < Late OE *cnawlœc* < *cnawan* (see KNOW) + *-lœc* < *lācan,* to play, give, move about] **1** the act, fact or state of knowing; specif. *a)* acquaintance or familiarity (with a fact, place, etc.) *b)* awareness *c)* understanding **2** acquaintance with facts; range of information, awareness or understanding **3** all that has been perceived or grasped by the mind; learning; enlightenment **4** the body of

facts, principles, etc. accumulated by mankind **5** [ARCHAIC] carnal knowledge:

see CARNAL —*SYN.* INFORMATION—**to (the best of) one's knowledge** as far as

one knows; within the range of one's information

At first glance, this entry might seem confusing, but each dictionary entry follows a pattern. Once you understand what information is listed where, most entries will become clear. For example, here is an explanation of the information about *knowledge* that appears before the definitions of the word:

- The main entry, the word itself, is written in boldface: **knowl·edge**
- Each syllable of the word is separated by bold, centered periods: ·
- The phonetic pronunciation follows, with a (´) over the accented, or stressed, syllable(s): (näl´ ij)
- The word's part of speech, in this case, is a noun: **n.**
- Finally, the etymology, or origin of the word, is also listed between brackets: [ ].

So before we read the definitions for this word, we know that the word has two syllables, that we should accent the first syllable when we pronounce the word, and that it is a noun. By referring to the usage guide for a list of abbreviations, we can also determine that the word has its roots in Old English (OE) and Middle English (ME). Knowing the etymology of a word helps writers understand its meaning more fully.

Following this information about the word are its definitions. Knowing how to define a word as it is used within a sentence or particular context is important. Some words have more than one meaning or sense, as *knowledge* does. Those multiple meanings are separated here by numbers in boldface. In some dictionaries, the different definitions are separated by a // or a double line. The five meanings of the noun *knowledge* provided in the definition above are as follows:

1. the act, fact or state of knowing; specif. *a)* acquaintance or familiarity (with a fact, place, etc.) *b)* awareness *c)* understanding

2. acquaintance with facts; range of information, awareness or understanding

3. all that has been perceived or grasped by the mind; learning; enlightenment

4. the body of facts, principles, etc. accumulated by mankind

5. [ARCHAIC] carnal knowledge: see CARNAL

In addition, this entry provides a **synonym**—the word *information*—and an example and explanation of an idiomatic expression or phrase that includes the word: **to (the best of) one's knowledge.**

Most dictionary entries will follow this basic pattern: the word, its pronunciation, its forms and part(s) of speech, the etymology, and the definition(s). The entry may contain other information, too. For example, you can use the dictionary to check the spelling of plurals (*pl.*), to find the comparative (*comp.*) and superlative (*superl.*) forms of modifiers, and to learn the various forms of a verb. If the verb will accept a direct or indirect object, that is also indicated by *vt.,* an abbreviation for *transitive verb.* The dictionary will also provide the correct spelling of the word with suffixes. Remember—if you are not sure what an abbreviation means within an entry, check the usage guide or list of abbreviations at the beginning of the dictionary.

COMPREHENSION AND PRACTICE B.1

Exploring the Usage Guide

1. Refer to the Usage Guide of your own dictionary and explain what *archaic* means in definition 5 of the word *knowledge.*

   _____

   _____

   _____

2. Using the Usage Guide, explain the following terms:

   obsolete: _____

   colloquial: _____

   rare: _____

COMPREHENSION AND PRACTICE B.2

Finding Additional Information

1. Look up the word *knowledge* in a dictionary that you use. How does the entry compare with the sample entry on pages 605–606?

   _____

   _____

   _____

2. Besides definitions, what additional information does your dictionary contain, such as maps, charts, or other reference information?

   _____

   _____

   _____

CHALLENGE B.1 **Searching the Library**

Visit your college or municipal library, and explore the section of the reference collection that contains dictionaries. What did you discover about the number and variety of dictionaries that are available? Select one or two specialized dictionaries that you find interesting or unusual. Write a paragraph describing the content of the dictionary, and explain why you found it intriguing. Share the results of your exploration with your classmates.

If you have access to the World Wide Web, your instructor may ask you to complete this challenge by identifying and exploring online dictionaries.

COMPREHENSION AND PRACTICE B.3

Exploring Etymologies

1. Find and write the etymologies of the following words:

   a. education:

   _____

   _____

   b. college:

   _____

   _____

   c. student:

   _____

   _____

   d. write:

   _____

   _____

2. Does your dictionary include any of the following words? Be sure to use the most current edition of the dictionary.

cyberspace	diskette
World Wide Web	online
digital	hypertext
technology	laser

3. Working with a partner, see what you can discover about the etymologies of these words. Be sure to explore how adding a prefix changes the meaning, multiple definitions, and references to the root of the word in your search. Share your results with the class.

CHALLENGE B.2 Playing a Dictionary Game

COLLABORATION

Play this game with four or five other students. Choose a word from the dictionary that you believe the students in the group do not know. Pronounce and spell the word for the group, distribute an index card or small piece of paper to everybody, and ask each person to write a definition for the word, including its part of speech. At the same time, you should write the correct definition from the dictionary on your own card. Collect the cards and read all the definitions. Ask each student in turn to guess which definition is correct. Students earn points by selecting the correct definition or by having their definition selected by another student. You earn a point for each incorrect answer. The game continues until every group member has a turn to choose a word.

Here is an example to get you started. Which of the following definitions is correct for the word *dibble?*

1. A dibble is a pointed gardening tool used to make holes for planting seeds and bulbs; it is a noun.

2. Dibble is an adjective that means small and without much worth.

3. Dibble is the technical name for the residue that remains after charcoal briquettes are burned. It is a noun.

4. Dibble is a verb that means to do something without much enthusiasm or seriousness.

After you've guessed, use the dictionary to find the right definition.

Rhetorical Index

Writers combine rhetorical modes to communicate their ideas in paragraphs and essays. Often, one mode is dominant, and one or more additional modes are used to provide illustration or support. To help you understand the characteristics of each mode, this index lists the paragraphs and essays in the text by chapter. Paragraphs and essays that contain characteristics for more than one mode are listed more than once, under the headings for each of those modes.

Paragraphs and Essays by Mode in Each Chapter

PART SEVEN Connecting: Responding to Reading

Credits

Text Credits

Greg Andree, "Fear Not." Used by permission of the author.

Judith Ortiz Cofer, "5:00 A.M.: Writing as Ritual." As appears in *The Latin Deli.* The University of Georgia Press, © 1993.

Susan Douglas, "Remote Control: How to Raise a Media Skeptic." Copyright © 1997 by Susan Douglas. As first appeared in Utne Reader (January/February 1997).

Paul Fletcher, "Nightwatch," published in the *Providence Journal-Bulletin,* 20 April 1990. Used by permission of the author.

Bob Greene, "Words, Good or Bad, Can Echo Through a Lifetime" from *The Chicago Tribune* (November 10, 1997). Copyright © 1997 by Tribune Media Services, Inc. All rights reserved. Reprinted with permission.

Stephanie Jezak, "Pride." Used by permission of the author.

Susan Messer, "Hit and Run." From *Chicago Reader,* December 10, 1999. Copyright © by Susan Messer. All rights reserved. Reprinted by permission of the author.

Lori Ann Moyer, "Home Schooling." Used by permission of the author.

Erica Nardi, "Two Peas in a Pod." Used by permission of the author.

Jane Patenaude, "Childhood—Then and Now." Used by permission of the author.

Diane Riva, "Exposed Toes." Used by permission of the author.

Amy Tan, "Fish Cheeks." Copyright © 1987 by Amy Tan. First appeared in *Seventeen* magazine. Digitalized with permission of the author and the Sandra Dijkstra Literary Agency.

Deborah Tannen, "Intimacy and Independence," from *You Just Don't Understand* by Deborah Tannen. Copyright © 1990 by Deborah Tannen. Reprinted by permission of HarperCollins Publishers Inc.

Josh Trepanier, "R-E-S-P-E-C-T." Used by permission of the author.

Naihsin Weng, "My Paradise." Used by permission of the author.

Photo Credits

11: Lonely Planet Images/Getty Images, Inc.; 27: Stone/Getty Images, Inc.; 49: Free Agents Limited/CORBIS; 77: Alison Wright/CORBIS; 89: K. Yamashita/PanStock/Panoramic Images/NGSImages.com; 98: Bob Krist/CORBIS; 107: Harvey Martin/Peter Arnold, Inc.; 115: Bill Brooks/Masterfile; 125: Taxi/Getty Images, Inc.; 135: Joel W. Rogers/CORBIS; 144: Kenneth Garrett/National Geographic Image Collection; 154: Keren Su/CORBIS; 169: Issei Kato/Reuters/Lando; 200: Charles & Josette Lenars/CORBIS; 205: Alamy Images; 208: Maynard Owen Williams/National Geographic Image Collection; 211: Richard Hamilton Smith/CORBIS; 214: Ron Watts/CORBIS; 217: Stephen St. John/National Geographic Image Collection; 220: Dave G. Houser/CORBIS; 224: Charles Philip Cangialosi/CORBIS; 227: The Imagebank/Getty Images, Inc.; 230: Chris Hellier/CORBIS.

Index